BOONE AND CROCKETT CLUB'S

21ST BIG GAME AWARDS

Boone and Crockett Club's 21st Big Game Awards

A book of the Boone and Crockett Club
containing tabulations of outstanding
North American Big Game Trophies
accepted during the
21st awards entry period of 1989-1991

Edited by
Gary Sitton
and
Jack Reneau

1992
The Boone and Crockett Club
Missoula, Montana

Boone and Crockett Club's 21st Big Game Awards

Library of Crongress Catalog Card Number: 92-071642
ISBN Number: 1-879356-19-8
Published 1992

Published in the United States of America by the
Boone & Crockett Club
250 Station Drive
Missoula, Montana 59801-2753

Foreword

Jack Reneau, Director, Big Game Records
Boone and Crockett Club

The Boone and Crockett Club proudly presents the *Boone and Crockett Club's 21st Big Game Awards* book to the hunting fraternity.

To those featured herein, recognition is given for an accomplishment of a lifetime. Even the smallest trophies listed in the trophy data sections are only a dream for most of us. All of us, however, can share in the excitement of 94 hunting stories told by the trophy owners in their own words. Hundreds of field and portrait photographs add to your reading pleasure.

To others, this book will be a "where-to-go" resource. These sportsmen and sportswomen will spend hours pouring over the data of 2,611 trophies to determine which areas are currently producing the records book trophies they are after, then using the data gleaned as the basis for planning future hunts.

Still others will settle down in a comfortable armchair to enjoy the experiences of others, while looking for valuable tidbits of "how-to" information that will enhance their own hunting prowess.

Novice and veteran hunters alike can experience the thrill of the variety of hunts featured between the covers of this book. For example, the reader relives Stephen A. Kroflich's muskox hunt on the beautiful and desolate Arctic landscape. In the same sitting, one travels to the hot and arid deserts of old Mexico with Robert L. Williamson in his quest for a trophy desert sheep.

Most importantly, this book is a testimonial to the past and present efforts of hunter-conservationists throughout North America. The records keeping efforts of the Club can actually be used as a barometer to measure the conditions of North American big game populations. Large numbers of trophy animals have long been equated with healthy wildlife populations.

The number of entries accepted by the Club increased dramatically during the last decade. A total of 947 trophies were accepted from 1980 through 1982 during the 18th Awards Entry Period. By comparison, 2,611 trophies were accepted for this book from 1989 to 1991, the 21st Awards Entry Period. This is an increase of 175% in just slightly over 10 years.

Theodore Roosevelt, the founder and first president of the Boone and Crockett Club, and his contemporaries were visionaries, men in the right place at the right time. They recognized exploitation of North America's wildlife resources as a serious problem and did something about it.

Take a moment now to put yourself in their place in the early to mid-1800s. Had you been there, you would have seen with your own eyes the vast herds of buffalo, pronghorn, elk, sheep and other wildlife that covered the vast plains. Had you also been there in the late 1880s, the absence of wildlife would have concerned you as much as it did the founders of the Boone and Crockett Club.

Returning to reality, however, we are fortunate to have been born in the twentieth century to see the re-establishment of our native big game populations. We, and the emphasis is on the we, are presently reaping the benefits of farsighted individuals like Theodore Roosevelt.

A debt of thanks is owed to past generations for their efforts to ensure that viable wildlife populations exist for our generation. We owe this same wildlife heritage to future generations. The Boone and Crockett Club started its leadership role in conservation of our wildlife resources in 1887 and continues that role today.

The magnificent bull elk print selected to grace the dust jacket is by well-known wildlife artist Ken Carlson. This print is from the Boone and Crockett Club's 1984 Conservation Stamp Print series. It is one of the series that commemorates North America's native big-game animals. Sales of the stamp prints help fund natural resource conservation research at the Club's Theodore Roosevelt Memorial Ranch.

The elk is appropriate for this book as it represents one of the successes of modern wildlife management. It has been estimated that there were less than 15,000 elk remaining in North America at the turn of the century. Elk presently occupy all available habitat and total well over 500,000 animals.

Thanks are due to a number of people who have helped with various aspects of the Club's records keeping efforts. The production of this book would not have been possible without the tireless efforts of the Club's staff during the last three years. Individuals deserving special recognition and thanks include Margaret Sefchick, Kelli Conner, Gene Harter and Jay Holland.

Special thanks are also due Walter H. White and members of the Boone and Crockett Club's Records of North American Big Game Committee. Members of this Committee, the governing body of the Club's records keeping program, volunteer their time, talents and resources to ensure that the Club's high ethical standards are upheld. Walter and his Committee are there whenever help and advice are needed.

The efforts of Buck Buckner, chairman of the 21st Awards Judges Panel, and the 15 other members who unselfishly volunteered their time and money to serve as judges are greatly appreciated. We especially thank the more than 700 sportsmen and sportswomen who serve as official measurers.

The Club thanks the Wisconsin Buck and Bear Club members who volunteered for all aspects of the 21st Awards display, auction and banquet in Milwaukee, Wisconsin, with a special thanks to the leadership and staff of the Milwaukee Public Museum for hosting the 21st Awards trophy display in Gromme Hall.

We hope you find success on all your future hunts.

Contents

The Stories Behind the Award-Winning Trophies

Illustrations

Boone and Crockett Club's
21st Big Game Awards

BOONE AND CROCKETT CLUB
NORTH AMERICAN BIG GAME AWARDS

This is to certify that the

non-typical Coues' whitetail deer 155

entered by

Charles E. Erickson, Jr.

in the 21st North American Big Game Awards
was awarded

Sagamore Hill Award

this 13th day of June 1992

_____
Director, Big Game Records

_____
Chairman, Records of North
American Big Game Committee

The Boone & Crockett Club Big Game Award Certificate. The Certificate and the Boone & Crockett Club Medal (pictured at the top of the Certificate) are both given to those trophies certified by the Final Awards Judges Panel for a place award. The Certificate only is given to trophies qualifying for other awards such as the Certificate of Merit and Honorable Mention.

A Profile of the Boone and Crockett Club

Stephen S. Adams
President, Boone and Crockett Club

An organization founded to champion a cause, take on the establishment, right a wrong, and challenge conventional wisdom is usually the brainchild of one passionate individual sufficiently disturbed over an injustice. By the same token, equally passionate support for the cause cannot be purchased, nor can the effort be strictly an intellectual pursuit. The movement's leaders must have the intestinal fortitude to persist through the months or even years of inevitable setbacks, constant frustrations and possible public ridicule. Such commitment can only come from the heart.

In 1887, a 29-year-old Theodore Roosevelt was an Easterner whose hunting and fishing experiences of earlier years in the West had captured his soul, changed his life, and altered the direction of his country forever. On a crisp December evening in New York City, Roosevelt gathered several of his prominent and influential friends for dinner. He preached to the choir as he conveyed his deep concern for the massive deterioration of the continent's wild game. All present were avid sportsmen who, during the previous 10 years, had witnessed the slaughter of some 60 million bison and what would become the complete annihilation of the passenger pigeon. Each knew all too well that the popularity of market hunting and the absence of game harvest restrictions would combine to cause continued depletion of the remaining wildlife populations, many to the point of extinction.

That evening marked the founding of the Boone and Crockett Club. The mission of the Club's membership was to do all in their individual and combined powers to stem the tide of this uncontrolled destruction and convince the nation's leadership that "fair chase" sport hunting was not only an ethical pursuit but a sound game management tool.

Since these early members had considerable political clout, a legacy was established with the Club able to initiate or influence a monumental volume of conservation legislation. Among the most notable were the protection of Yellowstone Park from commercial development and exploitation, the creation of Mount McKinley (now Denali) National Park, the formation of Montana's national Bison Range and Glacier

National Park, the preservation of the National Key Deer Refuge in Florida, and the enactment of the Lacey Act of 1900 (introduced by Iowa Congressman and Club member John Lacey), which outlawed the interstate transportation of illegally killed wildlife, the begining of the end for market poaching.

From 1901 to 1909, as the 26th President of the United States, Roosevelt became the most prolific conservator of natural resources in American history. Under his leadership, 150 national forests, 51 federal bird reservations, 21 reclamation projects, 18 national monuments, five national parks and four national game preserves were created—approximately 230,000,000 acres in all. Also during the Roosevelt Administration, four national conservation commissions were appointed and three national conferences on conservation held.

Even with the early successes, many Club members were still convinced that their generation of Americans would be the last to see the best examples of the big game animals that roamed North America. There was considerable evidence to support the belief that the largest, healthiest of the species would eventually be killed by poachers, market hunters and sport hunters leaving animals of inferior genetics to reproduce in the wild. Out of this fear, two projects were initiated that would come to significantly complement the Club's conservation efforts.

In 1895, with the assistance and support of many Club members, including the direct involvement of Roosevelt himself, the New York Zoological Society was founded. The Society would establish the New York Zoological Park, located on a 261 acre tract at the south end of Bronx Park. The Bronx Zoo, as it was to be named, was to become the home of North American game animals in simulations of their native habitats and a showcase for the principles of natural resource conservation advocated by the Club.

Club members then saw an opportunity to enhance what had been created and permanently preserve what they perceived as the few remaining examples of the "best of the best." In 1906, the National Collection of Heads and Horns was established, located in the Park, to provide a place for sportsmen to house their most outstanding trophies. It was to be a public display for examples of the majestic animals that once lived in the wild. (Note: The collection was moved in 1982 to the Buffalo Bill Historical Center in Cody, Wyoming.)

Then, in 1932, the *Records of North American Big Game* was published. Using the national collection as its base, the Club invited sportsmen to have their North American trophies measured, scored and ranked along side specimens of comparable quality. Again, the intent was to preserve for posterity the truly great examples of the continent's big game animals before they declined or disappeared forever.

In that first book, printed not knowing if there would be the need for another, editor Prentiss Gray, chairman of the Club's Editorial and Historical Committee, remarked that "certainly the best heads of bison and pronghorn are no longer available... [This] makes it difficult if not impossible for the sportsman of today to find trophies comparable with those taken by even the previous generation."

Fortunately, the fears were unwarranted. The conservaton legislation enacted in the early 1900's ended the decline of the large mammal populations. As a result, over the past half century, thousands of new entries have been added to the records program, attesting to the restored health of the game herds. Contrary to Gray's prediction, only one pronghorn listed in the early books is still ranked among the largest heads entered in the last ten years. Of the bison, the "old heads" represent only half of the top ten listed today.

The level of consciousness raised by the popularity of the records book has played no small part in causing those directly responsible for wildlife habitat conservation to continually reevaluate resource management practices. The program's strict requirement for a "fair chase" hunt, the concept originated by Roosevelt over 100 years ago, has been the primary cause for support from hunters and wildlife professionals alike.

In the 1952 records book, Club member Milford Baker wrote, "The awakened interest of North American big game should arouse sportsmen to the importance of wise conservation policies. The magnificent mammals inherited as a national wildlife asset by this generation should be given zealous protection by the sportsman and nature-lover lest future generations inherit a wasted natural resource."

The Boone and Crockett Club dedicates this volume to the natural resource management professionals of the public agencies and the private landowners throughout Canada, Mexico and the United States. These champions of stewardship - those who have taken special care to allow their lands to become more hospitable to wildlife - are the true heroes of the battle to restore health and vitality to the North American continent's game herds. Each must constantly weigh the pressure for multiple usage — the requirement for intelligently balanced economic development—with the necessity to sustain the productive viability of the resources under their management and control.

The 21st Awards Judges Panel, Standing, (l-r): Glenn E. Hisey, Minnesota; Philip L. Wright, Chairman Emeritus, Records Committee, Montana; Jack Graham, Alberta; Stanley R. Godfrey, Wisconsin; Dennis L. Shirley, Utah; Eldon L. Buckner, Chairman of Judges Panel, Oregon; Michael C. Cupell, Arizona; Walter H. White, Chairman of Records Committee, Wisconsin; Larry Streiff, Minnesota. Sitting (l-r): Jack Reneau, Director of Big Game Records, Virginia; C. Randall Byers, Idaho; William C. MacCarty III, Virginia; William L. Cooper, Georgia; John O. Cook III, Washington; Frank Cook, Alaska; James J. McBride, California; Howard Hanson, Saskatchewan; Bob Hults, Wisconsin. Photograph taken by Wendy Christensen-Senk of the Milwaukee Public Museum.

4

Legacy of Concern for Ethical Hunting

John P. Poston
Chairman, Ethics Committee
Boone and Crockett Club

The Boone and Crockett Club was created in 1887 to address the ethical concerns of its founders. Of particular importance to Theodore Roosevelt, George B. Grinnell, Francis Parkman, Carl Schurz, Albert Bierstadt, Philip H.Sheridan, William Tecumseh Sherman, and other early members, was the devastation of the West's big game herds by market hunters and the increasing exploitation of the many natural resources of Yellowstone National Park. These concerns were initially addressed by the Club in the drafting and support of two key Congressional Acts. The first of these acts, passed in 1891, authorized the President to set aside national forest reserves. The passage of the second, the 1894 Yellowstone Park Protection Act, gave the army the authority it needed to effectively protect the resources of the Yellowstone area. These early successes set the standard for the Club. Conservation and preservation remain the two primary goals of the Club today.

An additional goal of the Club is to constantly make every effort to maintain the integrity of its big-game records program. Full cooperation with state and federal law enforcement personnel is routine, and there is no hesitation to reject a trophy not taken in fair chase, or in violation of applicable game laws. On occasion, trophies have been removed from the records program because they were discovered to have been tampered with, fraudulently claimed, or taken in violation of the law. The Club pledges to work hard to protect, confirm and account for all trophies submitted for recognition in its record books. The integrity and vigilance of the Club is evidenced by the use of its data as a scientific base for the study and maintenance of wildlife.

Vital to the integrity of these records, and to the general purposes of the club as a whole, is responsible hunting. The Club has championed responsible hunting since its inception. Whether it was the drafting and promotion of a model act of game laws, or the support of the Lacey Act of 1900, which prohibits the interstate shipment of illegally killed wildlife, the Club members have used their considerable political influence to codify principles that promote and preserve the hunting heritage in a changing world.

Early on, the Club established rules of fair chase, which have been adapted to accommodate the advances of technology.

> The Boone and Crockett club does not accept in its records trophies obtained using the following methods of pursuit.
> 1. spotting or herding game from the air, followed by landing in its vicinity for pursuit;
> 2. herding or pursuing game with motor-powered vehicles;
> 3. using electronic communications to attract, locate, observe game, or guide the hunter to such game; and
> 4. hunting game confined by artificial barriers, including escape-proof fencing, or hunting game transplanted solely for the purpose of commercial shooting.

Of course, responsible sportsmen fully comply with all game laws.

The importance of compliance with these guidelines cannot be overstated. Each hunter ultimately must account for and be responsible for his or her own conduct. Hunting is, by its very nature a private endeavor. As Aldo Leopold, one of the Club's most distinguished professional members, said in his highly acclaimed *A Sand County Almanac*, "The hunter ordinarily has no gallery to applaud or disapprove of his conduct. Whatever his acts, they are dictated by his own conscience, rather than by a mob of onlookers. It is difficult to exaggerate the importance of this fact." Individual, personal responsibility of all hunters has always been, and continues to be, the goal of the Club.

Today, as hunting comes under increasing attack from antihunting extremists, it is the rare slob hunter who is their strongest argument. The conduct of an irresponsible few has stirred up emotions, providing press coverage and support for a cause that cannot find a rational basis for its argument. These extremists would like to portray hunters as the ultimate destroyers of wildlife, when in fact it is the sportsmen who, through their dollars, fund most of the current wildlife conservation.

In the end, the final arbiters will be the majority of Americans who do not hunt. If the public's impression of hunting is a negative one, they will not support the sport. **All** hunters individually must take it upon themselves to act responsibly and ethically. If they do not, we may someday lose the right to pursue the sport of hunting.

An Overview of the 21st Big Game Awards Program

Dr. Philip L. Wright, Chairman Emeritus
Records of N.A. Big Game Committee
Boone and Crockett Club

The 21st Awards Program had a total of 2,579 entries for the three-year period of 1989, 1990, and 1991. This was by far the largest number of entries, exceeding by over 400 the previous high of the 20th Awards period.

The top five trophies in each class were invited to be sent for judging to the Milwaukee Public Museum. The facilities at the Museum were excellent in every respect, for both the judging, which was conducted during the first week of May, and the display, which followed until the Awards Banquet on June 13.

The Wisconsin Buck and Bear Club actively supported all aspects of the program. A reception and two banquets were held. The first banquet was highlighted by a very successful auction of selected hunting trips, firearms, books, and sporting memorabilia, while the second featured the presentation of awards to the successful hunters.

Many hundreds of interested observers saw the extremely high quality of the trophies exhibited over the four weeks the trophies were on display. One hundred trophies were shipped to be judged. The panel of 11 judges and 4 consultants were working under new guidelines, which called for allowing the entry score to stand if the scoring teams felt that the trophy had been correctly scored prior to entry. This resulted in 34 trophies being left with their entry scores, although some shrinkage had occurred, and 12 were scored by the judges the same as their entry scores. Thirty-four scores were reduced and 18 were raised by the panel.

The previous grizzly bear Worldís Record was tied and 3 New World's Records were set. Detail about the awards made for 97 trophies follows. The huntersí stories of their hunts, which provide fascinating reading, follow. Clearly, trophy hunting is thriving throughout the ranges of our big game species.

There were good numbers of entries in all three active bear classes, with large specimens in each class. Most of the states and provinces now require a tooth to be saved from all bears killed, and some of this information is obtainable from recent entries. We know that bears continue to grow for many years and they are the longest-lived trophy animals we hunt. In the brown and grizzly classes, 20 entered bears were aged and 18 were over 10 years old, with two recorded at 28 years old.

In the Alaskan brown bear class, Kodiak or other island bears slightly outnumber the mainland or peninsula ones, 33 to 27. In the grizzly class, the previous World's Record held by two British Columbia heads, was tied by a trophy from mainland Alaska at 27-2/16, taken by Theordore Kurdziel, Jr. We had the first entry of a barren ground grizzly, 14-1/2 years old and taken on the Horton River in NWT by Vic Moss. It had been thought previously that bears from that area did not grow that large. Alaska and British Columbia were tied with 20 entries each, three were from Yukon and three from Alberta.

The 126 entries in the black bear class continue to come from all over the continent, with 22 states or provinces represented. The top black bear, scoring 22-13/16 came from California and is the largest trophy entered from that state. Alaska, with 18, and Saskatchewan, with 15, have the largest number of entries. Two came from the Queen Charlotte Islands, off the coast of British Columbia, the first entries from those islands. A picked-up head from Florida was the second entered from that state. Trophy black bears are usually over 10 years old, but they are not as old as those in the brown and grizzly classes.

A single jaguar, taken in 1971 in Mexico, before it was classified as an endangered species, was entered.

There were 96 cougars, by far the largest number ever entered in an Awards period. Every state or province within known cougar range is represented, except California, where cougars are not legal game animals. The top areas were Idaho, with 16 entries; Utah, with 13; Colorado, with 12; Alberta, with nine; Montana, with eight; and British Columbia, with seven.

In the typical elk class, the largest number of trophies, 14, came from Arizona, where Indian tribes are able to manage their elk herds to produce record-class bulls. In recent years, an increasing number of trophies from reservations are being taken and the tribes are to be complimented on their success. The more northern states and provinces, the traditional elk producing states, although producing large numbers of elk, have difficulty managing their herds to produce big trophies and as a result now have limited numbers of entries.

The non-typical elk class, first established in 1986, had 22 entries. A Manitoba elk taken in 1961 by James R. Berry, scoring 447-1/8, was designated by the judges panel as the New Worldís Record. Eight of the others came from Arizona. Although 13 of these trophies were taken earlier than the entry period, eight recently killed trophies were entered. This brings us to 37 animals in this newly established class. Earlier, it had been thought that only a handful of such trophies were in existence.

In the Rooseveltís elk class, with 25 entries, we have a New Worldís Record, scoring 3-3/8 points above the previous record at 388-3/8. This great trophy taken by Wayne Coe, came from Vancouver Island and is the first British Columbia Rooseveltís elk to come before a judges' panel. It is difficult for natives on the island to make arrangements with customs to ship their trophies to the Awards Programs in the U.S. The two previous World's Records in this class came from Oregon and Washington.

Columbia Blacktails continue to be entered, with the largest number, 44, from Oregon, 39 from California, and 20 from Washington. Mendocino County, Califorina, with 16 entries and Jackson County, Oregon, with 12 of these are the hottest areas.

In the recently established Sitka blacktail class, all of the top six trophies came from southeastern Alaska, with five of these from Prince of Wales Island. Previously, most of the top entries came from Kodiak Island. We had the first entry from the Queen Charlotte Islands. Sitka blacktails are abundant on these islands, having been transplanted from coastal British Columbia many years ago. Fourteen entries come from Kodiak Island, where the deer were transplanted from mainland Alaska many years ago, and 12 came from southeastern Alaska.

Whitetails were entered in unprecedented numbers, with over 900 entered: 540 typicals and 363 non-typicals. No less than 38 states and provinces were represented. The Iowa Big Bucks Club put on a drive to locate whitetail trophies, and they came up with 87 typical and 58 non-typical trophies. About half of these bucks were taken more than five years previously. There was only a single entry from Iowa in our 1958 records book. Minnesota, with 106 entries, Wisconsin with 87, and Illinois with 82, vividly show the tremendous rebound whitetails have made in these corn-belt states. Alberta had 34 entries, with first place awards in both the typical and non-typical classes, and Saskatchewan, with 24 entries, led the Canadian provinces.

In the Coues' whitetail classes, the Sagamore Hill Award was made for a non-typical trophy scoring 155, the largest ever recorded taken by a sport hunter. This great head was taken by Charles E. Erickson, Jr., in Gila County, Arizona, in 1988. Mr. Erickson had an opportunity to briefly describe his hunt to the audience at the Milwaukee banquet. The total number of entries was 11 each in the two Coues' deer classes. Although the Records Committee voted in 1990 to expand the boundary eastward in New Mexico for this class, no entries were received from this area.

Good numbers of moose continue to be entered in all three classes. In the Canada moose class, British Columbia leads the list as usual with 23 trophies, but the top trophy was taken in Quebec, which has not yielded any high ranking trophies in many years. Also surprising, the second and third awards were made to Ontario trophies, and there were three other entries from that province. Few records book moose have been entered from Ontario in recent years. New Hampshire authorized limited moose hunting in 1989, for the first time in 100 years, and a fine trophy scoring 208-2/8 was taken there in 1990.

Although no Alaska-Yukon moose trophies were sent to the Awards Program in Milwaukee, there were 45 entries in this class, with 38 from Alaska, six from Yukon, and one from NWT. In the Shiras, or Wyoming, class, Idaho, which has only recently resumed moose hunting, had the most entries with 14, followed by Wyoming with 13, Montana with nine, and Utah with eight entries.

Caribou continue to be entered in good numbers in all five of the classes. The most remarkable trophy displayed in Milwaukee was a mountain caribou taken at Fire Lake, Yukon, in 1989, by James R. Hollister with 73 countable antler points. Although a number of large caribou trophies are known with more than 50 antler points, mostly barren ground ones, and one with 61 points is listed, this head surpasses all others by 12 additional antler points. This almost unbelievable trophy scores 449-4/8 and is only 2-4/8 points below the current World's Record.

In the Central Canada barren ground class, which was first established in 1983, there were 72 entries during the period. When added to the 16 in the 19th Awards Program and 52 in the 20th, there are now 140 trophies in this class. This is far beyond what the Record Committee expected when this class was established, and it indicates that there is a healthy, huntable population in an area of many thousands of square miles which had only limited trophy hunting in earlier years. With the disqualification of the previous World's Record, a new record was designated by the panel. This fine trophy taken at MacKay Lake, NWT, by James H. Wooten in 1989 scores 412-6/8.

The number of pronghorn entries (278) was more than double the number entered in the 20th Awards Program. Fifteen states or provinces were represented, with Wyoming leading with 82 entries, followed by New Mexico with an all-time high of 52 trophies recorded. Nevada had 29, Arizona 28, and Montana had 22. Most of the largest antelope were taken in Arizona, New Mexico, or Nevada, as was true in the 20th Awards Program.

In the Rocky Mountain goat class, British Columbia continues to lead with 27 of the 56 trophies; Alaska followed with 15, and Montana with six, Washington with four, and Wyoming with one. The goats earning awards were all excellent trophies, with two scoring over 54 and ranking in the top 15 of all recorded trophies.

The muskox class is dominated by trophies from Northwest Territories, where 32 bulls were taken, with 16 from Alaska. The top trophy, taken in 1990 and scoring 125, is just 2/8 below the World's Record, which in turn was taken in 1988. Both came from Bay Chimo, NWT. Muskox are obviously thriving in NWT, and their tremendous recovery there is a significant highlight in the history of big game restoration.

In the bison class, only free-roaming animals from states which classify them as game animals are recorded. Eight of the trophies came from Custer State Park in South Dakota, where officials believe the animals are taken in fair chase. Seven animals came from Montana, where animals overflowing from Yellowstone Park have been legally hunted. This hunting has, as of 1991, been terminated by the Montana legislature.

Excellent numbers of bighorn sheep have been entered with 116 for this period, by far the largest number ever entered in a three-year period. This is largely due to the number of trophies, 66, from Montana. Most of these great trophies have come from herds that have been re-established by transplants, originally from the Sun River herd. In some cases, there were no remaining sheep living on these ranges when the transplants were made 15 or more years ago. There were two trophies from Blaine County, where the sheep have been reestablished in the Breaks of the Missouri River. A century ago Audubon's sheep occurred there.

Many of the transplanted rams grow horns at a rapid rate and some reach the 180 minimum score at six years of age. This rapid maturity and horn growth was unknown previously. Before the era of transplants, rams living on long established ranges had to be 10 years old or so before their horns reached record size, and many never grew that large, even at full maturity. This great success with bighorns has been due to excellent management strategies by Montana Fish, Wildlife, and Parks Department biologists, but the relatively mild winters over the past 13 years have also helped. Oregon also has a highly successful transplant of Rocky Mountain bighorns in the Wallowa Mountains, in the northeast corner of the state. This herd produced four entries in the 20th Awards period and 4 more big trophies in the 21st period. These bighorns also range across into Washington, and there was a single entry from that state. Bighorns have also been reestablished in eastern Arizona and western New Mexico, with the one entry, (the first), from each state. Alberta, with 18 entries, and British Columbia, with 19, have continued to produce record trophies in sizable numbers for many years.

The four bighorns seen at Milwaukee were: 11-1/2, 10-1/2, 10-1/2, and 8-1/2 years old, respectively, based on counting the annuli on their horns. Quite a few of 6-1/2-year-old rams are among the Montana entries and there are two judged to be only 5-1/2 years old. For some unknown reason, the annuli are more distinct on Rocky Mountain bighorns than on Dall's, Stone's, or desert sheep. The numbers of entries from Idaho, Colorado, and Wyoming, with three, one, and one entries, are reduced from recent entry periods.

In the desert sheep class, we have the first hunter-killed trophies ever listed from California; previously listed heads from California have all been pick-up trophies. Limited sheep hunting in that state was authorized by legislation in 1989, and three fine trophies taken in San Bernardino County were entered in the 21st Program. There had not been any legal sheep hunting in California for over 100 years prior to this recent hunt.

In the Dall's and Stone's sheep classes, good trophies continue to be entered. Eight of the 29 entries of Dall's rams were taken in the Mackenzie Mountains of Northwest Territories, three from Yukon, and the remainder from Alaska. Surprisingly five of the entries were taken in the Brooks Range. Two of the 16 Stone's rams were taken in Yukon, one each from the Anvil and the Pelly Mountains, the remainder from northern British Columbia. About half of the entries in both of these classes now include information about ages based on counting the annuli. The top trophies were 10 or more years old in each class, although two Dall's and one Stone's were 8-1/2 years old.

Since the first of the year, entries continue to come in to the office in good numbers for the 22nd Awards Program, to be held in 1995 at some as yet undetermined site. The Records Committee is anxious to receive invitations for appropriate sites to consider in advance. The Boone and Crockett Club's Executive Committee meeting in Milwaukee in June reiterated its strongly held conviction that the records and awards program is highly desirable in promoting first-class sportsmanship with strict requirements of fair chase and that it is totally in harmony with modern scientific game management.

11

Photograph by Wm. H. Nesbitt

WHITETAIL DEER, TYPICAL ANTLERS
FIRST AWARD
SCORE: 199-5/8

Locality: Edmonton, Alta.   Date: 1991
Hunter: Don McGarvey

WHITETAIL DEER, TYPICAL ANTLERS 199-5/8

Don McGarvey

As a lifelong resident of Edmonton, Alberta, I was aware of the trophy whitetail potential of the area surrounding my hometown, even prior to September 20, 1991. On that day, that trophy whitetail potential became trophy whitetail reality.

The area surrounding Edmonton, a city of 600,000 people, is a bowhunting-only zone and is comprised of farmland and woodlots. As a bowhunter for the past seven years, I was familiar with the area and had secured exclusive permission to hunt a certain parcel of land which I knew harbored a monster whitetail.

I had seen him twice during the 1990 season: once, in September, at 75 yards in a standing barley field; and another time in November, when I rattled him to within 12 yards. Unfortunately, the wily buck worked his way in behind the rattle to a position which afforded no shot. A brief change in wind direction allowed him to catch my scent, and he voiced his displeasure with my presence with an aggressive snort as he bolted away at top speed.

I have always bowhunted whitetails from treestands, usually placed at the edge of woodlots and along well-used transition routes between the bedding and feeding areas. My missed opportunity at 12 yards was the source of depression and frustration until the 1991 season began in September. Nothing was going to spoil another chance at the deer, or one of his brothers or cousins, which were undoubtedly in the area. I had seen many impressive whitetails in this area but knew that I would have to play my cards right and be extremely lucky to harvest one of these tremendous bucks.

From the opening of the 1991 season, I had watched the whitetails intensely and used my detailed deer diary to determine what stand locations would afford the best opportunity of harvesting a nice trophy. Quite frankly, I had never expected to see the big buck again. No one deserves three sightings of such a magnificent animal, and I thought I had my last chance in November 1990.

With the use of the deer diary, I realized that the deer were favoring a route across a barley field and into an alfalfa field to feed. This forced the deer to cross through a narrow 15-yard opening in a treeline separating the two fields. The conditions would have to be perfect to avoid being detected, since I intended my treestand to face north, the direction from which the deer would be coming.

I waited for a steady northwest wind, and as I sat in my office on September 20, 1991, I realized that this could be the day. I was anxious at work and could not concentrate, so I left the office in the early afternoon, showered and went to speak with the landowner and solidify our relationship. After chatting briefly with the landowner, I made my way on foot to the stand location with small portable stand under my arm and a series of tree steps. I found a favorable tree, hastily put up the treestand, and left the area to allow the area to settle.

The north wind had a bone-chilling effect, and I silently cursed myself for not bringing my gloves. I had been in my stand for about 20 minutes when I had my first sighting — an impressive whitetail buck, approximately 100 yards to the north. The deer was almost directly in front of my stand. I had positioned it in the southeast corner of the barley field, along the opening in the tree line which ran from east to west. The buck was not the one I had seen the year before, but it was nevertheless an impressive buck. I hoped for an opportunity.

After two agonizing minutes, the deer came at a trot along the edge, toward my stand. He stopped only when he was within 15 yards of the stand. Unfortunately, the angle was all wrong. His vital organs were not properly exposed, and it would have been a risky shot. I decided to wait, especially due to the fact that the foliage was heavy and I would have had to shoot through some leaves. I expected the deer to come directly in front of my stand through a patch of thistles and then through the tree line, but he had other ideas. He went into the brush to my right, through the treeline, and into the alfalfa field without offering me a shot.

Dejected, I turned to face northward, and the sight that awaited me was something I will never forget. A massive whitetail was working his way along the opposite edge of the barley field at approximately 200 yards. I entirely lost my composure. It is a wonder I did not drop my bow out of the tree but somehow managed to hang on. And thank God for safety belts! The time passed at an agonizing pace. As the buck worked eastward along the opposite edge, he came to the northeast corner of the barley field and then turned southward. He was on course to come along the same path as the previous deer.

Over the 15 minutes that it took the deer to carefully and cautiously work his way toward my stand, I slowly gained a measure of control over myself. Concentration began to take over as the deer approached the corner of the field, coming within 15 yards of my stand. He stopped. He was looking intensely down the treeline toward the west, but I could not risk turning and looking to see what was attracting its attention. He must have stood there for a good three to four minutes before deciding to move. I silently prayed that he would come toward my stand and not evade me as the previous deer had done.

The measure of luck that I had been dealt in seeing this deer three times was bigger than I deserved. The deer began to walk slowly thorough the thistle patch. As he did so, the buck reached a point where I lost sight of him momentarily due to a heavily leaved, overhanging limb. I used that opportunity to carefully draw my bow. As the deer cleared the overhanging limb, my 10-yard pin sought its vital area. I released my arrow as the deer was directly in front of me, at 10 yards.

I cannot remember being excited at the time. Another opportunity at this deer had forced me to concentrate. Luckily, the last thing I saw, before the deer bolted northward into the barley field, was the yellow and green fletching of my arrow as it entered the deer behind the shoulder. The deer turned to the north and ran only 60 yards into the barley field before it stopped, turned and went down.

Again, I was thankful for my safety belt; otherwise, I am sure I would have fallen out of the tree. As I had seen the deer expire, I could not wait the standard 20 to 30 minutes before going after the deer. I scrambled out of my treestand, raced out into the field, and admired my trophy.

I knew from the first time I saw the deer that it was an impressive animal. The magnitude of it all did not hit home until the next day, when I brought it to official Boone and Crockett and Pope and Young scorer, Ryk Visscher. After green-scoring the buck, Ryk felt that it was quite possibly the Number 2 typical whitetail ever taken with a bow and in the top ten for Boone and Crockett.

The phrase "deer of a lifetime" is perhaps a cliche, but it is certainly an accurate description of this deer. I will continue hunting whitetails as long as I physically can, but having taken this deer, I can only look forward to the thrill and excitement of being outdoors in pursuit of one of the world's most beautiful animals. If I do not shoot another deer for the rest of my life, I will not be surprised. However, I will always have this deer to remind me of how lucky the average hunter can be in the great outdoors.

Photograph by Wm. H. Nesbitt

WHITETAIL DEER, TYPICAL ANTLERS
CERTIFICATE OF MERIT
SCORE: 201-4/8

Locality: Hamilton Co., Iowa   Date: 1974
Hunter: Wayne A. Bills   Owner: Larry L. Huffman
(Hunting Story Not Available)

Photograph courtesy of Vernon Skoba

This typical whitetail deer was hunted in Day County, South Dakota,
in 1989 by Vernon Skoba. It scores 171-1/8.

Photograph courtesy of Dennis Schneider

This typical whitetail deer was hunted in Kankakee County,
Illinois, in 1988, by Dennis Schneider. It scores 171-4/8.

WHITETAIL DEER, NON-TYPICAL ANTLERS
FIRST AWARD
SCORE: 279-6/8

Locality: Whitemud Creek, Alta.   Date: 1991
Hunter: Neil J. Morin

WHITETAIL DEER, NON-TYPICAL ANTLERS 279-6/8

Neil J. Morin

The 1991 hunting season started early for me, with a great deal of excitement. It was still summer, and well before the opening of any season, when I spotted the whitetail buck that would keep me awake at night.

I was swathing a canola crop when I saw a whitetail come out of the brush and into the field. The buck paid little attention to the approaching swather. He stepped over to a slough and started drinking. As I passed within 40 yards of the buck, he lifted his head, and I got a good look at his antlers. He was in the velvet, and I knew that would make him appear larger than he really was, but he was still massive. I could see tines coming down off the beams and tall tines above the beams, lots of them.

After that sighting in the field and another, at a greater distance, while combining, I started reading as much material as I could on monster whitetail bucks. The pictures I saw of some of the top bucks were very impressive, but I felt the one I had seen would compare to them.

As opening day of the rifle season neared, I realized that I probably was not going to get out opening morning. I had decided to take care of some business with my parents in the nearest urban center. The early part of the season was difficult hunting and there was not much hunting pressure. For these reasons, I was not much worried about missing opening morning.

Even though I had been in the city, my mind was on the buck as we drove home. I was particularly alert as I approached the area where I believed the buck lived. I noticed a deer far out in a particular field of standing wheat. It was too far to tell if it was a buck, never mind the buck I wanted, but my curiosity was piqued enough to make me return with my rifle.

When I arrived at the place from which I had earlier spotted the deer, it was not in sight. It had been three-quarters of a mile from the nearest bush, so I did not believe the deer would have travelled that far without being spooked. At that point, I began to stalk toward where I had last seen the deer.

I had no problem staying concealed as I crouched and moved through the standing wheat. I knew I was getting close to the spot, so I slowed my pace and moved cautiously. Suddenly, a large buck stood up in the field, about 100 yards away. I dropped to my knees. My suspicions were confirmed as I saw the great antlers. The buck seemed nervous and appeared to be checking the wind and looking in my direction. The crouched walk and the sight of the antlers had made me incapable of a certain off-hand shot at that distance. Finally, the buck seemed satisfied, and incredibly, it bedded down again, out of sight.

I began stalking again, but at a painfully slow pace. I crept to within 30 yards of where the buck had bedded. I could see the tips of his antlers from a squatting position, but I knew all I had to do was wait for the buck to make the first move.

The next minute or so seemed to last forever. I felt fully prepared for anything that might happen. Of course, what happened next caught me by surprise. The buck exploded from its bed at a dead run. My rifle came up, I found the buck in the scope and squeezed the trigger. He kept going, so I shot again, and he fell. Later examination proved both shots to have been lethal. My Winchester Model 70 in .300 Winchester Magnum had done its job.

As I approached the buck, it really hit me that I had killed a very spectacular trophy. Its 14-inch brow tines and five drop-points made it extremely impressive. I counted 28 points.

I contacted Todd Loewen, a taxidermist I had met at a show earlier in the year, and asked him to mount my buck. When I took it to him, he rough-scored it at more than 274 points, Boone and Crockett. This gave me a good idea of how my buck would rank with the world's best.

As with most trophies, there is a lingering question: what if the drop-point on the right antler had not been broken off? Regardless of the broken tine, I feel privileged to have taken such an animal. It was truly a once-in-a-lifetime experience.

Photograph courtesy of Jeff D. Shrader

Jeff D. Shrader is all smiles with this typical whitetail he hunted in Coles County, Illinois, in 1990. It scores 170-6/8.

Photograph courtesy of Thomas D. Brittingham

Thomas D. Brittingham was hunting near Nuevo Leon, Mexico in 1990 when he killed this typical whitetail. It scores 183-1/8.

Photograph courtesy of Stan E. Christiansen

This typical whitetail was killed in 1990 in Barber County, Kansas by hunter Stan E. Christiansen. It scores 171-4/8.

Photograph by Wm. H. Nesbitt

WHITETAIL DEER, NON-TYPICAL ANTLERS
SECOND AWARD
SCORE: 259-7/8

Locality: Perry Co., Ala.   Date: 1989
Hunter: Jon G. Moss

WHITETAIL DEER, NON-TYPICAL ANTLERS 259-7/8

Jon G. Moss

Growing up in the rural South, I was exposed at an early age to the outdoors. I started deer hunting when I was 13 years old. Since my home county does not have the deer population that other parts of the country do, I was 22 years old when I killed my first deer. I had some luck hunting other game; the great North American whitetail always eluded me. Actually, I suspect the deer population has less to do with my frustrations than my inability to sit still.

The subject hunt started on Thanksgiving weekend of 1989. My brother-in-law, Bill May, had invited me over to hunt in Alabama. When I got there, he told me that a friend of his wanted us to go to Perry County. The friend, Hugh Thomas, had some land that I had heard about but had never had an opportunity to hunt. It was to be a work day, but Billy assured me that we would get some hunting done.

By the time we reached Perry County, it was 10:30 p.m. After a few minutes of planning, Billy and Hugh decided to ride around and look at all of the deer stands in order to determine which ones needed repair. Later, we would go back and work on them together. Since there were three people and only two three-wheelers, and we had to cover 5,000 acres, I decided my best bet was to sit in a tree stand, instead of bumping around on the back of a three-wheeler. I could join them later, when the repair work began.

Billy took me to an area that looked promising. There was a wooded strip about three-quarters of a mile long, 200 yards wide, and surrounded by soybean fields. I had heard Billy talk about the place so much that I was very anxious to get in my stand.

I selected a tree that was on the edge of the southernmost field. I positioned myself so that my back was to the edge, and I could look to my right or left, as well as directly down the treeline. In front of me, I could see down my side of the hollow and up the hill on the other side.

As I worked my way up the tree, I discovered a limb that blocked my way about 15 feet above the ground. I stopped there but later decided to break the limb, because my view was partially obstructed. I hated to make the noise, but I knew there were some places I could not see. I moved up to about 25 feet and settled in.

I had never used deer scent before, but had decided to give it a try. I had prepared the scent in advance by putting it on cotton balls and storing them in film canisters. I took out seven or eight cotton balls and dropped them around my tree.

When I got settled in, I looked at my watch. The time was 11:00 a.m. It was a sunny day but windy. The temperature had gotten down around 30 degrees the night before and had risen to about 45 degrees by late morning. At times, the wind made me feel cool, but I was for the most part comfortable.

After sitting in my stand for about an hour, I began to grow impatient, because I knew Billy would be coming to get me soon. An hour is not much time, but I had high expectations for the area. On several occasions, I had been told stories of seeing 15 and 20 bucks in a day.

I had a grunt call with me but had never used it, so I decided to wait until nearer to pick-up time to blow it. Thirty minutes later, nothing had happened. I knew Billy would be back soon, so I decided to give the call a try. I blew it five or six times, very lightly, trying for the deepest tone possible. I decided I would blow it at five-minute intervals. After three more grunting sessions and no results, I heard Billy coming on the three-wheeler. I could barely hear him, and I knew it would take him a few minutes to reach me.

I started down, stopping several times to listen and look. I was trying to be as quiet as possible. When I reached a point some five feet from the ground, I stopped and turned around with my back to the tree.

The years of plowing the field in the same place had allowed a wall of cedar trees to grow up along the edge. When I was up in the tree, I could see over them, but after descending below 10 feet, I could not see anything on the other side.

I paused for a moment and then hopped out of the stand. That hop set wheels in motion that would change the rest of my life.

As I left the stand, I twisted around, landing on my feet with my back to the edge of the field. The moment my feet hit the ground, I heard a crash behind me. Recognizing the sound that is characteristic of a startled deer, I brought my .30-06 to my shoulder as I wheeled around. I could hardly believe my eyes.

Flying through the air, no more than 15 yards away, was the most massive buck I had ever seen. He had apparently come down the tree line from my left as I was coming down the tree. I do not know why I did not see or hear him. My only explanation is that he came up on me fast, and we could not see each other after I descended below the tops of the cedar trees.

I have seen deer come out into a field and spook for a moment when another deer approached. That was the way he acted. He stopped and looked back at me as if he thought I was another deer. Then, things started happening so quickly that it has taken some time and a lot of thought to sort it all out.

When the deer landed, I immediately had my crosshairs on him. The problem was, I had turned my scope up to 9x to look across to the other side of the field. With the deer standing only 12 yards from me, I could not identify what part of him I was seeing in the scope. I moved the crosshairs up to the area that should have been his head. After locating his eye, I moved the crosshairs down his neck and pulled the trigger.

I know all of this sounds as if it took time, but believe me, it only took a split second. I still remember the anxiety and frustration that I felt, knowing that he would run at any second.

When the rifle fired, he went down like a rock. I then saw movement from my right. Another buck had apparently been following the one that I had just shot. He circled the downed deer and ran right by me. I put the rifle up to look at him through the scope. He was also a very large deer, with at least 10 points. A second later, I heard something over my left shoulder. I turned around to see a doe and a nice six-point go by. I turned back toward the big buck that had run by me. He had stopped about 100 yards away and was looking back at me. I started to raise my rifle for another look through the scope but heard another noise over my right shoulder. A doe came running by me. I looked back at the big buck just in time to see him going over the hill.

I had sat for an hour and forty-five minutes and had seen nothing. Then, I had seen three bucks and two does in less than 15 minutes.

I turned my attention toward my kill and began to count his points. I counted again and again and again. I thought, "This can't be right." I could not believe what I was seeing. The buck had more than 35 points, with more than 20 on one side.

Since that day, I have had time to think about the series of events that occurred. I do not think there was any one thing that made this event take place. I think the most important thing was that I was in the right place at the right time. I also believe that the scent and the grunting and the noise I was making, plus the deer's inability to see me, worked together to make him think I was another deer. Whatever the reason, I feel fortunate to have had the opportunity to take such a magnificent animal.

Photograph by Wm. H. Nesbitt

WHITETAIL DEER, NON-TYPICAL ANTLERS
THIRD AWARD
SCORE: 248-6/8
Locality: Warren Co., Iowa   Date: 1990
Hunter: Larry J. Caldwell

WHITETAIL DEER, NON-TYPICAL ANTLERS 248-6/8

Larry J. Caldwell

On Sunday, December 9, 1990, Larry Caldwell and his nephew, Lanny Calgiuri, were shotgun hunting during Iowa's second deer season. Early that morning, Lanny took a fine buck that eventually scored 170-7/8, Boone and Crockett. While they were field-dressing the deer, Larry suffered a serious knife wound to his thigh. After a trip to the emergency room in Des Moines for treatment and stitches, Larry thought his deer season was over. He could not have been more wrong.

Five days later, on December 14, Larry went hunting again. It was a day he will think about for the rest of his life.

The morning was slow. None of the five hunters in the party shot anything. They decided to drive to a timbered area where they had all taken deer before.

Larry was still hobbling around, so instead of being a drive, he took a stand. "I was walking like Chester from 'Gunsmoke'," Larry said. "All week long, I had waited on stand, instead of my usual walking...I prefer to walk."

Larry is a big man, and at 52 years old he had stayed in good shape by doing plenty of walking during other hunting seasons.

"After Lanny shot his big buck, I thought there was no way I was going to top that," said Larry. "We both let deer go by us during bow season if the rack isn't big enough. I figured I would do the same thing if I didn't get to shoot a mature whitetail. We were all feeling pretty good about someone from the party shooting one monster buck."

Larry had seen other deer escape from the stretch of timber in years past, so he knew where he wanted to stand. He moved in slowly, positioning himself up against a tree on the edge of the timber. From there, he could look out over a soybean field. He could not walk too far from the truck, so he knew he had to place himself in a well-used escape route.

It didn't take long for the action to start. The three drivers began to work through the long, narrow, hilly strip of brushy timber. Larry and another hunter guarded the escape routes.

"I could hear the other hunters getting closer, so I moved to another spot where I had seen deer move out before," Larry remembers. "They weren't shooting, so I didn't know if there were any deer in the timber."

The first time Larry saw the buck in the trees, it had its head and tail tucked low, so he didn't know how big a rack it was carrying. The deer had been pushed out of its sanctuary before and knew how to sneak out undetected, or so the big buck believed.

"I saw him come out of the timber and move across the soybean field toward a larger tract of timber. He was running full bore. It didn't take me long to throw my Browning autoloader to my shoulder. I knew if I didn't get him before he entered the big timber, I would never see him again."

"I knew I hit him, but he kept running," Larry said. "I was trying to run and reload my gun all at the same time, hoping to get off another shot. When I came over the little rise in the field, I knew I didn't need to worry about reloading. The buck lay a short distance away. It didn't take me long to get to the buck. I couldn't even feel my leg throb."

"I couldn't believe my eyes when I saw it. I started counting points — 10 points, 20 points, 30 points. I knew it had 30-something points. I had hunted 16 years, and I knew I had taken a big one, I didn't know it would score as high as it did."

Larry's non-typical whitetail rough-scored 250-2/8. Later, when it was officially scored by Dave Boland, it proved to be the fourth largest non-typical ever taken with a gun in Iowa. The big buck's main beams were 28 and 28-5/8 inches. The inside spread was 20-2/8 inches. There were 16 points on the right antler and 20 scorable points on the left antler.

Larry attributes his success to being in the right place at the right time: "I have hunted for years and have never seen anything like the buck that I shot. I knew where I wanted to stand, but if it hadn't been for Lanny stabbing me in the leg, I wouldn't have been standing where I was that particular day. I needed to be close to the pickup; that is why I stood where I did."

"But the buck is still mine!" he said with a smile.

Photograph courtesy of Terry L. Snyder

Terry L. Snyder was hunting in Madison County, Iowa, in
1989 when he got this typical whitetail. It scores 170.

Photograph courtesy of Rodney C. Chute

This typical whitetail was killed in 1989 in Schuyler County, Illinois,
by Rodney C. Chute. It scores 175-2/8.

Photograph by Wm. H. Nesbitt

COUES' WHITETAIL DEER, TYPICAL ANTLERS
FIRST AWARD
SCORE: 133

Locality: Pima Co., Ariz.   Date: 1990
Hunter: Michael E. Duperret   Owners: M.E. Duperret & J.K. Volk

COUES' WHITETAIL DEER, TYPICAL ANTLERS 133

Michael E. Duperret and Jeffrey K. Volk

It all began and ended with Bob Kramme.

I had known Bob long before I ever met him. To me, he was much more than a hard-working, gentle, ruggedly independent cowboy. Simply mentioning his name evoked thoughts of old-fashioned round-ups and mesquite corrals, wild canyons and lost mines, rugged hunts and huge Coues' whitetail bucks. I felt I had always known Bob Kramme, for he filled a place in my heart for the real old-time cowboy, the product of an era that had come and gone, never to be seen again.

In fact, I was thinking of Bob when I placed my Leitz 10x40 binoculars on the tripod that precious morning of November 17, 1990. I did not realize that a magnificent Coues' whitetail would soon enter my field of view, the buck of a lifetime, a buck that would have made Bob proud, if he had been alive to see it.

My hunting partner, Jeff Volk, who had introduced me to Bob Kramme only six years before, and I were on the eighth day of our nine-day November Coues' whitetail hunt in southeastern Arizona. We were physically and mentally exhausted, our feet were stone-bruised from the rugged canyons, and we had enough scratches from catclaw, cactus, and shindaggers to last a lifetime. We openly cursed the unseasonably warm weather, yet knew in our hearts that the hunting had been excellent despite it.

We had begun our hunt in a different hunting unit of southeastern Arizona. Friday night after work, Jeff and I had left Tucson for something we dream about all year long: our annual Coues' whitetail hunt. We drove into our hunting area, slipped on our backpacks, which contained provisions for a potential nine-day backpack hunt, and began our journey. A half-moon cast its silvery glow on the rugged maze of canyons as we silently passed through, guided by familiar nighttime landmarks. Thrilled about our upcoming hunt, the three-hour hike was quickly over, and we pitched our tent under the brilliantly starry Arizona sky. Anticipation hung heavily in the air, so sleep did not come easily.

The next morning found us high on a vantage point, glassing with our binoculars, as the flame-red glow of the rising sun cast hues of coral and buff on the deeply cut, jagged canyon walls all around us. The stunning sunrise illuminated the tan grassy slopes where we searched for the elusive Coues' deer, turning the slopes into golden, shimmering seas of desert grasses, accented only by an occasional stately yucca. Red-tailed hawks soared high above in the lavender-blue sky, hunting for rabbits and Gambel's quail, like those which noisily cackled from their roost below us. The quail were silenced only momentarily by the lonely howl of a solitary coyote who, like us, seemed moved by the stark beauty of the Sonoran desert at dawn. But the mysterious desert hid its secrets well that first morning; we saw only a few deer.

Four days of warmer weather followed, with surprisingly excellent hunting. We saw countless deer, glassing up as many as 60 in a single morning. We never saw another hunter, and each day we moved into wilder, more remote areas. The right buck for Jeff did not emerge from the manzanita thickets, grassy slopes, and cedar trees that we glassed. We saw some very nice bucks, but we were in no hurry to end our adventure with a shot from the .243.

On the fifth morning of our hunt, we glassed up a very large buck with an unusual, non-typical rack, watching him the entire morning from a strategic peak a mile away. That evening we made a long, difficult stalk, but darkness closed in before we could locate him in the thick brush. We had to bushwhack around a huge mountain to get back to camp, arriving two hours later, tired and dejected.

We located the same buck at dawn the next morning and Jeff led me a long, grueling stalk: we ran, climbed, and crashed through brush, making a huge loop which brought us to a high ridge above the buck. An hour later we arrived at the ridge, sweating, gasping for breath; we waited, hidden, intently glassing the cedar-choked ravines below us.

A tense half-hour passed; then, out into the open fed the non-typical buck and his two smaller companions. Jeff easily made the 300-yard shot using an 85-grain boat-tail handload from the .243.

The enjoyment of picture taking and well-deserved congratulations were followed by the meticulous work of field-dressing and boning the meat. By midmorning we were finished, and for the next eleven hours, we hiked out, finally arriving at the truck at 9:30 p.m., tired and sore. Midnight found us at the nearest town, icing down Jeff's deer and eating a very late dinner.

I held a permit for Coues' whitetail in a separate hunting unit, so we drove to my area late that night, slept for two hours, and made the long hike in. That first day in my hunting unit, we were tired but we hunted hard, happy to be in new country.

The following morning, the eighth day of our hunt, we were downright exhausted. We arrived at our vantage point late, and quickly set up our tripods to begin glassing. It was then that I began to think about Bob Kramme. I thought about Bob often when the going became tough, because life had always been difficult and challenging for him.

Fond memories of Bob wandered through my mind as I glassed the slopes below me: the respect and love he felt for his wife Romaine; the joy in his eyes when he reminisced about adventures with his son Kolin; the excitement of guiding big game hunts near Jackson Hole, Wyoming, many years ago; the pride he felt after a hard day's work at their ranch in the rugged Galiuro Mountains.

My memory of first meeting Bob at their ranch was nostalgic, yet vivid: his work-hardened frame sitting beside the old wood-burning stove; his sparkling eyes and warm, handsome smile; his tales of wild, remote places; his respect for the land and creatures that inhabit it.

I shivered beneath my warm jacket as I recalled the harsh drought that had begun in 1988. The Kramme's ranch was hit hard. The grass shriveled up and blew away like dust, stock tanks went bone-dry, and the Krammes had to sell off many of their cattle. All of this weighed very heavily on Bob. I could see the worried look on his wrinkled brow. On March 28, 1990, Bob died in his sleep. It was a huge loss and a shock to all of us. I felt shaken and hollow inside. One of the most special people I had ever met had died, and an era passed with him, an era never to be seen again. The world has seemed like a smaller place since.

After Bob's death the drought quickly ended. A few weeks later, while at the Kramme's ranch, we sat in the old stone house once again with the wood stove burning. Bob was not with us, and our hearts were heavy and sad. He had made a deep, lasting impression on all of us, and we talked for hours about him, as a huge rainstorm raged on outside. In our hearts, we each felt that somehow Bob was responsible for bringing back the rains.

The spring rains came and went, followed by the summer monsoons. I am not superstitious, but I unconsciously found myself thinking that Bob was watching over the desert, somehow bringing back the life-giving rains. The desert responded quickly to the long-awaited water and, by the time our hunt came around that November, the desert seemed almost lush by Arizona standards. The rocky, boulder-strewn saddle I was watching on the eighth morning of our hunt showed no signs of the drought. Long desert grasses and succulent green cacti poked up through the rocks. The desert canyon looked as it always had. Then, something happened that would change it in my mind forever.

Into my field of view stalked a huge, lone buck, carefully sneaking down the saddle with his head held low to the ground, as if avoiding some danger. I barely had time to glance at his dark body and magnificent rack before he disappeared into a manzanita forest. He was gone before I had time to share him with Jeff, put up the spotting scope, or fully evaluate his extraordinary rack.

What I did notice in those few short seconds from half a mile away was that his rack was extremely large and wide. How large I did not know, but my feeling was that he was bigger than anything I had ever seen before. Jeff sensed my excitement. Something very special lay hidden in the manzanita below us.

For the next two hours, we studied the huge thicket. The buck never left, convincing us that he was bedded there. There were two possible strategies: sneak closer and wait for the buck to reveal himself; or attempt a drive using Jeff as the "bird dog" to flush the buck toward me.

The debate of a lifetime ensued, but eventually Jeff's logic won out; we would attempt to flush him out, because he had already been alarmed by a hunter or lion and, therefore, might never show himself again. The wind was in our favor and the terrain was perfect for a deer drive. There was only one natural escape route, and overlooking it was a large, rocky outcropping from which to shoot. The only potential problem was that we had never, in all our years of hunting Coues' whitetail, attempted a deer drive. We had long since learned that these super-intelligent deer had a logic which far surpassed ours.

Nevertheless, desperate chances and uncertain outcomes are the fiber of an exciting hunt, and win or lose, we were thrilled with the prospects. Jeff set out on a hidden, mile-long loop to get to the far side of the manzanita thicket, while I set up for the shot. I found a strategic, comfortable vantage point and placed an 85-grain boat-tail round into the chamber of the .243. I swung the bipod down, cleared some obstructing grass in front of me, and breathlessly waited.

After an eternity, Jeff topped out on the far ridge, half a mile away, and slowly descended toward the manzanita thicket which lay between us. I had hoped the buck would slink out of the thicket toward me, offering a walking or standing shot from 200 to 300 yards. No such luck.

As Jeff entered the far side of the thicket, the buck exploded from the opposite end, sprinting for the small canyon below me. He leaped over 5-foot high manzanitas, twisting and turning as he ran. I followed him with the scope, amazed. The only whitetails I had ever seen run so swiftly and desperately were two does being chased by a mountain lion.

I carefully led the buck, and when he crossed the imaginary radius of 300 yards, I squeezed off a shot. The sight-picture looked perfect as the report broke the tranquility of the huge canyon, but the buck ran even faster. Quickly, I reloaded the bolt action, carefully aimed, and fired at about 250 yards. The buck twisted just as I shot and the bullet puffed harmlessly where I had hoped he would be. The miss did not matter, though, because the first shot from the .243 had connected. The buck crashed into a ravine 200 yards below me, never to leave it.

Jeff arrived at the deer before I did and met me just below the ravine where the buck lay. A large smile crossed his tired face and he said, "Mike, no matter how big you thought your buck was, he's bigger than you imagined. Congratulations." He held out his hand.

When I saw the magnificent deer, I was stunned and unsure what to think. The buck was huge, and he had the most incredible rack I had ever seen on a Coues' deer. Jeff watched silently, as I carefully examined the beautiful deer. We both knew it would be one of the largest Coues' whitetail bucks ever taken. I glanced up toward the saddle above me and felt sad that he had only a couple hundred yards to go to reach safety.

Time seemed to stop until Jeff broke the silence of the warm November day. "I never told you this, but Kolin gave me Bob Kramme's old camo hunting jacket after he died," Jeff said slowly, his voice unsteady. "This is the eighth day of our nine-day hunt. I figured we needed a change of luck, so I wore Bob's jacket this morning. For the first time ever. I guess Bob was smiling on us today."

Then I knew what to think. A trophy is much more than a big rack. It is a memory to be kept forever. I suddenly realized that, when I looked at this trophy, I would always recall our adventurous hunt, the huge buck, but most of all Bob Kramme.

We dressed the deer, carefully keeping all of the meat, the great rack, and the hide for a shoulder mount and flytying. Then, we hiked out of the ruggedly beautiful canyon with Jeff in the lead, carrying the rack. I glanced frequently at the old, faded camo jacket he wore and the huge rack in his hand. The connection between Bob and the buck seemed to be no accident. We hiked slowly, quietly savoring the experience. As the sun set, we somehow knew that we were a part of something bigger than ourselves.

We were humbled to be a part of it.

Photograph by Wm. H. Nesbitt

COUES' WHITETAIL DEER, TYPICAL ANTLERS
SECOND AWARD
SCORE: 120-3/8

Locality: Sonora, Mexico   Date: 1990
Hunter: J. Marvin Smith III

COUES' WHITETAIL DEER, TYPICAL ANTLERS 120-3/8

J. Marvin Smith III

A pink glow was beginning to appear behind the mountain that marked the entrance to the huge ejido (communal ranch) that we planned to hunt that day. It was my first hunt in the desert, and I was fascinated with the Sonoran terrain. The stark magnificence of the giant saguaros that towered over the lower vegetation stood in contrast to any landscape I had previously hunted. The beauty of the desert alone would have made the trip memorable.

My guide, Antonio, suggested that we leave the truck and walk down the road that rimmed the mountain to see if we could cut a fresh track. Several days earlier, we had crossed into Sonora through Nogales, heading south and then west. Since arriving at camp, we had followed a few tracks but had seen none promising enough to continue a long stalk. I held licenses for desert mule deer and for cola blanca (the desert whitetail described by Coues many years previously). I was particularly looking forward to the experience of tracking the deer in the desert. This was a talent for which Antonio was reputed to have some expertise. One hundred yards down the road, Antonio stopped. There, in the soft sand, was a fresh track leading off the mountainside onto the desert floor. He indicated that this one was worth following and appeared to him to be relatively fresh. We checked to see that we had all our necessary gear and started on a stalk that was to last for seven-and-a-half hours.

After following the track for half a mile, we came upon a flat impression beside a creosote bush, which I interpreted from Antonio's Spanish to be an area where the deer had been bedded. Antonio picked up some droppings, and after breaking them up and examining them, he indicated that the deer had left the bed some 45 minutes previously. It is an understatement to say that I was skeptical as to the accuracy of this assessment, but we pressed on. As we continued to follow this track, it occurred to me that the gender of this animal was still somewhat in doubt. Shortly thereafter, we happened upon a bush which had the branches broken off 2 to 3 feet above the ground. Antonio explained to me that the brush had been raked by the antlers of the deer. I was then convinced that we were following an animal of the right gender, and Antonio continually assured me that the track was that of a worthy buck.

It was apparent that the deer was wandering about, eating the small fruit on the top of the barrel cactus. It amazed me how this animal was able to reach in and pluck those morsels resembling miniature pineapples from among the fishhook thorns that surrounded them. Our quarry would sample eight to 10 of these little delicacies on the top of one cactus and then wander on to the next. There was a slow transformation from being skeptical concerning the success of this stalk to a confident feeling that we could continue to follow this animal until we found him.

The deer's walking track entered a barren area of the desert floor which had not a blade of vegetation in an area the size of two football fields. We quickly glassed the far brush line around the perimeter of this bare area, but saw no movement and no animals. As the track was heading straight upwind and was on barren ground, I thought we would be able to quickly gain on our quarry. Following the track at a fast walk, we reached the middle of the barren area. There, we observed the track stopping and backtracking at a 120-degree angle downwind, returning to the perimeter of the barren area. When we arrived at the brush line, the tracks in the sand told the story. The deer had been standing there, watching us expose ourselves, and had turned and run. We followed his running track for more than half a mile before it slowed to a walk once again. Antonio and I stopped to rest, having been on the stalk for nearly three hours at that time.

Twice more in this lengthy stalk, we evidently came close enough to the animal to cause him to run. Never did we see or hear him, but each time we would see where the walking track would break into a run and continue for a lengthy distance before resuming a walking pace. Each time we encountered this behavior, I became more committed to following the stalk to its ultimate conclusion. I glanced at my watch and realized we had been tracking this animal for nearly seven hours. A reasonable estimate was that we had covered 10 to 12 miles in a circuitous route without seeing our quarry.

Shortly thereafter, we crossed a dry arroyo and Antonio stopped to look at several spots of moist sand. After shifting the sand between his fingers and sniffing it, he looked at me and said "listo" in an imperative tone. I knew that he meant for me to be ready. I slipped the sling of my rifle off my shoulder and advanced in an alert fashion, one step behind and two to the left of Antonio.

We had advanced barely 20 steps when the sound of running hooves became audible. We had spooked the deer at 30 yards. I took two quick steps forward to put me ahead of Antonio. The 300 Winchester Magnum, which Bob Kleinguenther had made for me 12 years ago to take on my first Montana elk hunt, came to my shoulder with the same ease that my favorite 28-gauge side-by-side does upon a covey flush. The 3x9 Zeiss scope was on its lowest power setting, and the fleeing deer came quickly into view. The brush was 2-1/2-feet high, and the only parts of the fleeing deer that were visible were the erect head, the antlers and the white tail.

My eyes focused on the antlers, but there was precious little time to fully evaluate these. The deer was heading straight away and was fully ballistic, rapidly increasing the distance between us. After such a long stalk, taking this animal had become almost a matter of honor. The point of decision had been reached, and the 200-grain boat-tail was sent on its way. The gun recoiled upward, and instinctively, I worked the bolt to chamber another cartridge. As I brought the muzzle back down, all that I could see was a cloud of dust. I quickly recalled the sight picture that had been present prior to pulling the trigger. The crosshairs had been right on the back of the deer's head, the only clear target I had, just above the erect white tail. The deer had vanished.

After assuring myself that there was no longer a target in my scope, I dropped the gun from my shoulder and turned to look at Antonio. He gazed at me with big round eyes and tersely said, "Lo mato [you killed him]." This was quickly followed by his outstretched hand.

It was 104 paces from where I shot to the last running step the deer had taken. At the end of 30 feet of skid marks, he lay dead beneath a creosote bush. The bullet had entered the occiput and exited the right orbit. The skull plate was intact, because the bullet never expanded. Death had been instantaneous and unknown to this magnificent specimen of the desert whitetail.

As we stood over our deer, Antonio looked at me and said, "El que persite, mata venado [the persistent person kills the deer]."

To me, the manner in which we had pursued the stalk to a successful conclusion made the deer a great trophy. The last three seconds, after finally viewing our quarry, did not allow me to reflect upon how this animal might rank as compared to others, and it was not my primary concern. The fact that the deer's measurements also ranked it as a trophy was a bonus to the experience of taking my first Sonoran desert whitetail.

COUES' WHITETAIL DEER, TYPICAL ANTLERS
THIRD AWARD
SCORE: 119-6/8

Locality: Hidalgo Co., N.M.   Date: 1990
Hunter: Frank L. Riley

COUES' WHITETAIL DEER, TYPICAL ANTLERS 119-6/8

Frank L. Riley

Having always wanted to go kill a trophy buck of each North American species, I decided in the spring of 1990 to begin that dream by going west to hunt deer.

I live in the South, and I have hunted whitetails since I was 12. All of the magazines I read have always given a certain mystique to the Coues' deer. Called the gray ghost and a cousin to our whitetail, I wanted to hunt him first.

In the fall of 1989, I had been on a successful Alaskan moose hunt with my cousin, Lee Richardson. I called him to see if he wanted to join me, and he agreed. I started getting references and making inquiries to every outfitter and guide I could find. Several outfitters sounded good, but no one really made me enthused.

One day, I was reading the *North American Hunter*, a magazine published by the North American Hunting Club. I am a member of the club, and they had a membership drive going on, with donated hunts as incentives for recruitment. One of the donated hunts was given by Southwest Guide Service, Rt 1, Box 138, Duncan, AZ 85534. After writing, receiving their information, and thinking about their donation to help the NAHC, I decided to book my hunt with them.

I called Mike Pearce, co-owner & guide for Southwest Guide Service, several times. We talked, and I tried to build a relationship with him, since I was going to hunt with him. We were going to hunt in New Mexico, where deer tags were sold over the counter, so everything was set. About two months after booking the hunt, Mike called to say he had acquired two permits to take 30-inch-plus desert mule deer on private land. He gave us first choice on the permits, and we decided to take them.

Well, November came and we left for the desert. We met our guides and set up camp. Having never hunted in the arid Southwest, I wondered how anything could survive in such a dry place.

We hunted the private land for three days of the five-day season without spotting a trophy buck. Roundup was going on, and the ranch was using a helicopter. The chopper had scared the wits out of the deer, and they were low in the chaparral and greasewood. I had glassed until I thought I could not spot deer and wanted to change.

That night, I told Mike I had originally wanted to hunt Coues' deer and, with two days of season remaining, suggested that we move. We moved that night from rolling, rocky, open land to the foot of a mountain that looked pretty rough. The next morning we climbed up and over the mountain before first light.

At first light, I looked in a saddle and could not believe my eyes. Four eight-point bucks and a 10-point buck were making their way south. We tried to cut them off, but they got to patented land before we reached them. Two more eight-pointers were glassed by lunch time, and at 1:00 p.m., I heard my cousin shoot. At dark, he and his guide, Rex Jensen, came in with an 11-point buck that scored 106-1/8.

The next morning, determined to do something, Mike and I left camp. It was the last day of the season and time to succeed or bust. Around 10:00 that morning, Mike glassed a buck as it was bedding down. We waited for him to bed down and made our stalk to within 250 yards.

Trying to keep out of sight, we had slipped up on the buck by keeping a boulder between us. We did not know whether the buck had spooked or not. Around noon, the deer's antlers appeared over the boulder, and we both knew he was a fine trophy. I took my .240 Weatherby Magnum, shooting 100- grain Nosler Partitions, and let the legs of my bipod down.

At 1:10 p.m., the deer stood up broadside. I let out a breath, squeezed, and with the report, the deer bolted away. We climbed the canyon wall and could not believe how nice a trophy he was when we examined it.

This was truly a gratifying hunt that went to the last hour.

Photograph courtesy of Wayne W. Karling

This non-typical whitetail deer was killed near the Carrot River, Sask., in
1989 by Wayne W. Karling. It scores 198-1/8.

Photograph by William N. Toth

William N. Toth is the proud hunter of this non-typical whitetail deer near
N. Saskatchewan River, Alta., in 1988. It scores 188.

Photograph by Wm. H. Nesbitt

COUES' WHITETAIL DEER, NON-TYPICAL ANTLERS
SAGAMORE HILL AWARD
FIRST AWARD
SCORE: 155

Locality: Gila Co., Ariz.   Date: 1988
Hunter: Charles E. Erickson, Jr.

COUES' WHITETAIL DEER, NON-TYPICAL ANTLERS 155

Charles E. Erickson, Jr.

For several years, I had been helping a friend of mine by the name of Mick Holder with cow work and such on his ranch in Gila County, near Globe, Arizona. I have been in the cattle business most of my life and am an avid hunter. Until I met Mick, I had never been particularly interested in hunting the Arizona Coues' whitetail deer. He had hunted them all his life and had guided for Coues' deer and black bear for many years. He had reached the point in his life where he did not care to guide anymore. He just enjoyed hunting with friends and interesting people he had met through the years. Mick is one of the keenest and most knowledgeable observers of nature I have ever seen.

Coues' deer season in Arizona generally takes place during the last half of December. The weather is cool to cold, depending on weather systems moving through the state at the time. December of 1989 was especially good, because we had several storms and a fair amount of snow at the higher elevations. Conditions were perfect to start the Coues' deer into the rut.

We hunted a few days in rain and fog, seeing lots of deer. I had in the past killed several nice Coues' bucks and was only interested in a good trophy. The country we like to hunt is rough, steep, rocky mountain sides. They have a good combination of browse and grass but not too much brush. We like to use spotting scopes as much as possible to save time and movement. Many times, I have walked right by smart bucks and have learned to glass them up first.

We prefer to hunt with 7mm magnums, because they provide the advantage of flat trajectory for a long shot if you are unable to make a close stalk.

The fourth day of the season, I was moving through some very rough, rocky draws. I had not been able to find anything suitable with my scope that morning and had no choice but to start moving. The bucks were holding tight. Crossing the series of draws was not easy, since they are steep and remaining silent is almost impossible.

Sure enough, I heard a few rocks roll above and ahead of me and got a good look at a fine trophy buck moving out of sight in a hurry. A quick test for a records-book buck is whether his antlers are wider than his ears and his rear tines are more than 6 inches long. This buck had them but was moving fast. I could not get the shot.

I finished the day, met Mick that night, and told him what I had seen. We both agreed we should make another try for the buck the next day. There were no other hunters in the area, and we hoped he would stay close, so we could glass him up. We planned the hunt that night, though we could not agree on how to do it. We had both hunted this mountain several times. He had his ideas; I had mine.

The next morning, we were on the mountain before daylight and had another parley on how to hunt that day. Mick told me that, from his years of experience with Coues' deer, he really did not think the buck would be where I thought he would be. I finally had to modify my plan, and we started on up the mountain. I went high, and Mick stayed below me.

The higher I climbed, the more draws and other likely hiding places I wanted to check out. Anybody who has hunted whitetail deer very long knows they will hold tight. I did not follow our plan and got behind the sweep we had planned to make across the face of the mountain. I knew I was behind and was mad at myself, because Mick was out of sight, ahead and below me.

I had to cross a big, very steep rockslide. Trying to be quiet was almost impossible, but I crossed carefully and started to move forward. I had not taken three steps when a buck stood up. He was about 50 yards away and a little below me. He started running but not fast, down and away and to my right. When he first got up, I knew he was good, but when he moved a little and turned his head sideways, I could hardly see through his antlers.

Instantly, I sat down and took careful aim. My heart was in my throat as I squeezed off the shot. Click. I had forgotten to put a round in the chamber. I worked the bolt, thinking, "I'm going to get behind if I don't do it right." I took careful aim again, fired and bolted in another round. He was still moving and about 80 yards away. I fired again and bolted in another round. He kept running, but suddenly, he stopped about 125 yards away and looked back at me. I thought, "Boy, I've got to do it now." I fired again.

He turned and ran down the mountain into a draw, where he passed out of sight. I pulled one round out of my pocket and put it into the chamber, throwing the balance of the cartridges in my pocket out on the ground so I could reach them quickly if I needed them. I waited for him to show himself crossing the draw, but he did not and I moved to check for blood. I found the blood trail. He had run another 50 yards and was lying in some rocks and tall grass.

I cannot repeat the words I said, but I was literally awestruck when I saw the antlers. I just sat down and stared. Finally, I noticed that I had hit him with all three shots. That made me feel better, because I never knew whether or not I was hitting him while shooting.

I stood up and began examining his antlers. One major drop tine had been broken but was still attached by old velvet. He either broke it when he fell, or he broke it fighting. I knew it would hurt his score.

It took Mick a while to get to me. When he arrived, his mouth dropped open, and neither of us could say anything. Finally, he said, "Erickson, it looks like you have had a good December."

We finished field-dressing the buck and started off the mountain. I fell into some prickly pear on the way down, which marred a perfect day and brought me back to reality. Nothing is perfect. Of course, the argument about the buck I had seen the day before started again. I finally agreed that Mick was right, as usual, but look at the result of my disagreement.

COUES' WHITETAIL DEER, NON-TYPICAL ANTLERS
SECOND AWARD
SCORE: 132-3/8

Locality: Gila Co., Ariz.   Date: 1989
Hunter: Dale J. Little

COUES' WHITETAIL DEER, NON-TYPICAL ANTLERS 132-3/8

Dale J. Little

"When did ya get him?"

"Opening day."

"Had you seen him before the season?"

"No"

"Did you scout the area you hunted?"

"Well, kinda."

In all fairness, the Coues' whitetail I killed in December of 1989 did not come easily, but it did come with a measure of luck. In fact, luck seems to follow me when I am hunting the beautiful whitetail of the Southwest.

What else can you call it but luck when you shoot a near-record deer, after losing the trail and while trying to climb out of a box canyon before total darkness? That is just what happened a few years ago, the first time I hunted Arizona's Sierra Anchas Wilderness. That trip, with my good friend Tom Britt, now Region II Supervisor for the Arizona Game and Fish Department, introduced me to those rugged central Arizona mountains and to Leonard Cooper, who is the game department's wildlife manager for that area. Everyone took a nice buck on that trip, and it was largely due to Cooper's knowledge of the area and the deer.

All of Arizona's big game is managed on a unit by unit basis, and permit numbers are limited. Although frustrating for unlucky applicants, the system has been an undeniable success from a management standpoint. The trophy quality of the 10 species of big game is outstanding — particularly so when you consider the arid climate and often marginal habitat.

When I saw a photograph of a huge non-typical Coues' deer taken in 1988, in Unit 23, I decided then to try the Sierra Anchas again. I usually alternate mule deer one year and whitetail the next, and 1989 was a whitetail year. I discussed my plans with Tom Britt, who checked with Leonard Cooper for any tips he might have. He did not recommend the area we had previously hunted but had several other suggestions. Some were areas I was familiar with but some were not. My permit was for the last of Arizona's three whitetail seasons, during the last half of December.

After an early November mule deer hunt in Colorado, my remaining weekends were spent scouting the desert mountains. My son, Chad, and I combined the long Thanksgiving weekend into a combination scouting trip and Gambel's quail hunt. On the final scouting trip, accompanied by my horse and my hunting partner, Bob Dixon, we stood looking at a particularly rugged piece of real estate. Coues' deer live in a fairly narrow zone that seems to range about 4,000 to 6,000 feet above sea level. They are concentrated in the southeastern quarter of the state. The terrain does not get too rough or too vertical for these little gray ghosts. Bob and I had earlier spotted two small bucks near a water hole and were looking across a nasty 1,000-foot-deep canyon, up into some terrific Coues' country. Long grassy hogbacks broke in stair step fashion from the rimrocks 2,000 feet above us. As we sat and glassed, we saw no deer, but we agreed that they had to be there.

The day before the opener found me back in the same area Bob and I had glassed. After several days of mulling over the various areas we had scouted, I decided I just had to try those high grassy benches. After a few years of whitetail hunting, I have been able to define a certain type of terrain and habitat where they will be found. Whether this is true or not is not important, because when I see one of these spots I know the deer are there. It is that confidence that makes my feet climb mountains which otherwise might be beyond my endurance.

First light found me an hour away from camp and climbing. Although camping with friends is a treat of its own, I prefer hunting deer alone. This frees me to follow my own whims, instead of some pre-arranged schedule. My oversized fanny pack carried food, water, emergency gear and a Leupold 20 x 50 spotting scope. I carried my Leitz 10x40 binocular and my lightweight rifle. One of the early believers, I made up the fiberglass-stocked rifle in the late 70s. It has a Remington action, a Shilen barrel, a Brown Precision stock and is chambered for 7x57 Ackley Improved. I load with 139-grain Hornadys for deer. The scope is a Leupold 6x42. Good optics are very important for these 50 to 100-pound deer, since they are hunted more like sheep than deer. Many hours are spent behind the spotting scope.

The sun was well up before I reached my first objective. I had stopped several times to catch my breath and scan with the binocular but had seen no deer. Topping out on the first bench found me in tall grass and scattered evergreen oaks: perfect. Within five minutes, I located three deer, two does and a spike buck.

By 9 o'clock, I could see my second objective, a point from which I could glass an enormous amount of country, including a spectacular box canyon as wild and remote as I have ever seen. That was where I planned to spend the next several hours. During most of the year the search would be for bedded deer, but I hoped the rut was far enough along that deer might be active most of the day.

At exactly 9:30 a.m. two does came out of the head of a canyon and onto the face of a grassy hill about 800 yards away. Feeding slowly up the hill, they seemed unconcerned for several minutes. Then, one doe turned abruptly and went about halfway back to the canyon head. Switching to the spotting scope, I saw why. A buck stood 20 yards below her, and he was stretched out like a pointer. I could just imagine his lips curled back as he tested the wind.

This is the place where I tell you how I carefully judged the trophy quality and made a calculated decision. Wrong. The decision was immediate — big deer, heavy beams. How do I get closer?

The deer were going up the hill, with their backs to me, and there was good cover once I dropped off the point. I moved cautiously, stopping often and keeping the buck in sight. Nearing the last of the cover, I thought I was in range. I later paced the distance as 400 yards, instead of the 250 or 300 yards I thought it was. The buck was rubbing his antlers in some yucca, broadside and at the crest of the hill.

Decision time. Take off fanny pack and use for rest. Prone position best. Can't see him. Move and try again. Good view but slightly obscured by tall grass. Deep breath. Hold. Squeeze. Boom. Nothing.

Standing alert but not particularly concerned, the deer was untouched. Must have misjudged distance. Hold high on back. Squeeze. Missed again. At the second shot, the deer hesitated and then ran to the left, disappearing within a few yards. I quickly planned a route that would keep me out of sight until I reached a point above that from which the buck disappeared. When I could see where he had stood, I started forward very carefully. The hill was not large, and I knew it dropped off very sharply on the back side. My assumption was that he had jumped off the edge of the mountain, and I might be able to spot him when I reached the rim. As I neared the place where the buck had last been, he suddenly stood up. In characteristic whitetail fashion, he had hidden, instead of running. He had gone only 125 yards and had been lying in some oak brush. Instinct took over, and I very quickly shot off hand. At the shot, the deer jumped and disappeared behind the brush.

At that point, I really did not know if it as a hit, miss or wound, but all my senses were cued to the possibility of a running shot. Constantly looking ahead, I moved quickly until I suddenly saw a huge splash of blood on the flat stones at my feet. I was so intent that I had almost walked over the deer, which lay 6 feet behind me. I'll never forget the exact words that formed in my mind (or maybe I spoke them aloud): "There he is. Oh my God, he's beautiful."

Skinning the deer and leaving the meat in a tree, adrenalin took me down the mountain for the long drive back to Flagstaff and a belated appearance at my wife's office Christmas dinner. The next day, it was back up the mountain to pack out the meat. Even with Bob Dixon to help pack, it was still a chore on the steep rocky slopes.

In Flagstaff, the meeting place during hunting seasons is TR Taxidermy. Owner Tim Rajsich, who mounted my deer, is an official measurer for Arizona's Wildlife Trophies, as is my friend, Bob Dixon. We do a good deal of "hangar flying" there, with many a friendly six-pack wagered before the measuring begins. We green-scored my whitetail at least a dozen times because of the inevitable questions that come with non-typical antlers. It was finally decided the committee approach was best, with both Boone and

Crockett measurers and Arizona measurers. That way, it could go into both records books with the same score.

When the letter and score sheet came back from Eldon "Buck" Buckner, with a score of 137, I was elated. I only knew Buck by reputation, but he is known as quite a fan of the Arizona whitetail. The deer was honored by the Arizona Wildlife Federation as the annual award winner for the category, and the bronze statue that came with the award is a welcome addition to our home.

As I said, alternate years are for mule deer, so December of 1991 found me on the mountain again. At 9:32 a.m., the does came out of the same canyon. For three hours, I watched a very good buck follow the does and chase off two sub-dominant bucks. Deciding he was "King of the Hill" for that year, I made one shot count. Although short of the records with a green score of 101, his was a long- tined typical rack with almost perfect symmetry. He fell 165 paces from the location of the 1989 buck. Sometimes you just know they have to be there.

Billy Boston had the non-typical whitetail he took in Pike County, Montana, in 1990 mounted as a tribute to the trophy and the hunt. It scores 186 points.

This mule deer, typical, was killed by Jay M. Odgen in Mohave County, Arizona, in 1990. It scores 200-1/8.

Photograph by Wm. H. Nesbitt

MULE DEER, NON-TYPICAL ANTLERS
FIRST AWARD
SCORE: 264-1/8

Locality: Coconino Co., Ariz.   Date: 1989
Hunter: Gilbert T. Adams, Jr.

MULE DEER,
NON-TYPICAL ANTLERS 264-1/8

Gilbert T. Adams, Jr.

First through the binoculars, then a spotting scope. Yes. It must be him. The monster mule deer buck Jeff Warren caught a glimpse of the evening before.

When Kevin Harris and I came out of the mountains after dark, Jeff Warren met us at the designated rendezvous. Jeff was ecstatic. He said, "He's the biggest I've ever seen. It was almost dark and he was moving. I don't know how many points. I didn't have time to count them all. There are two huge drop tines coming off of each antler. There is a big bulb on the left drop. It's like dried velvet. He's in the mid-30s outside to outside."

For years Jeff, Kevin, Kim Bonnett and I have hunted out of the same camp. We have hunted trophy mule deer throughout the West. Jeff was not exaggerating. It takes a heck of a mule deer to get Jeff that excited. In camp that night, Jeff dropped his head and said, as if talking to himself, "I've always wondered if I would see one that big on the hoof. Now I have." We knew it had to be one of the biggest mule deer bucks seen in the Kaibab of Arizona for years.

After a hearty dinner, we carefully packed our daypacks. Intense planning and preparation for the next day's hunt kept the Coleman lanterns burning late in our tent. We reviewed the topo maps as a precaution. We estimated it would take at least an hour to get to where we would need to be by the first light of day. We hoped we would be able to relocate the monster as he fed on sage before slipping into the dense pinion-juniper to bed for the day. We set the alarm for 4:15 a.m., but anticipation made our sleep restless.

The next morning, through binoculars, Kevin, Jeff and I strained our eyes, trying to push back the darkness. Gradually the sunbeams came over the Royal Arches of the Grand Canyon. It was another breathtaking daybreak, but there was no time to see the sunbeams light up the Vermillion Cliffs. Total concentration was needed to literally take apart each pinion and juniper.

Suddenly, there was a terrific-looking buck on the horizon. With increasing light, Kevin was able to use his 20x50 spotting scope. The heat waves had the giant rack dancing on the head of the distant buck. After a mere glimpse of the buck through the scope, Kevin said, "I believe that's him. It must be him. Let's go!"

Feeding on sagebrush, moving toward a dense sanctuary of pinion-juniper some one-quarter mile away, was our quarry. Was it possible to close the distance in time? The wind was in our faces. Fortunately, the rising sun was on our backs, because time did not allow a cautious stalk. Things were going according to plan so far.

Where was he? Had the gray ghost given us the slip? After all, they do not get big by being stupid. A draw and a ridge lay just ahead. Could he be in the draw? A two-point appeared. Had the giant buck in the scope been a mirage? We were about to head in a different direction when we heard the tinkling of rocks. Running out of the draw with their afterburners ablaze, heading for the top of the next ridge, were four does. In seconds, they disappeared into the pinion-juniper cover. Then, two bucks appeared, running in the same direction as the does. Was the buck with the six deer? Yes, there he was. Unmistakably, El Muy Grande.

The two bucks were running through the first trees of the cover. There were only seconds left; they were 200 yards away. There was no time to look through the binoculars to count points, measure a spread, or field-score the buck. It would be the shot of a lifetime. The moment of truth had come. Would I go home with a trophy or an alibi?

In moments like that, you draw on the refined hunting instincts that you have developed through years of preparation and experience: the countless hunts for all sorts of game; the hours at the rifle range and at the computer with Bullet Simulator; the innumerable articles read; the fantasies and the physical training; and, of course, the many hunts when you came home with nothing, not because you did not see bucks, but because you did not find the buck that was a trophy in "your book."

I did not feel the recoil or hear the sound bursting from the muzzle of my Brent White Special .300 Weatherby Magnum, custom loaded to propel the 150-grain Hornady Spitzer at 3,315 feet per second. Through the 2.5- 8x Leupold scope, I saw the mighty buck instantly untracked from a headlong run in the window-like opening between two junipers. Big bucks are famous for resurrecting from the dead. After watching through my rifle scope and waiting for what seemed like an eternity, I was certain that this buck was down for the count.

A total rush overcame us as we reached the side of the incredible monarch. At first, we stared and then reverently touched the magnificent horns. There were two huge drop tines and points everywhere. The rack was dark in color, like smoked metal. There were rough, gnarled bases and bladed tines. The left drop tine was covered in rawhide velvet. There was even rawhide velvet on the back side of one bladed tine that the buck had never been able to scrape off. It was immediately apparent that we were looking at a "book head." The moment had sanctity that words cannot adequately express. Kevin, Jeff and I wanted to savor the moment for as long as possible. We knew that no matter how long we lived, no matter where we hunted, or how good we thought our skills were, there would not be another moment just like this one.

While the three of us revelled in the moment, we felt the presence of one whose physical absence was noteworthy. This person, a dear friend and hunting companion, was slowly recovering from a quirky, spontaneous tear in his lung, which had just weeks before brought him into the valley of death. That was the only reason he was not physically present. As we continued to study his rack, with its 14 points on the left, 15 on the right, and nearly 35 inches of outside spread, it seemed incredible that a buck could grow such magnificent antlers in a matter of six months. He would only have worn the regalia for another three months before returning it to nature. He was thin, without an ounce of fat. There was little hair on his knees or belly. It was obvious that he would have never made it through the winter. In 24 hours, he would weigh-in, field dressed, at 145 pounds. Later a careful examination of his molars would establish his age at 6-1/2 years.

A world's record of the species must always be carefully preserved and made available for general educational purposes, as well as for wildlife enthusiasts and admirers of mule deer to appreciate and study. With this object in mind, we were careful not to damage the hide or head while packing him out.

As soon as we could get to a phone, we placed a call to master taxidermist Ken Rowe, owner of The Arts of Wildlife studios in Phoenix, Arizona. He agreed to meet us at his shop. Ken's approach is that of a meticulous artisan. With detailed measurements, photographs and reference casting, Ken captured the unique qualities, features and attitude that is unique to every animal. The result is a beautiful preservation for posterity to see and enjoy.

A significant part of the hunting experience is knowing the hunting grounds. What is called Kaibab North is isolated and remote country, above the Grand Canyon in north-central Arizona. After the Pleistocene, many life forms became isolated on the plateau when the Colorado River formed the Grand Canyon barrier on the south side, and an arid climate produced desert conditions on the other three sides. The Kaibab Plateau extends 60 miles, north and south and approximately 45 miles, east and west.

While most of us think of the area as mountainous, in reality, the area lives up to its Indian name, kaibab, or "mountain lying down." Flatness dominates the area, with numerous volcanic peaks and hills haphazardly sliced by eroded canyons and large winter-range valleys. All but 120 square miles are above 6,000 feet elevation. The highest point is 9,200 feet and the lowest is about 3,000 feet.

Before the state of Arizona began enforcing the law north of the Grand Canyon, this was an area where outlaws hid from the law and lay in ambush for anyone daring to follow them. There has never been a large settlement of either Indians or white man in the Kaibab North.

Throughout the past century, there has been little change in the physical environment of the plateau, other than vegetative variations, due to drought, livestock and deer population levels. There have, for instance, been no significant farms, orchards, dwellings or other obstructions to alter migration routes. Except for an occasional roadway or jeep trail, a person exploring the Kaibab North will find it the way it was 100 years ago.

Even today, in an era of rapid transportation, the Kaibab is relatively isolated. A trip to the Kaibab North is a major undertaking for most hunters. However, more important than time is the requirement of winning the Arizona draw in order to obtain a hunt permit, the results of which are learned only weeks before the hunt begins.

There is a decided lack of available water in the area. If it were not for the man-made livestock and wildlife water catchments, much of the wildlife would not exist. Thus, biologists label the Kaibab North as "fringe country" in regard to wildlife. Wildlife must be carefully surveyed on an annual basis; game and livestock populations, and their general health, must be evaluated along with the habitat.

The North Kaibab is an area renowned for large bucks with many non-typical points. The habitat challenges, coupled with relatively sparse game populations, Arizona's restricted permit system, and dedicated management by the Arizona Fish and Game Department all combine to allow individual bucks to reach the maximum of their genetic potential. As a consequence, the Kaibab produces some of the largest racks on the North American continent.

There are two additional, significant factors that must have recognition. One is the proverbial hunter's luck. The other is the millions of hunters and wildlife conservationists, biologists and public officials, all of whom help make moments like this possible today, and most importantly, to occur in the future.

Photograph courtesy of Frank J. Cecelic

Frank J. Cecelic is all smiles with his typical Coues' whitetail taken while hunting in Gila County, Arizona, in 1989. It scores 108-1/8.

Photograph courtesy of Mitchell A. Thorson

Mitchell A. Thorson and friends with his typical Coues' whitetail from Sonora, Mexico, in 1988. It scores 109-3/8.

Photograph by Wm. H. Nesbitt

MULE DEER, NON-TYPICAL ANTLERS
CERTIFICATE OF MERIT
SCORE: 321-1/8

Locality: Umatilla Co., Oreg.   Date: 1925
Hunter: Albert C. Peterson   Owner: Don Schaufler

MULE DEER, NON-TYPICAL ANTLERS 321-1/8

Albert C. Peterson, hunter
Don Schaufler, owner

[This story was adapted from an account by Albert C. Peterson's great-grandson, David Ayars.]

At various times in his life, Albert C. Peterson was a trapper, stage driver, mail carrier, rodeo performer, businessman and rancher. He was also a hunter.

In 1926, Peterson and his wife, Ruth, were living on a ranch five miles north of Ukiah, California. Late in the fall of that year, he invited his brother-in-law, Bill Huddleston, to accompany him on a deer hunt. Before leaving on the hunt, he told several family members that he was going after a big deer, one he had heard of from friends and neighbors.

Peterson and Huddleston saddled their horses, shoved their Winchester .30-30s into the saddle scabbards, and left the ranch. After crossing a long valley, they climbed into a low range of mountains to reach an area known as the Sugarbowl.

Huddleston drove the rims of a canyon, while Peterson waited on stand. Within a short time, Peterson heard the crashing of a big buck, as it came through a brushy ravine. When the deer appeared, two shots from the .30-30 brought him down.

After field-dressing the deer, the two men returned to the ranch, arriving before dark. There, they told the story of the hunt to their very surprised wives.

Albert C. Peterson died in 1930, following an illness. When his wife died in 1983, the big buck was passed on to their only daughter, Dorene; she, in turn, gave it to her grandson, David Ayars.

61

COLUMBIA BLACKTAIL DEER
FIRST AWARD
SCORE: 170

Locality: Jackson Co., Oreg.   Date: 1989
Hunter: Wayne Despain

COLUMBIA BLACKTAIL DEER 170

Wayne Despain

Hunting and fishing has always been a major part of my life. I have lots of great memories of fun times with my dad, my brother and my Uncle Jay. For years, we have hunted all over the state of Oregon for elk and deer. We win some years and lose others, but no matter what the outcome, we have enjoyed the woods and each other through the years.

I have always been the lucky one, when it comes to hunting, or that is what people say. I agree, maybe because I feel so close to nature and the woods. I always have hunted hard when I did hunt, but I have paid my dues by going to the woods often, just looking for deer and elk.

My wife, Lyn, and I drive up into the mountains as much as possible to watch the game and learn their habits. I believe this gives me that small, extra advantage when it comes time for hunting season.

A few years ago, we lived in Alaska. During those years, I was not able to hunt, because I was too busy running the family business. It is really sad that I spent a great deal of time in that hunter's paradise and never fired a shot.

Needless to say, I was excited to move back to Oregon so that I could take early morning and evening drives to the woods, looking for deer and elk.

Since then, I have done some serious hunting, trying to make up for those years that I lost while living in Alaska, I have been very fortunate. I took my first Boone and Crockett buck, which scored 159-2/8, and a trophy Roosevelt's elk.

I have a good friend, Andy, who wanted a chance at shooting a nice buck, and he wanted me to share with him the secret of where they are found. I don't have to be asked twice if I want to go to the woods. The answer is always "yes."

One overcast October morning, just before dawn, we drove to my favorite hunting spot, in the Evan Creek area. Andy promised me that he would keep the secret of this hunting area between the two of us. We started hunting at daylight, going our separate ways.

After a while, we regrouped. We were not having much luck. It was then that I saw the buck. I could not believe my eyes. I slowly and quietly tried to direct Andy to the silhouette of the huge deer in the brush. I wanted Andy to get a shot at the trophy buck, but he simply could not see him.

The buck was coy. He had probably escaped many hunters in surviving long enough to reach his great size. He started walking away; then he began to run into dense timber. I decided to take my shot at him, since Andy still had not seen him.

I shot, and Andy yelled, "Did you get him?"

I told him I had and that the buck was up on the hill, in the brush. Andy ran to him first, and he was amazed; so was I. He kept saying, "Look at the size of his horns." My only regret was that Andy did not get the shot. We field-dressed the deer, packed it off the mountain, and headed home. I had another lucky day of hunting, and I feel fortunate to have killed another big buck within half a mile of where I killed my first Boone and Crockett records book buck. Many hunters spend thousands of dollars on guided hunts, and they never know whether or not they will have a fascinating story to tell when they return home.

I still am running a family business, but now I make sure to take time to hunt and enjoy the woods as often as possible.

Photograph courtesy of Ann F. Pope

This Columbia blacktail was killed in Jackson County, Oregon, in 1989
by hunter Ann F. Pope. It scores 130-6/8.

Photograph courtesy of Mickey C. Haynes

Hunter Mickey C. Haynes (left) and owner Travis J. Harver (right)
show their trophy Columbia blacktail from Jackson County,
Oregon, in 1989. It scores 160-3/8.

Photograph by Wm. H. Nesbitt

COLUMBIA BLACKTAIL DEER
SECOND AWARD
SCORE: 165-6/8

Locality: Curry Co., Oreg.   Date: 1988
Hunter: Si Pellow
(Hunting Story Not Available)

Photograph courtesy of Tami M. VanNess

This non-typical whitetail was taken by Tami M. VanNess in
Latah County, Idaho, in 1990, It scores 186-7/8.

Photograph courtesy of Richard C. Nelson

Richard C. Nelson was hunting in Provost, Alta., in 1990, where he took
this non-typical whitetail. It scores 230-7/8.

Photograph by Wm. H. Nesbitt

COLUMBIA BLACKTAIL DEER
CERTIFICATE OF MERIT
SCORE: 167-2/8

Locality: Lewis Co., Wash.   Date: 1976
Hunter: Maurice D. Heldreth

COLUMBIA BLACKTAIL DEER
167-2/8

Maurice D. Heldreth

The tail end of Washington State's 1975 elk season found me headed out of the high country south of the small town of Randle, in eastern Lewis county. It was late, but the cold and fatigue I had experienced earlier in the day had been offset in a way that only a large set of 7x6 elk antlers and a pickup load of elk meat can.

On the long drive out, I was brought back to reality by a large blacktail buck crossing the Forest Service road in my headlights. He was one nice buck. He scrambled up the bank on the uphill side of the road and was quickly swallowed by the inky blackness in the old-growth timber. The place where the buck had disappeared is called Blue Lake Ridge. I was very familiar with this particular ridge, because my father and I had hunted it off and on since 1946.

Over the years we had taken several nice bucks there. In 1951, I had killed a 3x4, and in 1955, I had shot a beauty of a 4x4. Both of them were heavy-horned old monarchs. Spurred by the sight of that nice buck, I made plans right then to hunt the top of Blue Lake Ridge on the season opener in 1976.

October 1976 found me headed south from my home in Puyallup. The evening before opening day, I slept in my Ford pickup at the Blue Lake Ridge trailhead. After a fitful night, I arose in the pre-dawn darkness to start my ascent of the ridge in order to be on top, where I wanted to start hunting, at daylight.

The season opener turned up lots of does and a couple of small bucks. Although I was primarily hunting for meat, I passed up the two small bucks. It was too early in the season, and I was having too much fun.

The second day again found me headed up the trail before dawn. The difference, however, was the presence of a skiff of snow. As I made my way up the trail, the snow gradually got a little deeper. The white stuff was almost 3 inches deep on top. As I neared the top of the ridge, I saw a large set of deer tracks. A buck had crossed the trail not long before. He had headed downhill through the old growth timber for quite a way before turning and roughly paralleling the main trail. At that point, his tracks became very hard to follow as he meandered through the timber, feeding.

Several deer had cut across the sidehill, and it was only a matter of time before I lost his tracks in the jumbled maze of deer sign. I finally picked out what I guessed to be his tracks where they came out on a small hogback in the timber. I had followed the tracks down the small ridge only a short distance when I jumped a heavy deer in the timber right in front of me.

I hot-footed it over to the south side of the hogback. I wanted to see if I could get a peek at the deer as he went off the back side. To my surprise, he was standing only a short distance from where I had jumped him. He was in a patch of small hemlock trees, with only bits and pieces of his body showing. I picked out the grey nose and one ear. When I put my scope on the deer to see if I could grow horns, I was rewarded with a glimpse of one large antler base protruding above the ear. That was enough for me. I slipped the crosshairs back to an opening in the hemlocks near his shoulders and sent a 150-grain Nosler on its way. The buck bolted at the shot and was quickly swallowed up by the trees. I jacked another cartridge in and went down through the trees where I had last seen him. He was piled up only 40 yards from where the bullet had taken him through both lungs.

What a deer! I have had opportunities to observe many large blacktail bucks in my life, both dead and alive, but nothing compared to the monster lying at my feet. He was a basic 4x4 with a few small kicker points thrown in, but the amazing thing was the heft of his antlers. Each point reminded me of a banana. After field-dressing the deer, I took his head and a load of boned-out meat and packed them back down to my truck at the trailhead. The next day I went back in and retrieved the rest of the meat before heading back home to Puyallup. I was one happy hunter.

Buzz Cook, a taxidermist and official scorer from Kirkland, Washington, did the taxidermy work on the deer for me. He also measured the antlers for the S.C.I. records book. The buck is currently listed as the top Columbia blacktail buck in the S.C.I. records book.

The head had bounced around with me for about 15 years, and the mount had suffered in the process. My son, Keith, had a friend in Olympia, Washington, Alden Johnson, who re-mounted the head with a fresh cape in 1991. At the same time, he took the buck's antlers back to Buzz in Kirkland to be scored for the Boone and Crockett records book. After the initial scoring, my buck's antlers were given a final score of 167-2/8.

Photograph courtesy of Kenneth N. Tucker

Kenneth N. Tucker is astride his typical mule deer from Pitkin County,
Colorado, in 1990. It scores 187-7/8.

Photograph courtesy of Thomas Aasbo

Somewhere in Kit Carson County, Colorado, Thomas Aasbo hunted
this typical mule deer in 1990. It scores 188.

COLUMBIA BLACKTAIL DEER
CERTIFICATE OF MERIT
SCORE: 160-3/8

Locality: Jackson Co., Oreg.   Date: 1989
Hunter: Mickey C. Haynes   Owner: Travis J. Harvey

COLUMBIA BLACKTAIL DEER 160-3/8

Mickey C. Haynes, hunter
Travis J. Harvey, owner

It was the day after Thanksgiving, 1989. You were two years and nine months old. We had had a delicious and enjoyable Thanksgiving with lots of company: great grandmas, grandpas, uncles, and cousins. I had been talking about going hunting the next day. You asked to go.

We got started the next morning around 8:30 or 9:00, after Nana Bon had made pancakes for breakfast and some snacks for your backpack. As we started to load up the old yellow truck, Nana Bon came out to take pictures. Then you wanted to take Gunner, our Australian shepherd.

As the three of us climbed into the truck, things started going through my mind. Do I need to take this old muzzleloading gun or just a walking stick? Would we see anything? Would it be right to shoot if we did? But then I decided that just seeing a deer would make a great day.

We drove a few miles up the road and parked at a fellow's place that bordered Bureau of Land Management land. I had seen a nice buck there the year before and had gained permission to go through the private land.

As we arrived, a light, misting rain started to fall. I loaded my .54 caliber muzzleloader and prepared it for wet weather. Fog hung to the trees so that the top of the ridge, three-quarters of a mile above us, could not be seen.

My plan was to climb to the top of the ridge and follow the trail along the top that led back down to the house.

Making our way to the top of the ridge became quite a challenge for you. The buck brush was so thick that, at times, we had to crawl. Broken limbs seemed like logs for you to climb over. A few times you slipped on the wet ground and rolled down the grade, at which point you would comment: "Mick, I can't handle it."

I could not help laughing, but all the while, I kept thinking that we were going to see a deer any minute. Not a chance though; Gunner had already been up the hill, to the right, to the left, and checked back in with us to see what was taking so long. Despite our difficulty, she was having a great time. About a quarter of a mile from the top, we caught a deer trail and you rode on my back the rest of the way up. I was beat, so we sat on a log for awhile and ate your snacks. The fog was lifting and it had stopped raining. The rest of the trail would be easy and a whole lot quieter.

We had not been walking long when I saw a big buck standing out on a point, looking down the hill. I knelt down on my knee and took aim, realizing that he was too far away. You asked, "Why didn't you shoot him Mick?"

I chuckled and told you he was too far away. The trail then headed downward, along the side of the ridge. The three of us quietly made our way down the trail and stopped about forty feet from where the buck had been standing.

I whispered: "Travis you hold Gunner, I'll walk ahead." I removed the sandwich bag that I used to keep my powder dry from the hammer. As I reached the point, I looked up the hill, and there, in an opening, stood the buck. He was only about 75 yards away, headed up the hill, with his big rack and head turned back, looking right at me.

I slowly pulled up, aimed and set the trigger, all at the same time. I could not shoot him in the head, so I decided to go for his neck. There was a thunderous blast, and when the smoke had cleared, I saw the deer angling up the hill in a trot. As he neared the top, he stopped, looked back and then disappeared over the hill.

I was shaking. Could I have missed? I couldn't have missed, but he was gone. Then, I turned back to check on you and Gunner. Gunner had vanished, and you were still grasping your ears. I walked unsteadily back to where you were, and asked if you were okay. You replied "Mick, you didn't tell me you were going to shoot!"

I laughed and called Gunner back. She was shaking as much as I was. Then I reloaded my gun, hoping the buck had not gone far. We walked out into the clearing, and I asked you and Gunner to wait for me once more. Not wanting to leave you alone long, I ran to where the deer had gone over the hill. I was ready and anxious to see him again. There was nothing in sight.

I walked down the hill a little further, checking for signs of a wound, but found nothing. But then, as I turned to head back, there he lay just ten feet or so from where he had gone over the top of the hill. I was really excited and amazed at the size of his antlers. He was the biggest buck I had ever shot.

I hurried back to get you and Gunner. It must have seemed like forever for you, although I had been out of your sight for no more than five minutes. You had tears in your eyes; the dog was still at your side. I picked you up and gave you a big hug.

You asked: "Did you see him Mick?"

I replied: "Oh yes, I saw him. He's just over the hill."

Still in my arms, I carried you to where the deer lay. As I set you down, both you and Gunner reacted in nearly the same way. She sniffed while inching closer, and you asked "Will he get up, Mick?"

After admiring the size of the deer and the large rack, the task of field dressing began. The 220-grain round ball had hit high on the right hip and stopped at the heart. It was a wonder he even took another step.

After disabling the gun, we both grabbed an antler and tugged the big buck back to the top of the hill. Though it was all downhill from there, the task wasn't quite that easy. I would carry you ahead, and then go back to drag the deer, all the while carrying the gun. On one steep, wet grade, the tables turned, and the deer was dragging me. You thought that funny as you watched from below.

After several hundred feet back and forth, I decided to hide the deer in the brush and go for help. There was still more than a mile between us and the house, so leaving the deer behind, we dawdled our way home, throwing some rocks, resting some, playing with Gunner, and talking about the deer.

We arrived at the house at 2:00 p.m., and I promptly phoned my brother for assistance. Your Uncle Frank and Aunt Diane drove us to where my truck was parked. Diane left, and the three of us returned for the deer. You talked the whole way, telling your uncle about what had happened.

After some explanation from Uncle Frank as to location on the ridge, you pointed up the hill with your stubby finger. We've laughed about that many times since that day. We took some pictures and headed home with our prize.

Travis, I've had many a memorable hunt, although to this date, this one tops them all. To you I dedicate the deer mount and this story. Remember, should you choose to be a hunter, always be safe, give fair chase, and if you elect not to pull the trigger, that will be okay, too.

Papa Mick.

Photograph by Wm. H. Nesbitt

COLUMBIA BLACKTAIL DEER
CERTIFICATE OF MERIT
SCORE: 159-2/8
Locality: Whatcom Co., Wash.   Date: 1963
Hunter: Paul A. Braddock

COLUMBIA BLACKTAIL DEER
159-2/8

Paul A. Braddock

The deer hunt was in 1963, during my tour of duty with the military, in the state of Washington. I enjoy hunting and nature very much, so the suggestion of a blacktail deer hunt with friends in the Mt. Baker Wilderness was exciting. I had no expectation of seeing a trophy deer, such as those shown in the brochures from the game commission, and I definitely did not expect to take one that would be recognized by the Boone and Crockett Club.

We set up camp near a trail, and that night we were engulfed by about 10 inches of snow. I prefer to hunt alone, so I told my friends I was going toward the top of the mountain to get away from other hunters and generally check the area for game.

About three hours later, I jumped a single deer that left big tracks a large bed. I was astonished at the size of the tracks and decided to pursue them, since the possibility of it being a buck was apparent.

After four hours of tracking through windfalls, circling and backtracking, I began to wonder who was hunting whom. The distance back to camp, with limited daylight remaining, was causing me concern.

While standing in place and contemplating the situation, I saw a movement about 45 yards away, coming toward me through the windfall. I could make out a large deer with antlers. He continued toward me, then stopped in a small clearing. The moment when I saw the size of his rack was one of the most beautiful experiences of my life.

I leveled the Winchester bolt-action .30-06 on the shoulder area and squeezed the trigger. The 180-grain bullet was accurate, and he dropped immediately.

Since I had no other means of taking the deer back to camp, I began the drag. Due to the windfall and other natural obstacles, it was a difficult and time-consuming task. After dark I hung the deer in a tree and marked my way back to camp.

When I informed my hunting companions of the buck's size, the disbelief was noticeable. Disbelief became amazement when I arrived in camp with the deer the following afternoon.

As we were leaving the area, we stopped for fuel near Everett, Washington, and I will never forget an older gentleman who looked at the deer and said, "You could hunt your whole life and never see another deer like that one." Still, I had no idea the buck was such a fine trophy until 28 years later. While in Joe Riggs Sporting Goods, in Waynesburg, Pennsylvania, looking at his copy of the Boone and Crockett Club's *Records of North American Big Game*, I mentioned the Columbia blacktail I had taken and said it looked a lot like the trophy deer pictured. Joe told me to bring the deer in for him to see. After he examined the trophy, he suggested having it measured for official scoring by the club, and I was, to say the least, very pleased with the result.

Photograph courtesy of Richard S. Mansker

Richard S. Mansker took this massive non-typical mule deer in Washington County, Utah, in 1990. It scores 251-6/8.

Photograph courtesy of Edward B. Franceschi, Jr.

This typical mule deer was killed by Edward B. Franceschi, Jr., in Kane County, Utah, in 1990. It scores 191.

Photograph by Wm. H. Nesbitt

SITKA BLACKTAIL DEER
FIRST AWARD
SCORE: 118-3/8

Locality: Prince of Wales Island, Alaska   Date: 1987
Hunter: Johnnie R. Laird

SITKA BLACKTAIL DEER
118-3/8

Johnnie R. Laird

The date was November 16, 1987. I walked from the house at around 9:00 a.m., as I do on such fall hunts. It was just getting light enough to see. The weather was cold and had been for several days, with the temperature around 20 degrees Fahrenheit for a daily high, a light snow drifting, and very little wind. Our season had a couple of weeks left in it.

I still had one harvest ticket left on the yearly bag limit of three antlered deer. It had been a good season for me, with a 3x4 in September and a 4x4 in October. Both were nice, sizable bucks. It seemed to be the year I was pulling the trigger on the big boys, though I usually pass up the larger bucks for a spike or a fork; the quality of the meat is better, and they are easier to get back home.

It was a good day for a hunt. The snow was not crusted over and noisy, but was powdery, dry and quiet instead. We are not used to such conditions in this usually wet, sea-level climate.

I started moving slowly as soon as I hit the trail because of fresh deer tracks in the powder. The deer are scattered that time of year and can be found anywhere from the beach to the upper elevations. The rut is just winding down. Browse and snow depth usually determine where the deer are, if the wolves have not been after them in a particular area.

I started my climb from the gradual grade of the abandoned logging road to the very steep game trail that seems like a million-step staircase, straight up. Because of the ice and snow, the footing was poor. I moved very slowly, looking over the hillside as I went.

Several deer had been through the area during the long fall nights as evidenced by their zigzagging tracks in the snow. The light snow drifted down through the canopy of spruce, hemlock and cedar, and as I continued upward, the snow gradually deepened. I like to take deer on the lower part of the mountain, because getting them home is less work, but there were none in that area.

I came to one of the hardest parts of the mountain, a series of 100 to 200-foot cliffs, with one steep game trail leading through the rocks and boulders. I decided to go on up and

81

over. Once on top of this difficult climb, the terrain flattens, with draws, small outcrops, good sized timber, windfalls, and a few openings grown in with berry bushes and devil's club. There were fresh deer tracks in the area. I have taken several nice bucks within a 200 yard radius in years past.

I moved over to an outcrop that I always check. I wanted to stop, take a rest and eat a snack. I noticed a fresh cedar top that had been snapped out of the tree by one of our latest big blows. Taking a closer look, I saw a mass of tracks and several beds in the immediate area. I still had not seen deer one and was beginning to think it was not the day.

I sat down on the fresh windfall and started munching on a frozen peanut butter, honey and chocolate chip sandwich. I tried my bleating deer call, making a series of calls while snacking and resting. It does not take long, once you quit moving, to freeze up, so my stop was short. It was about 1:30 p.m. by then — time to turn around and hunt back to the wood stove. Twilight and darkness come early on those short fall days.

I noticed a small draw leading around the devil's club patch I had just climbed through on the way to my perch. While down in the draw, I noticed a movement. Looking closer, I saw a big buck, about 25 yards away, with his nose buried in the thigh-deep snow. He was smelling my trail. I will never forget the eye-to-eye contact as he looked up, nose covered with powder to his eyes. He started and jumped behind a large spruce, totally out of sight.

I took a moment to clean my Leupold Vari-X II 2-7x, made sure it was on 2x, and checked for ice packed in the muzzle. I was ready.

He came stomping out from behind the spruce to check out the call I had just made, and my old .270 Winchester Model 721 Remington did the job again.

I did not realize the size and symmetry of the antlers at first. My main concern was to get the buck home before dark. After some very hard work, I was down to the level of the mountain where I could give my wife, Fran, a shout. By then, she knew I probably had a deer or I would have already been home. She was ready to drive the pickup closer and hike up the old logging grade, accompanied by our dog, Beaver.

I cannot remember the exact words she used to describe the deer when she saw it at the trailhead, but that was when I realized he was a dandy. Even though I am personally not much on mounted game, after having it scored by Bob Wood in Ketchikan, I decided to have Randy Jahnke of Southeastern Taxidermy make a shoulder mount. Now I have another excuse to pass up the 4x4s in those rugged, remote places if I do not think they will top a score of 118-3/8.

Photograph courtesy of Michael M. Golightly

Michael M. Golightly is holding his Columbia blacktail deer from Humboldt County, California, in 1990. It scores 135-5/8.

Photograph courtesy of Dean A. Bender

This Columbia blacktail deer was killed in Pierce County, Washington, in 1990 by Dean A. Bender. It scores 131-3/8.

Photograph by Wm. H. Nesbitt

SITKA BLACKTAIL DEER
SECOND AWARD
SCORE: 114-3/8

Locality: Hobart Bay, Alaska   Date: 1988
Hunter: Terry LaFrance

SITKA BLACKTAIL DEER
114-3/8

Terry LaFrance

O.K., say you are after a trophy whitetail. You have at your disposal thousands of articles of habits and hunting techniques. There is enough scientific data to keep you in school for four years.

When you are after a trophy blacktail, you find that there is not a lot in print about these ghosts of the dark, wet timber. Whether it is the Columbia blacktail of the Pacific Northwest or the Sitka blacktail of Alaska, nothing except a lot of time and effort in the woods will help you track down a good buck. I know, because I have been hunting these animals for the last 20 years.

In 1986, I found myself moving from Washington state to Hobart Bay, Alaska. Hobart Bay is a logging camp located 80 miles south of Juneau, on the mainland. I was cutting timber, and in the fall of 1989, I was cutting a right-of-way for a new logging road.

It was in August that I cut through a small saddle of a long ridge and found a lot of rubbed trees. I took some time, scouted up the ridge, and found that a very nice buck had been calling that place home for a long time.

Well, a few months passed, and the road was built into the area. I checked with a few of the truck drivers, and they confirmed that the buck was still around.

I was aware of what it takes to make the book, having taken a big 3x3 with a drop p int that green-scored about 107 points. I was ready to spend all of my time hunting the area of the rubs I had found in August, looking for "the big 4-point," as he had come to be known.

Camp had shut down in early November, so I spent a lot of time learning his area and his habits. It was not until Thanksgiving morning that all of my time and effort paid off. I left camp well before daylight, but the old truck I was using broke down about a mile from where I wanted to be at first light. Out I jumped and threw on my daypack and started hiking up the road. Six inches of new snow had fallen that night, which made a total of a foot and a half of prime tracking snow. The sky was just starting to clear up and the sun was hitting the tops of all the snow-covered peaks of Admiralty Island.

With one last look at daybreak, I stepped into the open timber and started still hunting.

Conditions were perfect: no wind, no sounds and the temperature was about 15 degrees. I dropped off the ridge into a small muskeg. I had found that the deer would feed along the thick huckleberry brush in the opening and bed in the dark timber. My plan was to skirt the feeding grounds until I cut his track and trail him in the deep snow.

I had a tough time getting through the head-high, snow-laden huckleberry brush. I jumped a lot of deer, and they all did the same thing. They took me through the thickest, wettest jungle imaginable before heading through an opening of felled timber to a brushy knob, where they were very safe. I was four hours into the game. My wool clothing was wet and heavy, and I still had not found his track. I took one more big circle back up to the ridge, and that is when I jumped him out of his bed.

He was not spooked, so I stayed off his tracks about 20 feet to the uphill side. I trailed him about 200 yards. Then, I caught him watching his backtrail, but I could not get off a shot.

We had seen each other and he wanted to lose me for good. I pushed him hard to make sure of his direction and then bailed off the ridge to a road down below. As soon as I hit it, I took off as hard as I could to try to cut him off before he made it to the brushy knob.

I slowed down to catch my breath as I approached the felled timber, where I thought he might cross. As I eased my way through the opening, I saw a deer, standing broadside, from the shoulders back. I raised up my .263 Saber, but through my 2.5-8x Leupold scope, I could not see the head; it was blocked by a big, snowy limb. Then, well above the limb, I made out the fork of an antler. I knew that this was not just a forked-horn buck but the back half of something big.

The crosshairs dropped to a point behind the shoulder, and I squeezed the trigger. The deer made one bound and all was quiet. I marked the spot and went to find the deer.

The snow was very deep, and I found neither deer nor blood. I returned to the site of the shot to check my position, but all was right. The deer should have been where I was, but it was not.

I did not think I could have missed a 70-yard shot. As I looked around, I noticed a black object under some brush and snow. In the buck's dying leap, he dislodged a lot of snow and completely buried himself, with just his back hoof showing.

I smiled, slowly started pulling him out of the snow, and got my first good look at his rack. He had height, width, a lot of mass, and the right number of points.

I then took a moment and gave thanks to the Good Lord for the hunt and the animal he had allowed me to take. I opened my daypack and took a few photos, notched my tag and field-dressed the buck.

After a short drag and an hour's drive, I was back at camp. The buck was quite run down from the rut. He weighed 120 pounds, and his teeth were very worn.

It was the best Thanksgiving I have ever had. In the spring, I sent the antlers to the fish and game department in Juneau. They scored 113-2/8, and that was enough to make the records book. The buck is hanging on my wall now, and the hunt is forever in my mind.

Photograph by Wm. H. Nesbitt

AMERICAN ELK, TYPICAL ANTLERS
FIRST AWARD
SCORE: 389-5/8
Locality: Park Co., Mont.   Date: 1990
Hunter: Butch Kuflak

AMERICAN ELK, TYPICAL ANTLERS 389-5/8

Butch Kuflak

This was my third hunt with Tom and Tim Wilkes and their Beyond Yellowstone outfit.

On arrival at the Gallatin Airport in Boseman, Montana, my friend and hunting partner, Dr. Jay Reno, and I were met by Bob Wilkes. After a few hearty handshakes, we collected our gear and were off to his house to meet his lovely wife, Judy. There, we enjoyed an excellent meal.

We had plenty of time to sight in our rifles and sort our gear before packing into the back country north of Yellowstone National Park the next day.

By 10:00 the following morning, the horses were taking us on a breathtaking 18 mile ride, deep into the snow-covered Absorka Wilderness. Jay's position behind me was never in doubt as the clicking of his camera gave him away. He would later confess that he had never taken so many pictures before in his life. It is beautiful country, postcard material. With all the preparations and anticipations of this type of adventure, it is a crime not to preserve these memories with a few photographs. Alas, I, too, plead guilty.

There was smoke rising from the wood-burning stove of the cook's tent as we rode into camp some six hours later. We savored the hot coffee as we unpacked our gear and rolled out our sleeping bags. Once again, I found myself with a good bunch of guys who very much enjoy the outdoors and the challenge of elk hunting.

Around 3:30 the next morning, Tom Wilkes poked his head into our tent and fired up the wood-burning stove. I greeted him with my usual salvo, "Hold the noise down!" He grinned when he told me I would be riding Widowmaker.

A few moments later, we were having a good, hot breakfast, prepared by Jane and MaryAnn Wilkes. This is a family affair, and you are part of it from day one.

Sunday was the first day of our hunt. Jay and I followed Tom into the darkness for a couple of hours before tieing up the horses and heading out on foot. Our plan was to try and cut some tracks as we climbed from the base of a mountain.

Jay and I both did our part to get ready for this trip. We ran and exercised for months in advance. For stealth and warmth, we were all wearing wool.

Tom did his part as well. Later in the day, he spotted two of bulls feeding on another mountain. It was too late to go after them, but we thought we might pay them a visit the next day.

As we rode into camp that evening, we were doing our elk chant, hoping all the powers that be would put us into the elk tomorrow.

Good luck had already arrived. Keith Pratt, from Pennsylvania, had put the super sneak on a heavy 6x6 bull, tracking him to where he had bedded. We were all happy for Keith, albeit a little envious, perhaps.

After a delicious meal and a good night's sleep, we were eager to find those bulls. As we criss-crossed the mountain, trying to cut their tracks, we finally stopped for lunch and did some glassing.

About mid-afternoon, Tom spotted a couple of bulls on the mountain we had hunted the first day. Again, it was too late in the day to reach them.

The third day found us on the same ridge as the day before. At about 10:00 a.m., Tom spotted some bulls feeding in the pines on a ridge across the valley. It was early enough in the day to go for them. Down the mountain, across the valley floor, and up the other side only took us four hours! But, we had closed to within 150 yards of the two bulls. One was a good 6x6, and the other was not yet showing the maturity we had in mind.

Jay moved into a good shooting position behind a rock and waited for a clear shot. The wind gusted but did not give us away. Jay put the crosshairs on the big fellow, and two reports from his .300 Winchester Magnum rifle gave him his first Rocky Mountain elk. Jay was all smiles as we took lots of pictures.

We field dressed the bull and headed back to camp. This time our elk chant had a special meaning. We were in camp less than an hour when we heard that chant again. The big smile on Lee Zartman's face told us another bull had been taken. It doesn't get much better than three bulls in three days.

It didn't for me, anyway. The cold I had been fighting forced me to take a camp day. I rested and was ready to go the next morning, Thanksgiving Day. What a day it would be.

Tom and I repeated the same strategy. As we were looking for tracks, I looked up a draw and spotted what I thought was the hindquarter of an elk facing into the trees. I reached for my binoculars, but I had left them back with the horses. Looking through my rifle scope, I was almost positive. Then, Tim confirmed it.

It was 8:00 a.m., and he was 500 yards away. We used some pine trees to conceal our approach. A light dusting of snow helped us with the wind, and we took advantage of it to gain some ground. The snow-covered rocks made the going tough, but by 9:00 we had closed to within 50 yards. Where was he? We looked back to check our bearings and found we were right on target. Unfortunately, the wind was softly blowing up our backs. Busted.

A few seconds later, Tom saw not one but two bulls. They were 125 yards above us and leaving. Their escape route was through the trees going left to right. We slipped and slid and crawled over the rocks to try and find a shooting lane. I took a position as Tom called their approach. I had maybe a three-foot lane if they continued on course.

As he peered through the binoculars, Tom whispered, "He's a 6-point, a real nice 6-point." As the first bull entered my lane, I found him in my scope.

Suddenly, Tom yelled, "Take the second one! Take the second one!"

A lot went through my mind in about a tenth of a second, but I was ready when the next bull stepped through the trees. The tops of his antlers were hidden amongst the trees, but the bottoms were most impressive. I waited for one more step and squeezed the trigger on my .300 Winchester Magnum. The first shot was solid, and I quickly followed up with another. The big bull collapsed instantly and came to rest about 25 yards down the hill. Until we could get to him, his true size was unknown.

Tom reached him while I was still 50 yards away. I watched him as he stared at the bull...and stared and stared. As I was about there, Tom spread his arms as wide as they would go and began to yell, "He's huge, he's just huge!"

The bass drum in my chest pounded heavily when I got to look at the animal. I was awe-struck. All I could say was "Wow!" I said it repeatedly.

Then, Tom and I joined in a chorus: "He's huge! Wow! He's huge! Wow!" I guess you get the picture.

We were pretty excited. This magnificent bull scored 336-3/8, S.C.I., and 395-7/8, Boone and Crockett He had 55-inch main beams and 24-inch swords. I will always be proud of this wilderness trophy and the special meaning of that Thanksgiving Day.

AMERICAN ELK, TYPICAL ANTLERS
CERTIFICATE OF MERIT
SCORE: 421-4/8

Locality: Gila Co., Ariz.   Date: 1985
Hunter: James C. Littleton

AMERICAN ELK, TYPICAL ANTLERS 421-4/8

James C. Littleton

I was not looking for just any elk. I had taken a 6x6 in 1984 on a hunt in Arizona. It made the Pope and Young records book, but that is another story altogether.

It was the last day of the hunt on the San Carlos Apache Reservation. The day was not extremely cold, but it was not warm either. My wife, Geraldine, had gotten a piece of glass in her foot and did not feel up to walking the mountains with Darrell Cassedore and me. She did insist on coming along and sitting in the Blazer. She loved to read, relax and enjoy the mountains.

Darrell Cassedore, my guide, was born and raised on the reservation, and he knew where to hunt. I was in good shape, and we had gone some distance before he decided to stop and glass the side of the mountain. After awhile, we saw one. Using Steiner 7x35 binoculars, we could see the bull had seven points on each side. He was about 300 yards from our position.

I was hunting with a Weatherby Mark V rifle in .300 Weatherby Magnum. The scope was a 3-9x Redfield. I used 220 grain Weatherby soft point bullets. The rifle was properly zeroed, and I felt confident of my shot. It was definitely not the time to miss or to make a bad shot. I pulled the trigger, and through the mountain air, I heard the bullet strike. It startled the elk, and with what life he had left, he made for the bushes. He didn't come out, though.

After waiting a little bit we started to the elk. I just knew that it was a clean kill. It was. It was a 7x7 and it looked big. At that point, I did not think I had a high-ranking trophy elk. I just knew it looked big.

I had no camera with me. I don't take pictures. Since my wife was not there, and she had already taken about 50 photographs of the 6x6 bull in 1984, I just thought that was enough. Many times I have regretted not taking a camera. As the weeks passed, I decided one day to measure the 7x7 bull. The score was high. I measured it again, and it was still high. I had the shoulder mount of the 6x6 bull taken in 1984, and it was too big for my house.

Two big bulls would definitely not fit, so I thought that I might as well have the bigger one mounted. I called my taxidermist and asked him if he could change the racks. He thought he could. As it turned out, this was not possible, but he told me he thought I had a record rack.

I got in touch with Mike Cupell. He had me bring the rack to his home. He scored it several times and it was a record—Number 1, in fact for Arizona. At that time, it was Number 3 in the United States. I could not believe it.

Mike asked if he could take it to the Rocky Mountain Elk Foundation in Prescott, Arizona. I told him to go ahead. When they brought it back, it became a place for Geraldine to hang clothes after ironing.

In all of North America, I don't believe there is a prettier place to be than the San Carlos Apache Reservation. The scenery is beautiful. You can go from desert scenes, mountains, lakes and big pines to rivers and streams, all in a day. There are still places where no white man has ever set foot. The eagles still soar in the mountains, coyotes still howl at night, wild geese and ducks still winter on the tanks, and of course, the elk, deer, antelope and wild mountain rams still run the same range as the cattle. It is a true dream land for the hunter, the photographer, or the person who simply wants to get away from the fast life. It makes you want to pitch your tent and never go home.

The Apache still use a lot of the spices, herbs and food that God gave them. They pick the acorns to flavor dishes, the pinon nuts to eat while walking, the century plant to bake over a campfire, and the prickly pear fruit for jelly.

Most of all, it is the quiet life that the cowboys and cooks learn to like. A cowboy's life is spent in the saddle, from daylight to dark. They live on the range.

Geraldine, my son Charley and I were invited to a dinner cooked over campfires, a way of life for the cowboys. It was like a banquet. Holes were dug in the ground and fires started in each hole. Each fire had it own special pot. One for the bean pot, another for potatoes, one for coffee, another for taco pie, and yet another for the golden-brown yeast rolls that would melt in your mouth. It was an honor to be invited.

The cowboys told stories of wild maverick bulls that, when caught, had to be tied for awhile before they could be handled. They spoke of wild horses that would come into camp and steal the mares if they could. They said there was even a kind of monkey that came over from Mexico to live on the land of the Apache; few people have seen these.

If some of the biggest elk in the United States do not bring you to the San Carlos, you might like fishing for some of the biggest catfish, trout, bass and other fish in the lakes or tanks. The Apache are proud of their land. They want to live on it as God intended.

Photograph courtesy of Jack Atcheson, Jr.

This typical American elk was killed in Petroleum County, Montana, in 1990.
by Jack Atcheson, Jr. It scored 378-3/8.

Photograph courtesy of David W. Kuhns

This typical American elk was taken by David W. Kuhns in 1989 in
Petroleum County, Montana. It scores 373-2/8.

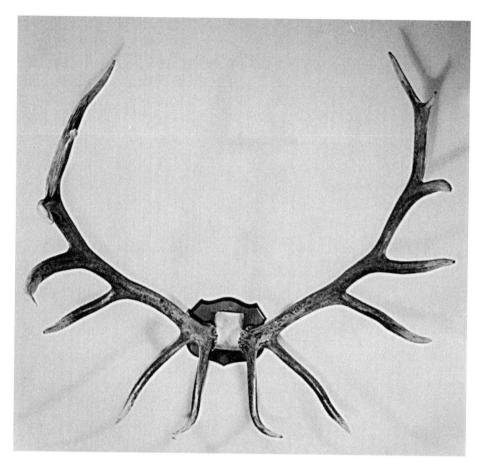

Photograph by Wm. H. Nesbitt

AMERICAN ELK, TYPICAL ANTLERS
CERTIFICATE OF MERIT
SCORE: 420-4/8

Locality: Yakima Co., Wash.   Date: 1990
Hunter: Charles F. Gunnier
(Hunting Story Not Available)

Photograph courtesy of Butch Kuflak

Butch Kuflak with guide Tom Wilkes and his typical American elk that scored 389-5/8. This elk was taken while hunting in Park County, Montana, in 1990.

Photograph courtesy of Gary Beley

While hunting in Park County, Montana, in 1964, Gary Beley killed this non-typical American elk. It scores 403-2/8.

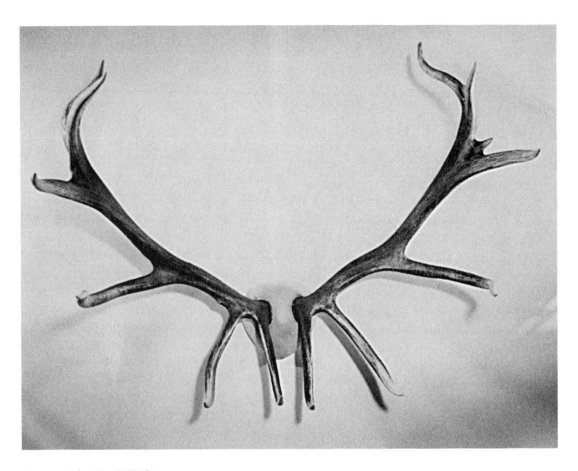

Photograph by Wm. H. Nesbitt

AMERICAN ELK, TYPICAL ANTLERS
CERTIFICATE OF MERIT
SCORE: 406-7/8

Locality: Duck Mountain, Man.   Date: 1980
Hunter: Herb Andres   Owner: Larry L. Huffman

AMERICAN ELK, TYPICAL ANTLERS 406-7/8

Herb Andres, hunter
Larry L. Huffman, owner

Recently, a huge elk rack was found sitting in an old granary, covered with old fertilizer cans and even an old lawn mower. It is believed to have been harvested around 1980.

The hunter of this fallen monarch is Herb Andres of Boggy Creek, Manitoba. John Reimer and Don Neufeld were visiting Herb one evening in September of 1989, while they were bowhunting for elk.

During their visit, Herb showed them a few racks he had around the farm. The first was a beautiful 6x6. Then, he pulled out another 6x6. John and Don knew that Herb had two racks that needed to be scored. They acquired permission to measure both for an official Boone and Crockett score.

Surprise, surprise. Both racks made the records book. The smaller antlers scored 377-4/8, and the larger set scored 413-4/8, which would place it seventh in the current Boone and Crockett ranking, first in Manitoba. On February 24, 1990, the Manitoba Big Game Trophy Association crowned this animal their new provincial record.

Herb Andres was afield on a beautiful high-pressure morning in September, an ideal morning for bugling elk. The high pressure system had come in during the latter part of the night, leaving a light frost in the MacCorkindale Prairie area of the Duck Mountains.

It was the second week of the early rifle season. Herb was restricted to hunting only during the morning, because he was working at a local shop. Due to the travel required to reach the hunting area, Herb decided to hunt every second day in order to keep his energy up and avoid fatigue.

The elk were very quiet that morning, even though conditions were right. Herb's game plan was to work the edges of some prime timber with his whistle pipe, hoping to lure a challenger bull into an opening.

Herb had been calling with very little success, so he decided to try a new location. A short walk later and Herb was in position. His first single call had an immediate response, and it seemed very close. The bull was on his way to check out his challenger.

Herb remembers seeing the antlers first, but antlers were not the main reason for the hunt; they would only be a bonus. Herb got ready for the advancing bull. He placed himself low to avoid creating a silhouette. His .308 Winchester Savage Model 99C was ready, loaded with 180 grain factory ammunition. He slipped off the safety.

Herb was hidden by the tall prairie grasses. At 20 yards, the bull had not picked Herb out of the foliage, and at that point it was too late. A single shot was all that was needed.

For at least 10 years, the antlers sat in a shed. Herb knew about scoring trophies, but this aspect of hunting held no real interest for him.

The inside spread of the rack is almost 49 inches. Both beams are over 54 inches, and G-3 measured 29-4/8 inches on the right side and 28-5/8 inches on the left. It has one abnormal point.

Herb was very late for work that day.

Reprinted from *Big Buck* Magazine, with permission, Vol. IV, No. 3, April 1991

Photograph courtesy of Michael S. Muhlbauer

Michael S. Muhlbauer took this typical American elk, scoring 375-3/8, while hunting in Apache County, Arizona, in 1989. Next to him is Si Muhlbauer.

Photograph courtesy of Robert M. Brittingham

Robert M. Brittingham is pictured here with the typical American elk, he took while hunting in Apache County, Arizona, in 1990. It scores 390-6/8.

Photograph by Wm. H. Nesbitt

NEW WORLD'S RECORD AMERICAN ELK,
NON-TYPICAL ANTLERS
CERTIFICATE OF MERIT
SCORE: 447-1/8

Locality: Gilbert Plains, Man.   Date: 1961
Hunter: James R. Berry

AMERICAN ELK, NON-TYPICAL ANTLERS 447-1/8

James R. Berry

When Jim Berry shot the big Manitoba bull on a wintry day back in 1961, he was just looking to bring home some meat for his family.

After taking a closer look at the elk he had just killed, he could see it was an impressive animal. Yet 30 years passed before he discovered it would be the largest non-typical elk ever shot.

Berry, of Langley, British Columbia, was in his early 30s when he shot the bull north of Riding Mountain National Park in southwest Manitoba. He had taken many elk and was not searching for a trophy at the time.

"I was just after meat to feed my family. I wasn't after the horns," he says. "Back then, you didn't look at the horns."

A scorer from the Boone and Crockett Club recently made an initial, measurement of the rack totalling 439-7/8 points. That would have earned the bull second place in the all-time records for non-typical American elk, only about five points less than the previous World's Record. That bull, scoring 445-5/8, was killed on the Fort Apache Indian Reservation in Arizona during 1984 by Jerry Davis of Katy, Texas.

Berry has carted the rack around through several moves, rightfully proud of the giant but unaware of its records-book potential.

"I knew it was big, but I never knew it was that big," Berry says. "It was just another elk to me. I mean, I had shot a lot of elk."

While many of the details of that day have faded with time, Berry remembers that he killed the animal with a single shot from his Winchester .30-30 carbine at more than 100 yards. He was hunting just outside of Riding Mountain National Park, on flat, brushy land cut by a few ravines. Today, that land has been cleared.

The bull weighed more than 1,200 pounds and provided Berry and his family with about 560 pounds of meat. After nearly three decades of drying, the 8x9 non-typical rack weighs 38 pounds, with 51-inch main beams and a 54-inch spread.

Following a move with his family to southwestern British Columbia, the lifelong hunter became involved with the Langley Rod and Gun Club. It was then that some of the locals found out about his 29-year-old antlers.

According to Berry, when some of his fellow club members bragged on big elk they had shot, he told them, "If you really want to see a big elk, I'll show you.'"

They were rightfully impressed. One fellow even offered Berry $1,000 and a rifle for the rack, but he refused to part with it.

"I didn't pack it around all these years just to sell it," he says.

Berry recently read of another non-typical bull taken near Riding Mountain National Park, scoring 397. It was billed in a magazine article as the largest non-typical bull ever taken in Manitoba.

He figures it is time to set the record straight.

EDITOR'S NOTE: James R. Berry accepted the Boone and Crockett Club's invitation to send his trophy to the 21st Awards Program held in Milwaukee, Wisconsin, in early 1992. The Judges Panel rescored Berry's massive bull at 447-1/8 points and declared it the New World's Record non-typical American elk.

Photograph courtesy of Richard P. Norrup

This typical American elk was taken in White Pine County, Nevada, in 1990, by Richard P. Norrup. It scored 363-2/8.

Photograph courtesy of Gordon J. Birgbauer, Jr.

Gordon J. Birgbauer, Jr. was hunting in Menzies Bay, B.C., when he killed this Roosevelt's elk in 1991. It scored 351-5/8.

Photograph by Wm. H. Nesbitt

AMERICAN ELK, NON-TYPICAL ANTLERS
CERTIFICATE OF MERIT
SCORE: 405-4/8

Locality: Granite Co., Mont.   Date: 1946
Hunter: Arthur W. Lundgren   Owner: Grace Lundgren

AMERICAN ELK, NON-TYPICAL ANTLERS 405-4/8

Arthur W. Lundgren, hunter
Grace Lundgren, owner

On a western Montana morning in 1946, my dad loaded up his .33 Winchester lever action rifle with 200 grain cartridges and told my mother and me that he was going elk hunting. It was November, cold and snowing.

As four-wheel-drives were rare in those days, the hunt would be on foot. The area he planned to hunt was about five miles from his house, all up hill. After about two hours of walking, he spotted a set of very large elk tracks leaving the timber and leading to an open hillside. As he moved closer to the opening, he could see a large bull elk pawing the snow to reach the grass. Just then the bull stepped forward enough to enable my dad to see his shoulder. As he squinted through the open sights of his rifle, he never realized that this could be a world-class bull. One shot dropped the huge bull in its tracks.

On approaching the bull it became apparent that he was a far larger animal than dad had realized. Then came the problem of transporting the bull home. It was far too heavy to lift, so dad decided to hike back home and get a team of horses and a stoneboat. The stoneboat is used to haul large stones off of fields and pastures and is only about a foot off the ground. This worked fine and we were able to roll the elk on to the stoneboat and transport it home. We had many fine steaks and roasts that following year.

My dad passed away in the 1960s and the antlers lay in my mother's garage until 1989, when my family and I talked her into having them scored by a Boone and Crockett Official Scorer. It was found that the bull would probably make the records book. If my dad were here today, he would be very proud as he was an avid hunter. The mount is on display at the Rocky Mountain Elk Foundation Wildlife Visitor Center in Missoula, Montana.

Photograph by Wm. H. Nesbitt

NEW WORLD'S RECORD ROOSEVELT'S ELK
FIRST AWARD
SCORE: 388-3/8

Locality: Tsitika River, B.C.   Date: 1989
Hunter: Wayne Coe

ROOSEVELT'S ELK 388-3/8

Wayne Coe

In 1989, I submitted an application for a limited entries permit for Roosevelt's elk on Vancouver Island. I was extremely pleased when I received a permit for the season commencing on October 7th and continuing until November 19th. Due to work commitments, and previously planned mule deer and moose hunting excursions, I was unable to set out in search of my elk until November 4th.

I contacted my hunting comrades to make plans for our venture. The four of us decided to depart from Union Bay in the early hours of the morning on November 4th. Our intention was to arrive at Eve River before first light.

Upon our arrival, we divided into two groups. Two of my cohorts (Fred Peters and Don Arthurs) decided to hunt the Eve River South main area. My partner, Sid McKay, and I elected to go to the Tsitka River area. Together, we drove to the end of the Tsitka River West main logging road. Once there, we scouted and hunted for signs of wildlife for several hours with no success. We discovered neither an animal nor a trace of tracks.

We returned to our vehicle and decided to search for Fred and Don to see if their luck had been better than ours. Approximately half way back down the Tsitka West main line, I saw what appeared to be the hind quarters of an elk. I promptly grabbed my binoculars and my .300 Weatherby Magnum. Next, Sid and I scrambled 300 yards up the brush covered hillside in an effort to get a better look.

Using my binoculars, I located the elk just inside some heavy timber, approximately 250 yards from our vantage point. Clearly, the animal in my view was a bull elk. I quickly concluded that I had better take advantage of this great opportunity as the season was soon to draw to a close. I told Sid that we ought to make an attempt at it.

I located a good, steady rest for shooting and patiently waited for the elk to turn broadside. All I could see in my scope was an area from the bottom of his ear to half way up his antlers. I waited for what seemed like an eternity. Eventually, I became anxious, considering the possibility that the elk might flee before I decided to shoot.

I told Sid I was going to attempt a shot at the elk's head. My first shot missed, but it did not cause the elk to retreat. Instead, he picked his head up a little more. I put the crosshair of my scope on the elk's ear and squeezed the trigger.

Sid exclaimed, "It's a hit!"

Together, we scrambled 250 yards or so up the hill to the place where the elk disappeared from sight. We found the bull dead, right where he had stood. Both Sid and I were shocked at his size. However, neither of us had any idea of the actual measure of my trophy.

With assistance from Fred, Don and two other fellow hunters who happened along our way, we were able to transport my trophy down the hill and into our vehicle. We arrived in Union Bay just before dark. We hung up the enormous bull elk at Don's place for skinning the next morning.

Throughout the next morning, several friends came to see my elk. I was told by some of them to have my trophy measured. Following the 60-day drying period, I did just that. I traveled into Courtenary to the fish and game association, where official scorers for Boone and Crockett measured my trophy at 390-5/8.

I awaited word as to whether or not my trophy would be invited to the final judging for Boone and Crockett's 21st Annual Big Game Awards with tremendous anticipation.

Public viewing of the 21st North American Big Game Awards exhibit took place at the Milwaukee Public Museum during May 16 - June 11, 1992.

photo 26B

Entrance to the trophy exhibit of the 21st North American Big Game Awards displayed in the Owen J. Gromme Hall, Milwaukee Public Museum.

Photograph by Wm. H. Nesbitt

ROOSEVELT'S ELK
SECOND AWARD
SCORE: 351-5/8

Locality: Menzies Bay, B.C.   Date: 1991
Hunter: Gordon J. Birgbauer, Jr.

ROOSEVELT'S ELK 351-5/8

Gordon J. Birgbauer, Jr.

In 1985, I was fortunate enough to take a records book woodland caribou in Newfoundland. I never dreamed that this would begin my quest for animals worthy of recognition by the Boone and Crockett Club in every category.

Having been invited to the 19th Awards, I have since taken four animals that qualified for listing in the Boone & Crockett records; four other trophies just missed. The pursuit of excellence that Boone and Crockett inspires has probably set my standards higher than I deserve. However, I have been very, very fortunate to meet many people all over the world and have had the adventures and trophies that would last most people a lifetime.

In 1990, I made a Roosevelt's elk booking for October of 1991. My choice of outfitters was Larry Dougan of Trophy West Outfitters. I basically put that hunt out of my mind until it was time to purchase airline tickets and proceed to Campbell River, Vancouver Island, British Columbia.

Larry picked me up at the airport. We proceeded to a local rifle range for sighting-in; then, we drove out to a farm on the chance that we might see an elk. The one thing we did see was a tremendous black bear, Unfortunately, I did not have a license at that time. We remained on stand for another hour. None of the elk came into the pasture, so we walked back and called it a day.

For the next five days, we got up at 4:00 or 5:00 in the morning and traveled north on Vancouver Island, approximately 60 miles each day. I was shown several bull elk, but Larry felt we could do better if we passed on them, and that is what we did.

The excitement of the stalk is probably the best part of the hunt. We glassed continuously from morning until night, watching the clear-cut areas that the foresters had provided. It is interesting country in the sense that the new growth makes walking virtually impossible. It is a matter of glassing all day long.

On the fifth day, we were walking into an older clear-cut area when we startled some cows. Lo and behold, behind the cows came a big bull elk. I shouldered my .300 Jarrett and, with a 180-grain Trophy Bonded Bear Claw bullet, took the animal with one shot at about 85 yards.

After 20 minutes or so of picture-taking, we proceeded to cape out the elk. Larry indicated that we had an exceptional elk. I debated about leaving the elk on the island for taxidermy work and measurement by a local Boone and Crockett scorer, but Larry talked me into taking the antlers home.

I was very lucky, as I switched planes in Vancouver, to avoid interference while carrying the rack through the airport. We got the rack safely back to Michigan and waited out the 60-day drying period. Just before the first of the year, I took it to Joe Newmyer, who did a super job of scoring. Everyone has certainly been most cooperative, and I would again like to congratulate the Boone and Crockett Club for the excellence of the standards they have established.

Photograph courtesy of George B. Putman

Mason County, Washington, was the scene of this Roosevelt's elk kill in 1900 (circa). Owner George B. Putnam and his trophy that scored 367.

Photograph courtesy of Ralph R. Van Beck

While hunting in Crook County, Wyoming, in 1989, Ralph R. VanBeck took this non-typical whitetail. It scores 200.

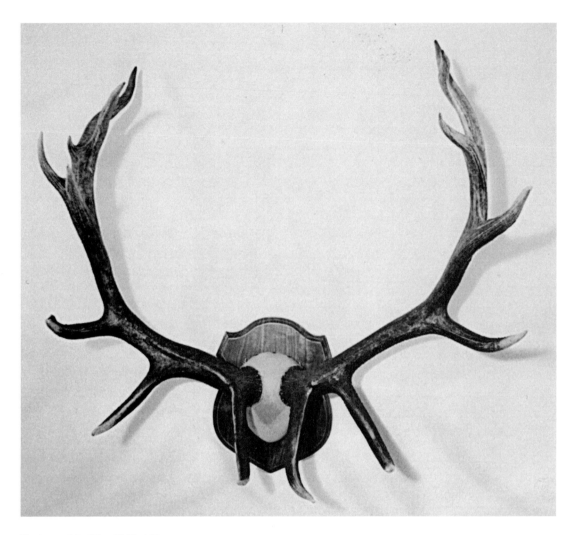

Photograph by Wm. H. Nesbitt

ROOSEVELT'S ELK
THIRD AWARD
SCORE: 341

Locality: Lewis Co., Wash.   Date: 1988
Hunter: Keith A. Heldreth

ROOSEVELT'S ELK 341

Keith A. Heldreth

The aluminum arrow's impact on the bull elk was both instantaneous and impressive. Of the nine elk that I had previously taken with bow and arrow, not a single one reacted quite the way this one did.

The bull had passed from right to left, moving steeply uphill from my position in a stand of alder saplings. His small band of three cows and two calves had come first, picking at the salmonberry and salal brush as they threaded their way up the steep, narrow draw. Close on their heels was the bull. With his head held low, his dark, heavy antlers swept back to just behind his shoulders. He was magnificent. He was also not very interested in salmonberry and salal brush. My mind was racing as the six elk unknowingly closed the distance between us.

When I first spotted the elk earlier that morning, they were bedded on the edge of a small opening in the alders. The cows and calves were content to lie placidly chewing their cuds. The bull was another story. He was obsessed with trying to demolish a red huckleberry bush growing from the side of an ancient cedar stump. He would hook his antlers into the bush and stump; then he would try to uproot the whole mess with a heavy thrust of his neck and shoulder muscles. Of all the things in the world that are impressed with a truly large bull elk, that old growth cedar stump was not one of them. I did not see that stump give up one inch of ground to the bull.

I had watched the elk with my binocular for about 15 minutes when the bull decided to look for something to pick on that was closer to his own size. That something came in the form of one of his lady friends, who had decided the siesta was over and breakfast was served. She browsed her way uphill to an old cat road, the bull firmly in tow. Not wanting to miss any of the festivities, the remaining four elk got to their feet, one by one, and followed suit.

I kept my binocular glued to the surrounding real estate for about five minutes before I spotted the elk again. They were loosely bunched and feeding through the corner of a stand of mature timber, slightly above and to the left of their previous position. I watched them for a few minutes longer until they came out of the timber and started working their way up an alder-choked side canyon. It was perfect.

The canyon they were in ended in a steep, narrow draw below a saddle. My preseason scouting had revealed two main elk trails crossing this saddle, both of which had their origin from the west side of the draw that the elk were now in.

I followed the old logging road around to the east side of the saddle. From there, I headed down the ravine to a point below the lower trail that afforded excellent shooting if they chose that route. I also had two small openings that I could shoot through to the upper trail. There was nothing to do now but wait.

The sounds of feeding elk drifted up the draw to me. They were very close, and I had a grand case of buck fever. As luck would have it, the elk chose the upper trail. It was not the best opportunity in the world, but an opportunity nonetheless.

As the cows and calves filtered through the first small opening, I tried to tell myself to calm down and pick a spot behind his shoulder. As the bull approached the opening, I gave a low cow call. It worked perfectly. Almost. The bull stopped with just part of his nose showing in the opening. At my call, the cows had stopped as well, trying to sort out where the mystery elk might be hiding in the thick tangle. A bird in the hand being better than two in the bush, the bull decided to stick with the birds he already had. He took a couple of steps farther into the opening and gave me the opportunity I needed.

The aluminum shaft flickered through the alders and disappeared just behind the bull's left foreleg. Expecting the elk to bolt and run, I was shocked to see him make one frantic lunge and then lose his footing on the steep sidehill. The bull went down heavily on his side and never regained his feet. His struggles ended against a log on the uphill side of the creek. It was in this position that I was finally able to get a good look at just how big an elk I had shot.

His antlers were even more impressive than I had imagined. They were heavy and as thick as my forearm, with seven points on the left side and eight on the right.

After the required 60-day drying period, I called Bob Mayton, an official scorer who lived out near the coast. Bob is an official scorer for both the Boone and Crockett Club and the Pope and Young Club. Bob told me that, if I could come right out, he would score my bull's antlers that very evening, along with another large bull taken on the Olympic Peninsula by another bowhunter named Larry Haddock. Preliminary scoring showed my bull to score 341. Bob told Larry and me that our bulls made the second and third times that the state archery record had been broken since the start of the season.

In early 1989, my elk's antlers were shipped to Boise, Idaho, for the Pope and Young Club's 16th Biennial Awards program. My wife and I were able to travel to Boise and enjoy the program and the dinner. My elk was panel scored at a final total of 343-2/8. It was the largest Roosevelt's elk in the recording period and is currently ranked in third place in the Pope and Young Club records book.

Photograph courtesy of James C. Littleton

In 1985, James C. Littleton killed this typical American elk in
Gila County, Arizona. It scored 421-4/8.

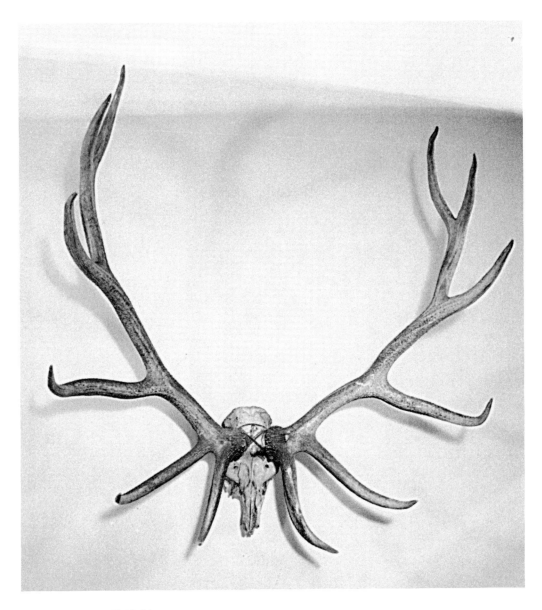

Photograph by Wm. H. Nesbitt

ROOSEVELT'S ELK
CERTIFICATE OF MERIT
SCORE: 367

Locality: Mason Co., Wash.   Date: 1900
Hunter: Unknown   Owner: George B. Putnam

ROOSEVELT'S ELK 367

George P. Putnam, owner

This set of Roosevelt's elk antlers has been in the Putnam family for about 90 years. My grandfather, William T. Putnam, homesteaded at Lake Cushman, Mason County, Washington (on the Olympic Peninsula).

The only information about the origin of these antlers that survives in memory is the "fact" that my grandfather paid fifty dollars for them at Lake Cushman sometime around the turn of the century. My father, W.T. Putnam, Jr., had first-hand information about the antlers, but he died in 1985. Whatever he told us about them, no one can remember anything other than their cost.

My mother, who is still living on the family farm near Hillsboro, Oregon, can only recollect that Dad remembered them from Lake Cushman when he was a small boy. He was born there in 1897. Since my grandfather operated a summer resort at Lake Cushman, it is likely that he purchased the antlers from one of his hunting guests from the East. This, however, is only a guess.

My grandfather and his family were forced out of Lake Cushman in 1923, due to the construction of Cushman Dam, which flooded their resort and farm. They moved to Hillsboro, Oregon, where they operated a 238 acre farm.

I remember the antlers from my boyhood. They were stored in an old granary, where we often played as kids. In the early 1960s, the granary was torn down and the antlers transferred to the basement of our home. They remained there, largely unnoticed, until the summer of 1990.

For several years, my mother insisted that she wanted to get rid of the antlers. She was using them as a hanger for the garden hoses during the winter. Since I live in Montana, I knew there would be greater opportunity to sell them here, possibly for knife handles. I did not realize their historical worth.

It is now my hope that these antlers can be returned to Mason County or to Olympic National Park, where they probably originated.

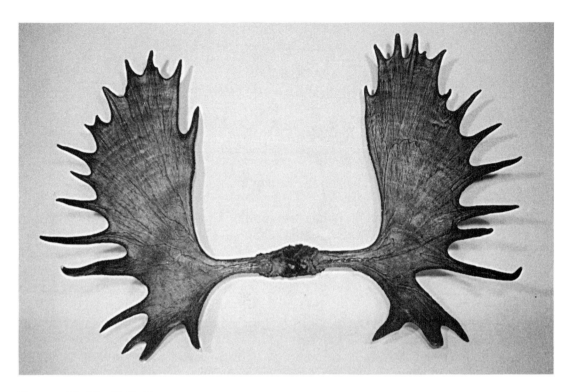

Photograph by Wm. H. Nesbitt

CANADA MOOSE
FIRST AWARD
SCORE: 221-4/8

Locality: Logan Mt., Que.   Date: 1988
Hunter: Charles R. Roy   Owners: C.R. Roy & R. Roy

CANADA MOOSE 221-4/8

Charles R. Roy, hunter
Charles R. Roy and Roch Roy, owners

It was October 1, 1988, the opening day for moose hunting with bow and arrow in Quebec's Gaspe Peninsula. The season takes place during the rut. Our outfitter was Le bloc Faribault, au pays des geants, which translates to "Faribault, the country for giant bulls." We were three hunters: my father, Roch Roy, my friend, Gerard Emond, and me, Charles Roy.

Just before sunrise, we took positions in our treestands. The sky was clear, and the temperature was around 35 degrees Fahrenheit. There was no wind. All the conditions seemed perfect for calling. My father imitated the cow call sometimes during this first day but nothing happened. It was like that until Wednesday, October 5, we heard some moose calling, but no bull came to us.

On Thursday, October 6, we went to a new spot, hoping the change would be successful, but it was not. Other parties who hunted on the outfitter's land were more fortunate than we were. Seven moose had been killed with bow and arrow since the opening day. One of the bulls had a rack with a 63-inch spread and another had a spread of 59 inches. We were encouraged by their successes.

Friday, October 7, brought rain and melting snow. The wind blew strongly. We decided not to hunt. At the end of the day, the rain turned to snow. I was slightly discouraged. My father, who acts as a guide for me, had 50 years of moose-hunting experience. He told me that after the storm, the weather would improve and the moose—bulls in particular—would be more active.

The next morning, my father got out of bed at 5:00. He was excited. Twelve inches of fresh snow were on the ground, the sky was full of stars, and the wind had stopped. We all agreed to hunt to the same spot as opening day.

We had to walk for about 30 minutes before reaching our treestands. During the walk, we saw some fresh tracks crossing our trail. We were very confident. We climbed into our treestands at 6:15. All of the trees were loaded with snow, and the woods were very quiet.

My father quietly imitated the cow call. Five minutes later, we heard a bull make a short call, then and another and another, until he had called five or six times. We had no doubt; the bull was coming to meet a cow.

After some minutes, which seemed like hours, the bull appeared, but he stopped immediately with his chest just behind a tree. I could see his head and his rack, and what a rack it was! My arrow nocked, I waited. I was ready. I could hear my heart. Suddenly, the bull walked slowly and stopped again. That was what I was waiting for. My arrow flew and penetrated the bull's body just behind the front leg, at the level of the lungs. The big bull began to run, crashing through the dense cover of snow-laden spruces. He disappeared.

I was sure of my shot. My father and Gerard told me they saw the arrow hit the bull in the chest. We waited 10 minutes. After that, it was easy to follow the big tracks in the white snow.

We found the big moose dead, 150 yards from where he was shot. We could all see at once that he was an enormous bull. We felt that he was a records book trophy, though not a New World's Record. I will never forget this hunt, early in the morning of October 8, 1988.

Photograph courtesy of Roger Mann

Roger Mann with the Canada moose he killed at Candle Lake,
Sask., in 1989. It scores 213.

Photograph courtesy of Dean A. Estes

Kakwa River, Alberta, produced this Canada moose scoring
203-7/8 for Dean A. Estes in 1987.

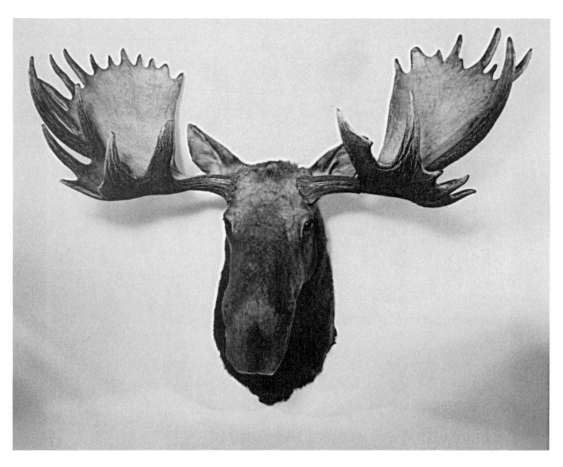

Photograph by Wm. H. Nesbitt

CANADA MOOSE
SECOND AWARD
SCORE: 219-7/8
Locality: East West Lake, Ont.   Date: 1989
Hunter: Kurt Skalitzky

CANADA MOOSE 219-7/8

Kurt Skalitzky

It was the spring of 1989, and already my cousin, Tim Sellnow, and I were anticipating the hunting activities of the fall. I recall the excitement I first felt when I was old enough to hunt with my father, and somehow leaving the United States to shoot my first moose parallels the memory.

We arrived at Gene and George Halley's camp in Ontario, Canada, late on the night of Saturday, October 7, 1989. It is located on the beautiful English River, 70 miles north of Kenora.

On Sunday, Gene packed the plane that would fly Tim and me to our destination, a secluded, remote area 50 miles north of the main camp.

When we arrived at the site, our guide, Randy Nordstorm, was busy setting up camp. Tim and I aided Randy by splitting wood and securing the two tents that would become our home during our 10-day hunt. The season did not officially begin until the following morning, so Tim, Randy and I decided to go fishing. We caught a few walleye, which became our supper. In anticipation of our big hunt, we turned in early.

After a sleepless night, I awoke at 4:00 a.m. Darkness surrounded our camp. We eagerly awaited daybreak. Tim pondered whether to take rain gear. Randy laughed at the idea, so we decided to take the advice of the professional and brought only the bare essentials — our guns and binoculars.

We departed from camp in a small aluminum motor boat. Soon Tim found the place perfect for him, a tall grassy meadow where Randy had seen a 40 to 50-inch bull prior to our arrival.

Randy and I continued down to the end of the East West Lake. There, we climbed over rugged rocks to watch yet another vast meadow. By 9:00 a.m., things looked bleak and suddenly worsened when a light mist of rain turned into a steady downpour. An hour and a half went by with no relief. Disappointment set in as the only game revealing itself to me were geese and mallard ducks.

Randy and I decided to dry off, so we headed back to camp, stopping along the way to pick up a frustrated and drenched Tim.

It finally stopped raining around 11:30 a.m., and we were dry and ready to stalk the game of choice — moose.

Randy decided to take me to a special area where he had previously sighted a very large bull. We hopped back in our boat and headed in the opposite direction from our morning hunt. We ended up at the north end of one of Ontario's finest meadows. As we walked along the river bed, it soon became apparent that history speaks for itself. A raging fire had engulfed the meadow six years earlier. New growth had spurted forth, producing vegetation approximately five feet high. This could make the hunt quite challenging.

I took my stand as time crawled. What seemed like eternity was in reality an hour. I tried not to make any noise, because it is so quiet when you are out in the middle of nowhere. Finally, I could not hold out any longer. I leaned my rifle against a small pine tree, got out my Copenhagen and took a pinch. I continued my watch, seeing only small game.

It was around 3:00 p.m. when, suddenly, I saw two massive antlers above the new growth. My first reaction was to grab my rifle. The moose was definitely close enough to shoot, about 150 to 200 yards away. However, his body remained concealed by the trees. I stood and watched him for half an hour. Then he disappeared into the brush.

At that moment, Randy came walking toward me with disappointment on his face. He had not seen a thing. I explained to him what I had just seen. A huge smile appeared on his face and he said, "That's him, let's go get him!"

I pointed out where I last spotted the bull, and we headed in that direction. We got about half of the way there, when Randy told me, "Watch your feet, so you don't make any noise." The aftermath of the fire made it difficult to walk through the cedar swamp. To get a better view, Randy climbed up a tree that was leaning at a 45-degree angle. He saw just what we had hoped to see. There the bull was, bedded down. We made our plan of attack. With the wind in our faces, we could circle in on him.

As we walked cautiously toward him, he must have sensed our presence. All of a sudden, we heard the electrifying crack and we froze. Not a second later we saw him thrashing toward us, thrusting his enormous rack against the trees. It sounded like a canoe paddle slapping against the water.

He was close enough to shoot, but the brush was much too thick. The moose was 50 yards away, glaring at us. He then turned broadside, took a couple of steps, and I raised my Browning .300 Winchester Magnum. I fired once, and he just flinched. I bolted another cartridge in, fired, and he spun to the ground. He was mine.

Randy hollered, "You got him, good hit!"

As we reached the bull, we realized his antlers were wedged at the base of the trees. Randy gave me a bear hug that was more like a tackle.

He said, "We got him! He's the biggest one I've ever seen!"

We admired his rack, took some pictures, and decided that we had only enough time to field dress the prize, because darkness was near. We took the heart back to camp knowing it would suffice as supper.

The next day we went back to skin and quarter the trophy. While Tim was clearing a path with the chain saw, Randy and I worked on the moose. It was only a quarter-mile to the canoe, but because of the mossy, bog-like terrain and the weight of the 1,400-

pound animal, it took us an entire day to get him back to camp.

Gene flew in to check on us. He couldn't believe the size of the rack. Measuring 66-2/8 inches wide, it amazed all of us. With considerable effort, we loaded the moose into Gene's plane, and he flew it back to the main camp.

Three days later Tim also shot a bull moose. A 10-day hunt that yields two moose within five days is not bad. To kill a moose with antlers scoring 225-2/8 is every hunter's dream. Now it is my reality.

Photograph by Wm. H. Nesbitt

CANADA MOOSE
THIRD AWARD
SCORE: 214-6/8

Locality: Red Lake, Ont.   Date: 1991
Hunter: Dan K. Brumm   Owners: D.K. Brumm & J. Krizsan

CANADA MOOSE 214-6/8

Dan K. Brumm, hunter
Dan K. Brumm and James Krizsan, owners

I never in my life thought I would be sitting here writing a story to be published by Boone and Crockett. After I returned from Viet Nam, I did not hunt for 15 years, when my son, Eric, became interested in hunting. Then, six years ago, my cousin, Dennis Vogel, invited me to go moose hunting in Canada.

We hunt at a spot about 25 miles west of Red Lake, Ontario. As the area is all lakes and islands, travel is by small, fishing-type boats equipped with 6 horsepower motors. Where we hunt, there is a base camp with one additional outlying camp known as the Trapper's Cabin.

On my third trip to Canada this past October, I was fortunate enough to kill this beautiful trophy moose. It has a unique story behind it, as well as three equally unique hunting friends: Jerry and Gordy Tionkowski, a father and son from Madison, Wisconsin; and Jim Krizsan, my hunting partner from Fort Allison, Wisconsin. I could not have gotten the moose back home without them.

Over the years, we have studied the movement patterns of these moose and found that, in a warm year, there is a lot of movement every three to four days. We had been hunting for three days and had not seen anything, so Jim and I decided to go to the Trapper's Cabin the next day. As I packed, I thought about the times I had been there on previous trips, but Jim had never been to this camp.

In the morning, Hugh Carlson, our outfitter and owner of Viking Outpost, flew us to the Trapper's Cabin in his Cessna 175 pontoon plane. When we arrived, we found a new cabin under construction, so we helped install four new windows before continuing with the hunt.

Hugh had told us there were three or four moose that had been seen around the camp during the summer. Jim and I started out in our boat to scout for places to hunt in the morning. We found the portage for Anchor Lake and were really excited as there was evidence of antler rubs and what looked like a bed. Our expectations rose.

However, the best laid plans went awry when I got my first look at this bull moose. It was the biggest moose I had ever seen, and he took me totally by surprise. He was probably a half mile away. At that distance, he looked like a giant standing there with his arms upraised. He was looking straight at us, so we could not see his body. The sun acted like a spotlight on his antlers and gave them a yellowish glow. It was a sight I will never forget.

I told Jim there was a moose dead ahead. Because he was looking over my left shoulder and couldn't see the moose, he told me it was a tree stump. I insisted it was moose and Jim finally repositioned himself so he could see around me to get a look at what I was seeing — a huge moose. All Jim could say then was, "Oh, my God."

We were in perfect position. The sun was in the moose's eyes and the wind was in our faces. He had his head down slightly, grazing at the shoreline. We had time to take the boat to the far side of the island in Anchor Lake. We worked our way across the island to where we could again see the moose. He was still grazing. The range was 300 to 400 yards.

Because Anchor Lake has an irregular contour, Jim and I discussed our options, hoping to get a closer shot. We decided to use the boat and take a chance on getting to the shore nearer the moose. We got out of the boat and still had about 100 yards of wooded terrain to work our way through to get a decent shot at the moose. We got to a point where we had about 250 yards of open water between us and the moose. We could go no closer. The moose had stopped grazing and was beginning to look around.

As I watched the moose through the Tasco 3x9 scope on my Husqvarna Model 9000 (7mm Remington Magnum) rifle, I could feel my heart pounding at a great rate. Jim kept telling me to take my time and make the first shot count. We were hoping to get the moose to give us a broadside shot, but then the moose twitched his ears. This told us he was going to make a move and make it fast. I let fly a Remington 175-grain bullet. The bullet hit. I was not quite sure where the bullet struck, but the moose rocked back, almost sitting down. I chambered another round. By this time, the moose had turned 180 degrees and was trying to get back into the woods. I took aim again and fired my second round, just as the bull went down.

Jim went back to the boat, while I kept an eye on the downed bull. Jim picked me up in the boat, and we went over to the moose. We were amazed by the size of him, and Jim kept saying, "Do you realize what we have here?"

I, in fact, did not realize what we had, but I was happy. It took about 10 minutes for everything to sink in. We shook hands, patted each other on the back, and then realized we were not really prepared to get the animal out of there.

We hurriedly field dressed the moose. The weather was fairly warm, and we had to get back to the cabin to make arrangements for flying the moose back to the base camp. By the time we got back to the Trapper's Cabin, it was close to 4:00 p.m. Hugh was glad for us. Then he delighted in telling us we would have to move the bull to the other end of the lake, so he could fly it out before the heat of the following day. He would need the full length of the lake in order to take off with a plane full of moose.

Jim and I went back to the moose, quartered the animal, and carried it 20 yards to where we could more easily get it into the boat. From there, we had to haul it to the sandy, far shore of the lake. By the time we were finished, it was getting dark. We were soaked, exhausted and concerned about leaving the meat out over night. Wolves and bear are known to be in the area.

Hugh arrived early the next morning to take the quarters out. It took him three trips to fly the moose, us, and our gear back to the base camp. None of us yet realized how big the moose really was.

The bull had obviously been in numerous fights, one quite recently. His left eye was swollen, and he had multiple scars about his head. As we finished cleaning the moose before hanging the meat in a screened enclosure, we found two cracked ribs on each side of his chest. We also found that my shot hit him in the left shoulder, shattering the shoulder, taking out the lungs and breaking two ribs, but never exiting. Because of the thick fur and hide, we could not find the exact point of entry. For the rest of the hunt, I was kidded about bagging a blind bull with broken ribs who probably fell over and died from a heart attack.

When I returned to Sheridan, Wyoming, I thought I would have the antlers mounted. After all, this was the biggest animal I would probably ever shoot. We still did not realize just how big these antlers were.

As I was showing the rack to my friends (and anyone else who would look at them), people started telling me to have them scored for Boone and Crockett. I thought they were kidding me.

I took them to Hartman Taxidermy, in Sheridan, and Greg Hartman, the owner, also asked if I was having them scored. Until then, I never took it seriously. Greg rough-scored the antlers at 222 points, but because he was not an official representative of Boone and Crockett, we had Ray Arzy do the scoring for us. Our final score was 218-6/8 points.

The hunt had been in October, and the deadline for applying for acceptance by Boone and Crockett was December 31, 1991. Everything seemed to be moving very rapidly. We received our official acceptance into the Boone and Crockett Club's records book on February 9, 1992. On March 6, I was both surprised and pleased to be notified the club wanted this trophy in Milwaukee by May 1st, because it was ranked in the top five in its category for the 21st Awards. I feel this is quite an accomplishment and honor for someone who had at one time quit hunting. I would like to thank everyone that helped me with this trophy, from the hunt through the mounting.

Photograph by Wm. H. Nesbitt

CANADA MOOSE
HONORABLE MENTION
SCORE: 208-3/8
Locality: Taku River, B.C.   Date: 1989
Hunter: Robert J. Matyas

CANADA MOOSE 208-3/8

Robert J. Matyas

It was the last hunt in October, near the Taku River in northern British Columbia. Moose were in the rut, and the snow was a foot deep. I had the pleasure to be hunting with Guy Anttila, the owner of Taku Safaris.

High up in the glaciers, the moose were feeding on browse, but I could not figure out how they were reaching the tops that were 10 to 15 feet from the ground. Guy informed me that, later that winter, the moose would be standing on 10 feet of packed snow and feeding on the alders.

The last few days had produced a nice 8-foot, 5-inch grizzly and a mountain goat. We had passed up a few nice moose while looking for Mr. Big. Moose in Guy's area run 50 to 55 inches in spread, with a few larger ones taken now and then. I had taken other good moose with Guy, but I wanted something special, along with a good supply of winter meat.

After packing supplies for a few days, we traveled to an area in the glaciers where Guy and I had taken a mean grizzly bear a few years before. It was a bright, sunny day, but there was a threat of snow in the air, as was the case there almost every day. We could have used snowshoes for some of the drifts, but I enjoyed walking and spotting in this majestic area with my .308 Winchester Model 70 on my shoulder. I do not know where in the world I would have rather been.

Following a concentration of tracks, we came into a thick area of alders where Mr. Big jumped up and started to run. I hit him in lungs with two shots at 100 yds. The moose had fallen into an indentation as we approached him. It was apparent that he was dead, but we poked him with the rifle to make sure. Without using the tape, we knew we had a trophy moose, but at the time, we did not realize just how big he was. Guy and I caped out the bull and started packing up the meat. He saw fresh grizzly tracks in the snow, and we were careful that we were not followed as we left a fresh scent, packing out the cape, antlers and meat.

A few days later, upon arriving at Whitehorse in the Yukon, I had a crate built for the antlers. At the airport, I was told that if the crate had been three inches bigger, it would not have passed through the cargo door of a Boeing 737 airplane. I would have had to truck it south to Vancouver for a DC-10 with bigger cargo doors.

Guy Anttila was given an award from the British Columbia Outfitters Association for the largest moose entered that year.

The moose was measured by a Boone and Crockett Official Measurer from the New Jersey Fish & Game Department in Clinton, New Jersey.

I'm proud to have this moose in my collection in Nazareth, Pennsylvania, and would recommend Guy as an outfitter.

Photograph courtesy of Robert J. Matyas

Robert J. Matyas in the field with the Canada moose he killed at
Taku River, B.C., in 1989. It scored 208-3/8.

Photograph courtesy of Daniel C. Boardman

This Alaska-Yukon moose was killed in the Alaska Range, Alaska, by
Daniel C. Boardman in 1974. It scored 218-5/8.

WYOMING MOOSE
FIRST AWARD
SCORE: 178-5/8

Locality: Sheridan Co., Wyo.   Date: 1991
Hunter: Jack A. Wilkinson

WYOMING MOOSE 178-5/8

Jack A. Wilkinson

On October 1, 1991, I was greeted at the airport by Randy Reese, my guide. I was to hunt the Big Horn Mountains, near Sheridan, Wyoming. As we headed for Randy's mother's house, he told me that he and his new bride had been scouting on the weekends for moose. Several large bulls had been seen in one particular drainage, and that was where we would be hunting.

Bright and early the next day, we were on our way to the hunting grounds. The day did not start out very well. After loading the horses into the trailer and stopping at the first stop sign, the bumper fell off the pickup. We unloaded the horses, got the bumper fixed, and we were on our way again. Then, on the way up the first grade, we lost the 4-wheel-drive hub on one side. It was not a great beginning.

After unloading all the horses at the bottom of each hill and walking them to the top, while Randy drove the truck and trailer, we finally reached camp grounds. We loaded all our of gear on three pack horses, saddled two riding horses, and hit the trail.

They say things happen in threes. That may be why one of the pack horses went crazy, rolled over and dumped his pack. An hour later, we were on our way again. After the third misfortune, I turned to Randy and said, "As you must know, when things start out badly, we are going to kill a monster."

That night, we got to camp about an hour after dark, tired but ready to go hunting. Camp was very comfortable and warm, and sleep felt good.

The next morning, we were up before daylight. The wind was blowing hard and it was cold. In the daylight, I saw our hunting area and it was spectacular. There was a very large drainage with a high pass at one end; a creek and meadows ran through the middle of the drainage. It was perfect area for moose to move through or hold in to mate. We hunted from daylight until 11:00 a.m. and then from 3:00 p.m. until dark. We saw nothing but heard a cow in a wooded area. It was pretty windy and not much was going on. We did lots of glassing and calling but had no luck.

The second day started off a lot better. During the night, we had gotten two to three inches of snow, and the drainage was just beautiful. I went to Lookout Rock to glass, and right away I saw a small 35 to 40-inch bull moose heading down the valley. I watched as he crossed, 75 or 100 yards below me. I probably dry fired on him 50 times, but he was too small. I had a good feeling about the day; things felt right.

About 10:30 a.m., Randy suggested we move about half a mile down the valley to another lookout. That was where he heard the cow the day before. As we got to the lower lookout, Randy went about 200 yards below me to call. Half an hour or so after leaving me, Randy came running back, all out of breath. He had heard two bull moose fighting, and by the sound they were probably good ones.

As my heart started pounding, we rushed to where he had heard the moose. When we got there, we heard nothing, so we decided to ease our way down the slope in the direction of the fight. On the first bench, I slipped on an icy spot, fell and hit my scope hard on a granite rock plate. I naturally began to worry, thinking, "What did I do to my scope? Is it still on, or did I knock it off?"

We then eased our way down to another bench, and Randy suddenly whispered and pointed to the bench below us. Standing at the edge of the trees, looking at us, was a very big bull moose.

As I took a rest to shoot, I thought of my scope. Taking aim with my .300 H&H Magnum, I put the crosshairs on the point of his shoulder (he was quartering toward me) and squeezed the trigger. I heard the bullet strike, and he just flinched. He moved behind a tree and I could not see him. Moving to my right, I shot again, and again I heard the hit. He just flinched and turned to go downhill. At the third shot, he dropped and we started shouting. I do not know which one of us was more excited.

When we got to the moose, we both realized we had a good one. After skinning, caping, and quartering the bull, we returned to camp and got ready to head out the next day. Back in civilization and 60 days later, we scored the moose. He scored 188-6/8. In February 1992, I received an invitation to the Boone and Crockett Awards Dinner in Milwaukee, Wisconsin, which to me is every hunter's dream.

Photograph courtesy of Michelle R. Liechty

Summit Co., Utah, was the setting for this Wyoming moose kill by
Michelle R. Liechty in 1989. It scored 155-5/8.

Photograph courtesy of William Ralphe Fleegle

William Ralphe Fleegle hunted the Mackenzie Mountains, N.W.T.,
to kill this Alaska-Yukon moose in 1988. It scored 215-3/8.

Photograph by Wm. H. Nesbitt

MOUNTAIN CARIBOU
FIRST AWARD
SCORE: 449-4/8
Locality: Fire Lake, Yukon   Date: 1989
Hunter: James R. Hollister

MOUNTAIN CARIBOU 449-4/8

James R. Hollister

When Jim Hollister of Boise, Idaho, booked a hunting trip with Teslin Outfitters in the Yukon, he wanted to shoot a nice caribou bull. The idea of bagging a trophy mountain caribou had never entered his mind, but after the hunt was over, Hollister packed out a huge caribou whose rack made veteran guides gape with awe. On this hunt, Hollister caught trophy fever.

The September 1989 trip was a combination caribou, Stone's sheep, moose and grizzly bear hunt. Hollister, a life-long sportsman, traveled to the Yukon Territory by himself. He flew into Watson Lake, ate a fine meal at the Watson Lake Hotel with some people he met on the plane, and got his tags and licenses from the fish and game department. On a Friday morning, he flew into Fire Lake, where the outfitter had set up base camp. Due to foggy conditions, it took the Cessna 206 two tries to reach the lake.

Upon arrival, Hollister discovered that the designated guide had twisted his ankle, which had been held together by pins. The pins were popping out and the guide was in excruciating pain. Luckily, another hunter had failed to show and an extra guide was available to lead Hollister on his hunt. The man's name was Leon, a Yukon native, who had only one good arm. "He only knew about 10 or 11 words, and most of them were 'hhhrrrumf,'" Hollister says, grunting to simulate Leon's vocabulary.

Leon told Hollister it would be a six-hour ride on horseback to the spike camp. "Well, it turned out to be a seven-hour ride, and it was raining or snowing most of the way. The thing that made me a little nervous was that we had gone all that way and we never saw any animals or cut any fresh tracks, other than a wolf track," Hollister recalls.

On Sunday, September 16, the first day of the hunt, Leon and Hollister woke up to pea-soup fog. They hung around camp until about 11:00 a.m., when the sky cleared enough to hit the trail. They left on horseback. After riding down the trail for about 45 minutes, Hollister saw his first caribou bull, just off the trail. "I was ready to shoot the first one. I was pretty impressed. But my guide just looked at me and laughed and shook his head and said, 'No good.'"

In the next hour or so, they saw about 30 mountain caribou, both bulls and cows. Then Hollister saw another group of animals go over a ridge into a bowl-shaped basin. As the animals filed by, Hollister saw the sun reflect on what appeared to be a large rack on one of the bulls. "Let's go take a look," he said to Leon.

With the naked eye, they could see nine cows and calves grazing in the left side of the bowl and behind them, they saw five bulls at the base of the far mountain. Hollister put his 15x60 Bausch & Lomb spotting scope on the bull with the big rack and said to Leon, "I don't know a lot about caribou, but that sure looks like a lot of points on that one."

When Leon peered at the big, old, wily critter, he remarked, "Many points — looks like 40 points!"

Hollister was really excited, but a 20-mph wind whipped across the basin from their backs, the worst possible direction. They forced themselves to sit tight for an hour or so to see if the wind died. It did not, but the animals started to move. Hollister and Leon had to stalk. They stayed in the timber surrounding the bowl and moved around the perimeter closer to the animals. By that time, Hollister had shed his extra layers of clothing and was ready to gallop after the bulls if they took off. Leon saw them start to trot away and signalled to the lean Boise man. Hollister bolted across the mostly open basin with his 7mm Remington Magnum in hand.

"It seemed like I ran for about half a mile and I could see the four bulls, but I couldn't see the big bull," he remembers.

Then he spotted it running at tree line, along the base of the mountain slope. Hollister hoped the bull would run toward the south end of the basin and into a clearing where he might be able to fire a shot.

"I kept running and finally he came out of the trees at a full run. I stopped and couldn't lie down because the brush was too high, and I couldn't shoot off-hand because I was breathing too hard, and it was 400 yards away. So I ran up about another 15 yards, and there was this spindly little pine tree with a diameter the size of a silver dollar. I leaned against that and I shot."

Hollister had no idea where the bullet hit the old bull, but he knew it made contact. The bull went down for a second, got back up, and just stood there. "I threw another round in the chamber of my Husqvarna and shot. He dropped where he was."

Hollister was using Federal Premium ammunition, with 160-grain Nosler Partition bullets. When he walked up to the animal, he discovered the first shot hit the bull in the shoulder, the second through the lungs. He paced it off: 409 long paces.

"I walked very briskly over to where the bull was, and by the time I was done inspecting him, I was one very happy person," Hollister says, grinning ear to ear. The normally silent Leon was falling all over himself when he saw the caribou's rack. "Lots of points! Many, many points!"

The two men counted more than 70 points on the incredible rack. They took several pictures, caped and field-dressed the animal, and prepared it for transport back to spike camp. Leon would not stop talking about the rack. "It could be a new world's record!"

A giddy Hollister shrugged and thought, "I don't know anything about caribou hunting, but I knew it was one beautiful animal."

Because it was so late, they had to leave the prize animal where it lay for the night. Hollister felt a little nervous about it, but he had no choice. "You never know, the grizzlies are thick in that country," he says. He could have returned the next morning to find the trophy destroyed by grizzlies, wolves or wolverines. But they lucked out, and the animal was still there when they arrived early the next day. They packed the antlers and the meat carefully to ensure the rack was not harmed in any way. At points on the trail where the trees narrowed to the width of a horse, the rack rubbed on the trunks, but no harm resulted.

Leon and Hollister remained in the Yukon backcountry for a few days and went moose hunting. The had no trouble finding moose. Hollister shot a fine bull with a 53-inch spread. "But all I could think about was that caribou back in camp," he says.

The men packed the game to base camp at Fire Lake, and all the guides and hunters went nuts about Hollister's mountain caribou. The guides agreed that Leon would win the belt buckle awarded each year by the Yukon Outfitters and Guides Association to the guide whose client bags the largest caribou, moose, sheep or bear.

Hollister flew back to Watson Lake, where the word had already circulated that someone was coming in with a phenomenal caribou. "I went to the taxidermist, and he wasn't quite sure he believed what he was seeing," Hollister said.

Hollister took the rack to the taxidermist to make sure it was packaged carefully for air transport. After he arrived home in Boise, Hollister waited two or three weeks for it to arrive. Still, no rack. He called the taxidermist to see what the problem was. The taxidermist said he had sent the rack by truck to Edmonton, Alberta, but not before about 40 or 50 rolls of film had been taken of it.

From Edmonton, the rack was supposed to go by air freight to Seattle, and then to Boise. But it almost got lost. It went from Seattle to Chicago to Denver, back to Chicago to Boise, back to Denver to Chicago to Denver, and finally to Boise. "I don't even want to talk about it, it was such a mess," Hollister says.

Finally, with rack in hand, Hollister could get it scored. It officially scored as the Number 1 mountain caribou rack in the SCI rankings. SCI awarded the rack 601-6/8 points. Hollister understands the rack has more countable, scorable points than any caribou in any category in the records books.

Hollister is so proud of the trophy that he commissioned Dennis Jones, the world-renowned wildlife artist in Joseph, Oregon, to craft a limited edition bronze of the caribou. The shiny bronze sculpture will be placed in a special area of the home he and his wife, Karen, are presently building.

The rack has won many other awards, including first place in the Yukon Outfitters and Guides Association big game awards for 1989, a gold award from SCI in 1990, the National Rifle Association's Leatherstocking Award in 1990, and an "Americas" award from SCI.

Jim says one of the most rewarding aspects of bagging a world's record caribou is that he has met all kinds of new people and made new friends. "I have met more people throughout the world through this deal than you could ever believe," says the owner of a Boise heating and air conditioning wholesale company.

Photograph by Wm. H. Nesbitt

MOUNTAIN CARIBOU
SECOND AWARD
SCORE: 440

Locality: Carcajou River, N.W.T.   Date: 1990
Hunter: David P. McBrayer

146

MOUNTAIN CARIBOU 440

David P. McBrayer

I awoke to screams: "Get out here! He's huge! You can almost shoot him from the tent!"

However, I was not leaving that tent until I was fully clothed and ready for at least eight hours of cross-mountain hiking. It was raining and snowing in the Northwest Territories mountain valley, about 15 minutes by air south of the Arctic Circle.

I had booked a 12- day hunt for mountain caribou and Dall's sheep with Stan Stevens' MacKenzie Outfitters. When I arrived at Stan's lodge, I admired the former Number 1 caribou mount over the fireplace and wondered if I could get one almost as large. Little did I know.

Stan flew another guide and me into an area with ten rams, but I turned the largest one down. When we returned, Stan asked me if I was willing to walk 20 miles for an old, heavy-horned ram. What could I say? Stan and the guide, Dynamite Danny Moore, were good to their word, and I got a 13-1/2-year-old Dall's ram. I also got to walk about 20 miles. This left only about three days for a mountain caribou, and I wanted one badly. On some previous hunts in northern British Columbia, I had seen Stone's sheep and mountain caribou. From those sightings, I developed a real desire to get this difficult and beautiful trophy that represents icy northland peaks.

Because time was short, Stan asked if I would mind doubling up with another hunter named Ike to hunt with guide Paul Weisser. Stan asked if I would allow Ike the first shot, because he had to get back to New York for his daughter's wedding. I said that would be no problem. I had read in Boone and Crockett's 19th Big Game Awards of John Kolnar's hunt with Paul Weisser. They took the First Award mountain caribou, and I felt we were really lucky to get Paul as our guide.

The next morning, Stan flew us into a mountain lake. On the way, we passed a bunch of big caribou bulls. Let me say that one reason you get game with Stan is that he can safely fly you into practically any place in practically any weather.

My pack got left at camp, but since I always wear enough clothes and hold my gun between my knees on a light aircraft, the loss did not worry me too much. We landed on a lake surrounded by caribou. However, Paul wanted the other hunter to have a chance at bigger bulls, so we headed up the valley, hoping that my pack would be waiting for us on the tundra, and it was. The next day we headed up a mountain valley and saw six big bulls. Ike shot one with heavily palmated antlers at about 500 yards. By the time Paul had skinned it and Paul, Ike, the pack dog and I had started over the mountain with the antlers, cape and meat, it was about dark at 11:30 p.m.

It was raining and snowing hard when we got back to camp. Paul pulled out about a quart of peanut butter mixed with jelly and smeared it on some bread. That was supper. We gulped it down and got into the tents.

The valley we were in was many miles long and wide. The valley floor was covered with brilliant green tundra, late fall flowers and berries. The mountains ringing the valley became snow-covered while we were there.

Sometimes fog, rain and snow can kill visibility and keep you in the tents for much of the day, and this is what happened just before the beginning of this story. When we pitched our tents, I thought, if a hunter stayed there long enough, a big caribou would come by, but I did not expect it to happen so quickly.

By the time I was fully awakened, fully dressed and got going, the bull caribou had moved about half a mile up the valley. Paul and I ran until we caught up with the bull in the low bush of the tundra. We had only a couple of little evergreen trees for cover, so we lined one up between us and the caribou and moved rapidly to it. Then, we moved to the second little tree and crouched down about 250 yards from the bull. All I could see at first were huge antlers over the bushes, but he soon moved and I had a fair shot at his shoulder. The .300 Weatherby Magnum recoiled, and there were the antlers still sticking up. The caribou had dropped in his tracks at the shot, but the antlers were so large that they still stood well above the brush.

The caribou was still in velvet as the hunt took place in late August of 1989. The antlers spread about 50 inches and they were approximately 55 inches long, with heavy beams and triple shovels. They were bigger than the rack in Stan's lodge. The bull's color was shiny dark gray-brown, with a light muzzle and neck. What more could anyone want from a caribou trophy?

When the bull fell, he ripped the velvet on one antler, so we removed the velvet. The antlers were still growing at the time, particularly on the left side where two more points were developing.

After we packed the meat, antlers and cape back to camp, Paul broke out the skillet and started cooking hotcakes. It was the first real meal in almost 38 hours. I got the first hotcake and deferred to Ike on the second in order to be polite. My only regrets on this trip were that I didn't take all the hotcakes I could get and that I could not immediately think of a trophy that would justify booking another hunt. This was the most beautiful area and the best hunt in 59 years of hunting.

Photograph courtesy of Karl H. Dore

This woodland caribou was taken at Grey
River, Newfoundland, in 1984
by Karl H. Dore. It scores 341-2/8.

Photograph courtesy of William S. Perry

William S. Perry (left) and friend show this fine mountain caribou that
was taken near Cranswick River, N.W.T., in 1988. It scored 382-2/8.

Photograph by Wm. H. Nesbitt

MOUNTAIN CARIBOU
THIRD AWARD
SCORE: 426-5/8
Locality: Pelly Mts., Yukon   Date: 1989
Hunter: Knut Wittfoth

150

MOUNTAIN CARIBOU 426-5/8

Knut Wittfoth

Finally, we had made it to camp. The orange tarp still stretched over the camp, keeping the light drizzle off the gear.

Byron, Dave and I pulled our Suzuki Quadrunner ATVs up to the trail's end and, with moans and groans, dismounted. We were happy that the 60 kilometers of swamps, mud bogs and face-whipping willows were finished. It was undoubtedly the meanest 60 km of overgrown exploration road ever travelled by man. Our camp was nestled into a stand of spruce right at treeline, next to Gold Creek. Three high basins stretched away from our location, two to the east and one to the west.

The week before, I had driven up the old exploration trail, which led high into the Pelly Mountains. There, I set up our camp and spent four days hunting the area before going out to meet Byron and Dave at the highway.

The year before, some friends and I had flown into Cabin Fever Lakes, and I noticed an old trail from the plane. I mentioned this to Byron one day in casual conversation, and he said he knew where the trail left the Campbell Highway. Well, our caribou hunting plans for the following year were set. We were going up the Moose Creek Trail into the Gold Creek country of the Pelly Mountains.

We quietly unloaded our bikes and tarped them over to keep them out of the rain. It would be backpacks and steep inclines from there. Dave fired up the stove, and Byron dug out some sheep steaks. A nice hot meal was just what we needed after the hellish, eight-hour ride. Then, sitting around the fire, I began relating stories to Dave and Byron of the four days of hunting I had done before they arrived.

I had spotted large numbers of caribou every day, missing one exceptional bull when he got my wind, and passing on several more. We sat up until late, talking and making plans for the next day. We headed for the tents, and large rain drops began pelting off our tarp. As I dozed into sleep, I hoped it would not be too wet to get an early start.

Morning brought clear skies and crisp, cool weather. Stars twinkled down from the heavens like jewels decorating the snowy crowns of the higher mountain peaks. It was a perfect morning to hunt caribou.

We had decided to pack up camp and head back to a basin at the end of a long, flat ridge, east of camp. So, after a hearty breakfast we began our attack on the ridge. After three hours of chest-high willows and alders, we staggered to the ridge top. The wind had picked up, and large white clouds went whipping by above us. I noticed large banks of clouds to the west, coming our way, but they did not look too serious. We still had to dress heavily against the icy wind, which gusted after us on our way along the ridge.

After three more hours of carefully moving down the ridge, I spotted two bull caribou, sparring and pushing about 60 yards ahead of me. I dropped to my knees, dropped my pack, and looked back at Dave and Byron. They had already done the same. I had first shot, so I looked the two nice bulls over and decided not to shoot. Byron also passed on the bulls. Dave looked them over and said Iíll take one, the one on the right.

At Daveís shot, both animals turned and ran for the edge of the ridge. Shoot again! yelled Byron.

Daveís next shot, even though unnecessary, dropped the caribou right on the crest of the ridge. Way to go Dave, nice first caribou, bud! , I exclaimed as we trotted over to see the bull up close.

Nothing could have prepared me for what I was about to see as I approached the downed bull. When I reached the ridge crest, I casually looked down into a small basin and promptly dropped like I had been shot. Below me, from 60 yards up to 200 yards, was an ocean of caribou, all feeding along below us.

Byron, over here, I hissed as I began scanning for a nice bull.

Just below and to my left, were four nice bulls. One of them was exceptional. That was the bull I levelled my Sako Deluxe in 7mm Remington Magnum on, and as the cross hairs of my 3x9 Leupold settled on him, I knew he was the bull to take. With a round in the chamber, I dropped the crosshairs behind his shoulder. I squeezed off one my 160-grain Nosler Partition handloads as soon as the bull stepped clear of the others. He hunched up, staggered around in a circle, and then stood facing the other way, with his head hanging down. One more round into the base of his neck and he was down.

As soon as my bull was down, Byron lined up on what we judged to be the next biggest bull and dispatched him with one neck-shot from his .270 Winchester.

Boone and Crockett was what we would talk about around the fire or in the bar, after a shift at work. Not once, since we left camp that morning, had the records book crossed my mind. But as I walked the 225 yards down to my bull, I began to see how big he really was.

After cartwheeling and dancing around the hillside, we all settled down to let things sink in. You know it was a good hunt when you knock down three monster bulls before you get to camp! exclaimed Byron, as he moved and twisted the rack on his beautiful bull to appreciate every angle of view he could get.

By then, the odd little hail storm was pelting us and the wind picked up considerably. It was time to get back to work.

We dressed out, caped and deboned all three animals in record time. Rather than stay on the mountain, we decided to take our trophies and gear back to base camp that night.

The next day, we made two more trips and got all our meat. It was a lot of hard work, but we all agreed it was well worth it. In the six years I have lived in the Yukon, September 26th, when I harvested my caribou, stands out as one of the most special days.

When we arrived back in Faro with our caribou, we got many a stare as people ogled the stack of racks in back of my truck. Dave's caribou scored 360-plus, Byron's totalled 390-plus, and mine officially scored 426-5/8.

That year, my caribou won first place among Yukon resident's mountain caribou. It received a gold medallion from SCI, scoring 495-2/8 and ranked fourth in their book at that time.

For a mechanic like me, working at Curragh Resources Lead Zinc Mine, this was a bit overwhelming. Receiving Mr. Reneau's letter from Boone and Crockett brought everything to a head. I cannot believe how lucky I am.

As I sit on the waste dump at work and look across the Tintina Trench and Pelly River at the majestic Pelly Mountains, I am thankful.

Thank you, Mother Yukon, for your wild and beautiful places, and thank you to my friends for sharing with me the wonderful memories of hunts and experiences.

Happy hunting from Faro, Yukon Territory.

Photograph by Wm. H. Nesbitt

MOUNTAIN CARIBOU
HONORABLE MENTION
SCORE: 392-2/8

Locality: Fire Lake, Yukon   Date: 1989
Hunter: Michael L. Haydock

MOUNTAIN CARIBOU 392-2/8

Michael L. Haydock

The hunt finally became a reality to me as we landed at Watson Lake, Yukon Territory. I had been to Watson Lake before, at the start of a trip to the Northwest Territories for Dall's sheep and mountain caribou. The excitement started to build as my partner and I checked in and then walked over to pick up our hunting licenses and tags.

The next morning found us at the Watson Lake Flying Service, ready for our flight into base camp. We were hunting with Doug Smarch of Teslin Outfitters. After loading our gear aboard a Beaver, we were ready to go.

The flight was smooth, and I found myself looking over the terrain, wondering what kind of game we would find on this trip. Looking down into the Pelly Mountains, and knowing there were Stone's sheep, moose, mountain caribou and grizzly bear down there made the trip seem to last only a few minutes. Looking down and hoping to spot something is fun but foolish, because it is difficult to spot game from the altitude at which we were flying. Then again, most of us in the hunting fraternity realize that the anticipation and other feelings help make the overall experience of the hunt.

My partner, Barry Baumann, and I unloaded our gear and met the guides and other people in camp. As it turned out, my guide was Leon Jules and Ivan Johnny was my partner's. They told us what had been happening on the previous hunts. After zeroing our rifles and eating an evening meal, we got ready for the ride to the spike camp from which we were going to hunt.

Early the next morning, we packed our gear aboard the packhorses and got our saddlehorses ready for the trip. If you have ever packed in before, you know that, until you get on the trail, the camp is like a three-ring circus, with all hunters and guides trying to get everything balanced, loaded and ready to move.

The ride in was up, down and around the snags, mountains, swamps, creeks and other obstacles along the way to our camp. About halfway in, we stopped for a sandwich. After getting all the pack horses lined up, we were ready to make the last ride to camp.

I am usually very lucky or absolutely snake-bit. After heading down the trail in the lead, one of the two pack horses I was leading went around the wrong side of a tree. I stopped, got the horse straightened out, and told my partner to go ahead. One of the animals I was after was an Alaska-Yukon moose. Guess what my partner ran into, 20 minutes down the trail?

Barry came back up the trail, leading the horses. He said, "Hold these. My moose is waiting for me about 200 yards up the creek, on a little knoll, just like a post card."

Ten minutes later, I heard the shot and walked the horses up to Barry and Ivan, his guide. They proceeded to tell me about this moose that decided to cross the river about the same time we did. Barry said not to worry; it was only a little 58-inch meat moose.

For those who have not had the chance to see a little meat moose like Barry's, let me tell you that it is a pretty impressive little moose.

We finally got into camp and settled in for the night. The location was beautiful. We were in a small stand of trees, close to a creek for water. There was a small lake just out of camp that was clear and deep. Across the lake was the face of one of the mountains we were going to hunt. We rode out of camp and found a few places where we could glass. We spotted some caribou and looked over the area pretty well.

The guides decided that we would split up and glass several different areas. Leon and I saw caribou almost all the time, as well as a few cow moose. We took our time during the next few days, heading out to a different area each day and glassing for game. It became apparent that my guide, Leon, could spot game and judge it long before I even found it. After seeing some average caribou, which did not excite either of us, and a grizzly that we could not catch up to before dark, we rode back to camp.

Late that night, my partner and his guide came riding back into camp, with a Stone's sheep, no less. About that time, I was starting to wonder if the trip was going to be one of those that starts slow and then tapers off.

The challenge of trying to show my partner that we were not just riding out and napping all day became a little more focused, especially whenever Barry reminded me of his success. To say we had a little friendly rivalry going would be an understatement.

Leon suggested that we try an area that had held some sheep on a previous hunt. The area we were in was rugged and steep, but the mountains were not as bad as they can be when hunting sheep. About noon, we reached the area we wanted to look over and, after an hour and a half of glassing, we had not spotted any sheep.

We took a break and had a sandwich, trying to figure out our next move. Below us was a little canyon with a small, shallow lake in it and plenty of grass. We decided to slowly work our way around the canyon on top to see if we could spot any sheep. We were about three-quarters of the way around when we finally saw a little area that had been hidden from view.

Leon and I looked at each other with big smiles. There were three caribou in the canyon, and one of them was an absolute monster. We decided the only way to get close enough to glass them, and possibly take one of them, was to climb back down to our starting point, get the horses, and ride to the opening of the canyon. From there, we would stalk on foot.

The adrenalin must have kicked in, because we made it around to the opening in no time. We tied the horses and started to walk into the canyon to look at the caribou.

As we entered, there were a few small points of rocks, as if some farmer had cleared a field and dumped the rocks in a sloppy fence. When we got close to the second point of rocks, we suddenly saw the tops of several caribou racks.

We hit the ground and crawled as fast as we could to the cover of the rocks. Once we got settled, made sure the caribou would not get our scent, and were pretty well hidden from their sight, we set up the spotting scope.

The three caribou were sparring with each other. The two smaller bulls would take turns jousting with the big bull. It was like watching a grown man play with some kids. The big bull would let the smaller bulls lock antlers with him and try to push him around. When he decided to show them who was boss, he just lowered his massive rack and shoved his challenger until the smaller bull turned and broke off the contest.

There was absolutely no doubt that this was a trophy bull. I asked Leon how big he thought it was. He said he was not sure, but it was as big as he had seen. The question was a formality, because he had already decided to take the big bull, if possible.

I had taken a mountain caribou in the Northwest Territories that scored approximately 385 in velvet. It would not make the book, so I kept it in velvet and had it mounted. This bull made it look small, and I wanted him.

We had one problem. We were approximately 600 yards away, and even though my .300 Weatherby was plenty of rifle, I wanted to make sure this one did not give us the slip. We decided to crawl to the next rock pile, trying to keep it between us and the caribou.

Luck was with us. The bulls continued to play their game of push and shove. Leon and I found a spot in the rocks that made a good rest, but there was a small mound about 75 yards in front of us, which hid most of the caribou if we stayed in the prone position. We decided to move a little to our left and see if we could get a better angle on the bulls from there.

We settled in, and everything looked fine. The big bull was about 300 yards out, but I knew the .300 Weatherby Magnum with 180-grain Noslers would be more than enough to do the job.

Leon watched through the spotting scope, while I got ready to shoot. The crosshairs were just behind the shoulder and steady as the rifle barked. It seemed as though it fired itself. The kick took the crosshairs up and away, and as they settled back down on the bull, I worked the action and was ready to fire again. The bull was hit hard, and my second shot was not really necessary, but it put him down for good.

We approached the big bull. It looked as big as it had through the spotting scope. We were like a couple of guys who had won the lottery. Smiles and congratulations took a few minutes. Then, we started to cape the bull and get ready to pack him out. It turned dark before we finished the job, and we went back to camp. We told Barry and Ivan about the bull, and they decided to come with us the next morning to give a hand packing it out. When we arrived, we all had turns, taking pictures with the bull and speculating about how big he was.

The rest of the hunt turned out very well for both my partner and me.

Barry took a beautiful caribou that had changed to an almost pure white color. He also took a grizzly that came to feed on what was left of his moose.

I was lucky too. We found a band of rams that had a dandy in it, a heavy, dark sheep that was definitely a real trophy. Unfortunately, after three days of trying to get close enough for a shot, he decided to move and we never saw him again.

I got a nice Stone's sheep on the next to the last day of our two-week hunt. The ram had more than a full curl, but he lacked the size of the dark ram. I swear that big ram had radar, because we wore out two pairs of hunting pants, crawling around trying to get close to him. We were never closer than 1,000 yards, and that is just not close enough.

We returned to base camp, and everyone congratulated me on my caribou. We swapped stories about our hunts and headed out the next day. We just beat a storm back to Watson Lake. We were lucky, and the shower and bed at the Watson Lake Hotel seemed like heaven.

After returning home to Wisconsin, I knew it would take some time to dry before my caribou could be officially scored. I made arrangements for the bull to be mounted and called Stan Godfrey to ask him if he would measure my bull. When the drying time had expired, Mark Zastrow and I took the rack over to Stan's for scoring. He confirmed our suspicions that it was a real dandy. The bull scored 426-1/8. Needless to say, we were all excited about the size of the bull. I think Stan was just as excited, measuring and scoring it, as I was. I do not know if I will ever be lucky enough to take another animal that meets Boone and Crockett standards, but it is exciting to make it the first time.

Photograph courtesy of Frank Entsminger

Frank Entsminger (left) is all smiles with hunter Bronk Jorgensen (right) with this barren ground caribou from Seventy Mile River, Alaska. Taken in 1989, Jorgensen's caribou scores 433-4/8.

Photograph courtesy of Bruce C. Wassom

This barren ground caribou belongs to Bruce C. Wassom after his hunt near Mulchatna River, Alaska, in 1991. It scores 429-4/8.

Photograph by Wm. H. Nesbitt

WOODLAND CARIBOU
FIRST AWARD
SCORE: 305-5/8

Locality: Long Range Mts., Nfld.   Date: 1989
Hunter: Collins F. Kellogg, Sr.

WOODLAND CARIBOU 305-5/8

Collins F. Kellogg, Sr.

The low clouds and fog made it almost impossible to see my son and hunting partner, Collins, Jr. (J.R.), and my friend and guide of many trips to Newfoundland, Clarence Childs. All three of us were sitting on a small outcropping on the side of a prominent hill, waiting for the fog to clear enough to give us another look at the fine moose that we had briefly glimpsed a couple of hours earlier. The moose was J.R.'s objective.

After staying for over an hour in that spot overlooking the obscured bogs and ridges, we decided the visibility was not likely to improve, so it would be best to head back toward camp and give up on the big moose for the day.

We started down the steep slope and had not yet gone 100 yards when a shifting gap in the mists revealed a ridgetop approximately half a mile away. As we progressed on down the slope, we suddenly saw the antlers of a huge caribou bull silhouetted against the clouds, above the rocky ridge. One look through the Leitz 10x40s and I knew that he was the animal for which I had come to Newfoundland. It was not even necessary to set up the spotting scope. There he was.

Our trip to Newfoundland came as the result of J.R.'s desire to take a good moose. Consequently, we planned a hunt with Gerry Pumphrey's Long Range Outfitters in Highlands, Newfoundland, for ourselves and several friends. We booked the hunt for the third week in September 1989, since that was the only time convenient for all members of the party. I would have preferred a mid-October hunt as that time would have been best for both moose and caribou. Having taken several moose and woodland caribou previously in Newfoundland, I opted for only caribou on this trip. The rest of the group wanted only moose. Since I had hunted with Gerry on several occasions, my wife and I knew that he runs a fine operation and has many outstanding eastern Canada moose and woodland caribou in his territory.

With a strong steady wind in our favor, Clarence led a beautiful stalk up and over the ridge. We crawled out to a point less than 100 yards from where the stag lay bedded down with two other large companions. I took a few moments at that closer vantage point to look over the fine caribou and decided that he would definitely make Boone and Crockett. The shot was an easy one. When the Ultra Light Arms .338 Winchester Magnum belched, the 210-grain Nosler Partition handload did its job. The bull's head simply dropped. He never moved. His two partners slept on through it all, never stirring until we approached to within 20 feet. Then, the two other caribou suddenly awoke and kicked turf in the air as they bolted away.

J.R. and I rough-scored the bull, as Clarence caped and quartered him. What a magnificent animal. He had a total of 34 points; two perfect, nearly-identical brow palms; exceptional bez formation; and long top points. The green score came out at 310 plus, more than enough for Boone and Crockett.

Two days later, Hurricane Hugo hit Newfoundland with excessively high winds, low clouds and driving rain, which lasted for the rest of our trip. J.R. took his bull moose in a 50-mile-per-hour gale. But that is another story.

It is always an adventure to tread the bogs and rocky ridges of that island and be with its great people. This hunt was especially memorable for me, because my son was with me when I took this magnificent trophy. It recalled another trip, 20 years ago, when we were together, and he took his first Boone and Crockett caribou at age 14. Now two generations of trophy hunters travel together regularly, throughout North America.

Photograph courtesy of Robert D. Lewallen

Robert D. Lewallen was hunting near Becharof Lake, Alaska, when he took this barren ground caribou in 1989. It scored 418.

Photograph courtesy of Jeff LaBour

Lake Clark, Alaska, was the site for Jeff LaBour's hunt for this barren ground caribou in 1991. It scores 405-2/8.

BARREN GROUND CARIBOU
FIRST AWARD
SCORE: 440

Locality: Mulchatna River, Alaska   Date: 1988
Hunter: Ted J. Forsi, Jr.

BARREN GROUND CARIBOU 440

Ted J. Forsi, Jr.

In 1972, I had the opportunity to move to Alaska. I have always had a passion for big game hunting, and I knew Alaska had some tremendous hunting opportunities. After living here two years and paying what I thought to be high costs for air charters, I signed up for flying lessons, and in the summer of 1976, I was a bona fide 90-hour, Super Cub-owning, fledgling bush pilot! I look back on those days with a smile on my face, to say the least.

Like lots of hunters, I dreamed about putting a barren ground caribou in the Boone and Crockett records book. I hunted caribou every year and glassed for that once-in-a-lifetime trophy. Most of my early hunts produced bulls that I thought were the biggest antlered game I had ever seen, and they were; but when it came to measuring up to Boone and Crockett standards, they just did not make it.

I spent many hours studying caribou antlers and finally, after several years, started to realize what it would take to make the book. Of course, long main beams are nice for starters. Double shovels help a lot, as do long bez and lots of points. I discovered that you need the two longest top points to be very long, and several top points are wanted.

In 1986, I started seriously hunting for a records book caribou. I had started an outfitting business and established a beautiful hunting camp northwest of Iliamna, near the Muchatna River. This caribou herd is very healthy at the present time and hunting anywhere in this area is excellent. I hunted about 15 days during the fall of 1986 and saw lots of big bulls, but nothing that I thought would score 400.

During the fall of 1987, I again made it my goal to find that trophy caribou. Again, even though I saw many big ones, I saw none that I was really sure would make the book.

The fall of 1988 was similar to 1986 and 1987. There were lots of big bulls, but I continued to pass. Toward the end of October, I was alone in my camp, taking down tents and buttoning things up for the winter.

There were lots of caribou moving through the area. I kept glassing from camp every hour or so, hoping against hope that I would spot a bull that would score 400 or more.

After two days, I was about ready to call it a season. After breakfast, I walked out of my cook tent and noticed a herd of about 125 animals, some 500 yards north of camp.

After getting my binoculars, I saw a beautiful bull near the end of the herd. He did not have the longest main beams, but I was impressed by the palmation of his upper beams. He looked like a moose on top, and his antlers were very symmetrical. I immediately decided to try for him. My .270 Winchester was in the cook tent, and I was soon making a short stalk along my bush airstrip.

At 150 yards, the bull saw me and stopped, standing broadside. It was a perfect shot, so I proceeded to miss. However, the next shot, taken as the bull was running at about the same range, was successful.

I knew I had a beautiful trophy caribou, but when he was scored two months later, his final score of 440 was a great surprise. I had covered many miles over three hunting seasons looking for this trophy, and I still smile a lot when I tell people that he almost walked into my camp!

Photograph courtesy of James A. Prince, Jr.

James A. Prince, Jr. is all smiles with his barren ground caribou
killed near Port Heiden, Alaska, in 1988. It scored 423-6/8.

Photograph courtesy of Debora D. Ford

This barren ground caribou was hunted by Debora D. Ford near
Mulchatna River, Alaska, in 1988. It scores 393-5/8.

Photograph by Wm. H. Nesbitt

BARREN GROUND CARIBOU
SECOND AWARD
SCORE: 434-6/8

Locality: Alinchak Bay, Alaska   Date: 1991
Hunter: Rodney R. Havens

BARREN GROUND CARIBOU 434-6/8

Rodney R. Havens

On the morning of October 2, 1991, I found myself in a local restaurant, having my last meal with my wife and daughter for the next three and a half weeks. I was leaving on the 9:15 a.m. flight from Kalamazoo, Michigan, to Anchorage, Alaska.

For nine years, I had been talking with my uncle, Jerry Meredith of Anchorage, a registered guide, about going on a brown bear hunt. Finally, in the fall of 1990, I contacted Jerry for a possible hunt in the fall of 1991. Being booked full, he invited me along to help set up his bear camp on the Alaskan Peninsula. We planned on hunting the last five days of season, after his hunters had left. This sounded like the ultimate hunt to me, since I have always wanted to see what life as an Alaskan guide is like.

The flight from Seattle to Anchorage was very interesting. I sat with a retired school teacher who lived at Lake Clark, 80 miles southwest of Anchorage. Living in Canada and Alaska all of his life, he had a vast storehouse of knowledge, which he shared with me.

Upon arrival in Anchorage, it was obvious that I was in a totally different environment. The trip to a local shopping mall to pick up some last minute perishables and hunting licenses was unique. Outside, there were beautiful snowcapped mountains; inside, things were very similar to the malls back home, except for the dog sled in one store and the abundance of mounted trophies.

After a delicious supper of deep-fried halibut, I retired for a very short night of restless sleep, awaiting that 5:00 a.m. alarm. At 7:15, Jerry and I were on a turboprop, headed for King Salmon, a small village on the Alaskan Peninsula. From there, we would take a bush plane to Alenchack on the Pacific Ocean, 80 miles from King Salmon.

Having never flown on a small plane before, I was headed for yet another new experience. As I observed our plane being loaded, I assumed the young man supervising was part of the ground crew. Wrong. He was our pilot.

The flight out to camp in the Cherokee 6 was below and through the intermittent fog and rain clouds so typical of this area. Our pilot maneuvered the plane to provide exceptional shots for my camera.

Circling Alenchack International Airport (the beach at low tide), I spotted my first brown bear. This is what I had been waiting for: wildlife, the fresh ocean air, and solitude.

As quickly as the plane had landed, it was unloaded and heading back to King Salmon. Only 30 hours from the high-tech automotive world, I was in a very remote area on the Alaska Peninsula.

Our camp and supplies for the next three weeks lay on the beach, covered with a tarp for protection from the intermittent rain showers.

While Jerry and I were getting ready to pack our second load up the 20-foot bank to the 150-yard trail to the camp site, he spotted a bear crossing the bay. Before long, the young brownie was headed our way, instead of going toward the salmon stream located 300 yards from camp. After a couple of quick pictures, we headed up the bank to stay clear of the rapidly approaching bear. In the pile of supplies that lay on the beach covered with a tarp was my rifle, still in its case. The bear stood on our supplies, as if to show me who was boss. He sniffed his new-found cache, pulled the tarp off, and pounced it flat. The 80-pound bag of salt used to preserve fleshed hides was his main interest. He rolled it clear of the pile as if it were a pillow. Even with the very explicit language we were using, he was not going to leave.

I ran back to camp and gathered Jerry's .338 Winchester Magnum rifle and headed back to the beach. Unwilling to leave, Jerry fired once over the bear's back with little effect. As the bear circled the salt, Jerry was able to fire a second shot under the bear's belly, throwing sand on him. Finally, he bolted, running about 30 yards down the beach, then slowing to a walk. Fortunately for all of us, that was the last we saw of each other. During the next three days, we spotted several bears and caribou while setting up camp.

Once again the Cherokee 6 circled the barren beach, this time leaving behind two hunters—Don Kress of Albuquerque, New Mexico, Jim Berg of Seattle, Washington — and assistant guide Ed Coleman of Wasilla, Alaska. After a couple of practice shots, we retired to camp for a hearty supper of homemade beef stew and an evening of swapping stories.

The next morning camp rustled with excitement. It was opening day of brown bear season. Plenty of game was spotted each day, including moose, caribou, and brown bear sows with cubs, but no large boars were sighted.

On the third day, at 12:30 p.m., Jerry spotted a large boar on a mountain ledge. By the time we readied the spotting scope, he had slipped into a heavily covered ravine. Jerry surveyed the canyon and located the best vantage point. Still, there were several paths by which the bear could escape from the canyon without being seen.

Four hours later he walked into an opening 70 yards in front of us. One shot from Don's .375 H&H Magnum anchored him; three more shots followed for safety. Don was the proud owner of a brown bear that squared 8-1/2 feet.

Two days later, Ed Coleman and Jim Berg returned from their spike camp with a fine caribou. After taking care of the meat and fleshing the cape, they returned to their spike camp, and Jim also took an 8-foot brown bear.

The next few days were spent close to camp due to inclement weather. During the breaks in the fog, we would glass from camp in search of a bear for me. We were able to venture out on a couple of days, but no bears were spotted. The weather had been turning colder each day, the ground had frozen, and the snow on the mountains was progressing downward.

Jerry had seen this before in the fall. He said, "When the ground freezes, bears hightail it to their den sites and dig in."

With this in mind, I thought I might "tag down" and take one of the nice caribou we had been seeing. In Alaska, you can use your tag on an animal of equal or lesser value if they are in season. In the area where we were hunting, you do not see a lot of caribou, but there are some nice ones.

One afternoon we spotted a good bull with about 15 cows. His long main beams and large, palmated tops stood out like beacons in the sporadic sunshine. We contemplated a stalk, but with the rough terrain and the distance, Jerry figured it would be dark when we got there. We did not pursue him.

The next day, we slowly worked our way to the same location, stopping frequently to glass for a bear. We glassed the same plateau and found that the small band of caribou was still there. We moved to the next vantage point for a closer look, and they were gone. After a couple of minutes of glassing, we found the problem. A brown bear sow and two cubs were climbing the mountainside toward the plateau.

The next day brought rain and heavy fog. Any glassing had to be done from camp. Four hours passed without a glimpse of anything. Ed came out to see if I had spotted anything and to confirm the fact that the plane would not be able to pick them up because of the fog. As we stood there talking, I spotted a movement in a clearing across the bay. Quickly focusing my binoculars on the movement, I saw a bull caribou disappear into the alders as rapidly as it had appeared.

I continued to glass the area, spotting the bull for the second time as he trotted through another small clearing. Once again he had disappeared as quickly as he had appeared. While I told Ed the bull was at least as good as the one we spotted yesterday, I was thinking I would try to take him.

We decided to go for him, slipped on our hip boots, shouldered our packs and rifles, and headed across the bay. It was low tide, so we were able to cut diagonally, saving a good deal of time. After climbing a seawall of stone, we entered the maze of alders. It was not long before Ed had us on a bear trail, which made for much easier and faster walking.

Suddenly, we were overlooking a large basin, and there stood my bull. He was 100 yards away, standing broadside, and looking at us.

As we dropped to the ground, Ed dropped his pack. I elected to keep my pack on in order to save a few seconds. That decision almost cost me my bull. When I tried to look through the 4x Kassnar scope, the crossbar on the pack pushed my hat over my eyes. I could not see. Removing my hat, I repositioned the .30-06 rifle. I exhaled, and the crosshairs found their mark on his shoulder.

At the instant I squeezed the trigger, the bull crouched, digging in for a fast exit. The

200-grain boattail went over his back. He was running then, and the second shot at 150 yards was a clean miss. The bull was in high gear, heading for the alder brush. Following the third shot, I heard a thud. The bullet had found its mark, and the bull was down, 200 yards away.

From our position, all I could see was antlers sticking up. We crossed the swampy basin. There he lay motionless, a mere six feet from a creek. Another shot was fired to make sure the bull was dead.

While shooting, I had been watching the animal, not his antlers. I had no idea how enormous the rack was until that moment. A foot of his 26-inch top tine was buried in the ground, showing the effectiveness of the spine shot. After several pictures, we began the chore of packing the animal back to camp. Four trips later the meat, antlers and cape were hanging neatly from the alders.

When we returned to Anchorage, Jerry measured the rack. He scored it, unofficially, at 438-4/8. For the first time, we knew it would make the records book and might make the top 50. That night, we prepared the antlers for the flight back to Michigan the next morning.

After waiting the 60 days required by Boone and Crockett, Mike Bowers of Albion, Michigan, officially scored the antlers at 440-4/8.

Memories of this hunt will never be forgotten or duplicated.

Photograph courtesy of Robert F. Hart

Robert F. Hart with his fine barren ground
caribou in 1990, while he was hunting
near Sharp Mountain, Alaska. It scores 385-6/8.

Photograph courtesy of Walter R. Willey

This barren ground caribou was taken near Moose Lake, Alaska, in 1991 by
Walter R. Willey. It scores 402-4/8.

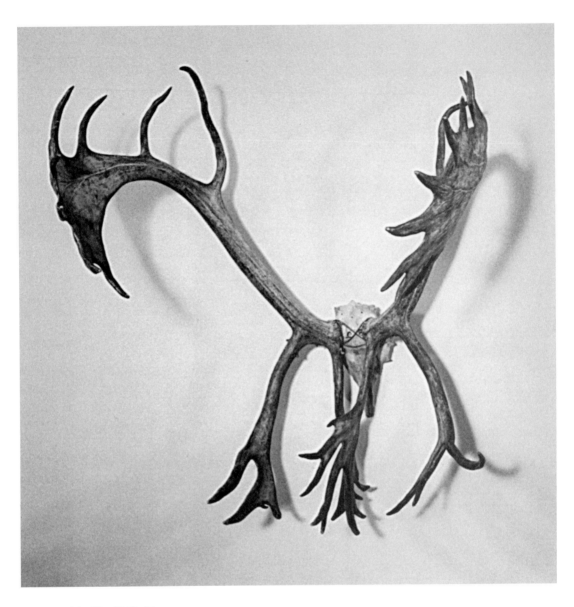

BARREN GROUND CARIBOU
THIRD AWARD
SCORE: 433-4/8

Locality: Seventy Mile River, Alaska   Date: 1989
Hunter: Bronk Jorgensen

BARREN GROUND CARIBOU 433-4/8

Bronk Jorgensen

Bronk Jorgensen, author and hunter, was 11 years old at the time of this hunt.

The Super Cub rolled to a stop and Frank Entsminger, one of the best hunters and taxidermists in Alaska, had a big smile on his face as he walked out from his camp to greet us. It would have to be a big old bruiser of a bull caribou to make Frank smile that big, so I was anxious to see it.

It all started when my dad had the local Wildlife Federation auction off transportation for a caribou hunt and Frank had purchased the donation. I had to pack out my whole Dall's sheep ram one week earlier, because Dad needed the time to get Frank out on the donation hunt. Now he was showing us the Boone and Crockett records-book caribou that he had already put the tape to. It was bigger than I could ever imagine. How I wanted one like it: beautiful, with heavy, wide-spread beams.

With a long weekend to hunt caribou and pick up Frank, I hoped it would be my turn to get a caribou around the Forty-Mile River. We had to cross several high divides that were well above timberline. The headwaters of these Arctic rivers are in remote country accessible only by aircraft or more than a week of travel on horseback.

We had flown over more than 150 miles of magnificent, roadless mountain country. The sun was getting low in the sky, and as we crossed a big, rocky divide on Iron Creek, we started to see more caribou. It was obvious that the fall migration was under way in the area. In the next 25 miles, we saw a lot of scattered caribou, but we did not stop until we reached Gold Creek, where Frank and his trophy waited. In a space more than 50 miles across, only two of the high, wind-blown ridges that we had flown over offered places to land. Both were marginal, and the sun was starting to get dim.

We quickly decided to go to the closest ridge. With the migration in full swing, we figured we could not go wrong, even if we had not been there. Dad flew me out first, along with the camp equipment. The hilltop was only 500 feet long, and the Super Cub's gear rattled and shook on the rocks as we landed. Dad quickly took the camp gear out of the airplane and went back to get Frank at Gold Creek. As I looked around, there were spruce trees on the sides of the mountains, and it was all tundra from several hundred feet below us to the peaks above. I took the tent down a steep bank to a sheltered spot in the willows. On the way down, a flock of ptarmigan flew noisily away. They were mostly white at that time of the year. I put up the tent and finished in time to hear the Cub coming back. I got my rifle and climbed back up the hill to meet them.

Dad took the airplane to a spot on the ridge where there was a dip in the ground. There, we rolled the big tundra tires into the depression to help keep the plane from blowing away. Frank and I were tieing down the left wing while Dad tied down the right wing, when out of nowhere, a small bull caribou was coming down the ridge toward us. He peeked out from a little hill, so I started stalking to see how close I could get. In a little bit, I was well within bow range. The caribou stood looking at me for about two minutes, wondering what I was. Then it snorted and ran down the hill.

We were hunting that country because my older brother had taken a big bull in the area several years earlier, while on a horseback hunt with our friend Mike Potts. The skull was broken, but many claimed it was a records book caribou. Several years later, Dad had seen another big bull as he was hiking cross-country on a grizzly hunt. He said it was huge in body and antler. More than once he expressed regret over not taking it, even though it would have been a three or four-day pack to get it out of the mountains. Dad thought these caribou summered in an area of tangled timber that cannot be hunted and migrated very late to the high country. As a result, he believed they were seldom hunted.

By the time we were set up, there were about 50 caribou high on the mountain, just coming into sight. As they came closer to us, we could see some nice bulls in the herd when their antlers were skylined in the setting yellow sun. They started to slow down, so we got a spotting scope to look at them. As Frank looked, he got more and more excited and had me look at some of the big caribou. As he explained, I could understand how to evaluate bull caribou to see if they might go in the records book. One had antlers with eight or nine points at the top, drop points, and a lot of points everywhere lower, but in the dim light, it was hard to see the brow tines. Another had tall antlers but very few points. A third bull had a good antler on one side, but the other was broken off about half way up the main beam.

The big bulls filled the evening with the noise of their fighting. We watched them move along the side of the hill until they went out of sight. I sure hoped some of them would be around there in the morning. We went down to our camp and put up Frank's tent.

We ate two Mountain House freeze-dried dinners as we listened to Frank's story of the records book bull he had shot after walking in 16 miles and glassing for five days. Packing it out alone, Frank had ferried meat, horns and camp in four-mile increments. Frank and his wife Sue are truly subsistence hunters, even though they like trophy hunting and enjoy Nature's majesty. Who else would pack the fatback and ribs for a winter feast, as well as the hide and antlers, over 16 miles of muskeg?

It had frosted in the night and it was chilly next morning. The soft snow from the night before was corn-flake crunchy and hard enough to hold up under foot. Most important, a nice day was on its way. I had not heard any caribou near the tent as I lay awake long before Dad and Frank awakened. One of the most exciting things about hunting caribou was the fact that they could sometimes be right around the tent in the morning, and you did not want to make any noise in the tent while putting on your boots. Memories of shooting my caribou from the tent, while in my stocking feet, were still vivid from the year before.

I carefully zipped the tent open, but there were no caribou in sight. After a quick breakfast, we were on our way to high ground. The ordinarily spongy lichens and mosses of the tundra were frozen hard, and we could really walk fast.

We glassed the immediate area for caribou and there were none to be found. Panoramas of frost in mountain valleys below, with the last of the bright fall colors fading or disappearing under the snow, ordinarily would have been breathtaking. A silver grizzly on the distant ridge looked for berries, but we saw no caribou.

Higher and higher we went. Finally, we could see more of the high country in a full circle. Two miles away, there were about 30 caribou. We hiked over to where the caribou had been the night before and up onto the jagged edge of a hill. There, we came to a promontory rock covered with a lot of different mosses and little plants. We looked the caribou over from that vantage, making sure that we had not missed any. I had already warmed up considerably, and we were starting to see scattered bands. Evaluating each migrating bull through the spotting scope, with Frank coaching, was starting to be fun.

There was a steadily upward incline in the tundra that led toward the next band of caribou. We followed it to a triangular butte and looked over the next basin. It was full of caribou: cows, calves and bulls in scattered bands. Through the binocular, five or six bulls looked big enough to make me happy, but a stalk on any of them would have been difficult with so many caribou in the basin. There were even caribou behind us on the trail.

It was obvious that Nature's camouflage worked for the caribou. The bulls have a rich, chocolate brown body with a white mane and rump patch in the late fall. How could we have missed them, even in the dim morning light? In the bright sunlight, they were easy to see and were everywhere, but those that walked into a mountain shadow disappeared. In dim light, caribou are like ghosts. All winter long, they match their surroundings as their coats change. We had just missed them in the early morning glow.

As the light got better, we could see more and more caribou, but the sun was causing shimmer in the scope, and it was hard to evaluate those that were a long way off. We looked over those that were the farthest away first. Dad would glass with his 10x40 Leitz binocular and point out the promising animals, while Frank and I put the 15-60x Bausch and Lomb scopes on each one.

One herd of more than eighty animals, with some coming and going all of the time, were in the center of the basin. The five or six bulls that I liked best were in this group, but getting to them would have been a problem.

Dad saw a lone bull on the near side of the herd, lying in a little depression. The top palms and points were big, and it looked like he had a drop point on the left antler, but the brow and lower points were hard to see. More caribou were grazing into sight, high up in Diamond Pass to the southeast. Even though they were miles away, the light was good and we could get a fair idea of their size.

Suddenly Dad whispered that the lone bull by the big band was standing, and he thought we should take another look. That look was convincing. It didn't take long for me to decide that was the one I wanted, but could we get to him? He was on the near side of a big tundra basin formed by the deltas of six or seven drainages. The deltas made a high curved basin, several miles across, that fell steeply off into Ynot Creek and the timber below.

We ducked back out of sight from our vantage point and went to our left, where he would be unable to see us. It seemed like it took forever to cover the two miles in the tundra as it was very hard to stay out of sight of the caribou herd. We had to crawl in some places and double back in others, and we were constantly coming into view of some part of the herd. Finally, it appeared impossible to go on without being in plain sight of what had become more than 100 caribou. We were so close that the scope was no longer needed to judge the big bulls in detail.

Was the big bull still there? Had he joined the herd or just moved on? Slowly, we crawled up toward a little spruce tree on a hummock. Beside the tree, there was a big clump of bunch grass that I could use as a rifle rest. Dad was behind the tree, so he raised up to look and couldn't see the bull. Any time our heads were up, we were in sight of the herd.

Then Frank said, "He is to the right and still a long ways out."

The bull was about 300 yards away, and we were pinned down with no terrain that would let us move closer, even by crawling. I asked Dad if I could use his .300 Weatherby Magnum, instead of my 6mm Remington, because of the range and the size of the animal. I had shot grizzly with the 6mm, but I had also used the .300 before. I placed my jacket on top of the clump for a rest and turned the Leupold up to 9x. I was sure the 180-grain Nosler bullets would do what I wanted if I could just stop shaking. I was so excited that I could hardly keep the crosshairs on him and that sure would not do.

The bull finally stood broadside to us, so I could make a good shot. I aimed a little low on the back at the shoulder and shot. He just walked a few steps toward us, and the big herd he was with was starting to move. He was still broadside to me so I shot again; that time he went down. He was a very big, beautiful dream bull. He had everything Frank had told me to look for: palms; top, drop and brow points; and shovels.

Most of the caribou in this valley were scared by the gun shots and ran over the pass out of sight. Some of them went into the timber.

We decided to take the cape from the legs up to the head for a pedestal shoulder mount. We split right up the back and stopped between the antlers. I took the spotting scope to see if there were some more big bull caribou or a bear around. Five caribou were already coming down the hill that we were going to hike up earlier. I watched them until they reached the bottom of the hill. From there, they must have smelled or spotted us, because they went back up the hill.

Dad and Frank had been boning-out the caribou. Frank was working on the head, so I went over to watch him finish caping it. The boned meat was packed into the backpacks, and the cape was tied on top.

I helped Frank and my Dad get their heavy backpacks on, and then I picked up the big caribou rack. They were not easy to carry with all the points jabbing me in back and sticking into the moss, because they are taller than I am. After a while, Dad tied them onto his backpack, and I carried the rifles for the long hike out of the mountains.

We had just started to walk on the muskeg near the plane when the wind started to pick up across the ridge and a few clouds could be seen. By the time we reached the airplane, the wind was blowing too hard to take off in the Super Cub. The wind kept blowing harder, so we tied down the airplane better to keep it from flying off without us. We put rocks in the plane, rocks in duffel bags tied to the wings, and rocks behind and in front of the wheels. I was not too disappointed over not being able to fly. It is sure more fun out there than it is in school, and I like school.

Frank said that he would like some ptarmigan in good shape for mounting, and I wanted a change from freeze-dried food, so we decided on another hunt. We walked about 200 yards and we spotted two birds. They were about 150 yards from us, right at the bottom of the hill, so we made our way down the hill toward them. As we got closer, we could see more of them. The ptarmigan stayed for a few seconds in the willows, so I gave Frank the gun. He shot, and it was a willow ptarmigan. After picking that one up, we found some fox tracks in the snow that went further into the willows. It was getting late, so we went down to the tents to spend the night. The wind was still howling up on the ridge.

In the morning, the wind was still blowing hard and it had snowed in the night. There were some ptarmigan below us, so I went hunting them. I shot two; they were rock ptarmigan. They are smaller and less common then the willow ptarmigan and they have black rings around their eyes. I could hear a lot more birds cackling down by the willows around the tents.

I decided to go glass the next valley. We went over to this jagged rock so we could get out of the strong wind to glass. There were no caribou in the country. Where had they gone?

In order to get out of the wind I would sit in the airplane. It would shake hard and it wanted to fly. The air speed indicator was up to 60 miles per hour. We put little spruce trees on the wings to break up the air flow. The Super Cub sure did look funny with trees on the wings, rocks in it, and wing covers that were blowing and flapping in the wind.

With the storm getting stronger, we went down to pack up the tents. We had to move camp down into the big spruce trees in the valley for more protection from the wind and snow. There was a small flat off to our right, and as we were going, I saw a white spot on the flat. I asked Dad whether it was a ptarmigan or just a patch of snow. The snow was all blown off from the wind. Dad said that it was a ptarmigan, so I walked over to it to try for it. I got it and went on back over to them and we kept on going.

The willows kept getting taller and thicker. It felt like you were enclosed in a box. The trees got bigger and thicker, and we came to a big spruce tree that provided good shelter. Frank put his tent up there, and Dad and I went over a little farther to set ours up under another huge spruce.

Both of our tents were lightweight, not too big, easy to set up, and water proof. A fire was soon crackling, so we could cook the ptarmigan and caribou steak. As we were eating, Frank told us that before he got his caribou, he got up one morning and watched a few wolves stalk and then chase after a small herd of caribou. He said it was very interesting. They worked the herd with one wolf hazing and the others chasing, but they went out of sight before they made a kill.

While looking for firewood, I found a nice big moose antler that had fallen off a moose the winter before. A big antler is a treasure to me as I make jewelry out of it to sell at tourist shops in Tok each summer. The moose had found the same shelter that we had from a winter storm. They drop their antlers here in December, when it is dark and 30 below zero. It is amazing that the mountains usually have a place out of the wind and secure, if you just know how to find it and take advantage of the shelter. That place was also full of good willows for a moose.

The next morning Frank and I went right up to the ridge, while Dad packed up camp. When we got up there, the wind was not blowing hard at all. We could fly, but we had to wait for Dad. There were not many clouds in the sky.

I got out the spotting scope and started to look around. When I looked where we had gone two days before, there was a beautiful cross fox running across the muskeg. I watched until it went out of sight over the hill.

The wind had slowly started to pick up again. I went to help untie the airplane so we could get on our way. We ferried the most important things with us to Gold Creek.

We had to walk up and get the rest of Frank's caribou. It took an hour to get up there and an hour to return. It was pleasant, with a slight cool wind. As we were walking we found dropped caribou antlers that I picked up and hauled back to use for jewelry.

The caribou racks were too big to put inside the airplane, so we had to tie them onto the struts. You could tell Dad was happy to have two records book caribou on the plane at the same time, and it was quite a sight. He took the antlers and the meat to town first. Then, it was a full day of flying for him just to get us in.

Both of the bull caribou were beautiful and both would go into Boone and Crockett. Frank was going to mount both of them. We were all tired. But we all had a lot of fun with the hunt and learned a lot about the wind.

Photograph courtesy of Paul E. Opfermann

This Central Canada barren ground caribou was killed near Courageous Lake, N.W.T., in 1988 by Paul E. Opfermann. It scores 361-1/8.

Photograph courtesy of Kent T. Michaelson

Kent T. Michaelson took this Central Canada barren ground caribou near Courageous Lake, N.W.T., in 1988. It scores 368-7/8.

Photograph by Wm. H. Nesbitt

NEW WORLD'S RECORD
CENTRAL CANADA
BARREN GROUND CARIBOU
FIRST AWARD
SCORE: 412-6/8

Locality: MacKay Lake, N.W.T.   Date: 1989
Hunter: James H. Wooten

CENTRAL CANADA BARREN GROUND CARIBOU 412-6/8

James H. Wooten

The basin before me was filled with caribou, but the huge bull that we had spotted earlier was nowhere to be seen. My spirits plummeted as I frantically searched the herd with my binocular. There were at least a half dozen bulls there that would have been records book contenders. Under other circumstances, any of those animals would have warranted serious consideration, but they paled in comparison to the bull that had been with the herd a couple of miles back.

The hunt really began earlier in the year at a fund raiser for various conservation and education projects. Thanks to the generosity of Gary Jaeb of True North Safaris, who donated a hunt for Central Canada barren ground caribou, I was hunting at MacKay Lake in the Northwest Territories of Canada.

This is a beautiful and rugged area on the tundra near the Arctic Circle, and well north of the treeline. MacKay Lake is almost 100 miles long, and the deep, clear water teems with huge lake trout. Some of these fish can attain weights of up to 40 pounds, and although the average weight is in the 8 to 12 pound range, some of the larger fish are caught each year. This can be a very nice bonus for the hunter who has filled his caribou tags early.

This particular hunt was run out of MacKay Lake Lodge, although Gary also has another camp on a different part of the lake, near Warburton Bay. The lodge is about 150 miles north of Yellowknife, Northwest Territories, and is only accessible by float plane. Due to the remote location, you might expect somewhat rustic accommodations, but this is not the case. Camp consists of several well-maintained cabins, a kitchen with dining area, and a separate recreation room. There are even hot showers and a generator for electricity. Transportation to the hunting area each day is by sturdy 14-foot aluminum V-hull boats with 25-horsepower outboards.

Along with my hunting partner A.L. Wilkes, and our guides, James Sangris and Jonas, I left camp the first morning with great anticipation. Within 15 minutes of our departure, we started to see small groups of caribou along the ridges near the lake. The first groups only contained cows and young bulls, but about five miles away from camp we spotted a group of six larger bulls. They were too far away to make any definite judgments as to antler size, but they certainly deserved a closer look, so we decided to try a stalk.

After following this group of bulls over three ridges, we got close enough to tell that at least two of the bulls were far better than average. Since this was A.L.'s first caribou hunt, we elected to let him try to get in position on the next ridgeline for a shot when the bulls moved in that direction. I was in perfect position to watch A.L. shoot from the top of the ridge, but I could not see the caribou. Since he fired only once, I was certain that he must have made a good shot, and I expected the other bulls to spook away from my position.

It was a great surprise when the other bulls came streaming around the ridge about 200 yards away. With my binocular, I could tell that one bull had much longer top points than the others. Since they were all were about the same in beam length and body size, I decided to take that bull. At the shot, he ran about 20 yards and fell.

The Remington Model 700 in .270 Winchester with 130 grain Sierra boattail handloads had done its job perfectly. My bull had seemed to have all the required attributes to score well, but I had been fooled by the fact that he had been with a group of bulls that were small in body size. He missed the book by less than five points. Still, with two nice bulls down the first morning of the hunt and five more days to fill our second licenses, we had to feel good.

The next day dawned to leaden clouds, high winds and intermittent rain. With the promise of several days of bad weather, the bulls of the first day were starting to seem better by the minute. We finally made it out of camp, and after fighting 4 to 6-foot swells for several hours, we started to see a few small groups of caribou on the ridges farther away from the lake.

It was nice to get off the lake after our somewhat hazardous trip. In the backs of our minds was the realization that hypothermia would set in within minutes if we were to capsize in the 40-degree water. We made a couple of stalks, but none of the bulls turned out to be noticeably larger than the ones we had already taken, so we passed them up.

The old saying "third time is the charm" never proved more prophetic than on this day. Our third stalk led to the situation described at the beginning of this article. We had spotted a large herd of caribou with several heads of records book quality in it. While trying to determine which bull would score better, our decision was made for us as another bull came into view from behind the ridge. There was no question that he was the largest caribou I had ever seen while hunting. I knew he would go very high in the book. Our only problem was how to get close enough for a shot, since they were moving away from us at a fairly brisk pace. After a short strategy session, we decided to circle a large point on the lake and try to intercept the herd somewhere on the other side.

When we finally got around the point and started inland over the first two ridges, we met the herd as it was filing through the large basin. It was at this point that panic began to set in, because I could see several larger bulls moving across the hill on the far side of the basin. Had the big one already crossed the hill before we arrived? Had I missed my opportunity for a truly outstanding animal?

There was a rock about 50 yards in front of me. Following a quick crawl to that position, I had a view of all the caribou in the basin. After what seemed an eternity of glassing the herd while the animals filed past as if on parade, I had almost given up hope of seeing the big bull again.

Just as I had decided to take an especially nice bull about 300 yards away, the big guy came ambling over the ridge with a group of about ten other caribou. Unfortunately, several of them were between me and my chance of a lifetime. I watched helplessly as the group started across the basin, never presenting me with an unobstructed shot. I was in a solid prone position with the bipod extended. The hills prevented the wind from being a factor, but the distance was rapidly increasing. The group was also heading toward a gully that would conceal them until they were far out of range.

At the last moment the other caribou parted, and I had an unobstructed shot at the big bull. He was already starting into the gully and half his legs were no longer visible. It was now or never. At the shot, he fell into the gully, almost completely out of view.

James and A.L. were watching this little drama unfold, and as it turned out, they were closer to where the bull fell than I was. As a result, they were first to reach him, and any concerns about his size were allayed when A.L. turned and gave a big grin and a thumbs-up sign.

When I got to him, I could see that he was as good as I had hoped. He had 50-inch beams, with longest top point being over 20 inches. His back points were over 10 inches, and the widest of the double shovels was over 16 inches. He scored 406-6/8 points Boone and Crockett, after the 60-day drying period.

It was amazing to watch James and Jonas prepare the meat for packing out to the boat. After removing the head and cape, the remaining part of the skin was used to wrap the meat and was tied together with a strong piece of cord. This bundle was then tied to a strap called a tumpline, which circles the forehead and supports the weight of the meat. To the hunter goes the honor of packing out the head, antlers and cape. It was one very happy hunter who headed back to the boat with his prize package.

By then, the weather was even more ominous than before, and we prepared for a very rough trip back to camp. We had been traveling for nearly an hour when A.L. spotted what he thought might be a caribou near the northern shore of the lake. Closer inspection revealed an old bull with beautifully palmated uppers and nice bez and shovels. After a short discussion, he decided to try a stalk. When close enough, he decided that with ever worsening weather, this caribou looked good enough to take. One shot was all that was necessary and soon we were taking pictures in preparation for caping and packing. As it turned out, that was a good decision, since rain and wind kept us in camp for the next three days.

On the night of our fifth day, the clouds cleared away long enough for us to watch an outstanding display put on by the Aurora Borealis, better known as the northern lights. The constantly changing colors and patterns entertained us for several hours and provided a portent of things to come on our last day in camp.

The dawn brought clouds and wind once more but not so much that we couldn't get out of camp to do some fishing later in the morning. We followed another hunter and his guide from our camp to the mouth of a small river that flowed into the lake. They were going farther inland to a crossing on the river where they would try to find a nice bull to fill the remaining license in camp. As we pulled our boat up on shore, we could see something dark running through the bushes on the other side of the river. They waved to us to come there. We found that they had run into a tundra grizzly along the stream, in the waist high bushes. Luckily, he had decided to head for the distant hills rather than dispute possession of that part of the stream.

This was a most fitting end to a fantastic hunt on the tundra of the Northwest Territories, and the fat lake trout that we caught later were almost an anticlimax.

We spent that evening preparing our gear for the long trip back home. That night, I lay there thinking that soon we would be back in the land of noisy automobiles, polluted air and masses of people hurrying from place to place. We were leaving a land of spellbinding beauty, a land of the tundra grizzly and the wolverine, of arctic wolves and the majestic caribou. Most of all, we were leaving a little part of our souls. Would I like to return to hunt in that magnificent country again? What do you think?

Photograph courtesy of Bruce E. Cepicky

Still in velvet, this Quebec-Labrador caribou was taken by Bruce E. Cepicky in 1988 near Ungava Bay, Quebec. It scores 379-3/8.

Photograph courtesy of Lorraine Harrison

Hunting in the Alaska Range, Alaska, Lorraine Harrison took this barren ground caribou in 1991, which scores 387-1/8. Her father, Henry Spivey accompanied her.

CENTRAL CANADA BARREN GROUND CARIBOU
SECOND AWARD
SCORE: 401-1/8

Locality: Courageous Lake, N.W.T.   Date: 1989
Hunter: Richard B. Limbach

CENTRAL CANADA BARREN GROUND CARIBOU 401-1/8

Richard B. Limbach

The idea of this hunt occurred about 1987, while I was hunting elk in New Mexico. I met Dennis Yost, who knew a caribou outfitter in the Northwest Territories. Dennis asked if I would like to go on hunt in late September for Central Canada barren ground caribou; he said he would arrange it.

We left on September 20, 1989, and arrived in Yellowknife the next day. We spent the night there and flew to base camp at Courageous Lake on September 22. There, we met the outfitter, Fred Webb, and his son, Martin. Since we could not hunt the same day we had flown, we settled in at camp.

After breakfast the next day, the guide took us out in the boat to a small river where we glassed for caribou. As we were sitting and watching the caribou, the wind came up and sleet started falling. The guide suggested we leave, because it was a two-hour trip back to camp. As we started out, the wind got stronger, the sleet fell harder, and the temperature was dropping fast. We made it back to base camp about four hours later, completely covered with ice.

During the night, the temperature fell below zero, the wind blew, and conditions were blizzard-like. By daylight, the storm had subsided, and shortly after breakfast, we again went out to look for caribou.

About two hours down the lake, we spotted a herd of caribou. As we rounded the bay, we saw approximately 10,000 to 15,000 animals. The main migration was on. Jerry, my guide, said we would go by boat toward the front of the great herd.

We pulled ashore, walked half a mile or so inland to a pile of rocks, and started glassing caribou. They split into two lines as they passed around the rock pile, and there were many, many good bulls in the herd.

After 15 minutes, I saw an exceptional bull. I turned to the guide and asked if he thought it was a records book animal. He said there could be bigger bulls in the herd, so I passed up that bull.

We lay there for another hour and a half, watching the caribou migrate past us. I probably saw three or four more trophy bulls before I spotted the one with the huge tops and bez. As I put the crosshairs on the animal, I asked Jerry if he had double shovels.

He said, "Yes, good double shovels."

Almost before he finished speaking, I pulled the trigger and the bull was on the ground. When we got to the bull, we took some pictures, took the head and cape, packed up the meat, and returned to the boat.

Back in camp, the wind started to blow again, and the temperature dropped. The outfitter called the airplane to come and pick us up early, since the weather was getting worse and he was afraid the lake would freeze. We left the next morning. All of the hunters had shot their caribou in two days.

After the 60-day drying period, I was very surprised by how well the bull scored. He was mounted, and when I got the mount from the taxidermist, I was thrilled to hang it on my wall, along with other animals I have taken in the last eight years.

Each time I look at the mount, I think back and reflect on the hunt. It was a great thrill to take this trophy animal.

John R. Young poses with this fine mountain caribou taken in the
Mackenzie Mountains, N.W.T., in 1985. It scores 390.

Cassiar Mountains, B.C., was the site of Peter E. Paulos' 1988 hunt for
mountain caribou that resulted in this fine animal that scores 412
points to qualify for the Awards records book.

Photograph by Wm. H. Nesbitt

CENTRAL CANADA
BARREN GROUND CARIBOU
HONORABLE MENTION
SCORE: 382-6/8

Locality: Rendezvous Lake, N.W.T.   Date: 1990
Hunter: James C. Johnson
(Hunting Story Not Available)

Photograph courtesy of Gary A. Jackson

This Central Canada barren ground caribou was
taken 1988 near MacKay Lake, N.W.T., by
Gary A. Jackson. It scores 363-6/8.

Photograph courtesy of Val B. Jones

This barren ground caribou was killed by Val B. Jones in the Taylor Mountains,
Alaska, in 1990. It scores 425-3/8.

Photograph by Wm. H. Nesbitt

CENTRAL CANADA
BARREN GROUND CARIBOU
HONORABLE MENTION
SCORE: 382-3/8

Locality: Courageous Lake, N.W.T.   Date: 1989
Hunter: Patrick T. Stanosheck

CENTRAL CANADA BARREN GROUND CARIBOU 382-3/8

Patrick T. Stanosheck

The hunt began as many have; my hunting partner, Richard Limbach, and I attended the FNAWS annual convention in Reno, Nevada, in 1989. There we met up with Dennis Yost, a friend from a previous hunt. Somehow, all three of us ended up in Fred Webb's booth with a beer in one hand and a deposit check in the other. The hunt was on for the third week of September 1989.

As usual, summer dragged along and the cool mornings of September finally arrived. It was time to get serious about getting ready. The bags were packed and the rifle was sighted-in. Before I knew it, September 20 had arrived and I was on a plane, heading to Edmonton, Alberta.

We all met in Edmonton, and after a restless night's sleep, we were on another plane destined for Yellowknife, Northwest Territories, early the next morning. After arriving in Yellowknife, we took care of the necessary paper work at the local game branch. Then we boarded a Twin Otter on floats and headed to a place called Courageous Lake. We were to find out why it was called Courageous Lake the next morning.

We were met by our outfitter, Fred Webb, his wife Irene, and their son Martin. After some hot coffee and fresh pie, we were situated in our sleeping quarters and spent the remainder of the afternoon making sure our rifles were still on target. That evening after supper, we were assigned to our guides and went off to bed.

The next morning after breakfast, Richard and I, along with our guide, Noel, boarded a 16-foot boat and went down the lake to a migration route. After about a two-hour boat ride, the wind picked up to gale force and it began to snow pretty hard. We went ashore for a short time and decided the weather was going to get worse as the day wore on, so back in the boat and back to camp we went. We had three-foot waves, and the snow was blinding if you were looking into it, which was the direction we had to go. Noel borrowed Richard's glasses so he could keep the driving snow out of his eyes. After four hours, we arrived back at camp. We were covered with ice from the water blowing into the boat, but after dry clothes and hot coffee, we were no worse for wear. We then understood why the lake was called Courageous Lake.

That night, the temperature kept falling and by morning the lake was beginning to freeze. The wind and snow, however, had stopped and we were ready to go hunting again.

Fred told us as we were ready to leave camp that we had better get our caribou that day because he was going to radio Yellowknife for the plane to pick us up the next morning. The lake was freezing up, and we did not want to spend the winter there.

The storm had started the caribou in motion. After about an hour's boat ride, we could see that the hills were covered with migrating caribou. Richard and I were in two different boats at this point and went ashore in two different spots, about half a mile apart.

After about two hours, I heard Richard shoot. Later, I learned that he had taken a tremendous bull. Noel and I moved to a little rock mound about a half-mile inland and were amazed by the number of caribou that just kept coming by us. I must have seen over 1,000 bulls. As the bulls passed, I kept trying to put the perfect rack together. When I saw one that looked particularly good, he would be surrounded by several others and there was no way to take a safe shot.

Finally, some four hours later, the herd started to thin out, and to keep things interesting, along came a barren ground grizzly, following the tail end of the herd and looking for an easy meal. I told Noel to keep his eyes on the bear while I kept looking over the caribou.

At last, the caribou started coming by us single file, and I spotted my bull about 400 yards away. I could see through my spotting scope that he was not especially big, but he had double shovels, very long top points and was well palmated on top. I let him come to within 125 yards or so. One shot with my Ruger .300 Winchester Magnum, and he was down. He was pretty much what I expected, because I had a lot of time to look him over as he came to us.

Following the picture taking, we caped and boned him out, hauled everything back to the boat, and headed back to camp. There were seven hunters in camp and we all got our bulls that day. The next morning we were on the plane and out of there before the lake froze-up completely. This was one of the best two-day hunts I have ever had. Thanks again to Fred Webb and his crew for another good hunt.

Photograph courtesy of Dan Brockman

Dan Brockman was hunting near MacKay Lake, N.W.T., in 1990 when he took
this Central Canada barren ground caribou. It scores 371-1/8.

Photograph courtesy of James C. Forrest

This barren ground caribou was taken in the Alaska Range, Alaska,
in 1988 by James C. Forrest. It scores 409-5/8.

Photograph by Wm. H. Nesbitt

QUEBEC-LABRADOR CARIBOU
FIRST AWARD
SCORE: 424-1/8
Locality: Serigny River, Que.   Date: 1989
Hunter: Brad Case

QUEBEC-LABRADOR CARIBOU 424-1/8

Brad Case

Your hunting dreams can come true; I know they can.

My particular dream was about a caribou hunt in Quebec's Ungava Bay area. In February of 1989, I attended the Eastern Sports and Outdoor Show in Harrisburg, Pennsylvania. I wanted to gather as much information on caribou hunting and outfitters as possible. With at least five pounds of pamphlets and booklets in tow, I still was not sure the trip would ever be more than wishful thinking.

For two months, I pored over each scrap of paper, read every pamphlet, and finally decided on an outfitter. The service was almost all-inclusive, to and from Montreal; just what I wanted.

Next, I had to decide when to go during the season. I noticed the outfitter was offering, at added cost, a trophy hunt during the last week of September. I felt that the larger caribou must be moving through the hunting area toward the end of the season, so I made a call and booked a hunt the week before their special trophy hunt on the chance the caribou migration would be a little early.

The really hard part was waiting for September to arrive. It finally did, and I found myself on a plane, headed for Montreal. Upon arrival, I met the outfitter and the other members of my hunting party. The other hunters were Bob Kane and his friend Alvin Mizelle from Virginia; Dave Bartlett, Sr.; his son Dave, Jr.; and their friend Dave Howe, all from Vermont.

In a fairly short time, our group seemed to jell, and we all got along famously throughout the trip. We gave the three Daves numbers: Dave #1, Dave #2 and Dave #3. Otherwise, every time someone called for Dave, half the camp turned around.

Well, we were out of Montreal in short order and winging our way to Schefferville, an exotic place I had only read about and imagined was just one step away from the edge of the earth. Since we arrived after dark, there was no time to look around as we were hustled through town to our lodging for the night. We were to fly to camp early the next morning. One thing did impress me, and that was the large number of empty homes on every street. Schefferville must have been a thriving city at one time, when it had an economy. Now it seemed only hunters like us were keeping it alive.

After a cozy night's sleep, our group was up early, eager to be on our way. A slight frost crunched under our feet as we walked from the cabin. After a quick but filling breakfast, we went to the dock, where our single-engine Otter was being deftly loaded with our small mountain of gear. The plane swallowed all of it, plus six hunters and the pilot, without protest.

As we chugged away from the dock, my thoughts began to focus on the week ahead, and I began counting caribou in my daydreams. The country from the air was magnificent. Shades of green and brown were interspersed with beautiful blue lakes of all sizes and shapes as far as the eye could see. Signs of civilization were quickly left behind. First the houses disappeared, and then the roads trickled out. Soon, there was only tundra, wild and pristine.

All eyes strained to pick up anything that looked like caribou below. Once, a couple of us saw what appeared to be several trees near the middle of a small lake. Strangely, there was a V-shaped wake behind them. Obviously, they were caribou swimming the lake, following an age-old migration route. Presently, the plane settled down gently on a lake of moderate size. As the pontoons knifed the surface, we got our first look at the tundra from ground level. What appeared as flat, barren landscape from the air was transformed into rolling hillsides. Great open areas were interspersed with trees that grew less than 15 feet tall.

This lonely picture was greatly improved when the outfitter's camp swung into view. The four tent structures that would house us over the next few days were nestled snugly beside a fishhook-shaped cove. A steep hillside offered necessary protection from the northern elements.

As soon as the plane touched the makeshift dock, unloading and reloading began. All hands pitched in to take off cargo for our party and load gear and game from the previous week's successful hunters. As I looked at the caribou racks being loaded, none looked outstanding, though all were respectable. Each hunter had apparently filled both his allotted tags. The pilot sent for a second plane to help with the load he could not carry. Afterward, we stood there and watched the plane taxi to the far end of the lake. As the engine roared and the plane slowly cleared the water's surface, a feeling of isolation crept up our spines. Then, our link to civilization disappeared over the ridge. We need not have worried. The camp was in daily radio contact with other camps nearby and a base station in Schefferville, 125 miles away.

After squaring away our gear and doing a few chores around camp, the rest of the day was spent checking weapons and scouting close to camp. Our two guides, Serge Gravel and Emil PeBenier, explained the migration routes through our area and generally gave us the lay of the land. The camp was placed purposely in a well-traveled migration area. That fact was evident by the camp log, which showed that nearly all the season's hunters had filled both of their tags. The icing on the cake came when the second pilot flew in to pick up the remaining cargo from the morning's activity. He told us about the many caribou he had seen moving toward our location. "Tomorrow will be a bang, bang day," he said.

I slept fitfully that night, but I was glad just to be in that wild place and to feel it around me, if only for too short a time. Next morning was one I will never forget.

The gray dawn greeted me with a crispness that hinted of coming winter as I struggled with my gear toward the boat that would carry me to the hunting area across the lake. I was stunned to see caribou on the distant hillside — not just one or two, but 10 or 20 were visible, making their way through the area where I was going to be. As I watched their shapes move across the tundra, I could hear the deep bellowing of the bulls echoing across the water to me. The place was alive with caribou.

I was assigned a stand against a large rock about 75 yards from the edge of the lake. It overlooked several trails and seemed like a natural funnel through which the caribou would move.

It did not take long for things to start happening. A group of cows trotted toward me down one of the trails to my left, passing me at about 15 yards. Each gave me the once over, but otherwise hardly paused at all. The migration was driving them. Shots rang out over the next ridge as other members of my party scored. Meanwhile, I watched a virtual parade of caribou pass by.

I saw one bull swimming across the lake in front of me, near its widest point. Through my binocular, it could be seen paddling steadily toward the far shore. Nearer, I could see bulls moving through the trees, but none offered a passable shot. Suddenly, straight ahead, I glimpsed splashing water and the movement of legs through a low-lying marsh about 100 yards away. Caribou, and lots of them, were coming at me. I got my scope up, intending to look each one over, but there were too many. I realized some were getting by when I heard the "tick tick" of their hooves to my right. I began to scan the herd, which must have contained 50 animals. My scope settled on several large sets of antlers in the rear as I tried to remember my homework: look for high antlers with symmetry, predominant bez tines and, most important, double shovels. No sooner had that thought finished than there he was.

My attention was immediately drawn to the high V-shape of the bull's antlers. The dark brown bez tines protruded forward, about two-thirds of the way down those arching scythes. I caught a glint of light as it shone through a one- inch gap between his double shovels. There was no doubt that he was master of the harem.

I moved the scope on my .308 Browning BLR to the three other bulls, but there was no comparison. Deliberately, the duplex crosshairs came to rest on the master's right shoulder. Time was running out and the bulls were closing. In single file they came, with the king bringing up the rear. I took the shot as he topped a small knoll in front of me. The 180-grain Winchester Silvertip pierced his chest, and he dropped in his tracks. The adrenaline chills shook through me and my mind raced as I paced off the distance — 30 steps. What a beautiful animal!

Shortly, my guide Serge appeared with Dave #1, and together we looked over my caribou. "That's a trophy for sure!" was all he could say. I was skeptical. It had been too easy. But Dave assured me, saying he had seen all the other caribou taken, and so far, this was the best.

Things slowed down considerably after that. Within 24 hours of the initial flurry of activity, the main herd had passed by. Those of us who had not chosen to fill tags in the first two days faced some hard hunting the rest of the week. The caribou became scare, but I did manage to take a young bull that offered me a challenging running shot about four days later. In the final tally, our group had taken 12 fine bulls, 11 with rifles and one with a bow.

Back in Maryland, two months after the hunt, I contacted a Boone and Crockett scorer out of curiosity. Initially, he was not too impressed, but when the numbers were tallied, they came to an amazing 424-1/8. The score was more than enough to make the all-time records book, and maybe good enough to place in the top 20. My dream of a great caribou hunt came true, and if I can do it, maybe you can too.

Photograph courtesy of W.I. Burns

MacKay Lake, N.W.T., was the site of W. I. Burn's hunt in 1991.
His Central Canada barren ground caribou scores 345 points.

Photograph courtesy of Thomas L. Vaux

This Quebec-Labrador caribou was taken near Lake Consigny, Quebec,
in 1988 by Thomas L. Vaux. It scores 392-6/8.

QUEBEC-LABRADOR CARIBOU
SECOND AWARD
SCORE: 416

Locality: Lake Consigny, Que.   Date: 1989
Hunter: Ricardo L. Garza

QUEBEC-LABRADOR CARIBOU 416

Ricardo L. Garza

I quickly released an arrow at my bull, only to get a sick feeling as the arrow passed over his back. Was this the way my hunt was to end? I hoped not.

After a year of planning, watching videos, reading articles and studying caribou antlers, my hunt was finally a reality. The outfitter we were hunting with was Safari Nordik. Our camp was on Lake Consigny, which is about 80 miles west of Fort Chimo, Quebec. Thanks to the videotape Henri Poupart had sent me, I already knew what to expect in the camp and the surrounding terrain.

When I arrived in camp, I met other hunters coming out to go home. One hunter had a big smile on his face. He told me he had shot a big bull caribou with his bow; it had rough-scored at 380 points. Wow! If only I could be that lucky.

After we settled in camp, Howard Biddle, a rifle hunter from West Virginia, and I went out and did some scouting behind our camp and along the peninsula. After walking about a mile, I spotted two bulls approximately 300 yards away. They were coming our way, angling toward the lake. I could not believe how big the rack was on one of the caribou. It was huge, just like in the videos. Well, that was Saturday, and I was excited about Sunday.

On Sunday, I walked and glassed, and walked and glassed, from the valleys to the mountain tops. All I saw the whole day were a few cows and calves.

On Monday, I hunted with my partner, Jerry Leair, also a bow hunter. The weather was rainy, cold and windy. We had set up on a ridge overlooking a narrow section of the southern end of the lake, where caribou had previously been seen crossing. Behind us was a heavily traveled trail through the woods.

At about 10:30 a.m., I spotted a medium-size bull coming down the trail. He was about 125 yards away. I quickly got into position. From a range of about 30 yards, I was able to harvest my first caribou bull. I was very proud of it. The bull had double shovels and would have scored 290 points or so. After that experience, I was determined to shoot nothing but a very big bull.

Tuesday started out to be a very beautiful day, with clear blue skies and a temperature in the mid-50s. Norman, our Inuit guide, said he was going to take us to the end of the lake, past the narrows where we had hunted the day before, to the place where the lake ended and the river started. As we were moving down to our destination, we spotted some big bulls on the side of the hill. Jerry and Norman got out there to hunt these big bulls, while I went farther down to the spot where Norman told me to go.

When I got there, there was action already. I went on top of a small knoll, overlooking a small lake and the woods on the other side of it. Sure enough, there was a herd of caribou with some nice big bulls going through the woods, and from what I could see, there were more coming down from the far lake to the tip of the end of the woods. That was where I would try to ambush them as they traveled by me.

Within minutes, I had caribou all around me. After that particular herd had left, I went down to the other side of the woods to see what I could see. All I saw were cows and smaller bulls. Just as I was about to return to my original spot, I saw him. There stood the trophy of my dreams, looking as proud as ever.

He was with another big bull. They were angling through the woods and down a slight incline toward the spot where I had been earlier. I started to run, and then crawl on my belly, parallel with them to intercept them where I thought they would come down.

After perhaps half an hour of stalking, they stopped and looked down to where I was. The smaller bull went back the other way. The larger bull stayed there, staring at me. I froze like a rock until he thought everything was safe. Then, whenever he put down his head to feed, I tried to crawl closer to him. He was then some 45 yards away. Suddenly, the smaller bull and some cows came up behind him and started walking my way. "My" bull decided to follow them, but he was very cautious. He came to within 20 yards of me, with a tree and bushes separating us, as the other caribou kept coming.

As they passed, they detected me and all hell broke loose. Caribou started running everywhere. I quickly released an arrow at "my" bull, only to get a sick feeling as the arrow passed over his back. Without thinking, I quickly nocked another arrow as the bull reached the point of the woods. He stopped briefly to look at me from a distance of about 65 yards. Then, everything went into slow motion. I raised my bow, roughly estimated the range, aimed, and released.

As my arrow appeared to reach the bull, I could no longer see it. The bull took off running toward the water before I saw the big red spot right behind the shoulder, dead center in the lungs. He ran about 85 yards, stopped and fell at the water's edge. I returned to my arrow to find that it went clear through both lungs — right through him.

As expected, my equipment worked flawlessly. I was shooting a Ben Pearson Renegade bow set at 58 pounds, with a Fast Flight string. My arrow was an Easton XX75 camo 31-inch shaft tipped with a 125-grain Thunderhead, which has always performed well. I have shot many big game animals with this broadhead traveling at 205 feet per second.

As I approached my bull, I could not believe how big he really was. He had huge 20-inch top points, a 50-1/2-inch inside spread and 21-inch double shovels. I rough scored him at 430 points. After the necessary drying period, I had him officially scored at 416 points. He entered the Pope and Young Club all-time records book as Number 3, with a panel score of 416-6/8. I hope he will rank fairly high in the Boone and Crockett records book.

Photograph by Wm. H. Nesbitt

PRONGHORN
FIRST AWARD
92-6/8

Locality: Coconino Co., Ariz.   Date: 1991
Hunter: Sam Jaksick, Jr.

PRONGHORN 92-6/8

Sam Jaksick, Jr.

Devoting the time required to collect an exceptional pronghorn trophy was relatively new to me. I have spent the majority of my hunting days over the last 20 years pursuing sheep and mule deer wherever the better trophies exist. Although I have shot several good pronghorn, none has quite made the records book.

In September of 1991, I had the opportunity to hunt Coconino County, Arizona, with a very knowledgeable guide, Tony Grimmett of Phoenix, Arizona. When I arrived in Phoenix, I was picked up at the airport by Tony. We then traveled to the area known as the Coconino Flat, which is renowned for consistently producing large pronghorn heads.

We set up camp and spent the next four days looking at as many animals as possible. Over that time period, we probably observed 30 to 40 bucks of various sizes.

The second day, we actually made an approach on one buck. Both of us were sure he would exceed the minimum score for the records book. However, since I had two weeks set aside for the hunt, I thought I should devote at least a few more days in pursuit of an exceptional head. It is funny how, on the way back to camp, you usually begin to question your judgement.

After four days at our original camp, we felt it was about time to move to a new location. It had been rumored by several archery hunters that during the archery season, an exceptional head had been seen at the opposite end of our area. Tony had previously seen several good bucks in that part of the area. We decided to break camp, relocate and search for the phantom pronghorn.

Once we arrived at the new hunting site, it became obvious to me that locating and observing heads from any distance was going to be difficult, mainly because of the rolling hills and junipers. On the other hand, once an animal was spotted, it would be much easier to approach.

As luck would have it on the evening of the second day, after walking several miles into a somewhat remote and desolate plateau, we came upon the pronghorn we felt certain was the animal we were seeking. The buck appeared very massive, with exceptional prongs.

Tony and I discussed the score and felt the head would exceed 88 points. It was a wonderful opportunity in that the wind was perfect, the sun was directly over my back, and there was a line of trees that, if my stalk went right, would put me within approximately 350 yards of the animal. Over and above these favorable factors, the buck was slowly feeding in our direction.

I knew that if the antelope spotted me during the stalk, it would immediately move off across the flat and into an area of dense junipers, thereby making it impossible to pursue. The buck had two does with him and they continually scanned the surrounding area. I was very concerned that once I began to move forward, I would be spotted.

Tony and I discussed the stalk and felt it was best to wait until the sun, which was already low on the horizon, was directly in the animal's eyes. At the proper moment, I began to crawl the approximately 200 yards to a pre-selected spot, where I planned to take my shot.

Everything worked perfectly, and just as the sun was about to set, I was able to touch off the shot using my 7mm magnum. When I again looked through my rifle scope, the buck was just standing there; he had not moved. I thought there was no way I could have missed that shot.

Tony yelled that he could see through his spotting scope where the pronghorn was hit, and it appeared the bullet had gone through the heart. In the past, with similar shots, the animal had at least moved, but this buck simply stood there. However, by the time I turned back from looking at Tony and prepared for a second shot, the buck had collapsed.

Tony then joined me, and we headed straight for the pronghorn. Once we got there, we realized that the head was even bigger than we had anticipated. It was an extremely massive head, with both prongs measuring in excess of 7-2/8 inches. Needless to say, Tony and I were very excited with the results.

Tony, who is also a taxidermist, skinned out the entire buck as I had some thoughts of a full-size mount of the trophy. After taking pictures, we carried the pronghorn back to the truck and headed to the nearest town for a steak dinner.

As soon as we had an opportunity, we rough scored the horns and came up with approximately 93. After the 60-day drying period, the head officially scored 92-6/8. It seems as though this was the biggest pronghorn taken in Arizona during the 1991 season.

Photograph courtesy of Christopher C. Hornbarger

Humboldt County, Nevada, produced this pronghorn, scoring 82-6/8.
Christopher C. Hornbarger killed it in 1989.

Photograph by Wm. H. Nesbitt

PRONGHORN
SECOND AWARD
91
Locality: Humboldt Co., Nev.   Date: 1990
Hunter: Steve W. Dustin

PRONGHORN 91

Steve W. Dustin

This hunt started in the summer of 1990, when I was anxiously waiting for the results of the 1990 trophy tag drawing in Nevada. While at work one day, I was called and told I had drawn a Nevada desert sheep tag; I just about fainted. Within a week I had drawn a desert sheep tag, a pronghorn tag for Nevada, and a muzzleloader elk tag for Idaho.

My main concern was the sheep tag, for there were only two non-resident tags for my area, and I was one of them. Next came the pronghorn, for which six tags were available, and then the elk hunt.

Living in Susanville, California, I am less than 200 miles from my pronghorn unit, 01-B, which is just north of Gerlach, Nevada. That gave my eleven-year-old son Matt and me a chance to go in and scout it. In mid-July that is just what we did. We packed up and went in for a three-day scouting trip. Then, the excitement of this hunt really hit me. It was not only the luck of drawing the tag, but the preparation for the hunt and sharing this with my son. We saw a lot of animals, including some good bucks, but nothing exceptional.

On August 16, two days before the hunt, my hunting partner Matt and I went to Nevada. Before going, I had talked to a friend of mine, Bob Roberts, who owns the Soldiers Meadows Ranch, which borders my unit.

Bob had told me to stay at the ranch and hunt from there. That is exactly what I did. What a beautiful place the ranch is. Seventy miles north of Gerlach, Nevada, it looks like an oasis in the middle of the desert.

We scouted for two days before the hunt and saw a lot of good pronghorn; but the morning before the hunt, Matt and I saw the one we wanted. He was a true high-horned giant. We figured his horns to be between 16 and 17 inches long.

The morning of the hunt produced a lot of good bucks. In fact, during one stalk I had nine good-sized bucks in my rifle scope at one time. Man what a sight!

At about 2:00 that afternoon, we saw the trophy we wanted and had scouted. We walked over a ridge and there he was, bedded down about 400 yards in front of us. He was looking right at us when we came over the ridge, so he had us pinned down. We could not get any closer, and I did not like the shot he gave me, so I let him trot away. Since we were the only ones hunting in the area, I figured I would give him a day to settle down and then go back and get him on the third day.

The afternoon of the second day of our hunt found us in another area we had scouted. While sitting on a ridge doing some glassing, Matt spotted four pronghorn about three-quarters of a mile away. Through my spotting scope, I could tell that one buck definitely was worth a closer look. They had not seen us, so we waited until they moved over a little ridge and out of sight. Then, Matt and I ran toward them to close the distance. One of the does saw us and ran, taking the others over a big, steep mountain. We just sat there and watched as the big buck reached the skyline. He stopped and looked back at us. I had my spotting scope on him, and I knew he was a very good buck, but when he ran over that hill, I really did not think we stood a chance of ever seeing him again.

Matt had other ideas. I think he wanted that buck more than I did. He had no intention of giving up, so up we went, with Matt leading the way to the top. On the back side, we slipped around a small hill and there they were, about 200 yards away.

They had not seen us. There was no breeze, and there was a light drizzle of rain coming down — perfect conditions for a perfect stalk.

I put one big sagebrush between me and the big buck. I had Matt stay put and told him not to move. I low-crawled about 30 yards closer. While I was studying the buck, a small stream of sunlight suddenly broke through the clouds. The bright sun highlighted the old buck's horns like a big diamond. I studied the buck for a good half-hour in my 3.5-10x Leupold rifle scope, trying to judge just how big he was. And then, the next time he turned broadside to me, I fired one 140-grain Nosler Partition from my 7mm Remington Magnum, placing it right behind the left shoulder. The buck went sideways but did not go all the way down. He was walking away when I put the final shot in his neck. I stood up, and Matt was running up to me with a big grin on his face, saying "Well, how big is he?"

I told him while we walked the 150 yards to our trophy that I did not know if he was going to make the Boone and Crockett book or not, but with the help of my good friend and taxidermist, Rick Sulvester of Sierra Taxidermy, he would look great on our wall.

The closer we came, the more the horns grew. We just stood there smiling, not saying a word for the longest time. It was truly a great feeling.

After high-fives and hugs, we took pictures. I just happened to have a tape measure in my day pack. I knew right there that he was 17-7/8 inches on one side and 17-5/8 inches on the other. I did not score him until after the 60-day drying period, when I found out he scored 92-1/8, with a final score of 91 after deductions.

We dressed out the buck and packed him very carefully back to the pickup, about three miles away. There, I put him on my camcorder, along with plenty of other pronghorn, deer, wild horses and burros. As I write this story I watch the videotape. The fact that I captured the perfect hunt on tape sends a chill down my back. I had a great scouting trip, an excellent place to stay, plenty of game to see, and most of all, a chance to share every bit of it with my hunting partner, my son Matt. I think that if it had not been for him, I would not have ever taken this buck or written this story.

Oh, on the other hunts, I did not fill my elk tag, but after 25 days of a solo hunt, I connected on a very impressive desert sheep. That is another story.

Photograph courtesy of Douglas J. Modey

This pronghorn was killed in 1990 by Douglas J. Modey
in Harney County, Oregon. It scored 84-2/8.

Photograph courtesy of Duane M. Smith

Duane M. Smith was hunting in Sweetwater County, Wyoming,
in 1989 when he killed this pronghorn. It scored 85-6/8.

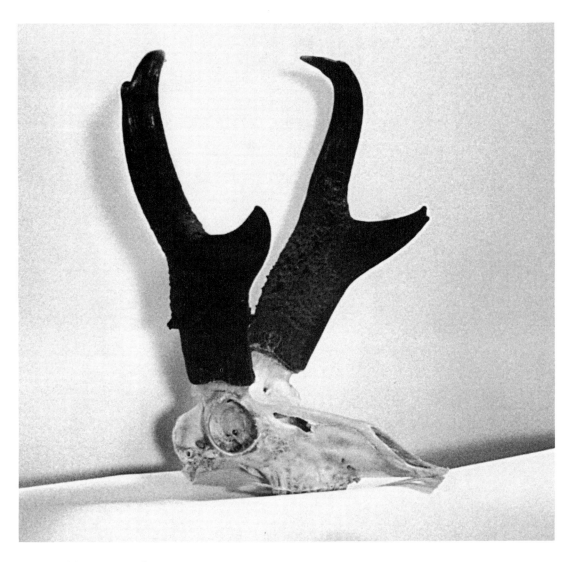

Photograph by Wm. H. Nesbitt

PRONGHORN
THIRD AWARD
90-6/8

Locality: Natrona Co., Wyo.   Date: 1989
Hunter: Richard J. Guthrie

PRONGHORN 90-6/8

Richard J. Guthrie

My pronghorn hunt in 1989 started like many other past hunts. I was hunting with a friend, Nick Vuicich, who is also from Fresno, California. We had drawn permits for Area 25, just north of Casper, Wyoming. We had hunted there many times before and had always seen nice trophies.

The area consists of large cattle and sheep ranches laid out in huge pastures. There is some BLM land, but all access is private, with permission readily available. The terrain is classic pronghorn country — gentle, rolling sage hills with large areas of sand dunes, bordered on the south by the Platt River. The habitat is excellent and usually holds a good population of pronghorn, plus an ever increasing herd of mule deer.

We arrived in Casper three days before the October 1 opener for our traditional pre-hunt scouting and fine-tuning of those old judging eyes. It was great to once again be under the spell cast by that wide-open prairie country. Its breezy, balmy days, open skies, and the parade of wildlife put you in a state of relaxation seldom equaled in today's world.

As always, three days was not enough. After the first day, all the bucks looked the same size. Though professed experts at field judging, we were short on agreement and long on laughter over our calculations. Oblivious to the real world, we pounded our way through every pasture we could gain access to, from daylight until dark.

Just before noon on the last day of scouting, I spotted a pronghorn buck that looked to be a real dandy. We were bouncing down a ranch trail that could scarcely be called a road, when I told Nick, "Here comes one that will go 20 inches."

After I slid down off the dash and the laughter died down, we got in some serious glassing. The buck was moving down a ridge at a good clip and crossed our trail at about 400 yards. He went to a small lake for water and then returned, at his nervous gait, back up the ridge to a doe herd he was tending. His horns, of course, were not that tall, but they sure were heavy. We watched him until mid-afternoon. That buck would not slow down long enough to give us a decent look. There was no pre-hunting activity in the area, so we left him in hopes that his herding would not move him too far overnight.

Opening morning arrived with a gusty, bone-chilling wind pushing dark, heavy clouds. They hung low in the sky and would not allow the day to begin. A cold drizzle began as we approached the buck's area from the south. Gaining a slight vantage from our trail, I spotted a distant buck. He watched us from over a rise, allowing only a glimpse before disappearing. It was enough to know that he had remained in the area. With the weather as it was, we decided to move down the trail a short distance to gain a better vantage of the lower terrain. From there, we could glass from the vehicle between showers. We felt the buck would remain in that part of the pasture.

An hour had passed when the buck appeared, coming over a ridge chasing several does. He crossed within 300 yards of us, but with his speed and the gusting wind, a shot would have been foolish. Again, he disappeared.

For another hour, we sat in the downpour with few opportunities to glass. It was during a break in the rains that we next saw him at over a 1,000 yards. That time, he created some anxiety. We had spotted a vehicle coming down a trail out of some distant sand hills. As it topped the ridge, the rig stopped and four hunters got out. I nearly croaked when the buck appeared 80 yards behind the group, chasing three does. He darted out of a sage pocket and, just as quickly, went into another. The hunters never knew he existed, and they were soon on the road again.

With the passing of another two hours, the sky had brightened considerably and the heavy rains had ceased. To our amazement, there was no hunting pressure yet. We had been able to glass the country thoroughly, with no sign of the buck, until I noticed a lone antelope, running at a tireless pace toward us from the hills to the east. He was a great distance away, but as he drew nearer, I recognized the heavy, forward-pitched horns. His route was direct and his attention seemed fixed on three does feeding on a ridge below us.

I left Nick to watch and slipped into a sage draw. I had a little time but none to spare. I was able to cover the quarter-mile and take a prone position well within the range of my .270. Those last seconds were nerve-racking, as I watched his final sprint to the does through my scope. The anticipated pause and head turn gestures never occurred but a chase did. I waited as he completed a sweeping circle and settled to a walk, quartering away. I took a good shoulder hold and let off, but the wind was too strong. The bullet missed, just off his rump. He was trotting, broadside, and again, with not enough allowance for the wind, I killed another piece of prairie. At 225 yards, going full-bore with a lead I could only guess, I fired my one remaining round. I could hear the hit as I felt the recoil. He went end over end, coming to rest in the sage.

Disgusted with my shooting and the wind, I walked back to Nick. Together we approached the buck for the first close look. He was breathtaking. We just stood there, looking with disbelief. The following silence, though shortlived, was a rarity for us. The relative calm came apart as I tagged the buck and began a serious bout with the shakes. It was very cold, but I have been a lot colder than that many times.

Nick suggested we hop in the truck for some hot coffee. When this did not help, I knew it was the adrenalin. Nick agreed, and I will admit that he was very calm when I handed him the broken door handle from his truck after rolling up the window. It just seemed to drop off in my hand, and so did the other one, from the driver's door, when

I entered the truck to load film in my camera 10 minutes later. It took awhile to complete the picture taking and dress the buck before leaving. Though the shakes had diminished, Nick declined my offer to drive. I could sense a sharpness in his voice when he told me not to touch the steering wheel. I was pumped!

Back in Casper, over the following week, the buck generated so much interest we had to display it at my friend Louis Ray's taxidermy studio. The parade of viewers included the local press, who ran a story with a photo. This put Louie to work full time, but he loved it. I had no idea that Wyoming had so many game wardens. They were great, green-scoring the buck and taking field information for their records. The buck scored in the low 90s, and an extracted tooth placed his age at 6.5 years. This hunt ended all too soon, but unfortunately, this story does not.

Back in California, two months later, I made the Boone and Crockett connection. On a sunny Saturday morning, I headed north to Sacramento for the appointment. I had no idea that it would be one of the worst days of my life.

As I drove up Interstate 5 just south of Stockton, my truck broke down, leaving me stranded. I diagnosed the problem as a faulty gas tank valve. Interstate 5 at this location is a six-lane freeway in a semi-rural commercial area. I felt comfortable with locking the truck at roadside and walking for gas. You can guess what happened next, but you can never in a lifetime imagine the feeling I had when I return to find my truck broken into and the horns stolen. I could scarcely speak when reporting the theft to the San Joaquin County Sheriff's Department. To this day, I cannot recall a single thing about the two-hour drive home. I was turned inside out as I drove away knowing that someone in the area had my horns. I was dysfunctional for the next three days, eating very little and unable to sleep. I just sat in my leather chair, mentally and physically exhausted.

I could not shake the memory of those horns. If my eyes closed, the horns would appear. I would wake with a start only to see the pronghorn trophies from previous hunts before me on my wall. I knew I could not let the depression continue. I tried to rationalize the theft. I had not lost a loved one. The trophy had brought me great personal enjoyment, and I still had those memories. I just no longer had the physical object. That is what the horns were, just a physical object.

I was not, however, about to simply say, "They are gone and that is that." By then, some of my emotion had turned to anger, and I wanted to avenge the loss. More important, the horns were out there somewhere and I had to try to get them back.

I made up about 400 fliers picturing the buck and offering a reward. I took three days from work and returned to Stockton. I contacted Detective F. Pence of the San Joaquin County Sheriff's Department. He had been assigned the case and had already alerted the Stockton Police Department, Cal Trans, and the California Department of Fish and Game. Additionally, he arranged an appointment for me with the local newspaper, The Stockton Record. The Record printed a great story of my misfortune. The fish and game department notified their officers who covered sporting goods outlets and taxidermy studios, statewide. I cannot thank these agencies enough for their help.

I then began a foot canvas of the area, posting and passing out fliers. With my time off ending, I felt I had accomplished what I could, so I went home. I could now accept whatever was to be.

Some three weeks later, the Stockton Police Department received a family disturbance call and dispatched a very observant officer. While handling the dispute, Officer G. Faselli spotted the horns in the back seat of a car parked at the home. He instantly recognized them and subsequently made an arrest. I was notified the next day of the recovery, which immediately restored my sanity. Upon the release of the horns to me, I completed the original trip to Sacramento. All the speculation over scoring was laid to rest. The buck was officially scored at 90-6/8. It had suffered some shrinkage, but that was secondary after all that had happened. During the next few weeks, I made two trips back to Stockton to give testimony in court. The case was closed with a guilty plea and a sentence of one year in the state penal system. In the years to come, I hope to return to those sand hills and sage draws. Although a lifetime could pass before finding another pronghorn of this quality, I will be happy to spend it trying.

Photograph courtesy of Steven J. Vanlerberghe

This pronghorn was killed in Sweetwater County, Wyoming,
in 1988 by Steven J. Vanlerberghe. It scored 85-6/8.

Photograph by Wm. H. Nesbitt

PRONGHORN
FOURTH AWARD
89-6/8

Locality: Colfax Co., N.M.   Date: 1989
Hunter: Hudson DeCray

PRONGHORN 89-6/8

Hudson Decray

The buck pronghorn had been slowly traveling with a doe when we first sighted it from the cab of Steve's pickup truck. Steve McClure and his family owned the ranch where we were hunting, almost 90,000 acres of rolling plains, near Springer, New Mexico. He had seen lots of pronghorn in his years and knew this was a good one. We dropped out of the cab and lay on the ground, while my wife and Steve's friend, Ed Roos, drove to a mesa about half a mile away to watch the stalk.

The two pronghorns followed the truck with their eyes and seemed satisfied they were out of danger. As they resumed feeding, we started what proved to be a very long sneak along a shallow ditch. Steve warned me to keep an eye out for the small prairie rattlers that can so rudely interrupt the meanderings of a horizontal pronghorn stalker. I was more preoccupied with avoiding little clumps of very uncomfortable cactus.

The pronghorn were soon out of sight, but Steve assured me that patience and favorable topography would put us back in touch with the pair soon enough. All we needed was a little bit of luck to back up his theory.

As we crawled along, I thought back to the previous January when I had first met Steve McClure. I had hunted the free-ranging Barbary sheep in the dramatic Canadian River Canyon, which forms one border of the Red River Ranch. The hunt had been a success, producing a 28-inch ram, the best to come out of that part of the canyon in several years.

Steve had taken me on that hunt and had proven to be a most enthusiastic companion, with uncanny hunting instincts. Nine months later and about 70 degrees warmer, there I was, crawling along in vastly different country, yet only a few miles from a remarkable canyon that is 800 feet deep and more than a mile across in some places.

My reflections were interrupted when Steve grabbed my ankle and pointed with his eyes at the two white and tan animals, the same two that we had lost sight of a half-hour earlier.

They had circled around to the left of us and were still feeding along, about 400 yards away. We crawled toward the pair for a few yards; then, Steve hissed at me to stop. He came alongside and whispered that we were about as far as we dared go. There was absolutely no cover remaining between us and the animals. No hills, no bushes, no ditches, just wide open space, with a slight contour downhill from us and then back up to the pronghorn.

Steve said it was time. The wind was blowing about 20 knots from right to left, the same direction in which the pronghorns were feeding, walking along slowly with the wind. I had zeroed my rifle in a similar wind a week earlier, back home in Bishop, California. At 300 yards, the bullet would drop about eight to 10 inches and drift almost two feet to the left. Steve asked where I would hold. I said about a foot over the buck's rump. Steve counseled me on the subject of how far to extend my lead on subsequent shots, presuming I would miss the first one. His confidence was less than overwhelming, but then he grinned and told me to relax and just go for it.

I could see the low afternoon sun's reflection off a side window of the pickup truck parked on the mesa to our right. I knew that my wife, Ruth, and Ed Roos would be watching with binoculars and our spotting scope. I also knew that my previous success at leading a running pronghorn at 400 yards, the length of a full-size sedan, was not the stuff of legends. This better be it!

I used a clump of bush and my cap for support, put the crosshairs above the hind quarter and touched it off. Steve yelled to shoot again, but there was no target. Nothing running, nothing period. And then he yelled again, because the buck was lying absolutely motionless on the prairie. We stood there for a minute or more. I had my scope trained on the unmoving form and Steve was watching with his binocular. It was over.

Steve wanted to pace it off and began taking long steps, counting. I was alongside and far too excited to count. I wanted to recapture the past few minutes and hold on as long as possible to all those little sensory details that would later fade from recollection.

My friend was approaching the 300 count when my reverie was interrupted by the appearance of the pickup truck beside the pronghorn, still a hundred yards away. Ruth, Ed and another friend, Bob Darmitzel, had watched the whole episode from beginning to end. They were whooping and hollering as if they had won the lottery.

Steve's final pace was number 410. There lay the buck with a single bullet hole high at the base of his neck. His horns seemed out of proportion to the size of the animal and, indeed, almost were, with a length of 19 inches. The horns were beautifully symmetrical and the buck was the finest hunting trophy I have ever taken.

I can relive the excitement of those ensuing minutes because Ruth had the foresight to bring a video camera along in the truck. I have almost worn-out the tape.

After the 60-day drying period, the pronghorn was officially measured at 89-6/8. My buck would be Number 11 if it were in the most recent Boone and Crockett records book, the 9th edition.

There have been newspaper and magazine articles, pictures, letters and phone calls from hunters, friends, and old acquaintances. The thrill of knowing my pronghorn will be duly recorded in a future edition of "the book" was a dream I could only hope to someday realize. But the essence of the whole, wonderful experience was a flickering moment sometime between Steve's "go for it" grin and when I squeezed the trigger. That is the moment I keep trying to hold on to.

Photograph by Wm. H. Nesbitt

PRONGHORN
HONORABLE MENTION
87
Locality: Chouteau Co., Mont.   Date: 1990
Hunter: Darrell J. Woodahl

PRONGHORN 87

Darrell J. Woodahl

I have always enjoyed hunting pronghorn, ever since I could hunt as a 12-year-old boy on my folks' ranch near Geraldine, Montana. The first buck I shot measured 15 inches, and it seems to have set a trend for me. My wife and I have enjoyed hunting pronghorn on her father's ranch, which is now owned by her brother and brother-in-law.

We have had some good bucks over the years. Now that my nephews, Steen and Henning, and their best friend Jay are working at the ranch, they keep pretty good tabs on the pronghorn.

My hunt actually started on October 13, 1990, one week after opening day. I had taken a married couple pronghorn hunting near Jordan, Montana. They had never hunted these animals before, so it was fun to guide them. As a result, my hunt began a week into the season.

I left Lincoln, Montana, where I live, at 3:00 a.m. for the four-hour drive to the ranch. I arrived at daylight and Henning and Jay were waiting for me. We got in the ranch pickup and headed out.

We spotted several small herds, checked them out, and kept going. We wanted to look at more animals if we could find them.

Henning drove to an old homestead. He said there was a decent buck hanging out there. He had seen the buck during the previous week, while he was looking over the cows. He had gotten within 50 yards of the buck, and he looked pretty good.

I spotted the buck a half-mile away. He was, in fact, decent but he looked to be only 15-1/2 inches, with good hooks. We drove to an old Quonset hut on the homestead and shut down the truck.

We got out and watched the buck and his does begin feeding as soon as we disappeared from their view. The buildings of the homestead are falling down, but they gave us plenty of cover.

Henning and I debated on how big the buck was. Henning could have taken him the previous week, but he decided to wait until I came down to hunt with him.

Meanwhile, the pronghorn were feeding toward us. I made up my mind to take him, so I lined up my Remington Model 700 Mountain Rifle in .270 Winchester and fired. They said I had missed, so I shot again, and the buck went down.

On the way to the ranch house, a herd of 10 pronghorn ran in front of us. Henning got out of the pickup and shot a nice 15-1/2-inch buck, so we had a good hunt.

My other nephew, Steen, and his wife had shown up at the ranch house. Steen measured the buck at more than 16-1/2 inches, so we knew we had a good pronghorn.

I stopped at a taxidermist in Great Falls, and he said it was an exceptional head. He rough-scored it and said it should rank in the top 20. I was planning on having my wife mount it for me when I got the cape back.

A year later, another taxidermist named Dusty Rollins got in touch with me and came up to Lincoln to see the buck. He asked to mount it. I have known Dusty for years, so off it went.

Harley Yeager of the Montana Fish, Wildlife and Parks Department measured the buck for Boone and Crockett after the 60-day drying period. The score came to 90 points, which put it Number 2 in Montana and way up in the all-time records book.

I think every person who ever hunts must dream of taking an animal that would qualify for the prestigious Boone and Crockett Club records book. I thank the Lord and my family for the enjoyment of all my hunts.

Photograph courtesy of Kevin L. Wieberg

Kevin L. Wieberg killed this pronghorn in Valley County,
Montana, in 1989. It scored 81.

Photograph by Wm. H. Nesbitt

PRONGHORN
HONORABLE MENTION
85
Locality: Coconino Co., Ariz.   Date: 1989
Hunter: John L. Neely

230

PRONGHORN 85

John L. Neely

My son and I had tried for 10 years to draw elk permits. He was drawn twice, but I never had been. In 1989, we decided to apply for both elk and pronghorn permits. With the luck of the draw, I received permits for both. An extra measure of luck was involved in the pronghorn permit, since there are only 20 issued for the large area bounded by Camp Verde, Flagstaff, Sedona and Clints Well of Arizona.

A week before the pronghorn season opened, my son and I scouted the area and saw one buck by himself and another running with about five does. Both bucks were large, so I would have been happy to take either one. Elk inhabit the same area in the Coconino National Forest, while the pronghorn were in more open terrain, among junipers.

The night before the season opened, on September 22, 1989, my son and I camped in the forest, near an open juniper area. We started walking at daylight, with juniper shrubs affording some cover. My son spotted the pronghorn first and motioned in the buck's direction. The buck stood up from his bed and saw us at about the same time we saw him. He was much closer to the forest than when we had seen him the week before.

I knelt on one knee and fired one shot at a range of about 150 yards. I was shooting 150-grain bullets from a Winchester Model 100 with a Leupold 3-9x scope. The rifle had been in our family for some 25 years and had produced a great deal of game. It is very accurate for a semi-automatic.

We walked to where the buck had gone down, hung him from a small tree, and were field-dressing him when the area game warden appeared. He had been on a nearby mountain and located us with a spotting scope.

We did not realize how good a trophy the pronghorn was until the warden took rough measurements. He told us it was a once-in-a-lifetime trophy, and he thought it had records book possibilities. He said that he had been stationed in Flagstaff for seven years and had never seen a buck that nice. The warden took several pictures of it, as well as a tooth and a piece of muscle from it. We did not have a camera, because we did not expect to bag an animal of such proportions.

We had the buck scored for Boone and Crockett by Mike Cuppel in Phoenix, and it is tied for eighth place in the all-time records for Arizona. The score of 89-6/8 was the highest in the state for 1989.

Photograph by Wm. H. Nesbitt

BISON
CERTIFICATE OF MERIT
SCORE: 128-4/8
Locality: Custer Co., S.D.   Date: 1989
Hunter: Stephanie Altimus   Owner: Wildlife Museum of the West

BISON 128-4/8

Stephanie Altimus, hunter
Wildlife Museum of the West, owner

The 1989 drawing for permits to hunt buffalo in Custer State Park, South Dakota, was September 17, 1989. I was notified the following week that my name had been drawn. I chose December 12, 13, and 14 for my hunt.

My guide would again be Fred Matthews. My husband Larry and I hunted with Fred in 1983 when I shot my first bison, an 8-1/2-year-old bull. Our guide then became our good friend, with whom we kept in touch. We were both very happy to be able to hunt with Fred again. He had worked professionally with bison for over 40 years and had been inducted into the Buffalo Hall of Fame in Missoula, Montana.

Larry and I drove from Montana to Custer State Park several days prior to my hunt in order to enjoy the country and photograph wildlife with still and movie cameras. The park borders the small town of Custer, South Dakota. Bison, deer, pronghorn, bighorn sheep, coyotes, and wild turkey inhabit its 73,000 acres.

Wednesday morning at 8:00, we met Fred at the Custer State Park office. Amid hugs, reminiscing and teasing, we planned my hunt. During the first two days of the hunt we enjoyed watching hundreds of bulls, cows and calves. The sound and sight of several hundred buffalo thundering across the prairie is indescribable. We scoped many bulls and narrowed my choice down to a mature bull with very long horns.

Fred still wanted to check out a remote corner of the park that was often a hide-out for large, solitary bulls. As we approached a canyon, we spotted what we hoped we would find — the tracks of a big, lone bull in the snow. The bulls we had scoped earlier had been in small herds, so the thought of a lone bull in this remote area was really making me excited. I hoped we would find that exceptional trophy every hunter dreams of at the end of the tracks. I knew Larry and Fred had the same hope. Suddenly, all talking ceased and the air was heavy with anticipation while we followed his tracks.

I think we all spotted him in the heavy dark timber at about the same time he spotted us. We froze, preparing to back off. The bull spun around and ran through the timber onto an open sunny hill dotted with younger pine trees. This gave us the perfect opportunity to set up our spotting scope and get a good look at him. I was really hoping to get an old bull with heavy horns, since we planned to mount my bull life-size and display him in the Wildlife Museum my husband and I built in our hometown, Ennis,

Montana. I also wanted my bull to have the contrasting golden shoulders and dark body and face for this mount.

As we spent the next half-hour scrutinizing this bison, I became certain he was the bull I wanted. Larry was sure he would score well in Boone and Crockett. It was late afternoon, and we all agreed to go after the bull first thing the next morning, because there was not enough time left in the day to skin the bull and care for the meat.

We backed away from him, hoping he would settle down and be in the same general area in the morning. My stomach was doing flip-flops as I wondered if he would stay put through the night. How close could I get tomorrow? Could I drop him with just one shot? Would Larry be able to film the stalk and kill? I experienced all the emotions and thoughts that race through a hunter's mind when the trophy animal is finally found.

That evening was spent with Larry and I recounting to each other what every inch of the bull's horns looked like, planning how close we wanted to get, and discussing where I wanted to place my shot. Even with 18 years of hunting experience behind me, the anticipation, excitement and nervousness was still part of the hunt.

We were up and ready to go early the next morning. The weather had become overcast and cold during the night, and as the three of us drove to where we had last seen the bull, it began to snow.

We spotted the bull in the thick, dark timber. Larry was able to shoot some movies of him before he ran up the hill and out of sight. I grabbed my rifle, a .308 Norma Magnum, and we started following his huge tracks in the snow. As we topped over the first small hill, we spotted him standing about 100 yards away, watching us. He spun and ran off again through the heavy timber. We continued slowly on the tracks for a few minutes and again spotted him about 75 yards uphill and ahead of us. We crept to within 50 yards of the bull. I knelt behind a tree. Larry was right behind me with the movie camera. The bull was standing broadside. He slowly turned his head to stare at us.

All of a sudden, 50 yards started to seem excessively close. His dark body against the snowy hillside looked immense. The only noise I heard was the pounding of my heart, which I was sure the buffalo could hear, too. Somewhere in the background I could hear the movie camera running.

I raised the rifle to my shoulder, looked through the scope, and waited for the huge bull to turn his head so I could shoot him behind the ear. My mouth was so dry I could not swallow. I tried to calm myself by taking several deep breaths. He slowly turned his head to face forward so his entire body and head were broadside to me. As I started to squeeze the trigger, he began to rub his forehead on a pine tree directly in front of him. His head was moving up and down, up and down.

I backed off on the trigger and released my breath. The rifle was getting heavy and my throat was getting drier. I could still hear the movie camera running. I held the rifle steady and continued to look through the scope at the spot I had picked out, right behind the ear. Suddenly, he stopped rubbing and stood still. At that instant, I squeezed the trigger on the .308 Norma Magnum. The bull's legs collapsed under him, and his huge body fell straight to the ground. Immediately, I put another round in the chamber and was ready for a second shot, although I really didn't think I would need it.

"Good job!" Larry shouted, "you got him with one shot!" The bull's tail slowly raised up a few inches, went back down, and that was it. At 50 yards I hit him right behind the ear; the 220-grain bullet had done its job perfectly. Even though this was my second buffalo kill, and I had been on other buffalo hunts with friends, I couldn't believe what a magnificent and awesome animal he was as we approached the bull.

Larry reached down and pushed the thick hair back from the base of the horns. He looked up at me, his eyes huge, and said, "Stephanie, I think you've got a lot bigger bull here than we originally thought!"

We were all smiles as Fred gave me a big hug and we examined the bull. We took picture after picture while we waited for help in getting the buffalo out of the field.

Checking park records, Fred determined my bull to be 11-1/2 years old. Following the 60-day drying period, Boone and Crockett measurer Fred King of Bozeman, Montana, measured my bull at 132-2/8.

My bull is mounted life-size in the bison diorama of our wildlife museum in Ennis, Montana. Thousands of people have been able to stand within 5 feet of this trophy bison. It is hoped that they have learned from the experience and gained a new appreciation for these magnificent animals, while coming to understand hunting as a management tool and an ethical sport.

Photograph by Wm. H. Nesbitt

BISON
CERTIFICATE OF MERIT
SCORE: 128
Locality: Custer Co., S.D.   Date: 1990
Hunter: Larry L. Altimus
(Hunting Story Not Available)

Photograph courtesy of Jed D. Topham

This bison was killed in Garfield County, Utah, by Jed D. Topham
in 1989. It scored 116-2/8.

Photograph by Wm. H. Nesbitt

BISON
CERTIFICATE OF MERIT
SCORE: 126-6/8

Locality: Garfield Co., Utah   Date: 1990
Hunter: Holland D. Butler

BISON 126-6/8

Holland D. Butler

A green island in the middle of rock and sandstone, the Henry Mountains of Utah are as unique as the land surrounding them. Found halfway between the Canyonlands and Capitol Reef National Parks, the Henry's Mount Ellen reaches almost 11,500 feet into the sky just north of Lake Powell.

Once the haunt of Butch Cassidy's outlaw gang, the Henrys were rumored to hide an old Spanish gold mine. Today, the Henry Mountains are famous for one of the last free-roaming bison herds in America.

The bison were never native to this area, and by 1835 the last of the species were gone from what is now Utah. During the 1950s, Utah's Division of Wildlife Resources transplanted a small group of bison from Yellowstone into the Henry Mountains area. As a result of careful management and loving care, the population was estimated to be 400 animals by 1990.

At the age of fifty-one, luck was with me in 1990. I drew one of Utah's coveted once-in-a-lifetime bison permits for the Henrys. Reared in a hunting family in Oregon, a love for the outdoors and respect for its creatures were lessons my brother and I were taught by our father. Since our move to Utah in 1975, I have been fortunate to draw both moose and desert sheep permits. Because I retired in 1985, I was able to concentrate completely on preparations for the bison hunt. The three weeks prior to the November 3rd opening were spent scouting. This familiarized me with the country and its bison; it also served as a conditioning exercise.

Being a firearms enthusiast, and a fan of pistols in particular, I naturally picked a handgun for the hunt, but only after extensive deliberation. A C. Sharps rifle in .50 caliber was my first pre-hunt choice. However, delivery would have taken 90-plus days. To stay with the traditional single-shot, falling-block action, a Ruger No. 1 in .458 Winchester Magnum was selected as my "buffalo rifle." For several years, I have hunted with a .45-70 single-shot pistol from M.O.A. Corporation. It is big, heavy and very accurate, so I included this one as well. My real love, though, is a Ruger single-action Bisley, skillfully and beautifully converted to .475 Linebaugh by John Linebaugh, the Cody, Wyoming, gunsmith. This revolver is fitted with a special 5-1/2-inch barrel and matching five-shot cylinder. The cartridge is based on the .45-70 case, trimmed and loaded with a cast LBT bullet weighing 430 grains. The muzzle velocity is 1,300 fps.

Millions of bison were killed on the plains of the West with rifles less powerful than this revolver. Practicing three times weekly, I had a sore hand and a keen eye.

Skookum is my partner. A wonderful Keeshond, she is always ready to go and never complains about the cook.

On our first scouting trip to the Henrys, Skookum and I started low on Stevens Mesa. Our first sighting of bison was memorable. A cloud of dust in the distance turned into a small herd of the shaggy beasts. We soon discovered that by using cover and being careful, approaching a group was not too difficult. We drifted along parallel to the feeding animals, down wind and using junipers to break our silhouette. Watching these animals, with the sun low behind them and hazy dust diffusing the soft evening light, I imagined myself in the company of Sioux or Blackfoot hunters as they stalked their traditional prey.

After three weeks of pre-hunt practice, we had a pretty good handle on what it would take to be successful during the November 3-16 hunt. Although these Henry Mountains bison are wild, they certainly are not as spooky as elk. They can be approached within pistol range if the hunter is careful, quiet and deliberate.

There are two types of bulls. The magnificent, shiny-black 5 to 8-year-old bulls generally stay together in groups. The old loners, out by themselves, join other animals only occasionally or during the mating season. It is among the older, blond-humped individuals that the largest animals are found, and of course these bulls are the most difficult to locate.

The week previous to the November 3rd hunt, we were comfortably camped near McClellan and Willow Springs. Our scouting had identified four different herd groups, one of which had several nice bulls. On Thursday before the Saturday opener, Skookum and I discovered an absolutely perfect specimen — completely coal black, very large, and impressive, shiny black horns. He was the one. The bull was feeding around a hidden watering hole and the situation seemed perfect. We would simply return on Friday, follow the great animal until dark, and he would surely be ours opening morning. Oh, yeah. Sure. You bet. We never saw a hair on Friday.

Saturday morning and dawn found Skookum and me in a cool canyon with a water hole at its upper end. We had found it and a small bunch of large bison about a week earlier. After a long, hard hike, we surprised 11 nice animals bedded around a seep. For me, it was adrenalin time, because to exit from this very narrow cut they had to pass within twenty feet of my position. Following the bigger ones with the muzzle of the .475, I decided not to shoot. Later that evening, we crawled up into a bunch of about 20 head, but we were so close and it was so dark that all we could do was crawl back out and wait for the next morning.

Sunday broke windy and cold, and we soon discovered other hunters were sharing that part of the mountain. After hearing shots, we departed.

Back at camp we packed enough food for a couple of days and a tarp in the Land Cruiser and started for Bull Creek Pass and Table Mountain. As we climbed higher, the snow got deeper. Deer were browsing the abundant plants, standing in belly-high grasses. This contrasted sharply with the lower elevations, where heavy grazing had left little feed.

It was soon apparent that the road was almost closed by drifted snow, and no one had driven the pass lately. I was surprised, because in almost a month I had never seen anyone on foot.

Near the top on the east face, we found a single set of large hoof prints. They meandered down the road, sometimes off into the brush, then across to another tidbit. Half a mile farther, the tracks stopped at a bed, right in the middle of the road. Well, big bulls are loners, and up there on Bull Creek Pass I was alone too, except for the wind and my dog.

I parked the Cruiser at a wide spot, buckled on the .475, shouldered a small pack, and went up the trail. We were in pine and aspen patches, with the south ridges bare. Thick, low brush grew in the gullies. It was fairly steep, and the tracks we had followed down turned to go up again. There were some snow patches in the shade so tracking the bull was not really difficult if I went slowly, watching carefully. By 3:00 p.m., we were in about 3 inches of snow, and from the tracks it appeared the bison had some place to go. I wondered if he had sighted us as we were driving down, because he was sure headed for the top.

It was 5:00 p.m., the sun was below the ridge in front of us, and the wind was really beginning to rise as the temperature rapidly fell. We broke out of the quaking aspens along the lower edge of a large hill, and there he was. All I could see was the top of a wooly hump. With only one small pine between the bull and us, Skookum and I started one-stepping it, hunched over and moving slowly toward the single patch of cover. The bison was feeding directly away from us. The range was about 150 yards. When we closed the distance to 100 yards, I realized I had nothing to judge this bull by, no points to count, nothing with which to compare him. So I added up what I knew: solitary bull, big tracks, horns curved, shaggy head and blonde hump equaled Old Bull. This was it.

Behind me, Skookum lay down in the snow while I pulled the .475 Linebaugh and tried to shrink into the sagebrush. I had only gone about 10 yards when the bull turned to his right, feeding directly broadside. The revolver came up. Too late. I was dead still as he fed directly toward the upraised muzzle. At about 60 yards, I knew it was time to do it. The plan is to slip a 430-grain bullet between shoulder and ribs, on a line with the heart. Careful. Careful. Sight picture, trigger, BOOM! I was watching the target so intently that I actually saw the hair part and dust rise from the exact spot the front sight had occupied. There was absolutely no reaction.

The bull wheeled around and started away at full speed. At 75 he turned slightly. I shot again. He never broke stride. The bull was going downhill, perhaps 100 yards away and nearing a grove of old pines and aspens, when he turned broadside. I was chanting, "Front sight, front sight." At the shot, the old bull pitched full-length and slid 20 feet on his left side.

I was running then, pushing out cases, and groping for ammunition. By the time I covered half the distance, he was back on his feet, but badly hurt.

I had just accomplished the goal of the hunt and was feeling elation and pride, but I also felt sadness, sympathy and admiration for that truly grand animal. A quick shot and it was finished for the old bison.

It was far from finished for this old hunter. What an animal! He was simply huge. It was almost dark, my feet were soaking wet, the temperature was in the 20s, and a hard, cold wind was blowing. Skooky and I ran about three miles down to the Land Cruiser. By dark, we had returned to the bison. I luckily found a dead pine stump and coffee and dinner were soon heating. By lantern and fire light, the cleaning and skinning chores started.

At midnight, the temperature was down to 10 degrees and one weary old man was done. Almost.

The first slug from the Linebaugh had penetrated between the shoulder and ribs as intended. When the first rib was hit, the big lead bullet didn't cut through. It was deflected slightly and caught the second rib edgewise, cutting it completely. Then, the bullet punched through half of a third rib and angled up and across, exiting after busting another rib on the far side.

The second, raking shot was too far forward, I guess my concentration was focused on the shoulder, because that's exactly where it hit. The angle was so acute that the bullet cut a six-inch furrow in the hide before entering behind the right ear. It was later found by taxidermist Sam Raby, just under the nose-pad skin.

My third shot broke the right femur, cut straight through a rib, ripped arteries from the heart and lungs, broke another rib, penetrated the shoulder bones, and disappeared into the woods. Big bullets do big work.

After the proper drying period, Dennis Shirley, an official Boone & Crockett Club scorer, measured the bull at 129. It presently ranks first among bison taken in Utah. It was also the first with a pistol.

Photograph courtesy of Thomas H. Coe

Thomas H. Coe killed this bison in Custer County, South Dakota, in 1991.
It scored 121-6/8.

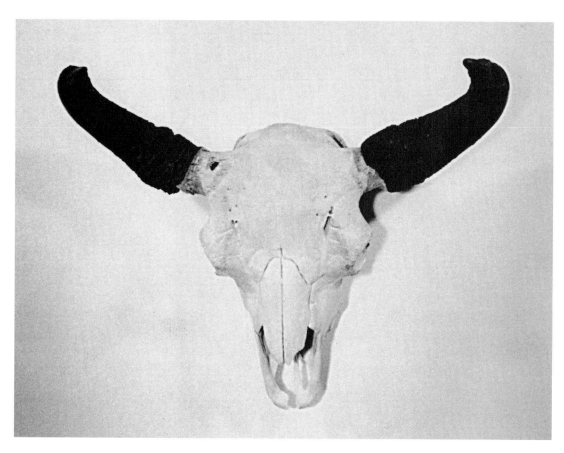

Photograph by Wm. H. Nesbitt

BISON
CERTIFICATE OF MERIT
SCORE: 125-2/8

Locality: Park Co., Mont.   Date: 1989
Hunter: Richard Olson

BISON 125-2/8

Richard Olson

A grey, dawning sky greeted me on the first (and probably the last) bison hunt of my life. It was January 31, 1989. The temperature was 45 degrees Fahrenheit and the wind was blowing 40 miles per hour, with gusts that shook my half-ton Chevy 4X4 like a baby's cradle. We knew a change in the weather was imminent, but the massive storm forecast was not supposed to arrive until the following day. Then again, when you have winds like those in Montana, they are usually the precursors of a storm front.

I hoped the meteorologist's prediction would be accurate. When we left home the previous day, it was 56 degrees (almost tee-shirt weather), so we shut off the furnace. Ten hunters, including me, along with friends, relations, and various state and federal game management people, waited for legal shooting light at the Corwin Springs Bridge on the Yellowstone River, seven miles north of Gardiner, Montana. My group, all from Helena, consisted of: me, a 45-year-old building contractor; my wife and loyal hunting partner, Linda; Charles (Chic) Barnett, a lifelong friend and hunting pal; and my older brother, Ted Olson. Everyone was keenly eager to go, as this would be a new and different experience for all of us. If I shot a bison weighing up to a ton, I would need help.

Ted parked his truck inches from mine, so we could roll down the windows and talk. We decided to drive two rigs for the obvious reasons: if one breaks down, you have a backup; if one gets stuck, the other can pull him out; two people ride more comfortably than four in the front seat.

With daylight gradually approaching, I had time to reflect upon what the wardens had said at the hunters' check-in meeting half an hour earlier. After showing our identification and paying our $200 tag fees, we were informed we would be hunting our 10 bison from approximately 70 head of cows and calves located on Church Universal and Triumphant (C.U.T.) property. My permit number was 195, listing me as the ninth of 10 shooters for that day. Although somewhat disappointed, I resigned myself to enjoy this trip to its fullest and to fill my freezer with whatever bison afforded me the chance for a clean, quick kill. We were also advised, if at all possible, to pinpoint the bullet's entry 4 inches behind the base of a horn, as this should stop one of these huge shaggy beasts instantly. It would be a judgment call. If a hunter felt comfortable with a head shot, fine. If not, he or she could opt for a heart or lung shot.

We watched as the first two hunters were ushered into a pickup. They traveled over the bridge and down the river, out of sight, apparently to rendezvous with the 70 cows and calves.

The emergence of full daylight brought with it a spectacular view of the Paradise Valley. On the hillsides nearby, there was an abundance of wild game. Across the river, at least 100 elk meandered single-file up a ridge toward their daytime bedding area. Two hundred yards north of the elk, in the midst of a rockslide, lay four respectable bighorn rams. A small band of mule deer browsed near the river. Directly behind us, some 300 yards away, five big bull elk were feeding in a large sagebrush park. To sit in one spot and observe such a variety of magnificent animals was a treat.

Another vehicle, carrying the second pair of hunters, disappeared following the same route north.

While having coffee, we continued to glass the surrounding area. Suddenly, a number of bison crested a low ridge about 600 yards south of us. These were the vanguard of 200 head, feeding as they moved in our direction. When they came closer, I was able to distinguish four large bulls to one side and near the front of the herd. I pointed toward the bulls and jokingly told my buddies, "I'm going to shoot that big black one."

The game wardens had returned, and the next two hunters were whisked away. It was nearly my turn to go, but all I could do was glass the bison in front of me and wish. We passed the next 10 minutes talking and sipping hot coffee. Several vehicles left our staging area. These were presumed to be helpers headed down the river to aid with field-dressing.

Shortly, two fish and game rigs returned to get the four of us that remained. We grabbed our packs and guns, jumped into the trucks and drove across the bridge. To my amazement, when we reached the other side we turned left to go up the river instead of down it. Evidently, we would be hunting our four buffalo from the herd with the bulls in it.

We drove as close as we could to the 200 head (about 150 yards) and left the trucks. The number six hunter was already there, and we watched the lead animal go down. This turned the main herd and they started back upriver; however, the four bulls paid no attention.

Adrenalin coursed through my veins as we walked within 70 yards of the bulls. I did not think I would get pumped up, but this was becoming far more exciting than I would have ever imagined. The seventh and eighth shooters put down bulls, each with one shot. It was my turn next.

As I squeezed the trigger on my .300 Weatherby Magnum, the realization that he was a records book bull never entered my mind. The bull never knew what hit him. The 180-grain Nosler struck precisely where I aimed. The last shooter did likewise, and our hunt was over.

I turned and looked toward the pickups at the bridge and could see Ted watching me through his spotting scope. I motioned for him and the others to join me.

Six or seven officials were with us at that point, and the activity was hectic around the downed animals. To be sure he would stay down for good, one bull had to be shot a second time. I overheard a warden say, "Those were the best four shots I've seen so far this year."

Then three different wardens came to tell me my bull would easily make the records book. I did not know Boone and Crockett had a category for bison. Talk about luck! Not only had I taken a bull, but he was one for the records book.

The minimum entry score in Boone and Crockett for bison is 115. My bull's score, after the 60-day drying period, was 128-6/8.

After picture taking, hand shaking and a kiss from Linda, we began field dressing and caping the bull. What a job! It took five men and Linda just to roll him from side to side. An outfitter with a boom truck arrived, offering to complete the process of skinning and quartering for $100. At that point, I would have paid him $500 and figured I was getting a good deal. With the boom, it was a simple matter to put the bull into my brother's rig. We then drove to the outfitter's ranch, where it took another couple of hours to accomplish this part of the task. With the buffalo hanging by one leg, I put a tape on him and figured he was nearly 12 feet from head to toe.

While waiting at the ranch, we turned the radio on and heard the ominous weather news. The storm was a day early. It had passed through Helena at 6:00 a.m., with blowing snow and the temperature dropping rapidly. At 6:00 a.m. it was 45 degrees; at noon it was 20 degrees below zero, with a wind chill index of 60 degrees below zero. In a 24 hour period, the temperature change was 76 degrees, a new record for Helena.

At 1:00 p.m., we were on the road, a little apprehensive perhaps, but having two four-wheel-drive trucks, we were not worried much. When we started our 170—mile trek north from Gardiner, it was still 40 degrees. By the time we reached Three Forks, with only 70 miles to go, the weather had turned "plumb grotesque." The temperature was below zero, with heavy snow and strong winds causing poor visibility. Our shortest route home would be through Toston and Townsend. We turned off Interstate 90 onto Highway 287 and proceeded. We sped along at 50 miles per hour for the first mile. Then we hit a ground blizzard cutting our vision to 8 or 10 feet, not enough to see the highway beyond the pickup. The only way to advance was to hang your head out of the window and watch the painted lines on the side of the road. Traveling another mile or so in this fashion, we came to the conclusion that we would never get home on that road. We backtracked to I-90 and headed for Butte. We meant to try Highway 69 to Boulder and then on to Helena.

There were moments of uncertainty, but we made it home at 5:30 that afternoon. Eight inches of snow had fallen and it was 26 degrees below zero, with a wind chill of 70 degrees below zero. Parking my pickup, I dashed into the house, running from room to room, turning on faucets and flushing toilets as I went. Linda and I were lucky no pipes had frozen. With the heat turned up and the oven on, it was 11:00 p.m. before our counter tops warmed up.

At 6:00 p.m. the next day, we took the meat to a local processor. I could not believe it. The quarters were already frozen solid. The next morning I contacted Bill Hilburn of Four Seasons Taxidermy in East Helena, Montana, to do a shoulder mount and tan the robe. As fate would have it, when the robe came back, I discovered I am allergic to its fine wool. It now adorns my brother's sofa. The meat, boneless and in little white packages, weighed 490 pounds. Its flavor was excellent, but I must admit the 12-year-old bull was somewhat chewy.

The bison is a genuine marvel and one of America's greatest conservation success stories. Brought back from virtual extinction in the 1880s, the bison has rebounded in dramatic fashion. At present, there are hundreds of privately owned herds with a dozen to 2,000 in each. Numerous government managed herds roam freely in places like the Black Hills, Alaska, Canada and Yellowstone Park.

Permits for hunting wild bison may still be applied for and drawn in the states of Utah and Alaska. However, in Montana the pressure brought by animal rights extremists has taken its toll. Hunters are no longer called upon to cull the herds, which are overpopulating and overflowing the boundaries of Yellowstone Park.

After the infamous ski-pole incident, when anti-hunters smeared blood on and stabbed a hunter with a ski pole, Montana's legislature and game management people, in their infinite wisdom, decided to end bison hunting in the state.

Indeed, this action by Montana's officials did quell the uninformed outcry of anti-hunters. However, this did not stop the problems of bison overpopulation and their natural disposition to wander. Therefore, during the winter of 1991, game wardens killed the bison migrating out of the park.

Whether they are shot because they pose the threat of transmitting brucellosis (a disease carried by Yellowstone bison that causes spontaneous abortion) to domestic livestock, or because game managers cannot allow wild bison to knock down fences and tear up private property, the solution is the same. Licensed legal hunting was stopped by a few vocal radicals, and the bison are still being shot as a management tool.

It is my hope that we will be able to maintain our hunting traditions, and that our grandchildren will also be able to enjoy hunting trophies like my bull well into the future.

Charles E. Erickson, Jr. receiving the Sagamore Hill Award for his Coues'
non-typical whitetail deer (155 points) from Stephen S. Adams (left),
President of the Boone and Crockett Club at the 21st Awards Banquet.

At the 21st Awards (Milwaukee, 1992), D. Alan McCaleb (left) accepts
Second Award (tie) from Walter H. White, Chairman
of the Records Committee, for his grizzly bear.

Photograph by Wm. H. Nesbitt

ROCKY MOUNTAIN GOAT
FIRST AWARD (TIE)
54-2/8

Locality: Yes Bay, Alaska   Date: 1991
Hunter: Wally L. Grover

ROCKY MOUNTAIN GOAT 54-2/8

Wally L. Grover

It was August 24, 1991, the fourth weekend of hunting season, when we decided to go after goats. Wally Grover and I had been climbing mountains on Prince of Wales Island, in southeast Alaska, to hunt the alpine country for Sitka blacktail deer on the previous three weekends. The weather had been marginal, but we managed to tag some beautiful bucks each weekend. We have a four-deer-per-year bag limit in this part of Alaska.

Wally and I both work in the timber industry, doing quality control work for a logging company based in Ketchikan. Much of our time is spent hiking through the woods and working with timber fallers. We have hunted together for several years and have had many productive and enjoyable trips.

We had talked about hunting Rocky Mountain goats each year but were not able to coordinate a trip to coincide with reasonable weather conditions. We prefer to access our hunting areas by boat, through the many saltwater channels and inlets in southeast Alaska. Not only does this save on expensive and uncertain airline charters, but it also allows us to choose mountains not easily accessible by air. This results in no hunting pressure, other than natural predators, and abundant game.

We knew there were goats on many of the mainland mountains surrounding our island, and we decided to talk to our friend Allan Merrill for advice. Al has hunted and fished this area for two decades when not busy working as a timber-falling foreman. Al told us the rugged, mountainous area between Ketchikan and Wrangell used to be his playground, and he had been on many successful goat hunts. He said that he had seen a possible world's record goat on a mountain near Yes Bay 10 years earlier but failed to get a shot. Since there were no lakes suitable for airplane access nearby, we figured the area had not been hunted much.

Normally we work six days a week, but we bargained with our boss, Chuck Lockhart, to take Saturday off and get an early start. We invited Joe Nichols, who is currently a partner in Alaska Wilderness Outfitting here in Ketchikan, to come along. He readily accepted the invitation.

We were all pretty excited when we left the dock in Ketchikan at about 11:30 a.m. The weather was overcast, the temperature was about 55 degrees, and the water was glassy as we boated up Behm Canal.

We could see the mountain range we had chosen as we neared Yes Bay, and we wondered if Al had given us a bum steer. There didn't appear to be any alpine country with the classic craggy peaks that goats are supposed to like. Although some of it was steep, there was timber all the way to the top. We checked our topographic map and sure enough, the highest peak was only 2,200 feet in elevation. Timberline is generally about 2,500 feet in these parts. We decided to go for it anyway, wondering about the prospect of hunting goats in the timber.

We arrived at our proposed anchorage about 1:00 p.m. Using nautical charts and our depth sounder, we located suitable water to allow for the tide and dropped the hook. After dismounting our 18-foot Coleman canoe from atop the 23-foot Olympic, we loaded our packs with overnight provisions and gear. We had enough on board for a week, which is a good practice when boating in southeast Alaskan waters.

We paddled to shore, gazing at our destination as just another mountain to conquer in quest of game. By 1:30, we had the canoe secured in the brush above the high tide line. I had located a probable access route on our maps and gave Wally the bearing. We all carry a compass, in addition to basic survival gear. I let Wally take the lead as he makes a good trail boss and usually sniffs out a good path.

I brought up the rear, hanging fluorescent flagging to mark our trail and I checked our back trail for landmarks. Our packs felt heavy at first, but we soon grew used to them. Wally was carrying his seasoned .270, a Remington Model 700, loaded with 150-grain Federal ammunition. Joe and I were both packing Rugers. Joe uses a No. 1 in the .375 H & H magnum caliber with 270-grain handloads. Mine is an old Model 77, chambered for .30-06, running 165-grain Federal Premium ammunition. All of our rifles are fitted with Leupold scopes.

We had to cross a mile and a half of rolling hills and little draws before we got to the base of the first mountain. It took us nearly an hour in the scrubby timber and thick brush, with only a couple of muskegs for easy going.

Around 2:30, we crossed the main drainage and began our ascent. The timber was thicker on the mountain and it was easier going without underbrush. However, the steep terrain required using both hands to grasp Devil's club while clinging to the mountain. We all wore top-quality caulk boots, which we feel are a necessity for sure footing and good support. We hit some sub-alpine muskeg at about 1,700 feet as we neared the top of the first peak.

After reaching the top of the first peak, we found a fairly large ravine separated us from the mountain we intended to hunt. It had not looked so big on the map, but they never do. We had to drop about 400 feet in elevation and found the game trail to do it.

By 4:00 p.m., we were back down to 1,300 feet and anxious to climb the last 900 feet to the top. The terrain was still steep and brushy, but it opened up into a series of broken muskegs, quartering up the hill and separated by scrubby timber. We had seen quite a bit of deer sign and expected to see some animals pretty soon.

We had our eyes peeled for goat sign and were hoping to spot some animals that we could stalk the next day. Wally spotted a small buck and a doe as we neared the top, and our spirits soared when he found some goat hair in a bed. The peak was not sharp, but rather flat with a long, narrow muskeg leading to the edge on the backside.

The light breeze was in our favor, quartering toward us from left to right. Wally had just started to peak-out in the semi-alpine muskeg when he ducked back and looked at us with bulging eyes. I could not believe my ears when he whispered, "There's a goat!"

When I looked down the narrow corridor of muskeg, I was instantly infected with goat fever. Not only had we found a mountain goat, but I knew he was a trophy billy. The long, black, curved horns were easily visible with the naked eye. He was lying down and quartering away on a small knob at the other end of the opening, with his nose to the wind, less than 100 yards away. Beyond the goat, the ground appeared to drop off immediately.

Since I had given Wally the pick of the bucks and first shot on two of the previous weekends, we had agreed that I would have the first shot. Wally and Joe took up positions just to my right as I slid down to a prone position, using my pack for a rest. The shot looked like an easy one, and I took my time as I centered the black crosshairs against the white hair just behind the shoulder.

At the sound of the shot, the big billy leaped out of his bed and dove over the nearly vertical edge. Wally managed to squeeze off a shot just before the goat disappeared from sight. We could not tell if the goat had been seriously hit. A second billy, noticeably smaller, burst out of the brush adjacent to where our trophy had been bedded and followed the leader.

We were all on the run an instant later, with Wally in the lead. I was trying to re-shoulder my pack as we raced across the lumpy muskeg. When we scrambled over the edge, hoping for a glimpse of the goat below, we noticed the torn-up ground where the goats had skidded before descending into the steep, rocky terrain. We did not see any blood or hair.

Wally and I descended, sliding and hanging onto small bushes to keep from crashing down the treacherous slope. Joe stayed at the edge on top. After only 100 feet, Wally skidded to a stop and raised his rifle. The goat had stopped just over the edge and was slightly above us, about 50 feet to the side. I was still sliding down the hill and stopped next to Wally, expecting him to fire. He lowered his rifle and fumbled with the scope. The power adjustment was still set on 9x from his first shot, and all he could see was hair.

After lowering the power to 3x, he re-shouldered his rifle just as the goat took off again. Joe had spotted the goat almost directly below him, but he was unable to get a clear shot. We could hear rocks rolling and brush crashing as the goat scrambled down through the boulders and scattered timber. The steep slope appeared to bottom out into a deep ravine 300 feet below. We could see a small, benchy muskeg opening on the other side so we stayed put, hoping that the goat would offer us one more chance.

We did not have to wait long before the goat appeared, crossing the opening and climbing for the far ridgeline. Wally was ready with a solid rest and touched off a shot. The crack of the rifle echoed a hit and we noticed the goat falter. He was still on his feet but had changed direction, going downhill. Joe and I also fired, and the goat went down. We made as rapid a descent as possible.

The goat was immense, between 350 and 400 pounds, with long, thick, curved horns. I knew immediately that he would qualify for the records book. Measuring the horns with a string and the ruler on my compass, we found them to be 12 inches long and nearly 6 inches around the base. The horns were fairly symmetrical, and I figured the goat would go high in the book.

It was 5:30 p.m., only four hours after we left the boat. We were all very excited about killing our first mountain goat and felt lucky to have found such a beautiful trophy.

We took some photographs and Wally and Joe proceeded with the skinning. The mosquitoes and whitesox were having a party, savagely attacking them as they worked. I helped them finish boning the carcass, and we loaded the meat sacks for the trip home. Hoping that no brown bears or wolves would show up that evening, we moved the meat and skin away from the carcass.

We found a windfall a little farther upwind. It took a little while to get a fire started as everything was wet from recent rains. Dinner around the campfire on the mountain was very rewarding. We were all very tired but knew our work was not over. Sleep came easily but was interrupted by a heavy rainfall at midnight.

By 6:00 a.m., we were up and loading our packs for the long trek home. I had planned a new route to the boat that would intersect our flagged trail about a mile from the beach and eliminate any uphill hiking. The packs were the heaviest we had carried all season, and we went cautiously to avoid a dangerous fall. It poured rain all morning, and the wind blew the treetops into a frenzy.

Just a mile from the beach and feeling pretty weary, we jumped a couple of deer. Wally decided we were close enough to the boat and dropped a nice, fat buck. Adding the extra meat to our already heavy packs, we trudged on.

We celebrated upon arriving at the boat at 1:30 Sunday afternoon, then headed for Ketchikan. By then, the winds were gusting to 45 miles per hour and a steady rain was falling. The boat ride home took four hours, compared to the hour-and-a-half it had taken to get there. The seas in Behm Canal were five to seven feet, and darkness came early that evening.

We took the horns and cape to Randy Jahnke of Southeast Taxidermy, in Ketchikan, and notified the Department of Fish and Game. Randy took some unofficial measurements and said it could be the largest goat killed in 25 years. After the 60-day drying period, Wally was notified that the goat had been entry scored at 56-6/8, tying the current world's record. It was celebration time again.

Note: Written by Ed Toribio with the help of Wally Grover and Joe Nichols.

Photograph courtesy of Michael L. Ross

Michael L. Ross (right) killed this Rocky Mountain goat at Bradley Lake, Alaska, in 1989 while accompanied by his brother, Joe Ross, (left). It scored 49-6/8.

Photograph courtesy of James L. Beskin

This Rocky Mountain goat was killed at Bradfield Canal, Alaska, in 1989 by James L. Beskin. It scores 50.

Photograph by Wm. H. Nesbitt

ROCKY MOUNTAIN GOAT
FIRST AWARD (TIE)
54-2/8

Locality: Mt. Meehaus, B.C.   Date: 1989
Hunter: Denis J. Chagnon

ROCKY MOUNTAIN GOAT 54-2/8

Denis J. Chagnon

Before we left Onaway, my partners and I decided to spend as little time as necessary getting to Iskut, British Columbia. After a drive of 2,700 miles, we still had a few days to exercise our legs and continue getting into shape. Within walking distance of the base camp was a pretty good rainbow trout lake, which I was familiar with from my hunt the previous year. We flogged that unnamed lake with all kinds of hardware, trying to catch a few trout. So far, the trip was grand.

Our hunt was to begin on September 15, 1989. On September 13, we arrived at Bruce's camp at Kinaskan Lake. We enjoyed the journey to the camp by way of the Cassiar Highway, which was dusty, sloppy, and full of unbelievably huge pot holes. Within a short time after arriving at camp, we were settled in and were getting reacquainted with the guides.

As I mentioned before, I had been a client of Bruce's the previous year and had already negotiated the details of the hunt that was ahead. I knew the hunt would entail a long, rough ride over some of the most beautiful country in the world; if it was anything like Lynx's camp on the Todigan River, we would be satisfied.

Preparing ourselves for our hunting adventure, we spent the remainder of the day sorting things out, repacking our gear, checking our supplies, and locating fishing equipment.

Ray was the first one up the next morning, eager to catch a batch of rainbows, and Wayne was not far behind. We started fishing about mid-morning, only to find the angling was a bit slow; but by noon, we had caught enough fish to put on a pretty good feed. We were informed by Bruce's wife, Louise, that we needed enough fish to feed ten people at dinner. Ray and Wayne anxiously filled the order.

That afternoon, Ray spent an hour or more cleaning fish, while Wayne and I helped two of the guides, Pye and Terry, round up and shoe a horse. Louise had told us at breakfast that Bruce and the cook had not arrived from Dease Lake yet, but she expected them before day's end.

Another hunter arrived at the camp during the afternoon. His hunt was for Stone's sheep. It was then that I was informed by Johnny, the camp wrangler, apprentice guide and cook, that there would be a change in the guides we were originally promised. In fact, the guide was already at Todigan Lake, waiting for the sheep hunter.

My heart sank, for I knew Bruce was excellent in high mountain hunting for such game as sheep and goat, but he left a lot to be desired when it came to moose, our primary objective. Wayne and Ray did not seem overly concerned about the change and had a positive outlook. The camp wrangler then told us how well the eight hunters at Forty-Mile Camp had done the previous year. I had seen the racks and conversed with those hunters, but they all attributed their success to the ability of Bruce's brother, Jerry, to call a moose. Unfortunately, Jerry would not be our guide. We spent the rest of the day preparing for the hunt, for the next day was September 15, when our hunt would begin.

September 15, 1989, we had a breakfast fit for a king —eggs, bacon, pancakes, hot coffee, and rainbow trout left over from the day before. We thoroughly enjoyed every mouthful and were filled with anticipation of the hunt. Bruce had arrived during the night, minus the camp cook. He thought all of us could pitch in and do the cooking. He also apologized for the change in guides, explaining to us that Jerry was guiding sheep hunts, instead of moose, and might eventually take over the whole operation.

At 10:00 a.m., we were on our way. We had to make one stop at Iskut, about 10 miles away, for food staples. We then continued to a site near the Stikine River, where we were to begin our hunt. The weather was cooperating, sunny and warm with a few clouds. It took several hours to unload and saddle the seven riding mounts and pack the remaining gear on three other horses. The guide was a real pro when it came to packing. When he threw that diamond hitch on that old pack horse and drew it up tight, it was tighter than a stave on a rain barrel.

There were six horses that had not had a rider since the previous hunting season. Naturally, they did not take kindly to us. They were pitching, turning, and humping, trying to launch us off their backs. At the same time, six more horses were trying to slide the panniers off their backsides. I must say the three packhorses were truly amazing. They resembled the sleigh on "The Grinch Who Stole Christmas." We were now headed to Forty-Mile Camp. This spike camp does not get its name from being just a few miles off the road; it was well after midnight when we arrived.

We were disappointed to find that nothing had been prepared for our arrival. I felt Bruce was neglecting his end of the bargain. He should have sent two of the guides up a day early to set up camp. To top things off, the weather had changed as we climbed the mountain. The sun turned to rain, and we fought it all the way to camp. We were drenched, as was all the gear.

It was 1:00 a.m. when we finally had two tents set up. We were exhausted as we crawled into our damp sleeping bags. Wayne and I slept pretty well; we had bags with synthetic insulation, and I had a polyfoam mattress. Unfortunately, Ray was not as comfortable; his goose-down bag had soaked up water like a sponge on the ride to camp.

At 7:00 a.m. the next morning, my Normark thermometer-compass read 17 degrees, which was quite a change in temperature from the day before. Ray was already up, trying to get a fire started so he could thaw his boots. Things only got worse from there.

As daylight became evident, so did the gaping holes in our tent. Luckily, with the aid of some plastic sheets and some twine, we were able to patch the tent before breakfast.

We all crowded into the cook tent to prepare for breakfast. The tent was in pretty good shape and was equipped with a heater. As we proceeded to cook our bacon and egg breakfast, we found that every egg that hit the frying pan was rotten. Needless to say, we ate bacon and bread that morning. We expressed our disappointment at not having a heater in our tent. The camp conditions were certainly not what I had had on my hunt the year before and bragged about to my buddies. I felt badly for my friends, who had expectations of much better conditions.

Later that morning, all the hunters and guides left together and rode from the camp to the top of the first summit. Bruce felt everyone should get the overall picture of the terrain. He told us later that he had not been at that particular camp in 20 years. The other two guides, Pye and Terry, admitted they had never been to the camp. It was Johnny's first experience guiding a moose hunt, but he had been to the camp the year before. Pye was the only guide who did not go with us that morning. He stayed in camp to organize the gear, chop firewood, and get things unpacked.

We returned to camp that evening to find very little done and Pye feeling sick. Despite our terrible fate thus far, we felt our luck was going to change. We all had seen some moose that day, even though they were several miles away and it was too late in the day to start to stalk them. Tomorrow was another day and we felt much more prepared.

It was September 17. Pye and Ray were both sick. Ray decided to hunt, regardless of being ill. Pye and Ray went to the same summit as the day before, following the peak to its farthest point. Terry and Wayne decided to go back down the mountain to the place where they had spotted a cow and calf the evening before. Bruce and I hoped to spot a moose and try to stalk it, once we reached the summit.

Sure enough, when we reached the summit, it was really easy to spot one of those big guys. Its polished white palms showed up like a drop of white paint on a green felt tablecloth. Spotting a moose from a summit is not hard, but stalking takes time and strategy. There are many variables to consider. Bruce knew we had to get behind the moose, which meant climbing down the mountain. We had to remember his last position and consider wind direction, so as to not spook him. The lower valleys looked like well-manicured lawns, but they were actually carpeted with brush 10 to 15- feet high. This made the ride on horseback through the valley very cumbersome.

By mid-afternoon, we were working our way down the face of the adjacent mountain. From time to time, we would get a glimpse of his white palms. We were then at the base of the mountain, not far from the huge animal. Unexpectedly, Bruce's horse went up to its belly in mossy green slime. The horse lunged and floundered until Bruce managed to get it under control. I was sure the commotion had spooked our prey, but we continued the hunt. We tied up the horses and began pursuing on foot.

It was late afternoon. Fresh moose sign was evident all around us. The smell of urine and fresh scrapes indicated that we were deep in their territory. We moved ever so cautiously, trying not to make the slightest noise. As the minutes ticked away, our odds grew slim. It was a long shot, but we continued to stalk the animal. When we had no luck, Bruce suggested we make our way back to the horses and hunt back toward the camp.

The weather was changing and storm clouds were moving across the mountains. The peaks were shrouded in gray and no longer were visible. We still had ample daylight, but we also had a long ride back to camp. I could see the concern in Bruce's face as we mounted our horses and started our ride. It was starting to snow and Bruce was wasting little time heading toward camp. I was finding it extremely difficult to keep his pace; he continuously urged me to move more quickly. I think he was hoping to outrun the storm, but we were running a losing race. The storm worsened as we pushed on. My horse fell three times. The storm lashed out at us like some angry god; I feared for our lives. The treachery of the steep mountain cliffs and the bitter, blinding snow left us helpless in the storm's path.

I pleaded with Bruce to stop and make a shelter in a crevice or large boulder formation. He feared that if we did not get down to the timberline, we would freeze to death, so we continued on.

Four hours had passed since sundown. We felt our way down the mountain, step by step, slipping and sliding, hoping the timber was not far off. I remember praying that if it was my time, let if be swift. I shuddered at the thought of falling into a deep ravine and being pinned under the horse.

Visibility was zero, and drifting snow covered the tracks behind us. Accidentally, we bumped into a small, wind-whipped tree. We knew the timber line was getting close and our spirits lightened somewhat. We knew we could find shelter until the storm subsided.

In a short time, Bruce found the right tree and used his short-handled ax like a lumberman. He knew exactly what to do to make an emergency shelter. He selected a very dense black spruce with branches that dropped to ground level and curled back up. I was amazed how the tree sheltered us that night. The snow sealed off the branches, blocked the wind, and the accumulation of needles from years gone by provided us with a soft cushion to lie on. As I think back, I feel pretty selfish for not sharing my emergency tarp with Bruce. I could not help but think of a story he had told me on my previous hunt. He said a hunter should always carry a bedroll and some supplies for the unexpected. I knew he did not practice what he preached when he commented that my canvas bedroll would be large enough for both of us. It was well after midnight, and we decided to go on two-hour shifts to keep the fire going.

Morning came. The snow had stopped, but a heavy fog had set in. We were confused and were not sure how far off course we were, or if we were even on the right mountainside. I was perfectly content to remain where we were until we could orient ourselves. I had water, shelter and few big blocks of Hershey's chocolate to sustain me until the fog lifted. The 10-hour nightmare of the previous evening was enough to make me a little fearful of another venture into the unknown.

It was 2:00 p.m. that day when the fog lifted and we finally left the protective custody of that ancient black spruce. I was more than anxious to get back to camp. We started back up the mountain so Bruce could get a feeling for the lay of the land. I had never seen Bruce use a compass. He usually had a pretty keen sense of direction. The storm had pushed us so far off course that we had stumbled to the backside of the mountain. Bruce figured we were about 10 miles from camp. We arrived back at camp late that afternoon. I will never forget the elation on Ray's and Wayne's faces. I could sense how they wanted to shake me in anger and frustration and hug me in relief and friendship.

Later that evening Wayne told me how he and Ray urged the guides to start a search. They had fired their rifles several times, hoping we would hear the shots. They never would have been able to find us in that blinding snow, and they knew we were on the adjacent mountain. By our very presence back at that camp, I felt we had avenged the fury of that mountain, but only with the help of God. I will never forget those twenty-four hours and all the emotions that went with that experience.

In the last few days of the hunt, Ray had become more feverish, and his cold was definitely getting worse. The lack of heat in the tent, coupled with a diet of canned food, was not helping Ray's condition. Bruce had expected to have a moose for camp meat by then. We were seriously considering aborting the hunt if we did not get some fresh meat and some heat in our tent. Over canned hash and coffee, we discussed this with Bruce. Johnny, the camp wrangler, informed Bruce of two other camp sites from the previous year that might have some items of use for us. Bruce was a second generation guide, as were his brothers, and I honestly believed they had a cache on every mountain.

Wayne and Terry were the first to leave the camp the next day. Ray had decided to hunt for part of the day in close proximity to the camp, since he was not feeling well. At 9:00 a.m., Bruce, Johnny, and I left camp. Johnny led the way, hoping to find a cache. We rode slowly, stopping every 300 to 400 yards to glass the landscape.

About an hour and half later, we found the first camp. A cache, wrapped in plastic and old canvas, was lashed tightly in a large black spruce. The contents of the bag included many different items: horseshoes, nails, farrier's supplies, Coleman fuel, and even pancake flour. We did find a stove, but it was not worth hauling back to camp.

We continued, hoping to find another camp. After two hours of searching, Johnny explained the location to Bruce. Bruce remembered being there as a young guide and knew the camp had to be closer to the ridges to the west, which were only about a mile away. As we rode toward it, we could see the camp site with the tent poles still standing, as if they were erected only the day before. That cache was in better shape. The tarp covering the goods was newer. We were thrilled to discover the stove and smoke pipes enclosed. After packing the stove up, Johnny headed back toward camp.

Bruce suggested that I follow a game trail to the base of the peak, leaving my horse at the bottom. The whole distance was about one mile and very steep. I was on top of the peak in a little more than an hour. The panoramic view was breathtaking. I had ascended to the southwest peak of Mount Meehaus. As I looked straight ahead, I could see the steep, icy, snowy slopes of Ice Mountain. The mountain was actually named

Mount Edziza, but the Indians called it Ice Mountain because of its appearance. The valley between Mount Meehaus and Mount Edziza was at my feet. The unobstructed view at that elevation made me feel small, insignificant, and dizzy.

As I regained my composure and my breath, I proceeded to glass the lower elevations for mountain goat. I spotted three goats immediately, lying on a rocky ledge below me. Tiny moisture droplets continuously formed on the lenses as clouds passed by.

Bruce arrived and set up his spotting scope. He confirmed it was a nanny and her kids. After taking a break to eat lunch, we continued to glass the area. Bruce suddenly stepped back, motioning me closer to the edge. As I peaked over, I could see a mountain goat feeding below. Momentarily, I turned to Bruce, commenting that we needed fresh meat for camp; he agreed. I did not mind using my tag for camp provisions since the mountain goat was a bonus objective anyway. The year before, I had been lucky enough to take a nice nine-inch billy.

Bruce and I crawled to the edge, being very careful not to cause loose rocks to fall. I felt somewhat like a tiger about to leap upon my prey. It amazes me how automatically one engages, applying skills acquired through years of practice.

Removing my hat, I shouldered my .338 Winchester Magnum. I slowly lifted the bolt, chambering one of my own reloads. I estimated him to be 300 yards away. He was feeding up the slope and toward me. He was cloaked in mist, which at that distance made it impossible for me to judge his size. Occasionally he lifted his head and looked directly at us. Knowing a goat has keen eyesight, Bruce inched his way out of sight and the goat resumed feeding.

I knew I could accurately shoot at that distance, but he was coming my way, so why not let him. At about 150 yards, I moved my safety to fire position, waiting for him to quarter once more. I know the importance of a well-placed first shot. I pondered the thought of a wounded goat diving over the edge of a mountain to a place where it would be unrecoverable.

Placing the crosshairs just a bit ahead of the shoulders and holding low, I would let this fellow walk right into eternity. As soon as the report sounded, Bruce was back at the edge. I was still working the bolt, making ready for another shot. I could see the goat rolling sideways down the mountain and disappearing into the mist, as if in slow motion.

We agreed that Bruce would go down for the meat and the cape and I would fetch the horses. It took me an hour and a half to return with the horses. As I sat waiting for Bruce, I snacked on a can of fruit cocktail. The gray clouds were beginning to make me very concerned. I did not want to sleep out again, and I knew we had an eight mile ride back to camp. It was at least 45 more minutes before Bruce, puffing like a steam engine, popped his head over the edge. He was trying to get his pack off and shake my hand at the same time, while saying, "Congratulations! You killed yourself a record book goat!"

I allowed him to unpack the cape and the head to show me, not really giving it much thought. I continued to insist that we get moving. It would soon be dark and I feared another storm.

It was not until that night, over dinner, that I began to comprehend my accomplishment. Conversing over coffee, Bruce claimed that, several years before one of his hunters had made the Boone and Crockett records book for mountain goat. He believed that my goat was larger.

That night, I reminisced about the months of preparation, only to have spent that investment in a few exhilarating minutes. I kept thinking of all the hours spent working up fast, accurate handloads. I had needed a bullet that expanded rapidly enough for a goat, yet penetrated deeply for a moose. I thought of my aching legs and feet from hiking and my saddle sores from riding that past summer. It all paid off. As I slipped into unconsciousness, my thoughts returned to the moose that eluded us earlier.

The next morning Ray was very sick with a high fever, coughing, and fever blisters. Even though the tent was somewhat comfortable with the stove, Ray's condition concerned us. After discussing and making decisions together, we decided to make our descent and start for home.

Photograph by Wm. H. Nesbitt

ROCKY MOUNTAIN GOAT
SECOND AWARD
53-6/8

Locality: Telegraph Creek, B.C.   Date: 1991
Hunter: Steven M. Gross

ROCKY MOUNTAIN GOAT 53-6/8

Steven M. Gross

My story begins with only the hope of ever taking a Boone and Crockett animal. I have been on many hunts, and before this trip I can honestly say that I had never seen a Boone and Crockett animal of any species. My hunts have taken me from Ontario's swamplands to the mountains of Colorado, Wyoming, and Montana. Throughout my travels, I have managed to bag three bull elk, four mule deer bucks, and a black bear, which fell just short of Pope and Young. Every hunt you go on seems to sharpen your skills and better prepare you for your next hunting opportunity.

I came close to seeing a Boone and Crockett animal when I shot a 59-inch Alaska-Yukon moose in 1989. That bull came up about ten points short of the minimum requirement. After seeing the size of that moose and knowing it was short of Boone and Crockett, I realized that it takes a tremendous animal to make the book.

We had failed to see a mountain goat on an earlier hunt to Alaska. Heavy fog and rain kept us from getting a chance to hunt. My hunting partner, Dave Patoka, and I planned a hunt in British Columbia. This hunt would be the hunt of a lifetime for me. This was a fly-in trip, with horses waiting on the other end to cover the long miles that normally wear you down to the bone. Dave and I decided, after weeks of ground work and several phone calls to various references, that we would go with Tahltan Outfitters of Telegraph Creek, British Columbia. Tahltan Outfitters have a very high success rate on mountain goats and a good following of repeat hunters. I also decided to hunt caribou on this trip, so I left a week earlier than my partner. He was to meet me at base camp after my caribou hunt was completed.

I spent a full year of planning, hiking and buying new gear to suit the hunt. As I stepped off that floatplane at Camp Island Lake, I knew it was worth it. This land can be considered God's Country. The only trails we found were those leading from our base camp to the hunting spots.

When I walked onto the landing pier from the floatplane, a man walked up and introduced himself as Rudy Day. He said that he would be my guide. We hauled my gear to a bunk house and got settled. Rudy and I then joined a couple of other newly arrived hunters for a quick check of our rifles. After four commercial flights and a floatplane trip, it is always necessary to inspect your rifle and reconfirm its sighting.

The first day of my hunt was actually more of a voyage into caribou country. After loading up an eight-horse pack train, we headed out at 9:00 a.m. I really had no idea what the trails ahead were like. For the next 10 hours, we stumbled along on wet, loose, rocky trails, with brush pounding on both sides of us. Every turn on the trail offered some kind of new scenery, from a deep canyon with a wide river to a beautiful meadow between some hills. We worked our way up to a campsite called Level Mountain. It was nearly to the top of a huge mountain range, where caribou usually spend their winter months. Rudy, along with two other hunters, had been at this campsite two weeks earlier. Both the hunters had killed nice caribou, one of which was Boone and Crockett-size. This really pumped me up for the next morning's journey to the top of that mountain.

When the next morning arrived, Rudy's wife Linda, our chief cook, whipped up some good old-fashioned bacon and eggs. Meanwhile, Rudy wrangled our horses for the hunt. We had about a three-hour ride before we would be in good caribou country. When we reached the top of the hill, my knees were shot from all the horseback riding, so I got off to walk around and loosen up for awhile. At that time, I realized how the mountain had come to be called Level Mountain; once you reached the top, you could see for miles. We walked for a couple of hours, occasionally stopping to glass some crevices and ravines that led us out of a huge plateau. Then we sat down on a rise that overlooked a large portion of land which surrounded us.

Rudy glanced over at me and asked "Where did all the caribou go? We have already gone further than those other hunters had to go to shoot their caribou."

Instantly, the wind started to cut through me. The temperature was less than 20 degrees. Suddenly I realized that the caribou picture looked pretty grim. Rudy finally spotted some caribou about three miles away, so we headed in that direction. With a three-hour ride back to camp, we had a lot of ground to cover in a short time.

The further we went, the more caribou we saw. Then, we spotted 30 to 40 caribou on a little ridge. Two nice bulls were going at each other like their lives depended on it. We were on our hands and knees, slipping along a grassy edge, while the bulls kept themselves occupied with each other. We had cut the range about 250 yards when some cows spotted us and began running away, spooking the others. The two bulls continued to tangle with each other, first wrestling to the ground and then resting a bit between lunges. Rudy said that was the best caribou fight he had ever seen in his 20 years of guiding. I wish I could have gotten it on video.

When the bulls finally split apart, I could not get a shot, because the other caribou were passing through my 3-9x Leupold scope. I finally focused the crosshairs on the bull that had been kicked out of the herd.

Rudy whispered "Shoot, shoot," so I cranked my gun back to the right, centered my crosshairs on the big bull, and squeezed the trigger on my Winchester .338.

"Too far back," Rudy said, so I then worked the bolt and let another 250-grain Nosler Partition fly. This time, the shot was good. He was a nice double-shovel bull, with a total of 34 points. Rudy caped the bull out, cut it up, and loaded it on the two pack horses. Horses really come in handy when you down an animal.

We spent the next day back at camp, preparing the cape and meat for the ride back to the base camp. The trip back to base camp did not seem as long as the trip out. It was the fourth day of my hunting expedition and I was heading down the hill with a nice caribou.

The fifth day was spent in base camp, fishing. I caught about 10 rainbow trout, which were eaten for lunch, and a landlocked salmon, a rare fish for that lake.

Around noon, Dave, my hunting partner, arrived by floatplane. I told him the story of the caribou hunt, the horseback riding and the distance we had to travel to find the caribou. He then sighted-in his rifle. After that, we packed our bags for the following day's ride to Goat Bluff, the breeding ground for the goats in that area.

The horseback ride to Goat Bluff was about 20 miles. The last five or six miles of the ride was over trails that are only used once a year. They were covered with brush and fallen trees. One of our guides was ahead of us, chopping and clearing out the bad spots. We had brought about 15 horses to make the trail passable heading in. We also had to cross the Chesley River, which is roughly 150 yards of fast water. If you fell in the river, you would go directly to Juneau.

We arrived at the Goat Bluff camp around 10:00 p.m. We unloaded the horses, covered our gear, and laid our sleeping bags under the stars to sleep.

Our crew consisted of four guides, four hunters, and a helper named Glenn. None of us felt like setting up tents. Unfortunately, it rained enough during the night to get everything wet. When morning came, the sky cleared off nicely, but the neighboring peaks showed signs of bad weather.

I saw my first mountain goat that morning, grazing on one of the cliffs. We spotted 25 to 30 goats on the hill we were about to climb. From bottom to top, it took about four hours to climb that hill. We instantly saw goats when we reached the top.

Dave, our guides Rudy and Dale, and I headed along the top of some steep cliffs, glassing down to scout the goats below us. As we followed along one ridge, we saw several good-looking billies, but none of them were shootable. As the day was coming to an end, we started back to a spot where a number of goats were grazing.

When we got there, three more billies had come out. One of the billies' horns appeared to be more than 9 inches long. When we were approximately 150 yards above them, Dave chose to shoot. He fired at the biggest one and finished him with a second shot. Dave and his guide, Dale, split off from us to retrieve his billy, which was down a steep overhang.

From the spot where Dave killed his billy, Rudy spotted a lone billy. He was back down the ridge, where we had spent most of the day glassing. Rudy asked me if I was interested in going back and trying for the goat. It would mean getting back to camp late or, possibly, sleeping under the stars. I instantly answered, "Let's go."

We had about an hour's ride back, including about half a mile of heavy pines and downed timber.

The lone billy was standing at the low end of the woods, where we had seen him last. We worked our way down through the woods. It seemed like we would never get to the end, but when we did, the goat was not there. We dropped down a couple of more humps and still no sign of the goat.

Then, Rudy walked up behind a couple of pines and the goat stormed out, running up to a little knob only 15 yards ahead of me. Rudy whispered for me to shoot. I already had my rifle up and had noted the size of him. I put the crosshairs on his shoulder, and the 250-grain Nosler did the rest. The billy goat fell over the hill and down about 40 yards, into some poplar trees.

When Rudy and I reached the goat, we could not believe how huge he was. Rudy measured his horn at just under 11 inches. He was truly a beauty. The goat was 12-1/2 years old and weighed around 350 pounds. I was never so happy to get an animal. I knew somehow that goat was special. We took lots of photographs. Then, Rudy began skinning the goat for a life-size mount.

We started on our long hike back up the hill to our horses. We finally reached our horses shortly after dark and headed back for camp. Snow began to fall and the wind was blowing hard, making it difficult to stay on the trails. It was a long ride back, but we arrived at camp about 2 a.m. That was certainly a long day of hunting.

The following day, I found out that Dave's billy had measured in at 9-2/8 inches long. Everybody kidded me about killing the grandpa goat, because he only had one tooth left in his mouth. Everyone knew he would score well, but exactly how high, we were not sure. The trip back to camp was much more enjoyable, even though we encountered bad weather for most of the ride.

We had a day back at base camp to salt the hides and prepare our gear for the long flight home. Everything went smoothly on my flights. However, my caribou antlers were two weeks behind me because of loaded planes.

I was not really sure how good my billy would score until I took it to Stan Godfrey, an official scorer for Boone and Crockett. After the 60-day drying period, Stan carefully measured the goat horns at a gross score of 54, with deductions of 4/8. This officially gave the goat a score of 53-4/8 inches, which placed it in the top 20 of all time.

It is a proud feeling to shoot a Boone and Crockett animal in a fair-chase situation. I hope that every hunter can have that feeling in their adventures.

I am really happy to be invited to the Boone and Crockett Club's 21st Big Game Awards in Milwaukee. I thank Boone and Crockett for making this a special time for me.

Photograph courtesy of Jerry E. Copenhaver

Jerry E. Copenhaver killed this Rocky Mountain goat, 47, in Chouteau County, Montana, in 1987.

Photograph courtesy of Roger L. Pock

This Rocky Mountain goat, 50-2/8, was killed by Roger L. Pock in the Sicintine Range, B.C., in 1988.

Photograph courtesy of Chris Guggenbrickler

Hunting on the Cleveland Penninsula of Alaska, Chris Guggenbrickler, killed this Rocky Mountain goat in 1987. It scored 54.

Photograph by Wm. H. Nesbitt

MUSKOX
FIRST AWARD
SCORE: 125
Locality: Bay Chimo, N.W.T.   Date: 1990
Hunter: Stephen A. Kroflich

MUSKOX 125

Stephen A. Kroflich

When I booked my hunt with Canada North Outfitters early in 1989, the excitement began early and never faltered. A year and a half would pass before the hunt took place, but to me it was the culmination of a lifetime of hunting. Having hunted virtually everywhere else in North America, this was to be my first, and possibly only, trip to the Arctic.

It was billed as a combination hunt in which I could purchase licenses and pursue muskox, barren ground grizzly, caribou, wolf, and wolverine. However, I had little interest in caribou, having lived in Alaska more than 30 years ago, and I already had taken two brown bears, which probably is one more than any single hunter should kill. Also, I had killed wolves for bounty in 1960 and had so little interest in killing any more that I did not bother purchasing the license for that species.

My first priority was a muskox, and I hoped for a respectable specimen. It was one of the few species of North American big game that I had not seen previously. I also hoped to bag a wolverine. Having graduated from Ohio State University and being a resident of Michigan, I had lived only 35 miles from our traditional rival, the University of Michigan, since 1964.

For previous hunts in Alaska and parts of northern Canada, I had preferred using my .338 Winchester Magnum, but for this trip, I opted for my 7mm Remington Magnum instead. The rifle weighs almost two pounds less than the .338, and that is a tremendous difference in burden, especially since the outfitter had already informed me that the hunt would entail walking a minimum of 15 to 20 miles each day across rough, uneven tundra. At age 53, expenditure of energy was a primary concern. I wanted to use 175-grain bullets, in that I had been told that the barren ground grizzly, although smaller than its southern cousins, was far more aggressive. My experience on bears was that penetration was perhaps the most important aspect of a hunting bullet. Little did I realize that the muskox would prove to be so difficult to bring down.

My rifle, a Ruger Model 77, was extremely accurate with 150-grain bullets, but I had difficulty in finding a consistent load with the larger slugs. After much experimentation, I did find an acceptable load using 65 grains of H-4831 powder and the 175-grain Speer Mag-Tip bullet. It chronographed at 2,900 feet per second, and shot into one inch groups at 100 yards.

In the months preceding the hunt, I concentrated on walking at least six miles per day at a pace of at least three miles per hour, and for the six weeks preceding departure, increased the effort by carrying a backpack with 35 pounds of books inside. Getting my legs and lungs in shape turned out to be an excellent idea.

The airline connections showed me how far from home this trip would be. I flew from Detroit to Edmonton on the first day, stayed overnight, and then flew from Edmonton through Yellow Knife to Cambridge Bay the following day. Finally, on the third day, a single-engine Otter dropped me off at the Innuit village of Bay Chimo, on the banks of the Arctic Ocean. We then traveled about 30 miles across the ocean, in small skiffs powered by outboard motors, to our base camp.

I was happy with my guide Philip Kadlun, a 38-year-old Innuit from Bay Chimo, who happened to be the chairman of the local hunters and trappers association. As it turned out, Philip was the guide for Don Nicholson, who had taken the World's Record muskox two years before from the same hunting camp. Philip was fine company. We walked and talked for 12 to 16 hours per day during the 15 days of the hunt, which allowed us to become well acquainted.

I had expected to see large herds of muskoxen. My hopes quickly were dashed, however.

On the second day, we finally saw a grizzly. We stalked to within 200 yards of the bear after two and a half hours of hard, sweaty labor. I took several photos and allowed the bear to walk away. That same afternoon we stationed ourselves on a high ridge, from which we watched six white wolves for several more hours.

It was the fourth day before we found our first muskox. It was a large, old bull with one broken horn. We stalked it awhile, then allowed it to pass as well.

Each day, we ranged farther from camp, seeing little more than the beautiful and desolate arctic landscape. We began taking Philip's skiff northward along the coast, pulling into secluded bays, and then hunting afoot from there. Still, we were unable to find game.

Then, on the seventh day, we stopped to visit with a friend of Philip's named Clarence, who lived in a remote cove with his wife and two granddaughters. We drank tea boiled in a pot over a propane stove and ate some tasty dried char, albeit I would have preferred to have a little salt to sprinkle over mine. Clarence told Philip of having seen two large bull muskoxen the previous day and gave him the location. It was too late to go there that evening, but we decided to try finding them the following morning.

On the eighth day, we left early, after a hearty, fat-laden breakfast. We cruised about 10 miles along the coastline, finally parking the skiff in a cove. We climbed a long, gradual slope from the shoreline. At the peak, a muskox could be seen in the valley below, approximately two miles away.

We began our stalk, and within an hour, we had positioned ourselves on a rocky outcrop within 400 yards of the animal. It was feeding on the lush summer grasses that were abundant there and gradually working toward us.

Philip had my Leitz 10x40 binocular, which left me with his, a tiny set of low-powered glasses similar to those often seen in opera houses. The prime advantage of using his glasses was that they kept the mosquitoes and black flies from flying into my eyes. As the animal neared, I asked Philip if the animal was a good bull. His eyes widened, and he said only two words, "Very large."

There was a large, steep rock wall across the grassy meadow from us, and the muskox was feeding, walking gradually closer to us, right at the base of the wall. I estimated that at the closest point it would pass about 175 yards from our position. I asked Philip in a whisper if he considered a high shoulder shot to be a good place to aim, and he nodded. It was 20 or so minutes later when the animal finally arrived at the closest point to present a shot. Placing my hat and gloves on the rock in front of me, I had excellent position to make an accurate shot. I fired, and the giant bull humped up, then spun around, seeming to be more confused than hurt. I fired again into his shoulder, and he began jumping up and down as if to shake off whatever was stinging him. My third shot was aimed at his chest cavity. The bullet entered his lungs, and he went down to his knees. I readied to fire again, but Philip stood and said that it would be unnecessary.

We began walking toward the animal. It rose to its feet and attempted to charge but could not. I put another shot into its shoulder, with no apparent effect, then aimed lower on the chest and placed a final bullet into its heart. It slumped and rolled over on its side, dead.

We approached the muskox carefully. Its horns were dug into the mud and it was impossible to see them well enough to determine their size. We began rolling it onto its back to begin skinning, but the two of us, working together, could not do so. After a great struggle, we finally worked it into position and Philip began skinning. I reminded him that he previously had told me that a mature muskox bull weighed in the area of 650 pounds. I was sure that this one must weigh close to 1,000 pounds. He looked up, smiled, and stated he thought its weight to be closer to 1,200. He then told me that it was the largest muskox he had ever seen. At that point, knowing that he had been the guide on the hunt when the World's Record was taken, I knew for the first time that I had something really special.

My elation was tempered during the next six hours, which I spent carrying meat on a pack frame back to the nearest point on the ocean, almost a mile away. It was very late when we finally returned to camp. The two other hunters, both from Minnesota, the British hunt manager for Canada North Outfitters, and the other Innuit guides all congratulated me on the fine trophy. I was too exhausted to care, preferring instead to drink several cups of hot tea, eat a little food, change my perspiration-drenched long underwear, and climb into my sleeping bag.

Upon my return home, my taxidermist measured the horns and informed me that I should take them to a Boone and Crockett measurer. He thought they would score very high. He introduced me to Cam Cogsdill, and Cam advised that I must wait at least 60 days to allow the horns to dry before he could do his measurements.

It was more than six months before I finally got around to taking the horns to Cam. He worked for two hours. He ultimately told me that he was unsure of the score, because the boss on my animal was so massive that he could not be sure that his measurement was correct. I took the horns back home and Cam contacted Boone and Crockett to verify how to assure taking the proper measurements. Several months later, I finally brought them back to him, and his measurement came to 127-2/8, a full two points higher than the current record.

I have been hunting for more than 40 years, and never previously had taken a single animal that even minimally qualified for Boone and Crockett. It should not be difficult to realize how I felt. I lost 15 pounds on this hunt, though I consumed upwards of 6,000 calories per day of fat-charged nourishment. It was one of my hardest hunts, but it was more than worth the effort. My only regret was that salt from perspiration damaged my camera batteries, and I managed to get only a few photos of my great trophy.

Archie J. Nesbitt killed this muskox on Kent Penninsula,
N.W.T. in 1989. It scored 114-6/8.

A hunt on Nunivak Island, Alaska, yielded David R. Lautner
this muskox in 1991. It scored 109-4/8.

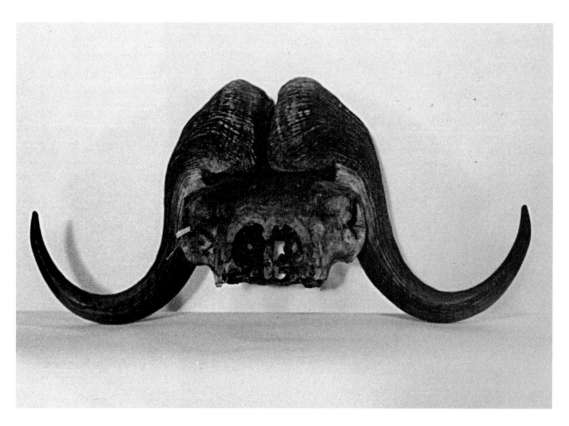

MUSKOX
SECOND AWARD
SCORE: 122-4/8

Locality: Rendezvous Lake, N.W.T.   Date: 1991
Hunter: William R. Powers

MUSKOX 122-4/8

William R. Powers

My hunt for trophy muskox began in 1990 at the Foundation for North American Wild Sheep Convention in Reno. I bought, at auction, a Rocky Mountain goat hunt with Collingwood Brothers, to be followed by a mountain caribou hunt with Jerry Geraci. Both hunts were in northern British Columbia. I took a nice goat, which measured almost 10 inches, and a mountain caribou that scored 387, Boone and Crockett.

My guide on the second hunt was a taxidermist from Missoula, Montana, by the name of Shawn Andres. During the hunt, he mentioned that eight muskox had come into his shop, seven of which made the records book, and all of the hunters were guided by Billy Jacobson, an Eskimo operating out of Tuktoyaktuk, Northwest Territories.

After some phone calls, the hunt was arranged with Billy for April 1991. My good friend Mark Adams, an electrical engineer from Bloomington, Indiana, booked to accompany me. Mark and I had been on many previous hunts together, and he was also anxious to take a trophy muskox.

Since we are both Hoosiers and basketball fans, we did not want to miss the NCAA tournament, so we arranged our trip to leave on Tuesday, April 12. That day, Indiana was warm and nice. We were soon winging our way north, toward much colder weather. We flew from Indianapolis to the Twin Cities and on to Edmonton, where we spent the night.

The next day, we flew north again, stopping in Norman Wells, where we got our first taste of snow — two to three feet and quite frigid conditions. We flew on and spent the night in Inuvick, Northwest Territories. We were surprised by how modern the town was, with a nice hotel and restaurants. It was the first time either of us had been in a community that lived on the permafrost. All the buildings were on pilings, and all of the city's facilities ran through above-ground conduits. At any rate, we spent the night there, got our licenses, permits and so forth, and left the following day by ski plane for Rendezvous Lake, about 180 miles to the northeast of Inuvick.

Billy and his delightful wife, Ilene, have a very well insulated mobile home at Rendezvous Lake, which serves as the base for Billy's caribou, muskox and arctic grizzly bear hunts. We had our own bedroom, Ilene is an excellent cook, and the conditions were incredibly comfortable for that hostile environment. Every day seemed to be sunny, with temperatures running between 16 and 18 degrees below zero in the daytime and dropping to 30 or more below at night.

We had seen muskox while flying in on the ski plane, and Billy, who had other hunters, had muskox located. He told us he knew where one bull was that would make the records book and if we were ready to go hunting, we should get changed and decide who would shoot first. So, with a flip of a coin—a lucky nickel, I might add—I won the toss.

We were soon in arctic coveralls and pac boots, traveling on the lakes and through the snowy scrub forest on snow machines. We had over-reacted to the thermometer and had so much clothing on that we could hardly walk.

We had probably traveled about 15 miles when we located the small valley that held the muskox. There were three bulls. We circled around as close as we could on the snow machines and made a short stalk with the spotting scope.

Billy picked the largest of the bulls, and at a distance of 200 yards, I squeezed the trigger on a .300 Winchester Magnum loaded with 180-grain slugs. The monster bull went down quickly; another shot was not necessary.

After taking several photos and a lot of hard work, the bull was completely skinned. We knew right away that I had quite a large bull, so I intended to have a full-body mount made. The pelt, horns and meat were put on a sled that we pulled behind a snow machine, and we returned to camp. There, Billy and Ilene measured and caped out the animal. According to the rough score in camp, the bull was 125 points, Boone and Crockett.

The next couple of days were spent looking for other bulls. Mark shot one that scored 111, also easily making the records book.

The rest of the time was spent with Billy, running his trap line. It was an incredible cultural experience to see both steel traps for martin and fisher and deadfall traps for arctic fox and wolverine. These traps, of course, have been in existence for centuries, but it was the first time I had ever seen the Native Americans use deadfalls and use them quite successfully. We also had a chance to see a lot of native wildlife, including ptarmigan, arctic fox and wolverine.

All in all, the hunt was a tremendous experience, not only for the hunt itself, but for the opportunities to see a community like Inuvick, meet Billy and Ilene, and be out on the arctic tundra. It is really a testimony to the human spirit that people live and enjoy their lives in such difficult surroundings. I will be hunting arctic grizzly with Billy in the spring of 1993.

Photograph courtesy of Tommy L. Ramsey

This muskox was taken at Cape Mohican, Alaska,
in 1990 by Tommy L. Ramsey. It scored 107-4/8.

Photograph courtesy of George P. Mann

This muskox was killed by George P. Mann at Bluenose Lake,
N.W.T., in 1990. It scores 105-4/8.

Photograph by Wm. H. Nesbitt

MUSKOX
THIRD AWARD
SCORE: 118-6/8

Locality: Bay Chimo, N.W.T.   Date: 1989
Hunter: Doyle V. Toliver

MUSKOX 118-6/8

Doyle V. Toliver

"I'm telling you, Doyle, this is the hunt of a lifetime." I kept repeating these words over and over as I drove to a construction site in Dallas, Texas, in the spring of 1989. I had just gotten off the phone with Jerome Knap of Canada North Outfitters out of Waterdown, Ontario. He told me he had two openings for an arctic bear, barren ground caribou and muskox hunt in the Northwest Territories, above the 69th parallel, that imaginary line separating the continent from the Arctic Circle.

What made this a "hunt of a lifetime" was the fact I would be in the second group of five hunters ever to hunt the area, other than the native Inuits. The first group of five hunters had done quite well, according to Jerome. By the end of the day, I made my mind up and committed myself to the hunt, which was scheduled for August of 1989. I also contacted a hunting friend in Dallas, and within two days, he also committed to the hunt.

When August finally rolled around, we flew from Dallas to Edmonton, on to Yellowknife and by prop jet to Cambridge Bay, Northwest Territories. Then we took an Otter with floats to the campsite on the Bathurst Inlet, south of Bay Chimo; this finalized the long trip to the beautiful area known as the Arctic Circle.

High winds and rain kept the five of us in our tents for two days. During that time, we got to know each other quite well. The other hunters were John Searles from Flint, Michigan; Chris Gutscher from Flushing, Michigan; Earnest Roberge from Waterboro, Maine; and Jim Hale from Dallas, Texas. The hunt manager was Tudor Howard-Davies, a delightful hunting guide from South Africa, who entertained us with his hunting stories about the Dark Continent. It was Tudor's first hunt in Canada.

On the morning of the third day, the storm broke and we left camp with our guides, going in different directions in search of the three species we were there to hunt. My guide, Phillip Kadlum, and I left by boat to hunt on the Banks Peninsula in Bathurst Inlet, near the James River and approximately 125 miles north of the Arctic Circle.

The three trophies I was hunting were the barren ground arctic grizzly (*Ursus arctos*), barren ground caribou (*Rangifer tarandus graenlandicus*), and Muskox (*Ovibos moschatus*).

The grizzly of the arctic is a smaller version of the grizzly found in the interior of Canada and Alaska and is small compared to the coastal browns found in Alaska and Siberia. What it loses in bulk, it more than makes up in sheer beauty. A kaleidoscope of colors make this bear the most beautiful, and possibly the most difficult to hunt, because of its ability to blend into the tundra.

The Canadian barren ground caribou number approximately 1,000,000 and are divided into five herds throughout Canada and the Northwest Territories. I was hunting the Bathurst barren ground caribou herd, which numbers well over 150,000 animals.

These animals, members of the deer family with massive antlers, may weigh 250 to 300 pounds and are the mainstay of the Inuits' diet. Each person in Bay Chimo may eat five caribou per year and may supplement his diet with muskox and arctic char. The caribou are very important to these people.

Now we come to the muskox, "the bearded one," as the Inuits call this, the strangest looking animal one would ever want to see. This animal, weighing as much as 1,000 pounds, is very difficult to hunt during the summer months. Unlike the bear, which covers a vast area in search of food on a daily basis, and the caribou, which is in perpetual motion due to its migratory habits, the muskox does not migrate, has an available source of food in nearly any direction, and therefore moves very little on a day-to-day basis. In an area of 250,000 square miles, a great deal of luck is needed to find one of these gregarious animals, particularly since the benefits of snow machines are lacking during the summer months; the hunter must walk to search for these animals.

The muskox (or tundra buffalo as they are often called) shares a sad history with the American bison. They were hunted to near extinction during the early 1900s, and in 1917, they were accorded full protection by the governments of Greenland and Canada. The Boone and Crockett Club records book still contains turn-of-the-century muskox entries, but there is a break of nearly 50 years with virtually no entries.

Greenland and Canada have rebuilt their herds and they are believed to number in excess of 50,000. This long-protected, horned animal from the Bovidae family is now available to a few lucky hunters. I was one of the few, and luck was to play a large part in my taking this most unusual animal.

Of the three, the animal I wanted the most was the arctic bear, for I had taken a barren ground caribou on the Alaskan Peninsula in 1985. I also had the good fortune to take a muskox on Ellesmere Island, while hunting polar bear in 1986. However, fate was to play a big part on this trip, for the muskox was to be the highlight of the hunt.

When the weather broke, Phillip and I headed for the James River, an area that is known for its large concentration of bears. The James River was approximately eighty miles from our base camp, so we used the boat and outboard motor. We were at the mouth of the James in approximately six hours, made camp and prepared to hunt the following day.

The next morning, upon entering the mouth of the James, we had not progressed more than a mile when a large bear got up from the alder bushes and took off running over the tundra as only a grizzly bear can. We immediately went ashore in hot pursuit of the bear.

While moving through the tundra, running and walking, I lost my Nikon waterproof camera. Since no tracks are left in the tundra, searching for the camera was useless. Someday, 100 years from now, someone may find that camera with the exposed film still intact due to its waterproof construction.

Two miles inland we gave up on ever seeing the bear again. After a warm meal and some hot tea, Phillip and I had a camp meeting and decided that life was not too bad after all. We decided to stay with the bear hunting and forget caribou and muskox altogether. So, the next morning we headed back to the James River for bears and a short walk into the tundra, along the route where I lost my camera.

Climbing the highest hill available, we had a lunch of freeze-dried food and wonderful Inuit tea and began glassing our surroundings in earnest. About 1:30, Phillip said, "I got your bear."

I turned and watched as he looked through the Leupold 30x spotting scope at the animal in the distance. He said, "I'm quite sure it's a bear, and he is about five to six miles up the shoreline. It appears he is moving this way."

I asked to take a look, and sure enough, I could see a dark speck moving very slowly down the shoreline. "Let's go," Phillip said, as he started for the boat, approximately a mile away.

When we were in the boat and headed up the, inlet Phillip said, "Let's stop at camp and get some fresh water." I agreed, being thirsty from the run to the boat. Our camp was on the way to the last known position of the bear, or at least what we thought was a bear.

When we went into camp to get water, Tudor, our hunt manager, asked if he could go with us and neither Phillip nor I had any objection. It was a good thing he did, for as we were running at high speed toward the bear's last known position, he tapped Phillip on the shoulder and pointed toward land. Phillip shut the engine down to determine what Tudor had seen on the shoreline, approximately a mile away. When the boat finally settled down, we were able to get our binoculars on the animal. Phillip said it was a muskox and must be the object we saw earlier and assumed was a bear. It had taken us a good hour or more to reach that point, and in the interim the muskox had moved about two miles down the beach.

It was decision-making time. What to do? Phillip said to me, "Do you want him or do you want to continue hunting bear?" He explained it would probably take a day to cape him and bone out the meat. I had a decision to make, since I had already taken a muskox on a prior trip and could not afford to lose any more time if I wanted a good bear.

While I was mulling it over, Phillip said he was probably a good bull that had been kicked out of the herd by a younger muskox. This suggested he is probably very old and very big. That one statement is the reason I am writing this story. I probably would have let the muskox go and forfeited my chance at having a trophy animal in the Boone and Crockett records book if my guide Phillip Kadlum had not used those words, "He is probably very old and very big."

The decision was made. We were at least going ashore to look him over, but that was not as easy as it sounds. We were approximately a mile from shore and completely exposed to the muskox. After a hasty discussion, we agreed to turn around, go back toward our camp for a mile, and then go ashore, set up, and let the muskox come to us. The time was 3:30 to 4:00 p.m.

When we got closer to shore, we saw a small freshwater creek coming into the shoreline, and it looked large enough to hide our boat. In the meantime, the muskox was about a mile up the coast, making his way slowly toward us. We settled in below a small mound of tundra for the chance to get a look at what we hoped was a very old and very big muskox.

The good news was we were well-hidden. The bad news was we were lying in an area that was very wet. When we lay down, we did not realize we were going to be in that area for a long time. Some 30 minutes after we set up, the muskox moved to within 500 to 600 yards of us and settled in, grazing and resting for the next five hours.

We were committed. We could not move without being seen, so we were three wet puppies when, at around 9:00 p.m., he began to move down the shoreline toward us.

When the bull came within 300 yards, Phillip whispered to me, "He is a monster." Those were the last words anyone spoke.

He was on the move and would walk right over the top of us if we let him. I had made up my mind to take him, and it was just a matter of when, for on he came.

Phillip was lying to my left, just inches from my left shoulder, and I could tell he was very nervous, for the muskox was about 50 yards away and coming. I could not find a shot. He was coming with his head down, completely covering his chest area, and his legs were so short that there was nothing to shoot at except the boss of his horns. My .340 Weatherby Magnum was resting on my backpack, and my eye was glued to the scope. The safety was off and my finger was on the trigger, but I could not shoot.

I began thinking of alternatives to the problem. I decided that, if he had not afforded me a shot by the time he came within 25 yards, I would yell and hope he would react by turning or raising his head.

At 25 yards, the 1,000 pound muskox looked like a train engine, one that would run right over the top of anyone in its way. I knew Phillip was silently willing me to shoot, and Tudor was probably thinking how he could be in a warm tent, drinking hot tea, instead of in danger of being trampled by an enraged, half-ton muskox.

These thoughts were going through my mind when the muskox turned his head. He looked out to sea, and I took him with one 250-grain Nosler in the chest.

The next thing Phillip said stopped all of the cold and discomforts. "He's the biggest muskox I've ever seen."

Phillip was right. It was a very big muskox, indeed. The next day was devoted to caring for this massive, beautiful animal that I shall remember all my life.

After the muskox was boned and the cape secure, we had three days left to hunt. Lucky hunter that I am, I harvested a bear and a respectable caribou during the remaining time.

When the five of us met at Umingmaktok, the Inuit name for Bay Chimo, which in their language means "place of the muskox," we knew we had been part of something special. We thought the bull would make the Boone and Crockett records book. No one knew just how big he was until later, when he was measured by Dr. Phil Wright of Missoula, Montana, who scored him at 117-6/8.

On the long flight home, I kept reflecting on the beauty of the country, the soft, unassuming demeanor of its people, and especially Phillip Kadlum, who is probably the best hunting guide I have had the opportunity to meet. And yes, it was the hunt of a lifetime, up until now.

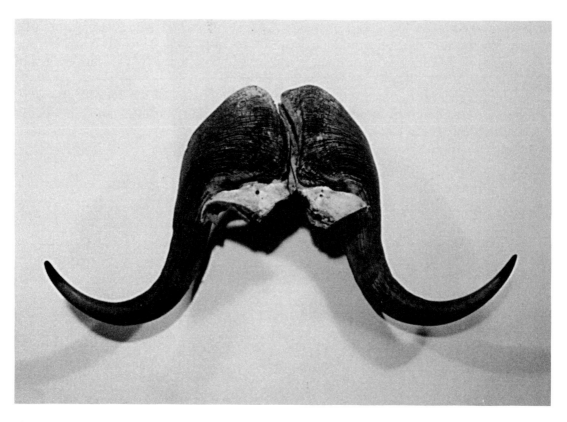

MUSKOX
FOURTH AWARD
SCORE: 118-4/8

Locality: Perry Island, N.W.T.   Date: 1990
Hunter: Lawrence T. Epping

MUSKOX 118-4/8

Lawrence T. Epping

Day 1 (Sunday, April 1)

I took a flight from Portland to Spokane, then to Calgary and on to Edmonton, where I stayed overnight.

Day 2 (Monday, April 2)

I flew to Yellowknife, Northwest Territories. Bill Taite, a partner in Canada North Outfitters, met me in Yellowknife, and I also met some of the other hunters who would be in the same camp. One, named Sonny, was from Thailand. We flew to Cambridge Bay, which is on Victoria Island in the Arctic Ocean, north of the N.W.T. mainland.

There, we were met by Bob, who, after we got licenses, lined us up with a flight on the Twin Otter to Perry Island, about 140 miles southeast of Cambridge Bay.

We arrived at Perry Island only to find the ice and drifted snow was too rough at the camp to land. We flew around for 15 minutes and found a lake about 5 miles from their camp. We landed there and the Inuits came out on their snow machines and sleds to pick us up. We got settled in our plywood cabin, where we had an oil heater and a Coleman lantern. There would be no roughing-it in an arctic tent on this trip.

Day 3 (Tuesday, April 3)

After a hot breakfast, my Eskimo friend George and his partner, Peter, Sonny and I took off on two snow machines, each with a sled. We were hunting in an area that is over 100 miles from the nearest human being. The terrain in the arctic is not mountainous, but rolling hills and ridges with drainages sloping to the north, into the Arctic Ocean. Because of the possibility of trouble, the hunts are most always conducted with two snow machines and two Eskimos for each hunt. George said the temperature was more than 30 degrees below zero Fahrenheit, so we were accordingly dressed in down clothing. Even then the cold gets to your nose, hands and feet.

We spent the entire day glassing and looking for muskox. Sonny and I needed to alternate on our choice to shoot. We glassed and passed-up about five groups of muskox during the day. We hunted about 20 miles south of our camp. It was a pleasure to get back to a semi-heated shack, warm up and dry out. It was quite a contrast to some arctic hunts during which I have stayed in a tent.

Day 4 (Wednesday, April 4)

The day was a duplicate of the one before until we spotted a herd of bulls, one of which was a pretty fair 115-point Boone and Crockett muskox. George said it was the same herd that we passed on the preceding day. As we watched the herd, the biggest bull split off and went up a ridge. Sonny and his guide, Peter, trailed the bull and were able to close to within 250 yards for the kill.

After dressing out the muskox, we hunted the rest of the day in the area, about 20 miles from camp. We saw and scoped three other herds, but the bull I wanted was not there.

While George and I were on a lookout point, three very curious arctic hares came to within 10 feet of us. After satisfying their curiosity, they finally hopped away. George said that in all his years in the arctic, he had never seem them do this before and it was "a good hunting omen."

Day 5 (Thursday, April 5)

A gale-force arctic storm started in the night and continued for 24 hours. We stayed in camp all day, watching the storm through the windows. We computed wind chill factor to be 70 degrees below zero Fahrenheit. Conditions approached a complete whiteout.

Day 6 (Friday, April 6)

The wind was still blowing, but with less force, so we headed out to hunt. About 14 miles from camp, the wind picked up and the visibility dropped to approximately 100 yards. About 1:00 p.m., we went back to camp to regroup and wait for better weather. Time was running short. The forecast on the our battery powered radio was for more of the same weather.

Day 7 (Saturday, April 7)

The arctic wind blew all night long. We were going into the third day of the storm. Visibility was just about a whiteout. The dim outline of our cook shack was seen through the blowing snow at 20 yards. We were told that a few weeks earlier, it stormed for 11 days running. We were 140 miles from Cambridge Bay, and no planes could fly until the weather cleared. And no hunting for the big bull muskox. I put my "mind over matter" into effect to hibernate or "hole up" like the other animals do. Some of the hunters are starting to get cabin fever. I will not let it affect me.

Day 8 (Sunday, April 8)

We were up at daylight, 4:00 a.m. George and I went alone for our last try. A 15-knot wind was blowing. It was time to get the job done, since the Twin Otter was scheduled to come in that afternoon and take us back to Cambridge Bay. George and I were all alone, with no back up snowmobile, but we had the life saver of the arctic, a two-way radio.

We were heading for an area George called "muskox ridge," which was east of Perry Island at a somewhat higher elevation. In the previous two years, three trophy muskox had been taken from that area. It was 25 to 30 miles from camp. I had learned to ride the sled by relaxing, but even so the whole sled was sometimes air borne and hit bottom with jarring force. As the wind drifted the snow, it formed and small, parallel snow ridges like waves on the ocean. The wind was picking up again, so drifting, blowing snow was reducing the visibility to about one mile.

We stopped at a high point and crawled to the top for a look. George saw something he thought were black rocks. He pinpointed the formation and continued looking elsewhere. When he looked back later, one rock in the formation was not in the same location, so we knew we had located some muskox. They were about two miles away. We took off on foot to pull our sneak on them.

We crawled out on a knoll about 250 yards from them. George and I set up the spotting scope that I gave him on our last hunt together. There were two good bulls in the herd of four, and one was considerably larger than the others. We estimated him to be 117 points, Boone and Crockett. I was originally planning on a bull scoring over 120 points, which would have put him in the top ten of Boone and Crockett and might have been a world's record muzzleloaders, but time was short. The wind was blowing 30 knots, and the wind chill factor was more 60 degrees below zero.

Because of the wind drift of the muzzleloader bullet, I told George we needed to be as close to downwind as possible. We got downwind and started our sneak, hoping to get within 100 yards. We slowly walked, hunched over and single file to resemble wolves. When they stopped feeding, we halted, and when they started feeding again, we moved forward. At 150 yards, we got down and crawled on hands and knees. At 115 yards, they were getting nervous, so I decided to go for the big one. At that moment, an arctic hare ran to our left, from under the feet of the big bull. I knew that I had found my trophy.

With the wind and snow and all of my arctic clothing, including the face mask, it was difficult to get a decent sight picture on the bull. I needed to stand up and shoot off hand. He was facing me, so I aimed for his brisket and fired. I heard the bullet hit and the herd took off, running.

They went behind the next ridge, so we sneaked up behind it. I got another shot, at 120 yards in the cross wind, but missed. I used the backup muzzleloader, which was difficult in the wind. When I had reloaded, we made the final stalk and gave him the finishing shot.

We walked up to him, a huge-bodied bull muskox, which made his horns larger than we had estimated. We hurriedly skinned and quartered him, and away to camp we went, hoping to catch the plane.

We measured the bull back at camp, and with deductions, he scored 121-1/8. The weather cleared up some toward evening, and the wind slackened. The Twin Otter came in and transported us back to Cambridge Bay. So ended a very successful hunt, which allowed me to accomplish my goal of a green-scored muskox of 120 or more.

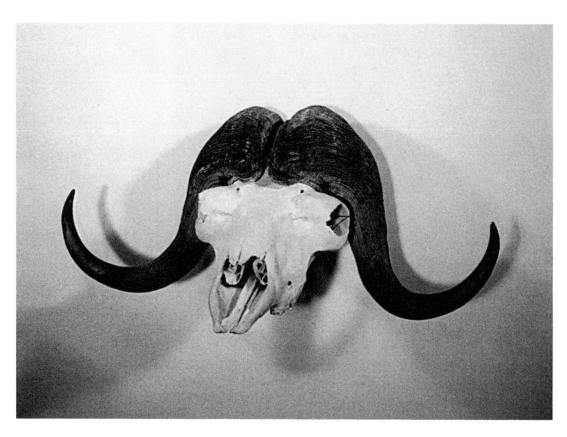

Photograph by Wm. H. Nesbitt

MUSKOX
FIFTH AWARD
SCORE: 117

Locality: Perry Island, N.W.T.   Date: 1989
Hunter: Robert D. Jones

MUSKOX 117

Robert D. Jones

Late March of 1989 found me and some of my hunting partners camped at the old Hudson's Bay Post of Perry Island, Northwest Territories. We had come to the high arctic on a spring muskox hunt. Several of us had been there the year before, and that experience and the country had called us back. I had taken the Boone and Crockett Number 2 muskox on that trip, and that bull later received the Second Award at the Club's 20th Big Game Awards in Albuquerque, N.M.

George Angiahitok, my guide, and I set out to find an old bull that would score in the 120 point range. We knew a bull of that size would require a lot of luck, and we might not see anything in that class. We spent our first two days on the upper Perry River and saw few muskox and few tracks. The evening of the second day, we studied our topo maps and decided to spend the third day of the hunt along the arctic coast.

Sometimes, if undisturbed, the muskox herds will gather along the sandy dunes to feed on grass that is blown free of snow. George got our snowmobile running in the minus 32-degree temperature of the morning. The days were bright and sunny, and temperatures were getting up to minus 10 degrees, with little wind.

Late in the afternoon of that third day George came across the tracks of five muskox traveling north across the base of Whitebear Point, a small peninsula jutting out into the frozen Arctic Ocean. We traveled west across the peninsula, and the tracks never came back south, so we climbed to the top of a small hill to glass.

We spotted the muskox feeding in some dunes about a mile from our vantage point. George got his spotting scope set up and we glassed what looked to be a very good bull with two smaller bulls and two cows. A slight breeze was blowing our way, so we began a slow, easy stalk to determine if the bull was as good as we thought he could be.

George is an excellent judge of trophy muskox and he said he thought the bull would score in excess of 115 points. I asked if he thought we could find a better one. Then I said, "If anyone ever asks you to find him a bull that scores over 115, when one is standing 200 yards away, you want to smack him over the head with you spotting scope!" I used my backpack for a shooting rest and killed the bull with a 150-grain Nosler through the lungs from my .270.

The bull green-scored about 120 points, and scored 117 when officially measured for entry a year later.

MUSKOX
HONORABLE MENTION
SCORE: 113-4/8

Locality: Bathurst Inlet, N.W.T.   Date: 1988
Hunter: George R. Skaggs

MUSKOX 113-4/8

George R. Skaggs

Little did I know an 18-day adventure in Canada's Northwest Territories would turn out to be one of my best and most successful hunts.

It was the third week of August 1988. I was in Cambridge Bay, a small town situated on the south side of Victoria Island. There, I met the group I would be hunting with: Don Nicholson of Corsicana, Texas; Allen DeArmond of Baton Rouge, Louisiana; and, a hunt representative for Canada North Outfitting, Steve Cooke of Clinton, Ontario, who would do the cooking honors and oversee the hunt.

We purchased our hunting licenses and last-minute supplies. Then we boarded a single Otter, bound for the western shore of the Bathurst Inlet, 100 miles southwest of Cambridge Bay.

The spike camp was located on the shore of a small bay. We met our Inuit guides; Kegeona—Clarence was his Christian name—was to be my guide. Quarters were a bit spartan but comfortable, consisting of one tent for the hunters, one for the guides, and a well-stocked cook tent. Although my original quest was for muskox, the hunt turned into a mixed-bag affair. Besides muskox, I would be hunting Central Canada barren ground caribou, as well as barren ground grizzly.

I am sure glad I upgraded the hunt. With help from my guide, Clarence, and some luck from the hunting gods, I downed a beautiful blond grizzly the second day into the hunt.

The fourth day, Clarence and I hunted all day and into the late evening with light from the long arctic sun. While hiking back to the boat, a good caribou walked right in front of us. I immediately recognized the bull was a trophy. I chambered a round and fired. The big bull took one limp step and toppled.

Hunting fortune continued on the sixth day, when I filled my second caribou tag with a nice double-shovel bull. A few months later, the caribou was scored at 356-4/8, making it eligible for the all-time records book.

Having had success on caribou and grizzly, we decided to move camp to Chimo, the home village of our guides. There we hoped to find better muskox hunting. Don Nicholson had left for Chimo a few days prior to our departure.

Arriving in Chimo, we learned Don had killed a huge muskox. It was later scored at 125-2/8. At the 20th North American Big Game Awards, Don's muskox would

293

become a New World's Record. It was hard to believe the hunting bonanza we were enjoying.

My guide wanted to hunt muskox north of Chimo, but the seas were too rough for travel in our 18-foot boat. For the next two days, we hunted the Chimo Area with no luck.

At last the winds subsided enough to permit navigation. A small tent, a stove, food, and a radio were loaded in the boat, and we departed. We motored north, along the coast, for 50 miles, pulled into shore, and set up our spike camp. While Clarence was preparing dinner, I wandered down along the beach. It was exhilarating, looking out on the sea with the barren tundra at my back. It was a magnificent land. After dinner, I lay back in the comfort of my sleeping bag and drifted off to sleep, with the rhythm of the surf breaking against the shore in my ears.

We set out in the morning, traveling two miles inland and glassing along the way. "There big bull," said Clarence, pointing off into the distant tundra.

I quickly set up my spotting scope, aiming it in the direction my guide had pointed. The muskox had to be a good mile away. As we looked the animal over, I asked Clarence how large the horns were. He simply replied, "Good bull." At the time I didn't realize what an understatement that was.

We started our stalk, staying out of sight and periodically checking the bull's position. By the time we were within 300 yards of the animal, it had bedded down. We held our position and again judged the large bull's horns. The muskox occasionally raised its head to survey the surrounding tundra. Then, he would drop his huge head back down and rest.

I wanted to get closer, but there nothing to use for cover. I told Clarence to stay behind, while I attempted the final stalk. With no cover, I had to crawl when the bull's head was down. When he raised his head, I stayed still. The plan put me within 100 yards of the bull.

With a good rest, I aimed for the left shoulder. The next time he raised his head, I fired. The 250-grain Nosler found its mark. The muskox managed to stand up, turning broadside. I chambered another round and fired again, this time striking the bull in the right shoulder. The big bull staggered several feet and fell.

My guide walked up, congratulating me. When we approached the animal, Clarence reached over and took hold of a horn. To our amazement, the bull we thought dead suddenly came alive. We both retreated several steps rather quickly. I raised the .338, worked the bolt, and fired the finishing shot.

We took the usual trophy pictures and started caping the animal. If you ever have the opportunity to cape a muskox, you will find it is a tougher task than caping usually is. It was cold and the arctic winds were blowing hard, making the chore even harder. We managed to get the job done and pack the animal back to camp by evening.

With the muskox caped and the winds calmed, Clarence suggested we break camp and head for Chimo. The going was good for 20 miles or so. Then, as the small craft motored out of a channel, we encountered six foot swells. The winds had again picked up. It was too much for the small boat, and we had to head for the safety of shore.

Out came all the gear we had earlier loaded. Setting the tent up in the high winds was no easy task. With everything secured, we settled in to wait out the storm. A day and a half had passed before the winds finally died down enough to allow travel. We quickly packed the boat and made a run for Chimo.

The seas were just starting to pick up again as we arrived in Chimo. Don and his guide were still spiked out, hunting caribou. Later, I learned he had filled his tags, but he and his guide were also sitting out the weather. Al and his guide were still out too, hunting muskox. They all returned within a few days, Don with two fine caribou and Al with his muskox.

The next few days were spent working on capes and drying meat. We also spent time with the Inuit of the small village. It was an experience to observe their customs and everyday lifestyle.

As I stated in the beginning of this story, this was one of the best and most successful hunts I have had. Three hunters took three grizzly, three muskox, and six caribou. I met, shared camp and made friends with some fine people. After having my trophies scored, I had a caribou that would make the all-time records book and a muskox that has a chance of placing in the top ten of the all-time records book, What a hunt!

MUSKOX
CERTIFICATE OF MERIT
SCORE: 119-4/8

Locality: McNaughton River, N.W.T.   Date: Picked Up, 1991
Owner: Robert D. Jones

MUSKOX 119-4/8

Robert D. Jones

I had hunted for trophy muskox in the high Canadian Arctic in 1988 and 1989. These were very high-class experiences for me, and I had been fortunate enough to take outstanding trophies on both the Perry and Ellice Rivers on these trips.

The bull of 1988, taken on the Ellice River, had placed second at the 20th Big Game Awards in Albuquerque, with 124-6/8 points, and the bull of 1989, from the Perry River (Whitebear Point), was officially scored at 117 points.

In 1991, a new area east of the Perry and Ellice Rivers was being opened to sport hunters, and I very much wanted to be part of it. This new area was thought to be habitat for muskox of the Perry/Ellice gene pool, which are the largest in North America.

The sport hunting area was established along the McNaughton River, a rugged 140 miles snowmobile and komatik ride each way from the access point of Goa Haven, Northwest Territory.

Lack of proper equipment from our outfitter and guides, who were not well versed in sport hunting, contributed to a situation where hunting opportunities were very limited. Fourteen days in the area resulted in about two days of actual hunting, and no trophy muskox were seen.

During the hunt, my guide and I came across two natives who were camped on the upper McNaughton River on a meat hunt for muskox. They had taken four bulls, and one of them was a dandy. I was taking photographs of these animals when the younger native told me of a large skull he had seen on a ridge above the river, about five miles from that point. I talked him into taking our snowmobiles to the area, and he showed me the skull of a tremendous bull that had died several years earlier on that ridge, about one mile west of the McNaughton River.

I brought the skull out, and it officially scored 119- 4/8 Boone and Crockett points.

BIGHORN SHEEP
FIRST AWARD
SCORE: 200-7/8
Locality: Deer Lodge Co., Mont.   Date: 1990
Hunter: Lester A. Kish

BIGHORN SHEEP 200-7/8

Lester A. Kish

To say that hunting is a sport of luck is an understatement. In 1990, I had the good fortune to draw a bighorn sheep permit in Montana's Unit 213, near Anaconda. With odds exceeding 100 to 1, just drawing the permit was an incredible stroke of luck.

Unit 213 has a transplanted herd that originated from sheep trapped in Montana's Sun River area. In a little over 20 years, the herd had become a producer of super rams, with the herd consisting of over 400 sheep.

Then, late in the summer of 1991, the population crashed due to an epidemic of *Pasteurella pneumonia*. Writer Duncan Gilchrist and I visited the area in February 1992. Range that supported upward of 150 rams during the winter of 1991 contained only 22 sheep. While later counts were a little more encouraging, the total herd had been reduced to about 30percent of pre-*Pasteurella* levels. In addition, the majority of the big rams perished during the epidemic.

I would not be able to write this story if my permit were for 1991 since most of the big rams had died prior to the hunting season. What a difference a year makes.

During August and September of 1990, I made several scouting trips to the area. Sheep were plentiful, and I was able to find the favored haunts of the rams. One day, more than six hours were spent watching a group of 14 rams. Two of the rams were huge. One sported a massive, deeply dropping, heavily broomed set of horns. The other ram was even more incredible. He had it all. Built like those of an argali, the horns were long, massive, relatively unbroomed, and flared. I would later learn that this ram had been observed, photographed, and even videotaped by Duncan Gilchrist and others during previous winters. The ram had aptly been nicknamed Flare. The shadows lengthened and darkness fell as I walked off the mountain. Sheep season was still three sleepless weeks away.

September 15, 1990, finally arrived and with it the opening of the Montana sheep season. Ironically, I had scheduled my vacation for this date. Imagine, nine whole days to hunt ram.

The weather was superb, though actually too warm during the first days of the season. My hunting partner, Jo, accompanied me the first two days. We saw lots of country and quite a few sheep, but nothing exceptional, so the hunt continued. I was glad that Jo had the opportunity to share the thrill of glassing for rams in the high country. Few people have been so fortunate.

From the third day on, I would be hunting alone; Jo had to be back to work. Early that third morning, I climbed out of Lost Creek Canyon. From my vantage point, I could see an expanse of rock and timber. Occasionally a ram or two would appear briefly in an opening and then disappear. Some rams were respectable yet not tempting enough to make me want to end the hunt of a lifetime. Vivid memories of those giant rams seen during preseason scouting kept me from getting too excited about taking an average ram.

That afternoon, I hiked out and moved camp to another area. I would concentrate on the area where I had earlier seen Flare. With camp moved, I did some hiking and scouting. Around dusk, several rams were spotted, miles away. While I could not be sure, I had a feeling that they might be the same bunch that I had watched for six hours during the preseason. Would the big rams still be with them?

For some reason, I did not get any sleep that night. I almost wore out the switch on my flashlight by checking the time every few minutes. At 4:00 a.m., I couldn't stand the waiting so I got up and made some coffee.

Soon after, flashlight in hand, I was hiking up the ridge toward the rams, hoping they were still bedded. I knew my intended approach well. I had worked and reworked the stalk during the sleepless night. The rams were approachable, provided that they stayed put.

What were the odds that this was the same bunch of rams that I had glassed for hours during the preseason? Better yet, what were the odds that the old argali named Flare would be with them? It just had to the same bunch. I knew it was the day for a big ram.

The sky brightened. Soon, the first rays of morning sunshine would illuminate the neighboring peaks of the Pintlars. Spectacular scenery is usually available on demand when sheep hunting, and the Pintlars obliged each time I looked over my shoulder.

Only the sheep hunter knows the inexorable lure of hunting the high country. While I had spent years stalking the Rockies for other mountain game, those experiences paled in comparison to this hunt. The sheep hunting mystique was real; Jack O'Connor was right. Once you contract sheep fever, you are a goner.

At first light, I reached a vantage point overlooking the head of the drainage. Out came the spotting scope. Were the rams still there? You bet! There were twelve rams in all, with the big argali lying in the center. It was a most incredible sight.

I packed away the scope. It was crunch time. The rams were a little over a half-mile above me. I backed out of sight, threw the old legs into gear, and headed up the mountain.

I soon reached the lodgepole timber. Continuing on, I made sure that I was well above the rams. Then I cut across the slope in their direction.

Eventually, I reached the drainage head. Grass appeared through the timber but I saw no rams. Like a snake in the grass, I bellied down the slope. A single horn appeared. More slithering, and more horns popped into view.

They were only 70 yards away. From a prone position, I could not see the rams. The grass was too tall. Up on my knees, I could only see heads and necks — not enough for a shot.

The biggest sheep on the mountain was right in front of me, and I could not do anything. Man, was I nervous. I waited an honest 20 minutes as rams started getting up to feed. Finally, the big one got up. Caught in the open, I had to shoot offhand. Deer and elk running through the timber seem to be easy targets to me, but a huge ram, standing in the open, was almost impossible.

Every ram but Flare was staring at me. I shot, missed, and all hell broke loose. The stampede was on. Just as he was about to disappear into a gully, I broke his back. I could hear rocks rolling. Then the ram appeared down below, and he was trying to get up. I put two more shots into the rolling ram. All was quiet.

When I reached the ram, I was shocked. He was the most incredible animal I had ever seen. Unfortunately, I did not take much time admiring him. It was only 7:45 a.m. but the sun was already starting to feel hot. Hastily, I took some pictures and set about the caping and boning chores.

The next twelve hours were pure hell. It was hot and dry. I ran out of water. I wanted to get the meat and cape off the mountain in a hurry. By maintaining a relentless pace and leapfrogging loads of meat and the head for short distances, I got closer to the car with each load. That way, I did not have to hike all the way back to the kill site once any one load was all the way out.

I got back to camp with the last load just as it was getting dark. Rather than spend the night, I packed up my gear and drove home.

When I pulled in late that night, Jo was up in a flash. The smile on my face said it all. Yes, I got one, a pretty good one.

"You look worse than the sheep," Jo said. "You certainly smell worse."

I was all scratched up and had a chunk of hide rubbed off my back from the friction of the packframe. In addition, I had lost 10 pounds in four days of hunting.

Next morning, I went down to fish and game headquarters to get the horns plugged. Fred King, a scorer for Boone and Crockett, was in the lobby. When I walked in, he asked how the sheep hunting was going. "Come out to the car and take a look," I said. The reaction when I opened the tailgate was, "Oh my God!" We carried the head into the lab. Soon, people were popping out of the woodwork to admire the sheep. "Is he a big one?" someone asked. "Yes, he certainly is. Maybe a new record!"

He was plugged as 80 MT 361. When the tape hit the left horn, it stretched to 20 inches, 30 inches, and then 40 inches, with more to go. The tape finally stopped at 49-2/8 inches. Even the short horn measured 45-5/8 inches. Geez, what a sheep!

Sixty days later, he scored 200-7/8, thus making him the new state record for Montana, the land of the giant rams.

Friend and taxidermist Dale Manning from Missoula, Montana, did a superb job on the shoulder mount. Now, when I look at old Flare (or Oscar, as I prefer to call him), I relive the excitement and rigors of the hunt. I also dream of the day when I again can pursue great rams in the high country.

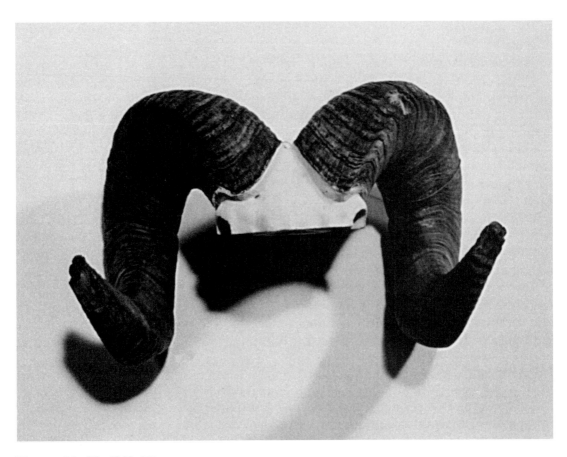

BIGHORN SHEEP
SECOND AWARD
SCORE: 197-5/8

Locality: Deer Lodge Co., Mont.   Date: 1987
Hunter: Arthur R. Dubs

BIGHORN SHEEP 197-5/8

Arthur R. Dubs

During a previous hunt in Montana in 1986, I had set a goal for myself: a 200 point Boone and Crockett ram. I passed up several rams which I knew would score in the 190s, but I was not sure any of them would exceed 200 points. I hunted very intensively over a period of five weeks, from Anaconda, Rock Creek and Petty Creek to the high Cabinet Mountains, 250 miles to the north.

On one occasion in the Anaconda area, I stalked to within 200 yards of three large rams. One of the rams in particular was very massive and heavily broomed. I knew he would come close to fulfilling my goal, but I was not certain. After watching and debating on whether or not to shoot for more than a half-hour, I watched as the rams finally walked up and over a high ridge, leaving the country. My time was running out and four days later, just prior to the closing of the season, I settled for a lesser ram.

The first of the 1987 season found me back in the Anaconda area, where I had last seen the big ram. I knew that if he made it through the winter, he would be worth looking at again.

On the fourth day, at sunrise, I was glassing a far basin, below timberline, from a high rimrock. I picked up a band of seven rams on the far side, weaving their way through the stunted firs. They appeared to have been spooked. I could see that the ram leading the pack carried an extremely massive set of horns. Upon closer observation through my spotting scope, I was surprised to see that it was the same heavily broomed ram I had passed up the year before.

Watching them, I took a few quick pictures with a long telephoto lens as the group continued through the basin. The big ram would stop occasionally and then cautiously move on.

After making a half-mile circle around the basin, the big ram stopped, but he seemed uneasy. A few minutes passed, and a couple of his smaller companions lay down. I was wishing the big one would do the same, but he took a few steps and disappeared into the scrub pines at timberline.

Checking the wind, I avoided all possibility of the sheep seeing me by making my way down from the rim through a crevice in the rocks. Reaching the edge of the timberline, I had more cover. The wind was in my favor, so I carefully moved through the pines, stopping often to glass through the thick foliage in search of the big ram. I knew he would not have gone far with the other rams close by, but I could not locate him.

I kept easing along very slowly, glassing every inch of the terrain, and I finally picked up movement. I could see the ram's head and one horn under a bush, not more than 100 yards away.

I immediately set up my spotting scope. Unfortunately, I could only see the ram's right horn, which was broomed off quite heavily. I estimated the horn to be 42 inches in length, with a 16-inch base. I knew he was extraordinary, but I wanted to be sure he would satisfy my goal of 200 points. As close as I was to the ram, and despite my fear of the ram and his companions getting my scent or seeing me, I made myself comfortable. I took more telephoto pictures and decided to wait him out. I wanted a good look at his left horn before making a decision to shoot. I knew he would be moving sooner or later, either to change positions or to feed.

At 2:00 p.m., seven hours from the time I first spotted him, the big ram finally stood up, took a few steps as he nibbled on tufts of green grass, turned and walked straight away. He was going uphill, toward heavier cover. I then got a glimpse of his left horn, which appeared to be as long as his right side. The other rams were all on their feet as well, watching their commander. If I wanted him, I had to shoot quickly, but I was not sure. Could I find a larger one?

I chambered a 180-grain softpoint in my .300 Weatherby Magnum and placed the crosshairs just over the ram's tail bone. As he took his last step into a thicket of scrub pine, I squeezed the trigger. The ram's legs buckled and down he went, sliding a few feet back down the slope. He regained his feet, I fired again, and he was down for good.

While waiting for the Boone and Crockett Club's 21st Big Game Awards in Milwaukee, Wisconsin, June 13, 1992, I was informed that a panel of judges had confirmed the ram's final score to be 197-5/8. The left horn measured 42-4/8 inches, and the right was 41-1/8 inches. The average circumference of the bases was 16 inches, and the circumference of the third quarters averaged slightly more than 11 inches.

He did not break the 200 point mark, but he was truly a great ram. He matches beautifully with the largest slam that I have taken of North American wild sheep.

Photograph courtesy of Carol K. Chudy

Carol K. Chudy killed this bighorn sheep, 186-6/8, in
Granite County, Montana, in 1991.

Photograph courtesy of Alan E. Schroeder

This bighorn sheep was killed at Cougar Mt., Alta. by
Alan E. Schroeder in 1989. It scored 186-1/8.

Photograph by Wm. H. Nesbitt

BIGHORN SHEEP
THIRD AWARD
SCORE: 197-1/8
Locality: Granite Co., Mont.   Date: 1990
Hunter: Lee Hart

BIGHORN SHEEP 197-1/8

Lee Hart

As a boy growing up on my father's Montana ranch, I watched with awe the bighorn rams that wintered along the Gallatin River. I remember picking up the horns and skulls of the unfortunate ones that did not survive the particularly harsh winters. The weight and mass of the horns those mountain kings grew always amazed me.

One unusually chilly fall, I was helping neighbors gather cattle from the foothills north of the Spanish Peaks when, out of nowhere, a lone bighorn ram took up residence with the cattle. For two long days, the ram created mass confusion in the sorting pastures, running from one group of cows to the next, a castaway desperately seeking acceptance. One of the cowboys remarked, "That's the price you pay for eating wild onions; nobody wants anything to do with you."

At supper that evening, one of the owners decided that if the "nuisance" was still there in the morning, he would see if bighorn sheep were really as good to eat as people said. He didn't think the old boy would survive the winter anyway. The theory around the table was that he was an old ram, defeated by his comrades. A slight limp from a shoulder injury supported the theory.

Frost was still on the ground the next morning when I arrived to find the ram already field dressed. Even with the tips broken off ("broomed," I later learned), the horns extended several inches beyond the bridge of his nose. A ranch hand placed a lariat loop around the base of the horns and Old Nip, a big gelding, headed for the ranch buildings, dragging the ram over the frozen ground. Whichever horn happened to be on the bottom gouged into the earth, occasionally splintering the horn.

Nearly 25 years later, I discovered the skull of that ram hanging in the hayloft of a barn on the same ranch. From my boyhood memory, I estimated seven or eight inches had been broken from each side. Still, the horns measured 16-5/8 inches and 16-6/8 inches around the bases. Leaving the horns of the great mountain king to collect dust in a hayloft struck me as a shameful waste. How could anyone carelessly break his horns? If only there had been some way of preserving this fallen monarch. It was then I made a vow to myself that if ever I had the fortune to harvest a similar ram, he would be given proper respect. Appropriately mounted, he would be hung high on a wall overlooking everything, just like that rocky outcropping on the mountain where he stood so many times overlooking the vast valley below. He would forever be a mountain king that many people could see and enjoy, rather than that small handful who had been lucky enough to see him in the wild.

During the intervening years, I contracted "sheep fever." Like any hunter, I dreamed of taking the big one and yet that did not seem to be a high priority. More important was the challenge of studying them, learning their habits, where and when they feed, and where they go when disturbed. I spent endless hours looking through a spotting scope, learning to distinguish a good ram from a mediocre one, a 180 ram from a 175.

In 1969, I acquired my outfitter's license and started guiding others in their quests for bighorn sheep. I've learned to respect every ram on the mountain; whether big or little, each ram is a trophy. I had been involved in the taking of numerous rams, as well as the completion of several Grand Slams, but it was always the other guy who got to shoot. Always a bridesmaid and never a bride, always a guide and never a hunter.

For several years I had applied in my home state for a sheep permit of my own. I personally knew of some great rams that existed in a couple of areas; all I had to do was live long enough to draw the permit.

It was early August. I had just turned 50 and was suffering from "over-the-hill syndrome." I was sorting the day's mail (bills vs. Ed McMahon's opportunity to be a millionaire) when one particular envelope caught my eye. Must be my refund check, I thought. But wait, there had obviously been a computer malfunction because it was not a refund, it was a sheep permit! In a matter of minutes, I turned 25 again.

The day before the season opened, my son-in-law and I headed into the area with a couple of pack animals. Having just completed eight days of guiding sheep hunters in a different area, there had been no scouting time. The next three days on the mountain did not show me quite what I wanted. A few 3/4 curl rams were spotted, several with 30 or more inches of horn, but, when viewed through the spotting scope, they were only 3 years old. That's 10 inches of horn growth each year and it proves the area is capable of producing some giants.

I knew there were 8 to 10-year-old rams in the area. The weather at the time was very hot and dry, so we decided to go home and try later in the season, closer to rut time. The schedule for the fall was very tight. Prior to receiving the sheep permit, I had booked a full hunting season of elk and deer hunters. They would start arriving in late October. There would be no time for me to play around sheep hunting once the elk season opened.

With a lot of help from some "city cowboy" friends, and after several long days, we got all the trails cleared, horse feed packed in, firewood cut, and tents up. I had just five days left to hunt sheep before the first elk hunters arrived. At the pace I had been living, that seemed like time enough to circle the whole state on a flat-footed horse. After all, you only need one day if you are lucky (something I had never been long on).

I called up my good friends Larry and Barbara Clark, whose ranch adjoins a portion of the sheep country I wanted to hunt. They invited me to come stay at their house, hunt from there each day, and Larry would help me find a ram. The catch was that I had to deliver to their ranch a registered Charolais bull, a 4-H project my youngest daughter was selling. Sounded like a good deal to me — free sheep hunt, free board and room at the Clarks', and no more drain on Dad's grain bin by a gluttonous 4-H animal.

I arrived at the Clark ranch late that evening and deposited Toro the bull in a corral, then went inside to retire to a soft bed and let the few remaining hours of darkness pass. In the two minutes it took me to fall asleep, I remember thinking something was wrong. Sheep hunting involves extensive packing into the high country, enduring the elements, getting wet and cold, and going hungry for a day or two. And there I was, living like a king at the Conrad Hilton.

The smell of Barbara's breakfast came early the next morning. Larry thought we would start by taking his 4x4 limousine up an old logging road and doing some looking with the spotting scopes. He knew some good vantage points. Immediately, we were looking at several scattered bands of ewes and lambs, one bunch with more than 75 head in it. From the distance of 1-1/2 miles, they could almost have been mistaken for domestic sheep.

Finally, three rams were spotted in a grassy clearing high on a distant ridge, so far away that the 40x scope barely showed them to be rams. Larry thought this was a good place to head as the ridges adjacent to the three rams had always been good ram country in the past.

Driving to a trail head that led into the area, we went up the mountain with day packs and lots of enthusiasm. On the first open hillside, about 15 ewes and lambs were feeding, along with a couple of half-curl rams. Then, suddenly, an echoing "whack" came from farther up the canyon. The big boys were apparently up ahead somewhere, trying to establish a pecking order. Only two rams crashing their heads together can make that sound.

After nearly three hours of climbing, we approached the ridge opening where the three rams had been spotted earlier. We circled the clearing like nervous mice, but the rams had seemingly left. Freshly barked spots near the base of two pine trees indicated we were in the right place.

Then a white patch appeared through the trees, and we froze in our tracks. With the help of binoculars, we made out the details of all three rams, lying down and chewing their cuds, not 40 feet away. As we inched forward in super-slow motion, I was able to study their horns — nearly full curls with a little brooming on the ends. Pretty good sheep, but the rings showed they were only 3-1/2 years old. I had guided hunters in other areas that would have traded their wives for a shot at something like that.

At that point, Larry had the video camera running. The sheep got to their feet, gave us a quick stare, and headed for safer timber.

Candy bar time. That was fun! Several minutes passed as we sat, munching on half-melted granolas. Then, there it was again — "whack." Though still a long way off, that unmistakable sound did more for a tired body than ten candy bars. We agreed on the general direction the sound came from and headed that way. For the next two hours, we continued to climb, the blind leading the blind because without another "whack" for direction it was nearly impossible to locate the rams in the heavily timbered canyon.

It was 2:00 P.M. and dead silence prevailed over the canyon. We came to a clearing and decided to eat lunch. In that part of the canyon, a "clearing" is any opening large enough to admit sunshine.

An hour passed. We had just eaten. It was warm out and both of us were plagued with heavy eyelids. More time passed, then "whack!" We sprang to our feet like bounced rubber balls. That was what we had been waiting for and this time it was no more than 200 yards away. The little bit of air movement there was seemed to be coming straight toward us, so we cautiously headed in the direction of the sound. As we topped a rise on the hillside and looked across a slight draw in front of us, I saw the top of a small lodgepole pine whipping back and forth like something was trying to uproot it. That had to be our sheep.

Step by step, inch by inch, we moved closer. At the base of the whipping pine, we saw legs moving. Then, off to our left, there was an entirely different ram in nearly full view, half asleep on his feet. A good ram, at least 185. Larry started the video camera running. For the next 25 or 30 minutes we remained nearly frozen in our positions, studying every detail.

We counted nine rams, every one would make the book; two of them in the mid 180s and the rest over 190. Two rams grazed nonchalantly until suddenly, as if by command from their leader, they turned on each other, came up on their hind legs, and with all the weight and power they could put into it, collided head-on. Both looked half stunned for a few minutes, then resumed eating as if nothing ever happened. Larry got it all on tape.

At times there were rams within 40 or 50 yards of us, and yet the trees are just thick enough that I could never see more than two rams at any one time. For some reason, sheep never seem to line up side by side, left view, right view. It's not like a police "lineup." You have to know how to judge each ram individually, on his own merits. It was time for those countless hours of studying rams with a spotting scope to pay off.

One particular ram impressed me more than the others. His horns had tremendous mass that carried well out to the heavily broomed ends. Over the course of our watch, this ram reappeared three or four times. I had viewed him from all sides, and his horns appeared to be extremely even. I judged him to be at least 195. Twice I put the crosshairs on him. What to do? I had four more days to hunt, and it was the first day out. Were there other rams in front of me that I had not yet seen? Was a bird in the hand better than two bigger ones in the bush? I knew the area could potentially produce a new state record, and this ram probably wouldn't quite do it. I knew that when I squeezed the trigger, my once-in-a-lifetime permit was used. What a dilemma for a hunter!

Once again the big boy showed through the trees. I removed the safety as he turned broadside and I took another view through the scope. The crosshairs were right on the heart area, just behind the shoulder. It would be a clean shot. Bang! The decision had just been made; I hoped it was the right one. A mountain king had just fallen, but best of all it was instantaneous, no suffering.

With the video camera still running, the other rams started milling around, not knowing what had happened. Then, in single file, they went bounding down the hill. Five more rams came running by from higher up, five we hadn't even seen yet, and every one of them would easily have made the book. Fortunately, the video replay showed none of them to be quite the equal to the ram of my choice.

With everything once again quiet and peaceful on the mountain, we approached my ram to see what kind of decision I had made. Wowee! I quickly ran a tape measure over the horns, and being a little conservative, came up with 196-4/8. I thought I would keep him!

My mind suddenly raced back to my boyhood and that first fallen mountain king whose horns hung in a hayloft for 25 years. Here was my opportunity to fulfill the personal vow I had made then. So, with pictures taken and amazed looks on our faces, we proceeded to cape out the ram for a life-size mount. I figured mounting him as if he were still standing in his natural setting would be the greatest tribute I could make to the massive ram.

I selected a fellow sheep hunter and noted taxidermist, Lorraine Harrison, to do the taxidermy honors. The sheep was killed October 11, 1990. Lorraine had the life-size mount completed in four months and ready for display at the February, 1991, FNAWS convention in Reno, Nevada. I entered the ram in the FNAWS Ram Award Contest, winning the Gold Award for Rocky Mountain Big Horns and the Award of Excellence as best overall ram taken that year. Additional first place awards went to Lorraine for her taxidermy work, including the coveted People's Choice Award.

The official Boone & Crockett entry score turned out to be 197-1/8. But more important than the score is the fact this ram will be made available to thousands of people to view and enjoy, hunters and non-hunters, school children and seniors. It is my way of sharing with others the great experience and the good fortune I had on the mountain. It is my way of paying a lasting tribute to a truly grand mountain king.

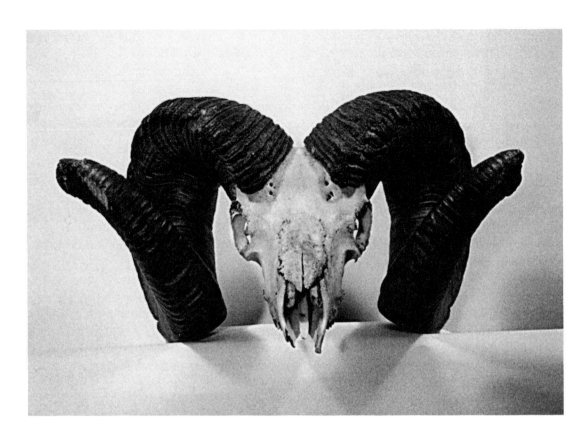

Photograph by Wm. H. Nesbitt

BIGHORN SHEEP
CERTIFICATE OF MERIT
SCORE: 202

Locality: Canmore, Alta.   Date: Picked Up, 1987
Owner: Alberta Fish & Wildl. Div.

BIGHORN SHEEP 202

Alberta Fish and Wildlife Division, Owner

This ram was killed by a truck on a highway, near Canmore, Alberta. The sheep winter in this area. The ram became the property of the Alberta government since it was killed on the highway. A life-size mount of the animal is used in public education programs.

DESERT SHEEP
FIRST AWARD
SCORE: 197-1/8

Locality: Graham Co., Ariz.   Date: 1988
Hunter: Arthur R. Dubs

DESERT SHEEP 197-1/8

Arthur R. Dubs

At the auction of the Foundation for North American Wild Sheep in February of 1988, I obtained a permit to hunt desert sheep in Aravaipa Canyon, an eight-mile gorge that slashes through some of the most rugged country in southwestern Arizona.

As I have done in the past, I wanted to capture the excitement and spectacle of the hunt on film. I could not wait to pack my camera, along with my .300 Weatherby Magnum rifle, and head for Arizona. I was determined to search out and take the largest desert ram in Aravaipa Canyon and to share the experience with my fellow sportsmen.

My guide, Floyd Krank, who lives in Globe, Arizona, had been hunting and scouting the area since the Arizona Game and Fish Department opened it to hunting in 1980. Three years prior to my hunt, Floyd had spotted a huge ram and named him Chiphorn, because a large piece was missing on the back side of his left horn. In succeeding years, while Floyd was hunting with clients, the old ram managed to escape all efforts to track him down. Floyd finally caught another glimpse of the ram on a scouting trip the previous summer, during the height of the rutting season. The ram was lean and haggard from running off young upstarts. At the time, Floyd had serious doubts whether Chiphorn would be able to make it through another winter.

I arrived in Aravaipa Canyon on December 1, 1988, and met Floyd a day before the season opened. He had already set up a comfortable camp and we both had a serious dose of sheep fever. We sat up late that night, exchanging ideas on how we might be able to outsmart the ram. If he was still alive, we had 21 days to find him before the end of the season.

Five o'clock came early. Before sunrise, Floyd and I were dodging cactus and slipping on rotten volcanic rock as we made our way through the jagged rims overlooking the canyon. Soon, golden rays of sunlight spread a brighter path for us to follow along the canyon rim.

As we cautiously peeked over the edge, we were treated to a spectacular view of the canyon, and we could hear Aravaipa Creek bubbling 2,000 feet below us. A group of a dozen ewes and lambs grazed contentedly on an outcropping only a few yards from us. We skirted around them, leaving them undisturbed as we kept moving under cover of the rocks, glassing every draw and crevice. The sheep were scattered and we saw several small rams. We arrived back at our cozy camp two hours after sunset with new scratches and an accumulation of cacti.

After three days of hunting from daylight to dark, we ended up with no leads on Chiphorn. Floyd and I were beginning to wonder if the old ram was still alive. We had photographed and passed up several trophy rams that would have scored well up in the records book, but we saw nothing that approached the stature of Chiphorn.

It was a nice awakening when, at sunrise on the fifth day of the hunt from the top of the rim above Aravaipa Creek, we spotted a heavy-horned ram with a group of other sheep. They were more than a mile away, at the head of Javelina Canyon. The ram was on a talus slope, feeding on a barrel cactus.

We rushed to set up our 60x spotting scope. There was no question of identification. Even from the great distance, we could see the ram's massive, broomed horns. We knew we were looking at one of the largest desert rams on the continent.

The ram had not only survived the summer's rutting season, but he had bulked up considerably and was robust and healthy. He was banging heads with two younger rams, showing his prowess in view of a half-dozen ewes and one small lamb. He looked out of proportion, holding up his huge load of yellowish horn. We were amazed by his ability to carry such a heavy set of horns with such agility.

We quickly took a series of telephoto film sequences. Then, we wasted no time in moving around the rocky rim to get closer to the old ram. After an hour of weaving around the heads of several scabrous side canyons, we still found ourselves 600 yards away, looking down on Chiphorn 1,000 feet below us.

We went around the last possible side canyon in the vicinity of the ram. Again, we were overlooking the ram, but the range was no more than 250 yards. Luckily he was still with the other sheep, continuing to dominate the herd and flirting with the same ewe.

I quickly placed my tripod and camera in position and ran off a few feet of movie film. Then, the thought struck me: I had an opportunity to bag the largest desert ram I would ever see, but how would we retrieve him if I shot him? We agreed that even if we had to resort to mountain climbing equipment, we were not going to pass him up.

I quickly chambered a cartridge and carefully crawled out as far as possible over the edge of the rim. I steadied my rifle on a rock. The crosshairs of my scope found the great ram, and I squeezed the trigger. As the rifle roared, the ram dropped in his tracks, never flinching.

Floyd yelled, "You got 'em!" as the echo of the shot bounced off the canyon wall below us. The rest of the herd scattered and disappeared.

Congratulations were followed by the challenge. We had to climb down to the talus slope to retrieve the ram. After attempting to backtrack through several side canyons and changing our route several times, we discovered a faint trail that revealed fresh sheep tracks. I have taken several bighorn sheep, but the tracks Floyd and I found were as large as any we had ever seen. We knew they had to have been made by Chiphorn and his band. We followed the tracks through a narrow passage hidden by boulders and continued by crawling through a jungle of undergrowth. We knew that if Chiphorn and his entire band, including the small lamb, had made their way through the canyon and onto the talus slope, we had a chance to do so as well.

We continued our descent through the rocky passage and finally broke out into some of the most beautiful terrain we had encountered in Aravaipa. There were several water holes. The canyon was an oasis, a paradise for birds and sheep and rattlesnakes too, for we met some of them.

It had been almost three hours since the shot. Soon, we rounded the last talus slope and saw the fabulous desert ram.

I broke out my measuring tape. Both of the horns measured more than 42 inches in length. More impressive still was the massiveness of the horns. They were broomed off as big as coffee cups, with 11 inch third quarters and bases of more than 16 inches. He had only four teeth left and all but one were extremely loose. We aged him at 12 years old. Yet the muscles still rippled over his dark-furred body. We concluded that his enormous front hooves were essential to support the weight of his horns.

We took a complete set of field measurements before field-dressing him. I wanted the end result to be the truest representation possible of a ram in a full mount, as he appeared in the wild.

A few days later, the horns green scored 198-5/8 when measured by an official Boone and Crockett measurer in Tucson, Arizona. On May 20, 1992, I was informed that a panel of Boone and Crockett scorers had officially confirmed the score at 197-1/8 points. I was delighted that I had shot the largest desert ram ever taken by a sportsman in fair chase.

Photograph by Wm. H. Nesbitt

DESERT SHEEP
SECOND AWARD
SCORE: 186-3/8

Locality: Gila Co., Ariz.   Date: 1990
Hunter: Steven E. Wright

DESERT SHEEP 186-3/8

Steven E. Wright

Since I start thinking about next year's hunting seasons as soon as the previous season is over, August is a long time to wait for results from my hunting applications. Big game permits in Arizona are limited for most hunts and are awarded by a computerized drawing.

On that August day in 1989, I remember standing in front of my mailbox with high hopes of drawing at least half of the permits for which I had applied. My face must have looked like I had just lost my best friend when I opened my mailbox and saw all the pink rejection slips mixed in with the other mail. I sorted through the mail, setting aside the pink slips. Elk, deer, antelope; the sinking feeling in my stomach increased with each one. I halfheartedly sorted the rest of the bills and junk mail. Then I came across an envelope from the Arizona Game and Fish Department. It did not dawn on me what it signified until I actually pulled the permit out of the envelope and read the label. I had just been drawn for a desert sheep permit!

Considering it was only my third try, the chance of being drawn was about as good as winning the lotto. I was overwhelmed. In fact, I am surprised I did not start dancing and jumping up and down, right there in the post office.

August and the first few weeks of September quickly melted away, with only one short scouting trip made to my sheep unit. I was not concerned, however, because I thought I had the entire fall to locate a nice ram.

My nephew Eric was living with us for the school year, and I was trying to spend some time with him, showing him the wondrous outdoors. I promised him a trip to call and video some elk, and he was quite excited. Between Eric and my two-year-old son blowing elk calls over a period of several weeks, my wife was just about ready to pull out her hair.

We left for our outing on Saturday, with a promise to be back in time for a neighborhood barbecue the following afternoon. We saw about 100 elk and had numerous cows and bulls within 15 to 20 yards of us. My nephew was quite impressed, especially when four small bulls almost ran right over us while hurrying to my cow call.

We should have stayed in the woods, because the barbecue ended in a disaster. While playing volleyball, I blew out the cruciate ligament and tore cartilage in my left knee. Having been subjected to two previous reconstructive surgeries on my right knee, I knew there was a chance that I would not be going on my sheep hunt at all.

The earliest I could schedule my surgery was the middle of October and I knew that only six weeks of rehabilitation would hardly be enough to get me ready to tackle sheep terrain. Thank goodness surgical methods and the treatment of knee injuries have changed. With my first surgery 10 years ago, I was in a full leg cast for eight whole weeks. With this last surgery, the physical therapist came in the very next morning and began the daily routine to get me back on my feet. With the goal of being able to fill my sheep tag, I worked extra hard at rehabilitation.

The Arizona Game and Fish Department and the Arizona Desert Bighorn Sheep Society have done a tremendous job of re-establishing bighorn sheep in the state. The numbers of sheep have increased dramatically and so has the quality of the rams. My permit was in Unit 22. The sheep are concentrated in the southern end of the unit, along a series of small lakes created by dams in the Salt River drainage. The Mazatal Mountains jut and crash into the Salt River drainage, creating peaks, canyons, and cliff faces that are breathtaking. Most of the sheep are located in the Four Peaks Wilderness Area, and motorized vehicles are not allowed.

The easiest way to access the wilderness area is by boat, across the small lakes. With a 14 foot aluminum boat and a small outboard that I use for fishing, I was all set. I contacted the game manager in Unit 22, and he told me that two Class IV rams had been spotted during October, when the game and fish department flew the unit for a sheep count.

Several years earlier while on a fishing trip, I saw where a nice ram had been taken. I knew where I wanted to set up camp and start my hunt, but I had one more doctor's visit to pass first. My appointment was scheduled the day before the hunt started. By that time, I could peg-leg along quite nicely with my leg brace. At my appointment, the surgeon checked my leg and said I was coming along fine. I did not tell the surgeon what I had planned for the next two weeks, and I did not want to hear his reply.

My brother Serge was my partner on this hunt. He is a good extra set of eyes to have along. We do most of our hunting by glassing and stalking, so we felt fairly confident we would find a nice ram before the hunt was over.

After the first two days, we were not quite so optimistic. We hiked and glassed continuously, trying to locate the sheep. We saw mule deer, Coues' deer, javelina, and the ever present scourge of sheep country, burros, but the sheep were winning at hide-and-seek.

The weather could not have been more cooperative. It usually warmed up enough by the middle of the afternoon to peel off everything but a Tee-shirt.

When I referred to the area as breathtaking, I was not speaking only of the scenery. By the end of the second day of hiking in and out of canyons and climbing to vantage points for glassing, I was one tired puppy. My leg did not bother me too much during the day, because I was too busy trying to find sheep. Back at camp at night, it would constantly remind me that my rehabilitation was not quite complete.

After the second long, discouraging day, we decided to camp out of the boat for a few days in a new location. We piled our camp gear and several ice chests in the boat and headed out for the opposite shore. We decided to try a new series of canyons farther south from our camp.

After climbing and finding a good vantage point, we began the routine of trying to locate some sheep. We were across a large canyon from a large cliff face, which tapered off into several smaller canyons.

We must have spotted the rump at the same time, because we both started babbling at once. Having confirmed that, yes, it was a ewe, we began looking for rams. We spotted seven more ewes and a small ram farther down the cliff, on another ledge. Then I saw my ram.

The ram was standing on the uphill side of a saguaro cactus, eating. He had either eaten or torn off the top of the cactus, revealing the white fleshy pulp. The sheep did not seem to be in any hurry, so I pulled out my spotting scope to get a better look. One look confirmed what I already knew; I wanted that ram. He turned to walk uphill and the angle really showed how massive his horns were.

We studied the cliff face, trying to find the easiest way to approach the big ram and still avoid spooking the other sheep. Normally I would not have worried about following them all day, if needed, but I did not know if my leg would hold up. The ram and a single ewe were several hundred yards above the other sheep, feeding toward a canyon. I started down to cross the main canyon and work my way up the other side, and my brother stayed to observe and give me directions in case the sheep spooked.

I have shot a Remington Model 700 BDL in .30-06 for the past 17 years. Three years earlier, I had placed a synthetic stock on my rifle and began handloading 165-grain Hornady boat-tails in front of 57 grains of IMR-4350. My rifle is topped with a Leupold 3.5-10x scope, and I knew from the past that it handles anything.

Upon reaching the other side, I went up a small rock chute I had selected earlier. It put me directly in the path of the big ram. I worked my way up with my rifle over my back, clawing and pulling at the brush and whatever small rock outcroppings I could grab. I emerged at the top of the chute and could see the ewe less than two hundred yards away. I could not see the ram, but I knew that he had to be somewhere close by. I eased forward, trying to find a good position to take a rest for a shot. Unless I wanted to look like I had slept with a porcupine, lying prone was out of the question. There was too much cholla and other cactus in the area.

I finally found a rock I could use for a rest that gave me a good view of the area. I still could not see the ram, but the ewe must have spotted me because she was turned facing my direction. I finally spotted the ram coming out of a small swale, and he worked his way in between a couple of scrub bushes. I slowly eased a cartridge in the chamber, waiting for a clean shot. After what seemed like an eternity but probably was not more than a couple of minutes, the ram finally moved enough to give me an unobstructed shot at his chest.

I centered my crosshairs and shot. The ram wheeled around, stepped out on a small boulder, and looked down at me, acting like he had not been hit at all. My mind started racing as I cranked another shell into the chamber, wondering when I had bumped my scope enough to cause a miss. I put my scope on the ram again, just in time to watch him topple over like a felled tree.

After the required photo session, the work really started. We butchered the ram on the spot, carried it down the cliff with a pack, and then hauled it out the canyon to the waiting boat. Let me tell you, a place to sit and prop up my leg never looked so good!

Photograph courtesy of Michael A. Gwaltney

This desert sheep was killed in Mohave County, Arizona, in 1990.
by Michael A. Gwaltney. It scored 171.

Photograph courtesy of Louise B. Ellison

Louise B. Ellison killed this desert sheep in Mohave County,
Arizona, in 1984. It scores 168-4/8.

Photograph by Wm. H. Nesbitt

DESERT SHEEP
THIRD AWARD
SCORE: 185-3/8

Locality: Baja Calif., Mexico   Date: 1987
Hunter: Robert L. Williamson

DESERT SHEEP 185-3/8

Robert L. Williamson

It was the night of Friday, December 11, 1987, as I gazed up at the vaguely tinted, twinkling stars. I was in my partially open sleeping bag that mild night, in the northern Baja of Mexico. More specifically, I was hunting the La Palmita Norte area of Arroyo Grande, an area which had reportedly had no legal hunting pressure during the past few years.

I was filled with anxiety about our plan to pursue two desert rams the next day. They had eluded us for two days. The anxiety was high, partly because I was attempting to complete my Grand Slam of North American Sheep before the age of 40. I was 39, but I was also anxious because of the hunt itself; we were having such a great time!

I am a geologist and an independent oil producer in Shreveport, Louisiana. I had been fortunate enough to take a Boone and Crockett Stone's sheep in 1981 in British Columbia, a Dall's sheep in 1982 in the Northwest Territories, and a Bighorn in 1986 in the Wind River Mountains of Wyoming. After considerable thought, I decided to attempt a desert sheep hunt in Mexico while I could choke down the cost and my health was good, rather than continue with the lottery system in the United States. I consulted Michael Valencia in Los Angeles for some advice on procedures, and months later, I found myself scheduled for the first hunt of the season.

I arrived at the Imperial-El Centro Airport in extreme southeastern California. I was met by Hector Gracia Galvan, the local Mexican Consulate living in San Diego, and Edwardo Menendez Acosta, a biologist and the Technical Director of the Consejo Nacional de la Fauna (CNF) from Mexico City. Michael had arranged the unusual service, which was more convenient because they were in the area for a ceremony scheduled the next day. We crossed the border into Mexicali with ease and checked into Hotel Lucerna.

There, I met Jerry Olsen from White Bear Lake, Minnesota, and two Mexican nationals who would be hunting the "opening." Hotel Lucerna was alive with activity, and we seemed to be the center of attention.

The next morning (Sunday), we were escorted to a press conference at the local Committee of Tourism and Conventions for the introduction of the new CNF Department and the dedication of brand new hunting equipment to be used in hunting *borrego cimarron* (desert sheep). At the press conference, I met my head guide, Lupe, and saw the small fleet of brand new Dodge Ramcharger four-wheel-drive vehicles that the Department had purchased, primarily for sheep hunting.

The only hitch in my whole trip came at mid-day, when we tried to obtain gun permits from the general at the military garrison. Apparently, he could not be located and I finally received the permit on Monday afternoon. The CNF seemed embarrassed by the delay and actually paid for my extra night's lodging at Hotel Lucerna. Jerry and I became well acquainted during our 48 hours together and wished each other the best as we packed up with our guides.

Finally, I was on the road late Monday. We drove south to San Felipe, then inland to Arroyo Grande, and on into our base camp about midnight.

The next morning we awoke for breakfast and met Abraham, a warden who verified my paperwork and sent us off south across Arroyo Grande. My entourage included three wardens, Lupe, Modesto, and Gorgomio, along with two packers, Armando and Pablo. We had two new four-wheel-drive Ramchargers, new tents, camp stoves, lanterns, binoculars, spotting scopes and packframes. The wardens had new uniforms and boots. Modesto always wore his pistol and always stayed with the vehicles. Lupe was in charge; Gorgomio was big and contagiously happy; Armando was the appointed cook; and Pablo, a plump, ever-pleasing, blue-eyed kid with an infectious grin, was in great need of a bath.

After hours of driving through desolation, we found ourselves at our campsite in a range of low mountains bordering Arroyo Grande, where we would be for two nights. Modesto stayed at camp, while we walked about a mile up a narrow arroyo to an area they knew to glass for the remainder of our daylight. Nothing. No sign of life at all.

Dinner was grilled beefsteak, tortillas, and fruit. Breakfast was tortillas, eggs, and fruit. Following breakfast, we hiked and climbed to an area in which we spent the day carefully glassing. We split up later, and Lupe did manage to see a ewe during the day. The area was bleak and after dinner, they decided we would break camp tomorrow for a hard-to-reach range of mountains on the north side of Arroyo Grande.

Our vehicles crept over and around rocks, boulders, cacti, thorns and washouts to a location about a mile from the base of the rugged mountains. We sorted gear for our backpacks and took enough food and water for two nights. All I packed in addition to my rifle were personal items, ammo, snacks and water. The packers carried my sleeping bag and pad, as well as supplies.

We left Modesto to glass from the vehicles as we streaked directly to a large shadow area at the mouth of an arroyo. The mid-afternoon sun was hot, and the pace had my pulse rate at a record high. We took a breather, and then began a slow walk-and-glass routine to the head of the arroyo. This area seemed more alive and the anticipation was building.

Then we carefully climbed up the steep mountain to a saddle along the ridge crest. We dropped over the saddle and settled in for some glassing. Immediately, Gorgomio spotted a ewe down the ridge and below us. He spied another one above us and up the ridge.

The sun was already down when Gorgomio excitedly whispered for me to join him, and he pointed to a ledge that overlooked our trail up the mountain. There, silhouetted, were two rams looking away from us. One was definitely trophy class with heavy horns, which were high and deep with some flare at the broomed tips. Then the sheep suddenly bailed off and disappeared from sight. Lupe decided we would camp there and go after them in the morning. I had never camped in the middle of sheep before, but I reluctantly went along with the plan. Even though I did not prefer our campsite, we had an enjoyable evening under the stars.

The next day, we broke camp after breakfast and went after the rams. We never spotted any sheep, but the guides cut tracks which they were convinced belonged to the rams. These tracks led right off the mountain, down the arroyo, and right to where we had entered the day before. The day was almost gone so we headed for the vehicles. When we arrived, we reported the events to Modesto. He immediately picked up his binoculars, found a vantage point, and began glassing the mountain front. I was finishing washing up after the grueling day-and-a-half when Modesto found the rams to the right of the arroyo and near the valley floor.

We had obviously spooked them out of their territory late yesterday, but they were feeding and working their way higher. They were slightly above the arroyo as darkness fell. We had another dinner of beefsteak, tortillas, and fruit before unrolling our sleeping bags under the stars.

We were up early, and the mood around breakfast was excited. The moon was still out so we were able to make it safely to the arroyo before daylight. We began hunting ever so carefully up the arroyo, then climbing to the right. An hour or so passed with no sight of the rams. The farther we traveled, the more likely it became that the mountains had swallowed the rams.

The five of us were partially exposed when Lupe pointed to the rams. They were ahead of us, watching our every move. Fortunately I dropped right behind an outcrop that made a perfect rest. The rams were facing us at our level and about 250 yards away. This was an exact range that I had practiced with my .280 Remington and its 6X Leupold scope. I had a Ruger Model 77 action, which I had glass-bedded and free-floated the barrel. I was shooting 140-grain Nosler Partition handloads with 55.3 grains of IMR-4350 powder. Lupe made sure I was shooting at the largest ram, even though there was no comparison. He wanted me to wait until I settled down before he said okay. The ram was facing us but was turned slightly to his left, and I held right on the top of his right shoulder. When the bullet struck, the ram spun in a half circle, went down and began sliding down the slope. I was ready to fire again, but they insisted it was unnecessary. The ram kept moving slightly and sliding down until he went out of sight.

Gorgomio scrambled after him, as I tried to walk. My legs were like rubber, and I had to sit down for a moment before slowly proceeding. The emotion of finishing my Grand Slam—and with such an obviously fine trophy ram—was overwhelming.

Gorgomio reached the ram which had, without our knowing it, fallen 150 vertical feet. By some miracle, his massive horns were not broken but they were splintered on both tips. A fresh triangular piece was missing near one base, on the seemingly inaccessible inside curve.

We were all elated as we enjoyed backslapping and handshakes. Then we posed for pictures before they began the task of skinning, quartering and caping the head. Lupe, as head guide, had the honor of packing out the head as Gorgomio led us down and out to the vehicles. Lupe also had the honor of killing the only rattlesnake we saw on the hunt as we walked back to show the head to Modesto. We joyfully rode back to our base camp where Abraham measured the ram for his records. Following a late lunch, we headed back to Mexicali and I was home late the next night.

The ram was a monster and it won the Silver Medal at the 1988 Foundation of North American Wild Sheep Convention in Reno. After the required 60-day drying period, Marlin Mann scored the ram at 185-3/8. A twist to the story is that my first submittal of this score in 1988 to Boone and Crockett somehow went to their former address and was then returned to my office. It was mailed again and apparently lost in the mail. The ram also helped me receive another outstanding award at the 1988 FNAWS Convention. I was one of the 15 honored as having the largest combined Grand Slam scores ever recorded.

Photograph courtesy of Richard L. Dean

This desert sheep, scoring 168-1/8, was killed in Clark
County, Nevada, in 1988. by Richard L. Deane.

Photograph courtesy of Alfred L. Raiche

Hunter Alfred L. Raiche (left) and Kerri Raiche (right) killed this
desert sheep in Nye County, Nevada, in 1988. It scored 184-6/8.

Photograph by Wm. H. Nesbitt

DESERT SHEEP
CERTIFICATE OF MERIT
SCORE: 190-3/8
Locality: Arizona   Date: 1903
Hunter: Unknown   Owner: Bruce R. Kemp, Sr.

DESERT SHEEP 190-3/8

Bruce R. Kemp, Sr., owner

In 1959, while I was serving as a sheriff's deputy and constable in eastern San Diego County, my trophy was given to me by the widow of a reserve deputy. The trophy had been given to them by the previous owner of a store they had purchased some years before.

Legend has it this man was in a hunting party with Kermit Roosevelt in 1903. They hunted near Yuma, Arizona. Referring to Kermit Roosevelt's book, *Happy Hunting Grounds* (Scribners, 1920), we find an account in the third chapter which may be relevant. Kermit named his hunting companions as Mr. Charles Utting, clerk of the District Court and former Rough Rider; Mr. Win Proebstel, ranchman and prospector; and Mr. Proebstel's brother, Ike. Cipriano Dominguez and Eustacio Casares were engaged for the hunt. They left Wellton, 40 miles east of Yuma, on August 10. Since daytime temperatures were 140 degrees, they left by full moon, traveling east to a water hole. After resting for a few hours, they loaded their outfit on pack mules and proceeded to the Tinajas Atlas, about four miles from the Mexican Border. Below the natural tanks, which collect rainwater, were some 150 graves of those who, crossed the desert and found the tanks dry. Roosevelt tells the story of a Mexican outlaw named Blanco, who arrived at the tanks ahead of 46 unfortunates on a journey to the United States from Mexico. The outlaw scooped out water for himself, watched the travelers die, robbed them, and escaped. The book contains numerous other stories of tragedy and hardship associated with the area.

The hunt began at 3:00 a.m. and produced a lot of shooting. The hunt took many twists, with most animals being taken at between 200 and 300 yards. On Page 91, Roosevelt gives the measurements of a ram's horns as being 16-3/4 inches around the base and 35 inches long. They were described as larger in circumference, though shorter, than another specimen he took earlier. On Page 97 there is an unidentified trophy which could possibly be mine. The enclosed photo is a poor enlargement, but

I give thanks to Dr. Lorin Lutz, president of the Society for the Conservation of Desert Bighorn Sheep, and Dr. Ken Staeger, Los Angeles County Museum of Natural History (retired), for their valued assistance in bringing "Kermit," as my children call him, to his place of honor with the Boone and Crockett Club.

Photograph by Wm. H. Nesbitt

STONE'S SHEEP
FIRST AWARD
SCORE: 176

Locality: Tuchodi Lakes, B.C.   Date: 1989
Hunter: Terry Filas

STONE'S SHEEP 176

Terry Filas

The first hunt of the season has its advantages, or so they say. My outfitter, Ross Peck, must have believed it, because my hotel reservation had been cancelled when I arrived in Fort St. John, British Columbia. I was told Ross wanted me in camp that night so we could be in the mountains, ready to hunt, on opening day. The flight to Ross' camp seemed to last mere minutes. Soon after landing, my bags were unloaded (except for the sleeping bag that never arrived in Fort St. John), Ross introduced me to the staff, and I was in my cabin.

Over dinner, Ross explained that he wanted me to leave early the next morning for spike camp. Ross' brother, Timber, and an Indian guide, Ted Metecheah, would accompany me. Timber and Ted had seen some big rams in the area and they wanted to be able to hunt them on opening day. After dinner, I was instructed to pack light for the five-day trip and I was delighted to receive the loan of a sleeping bag.

Immediately after breakfast the following morning, we headed out for spike camp. After a long day's ride, the sight of camp was a welcome relief.

Getting up in the morning was not difficult. After waiting a year for the hunt, I was the first to awaken. With fresh horses, we were soon out of camp. Half-way up the mountain, Timber suggested that we begin climbing on foot. Since it was a warm August day, we stripped down to light clothes and began moving higher.

After walking and glassing for a few hours, we climbed a very steep incline above a beautiful, lone ram. Timber said he was of legal size. He also said it was my call. People had told me about first-day rams. If the ram is nice, the story goes, you had better take it. Otherwise, you might well kick yourself later.

As we inched our way down the slope, we lost sight of the ram. I looked at Timber and he signaled, indicating that the ram should be just below us. We carefully moved down a few more yards. No ram. Timber signaled again. Still no ram. This sequence was repeated several times. Finally, we decided the ram had grazed out from under us.

As soon as Timber and I let our guards down, the ram walked out about 75 yards below us. I readied myself to shoot, pulled the trigger, and sent a shot flying over the ram's back. The ram took off, never to be seen by us again. I looked at Timber and felt like a real jerk. The night before, I had talked about my past hunting accomplishments, and now Timber wondered whether or not I knew how to shoot. He reassured me, saying it was still early in the day and there was no reason to let the miss get me down.

We checked the area where the ram had been when I shot, just to make sure that he was not hit, then started our climb back up the mountain. Waiting at the top, Ted said he had seen the ram take off after the shot, unhurt. He explained that the ram was so scared and running so fast that he probably wound up on the next mountain range. I think they were trying to make me feel better. Knowing that the ram was not wounded did put me at ease.

After lunch and a brief nap, we headed over to the other side of the mountain and started glassing. Ted took off to check out another area.

Meanwhile, Timber and I were having no luck. After an hour or so, Ted came back and we started to discuss our plans for the second day. Not far away were huge black storm clouds heading in our direction. The way the day was going, I knew this storm was not going to blow by us. It did not even take 30 minutes to reach us. The cool shower felt nice at first; then the storm produced heavy rains, accompanied by hail. The three of us ran to take cover as best we could. I would have given anything for my rain suit, but it was tied on the saddle of my horse many miles away. After 20 minutes, the storm passed, leaving us soaked to the bone. We tried our best to dry out on our way down to spike camp.

The next morning we headed back to the same area. Once on top, Timber and Ted went scouting for about an hour. While they were gone, I glassed the area, thinking about the ram I missed, wondering if I would ever get another chance. Timber and Ted returned with smiles on their faces. They had discovered four nice rams positioned on a finger of the mountain. Getting down to them would be difficult because there were several cautious ewes and lambs on the opposite slope.

Our plan was to stay as low as possible and still get there quickly. Two hours of stalking was halted by a narrow, open crossing between us and the finger leading to the rams. We were pinned down and being watched by the ewes and lambs above us. The only easy way across this natural land bridge was too apparent; the sheep would surely catch us. We looked over the side ledge that went straight down about 50 feet. On that ledge was a 6-inch shelf tucked down far enough that the sheep would not see us crossing. Timber went first across the 25-foot stretch and climbed up into some low brush. He then motioned for me to do the same. While I was looking down at the 50-foot drop below the narrow shelf, I gave Timber a dirty look with words to match. Holding on to the top of the ledge with my fingers, I carefully lowered myself across the stretch. My heart was pounding hard as I pulled myself up into the brush next to Timber, repeating my previous words. Then, Ted climbed across the dangerous shelf. We decided to slide on our butts for the next 75 yards in order to reach a group of small pine trees. Once we made it to the pines, we were able to see the rams about 150 yards away.

Three rams were standing and one was lying down. They were all legal rams but Timber noted that the one lying down was the biggest. I used the pine tree in front of me for a rest to steady my shot. I did not want to miss this one. As I was getting ready to shoot, Ted whispered loudly, "Wait, I see a bigger one behind the rock." Sure enough, you could just see part of his horn sticking up above the rock. The fourth ram was lying down, keeping guard on the other side of the rocks.

We waited for what seemed like hours for the ram to stand. By luck, two of the other rams started to fight, which caused the big ram to stand up. As I was looking through my rifle scope I heard Timber say, "When he gets in the clear, take him." That was all I needed to hear. As the ram broke into the open, I pulled the trigger.

"You hit him!", Ted said, "shoot him again." The ram stumbled back around the rocks and we lost sight of him. We were close to the tree line and did not want to lose him in the pines, so we started running down to where he was when I shot. The other rams saw us coming and ran. Timber ran to the rocks and yelled that the ram was down near the creek. I saw the ram stumbling down the hillside, some 250 yards away, and I shot again, hitting him in the foreleg. Quickly I fired a third time and he fell between some rocks in the creek.

When we came up on the ram, Timber said it was the largest of his guiding career. He thought it would go well over 40 inches.

After caping and packing up the meat, we decided that Timber would go back for the horses. Ted and I would follow the creek down to the main river follow that back toward camp and meet Timber half-way with the horses. It sounded pretty easy since it was my idea. We put the pack with the meat in the creek to keep it cold and took the cape with us. I was not going to let that head out of my sight.

We hiked for a few hours in the waning daylight and saw no sign of Timber. Ted decided that with the bit of daylight left, we had better get some firewood and build a fire on the river bank. Ted and I split a candy bar for dinner and spent the night curled up by a fire. It wasn't hard getting up at daylight, and the two of us were off, hiking to spike camp. Ted figured we were within three hours of camp. When we arrived, Timber was packing up camp. He had spent the night in the woods with the horses. We had breakfast, packed up and headed for main camp. The trip back to main camp was the best ride ever, watching the huge horns of the ram on the pack horse in front of me all the way to base camp.

Ross and his wife Deborah greeted us coming into camp. After measuring the horns, there was no doubt that we had a very big, records-book Stone's sheep. I left for home the next morning on a supply plane. Once in the air, the pilot asked if I had a good hunt. Yeah-ahh, it was a great hunt, thanks to Timber and Ted.

Photograph by Wm. H. Nesbitt

STONE'S SHEEP
SECOND AWARD
SCORE: 174-5/8
Locality: Prophet River, B.C.   Date: 1989
Hunter: Craig R. Johnson

STONE'S SHEEP 174-5/8

Craig R. Johnson

Almost every year, it seems that at least one of the three largest Stone's sheep in the awards competition of the Foundation for North American Wild Sheep comes from the Muskwa/Prophet area outfitted by Garry Vince, Muskwas Safaris Ltd. With this in mind, I approached Garry at the October 1988 meeting of the FNAWS board of directors and asked about openings or cancellations for the 1989 season. Garry and I sit on the board, where we volunteer our time, trying to guarantee a future for wild sheep and sheep hunting for future generations. He was fully booked at that time but his wife Sandra called just before Christmas to confirm that I could have one of the two additional permits they had been granted because of the average old age of the rams they were taking. My hunt would begin on the season opener, August 1. Needless to say, I jumped at the chance.

I had previously taken an old, although light-horned, Stone's ram in 1977 on the 12th day of a 14-day hunt, this after hunting for 15 days unsuccessfully in 1975. Since I had already taken this ram, I decided in 1989 that I might not take a ram. If I did, he would have to be a good one.

Four days before the season opener, I was met at the airport in Fort Saint John, British Columbia, by Sandra Vince and driven approximately 200 miles up the Alaskan Highway to a roadside strip. There, Garry was waiting to fly us to his beautiful Muskwa River ranch. At the ranch, I met my head guide, Sandra's brother Marlin Watson, as well as the assistant guide, Brent Reile, and the horse wrangler, Denny. The next day, after checking the zero of my rifle, Garry flew us into bull camp, where Marlin had previously trailed our packstring. A ride of approximately four hours the next morning brought us to a beautiful spike camp. We soon spotted rams on the adjacent mountains. Our camp consisted of a tarp tied horizontally between the trees, with our sleeping bags scattered underneath. On July 31, the day before the season opened, we climbed high into the surrounding mountains, scouting for a big ram. This proved to be the only day that we did not see legal rams.

That evening, shortly after we crawled into our sleeping bags, Marlin's dog made a muffled growl. In the fading daylight, we suddenly spotted two nearly full-grown grizzly cubs some 20 yards from our camp. They made a hasty retreat in the same direction from which they had come. This was fortunate inasmuch as "mama" was trailing along behind. It was quite a while before my heartbeat settled down to normal so I could get some sleep.

For the next two days, we hunted out of that spike camp, climbing high into the surrounding mountains. Each day, we spotted and walked away from mature rams that we estimated would score more than 160 Boone and Crockett points.

Marlin decided to move our camp to Horn Creek so we could explore some new country. The next day we climbed a long mountain near our new camp. It was literally crawling with sheep, including 30 rams. At one point, two 160-plus rams walked leisurely below us at about 60 yards but I still did not chamber a cartridge. I was enjoying the hunt too much to end it.

On August 5, we put an extra sandwich and a can of fruit into our day packs, with the intent of spending the night on top of a long mountain stretching toward the Prophet River. In that area the big, old rams will often bed during the day in the junipers and heavy buck brush, making them almost impossible to locate. If we were in position above likely habitat during the late evening and early morning hours, we felt we might spot an old buster while he fed.

About halfway to our destination, while moving just below the ridgeline, we sat down for a short rest and also to do some glassing. It was close to noon when Marlin crept up a few feet to look over the top of the ridge. Suddenly, a pebble hit me in the back and a quick glance showed Marlin and Brent smiling and giving the "ram" sign.

Bedded on a shale slide about 200 yards from us were six rams with four or five ewes, an unusual mix at that time of year. Two of the rams were legal, with one being a heavily, broomed ram. Through the spotting scope, we aged him at 8-1/2 to 10-1/2 years. The sheep were completely oblivious to our presence as we debated their qualifications and thoroughly enjoyed watching them.

After 20 minutes, Marlin whispered, "You could probably hunt a long time to find a better one."

It was time to end the hunt. At my shot, the ram kicked enough to begin rolling over and over down the shale slide, finally coming to rest approximately 400 yards below his initial bed.

We sat down to eat our can of fruit and savor the moment. We would not be spending the night on the mountain after all. I then began picking my way down to the ram, with Marlin and Brent literally flying down the mountain. They had reached him, taped him at 39-4/8 x 15 inches, and pronounced him a "book" ram while I was still well up the mountain.

After picture taking, caping for a life-size mount, and boning the meat, we began the long walk back to camp. It proved to be pretty comfortable in our warm sleeping bags in a dry tent that night while the thunder roared and the rain poured down, rather than shivering in my rain gear on top of the mountain. It was doubly satisfying to look through the tent flaps and see my ram's horns hanging in the tree during each flash of lightning.

We proceeded to trail out the next day to the Prophet camp, where Garry picked us up and flew us back to the Muskwa ranch. Upon reaching home, my ram was green-scored for FNAWS at 175-2/8 and officially scored three months later for Boone and Crockett entry at 174-5/8.

What a great hunt with an outstanding outfitter, excellent guides, beautiful country, and a magnificent ram!

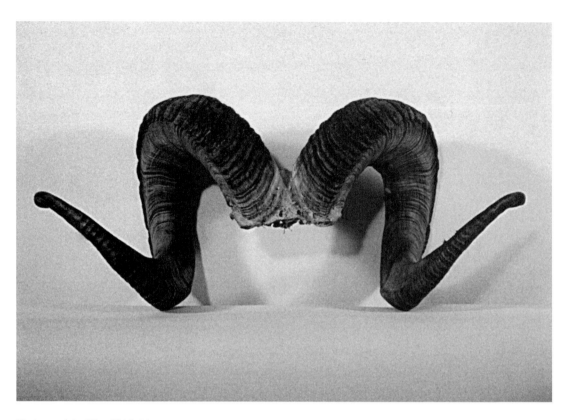

Photograph by Wm. H. Nesbitt

DALL'S SHEEP
FIRST AWARD
SCORE: 180-3/8

Locality: Hartman River, Alaska   Date: 1989
Hunter: Carl E. Jacobson

DALL'S SHEEP 180-3/8

Carl E. Jacobsen

I suppose I was not terribly surprised when the pilot on my commercial flight from the Bay Area came on the public address system as we approached the Anchorage airport. According to the announcement, the area was in the midst of a record rainfall that showed no signs of letting up. I was going to Alaska to hunt Dall's sheep; the lousy weather was not the first, nor would it be the last, obstacle I would have to overcome in pursuit of this trophy.

I had hunted with Scott and Bettina Miluer of Fair Chase Hunts in Palmer, Alaska, in 1986 and decided to return in 1988 for a 40 inch ram. However, due to circumstances beyond my control, the hunt was delayed until 1989.

The hunt was supposed to begin on opening day, August, 10, 1989, in the Brooks Range. However, I was injured in an accident at home. Rather than cancel, we decided to postpone the hunt for a couple of weeks until I was physically fit. The Brooks Range would be out of the question by then but Scott convinced me that an exploration in the Alaska Range was worth the trip.

I met Scott and Bettina, his wife and able assistant, in Anchorage on August 17, 1989, amidst heavy rain and wind. We spent two days pinned down by a deluge that would have made Noah nervous. Finally, early on the 19th, the rain eased just enough to allow our bush pilot to fly us into the uncontrolled area of the Alaska Range where we were to hunt. We were so relieved to be under way that we did not much mind the cold and bumpy ride.

Landing in the area of the Hartman drainage, we began to set up camp in the alders for protection against the constant storms. The river was rain-swollen and dangerous, so we felt it safer to camp above the high water mark of the spring floods.

Scott, Bettina and I set off in the continuing rain to scout the main drainage. While glassing, we spotted what I judged to be about a 38 inch ram. He was just below the cloud line. Scott and I were convinced that we could do better but we designated the ram as a backup target in case our further explorations were unproductive. The following day, wind and rain kept us in camp.

On the 20th, the weather cleared enough for us to set out on our backpack hunt. From the 20th through the 23rd, we covered the entire area within a radius of approximately 10 miles from our base camp. We also encountered grizzly, black bear and several moose. Late on the 23rd, we headed back toward base camp. On the way down the mountain, we kept an eye out for our 38-inch backup ram, but he was nowhere to be seen.

The rain, which had continued intermittently since we first arrived, was again becoming heavy. We crossed waist-high water that soaked our clothes and then made a discovery that dampened our spirits as well. As we approached camp, we saw that a resident plane was tied and the party had set up camp across the way from ours. They returned later that night and said they had not seen any rams that day.

Deciding that the drainage was not big enough for both of us, Scott radioed our pilot to come in and move us to a new area. The pilot said he would let us know when and if he could make it in due to the rotten weather conditions.

We had brought food for a ten day hunt, and our provisions were running low on the eighth day. The next day, the residents shot a caribou and offered us the liver, which was gratefully accepted. On the 10th day, I shot a caribou, and there was fresh meat in camp. Throughout the whole time, the weather had us pinned in camp and not a single sheep was seen.

I should mention here that we were then in the 10th day of what was planned to be a 10 day hunt. Scott and Bettina were willing to stretch it out a few days longer and I gratefully accepted their offer.

On the morning of August 28th our pilot decided to pluck us out in spite of the continuing downpour. He flew in under the cloud cover, dropped down to pick us up, and deposited us some five to 10 miles downriver.

Later that afternoon, the new camp was made and our enthusiasm returned. Bettina looked across the river and thought she saw up to five sheep fading in and out of the fog. She felt one of them would be over 40 inches. I was unwilling to attempt a crossing with the river at flood stage. If you had seen the small yellow raft that we had to use for the crossing, you would understand my caution.

The following day, we crowded into our little yellow raft, paddled across the less-than-calm water, and the ascent began. From there, we made the tough, slow, bruising climb up a creekbed densely overgrown with willows, devil's club and alders. I was not fully recovered from my earlier injury and was nearing the point of physical and mental exhaustion. As I watched Bettina forge ahead without faltering, I was both embarrassed and inspired by her stamina. And so we struggled on.

Around 11:00 a.m., we broke through the worst of it, and the ground was no longer brush-choked. We had reached sheep country. Shortly thereafter, we glassed some sheep, up where a small canyon opened into an alpine basin of sorts. There were several rams, one of which I judged to be over 40 inches. We set up the spotting scope to get a better look and we spotted five more rams at the head of the main drainage.

At that point, Scott and I planned our stalk and set off with Bettina to go around the back side of the mountain. We topped out after climbing several hundred feet. Scott then scooted out over a ledge to glass the sheep from a distance of about 800 yards. Scott turned to me, a little wide-eyed, and said that the 40-incher we had spotted was not the biggest in the group. There was a much bigger ram bedded down to the left of him.

In a small ravine was a ram that had appeared in my dreams. The heavy horns had to be in excess of 43 inches, and they curled beyond his ears. For the next several minutes, we took turns with the glasses while we discussed how to get closer. The adrenaline was pumping, and the tired legs were a distant memory. We mapped out a route that would take us to within 300 to 350 yards of our quarry.

At 4:00 p.m., there was a total of eight rams in the group, including the big ram. He was bedded, facing away from me. I did not feel comfortable about trying a long shot in those wind conditions.

About 5:30, three small rams got up from the main group and began grazing. They went across the basin and then came back to within 200 yards of me, on the far side of a little knob. The big ram stood once, stretched, and then went back down.

Shortly after 6:00, the big ram rose and began to graze toward us and the knob. When the knob obscured him from our vision, Scott and I ran to the outcrop to cut the distance down. The final few feet, over the wet shale, still had to be traversed before I would see the sheep.

Scott started our final crawl. The three smaller rams just looked at us and did not spook or alarm the big one. There, about 150 yards away, the big ram was grazing toward us. His head came up and he looked right at the intruders to his secret basin. The crosshairs settled on the "sticking pin" spot and a moment later, the .300 Weatherby Magnum roared. The great ram was down.

We had less than an hour and a half until sunset, and we had to get off the mountain with the ram. As we hurriedly caped the ram, Bettina took a tape to the horns. "Carl, they're both over 44 inches! Congratulations!"

The ram of my dreams was mine. We packed off the mountain, arriving at the riverbank at about 11:00 p.m. We stopped there for the night, because we did not want to attempt a river crossing in the dark. After dawn, we climbed into our little toy boat with the added burden of 150 pounds of sheep and paddled across the river.

We arrived at camp around 8:00 a.m., and I was finally relaxed enough to take another look at the horns. I ran the tape around the horns and came up with 46 inches. He one of the most magnificent rams to come out of Alaska in almost 20 years.

The next day, we radioed for our pilot and broke camp. The sky was still ugly and the flight there, according to the pilot, was "next to horrible." The flight out was worse. Take my word for it. But somewhere amidst all the trials and tribulations, somewhere between the bumps and bruises, somewhere between downpour and deluge, the clouds parted briefly, and Diana, Goddess of the Hunt, smiled upon us.

Photograph Courtesy of Robert A. Klicker

COUGAR
FIRST AWARD
SCORE: 15-14/16

Locality: Walla Walla Co., Wash.   Date: 1988
Hunter: Robert A. Klicker

COUGAR 15-14/16

Robert A. Klicker

December 17, 1989 was one of those beautiful, relaxing Saturdays that are just right for a short hunt. It was also a good time to check the mountain for cougar tracks. We had traveled about two miles in our hunting area and were going through timber when Claude Scott said, "Whoa! I believe I saw a fresh cougar track. Let's use Murphy. He's my best tracking dog."

He put the dog on a leash and down through the timber we went. Shortly, Murphy started baying and Claude turned him loose. You could hear him bay as he went down the canyon, up over the ridge, down through another canyon, and over another ridge. We traveled two-and-a-half miles before we heard sounds indicating where he had treed the cougar, about a half-mile down in Sheep Springs Canyon.

With a foot of snow under foot, I followed behind my son Mark and Claude, our guide, and two more dogs as we worked our way down through brush and large timber. I took the lower trail and about 100 yards before I reached the tree, I started following huge cougar tracks. My heart started racing, and the adrenaline shot through my body.

As I came into a small open space, Mark and Claude said, "A big cougar is just above you on the bottom limb of the fir tree! Climb up the hill quickly, because if you shoot from there he will leap on you."

While climbing up the hill, I felt scared as I looked up about 20 feet into the tree to see him hunched on a limb. Just as I turned around, the cougar was ready to leave the tree. Claude ordered, "Shoot now!"

I shot, and the cougar leaped out of the tree, landing on the spot where I had been just 30 seconds before. The big cat took one more leap and disappeared.

Claude yelled, "Turn the dogs loose!"

With that command, the dogs knocked me down as they frantically took off after the cougar. I picked myself up out of the snow and ran through the brush after Mark, Claude, and the dogs. Fifty yards down the hill, I came upon the dogs. They were chewing on a dead cougar and as I approached, Claude exclaimed, "Wow! He's a good one!"

After the dogs had chewed on the cougar for a few minutes and we had calmed down, Mark climbed back up the mountain, then drove 12 miles off Klicker Mountain and back up the canyon. Meanwhile, Claude and I pulled the cougar a mile down the canyon to meet him.

I was born and raised on my Grandmother Klicker's homestead on Mill Creek in the Blue Mountains, 14 miles east of Walla Walla, Washington. Klicker Mountain is where my grandfather's and my father's homesteads are located. Eventually, the Klickers bought the surrounding mountain land, which now pastures cattle in the summer and elk and deer in the winter. During the past 64 years, while raising cattle on the land, it has been my home and hunting paradise. It was always exciting to watch other hunters bag trophy elk, deer or bear, but I had no desire to shoot a trophy. All I wanted was a spike elk for good eating.

In the last few years our cougar population has increased dramatically and because a mature cougar will kill a deer or an elk or a domestic calf each week, I decided I would apply for a cougar tag and help protect our wildlife and cattle. We knew of at least nine different cougar in our 10 mile area.

Also, when I was ten years old, three of us boys had been stalked and screamed at by a cougar in a deep canyon. This, of course, scared us so badly that we didn't go back to that location for two years. It was then that I decided that someday I would shoot a cougar. Fifty-two years later I did.

The mounted cougar is now standing in Drumheller's Sporting Goods Store in Walla Walla, Washington. There, everyone can see a mature cougar with its majestic beauty and impressive size.

I will always remember this powerful cougar as it leaped out of the tree and, with one more leap, disappeared. He was a beautiful animal and one to respect. Now as I hunt, ride for cattle, or cruise timber, I always watch the low limbs in the trees and periodically glance behind me. Quite often, I get the feeling that I am being watched, and the feeling causes the hair on my arms to stand on end.

Photograph courtesy of Rick Bergholm

On his bow hunt, Rick Bergholm killed this cougar in Bear Lake County, Idaho, in 1990. It scored 14-15/16.

Photograph courtesy of Darrell G. Holmquist

Darrell G. Holmquist hunted in Shoshone County, Idaho, in 1990 to find this cougar that scored 15-4/16.

Photograph courtesy of Donald G. Thurston

This cougar, 15-5/16, was killed in Boise County,
Idaho, in 1991 by Donald G. Thurston.

Photograph courtesy of Ed J. Strayhorn

Ed J. Strayhorn killed this cougar in Elmore County, Idaho, in 1989.
It scored 15 points.

COUGAR 15-11/16

SECOND AWARD

Layne K. Wing

It was January 15, 1990, and I had found the same huge lion track for the fourth time in about six weeks. The first time I cut the track in the Sheep Creek drainage early in December of 1989, I felt that it was four to five days old and did not even turn the dogs loose on it.

The second time I found the track, on January 6, 1990, it was again in Sheep Creek, and I estimated it to be two or three days old, so I decided to see if the dogs could work it out. I put two of my Walker hounds, Daisy and Buck, on the track and they cold-trailed it for approximately two miles before losing it. Snow conditions were poor and a large herd of elk wintering in the area had obliterated any sign that was left.

The third time, on January 11, it was leaving the Sheep Creek drainage and heading northwest toward the base of "W" Mountain. I was checking bobcat traps and had brought three hounds with me just in case I found a lion track. It was 2:00 in the afternoon and the skiff of snow that had fallen the night before had all but disappeared from the south-facing slopes. The dogs, Daisy, Buck and Ben, cold-trailed slowly across the open, rocky ground but they made fairly good time when the track moved around to the shaded, north side of a slope or down into a creek bottom. They were progressing steadily and I felt they had a decent chance of jumping the lion before nightfall if he had not traveled too far. But it was not to be that day either. Darkness overtook me and the dogs on a cold, windswept ridge, so I called them in and started the long walk back to the truck. I was beginning to wonder if I would ever get a look at the lion that was leaving his enormous tracks in the terrain east of my house.

As I mentioned at the beginning, I found the track again on January 15, 1990. It had snowed about half an inch the night before, and I was checking coyote and bobcat traps in the Sheep Creek drainage when I came upon the huge lion tracks for the fourth time. I hadn't brought any hounds with me that day. I had planned to check my traps and hurry home to get some other work done. But when I saw those tracks, my plans changed in a hurry. I quickly checked the last few sets and made a beeline home to pick up a few hounds.

I let Buck and Daisy out of the kennel, loaded them in the dog box, and was back to the track by 12:20 p.m. When I unloaded them from the truck, they stuck their noses in the track and let me know that they were going to do their best to put this big bruiser up a tree so I could get a look at him.

They quickly disappeared up and over the first ridge, so I shouldered my day pack, strapped on my Smith and Wesson .357 Magnum revolver, and started the long climb to the ridge top. When I made it to the top, I stopped to listen. I could hear the dogs. They were still moving and about to go out of hearing over another ridge. The excitement of the chase was building as I hurried to the bottom of the canyon and started up the other side.

Just before the dogs went over the second ridge, I heard all hell break loose and knew they had jumped the lion. I knew that when I made it to the top of the ridge, I would be treated to the music that every houndsman loves to hear, the sound of hounds treed up solid, the sound of hounds saying, "C'mon boss, we've got him."

When I got to the tree at 2:45 p.m., Daisy and Buck were doing their job perfectly. They were standing on the tree, looking up and barking with every breath. After admiring them for a few seconds, my attention shifted to the lion. He was standing on a large limb, about 20 feet up in the Douglas fir.

What a sight to behold: a huge tom, snarling defiantly at his pursuers. I moved back from the tree, cleared some snow from a fallen limb, and sat down to take it all in. I was greatly impressed by the size of the lion and decided to take him. At the time, I really did not think he would make the records book but I felt he would be close.

I tied the dogs back out of the way and brought the revolver up slowly. As the sights settled on his chest, I cocked the hammer and squeezed the trigger, sending the 158-grain bullet on its way. At the impact, the lion climbed higher in the tree, so I fired a second round and down he came.

I took some pictures of him and the dogs, then started skinning. It was almost dark by the time I finished, and I still had to walk back to the truck. It was a long hike but I was literally skipping along, praising the dogs and feeling very lucky. I got home at 9:00 p.m., took care of the dogs, ate dinner, and fell asleep thinking about the day's hunt.

The next day, I took the hide and head to Slim's Taxidermy in Glenwood Springs, where owner Don Waechtler said that he felt that the lion would make the book.

After the drying period, Hal Burdick, an official measurer for the Boone and Crockett Club, scored the skull at 15-11/16".

Photograph courtesy of David K. Mueller

This cougar was killed in Shoshone County, Idaho, by
David K. Mueller in 1988. It scored 15-1/16.

Photograph courtesy of Kendall Hamilton

Montrose County, Colorado, was setting for this cougar killed in
1988 by Kendall Hamilton. It scored 15-8/16.

Photograph Courtesy of Randy L. Waddell

COUGAR
THIRD AWARD
SCORE: 15-9/16

Locality: Idaho Co., Idaho   Date: 1990
Hunter: Randy L. Waddell

COUGAR 15-9/16

Randy L. Waddell

As a hunter, you always dream of that perfect hunt where you will bag the big buck with huge antlers or the monstrous 6x6 bull elk. In my case it started when I was seven years old. My father would take me to the local hardware store, where the owner had huge bull moose, elk, bear and caribou hanging from his wall. From that experience and my first Daisy BB gun, I was hooked on the sport of hunting. Little did I know that some 22 years later, I would even be considered for one of the greatest thrills a hunter could ever wish for: recognition in the Boone and Crockett records books.

For the past ten years I have had some great hunts and some great opportunities to hunt big game. I have taken elk, caribou, whitetail, mule deer, pronghorn, black bear and wild turkey with a bow and a rifle. All were trophies in my mind, and each animal was very special to me, especially the mountain lion I bagged on February 4, 1990.

I planned for almost a year in advance to hunt with an outfitter in Idaho. I had heard a lot of good things about him, and I was interested in hunting cougar. After a few phone calls to Rick Hussey, owner and operator of Quarter Circle A Outfitters in Salmon, Idaho, I booked the hunt for February 1990.

After practicing through the fall and winter with my bow, we left Pittsburgh Airport on January 30, 1990, and landed in Missoula, Montana, that same evening. A bad snowstorm stranded all airplanes for the next 24 hours at Missoula. The storm finally broke and we left Missoula on February 1, flying into the Selway. This was an experience on a very small plane with skis on the landing gear.

A couple of hours later, we landed on a homemade runway at Rick Hussey's tent camp in the Selway Wilderness. Roy and I were ready to go. With two feet of snow on the ground, and most of it fresh, all we wanted to see were tracks.

We unloaded our gear and met Rick Hussey and dog handler Les Udy. We followed Rick up a snow-packed trail to see the tent where we would be staying for the next seven days. We heard the three Plott hounds bellowing and barking down below the tent. They knew what was happening. Soon, it would be time to hit the trail and they wanted to go.

Rick and Les told us of fresh tracks they had found earlier that morning, not too far from the tent camp. "What are we waiting for?" I asked. We got our gear all unpacked and got settled in, put our hunting gear on, took some practice shots with our bows, and took off.

We hit the tracks a half-hour after we left the tent camp. The dogs were barking treed not too far from us. When we got there, the dogs had a beautiful 7-foot female treed. Roy and I flipped for the shot and I won but deferred to him. I was after a tom.

Roy was pleased and prepared for a shot. The cougar fell fast as Roy placed a beautiful shot through both lungs. The cat expired within seconds of the shot.

What a day. We had just arrived, and within three hours we had a mountain lion. Back at camp we skinned Roy's cat, got something to eat, talked a lot about what was ahead, then went to sleep.

After a restless night, we got up early, ate breakfast, and got ready to go hunting. After hiking all morning, afternoon and evening over rock ledges, mountains, valleys and river bottoms, we had cut only old tracks. Rick and Less thought it would be best to go back to camp, rest up, and go out the next day.

We followed the same routine, ate breakfast and then went hunting. It was dinner time before we knew it. We sat down and ate some sandwiches. Again, all the tracks we had been seeing were old. Rick decided to split-up and try to find fresh tracks before dark.

Roy and Les went up one valley, while Rick and I headed for a place called Crow's Nest. Halfway up the valley, Rick and I could not believe our eyes. Rick yelled, "What a track. Look at the size of the track."

I was excited, but by then it was late, very late. Rick decided to go back to the tent camp, rest up, regroup and get on the track first thing in the morning.

I will never forget what happened on February 4, 1990. I did not sleep the night before because of the size of the track we had found. I worried if the track would still be there. Would it snow over them, or rain? Finally it was morning, and the weather was nice — no rain and no snow. I was ready to go.

We left camp with the dogs, our back packs, and a lot of anticipation. As we climbed the same valley we had left the night before, I could not wait to see the track. Rick said, "There it is."

The dogs got a whiff of that cat and went nuts. They wanted to get after that cat badly. Rick unleashed those Plott dogs, and they were gone.

We followed the dog and cat tracks for five hours. I was exhausted, along with Rick, Les and Roy. All of a sudden, down in a valley, Les said "Listen, listen, the dogs are barking treed."

It sounded so far off, and after all that time of going up hills, down hills and sideways, I wondered if this was it. My heart pumped more with joy than from fatigue. Off we went to the sound of those beautiful, barking dogs.

It took us awhile to get to that enormous pine tree, but we made it. Words cannot describe what I saw on the side of that mountain. I had to stop to get my breath and gaze at that huge cat. I have never seen anything like it.

There he was, a huge male mountain lion. Rick was yelling at me to get where I had a good shot. I found it on the side of that snowy hillside. I pulled my bow off my side and drew an arrow out of my quiver. I rested and shot, a clean miss. The cat was treed about 70 feet up in the huge pine. I drew another arrow and shot, another clean miss. I began to wonder what was wrong. Back home, I had practiced so much, and it was an easy shot. As I drew back the third time, I aimed lower. Both of the previous shots had been about a foot high. I made a mental calculation and shot. It was a hit, right through both of his lungs. The cat scrambled high into the tree. I was hoping he would not go up there and die. He did not present another good shot. I knew the cat was getting weaker, but he was so high, with branches all around him. I shot the fourth arrow at him, just to make him move. He moved all right, straight down, fast and hard.

Rick Hussey was standing right beside me. He yelled, "Randy, shoot him, shoot him, not with your bow." With this, he handed me a Ruger .22 Magnum.

Like lightning, the mountain lion was at the base of the tree. Things were happening fast. I aimed and shot, hitting the cat square in the chest and killing him instantly. It was over. What a mountain lion!

Rick later said, "Randy, I wanted that big, ole boy dead fast, and that is why I handed you the pistol."

Rick knew what that cat was capable of doing, especially with an arrow through both lungs. Sure, I would have sooner let him die with just another arrow or let him expire on his own, but at that big pine tree we only had seconds. At the time, we were not thinking about records books.

I was curious why I had missed the cat on the first two shots. Back at camp, I discovered that my sight pin was bent. You could not notice it by looking at it, but rolling it on a flat surface revealed the problem. Somewhere during that long, hard hike after that tremendous cat I had bumped the sight pin on my bow.

Records books never crossed our minds until we began looking at how huge this cat really was. Back at camp, we rough-measured the cat's skull and came up with approximately 16 inches. He was 8-1/2-feet long and he weighed 190 pounds. It was remarkable, especially when the huge lion was placed next to my buddy's 100 pound female. We knew that 16 inches would put him very high in the records books.

Clouds moved into the valley of our tent camp and it began to snow. The fog came in and it was very hard to see. We were stranded for four more days. The weather was so bad that the plane could not fly. To pass time, we took hikes and talked a lot and ate often.

After bringing the skull back home and letting it dry for 70 days, I had it officially scored in Harrisburg, Pennsylvania, by Carl Graybill of the Pennsylvania Game Commission. The score was 15-9/16, placing it third or fourth in the world, Pope and Young. It should also rank in the top 15 of Boone and Crockett.

I am very thankful for my mountain lion. The trip will always be remembered as a once-in-a-lifetime hunt, and I am glad I was able to share it with you.

Photograph Courtesy of John Cassidy

COUGAR
CERTIFICATE OF MERIT
SCORE: 15-11/16
Locality: Fisher Creek, Alta.   Date: 1985
Hunter: John Cassidy

COUGAR 15-11/16

John Cassidy

This hunting story must start from the very beginning. My father and I would go west of Calgary for Christmas trees every year, and while in the area we would stop in on Dad's old hunting partner, Ole Olson. Ole ran a saw mill and hunted cats.

One day we arrived to find three cats hanging on Ole's shed. With his Norwegian accent, he said, "Jon, come in and I'll tell you all about them."

As a 14-year-old boy, I was hooked on cat hunting right there and then.

At that time cougars were considered predators and Ole hunted them for a bounty paid by the Alberta government. Years later I got my first hound. I thought I would tree every cat in the country. Three years later, I managed to tree my first cat, a female, and it was back to Ole for more advice, time and time again.

On one of my visits, Ole introduced me to a young sawyer named Mark Tannas. He also had the "cat bug." From that day on, Mark and I teamed up and guided for more than 60 cougar, five of which made the Boone and Crockett records book. The largest cat, killed by Bob Bryant from Stoney Plain, Alberta, scored 16-1/16 (Boone and Crockett, 15-14/16) while still green.

To get down to the story at hand, it happened a few years ago, but you never forget. Mark and I had spotted a track going south on the Fallen Timber Road. Looking at the 3-1/2 inch pad, we knew it was definitely a large tom. He was heading into an area without roads or cutlines to follow. The track was no more than two days old.

I turned to Mark and said, "This might be a long day."

Lions can travel great distances overnight. We tracked him for three or four miles and then let the hounds go. They could cover more ground without us hanging on to them.

The hounds, three redbones—Trapper, Sounder, and Mark's young dog T.G.—went straight south, moving eagerly on the track. We followed all day.

With only two hours of daylight left, Mark said, "We can't hear the hounds. Let's call it a day and start fresh tomorrow."

Back at the truck, I left my jacket for the hounds if they decided to come back. Stiff and sore, we got back to the ranch at 11:30 that evening.

The next morning, we awoke to a fresh snow fall. "Damn it," Mark said, "We'll be lucky to find the hounds."

We loaded the snowmobiles and headed up the road. When we arrived at the drop off point, we found three tired hounds curled on my coat. They were weary and glad to get back in the truck, fully anticipating a warm bed and a long rest.

By then we had at least two inches of snow on the ground, and it was still coming down. The cat hunting was over for that day and we headed home.

The truck tracks were already filling with snow when Mark hollered, "Whoa."

I already had the brakes on; we had both seen the track at the same time. A large male, 3-1/4-inch pad, smoking hot, had just crossed the road. We had to coax the stiff hounds out of the vehicle, but once on the cat track, they needed no coaxing.

The chase was on. Straight up the ridge they went, with T.G. way out in front. What a racket!

"They've got him lined out," I said. "I think they've topped the ridge."

Close to the top, I asked Mark to stop the machine so I could listen for the dogs. Much to our amazement the dogs were barking less than twenty feet away. It was one of those easy ones. On another hunt, we tracked a tom for seven days — he never made a kill and we never got him either.

My tom had run up a broken poplar. He was only 6 feet off the ground. The hounds were whirling around right under him.

"Mark," I said, "get those hounds before the cat gets them."

"You get them. I'm not going under there," he replied.

I coaxed them out, one by one, and tied them up. The tom looked down from his low perch. Why he didn't bail out, I'll never know. We studied him for what seemed like an eternity, admiring his size and tawny red color. He had porcupine quills on one side of his face, and the tip of one ear was frozen off, but he was otherwise unblemished and magnificent.

Some old toms are pretty beat up from fighting other toms. They lose their ears and tails to freezing, and they are injured by hooves and horns. Sometimes they get slammed into trees while pulling down their prey; some are even killed.

I killed this tom at twenty feet with a .264 Winchester Magnum, one shot through the lungs. He ran 75 yards. He scored 15-11/16, Boone and Crockett. He was 7 feet 8 inches in length and weighed 165 pounds. I have weighed lots of cats. Males usually weigh between 135 and 145 pounds; females will ordinarily scale from 95 to 110 pounds. The only tracks we follow are those over 2-1/2 inches, and the probability of treeing only males is very high.

We had just loaded up when two men who were working at the government ranch that supplies horses for the Banff National Park, stopped to talk. One of them, a man named Cal Hayes, said, "That's the biggest cat I've ever seen." He was glad his horses wouldn't be bothered by the cat again.

Cougars are very good at killing their prey, which can be anything from a 3 pound rabbit to a 1,200 pound moose. One tom we got killed two whitetail fawns, a coyote and a cow elk in a three day period.

I could go on and on about this magnificent green-eyed predator, which I believe to be one of North America's finest trophies. By the way, the tom with the 3-1/2-inch pad that was going into the roadless area is still roaming out there somewhere. I hope we will cross paths again.

Photograph Courtesy of Loren C. Nodolf

BLACK BEAR
FIRST AWARD
SCORE: 22-13/16
Locality: Ventura Co., Calif.   Date: 1990
Hunter: Loren C. Nodolf

BLACK BEAR 22-13/16

Loren C. Nodolf

I started bear hunting in the spring of 1985 in Wyoming. My hunting partner, Bob Carlson, and I learned a lot about bears that year. In 1986 I harvested a nice spring trophy.

In September of 1990, I applied for the $18.50 bear tag in California, knowing the outcome depended upon a court decision in October. The previous year's hunt had been stopped by anti-hunters. Needless to say, I was excited when my tag came in the mail.

My plan was to hunt locally in Ventura County by glassing hillsides and still-hunting. Using a backpack allows me to carry enough food, water and gear for a full day of hunting; it also gives me the option of camping overnight, if necessary.

My first few trips in the field produced no sightings and I found little fresh sign. I did not expect quick success, because less than 10 percent of bears harvested are taken without dogs.

My friend, Tim Batta, and I were reloading ammunition for my Ruger Model 77 in .300 Winchester Magnum in preparation for hunting the next day. My load of choice is the 150-grain Nosler Partition bullet with 76 grains of Accurate 3100. Tim had a deer tag for Area D-13 and suggested I hunt this area for bear, too.

The morning of October 28th was dark and quiet as we pulled into the campground a few miles from Interstate 5 in the Los Padres National Forest. We loaded our backpacks and got out a flashlight as we prepared to leave the vehicle. The sun was coming up when an hour later we came to a trail junction. Tim stayed back, glassing some ridges, while I headed up a trail that wound along the side of a hill. I was optimistic, since bear scat and tracks were plentiful.

Still-hunting along, I heard some rustling in the ravine below me. Manzanita and brush prevented me from seeing the source of the noise coming from under a large oak tree. It had to be a bear eating acorns, I thought. I watched a small clearing below the tree and waited.

About 10 minutes later, the sounds of breaking branches stopped and a large bear swaggered into the clearing. Its brown coat rippled and shimmered as it moved. I squeezed off a 75 yard shot, aiming behind its shoulder. The bear's head looked as big as a bushel basket as it spun around and went back into the brush. I knew it was a good hit and the sound of labored breathing quickly ceased.

I picked my way down the ravine and found the dead bear about 30 feet from where I had shot him. His sheer size and large head amazed me. I knew he would be a special bear for me.

The work had only begun. Skinning the 8 foot bear took me most of two hours. Tying the hide to my packframe, I crawled into the straps as the pack rested on the ground. Tim assisted me to my feet and loaded the rest of my gear and water on his pack. We made frequent stops during the four mile hike back to the pickup because the temperature had warmed to 80 degrees. Later that night, with the help of three friends, we salvaged as much meat as we could carry.

After the drying period, a measurer scored the skull at 22-11/16. Placing a trophy near the top in Boone & Crockett's records book has been a dream come true for me. The bear's life-size mount is on loan to the club's National Collection of Heads and Horns in Cody, Wyoming. My special bear also allowed me to receive the 1991 Leatherstocking Award from the National Rifle Association.

I know the 21st Awards banquet and the chance to talk with other trophy owners will be memorable experiences.

BLACK BEAR 22-2/16

SECOND AWARD (TIE)

Craig N. Beachy

To tell the truth, this is not much of a hunting story because I was not really hunting.

I have lived in the village of Port Clements on Graham Island, one of the Queen Charlotte Islands, for 15 years. From time to time while going to and from work in the bush, I see black bear. Once in a while, I have seen really big black bears, the kind that look as tall as the hood of my Ford 4x4 when they cross a logging road in front of me. So for the last 10 years or so I have bought a bear tag, just in case I get an opportunity to get a good shot at one of those big ones.

I finally got my chance. It was a Sunday afternoon in June of 1988. My father, Glen Beachy, two friends, Kurt Saffarek and Henry Reimer, and I drove to the Honna River road to take a look at a bridge building job. Henry brought his rifle along, just in case we saw a deer or a bear.

On the way home, we were passing a logging slash and there he was, one of the biggest black bears I have ever seen. Henry said, "There is a record book bear, if you want one," and passed me the rifle.

His rifle was a 7mm Remington Magnum loaded with 168-grain Sierra Match King handloads. I got out of the truck, put the crosshairs on his chest, and pulled the trigger. The bear collapsed and did not even move.

When I got it home and cleaned the skull enough to get a rough score, I realized it was even bigger than I had thought. I finally had the bear I had been waiting for.

Photograph courtesy of Gary G. Dumdei

This black bear was killed by Gary G. Dumdei by the Smoky River,
Alta., in 1989, and it scored 21-7/16.

Photograph courtesy of Rodney S. Petrychyn

Rodney S. Petrychyn was hunting in Canora, Sask., when he killed this
black bear in 1991. It scored 21-3/16.

BLACK BEAR 22-2/16

SECOND AWARD (TIE)

Danny R. Thomas

I live in Glennville, a small town northeast of Bakersfield, California, which has a population of 103. I have been shooting and small game hunting, off and on, for most of my life. But I did not begin to big game hunt until 1980. I have killed a few bucks with both rifle and archery equipment. I was even lucky enough to draw a pronghorn tag in 1984 and was successful with a 14-6/8-inch buck. That, along with hunting elk, mule deer and bear, had always been a dream of mine.

This brings me to my bear hunt. In between my hunting trips, work, and chores around the house, I find time to cut firewood. Early in 1988 while cutting wood, I began noticing a lot of bear sign, more than I ever had before. I even saw a couple of bears. I decided to apply for a bear tag again. I had applied several times before but had never been successful in taking a bear. And, although I had never dreamed of having the chance to shoot a records book animal in any category, on October 28, 1988, it happened.

My friend Scott McGowan and I went hunting for bear that day. We spent most of the day walking ridges and checking draws around the area where I had seen bear sign. We did not find any bears or fresh sign.

The day was starting to come to an end, so we made our way back to my truck. We wanted to go check-out another area before the end of the day. We were driving into that area when I noticed a bear walking on a small ridge, about 130 yards away.

I stopped the truck, got out and grabbed my rifle from the back of the truck. I loaded it and looked back toward the bear. He was walking along, then he stopped and looked in our direction. I brought my rifle up and took careful aim. The bear just stood there. I squeezed off the shot and the bear dropped. He did not move at all. The shot was placed between the shoulder and the neck.

I had never shot a bear nor had I been around anyone who had shot one, but I had been told some pretty exciting stories. To be truthful, I was very shocked that he did not even move. I shoot a .270 Winchester with 150-grain Speer boat-tail softpoint handloads and they worked fine.

Scott and I made our way up to the bear. It was a very tense and exciting moment. I reached out and nudged the bear with my rifle. He did not move. I handed Scott my rifle, then reached out and touched the bear with my hand. He moved down the hill a little and made a grumbling sound. We both jumped back but he was dead.

Scott and I were able to get him loaded into my Toyota truck. He filled up the whole bed. We took him by Jeff Bowen's house. Jeff suggested that we weigh the bear on the nearby cattle scales. Off we went. The bear weighed in at 402 pounds.

From there, we took him in for skinning. I wanted to make a rug of the hide, so we were careful skinning it. I decided to leave the skull in the hide. Neither of us had ever caped a bear out and I did not want it ruined.

The next day at work, I talked to a friend of mine, Dave Tilly, who did taxidermy on the side as a hobby. I asked him if he would come up and show us how to cape the bear. He did, and that is when the first mention of Boone and Crockett came up. When Dave got the skull out he said, "This is a good-size bear. It might be close to making the book."

I got excited and asked him how to check it. He told me to clean the skull, measure the length and width, and add them together. Jeff and I cleaned it, then took some outside calipers and measured it. We came up with 22-8/16 inches. At the time, we still did not know what the minimum score for the records book was.

I went to work the next day and told Dave about our measurements. He replied, "No way. Twenty inches is the minimum for the book." I went home that night to recheck it and came up with the same thing. The next day I told Dave and he still did not believe it. He came up and checked it himself. His measurements matched ours.

I went to a gun shop in Bakersfield and looked at the Boone and Crockett records book there. The score of 22-8/16 ranked very high among the 170 bears listed.

I had to wait for the drying time to pass before having the skull officially scored. Meanwhile, I began searching for an official scorer.

I located one about 300 miles away. While at work one day, I was talking with a friend, Gary Powers, who was getting ready to go up that way on a vacation. I asked if he would take the skull and have it re-measured. He did, and when he returned, I was tickled to death to find out it measured 22-1/16 inches.

I sent my score off to Boone and Crockett and, to my surprise, received a certificate of entry. The accompanying letter stated that if the score was high enough at the end of the entry period, I could be invited to a banquet. I never thought it would happen, but I was very proud of my entry certificate.

On March 2, 1992, I received a package from Boone and Crockett with an invitation to the banquet. They asked me to send the skull for final measurement. I was nervous about that, to say the least. Milwaukee a long way from my home in California, so I was very hesitant. Nevertheless, I sent it off.

Last week, I received the official confirmation of my final score for black bear skull. I was amazed to learn that it measured 1/16 inch larger than the entry measurement.

I am very excited about going to Milwaukee to see the skull on display with all the other fine trophies. It may seem that I take full credit for all my hunting successes, but I do not. I give all the glory to God. He guides and leads me each day, and I praise Him for the success he has given me.

Photograph courtesy of Patrick G. Povah

While hunting in the Pasquia Hills, Sask., in 1989, Patrick G. Povah
took this black bear. It scores 21-4/16.

Photograph courtesy of Tim P. Matzinger

Prairie River, Sask., was the place where Tim P. Matzinger took
this black bear, in 1989. It scored 21-10/16.

Photograph Courtesy of Steven J. Stayner

BLACK BEAR
THIRD AWARD
SCORE: 22

Locality: Gila Co., Ariz.   Date: 1991
Hunter: Steven J. Stayner

BLACK BEAR 22

Steven J. Stayner

The black bear is a magnificent and noble animal. He is difficult and challenging to hunt when met on his own ground, especially when you are not using dogs or bait. If you throw in a self-imposed requirement of taking a trophy class animal or nothing at all, you have exciting possibilities.

Early August of 1991 found me scouting in the rugged mountains of central Arizona. Each weekend, I headed out with a couple of different friends. We would backpack to get away from the roads and then find a high spot from which to glass. We had run-ins with gnats, mosquitoes, scorpions, rattlesnakes and sunburn, but saw no bears. The country was steep, rough and incredibly brushy, which made it difficult to see. The sign was there in the canyon bottoms however, and we did not lose faith.

When the season opened in September, my good friend Glade Taylor and I started hunting in earnest. We backpacked into canyon after canyon. We were seeing bears, but for one reason or another, we could never get to them. The distances and terrain were such that we always seemed to run out of time.

Finally, we packed onto a long, high ridge that was cut with canyons that ran to the north. It was a long, up-hill hike of about six hours. The weather was so hot that we were exhausted by the time we rolled out our bags to make camp on a point between two canyons. We set up our binoculars on tripods and glassed until dark but saw nothing except a couple of good Coues' deer bucks.

The next morning was a repeat of the previous evening. Nothing. After a mid-morning lunch, we packed in another couple of hours and set up once again with two canyons to glass. Glade and I decided to split-up and cover different areas. I went a half-mile or so to the southeast and put up the tripod where the canyon made a big bend.

It was about 4:00 p.m. when I spotted him. He was in a little clearing at the bottom of the canyon, about a mile away. I took the binocular off the tripod and snapped on the spotting scope. He looked big. He was tall as well as wide, and every move he made looked as though he was locked in slow motion. His body would roll each time he took a step with that pigeon-toed gait that always seems exaggerated in large bears. The ears were set wide apart and looked small in comparison with his head. He was big.

The bear was feeding and seemed to be going nowhere in particular, but a quick assessment of the terrain made the situation look hopeless. There was a point of rocks down the canyon that would cut the distance in half but the brush was so thick I could not see any way of getting closer.

It took an hour to get down to the rocks I had seen from the top. They turned out to be closer to the bear than I had originally thought. The clearing where the bear had been was about 800 yards below me but the bear was not there. Another half-hour of glassing not only failed to locate the bear but also confirmed the fact that there was no way to get closer, or even gain a better vantage point.

I had not seen the bear for an hour and a half. The afternoon was passing into evening. As a last resort, I took out my predator call and started to blow. After calling for five or six minutes, I saw the bear's head pop up in the scrub oak about 250 yards below. He was in sight for just a couple of seconds as he stood on his hind legs to take a quick look around. He was coming.

I expected him to come up a little ravine to my left, so I set up to shoot in that direction. After 10 more minutes of calling (which seemed like 10 years), he showed up off to my right, 125 yards out. He was down on all fours in one of the few small openings on the entire hillside. Because of the way I was sitting, I had to twist around awkwardly to get on him. The crosshair settled on his chest, and as I touched off the old .30-06, he rolled over backward and ran downhill. All I got was one more hurried shot as he ran through the brush.

There is nothing worse than wounding an animal. As I sat watching the canyon, I was heartsick. The shot had felt good but maybe in the excitement I had pulled off. The only thing to do was go in after him.

At the edge of the opening there was blood. It was a good trail that led down into the canyon. When it hit the bottom, the trail turned upstream. I was going very slowly and watching ahead with about as much intensity as a guy could have. I must admit the adrenalin was flowing. I would not say I was scared, but if a quail had flushed, I might well have fainted.

Suddenly, there he was, 20 yards from me. He was in the middle of the stream, facing away. Only his head presented a clear shot, so I backtracked and went up the side bank to get a better view. When I shot, he fell into the water and never moved.

There was no moving the bear. He was so big I could not budge him. I was not sure what to do and was really happy to hear Glade holler down from the rim. He had heard the shooting, grabbed a backpack, and came looking for me. Between the two of us, we were finally able to roll the big boar onto the stream bank. It was then we discovered the camera was in the other pack, back at camp, so we started skinning, trying to beat the sunset.

The dressing chore took a couple of hours, and our examination of the carcass revealed that the first bullet was a little off center. We found the 150-grain Hornady just behind the last rib on the far side. It had angled through the left shoulder and the back edge of the lungs. The shot taken as he ran through the bushes only made a 3-inch crease across his back. It cut the skin but didn't break it.

It was about 10:30 p.m. when we fought our way back to the top of the ridge by the light of a nearly full moon. We were soaked with sweat and dead tired. After another 45 minutes, we reached camp and fell into our sleeping bags, exhausted.

The next morning, before we started home, we glassed again from camp. Almost immediately, Glade spotted another jet-black bear in the canyon west of us. The spotting scope showed him to be as big as the one we had. The bear was moving, but Glade made a valiant effort to get to him while I stayed on top to give hand signals. It was not to be. He never stopped and was over the top into the next canyon before Glade got to the bottom.

We made our long, hard walk out with the heavy load and the big bear made the Boone and Crockett records book. I'm glad he made the book—he deserved it—but that was only icing. The satisfaction of a good, hard hunt for a magnificent animal is what really makes it worthwhile.

Photograph Courtesy of Theodore Kurdziel, Jr.

WORLD'S RECORD GRIZZLY BEAR (TIE)
FIRST AWARD
SCORE: 27-2/16

Locality: Inglutalik River, Alaska   Date: 1991
Hunter: Theodore Kurdziel, Jr.

GRIZZLY BEAR 27-2/16

Theodore Kurdziel, Jr.

On April 16, most people still have their minds on income taxes. On that day in 1991, I found myself scooting on a snowmobile across the frozen landscape near Koyuk, Alaska, looking for grizzly tracks in the snow. My guide was Steve Brady, and my outfitter was Bob Hannon. I had intended to take my bear with a bow and arrow, and Bob had reluctantly agreed to let me try.

In the morning, Steve and I covered many miles on our snow machines, finding no tracks at all. At about 10 a.m., we came across a huge set of prints. As we strapped on our snowshoes, I pondered whether to carry my bow or my .300 Weatherby Magnum rifle. I decided that a bow would probably not be a wise choice as a weapon, so I left my bow on the snow machine and slung my rifle over my shoulder. Little did I know that this decision would probably save my life.

The tracks were enormous and Steve felt confident that the bear would be exceptionally big. We started tracking and Steve told me to be prepared to hike all day long. The snow was cold and hard and it was easy to walk on the crust, but as the spring sun warmed the Arctic air to about 60 degrees, the snow became mushy.

The ground was relatively flat, with rolling hills covered with spruce or tundra. We followed the tracks like a couple of hounds, pacing ourselves. All of our camping gear was on the snowmobiles.

After five or six hours, we were tired. Steve was continually telling me to stay on his heels, but I had a strange feeling that I wanted to hold back a little. I felt I wanted a better view of the whole situation in case the bear turned and came after us.

Soon, the track started zigzagging and Steve said the bear knew we were on his trail. Steve began crashing through a thicket and I waited, wondering how far the bear was from us.

Suddenly the bear appeared about 40 yards ahead, running for me at full speed. Steve could not see him from his position. The bear, his hackles raised, looked as mad as a guard dog protecting his turf. I shouldered my rifle and found the grizzly in my scope. The only shot I had was at the bear's head, so I held off until the bear was about 20 yards away. At that point, he stumbled momentarily and exposed his chest, and I fired instinctively. The bear spun around like a top and ran uphill, more or less angling toward Steve. I shot again, hitting the bear in the neck.

When we walked up to that mountain of a bear, we were awestruck by his size. I really did not care at that point whether he was a Boone and Crockett bear or not. All I knew was that I had experienced a close-range encounter with one of the most imposing and gorgeous creatures on earth, and I had survived.

GRIZZLY BEAR 26-14/16

SECOND AWARD (TIE)

Denis E. Schiller, hunter
D.E. Schiller & K. Karran, owners

On the evening of May 14, 1990 Ken Karren, my father-in-law, phoned and asked if I wanted to hunt a grizzly bear. Would I? I got excited just thinking about it. I had no idea the bear would bring an added bonus — a spot in the Boone and Crockett records book.

Ken had seen the bear tracks on his newly seeded hay meadow and figured he was a big one. He later spotted the bear about 200 yards from his corrals. That is when he gave me a call.

I left immediately for Ken's ranch which is located 30 miles from Anahim Lake on the Dean River.

About a half-hour after I arrived, while looking out from the living room window, we spotted the bear as he crossed the meadow on the far side of a small creek. He was plodding along, occasionally stopping with his nose in the air, sniffing. Ken had some mares and newborn foals in a field nearby and we wanted to stop him from getting a taste of tender horse meat.

We slowly made our way toward the bear, and from about 100 yards away, I shot him. In no time at all, he was across the water and coming fast. At about 60 yards I fired again. The bear turned and took cover in the thick willow brush. I was not impressed with my .270 rifle.

Ken whistled for his dog Buddy. The small collie came running and Ken told him to "get him out of there," as if the bear had been a range cow hiding in the brush.

Soon, the dog had the bear thrashing through the willows in our direction. Ken quickly put the bear down for good with his lever-action .30-06.

The old boar had only one ear. Some of his teeth were missing or broken. The wildlife department of British Columbia estimated him to have been 28 years old. The skull measured 26-14/16, earning the bear a high place in the Boone and Crockett records book.

Photograph Courtesy of D. Alan McCaleb

GRIZZLY BEAR
SECOND AWARD (TIE)
SCORE: 26-14/16
Locality: Teklanika River, Alaska   Date: 1989
Hunter: D. Alan McCaleb

GRIZZLY BEAR 26-14/16

D. Alan McCaleb

For four years my hunting partner, Butch Killian, and I had seen those bear tracks, the largest we had ever seen while we were moose hunting in the fall.

In the spring we would go back to that area and look for that large bear, or any large grizzly bear, as we knew that there were some big ones around.

We talked about hoping to get just a glimpse of that big bear or having just one crack at shooting it. We sat for hours and got excited like all hunters do about the prospect of shooting a trophy size bear.

My partner and I have hunted big game together in Alaska for 10 years, and during that time, we have bagged a number of trophy-size animals. We are both avid hunters and have lived in Alaska most of our lives. In our opinion there is no place on earth that a man who hunts would rather be than here. Every year, we take time off from work to go spring bear hunting, and in the fall, we take off for moose, caribou, sheep and bear hunting.

The spring of 1989 proved to be different from our other hunts. In the past we had fought crossing the rivers in our Argos. We had been soaked by drenching rains and had literally spent days when we could not get out of our wall tent due to extreme weather conditions.

It was a beautiful day when Butch, his son Ray, and I headed out once again to look for that big bear, or a bear that would at least square 7 feet. We live in Healy, 110 miles south of Fairbanks, and to get to our hunting ground, we traveled all day by Argo (an amphibious, 8-wheeled vehicle), so it was evening by the time we reached our destination and set up our camp.

That first day out, we established camp in our regular spot, overlooking a view of the river drainage and its tributaries. We spent the evening relaxing, checking the river bottom, and spotting the drainage for fresh sign.

Not finding much fresh sign, the next morning we decided to do something we had never done before; we headed farther back to another drainage. The decision proved to be disastrous.

The land had not been touched by many motorized vehicles, largely due to the river that had to be crossed. The river is too swift for a vehicle that will float and too deep for one that will not. An Argos is amphibious, but it is definitely not intended for swift

377

water. We had sunk one in the past and had many other dangerously close calls.

We crossed the river with no problems, but we had virtually no idea of what we were getting into, even though we had looked at maps of the area. There were no trails, so we had to follow game trails where we could. The alders were dense, the ground was swampy, and the mosquitoes numbered in the millions. Since we had not taken on extra fuel for this time-consuming exploration, we headed back to base camp, tired and disgusted.

Just before reaching camp, I spotted a moose that was acting very peculiar and I drew Butch's attention to that sight. Unknown to us at the time, it is entirely possible that moose was being stalked by my bear.

We went back to camp, set up our spotting scopes and made dinner. After having spent 12 hours in the Argo, it felt good to be able to relax. The coffee was hot and dinner tasted great. We had been spotting for awhile when we noticed the wind was picking up and starting to blow. Butch and Ray decided to go inside the tent to take a nap. I sat out on a point overlooking the drainage, spotting, and then my eyes started growing heavy. I fell asleep too.

Butch was the first to wake up, and he came out to see if I had seen anything. I woke up and we spotted together for about 10 minutes before Butch said he was going to go back to bed. The wind was blowing pretty hard by then. The time was about 9:30 p.m. We talked it over and decided we would get an early start in the morning.

As Butch got up and started walking back to the tent, he noticed a bear coming out of the brush where we had previously seen the moose. He said, "Is this bear big enough for you? If not, I'll go wake up Ray, so he can shoot it."

You see, since we hunt together all the time, we have worked out a system so that neither one of us would ever have hard feelings about shooting specific animals. From year to year, we have the option to shoot or to pass the shot. If, for example, I shoot the biggest moose one year, Butch gets to decide whether he wants to shoot the first moose we see the next year. If not, I am obligated to shoot that moose for the meat. We use this same system for everything we hunt. Since Butch had already shot a grizzly bear, we were basically hunting for me and it was my option to shoot this bear or pass the chance to Ray. I told Butch, "Go ahead and wake up Ray while I look this bear over."

The wind was blowing in our favor and the bear was heading straight down the drainage toward us. At that point, the bear was probably 400 yards away. While I was looking the bear over, I noticed he was walking pigeon-toed. I had heard that the more pigeon-toed a bear was, the bigger he was. Judging by everything I could see and the numerous bears we had encountered in the past, I knew this bear would square at least 7 feet, and that was big enough for me!

By the time Butch and Ray got back to me I had already headed upstream to get a good broadside shot. The three of us lay down on the bank and waited. Putting the scope of my Winchester Model 70 in .300 Weatherby on the bear while I waited for it to get closer, I realized the bear was magnificent. The bear's dark spring coat shone with the setting sun on its back. It was moving fast toward me and doing very little grubbing.

The excitement of the wait was overwhelming. My heart was pounding with excitement and a bit of nervousness. I had waited four years for that moment.

We had decided while talking among ourselves that as soon as the bear was directly in front of me, I would shoot. If I had any problems knocking it down, I would call for Butch and Ray to shoot. We did not want a wounded bear to get away. We were all in position.

The range was 125 yards when I fired the first shot using a 180-grain bullet. There was no doubt I had hit the bear hard. It went down in a cloud of dust. As soon as it hit the ground, I jacked another cartridge into the chamber. As the bear started to pick itself up, Butch yelled, "Shoot it again."

I shot again. Both bullets hit the bear's spine, paralyzing him behind the shoulders and immobilizing him. The bullets lodged only inches apart. Not wanting to let it linger, I went for a good heart shot. After that third and final shot, the bear did not move.

Butch headed for the bear and I held my shooting position. When Butch reached the bear and was in position, he called for me and Ray.

As I walked out of the brush behind the bear, I thought the animal looked like the pictures I had seen of brown bears. It was definitely the biggest bear I had ever seen. The bear measured 10 feet, claw tip to claw tip, and 8 feet 7 inches from the tip of the nose to the base of the tail; thus, it squared out at 9 feet 3-1/2 inches. It was plenty big enough for me. I had never seen or heard of a grizzly bear being that big before. Ray and I started the job of skinning the monster and Butch went back to camp for the Argo. It was then around 10:00 p.m.

The next morning, we broke camp and headed home. The temperature was in the 70s and we did not want the hide to spoil in the heat.

After returning home, a friend mentioned that I ought to have the bear scored, because it might make the Boone and Crockett records book. Until then, I had never thought about that possibility.

The bear finally scored 26-14/16, which placed it well up in the records book. From the size of the bear, I am sure we bagged the big one that had been making the tracks all those years, for we have never seen them in our hunting area again.

Photograph Courtesy of Mrs. William H. Green

GRIZZLY BEAR
THIRD AWARD (TIE)
SCORE: 25-15/16

Locality: Tatlawiksuk River, Alaska   Date: 1988
Hunter: William H. Green   Owner: Mrs. William H. Green

GRIZZLY BEAR 25-15/16

William H. Green, hunter
Mrs. William H. Green, owner

[This story is told in the words of Denie Harison, who was the guide on this hunt. William H. Green lost his life in an airplane accident in July of 1990.]

We were not comfortable by New England standards, but we were not in New England. Big Bill Green and I sat in a quick-made spruce cubbie beside a creek at treeline in western Alaska. Bill kept feeding the fire with dead wood gathered from a near-by beaver dam. He was smiling. Thinking about our day of bear hunting made me smile too.

We had flown in to our mountaintop spike camp from Stoney River Lodge the day before, with master guide Curly Warren. It was a brisk, late-fall day, with skim ice starting to form along the edges of the beaver ponds. Bill was looking for a trophy grizzly bear and I was his guide for the hunt.

We unloaded our gear from the Super Cub and hauled it down the hill from the mountaintop landing area to the 10 by 12-foot wall tent. With bunks, a wood stove and a door, we were quite snug and comfortable despite the stiff breeze outside. After getting settled in and a lunch of moose meat sandwiches, we set out to stretch our legs and select a spot from which to glass for our bear the next morning.

Bill, having hunted from the camp before, was showing me the sights as we topped a ridge about a quarter-mile north of camp. We sat to take a breather, looking out across the steep valley with its scattered alder brush patches and small beaver dammed creeks.

Discussing the merits of various vantage points, we selected a low, bald-topped ridge about four miles north. It would give us a good view of our valley, as well as the next valley over which had a larger creek. Directly across from us, about half a mile away and walking out of an alder patch, was a bear.

We watched as he came down to the creek below and downstream from us, and proceeded to swim in a beaver pond as darkness began to fall. After a while, the bear shook the water from his golden brown fur and ambled over the ridge to our east.

We went back to camp and talked half the night about bears. That bear had been nice, but not that nice, and Bill wanted a trophy.

We were up at 5:00 a.m. for coffee and breakfast. With lunch packed, we were out the door just as it was getting light. Climbing the mountain next to camp to get to our glassing spot was not Big Bill's idea of fun. However, the sighting of the night before and the prospect of the commanding view provided plenty of fuel for the job. Once on top of the mountain, with the side-hilling climb behind us, Bill got his smile back and we picked up the pace, heading down the ridge to our destination.

It was still early in the morning when we saw a herd of caribou, about 30 in all, moving up from the valley to the relative safety of our open ridge. With the breeze blowing on top, they bedded down in the spruces. Bill had a caribou tag but none of the herd was trophy size. Besides, he could not get his mind off that bear.

We made it to our vantage point just before lunch time. It had the view we had hoped for, and we sat down to glass for the rest of the day. I set up my Simmons 25x50 spotting scope and we glassed, had lunch, glassed, took a short nap, and glassed.

By late afternoon, our eyes were getting sore and so were our backsides. We got up and stretched, packed our gear, and stood there talking about bears. From our position, Bill decided that we could see anything moving below us with the naked eye. He said we did not need all of the equipment I was packing. Then, he said, "Like that black bear right there."

Well, there was a bear there, all right. It was about three miles to the northeast of us and heading west. Going back to the spotting scope, we determined that it was no black bear. It was not the "nice" bear we had seen the night before either. It was very dark and very large and very grizzly. Big Bill stood by impatiently while I did the looking and calculating I am required to do by Curly Warren. I came to the conclusion that yes, it was a good bear.

With the breeze blowing down the valley and the bear walking up, Bill and I considered our situation. We were at least four miles from camp as the crow flies. Since we were not crows, the distance was probably six miles — about three hours of walking. The bear was about an hour and a half down the hill at a fast walk and he was in no hurry. It was getting late in the day and we do have long days at that time of year. Big Bill wanted that bear. So with the understanding that our tent camp would "still be there tomorrow" and "it wasn't that cold last night," we headed down the mountain.

I called him Big Bill because he was a big man, but the biggest part of him was his heart. The guy had a lot of heart.

We proceeded down the hill at a pretty good gait, quartering to the left and trying to get a couple of miles ahead of the bear so we could intercept him. The bear was not stopping for anything. He was just plodding along.

Bill and I dog-trotted down the level part of the grade. Then the hill started to get a little steeper and we slowed to a walk for safety's sake. It seemed like we walked and skidded and slid down the better part of it, probably 400 or 500 yards, before it leveled out into an extremely large patch of tussock. These clumps stand about pants-pocket high on a man. They range from the diameter of a five-gallon can to that of a small kitchen table. A man has to either walk on top of them, which is best done by an acrobat, or worm his way around them, which a moose prefers to do. Imitating the moose is very difficult, since they have about twice as much leg as we do. The going was slow and we kept at it for about an hour. As I looked back at Bill, I could see he was doing fine. He was breathing hard and sweating, but he was still with me.

We spotted the bear and he had done just what we hoped he would do, which was slow down and start to feed. At that point we were still an hour from getting into a good shooting position.

When we crested a ridge, the bear was some 250 yards off to our right in the middle of a beaver pond. He was just playing and swimming in the water. Bill got into the prone position and took a minute to catch his breath and steady himself.

We had gone as slowly and as quietly as possible, but suddenly, the bear stuck his nose in the air; he was smelling us. "Shoot," I said and Bill fired.

The bear was on a mound, and with the shot, he fell backwards but up he came. "Shoot," I said, and Bill emptied his .300 Weatherby Magnum. Then he realized he had lost his spare ammunition during the stalk. He reached into his top pocket and found one desperately needed cartridge.

We could no longer see the bear. We knew he was hit but we did not know how badly he was hurt. After impatiently waiting for him to appear, we began to circle to the left and climbed up on a beaver lodge.

Thinking the bear was much more to our right, we were startled when the bear bolted at us from 25 yards away. Bill fired his last shot and the bear dropped about 25 feet from us. He did not come up.

It was beginning to get dark and we realized we were there for the night. Keeping an ear and an eye on the bear, we began to look around (with our eyes only) for some kind of shelter. After a while, which seemed like hours to us, we crept up on Big Bill's grizzly. He had fallen in the pond and was dead.

We were both too tired to make the long trek back to camp. We were even too tired to go back and find our packs, which had our food, extra clothing and necessities, so we decided to sack out with the bear.

Shelter was a must. We gathered some branches and beaver-cut sticks and built a fire. Of course, the beavers were pretty mad when Bill stole some of the wood from their dam. All night long, we took turns stoking the fire.

The next morning, we got to skinning the bear and he was a big one, a regular monster. By that time, he was covered with ice crystals. We were both strong men, but it took all the strength we could muster to move the bear in order to cape him. We stood knee-deep in mud and water, skinning that big grizzly. It was obvious to me that Bill was proud, happy and more than satisfied with his new trophy.

It was a long 12-mile hike back to camp. I kept the hide whole and packed it out five miles to an area where the plane could land the next day and pick it up. There were many rest stops along the way. I would sit down, leaning against a tree, and Bill would help me to get up and moving again. We were completely worn-out when we reached out tent camp and spent the rest of the day catching up on our much-needed sleep.

The Super Cub arrived the following day to take us back to the main lodge. That is where Bill happily discovered his grizzly squared approximately 9-1/2 feet!

Photograph courtesy of Harry A. Knowlton

Toad River, B.C. was the location of the hunt for this grizzly bear killed in
1990 by Harry A. Knowlton. It scored 23-12/16.

Photograph courtesy of Walter J. Miller

Walter J. Miller killed this grizzly bear that scores 24-5/16,
near Squirrel River, Alaska, in 1990.

GRIZZLY BEAR 25-15/16

THIRD AWARD (TIE)

Josef Martinek

The fall hunt of 1991 is one that I will remember for the rest of my life. On October 3rd, at about 6:00 a.m., I left Prince George for a trip to one of my favorite hunting areas deep in the Coastal Mountain Range of British Columbia, at a place called Morrice Lake.

On the way there, everything went well and as I got closer, I could feel the excitement starting to build. Even my little terrier Rocky seemed to sense that we were going on another bear hunt. On a previous occasion, he had chased a small black bear up a tree.

That afternoon when we arrived, the weather was just perfect for hunting. By the time I had set up camp and put the boat in the water, it was about 3:00 p.m. and nearly four hours remained before sunset. I placed the 3-9x Bushnell scope on my .300 Winchester Magnum Ruger Model 77 and packed a box of handloaded ammunition (I use 200-grain Sierra spitzer boat-tail bullets with 67 grains of IMR-4350 powder) into the packsack, along with my Bausch & Lomb 7x35 binoculars, a camera and a bite to eat, and left the camp. After some time I moored the boat and started to walk slowly on the shore, checking for signs of bear on the sandbar. Following the game trails, I went about a mile and then decided not go any farther since I wanted to get back to camp before dark.

The next morning after breakfast, I packed a lunch as I planned to stay out until that night. This time, I went with the boat but not as far as the previous day. After a bit, I took out my fly fishing rod and did some fishing, hoping to catch a rainbow trout. Sure enough, about 15 to 20 minutes later my rod bent and my line started going out. About five seconds later, he was right out of the water, then back in and out once more. This went on for about 10 minutes or so and then he finally started giving up. I carefully released him and he disappeared slowly into the lake.

After a quick bite to eat and some coffee, I went farther along the shore, looking for some sign of bears. The weather was fine and yet I did not see any fresh sign or movement anywhere. It was well after 7:00 p.m., so I headed back to camp.

The next day was pretty much the same and I only saw a black wolf, which crossed at an open point and quickly disappeared into the timber. Back at camp that evening, I made myself a drink and thought about the big grizzly that came almost every year to the slides along the lake shore. Several times before, I had seen a large grizzly bear high up on the mountains but he always disappeared before I could climb up there. I remembered seeing those big tracks deep in the mud by the shore and I wondered if, perhaps, someone had already shot him or if he had died of old age.

The following day, other hunters and fishermen came but they had only a canoe. I knew I would be undisturbed on the water because the lake was too rough for the canoe. It was October 6th, and I did almost exactly the same thing as I had done the day before. I beached the boat in the little cove and walked for about a mile, checking the shoreline for signs of game, then walked back again. I had something to eat and then went about a mile in the opposite direction, but to my disappointment, there were no signs of game. I went back to the boat.

It was about 5:00 p.m., so I took my fly rod and started fishing. After about an hour, I got a bite, a really big one. When the fish leaped out of the water, I knew that it would weigh at least 3 or 4 pounds. Just at that moment I could hear branches breaking not too far behind me, and as the fish came up for a second time, I unfortunately lost him. I put down the rod and picked up my rifle. My terrier heard the noise too and went rushing into the bush, barking loudly, and returned immediately with his tail down.

On one side of me was a trail. How lucky for me. The only place where I could see clearly was where he appeared. I had goose bumps on my back, or perhaps a cold sweat. I shot. He roared and jumped away. I did not see anything and heard only the roars and a noise like someone chopping trees. This lasted only a couple of minutes and then everything was still.

I waited there holding Rocky, but after a few minutes, I knew I would have to go and see what had happened before it got too dark. I started very quietly, with Rocky on the leash. When we got to the place where I shot him, I could see some blood. A few yards farther on, I could see a circle about 5 yards across, all cleared, and he was in the middle of it.

When I saw the size of him, I was really afraid that I would not be able to skin him by myself. I tried to move him, but I had no chance. The beast must have weighed over 1,000 pounds. I had to leave him where he was and return to camp as it was already getting dark.

When I got back to camp, I saw that some more people had arrived and I knew I would get help the next day. When I asked in the morning, a party of four offered to help.

When we arrived at the bear, he was just as I had left him. The guys could not believe how big he was and said, "Now we know why you need help."

After about five hours, the job was done. I then asked one of the fellows to help me pack it into the boat, which was not easy either. I was glad it was not too far back to the boat.

When I arrived back at the camper there was another party from Prince George, all of whom I knew. They were just returning from a successful hunt for Rocky Mountain goats on the other side of the lake.

We compared our trophies, and after a few pictures and some measurements of the hide, they all agreed that this was the true "King of Morrice Lake." He was nearly nine feet long, from tail to nose. His front paws were 7 inches across and his hind feet were 11 inches long.

Seventy days later, when the skull was boiled and cleaned, it measured 25-15/16 inches, a truly nice trophy.

Photograph courtesy of Charles L. Fuller

In 1988, Charles L. Fuller killed this grizzly bear near
Christmas Creek, Alaska. It scored 24-3/16.

Photograph courtesy of William M. Eubank

This grizzly bear was killed by William M. Eubank, near
Squirrel River, Alaska, in 1988. It scored 24-14/16.

ALASKA BROWN BEAR 29-8/16

FIRST AWARD

Martin H. Shaft

On March 30, 1990, my brother-in-law, his son and I flew to Anchorage, Alaska. After staying the night, we left for Kodiak Island, only to circle the airport for an hour and return to Anchorage until the weather changed. Later that afternoon, we finally landed in Kodiak. We were rushed onto a Grumman Goose for the flight to Kaluqnak Bay. There, we were greeted by our registered guide, Gus Lamoureux of Ugashik Lakes Lodge, plus guides Randy Moore, Fred Cook and Daniel Nicolai. Daniel was to be my guide for the hunt.

The accommodations were entirely adequate, the food was superb, and the atmosphere lived up to my expectations. The weather consisted mostly of drizzle, with some sunny moments, and the temperature ranged from 36 to 76 degrees.

We hunted long and hard and saw quite a few bears. The other client, Don Grimes, got a nice 8-1/2-foot bear on the fifth day.

My brother-in-law, John McIntosh, Jr., and his son, John III (also known as J.J.) hunted together. On the 10th day they saw a large paw print. We nicknamed the bear with the large print "The Trackster."

On the 11th day John and J.J. went looking for The Trackster but they had no luck. They spotted a bear across the bay, pursued it and were successful, taking a beautiful 7-1/2 foot blonde bear.

The 12th and last day came and I was still without a bear. J.J. offered to go with Daniel and me to look for The Trackster. He had hunted in the same area in 1987 and took an extremely nice 9-1/2 foot bear, so he was on the trip as a packer.

We left camp at 6:00 a.m. and arrived at the place where the large prints had been sighted. There, we started to glass the area. Around 8:00, I spotted a large bear as it went over a distant knoll. Since it was the last day, we decided to go for it.

At about 11:00 a.m., we crossed the knoll and saw that the bear had gone through a cut in the rock ledge, heading east. We followed and eventually spotted him about a third of the way down the valley.

After some deliberation on my part, we decided to try to stalk him. Forty-five minutes later we were within 125 yards of the bear. It was then that we realized he was really The Trackster. We watched and at the right moment, he stood up. I fired, taking four shots to put the magnificent animal down.

We spent three and a half hours getting the bear back to camp. It was a great thrill but also a great loss. He was a magnificent animal and I hope his offspring will carry on his genes. We were up until 3:00 a.m. the next day, preparing my trophy for the flight home.

I had the hide made into a rug. It will always remind me of the great animal he was.

Photograph courtesy of John D. Teeter

This Alaska brown bear was killed by John D. Teeter near Cold Bay,
Alaska, in 1988. It scored 28 points.

Photograph courtesy of Andrew J. Fierro

Andrew J. Fierro was hunting on Kodiak Island, Alaska, when
he killed this Alaska brown bear in 1991. It scored 28-8/16.

Photograph Courtesy of Robert L. Coleman

ALASKA BROWN BEAR
SECOND AWARD
SCORE: 29-5/16

Locality: Braided Creek, Alaska   Date: 1991
Hunter: Robert L. Coleman

ALASKA BROWN BEAR 29-5/16

Robert L. Coleman

Earlier this year, I was looking for a barren ground caribou hunt. When I found Katmai Guide Service was a donor to the Flint S.C.I. Fund Raiser that I attended, I called Joe Klutsch who owns the outfit.

During our conversation, Joe asked if I had any interest in brown bear. I told him I had but there seemed to be a two to three year wait for a good outfitter and I hadn't started that process yet. He said he had a similar waiting list but he had just received a cancellation for the fall of 1991. After checking references, I booked the hunt for October of 1991.

It was my second trip to Alaska in as many months. I spent one night in Anchorage and flew Reeve Aleutian Airways to Port Heiden the next morning. Port Heiden is located on the Alaska Peninsula, directly west of Kodiak Island.

I was met there by the pilot, who flew us to base camp. After a quick lunch and sighting in my rifle, he flew me to a landing area. My guide, Mark Knapp, was waiting for me.

We spent the night there. Early the next morning, Mark was glassing he area where we meant to make a spike camp when he spotted a good sized bear. We packed up and headed out.

Two hours later, we reached the area where we set up our spike camp. After lunch, we headed for a hill to glass for bear. We saw six bear before returning to camp for the night. We left camp early the next morning for another hill, one that was higher and allowed us to cover more area by glassing.

The weather had been fantastic for the peninsula, with sunshine and little wind. However that morning we got the more typical rain, snow, and wind. We climbed the hill, but the weather was so bad that at times we could barely see 50 yards. I learned quickly that GORE-TEX and down were not intended for that climate. I was soon wetter than I had ever been. If you go for brown bear, invest in wool clothing and real waterproof rain gear.

We spotted a sow and a very large cub in the first few hours, along with some gigantic moose and wolverine. About noon the weather got so bad that we decided to pack up and head back to our spike camp. We had gone as far as pouring out our water bottles— the very last thing you do before climbing down, so as to reduce weight—when there was a very slight break in the weather. Mark decided to go to the other side of the knob and glass one last time before quitting. This resulted in several more hours of glassing during breaks in the weather.

Late that afternoon I was on the back side of the knob when Mark came running around and said, "Put everything in your pack quickly. There is a big boar down there!"

We didn't have a lot of daylight left. Mark anticipated where the boar would come out and we began an hour of stalking. The bear was feeding on salmon and working down the river. About 75 yards before we got to where we thought we might intercept the bear, we dropped our backpacks for the final stalk.

We came to a bend in the river. Mark pointed and said, "He should come out right about there."

As the anticipation grew. I noticed a movement in the opposite direction. Some 200 yards away on a gravel bar, the big bear had just flipped a salmon out of the river. He had beaten us to our expected interception point.

I pulled up my Mag-Na-Ported .375 H&H Sako and fired. The large bear spun around and fell at the same time. He then got up and crashed into a heavy thicket. I threw a quick second shot after him and watched him disappear.

We had about 15 minutes of daylight left when we started to follow his blood trail. We only went a few yards when Mark said he could see something. Due to the approaching darkness, he had to use binoculars to identify it. It was a bear. After an insurance shot, we made our way over to the bear. He was dead.

It was dark and we used our flashlights to skin him out. We finished the work at about 1:00 in the morning. We were two and a half hours from our spike camp, so we decided to spend the night right there. We were concerned that wolves or another bear might eat my trophy, and I didn't want to take any chances.

Mark took rough measurements of the bear and was very impressed with its size. He said it would square over 10 feet.

It snowed over 3 inches that night. We were able to get a small fire started by using a piece of rubber that Mark cut from his waders. We burned bear fat all night. Needless to say, we got no sleep.

The next morning, packing the bear out to where we would meet the plane took five-and-a-half hours. We had to go back the next day to retrieve our spike camp.

When we made it back to the main camp, we fleshed the hide out. It squared 10 feet 9 inches. After the 60 day drying period, the bear measured 29-11/16 S.C.I. and 29-5/16, Boone and Crockett.

Joe Klutsch has a reputation for large bear in his area and Mark Knapp certainly knows how to identify them. The caribou weren't in the area, but it didn't seem to matter after an exceptional bear.

Photograph courtesy of Bruce T. Berger

Bruce T. Berger killed this Alaska brown bear on Kodiak Island,
Alaska, in 1988. It scored 28-1/16.

Photograph courtesy of David B. Colclough

This Alaska brown bear was killed near Olga Bay, Alaska,
by David B. Colclough in 1989. It scored 28-3/16.

Photograph Courtesy of Peter Ma

ALASKA BROWN BEAR
THIRD AWARD
SCORE: 29-3/16

Locality: Alaska Pen., Alaska   Date: 1990
Hunter: Peter Ma

ALASKA BROWN BEAR 29-3/16

Peter Ma

Wind whipped the Aleutian coastline of the Alaska Peninsula as Peter Ma approached the remote spike camp where he would begin his hunt. The red and white Piper in which he flew with guide Butch King would soon be landing The right tundra tire was first to touch down on the steep beach. The second tire began to track as the Piper rolled above the tide line toward a sandy flat area in front of the spike camp. The propeller whirled to a stop, as Peter swung the door open. He was introduced to King's assistant, Mike McKary, who would be Peter's guide as he spent the next week hunting for a trophy Alaska brown bear.

While his gear and supplies were unloaded, Peter discussed the strategy of hunting this area with Butch and Mike. Butch had seen several bears while scouting the area earlier in the season.

"There has been an exceptionally big bear working the beach a few miles south of your camp," Butch told Peter and Mike. "He's well over 10 feet and the one to look for. There's only one thing that bothers me; he's never alone. There is an 8-1/2-foot sow with him, and another boar doesn't seem to wander too far. They've been a threesome since the beginning of the season."

It sounded to Peter like jumping in the middle of three bears could be risky, but if this one was really big, the reward would be worth the risk.

Lining up with the rapidly shrinking beach, the Piper bounced between the seaweed and driftwood, then hopped off as the incoming tide washed the wheel marks from the sand.

This was Peter's first hunt in Alaska. He had previously hunted big game in the deserts of Sonora, Mexico, with his friend Ernesto Zaragoza and found the experience exhilarating. Afterward, he and Ernesto had planned an Alaskan hunt. Now, in separate spike camps, they were ready to search out the Alaska brown bear.

After breakfast, Peter and Mike went hunting. By 5:00 a.m., they were two miles south of the spike camp, glassing the windswept hillsides of the Pacific coast.

"We'll need to pass through a patch of alders if we're going to get to where the bears have been working the beach," Mike whispered soberly.

Peter chambered a round in his .300 Weatherby, while Mike did the same with his .375 H&H Magnum. With the wind in their faces, one step at a time, they worked through the tangled patch, stopping only twice to listen and sniff the air for the foul odor of the bear.

As they broke out of the brush, the bite of morning chill was slowly wearing off. They crested a grassy knoll and viewed the rolling hills standing sentry above the coastline.

The beach below hosted quite an array of bird life including seagulls, cormorants and bald eagles. Sea ducks and a few puffins bobbed in the water offshore.

The only sign of brown bear was a single set of staggering tracks, and they were rapidly being erased by the surge of an incoming tide.

Swinging his compact scope slowly to the hillside which towered above the beach, Mike spotted the bear, only slightly darker than its surroundings. Peter, in turn, gazed through the scope.

"That's not one bear," observed Peter. "There are two bears."

After determining the best approach, Peter and Mike set out to get as close as possible to the sleeping bears. From the next ridge, they could confirm that this was the huge animal they were after. They could not find the smaller boar that Butch had warned them about and that bothered them.

Crawling like snakes through the tall, wet, amber stalks of last season's eel grass, Peter and Mike closed the distance between them and the bears. As they eased to the top of the last ridge, they found what they had been missing. The third bear lay just 60 yards ahead. They had it dead to rights if they wanted it.

With its head up, it was only 40 yards from the monster and the sow. The smaller bear was slowly swinging his head from side to side. Its large, black nose was working overtime to scent approaching danger. The offshore breeze kept Peter and Mike's position concealed for the time being but the brownie was getting more nervous by the minute.

With all three bears in plain view, Peter steadied his rifle on Mike's pack. Peter was momentarily tempted to go after the smaller bear, because it was much closer than the others. The thought of the reward of a large trophy quickly changed his mind.

Peter silently leveled his Weatherby on the larger boar. The huge bruin lay flat on his back. His legs were in the air, and each was as big around as a man's chest. Both men knew they were in the middle of what could be a very dangerous situation. The only chance Peter figured they had was to hit the big bear and hope the other two would clear out when the shooting started.

The monster bear suddenly sensed danger and struggled to rise. Peter's .300 roared as the bear came to a full sitting position. The 180-grain Nozler drilled through the bear's front paw and into his chest, sending him into a spin. Peter proceeded to empty his Weatherby into the bellowing brown fury. The bear tucked his head and attempted to somersault out of the line of fire as Mike's gun joined in the shooting. The huge beast came to rest some twenty yards below the hole where it had been lying with the sow.

Peter knew the action was just beginning. They were not out of danger until they were sure of the location of the other bears.

The sow had left the boar during the shooting and had disappeared over the crest of the hill. The men scanned the area.

"Here he comes," warned Mike.

The smaller boar was headed their way, looking over its shoulder at the downed bear. Unaware of the hunters position, the bear was rapidly closing with them. When the bear finally saw the men poking above the tundra, he stopped in his tracks.

Standing on hind legs, the smaller boar made an unsuccessful attempt to sample the air for a whiff of the intruders before him. A few seconds seemed like a lifetime as the hunters and the bear stared into one another's eyes, each looking for a weakness or an indication of what was going to happen next.

The brownie yielded first. He dropped to all fours and skirted the hunters in cat-like bounds until he caught their scent, which sent him racing off.

"Let's get a look at your bear, Peter," Mike exclaimed.

They had taken only a few steps in the direction of Peter's downed trophy when the sow came busting over the ridge above them as if shot from a cannon. Peter screamed a warning as Mike raised his rifle. Peter could see the breath from the bear's nostrils and the glint of her eye as she rapidly approached.

Mike said, "I'll shoot a warning shot just to the right of her head and you shoot to the left." The .375 bellowed. The sow changed direction slightly, and the charge broke to a bewildered gait. At 20 yards, there was no time to shoulder the rifle. The second warning shot exploded over the bear's head, sending her in the other direction. Peter and Mike watched her until she disappeared over the ridge.

The strange, foggy mist of an Aleutian storm was rapidly approaching from the southeast. Considering the events of the past few minutes, it seemed only appropriate.

Peter and Mike cautiously approached the downed bear, not yet knowing it would square just under 11 feet and score an even 30 inches, making it the new #3 Alaska Brown Bear in the S.C.I. records book.

Photograph courtesy of Joe B. Owen

Joe B. Owen killed this Alaska brown bear near Beaver Bay,
Alaska, in 1989. It scored 27-8/16.

Photograph courtesy of Chung C. Huang

Chung C. Huang killed this Alaska brown bear, in 1990 near
Muddy River, Alaska. It scored 28-14/16.

ALASKA BROWN BEAR 29-1/16

FOURTH AWARD

Randy D. Klingenmeyer

Randy Klingenmeyer of Anchorage, Alaska, began his Alaska brown bear hunt in late April of 1991. Like many Alaska residents, he is skilled enough to guide himself on hunts, even for big brown bear on famed Kodiak Island.

Klingenmeyer arrived on Kodiak on April 26. His mode of travel was the Alaska version of the automobile, the float plane. And, a boat and good-sized outboard motor made it easy to charnge location when needed.

Klingenmeyer killed his big bear on April 30, near Fraser Lake, at a distance of 90 paces. He used a .375 H&H with Federal 300-grain Nosler bullet. The wind, as usual was blowing (about 40 mph) but it was sunny and clear at the time of the kill. About three feet of snow was on the ground where the bear was shot, some 2,700 feet elevation on the mountain.

Klingenmeyer's very successful hunt ended when he was flown-out from Kodiak on May 7.

Photograph Courtesy of William G. James

ALASKA BROWN BEAR
HONORABLE MENTION
SCORE: 28-14/16

Locality: Olga Bay, Alaska   Date: 1989
Hunter: William G. James

ALASKA BROWN BEAR 28-14/16

William G. James

I had heard about 10 foot bears, but I had no appreciation of what they were like. I discussed this subject with Fred Moseley, a long-time hunting friend from Anchorage, Alaska. He suggested that I go to Kodiak Island if I really wanted a giant bruin. He also recommended Bill Pinnell and Morris Talifson, master guides with 120 years of guiding experience between them. They have put more hunters on to giant browns than any other outfitters in Alaska.

I took Fred at his word and called Bill Pinnell and booked a hunt for the following spring of 1989. I was fortunate to get an opportunity so soon. There had been a cancellation and my timing was perfect.

In the next seven months, I had many telephone conversations with Scott Mileur, the field guide, to go over all of the details of the hunt. The time went by very quickly and before I realized it, I was at O'Hare airport saying good bye to the family.

The flights to Anchorage and on to Kodiak were as uneventful as you would like them. However, I could feel the excitement that every hunter feels as his hunt starts to unfold. That evening I had dinner with Bill Schmoe (former president of Remington Arms, now retired) from Jackson Hole, Wyoming. Bill had also booked with Pinnell and Talifson and was as excited as I was about what lay ahead of us during the next 15 days.

We purchased some supplies the following morning and about noon, we met our chartered flight. An hour later, we landed at Olga Bay, the base camp for Pinnell and Talifson's operations. The camp was an old salmon cannery dating to before World War II. The accommodations were very comfortable and the food was as good as anyone could want. After dinner, Bill Pinnell, age 93, and Morris Talifson, age 81, entertained us with stories of bear hunts they had guided during the past 60 years. We quickly realized why these two fine gentlemen are known as "The Last of the Great Bear Hunters."

Bill and I were up early the next morning, ready to begin our adventure. Scott and Bill Schmoe headed west toward the Red Lake area, while my guide, John Twardowski, and I headed straight south to Karluk Lake. We walked a few miles, to an old boat and a motor that had been dropped earlier and crossed the lake. We then climbed half way up the mountain to the east and set up our scoping operations. The walking would not have been bad except for the hip boots needed to negotiate the boggy tundra. We were right on the snow line of the mountain as we dug in to scope for the giant bears. We glassed all day but only saw a sow and two 7-foot cubs, four miles away.

I asked John how we would know when we spotted a 10-foot bear. He said, "Don't worry. You will know when you see him," which left me a little bit puzzled. As darkness fell, we headed back to camp. We enjoyed another fine dinner and more bear conversation from our senior hosts.

The next two days were more of the same. We spotted a number of 7 or 8-foot animals but saw nothing interesting. The fourth day, we awoke to a real blizzard that grounded our hunting. Bill and I explored the huge cannery and listened to more impressive bruin stories that evening.

The following day the snow had stopped. Bill Schmoe killed his bear in the morning with his .416 Remington. The bear squared 9 feet 3 inches and was a real trophy. That evening we had a new orator at dinner.

The next three days brought more snow and poor visibility. The walking got tougher because of the snow and mushy tundra. During the evening of the seventh day, I told Bill Pinnell that I was losing my confidence in getting a big one. I had not even seen anything that we could put a stalk on. He just smiled and said, "Don't give up and keep going." I thought that was easy enough for him to say, sitting next to that warm, old wood-burning stove.

The next morning John and I got an early start back to Lake Karluk. The going was slower and the snow line had moved to the base of the mountain. Slowly we climbed the slippery and very soggy mountain to set up our scoping operations in our regular position. We scoped all morning and saw six bears, all 8 feet or less and most of them rubbed badly.

After lunch, I spotted something black about five miles away, directly to the west. As soon as I saw it, I knew it was a 10-foot bear. He was lumbering across the mountainside opposite from us. As he walked in the golden grass, it was easy to follow him with our 20x spotting scope. After 20 minutes, he did what you hope all bears will do; he lay down and appeared to go to sleep. We gathered up all our gear, made a good mark on where he was, and started our stalk. We got down the mountain and into the old wooden boat quickly. John said he did not seem to be rubbed and assured me he would be a fine trophy animal. I did not feel the cold spray as we headed across Lake Karlack.

Once we reached the other side of the lake, the object was to climb the mountain, trying to stay down wind from him. John and I quickly went through about 400 yards of the thickest bunch of alders I have ever seen. There are no trees on the island, but there are large patches of alders with the rest being filled in with waist-high, golden brown tundra grass.

John kept pushing me, saying, "Hurry or he might move on us." We had lost sight of him as we began our climb. I took a number of rest stops, but we finally broke out in a grassy opening where John thought the bear was.

We sat down and started looking for him. I was wet to the skin from crawling the last 300 yards. We did not want to go any farther for fear of coming right up on him as he slept in the tall grass. The advantage would have then become his.

After twenty minutes, which seemed like forever, we heard a noise about 125 yards in front of us. John said, "Get ready, because he could be close." I took the safety off my .300 Weatherby, awaiting the shot of my dreams. The noises grew louder and louder. Finally two boars, both about 9 to 9-1/2 feet, broke out in the open and started a fight that set the hair on the back of my neck on end.

John said, "Don't shoot." They were slightly over 100 yards away and I was ready to take either one for my trophy. Quietly, John said, " I don't think that either of these bears is the bear that we are stalking." We watched in awe as these monsters tore into each other. You could see their blood soaked wounds and hear the deafening cries of battle. If only I had my video recorder. As I reached for my camera, John told me not to move or they might sense us and charge. As we watched this battle of the giants, I suddenly noticed movement about 250 yards to our right and slightly above us. When I pointed it out to John, he said, "I knew these two bears were not the bear we scoped." We patiently waited until this bear decided to find out what all the noise was about.

When he broke through the alders and started walking toward the two bears in combat, I knew what a 10-foot bear was! He was massive in body and he lumbered back and forth with every movement. John estimated the range at about 200 yards and told me to take him when he hit the middle of the opening. He also reminded me to make sure the first shot was good because the bear would charge down the mountain like a locomotive and would cover 100 yards before I was ready to fire the second shot. The third shot, he said, was to be saved to put in his mouth or mine, whichever I chose.

The bear hit the middle of the opening and the crosshairs of my 9x scope were right on his shoulder. I squeezed off the shot. The bullet hit the bear with a solid thud but he only quivered slightly. The bear did exactly what had John said he would do. He came charging like a locomotive and John hollered, "Shoot again!" The second shot caught him in the chest at 100 yards and sent him rolling in a thicket. We could hear him thrashing around but could not see him. John watched the other two bears disappear.

As we tentatively walked up to the massive beast, we were in awe of his size and the strong fish smell the older boars have. We approached cautiously, but he was dead. The pounding in my chest proved that my bypass surgery had been done well.

It took us four hours to skin the bear and another two hours to pack out 180 pounds of skull and hide. I don't even remember the five mile walk back to camp, for I was reliving the great events of the day.

Once in camp we stretched the hide and took a preliminary measurement on the skull. The hide squared slightly over 10 feet, while the skull measurement was 29-8/16 inches.

Bill Pinnell told me I would get a good bear because I was in the best bear country. He was surely right. Bill and Morris made my trip of a lifetime come true.

Tabulations of Recorded Trophies
21st Awards Entry Period
1989-1991

The trophy data shown herein have been taken from score charts in the Records Archives of the Boone and Crockett Club for the 21st Awards entry period, 1989-1991. Trophies listed are those that meet minimum score and other stated requirements of trophy entry for the period. The final scores and rank shown are official, except for trophies shown with an asterisk. The asterisk is assigned to trophies whose entry scores are subject to certification by an Awards Panel of Judges. The asterisk can be removed (except in case of a potential World's Record) by the submitting of two additional, independent scorings by Official Measurers of the Boone and Crockett Club. The Records Committee of the Club will review the three scorings available (original, plus two additional) and determine which, if any, will be accepted in lieu of the Judges Panel measurement. When the score has been accepted as final by the Records Committee, the asterisk will be removed in future editions of the all-time records book, *Records of North American Big Game*, and other publications. In the case of a potential World's Record, the trophy <u>must</u> come before a Judges Panel at the end of an entry period. Only a Judges Panel can certify a World's Record and finalize its score.

Asterisked trophies are shown at the end of the listings for their category. They are <u>not</u> ranked, as their final score is subject to revision by a Judges Panel or by the submission of additional official scorings, as described above. Note that "PR" preceding date of kill indicates "prior to" the date shown for kill.

The scientific and vernacular names, and the sequence of presentation, follows that suggested in the *Revised Checklist of North American Mammals North of Mexico*, 1979 (J. Knox Jones, <u>et al</u>; Texas Tech University, 14 December 1979.)

Trophy Boundaries

Many of the categories recognized in the records keeping are based upon subspecies differences. In nature, subspecies freely interbreed where their ranges overlap, thus necessitating the setting of geographic boundaries to keep them separate for records keeping purposes.

Geographic boundaries are described for a number of categories. These include: brown and grizzly bear; American and Roosevelt's elk; mule, Columbia, and Sitka blacktail deer; whitetail and Coues' deer; moose; and caribou. Pertinent information is included in the trophy date listings that follow, but the complete, detailed description for each is to be found in the latest edition (9th. Ed., 1988) of the all-time records book, *Records of North American Big Game*, and also in the "how-to" book, *Measuring and Scoring North American Big Game Trophies*.

In addition to category specific boundaries, all trophies must be from North America, north of the south border of Mexico, to be eligible. For pelagic trophies, such as walrus and polar bear, they must be from the U.S. side of the International Date Line to be eligible.

Trophy boundaries are set by the Boone and Crockett Club's Records of North American Big Game Committee, working with the latest and best available information from scientific researchers, guides, hunters, and other parties with serious interest in our big game resources. In general, boundaries are set so that it is highly unlikely that specimens of the larger category can be taken within th eboundaries set for the smaller category, thus upsetting the rankings of the smaller category. Trophy boundaries are revised as necessary to maintain this separation of the categories.

Black Bear

Ursus americanus americanus and related subspecies

Minimum Score 20 World's Record 23-10/16

Score	Greatest Length of Skull Without Lower Jaw	Greatest Width of Skull	Locality Killed	By Whom Killed	Owner	Date Killed	Rank
22 13/16	14 1/16	8 12/16	Ventura Co., Calif.	Loren C. Nodolf	Loren C. Nodolf	1990	1
22 2/16	13 14/16	8 4/16	Queen Charlotte Islands, B.C.	Craig N. Beachy	Craig N. Beachy	1988	2
22 2/16	13 12/16	8 6/16	Kern Co., Calif.	Danny R. Thomas	Danny R. Thomas	1988	2
22	13 12/16	8 4/16	Prince of Wales Island, Alaska	George P. Mann	George P. Mann	1991	4
22	13 10/16	8 6/16	Gila Co., Ariz.	Steven J. Stayner	Steven J. Stayner	1991	4
21 15/16	13 12/16	8 3/16	Clearfield Co., Pa.	Dwayne B. DeLattre	Dwayne B. DeLattre	1987	6
21 15/16	13 12/16	8 3/16	Gila Co., Ariz.	Thomas Alvin	Thomas Alvin	1990	6
21 15/16	14 6/16	7 9/16	Birdtail Creek, Man.	Barry Minshull	Barry Minshull	1990	6
21 14/16	13 9/16	8 5/16	Luzerne Co., Pa.	Adrian C. Robbins	Adrian C. Robbins	1989	9
21 13/16	13 4/16	8 9/16	Menominee Co., Mich.	Andrew M. Bray	Ray Bray	1989	10
21 12/16	13 4/16	8 8/16	Huerfano Co., Colo.	Harvey R. Newcomb	Harvey R. Newcomb	1988	11
21 12/16	13 5/16	8 7/16	Lily Lake, B.C.	James W. Zevely	James W. Zevely	1990	11
21 12/16	13 8/16	8 4/16	Makinak, Man.	Wendell Hanson	Wendell Hanson	1991	11
21 11/16	13 7/16	8 4/16	Queen Charlotte Islands, B.C.	Kurt M. Saffarek	Kurt M. Saffarek	1988	14
21 11/16	13 6/16	8 5/16	Prince of Wales Island, Alaska	Richard J. Asplund	Richard J. Asplund	1990	14
21 11/16	13 15/16	7 12/16	Porcupine Hills, Sask.	Richard K. McLean	Richard K. McLean	1990	14
21 11/16	13 5/16	8 6/16	Ventura Co., Calif.	Marsha Vaughan	Marsha Vaughan	1990	14
21 10/16	13 12/16	7 14/16	Piscataquis Co., Maine	J.D. Flowers	J.D. Flowers	1980	18
21 10/16	13 9/16	8 1/16	Prairie River, Sask.	Tim P. Matzinger	Tim P. Matzinger	1989	18
21 10/16	13 2/16	8 8/16	Gila Co., Ariz.	John F. Peters	John F. Peters	1989	18
21 10/16	13 10/16	8	Alcona Co., Mich.	Randy Schultz	Randy Schultz	1989	18
21 10/16	13 7/16	8 3/16	Graham Co., Ariz.	S. Kim Bonnett	S. Kim Bonnett	1990	18
21 10/16	13 6/16	8 4/16	Bucareli Bay, Alaska	Dwight B. Leister, Jr.	Dwight B. Leister, Jr.	1990	18
21 9/16	13 11/16	7 14/16	Tyrrell Co., N.C.	Larry D. Bailey	Larry D. Bailey	1987	24
21 9/16	13 13/16	7 12/16	Collier Co., Fla.	Picked Up	Florida Game & Fresh Water Fish Comm.	1988	24
21 9/16	13 2/16	8 7/16	Thorne River, Alaska	Ernest W. McLean	Ernest W. McLean	1989	24
21 8/16	13 8/16	8	Lincoln Co., Wyo.	Picked Up	Matt Failoni	1965	27
21 8/16	13 6/16	8 7/16	Sarkar Creek, Alaska	Robert F. Ellebruch	Robert F. Ellebruch	1988	27
21 8/16	13 10/16	7 14/16	Lake Co., Fla.	Picked Up	Flordia Game & Fresh Water Fish Comm.	1989	27

409

Black Bear - Continued

Score	Greatest Length of Skull Without Lower Jaw	Greatest Width of Skull	Locality Killed	By Whom Killed	Owner	Date Killed	Rank
21 8/16	13 5/16	8 3/16	Gila Co., Ariz.	Don Hoey	Don Hoey	1989	27
21 8/16	13 4/16	8 4/16	Stove Lake, Sask.	David Prince	David Prince	1990	27
21 8/16	13 3/16	8 5/16	Clinton Co., N.Y.	Todd F. Rabideau	Todd F. Rabideau	1990	27
21 7/16	13 2/16	8 5/16	Somerset Co., Pa.	Ralph T. Myers	Ralph T. Myers	1987	33
21 7/16	13 9/16	7 14/16	Smoky River, Alta.	Gary G. Dumdei	Gary G. Dumdei	1989	33
21 7/16	13 7/16	8	Kupreanof Island, Alaska	David K. Mueller	David K. Mueller	1989	33
21 6/16	13 2/16	8 4/16	Prince of Wales Island, Alaska	John Stubbs	John Stubbs	1973	36
21 6/16	13 3/16	8 3/16	Klawock, Alaska	Tom R. Engel	Tom R. Engel	1987	36
21 6/16	13 6/16	8	Grant Co., W.Va.	Carnie Carr, Sr.	Carnie Carr, Sr.	1988	36
21 6/16	13 7/16	7 15/16	Graham Co., Ariz.	Timm J. Haas	Timm J. Haas	1988	36
21 6/16	13 8/16	7 14/16	Cattaraugus Co., N.Y.	John M. Abrams, Sr.	John M. Abrams, Sr.	1989	36
21 6/16	13 5/16	8 1/16	Potter Co., Pa.	Earl E. Carolus	Earl E. Carolus	1989	36
21 5/16	13 5/16	8	Potter Co., Pa.	Gary R. Sellers	Gary R. Sellers	1989	42
21 5/16	13 8/16	7 13/16	Hudson Bay, Sask.	Jim Strini	Jim Strini	1990	42
21 5/16	13 3/16	8 6/16	Swan River, Man.	Linda A. Nuss	Linda A. Nuss	1991	42
21 4/16	13 2/16	8 3/16	Swan River, Man.	Richard C. Weber	Richard C. Weber	1987	46
21 4/16	13 4/16	8	Mille Lacs Co., Minn.	Timothy J. Dusbabek	Timothy J. Dusbabek	1988	46
21 4/16	13	8 4/16	Greenlee Co., Ariz.	Bart Bledsoe	Bart Bledsoe	1988	46
21 4/16	13 1/16	8 3/16	Catron Co., N.M.	Gary L. Raney	Gary L. Raney	1989	46
21 4/16	13 2/16	8 2/16	Pasquia Hills, Sask.	Patrick G. Povah	Patrick G. Povah	1990	46
21 4/16	13 2/16	8 2/16	Aroostook Co., Maine	John S. Drost	John S. Drost	1990	46
21 3/16	13	8 4/16	Shasta Co., Calif.	Rick Moore	Rick Moore	1988	52
21 3/16	13	8 3/16	Red Deer River, Sask.	Gordon Paproski	Gordon Paproski	1989	52
21 3/16	13 2/16	8 1/16	Kuiu Island, Alaska	Michael D. Speigle	Michael D. Speigle	1990	52
21 3/16	13 3/16	8	Prince of Wales Island, Alaska	George P. Mann	George P. Mann	1991	52
21 3/16	13 1/16	8 2/16	Catron Co., N.M.	John M. Burton, Jr.	John M. Burton, Jr.	1991	52
21 2/16	13 7/16	7 12/16	Canora, Sask.	Rodney S. Petrychyn	Rodney S. Petrychyn	1988	57
21 2/16	12 13/16	8 5/16	Pencil Lake, Ont.	Michael F. Gerber	Michael F. Gerber	1989	57
21 2/16	13 4/16	7 14/16	Turtle Lake, Sask.	Tony L. Johnson	Tony L. Johnson	1989	57
21 2/16	13 2/16	8	Cold Lake, Alta.	Dean Herron	Dean Herron	1990	57
21 2/16	13 3/16	7 15/16	Bjorkdale, Sask.	Clayton R. Shiels	Clayton R. Shiels	1990	57
21 2/16	13 1/16	8 1/16	Moresby Island, B.C.	Roger W. Robinson	Roger W. Robinson	1991	57
21 1/16	13	8 1/16	Piscataquis Co., Maine	J.D. Flowers	J.D. Flowers	1966	62

				Owner	Hunter	Year	Score
21 1/16	12 14/16	8 3/16	Cook Co., Minn.	Kevin R. Johnson	K. Johnson, G. Bjerkness, & S. Borud	1986	62
21 1/16	13 1/16	8	Charlaroix Co., Mich.	Gerald L. Fuller	Gerald L. Fuller	1988	62
21 1/16	12 14/16	8 3/16	St. Louis Co., Minn.	Jonathan E. Polecheck	Jonathan E. Polecheck	1989	62
21	13 2/16	7 14/16	Ostenfeld, Man.	Erik Thienpondt	Erik Thienpondt	1983	66
21	13 6/16	7 10/16	Muriel Lake, Alta.	Edward R. Rempel	Edward R. Rempel	1988	66
21	13 2/16	7 14/16	Gates Co., N.C.	John W. Whitehurst, Jr.	John W. Whitehurst, Jr.	1988	66
21	13	8	Carbon Co., Utah	Lonnie K. Bell	Lonnie K. Bell	1989	66
21	12 13/16	8 3/16	Iron Co., Wisc.	Todd J. Brauer	Todd J. Brauer	1989	66
21	13 2/16	7 14/16	Peace River, Alta.	Danny de Melo	Danny de Melo	1989	66
21	12 15/16	8 1/16	Brokenhead River, Man.	Michael E. Vandenbosch	Michael E. Vandenbosch	1989	66
21	13	8	LeDomaine, Que.	Anthony Becciro	Anthony Becciro	1990	66
21	12 10/16	8 6/16	Greenlee Co., Ariz.	Robin W. Bechtel	Robin W. Bechtel	1990	66
21	13	8	Beaufort Co., N.C.	Marlow V. Jones	Marlow V. Jones	1990	66
21	12 12/16	8 4/16	Peace River, Alta.	Kent S. Anderson	Kent S. Anderson	1991	66
20 15/16	12 15/16	8	Iron Co., Wisc.	Steven D. Markham	Steven D. Markham	1987	77
20 14/16	13 4/16	7 10/16	Centre Co., Pa.	Carroll G. Heckman	Carroll G. Heckman	1985	78
20 14/16	12 14/16	8	Okanagan Lake, B.C.	Steven O. Townsend	Steven O. Townsend	1991	78
20 13/16	12 13/16	8	Red Deer River, Sask.	David Schmidt	David Schmidt	1985	80
20 13/16	13	7 13/16	Greenlee Co., Ariz.	Robert R. White	Robert R. White	1988	80
20 13/16	13 1/16	7 12/16	Westmoreland Co., Pa.	Robert Forish	Robert Forish	1989	80
20 13/16	13 1/16	7 12/16	Loon Lake, Sask.	Gregory D. Gille	Gregory D. Gille	1989	80
20 12/16	13	7 13/16	Northbrook, Ont.	George J. Hubal	George J. Hubal	1989	80
20 12/16	12 10/16	8 2/16	Boise Co., Idaho	Charles S. Barto	Charles S. Barto	1988	85
20 12/16	12 15/16	7 13/16	Rappahannock Co., Va	John W. Merchant	John W. Merchant	1989	85
20 11/16	12 11/16	8	Shasta Co., Calif.	Kevin D. Sanders	Kevin D. Sanders	1990	87
20 10/16	13 2/16	7 8/16	Centre Co., Pa.	S. Elwood Homan	S. Elwood Homan	1989	88
20 10/16	13	7 10/16	Piwei River, Sask.	Adam Shawaducki	Adam Shawaducki	1989	88
20 9/16	12 14/16	7 11/16	Duncan Canal, Alaska	Wayne G. McCaulley	Wayne G. McCaulley	1990	90
20 9/16	12 7/16	8 2/16	Warren Co., Pa.	James M. Mele	James M. Mele	1990	90
20 8/16	12 11/16	7 13/16	Becker Co., Minn.	Kurtis D. Fischer	Kurtis D. Fischer	1989	92
20 8/16	13 2/16	7 12/16	Clearwater Co., Minn.	Michael D. Aakhus	Michael D. Aakhus	1990	92
20 8/16	12 12/16	7 12/16	Iosegun River, Alta.	Terry B. Upright	Terry B. Upright	1990	92
20 7/16	12 11/16	7 12/16	Essex Co., N.Y.	John W. Phillips	John W. Phillips	1988	95
20 7/16	12 12/16	8	Rappahannock Co., Va.	Collis W. Dodson, Jr.	Collis W. Dodson, Jr.	1989	95
20 7/16	12 7/16	7 13/16	Price Co., Wisc.	Paul F. Gehrke	Paul F. Gehrke	1989	95
20 6/16	12 10/16	7 9/16	Catron Co., N.M.	Kenneth L. Buholtz	Kenneth L. Buholtz	1989	98
20 6/16	12 13/16	7 13/16	Chippewa Co., Mich.	Robert M. Dicus	Robert M. Dicus	1989	98
20 6/16	12 9/16	7 11/16	Georges Lake, Nfld.	Melvin P. Locklyn	Melvin P. Locklyn	1989	98
20 6/16	12 10/16	7 12/16	Prince of Wales Island, Alaska	Lucretia Y. Mann	Lucretia Y. Mann	1990	98
20 5/16	12 12/16	7 12/16	Kuiu Island, Alaska	Keith B. Shoaps	Keith B. Shoaps	1990	102

Black Bear - *Continued*

Score	Greatest Length of Skull Without Lower Jaw	Greatest Width of Skull	Locality Killed	By Whom Killed	Owner	Date Killed	Rank
20 5/16	12 7/16	7 14/16	Vancouver Island, B.C.	Jack L. Covington	Jack L. Covington	1991	102
20 4/16	12 8/16	7 12/16	Sioux Lookout, Ont.	William K. Yeiser	William K. Yeiser	1985	104
20 4/16	12 14/16	7 6/16	Temiscamingue Lake, Que.	Cyril H. Sykes	Cyril H. Sykes	1988	104
20 4/16	12 3/16	8 1/16	Sullivan Co., Pa.	Guy R. Bieber	Guy R. Bieber	1989	104
20 4/16	12 5/16	7 15/16	Athapapuskow Lake, Man.	Dean K. Reidt	Dean K. Reidt	1989	104
20 4/16	12 15/16	7 5/16	Garfield Co., Colo.	Robert J. Witt	Robert J. Witt	1990	104
20 4/16	12 11/16	7 9/16	Leaf Lake, Sask.	David Schmidt	David Schmidt	1991	104
20 2/16	12 10/16	7 8/16	Prince of Wales Island, Alaska	John J. King	John J. King	1987	110
20 2/16	12 14/16	7 4/16	Pine Co., Minn.	Brian D. Scarnegie	Brian D. Scarnegie	1988	110
20 2/16	12 10/16	7 8/16	Baker Co., Oreg.	Craig L. Dolby	Craig L. Dolby	1989	110
20 2/16	12 5/16	7 13/16	Marinette Co., Wisc.	Mark D. Wolf	Mark D. Wolf	1989	110
20 2/16	12 10/16	7 8/16	Idaho Co., Idaho	Robert J. Kaminski	Robert J. Kaminski	1990	110
20 2/16	12 7/16	7 11/16	Prince of Wales Island, Alaska	Thomas A. Kooistra	Thomas A. Kooistra	1990	110
20 2/16	12 10/16	7 8/16	Latah Co., Idaho	Patrick M. McCullough	Patrick M. McCullough	1990	110
20 2/16	12 9/16	7 9/16	Langlade Co., Wisc.	Robert R. Baker	Robert R. Baker	1991	110
20	12 14/16	7 2/16	Snohomish Co., Wash.	Mark Felz	Mark Felz	1988	118
20	12 12/16	7 4/16	Idaho Co., Idaho	David C. Huber, Sr.	David C. Huber, Sr.	1988	118
20	12 11/16	7 5/16	King Co., Wash.	Brent R. Perschon	Brent R. Perschon	1988	118
20	12 2/16	7 14/16	Nameigos Lake, Ont.	Brian D. Girdley	Brian D. Girdley	1989	118
20	12 5/16	7 11/16	Iron Co., Wisc.	R. Joe Maciejewski	R. Joe Maciejewski	1989	118
20	12 11/16	7 5/16	King Co., Wash.	Matthew J. McCoy	Matthew J. McCoy	1990	118
20	12 10/16	7 6/16	Aubichon Arm, Sask.	Michael D. Tofte	Michael D. Tofte	1990	118
20	12 12/16	7 4/16	Bill Lake, Sask.	Anthony M. Sciascia	Anthony M. Sciascia	1991	118
22*	13 14/16	8 2/16	Prince of Wales Island, Alaska	Stanley L. Parkerson	Stanley L. Parkerson	1991	118

* Final Score subject to revision by additional verifying measurements.

412

Grizzly Bear

Ursus arctos horribilis

Minimum Score 23

Score	Greatest Length of Skull Without Lower Jaw	Greatest Width of Skull	Locality Killed	By Whom Killed	Owner	Date Killed	Rank
27 2/16	17 3/16	9 15/16	Inglutalik River, Alaska	Theodore Kurdziel, Jr.	Theodore Kurdziel, Jr.	1991	1
26 14/16	16 14/16	10	Teklanika River, Alaska	D. Alan McCaleb	D. Alan McCaleb	1989	2
26 6/16	16 6/16	10 8/16	Anahim Lake, B.C.	Denis E. Schiller	D.E. Schiller & K. Karran	1990	2
25 15/16	15 15/16	10	Tatlawiksuk River, Alaska	William H. Green	Mrs. William H. Green	1988	4
25 15/16	15 13/16	10 2/16	Morice River, B.C.	Joesf Martinek	Joesf Martinek	1991	4
25 13/16	16 4/16	9 7/16	Knight Inlet, B.C.	Charles E. Gromatzky	Charles E. Gromatzky	1988	6
25 11/16	16 2/16	9 9/16	Babine River, B.C.	Robert V. Ellis	Robert V. Ellis	1991	6
25 11/16	15 5/16	9 14/16	Skeena Mts., B.C.	Thomas J. Grogan	Thomas J. Grogan	1989	8
25 7/16	16 2/16	9 2/16	Dazell Creek, Alaska	Armand J. Giannini	Armand J. Giannini	1988	9
25 4/16	16 4/16	9	Trapper Lake, B.C.	John Kloosterman	John Kloosterman	1991	9
25 4/16	15 6/16	9 12/16	Dease Lake, B.C.	John Flynn	John Flynn	1988	11
25 2/16	16 2/16	9	Noomst Creek, B.C.	Marc A. Laynes	Marc A. Laynes	1988	11
25 2/16	16 9/16	8 7/16	Chincaga River, Alta.	Bernd Licht	Bernd Licht	1989	13
25	15 7/16	9 8/16	Maroon Creek, B.C.	Roger M. Britton	Roger M. Britton	1988	14
24 15/16	15 4/16	9 10/16	Squirrel River, Alaska	William M. Eubank	William M. Eubank	1988	15
24 14/16	15 8/16	9 9/16	Grayling Fork, Yukon	Michael L. Rogers	Michael L. Rogers	1991	15
24 14/16	15 15/16	8 13/16	Teklanika River, Alaska	Kenneth E. Abel	Kenneth E. Abel	1990	17
24 12/16	15 13/16	8 14/16	Moses Inlet, B.C.	Robert E. Johnson	Robert E. Johnson	1989	18
24 11/16	15 14/16	9 2/16	Muskwa River, B.C.	Benjamin F. Kirkham	Benjamin F. Kirkham	1990	18
24 10/16	15 14/16	8 12/16	Swan Hills, Alta.	Henry H. Foisy	Henry H. Foisy	1988	20
24 10/16	15 12/16	8 14/16	Mt. Miller, Yukon	Doug White	Doug White	1990	20
24 8/16	15	9 8/16	Buckland River, Alaska	Curtis R. Cebulski	Doug Christiansen	1988	22
24 8/16	15 6/16	9 2/16	Norton Sound, Alaska	Jerry W. Peterman	Jerry W. Peterman	1988	22
24 8/16	15 2/16	9 6/16	Bowser Lake, B.C.	Raymond J. Kotera	Raymond J. Kotera	1990	22
24 7/16	15 6/16	9 1/16	Dore River, B.C.	Brian C. Jeck	Brian C. Jeck	1987	25
24 6/16	15 6/16	9	Willow River, B.C.	Eric Hanet	Eric Hanet	1962	26
24 6/16	15 7/16	8 15/16	Poutang Creek, B.C.	Irvin H. Brown	Irvin H. Brown	1990	26
24 5/16	15 3/16	9 2/16	Poktonik Mts., Alaska	John W. Bania	John W. Bania	1989	28
24 5/16	15 6/16	8 15/16	Squirrel River, Alaska	Walter J. Miller	Walter J. Miller	1990	28
24 5/16	15 6/16	9 1/16	Horton River, N.W.T.	Victor E. Moss	Victor E. Moss	1990	28

Grizzly Bear - *Continued*

Score	Greatest Length of Skull Without Lower Jaw	Greatest Width of Skull	Locality Killed	By Whom Killed	Owner	Date Killed	Rank
24 4/16	15 1/16	9 3/16	Knight Inlet, B.C.	Steven C. Gromatzky	Steven C. Gromatzky	1988	31
24 4/16	15	9 4/16	Gathto Creek, B.C.	James I. Scott	James I. Scott	1988	31
24 3/16	15 6/16	8 13/16	Christmas Creek, Alaska	Charles L. Fuller	Charles L. Fuller	1988	33
24 3/16	14 14/16	9 5/16	Henry Creek, Alaska	Ray S. Smith	Ray S. Smith	1990	33
24 3/16	15 2/16	9 1/16	Nuka River, Alaska	Gene Hynes	Gene Hynes	1991	33
24 1/16	15 5/16	8 12/16	Little Red Rock Creek, Alta.	P. Casey & B. Winters	Patrick Casey	1987	36
24	14 14/16	9 2/16	Nome River, Alaska	Samuel J. Nicolosi, Jr.	Samuel J. Nicolosi, Jr.	1990	37
24	14 8/16	9 8/16	Koyuk River, Alaska	Thomas A. Vaughn	Thomas A. Vaughn	1990	37
24	15	9	Caribou Creek, Alaska	Lee M. Wahlund	Lee M. Wahlund	1991	37
23 12/16	15 4/16	8 8/16	Toad River, B.C.	Harry A. Knowlton	Harry A. Knowlton	1990	40
23 8/16	14 9/16	8 15/16	Kokokik River, Alaska	Louis B. Mann	Louis B. Mann	1989	41
23 6/16	14 6/16	8 14/16	Shaktolik River, Alaska	Walter A. Tilley	Walter A. Tilley	1988	42
23 6/16	14 7/16	8 13/16	Eureka Dome, Alaska	Lawrence J. Bess	Lawrence J. Bess	1991	42
23 2/16	14 4/16	8 14/16	Killik River, Alaska	Gene B. Wolstenholme	Gene B. Wolstenholme	1991	44
26 2/16 *	16 9/16	9 9/16	Washwash River, B.C.	Bruce A. Simon	Bruce A. Simon	1989	

* Final Score subject to revision by additional verifying measurements.

Alaska Brown Bear

Ursus arctos middendorffi and certain related subspecies

Minimum Score 26   World's Record 30-12/16

Score	Greatest Length of Skull Without Lower Jaw	Greatest Width of Skull	Locality Killed	By Whom Killed	Owner	Date Killed	Rank
29 8/16	18 1/16	11 7/16	Kaiuguak Bay, Alaska	Martin H. Shaft	Martin H. Shaft	1990	1
29 5/16	18 1/16	11 4/16	Braided Creek, Alaska	Robert L. Coleman	Robert L. Coleman	1991	2
29 3/16	18	11 3/16	Alaska Pen., Alaska	Peter Ma	Peter Ma	1990	3
29 1/16	17 12/16	11 5/16	Fraser Lake, Alaska	Randy D. Klingenmeyer	Randy D. Klingenmeyer	1991	4
29	17 8/16	11 8/16	Middle Bay, Alaska	Royal V. Large, Jr.	Royal V. Large, Jr.	1990	5
29	17 5/16	11 11/16	Kodiak Island, Alaska	James D. Nyce	James D. Nyce	1990	5
29	18 3/16	10 13/16	Karluk Lake, Alaska	Robert W. Stevens	Robert W. Stevens	1990	5
28 15/16	17 5/16	11 10/16	Kodiak Island, Alaska	Geoffrey H.S. House	Geoffrey H.S. House	1989	8
28 15/16	17 6/16	11 9/16	Dog Salmon River, Alaska	John H. Sholtiss	John H. Sholtiss	1989	8
28 14/16	17 3/16	11 11/16	Olga Bay, Alaska	William G. James	William G. James	1989	10
28 14/16	18 5/16	10 9/16	Muddy River, Alaska	Chung C. Huang	Chung C. Huang	1990	10
28 14/16	17 12/16	11 2/16	Meshik River, Alaska	R. Jackson Willingham	R. Jackson Willingham	1990	10
28 14/16	18 11/16	10 3/16	Cold Bay, Alaska	Dick A. Jacobs	Dick A. Jacobs	1991	10
28 12/16	17 3/16	11 1/16	Deadman Bay, Alaska	Marvin Shick	Marvin Shick	1989	14
28 11/16	17 1/16	11 3/16	Kodiak Island, Alaska	Terry M. Webb	Terry M. Webb	1986	15
28 11/16	17 13/16	10 14/16	Cold Bay, Alaska	Simon Aragi	Simon Aragi	1988	15
28 11/16	18 3/16	10 8/16	Littlejohn Lagoon, Alaska	Anthony C. Henry	Anthony C. Henry	1990	15
28 10/16	17	11 10/16	Kaguyak Bay, Alaska	Robert W. Bundtzen	Robert W. Bundtzen	1989	18
28 10/16	17 2/16	11 8/16	Kodiak Island, Alaska	John D. Powers	John D. Powers	1989	18
28 10/16	17 14/16	10 12/16	Alaska Pen., Alaska	James L. Kedrowski	James L. Kedrowski	1990	18
28 9/16	17 6/16	11 3/16	Talkeetna Mts., Alaska	Max C. Schwab	Max C. Schwab	1987	21
28 9/16	17 2/16	11 7/16	Sitkalidak Island, Alaska	Travis L. Barber	Travis L. Barber	1989	21
28 8/16	17 4/16	11 4/16	Viekoda Bay, Alaska	Houston Smith	Houston Smith	1989	23
28 8/16	17 8/16	11	Kodiak Island, Alaska	Andrew J. Fierro	Andrew J. Fierro	1991	23
28 8/16	16 15/16	11 9/16	Deadman Bay, Alaska	John L. Spencer	John L. Spencer	1991	23
28 7/16	17 8/16	10 15/16	Uganik Bay, Alaska	Mark T. Jacobson	Mark T. Jacobson	1989	26
28 7/16	18	10 7/16	Cold Bay, Alaska	George A. Bettas	George A. Bettas	1990	26
28 7/16	17 14/16	10 9/16	Karluk Lake, Alaska	Stanley N. Kaneshiro	Stanley N. Kaneshiro	1990	26
28 7/16	17 4/16	11 3/16	Uganik Island, Alaska	David S. Collett-Paule	James J. Brooks	1991	26
28 7/16	17 8/16	10 15/16	Unimak Island, Alaska	Danny V. Grangaard	Danny V. Grangaard	1991	26

Alaska Brown Bear - *Continued*

Score	Greatest Length of Skull Without Lower Jaw	Greatest Width of Skull	Locality Killed	By Whom Killed	Owner	Date Killed	Rank
28 6/16	17	11 6/16	Olga Bay, Alaska	David B. Colclough	David B. Colclough	1989	31
28 6/16	17 15/16	10 7/16	Pavlof Bay, Alaska	John R. Sullivan	John R. Sullivan	1989	31
28 6/16	17 2/16	11 4/16	Karluk River, Alaska	Terry J. Leffler	Terry J. Leffler	1990	31
28 5/16	17 4/16	11 1/16	Captain Harbor, Alaska	Tarleton F. Smith	Michigan State Univ. Mus.	1949	34
28 5/16	17	11 5/16	Kaguyak Bay, Alaska	Arnold F. Thibault	Arnold F. Thibault	1989	34
28 5/16	17 4/16	11 1/16	Kodiak Island, Alaska	J. Dorsey Smith	J. Dorsey Smith	1990	34
28 4/16	17 15/16	10 4/16	Cold Bay, Alaska	Carlos F.S. Schutz	Carlos F.S. Schutz	1990	37
28 3/16	17 1/16	11 1/16	Afognak Island, Alaska	Donald E. Peterson	Donald E. Peterson	1984	38
28 2/16	17 12/16	10 6/16	Meshik Lake, Alaska	Richard L. DeFelice	Richard L. DeFelice	1989	38
28 2/16	16 6/16	11 12/16	Uyak Bay, Alaska	Picked Up	Randy C. Arsenault	PR 1990	38
28 2/16	16 15/16	11 3/16	Karluk Lake, Alaska	Robert W. Stevens III	Robert W. Stevens III	1990	38
28 2/16	17 4/16	10 14/16	Akwe River, Alaska	Roger R. Reck	Roger R. Reck	1991	38
28 1/16	17 6/16	10 11/16	Kodiak Island, Alaska	Bruce T. Berger	Bruce T. Berger	1988	43
28 1/16	17 12/16	10 5/16	Cinder River, Alaska	Keith Pilz	Keith Pilz	1989	43
28	17 9/16	10 7/16	Cold Bay, Alaska	John D. Teeter	John D. Teeter	1988	45
28	17	11	Sulna Bay, Alaska	Theodore A. Mallett	Theodore A. Mallett	1989	45
28	17	11	Uganik Bay, Alaska	Donald M. Sitton	Donald M. Sitton	1990	45
28	16 12/16	11 4/16	Uganik Bay, Alaska	Gene J. Brzek	Gene J. Brzek	1991	45
27 15/16	17 4/16	10 14/16	Uganik Bay, Alaska	Christopher L. Tillotson	Christopher L. Tillotson	1991	49
27 11/16	17 4/16	10 10/16	Fox River, Alaska	Anthony J. Zucco	Anthony J. Zucco	1989	50
27 8/16	17 2/16	10 6/16	Beaver Bay, Alaska	Joe B. Owen	Joe B. Owen	1989	51
27 4/16	17 1/16	10 3/16	Alaska Pen., Alaska	Joseph J. Roscioli	Joseph J. Roscioli	1968	52
27 4/16	16 6/16	10 14/16	Kaguyak Bay, Alaska	Bill Davis	Bill Davis	1990	52
27 2/16	15 14/16	11 4/16	Wild Creek, Alaska	Larry L. Prine	Larry L. Prine	1990	54
27 2/16	16 12/16	10 6/16	Uyak Bay, Alaska	Michael P. O'Neill	Michael P. O'Neill	1991	54
26 14/16	17 2/16	9 12/16	Cold Bay, Alaska	George A. Bettas	George A. Bettas	1982	56
26 14/16	17 4/16	9 10/16	Bristol Bay, Alaska	Richard C. Klimes	Richard C. Klimes	1990	56
26 10/16	16 6/16	10 1/16	Nukakuk Lake, Alaska	Christian J. Mangels	Christian J. Mangels	1990	58
26 6/16	16 6/16	10	Uganik Bay, Alaska	Michael J. Jacobson	Michael J. Jacobson	1989	59
26 3/16	15 14/16	10 5/16	Deadman Bay, Alaska	Lonnie L. Ritchey	Lonnie L. Ritchey	1990	60

Jaguar

Felis onca hernandesii and related subspecies

World's Record 18 7/16

Minimum Score 14-8/16

Score	Greatest Length of Skull Without Lower Jaw	Greatest Width of Skull	Locality Killed	By Whom Killed	Owner	Date Killed	Rank
16 13/16	10 4/16	6 9/16	Tabasco, Mexico	Watson T. Yoshimoto	Watson T. Yoshimoto	1971	1

Cougar or Mountain Lion

Felis concolor hippolestes and related subspecies

Minimum Score 14-8/16   World's Record 16-4/16

Score	Greatest Length of Skull Without Lower Jaw	Greatest Width of Skull	Locality Killed	By Whom Killed	Owner	Date Killed	Rank
15 14/16	9 2/16	6 12/16	Walla Walla Co., Wash.	Robert A. Klicker	Robert A. Klicker	1988	1
15 11/16	9 3/16	6 8/16	Fisher Creek, Alta.	John Cassidy	John Cassidy	1985	2
15 11/16	9 4/16	6 7/16	Eagle Co., Colo.	Layne K. Wing	Layne K. Wing	1990	2
15 9/16	9 2/16	6 7/16	Idaho Co., Idaho	Randy L. Waddell	Randy L. Waddell	1990	4
15 8/16	9 4/16	6 4/16	Montrose Co., Colo.	Kendall Hamilton	Kendall Hamilton	1988	5
15 8/16	9 2/16	6 6/16	Clallam Co., Wash.	John M. Rawlings	John M. Rawlings	1990	5
15 7/16	9 1/16	6 6/16	Pend Oreille Co., Wash.	Wesley M. Kreiger	Wesley M. Kreiger	1988	7
15 7/16	8 15/16	6 8/16	Ferry Co., Wash.	John P. Peruchini	John P. Peruchini	1989	7
15 7/16	9 4/16	6 3/16	Colfax Co., N.M.	Robert M. Werley	Robert M. Werley	1989	7
15 6/16	8 14/16	6 8/16	James River, Alta.	Susan M. Geduhn	S. Geduhn & F. Geduhn	1989	10
15 6/16	8 15/16	6 7/16	Nez Perce Co., Idaho	Rob Courville	Rob Courville	1990	10
15 5/16	8 15/16	6 6/16	Dutch Creek, Alta.	Darryl C. Naslund	Darryl C. Naslund	1988	12
15 5/16	9 2/16	6 3/16	Ravalli Co., Mont.	Edward J. Pines III	Edward J. Pines III	1988	12
15 5/16	8 15/16	6 6/16	Boise Co., Idaho	Donald G. Thurston	Donald G. Thurston	1991	12
15 4/16	8 15/16	6 5/16	Cassia Co., Idaho	Charles W. Eagleson	Charles W. Eagleson	1988	15
15 4/16	8 15/16	6 5/16	Wallowa Co., Oreg.	Mark D. Armstrong	Mark D. Armstrong	1989	15
15 4/16	8 14/16	6 6/16	Shoshone Co., Idaho	Darrell G. Holmquist	Darrell G. Holmquist	1990	15
15 4/16	8 15/16	6 5/16	Whaleback Ridge, Alta.	Sally A. Kloosterman	Sally A. Kloosterman	1991	15
15 3/16	8 13/16	6 6/16	Clearwater Co., Idaho	Mike T. McCain	Mike T. McCain	1988	19
15 3/16	8 14/16	6 5/16	Lincoln Co., Mont.	Jon G. Clark	Jon G. Clark	1989	19
15 3/16	9 1/16	6 2/16	Mt. Thynne, B.C.	Cliff C. Cory	Cliff C. Cory	1989	19
15 3/16	8 13/16	6 6/16	Porcupine Hills, Alta.	Sidney Websdale	Sidney Websdale	1989	19
15 3/16	8 15/16	6 4/16	Idaho Co., Idaho	Stephan Galles	Stephan Galles	1990	19
15 3/16	8 11/16	6 8/16	Larimer Co., Colo.	Peter A. Larson	Peter A. Larson	1990	19
15 3/16	9 2/16	6 1/16	San Miguel Co., N.M.	Robert J. Seeds	Robert J. Seeds	1990	19
15 3/16	9 1/16	6 2/16	Archuleta Co., Colo.	Charles T. Ames	Charles T. Ames	1991	19
15 3/16	8 15/16	6 3/16	Coleman, Alta.	Jerry Fisher	Jerry Fisher	1991	19
15 2/16	8 13/16	6 5/16	Clearwater Co., Idaho	Michael J. Kennedy	Michael J. Kennedy	1987	28
15 2/16	8 13/16	6 5/16	Union Co., Oreg.	Francis G. Culver	Francis G. Culver	1988	28
15 2/16	8 12/16	6 6/16	Lake Co., Mont.	Kevin J. Warning	Kevin J. Warning	1989	28

15 2/16	9 1/16	6 1/16	Woods Lake, B.C.	S. MacKenzie & B. Jaeger	Sean MacKenzie	1990	28
15 2/16	9	6 2/16	Taos Co., N.M.	William L. Porteous	William L. Porteous	1990	28
15 2/16	8 15/16	6 3/16	Park Co., Colo.	Jack P. Van Vianen	Jack P. Van Vianen	1990	28
15 1/16	8 13/16	6 4/16	Idaho Co., Idaho	Ronald R. Feist	Ronald R. Feist	1987	34
15 1/16	8 11/16	6 6/16	Shoshone Co., Idaho	David K. Mueller	David K. Mueller	1988	34
15 1/16	9	6 1/16	Missoula Co., Mont.	Kenneth P. Schoening	Kenneth P. Schoening	1988	34
15 1/16	8 13/16	6 4/16	Clallam Co., Wash.	John R. Franz	John R. Franz	1989	34
15 1/16	8 14/16	6 3/16	Daggett Co., Utah	T.C. Benson & L.V. Massey	Todd C. Benson	1990	34
15 1/16	8 11/16	6 6/16	Utah Co., Utah	Mary L. Brooks	Mary L. Brooks	1990	34
15 1/16	8 14/16	6 3/16	Rio Blanco Co., Colo.	Gerald L. Dowling	Gerald L. Dowling	1990	34
15 1/16	9	6 1/16	Millard Co., Utah	Edwin A. Lewis	Edwin A. Lewis	1990	34
15 1/16	8 13/16	6 4/16	Dolores Co., Colo.	Anthony S. Wagner	Anthony S. Wagner	1990	34
15 1/16	8 14/16	6 3/16	Latah Co., Idaho	Stephan D. Galles	Stephan D. Galles	1991	34
15	8 11/16	6 5/16	Ashnola River, B.C.	Bill Bryant	Bill Bryant	1985	44
15	8 11/16	6 5/16	Columbia Co., Wash.	David N. Bowen	David N. Bowen	1988	44
15	8 12/16	6 6/16	Big Horn Co., Wyo.	Brant Z. Hilman	Brant Z. Hilman	1988	44
15	8 13/16	6 4/16	Summers Creek, B.C.	Jack Sprayberry	Jack Sprayberry	1988	44
15	8 12/16	6 3/16	Clear Creek Co., Colo.	Garry E. Fry	Garry E. Fry	1989	44
15	8 13/16	6 4/16	Pillow Co., B.C.	K.T. Michie & T. Wasylyszyn	Kent T. Michie	1989	44
15	8 12/16	6 3/16	Porcupine Hills, Alta.	Dennis M. Olson	Dennis M. Olson	1989	44
15	8 14/16	6 4/16	Rio Arriba Co., N.M.	Robert J. Seeds	Robert J. Seeds	1989	44
15	9	6 2/16	Elmore Co., Idaho	Ed J. Strayhorn	Ed J. Strayhorn	1989	44
15	8 11/16	6	Cotton Creek, B.C.	Ed Swanson, Jr.	Ed Swanson, Jr.	1989	44
15	8 11/16	6 5/16	Bob Creek, Alta.	Tom Ellis	Tom Ellis	1990	44
15	8 15/16	6 5/16	Grand Co., Utah	Darin King	Darin King	1990	44
15	8 14/16	6 1/16	Carbon Co., Utah	Roy R. Wheeler, Jr.	Roy R. Wheeler, Jr.	1990	44
15	8 12/16	6 2/16	Kane Co., Utah	Robert A. Carlson	Robert A. Carlson	1991	44
15	8 10/16	6 4/16	Granite Co., Mont.	Hal W. Johnson	Hal W. Johnson	1991	44
15	8 13/16	6 1/16	Eagle Co., Colo.	James R. Johnston	James R. Johnston	1991	44
15	8 15/16	6 3/16	Duchesne Co., Utah	Lonnie L. Ritchey	Lonnie L. Ritchey	1991	44
15	8 11/16	6 1/16	Fergus Co., Mont.	Charles R. Taylor	Charles R. Taylor	1991	44
14 15/16	8 12/16	6 5/16	Coconino Co., Ariz.	Billie F. Bechtel	Billie F. Bechtel	1987	62
14 15/16	8 11/16	6 3/16	Park Co., Mont.	Patrick J. Gilligan	Patrick J. Gilligan	1988	62
14 15/16	8 14/16	6 1/16	Carbon Co., Wyo.	James White	Clifford White	1989	62
14 15/16	8 13/16	6 2/16	Bear Lake Co., Idaho	Rick Bergholm	Rick Bergholm	1990	62
14 15/16	8 10/16	6 5/16	Union Co., Oreg.	Bernie Van Dyke	Bernie Van Dyke	1990	62
14 14/16	8 13/16	6 1/16	Wasatch Co., Utah	Gordon P. Mitchell	Gordon P. Mitchell	1989	67
14 14/16	8 11/16	6 3/16	Clark Co., Idaho	Hughie R. Lepage	Hughie R. Lepage	1990	67
14 14/16	8 13/16	6 1/16	Rosy Lake, B.C.	Keith A. Heldreth	Keith A. Heldreth	1991	67
14 13/16	8 11/16	5 15/16	Wallowa Co., Oreg.	David S. Squires	David S. Squires	1990	70
14 13/16	8 11/16	6 7/16	San Miguel Co., Colo.	Tommy L. Winters	Tommy L. Winters	1990	70

Cougar or Mountain Lion - *Continued*

Score	Greatest Length of Skull Without Lower Jaw	Greatest Width of Skull	Locality Killed	By Whom Killed	Owner	Date Killed	Rank
14 12/16	8 10/16	6 2/16	Lemhi Co., Idaho	Gary A. Laatsch	Gary A. Laatsch	1988	72
14 11/16	8 10/16	6 1/16	Custer Co., Idaho	Steven D. Bacon	Steven D. Bacon	1985	73
14 11/16	8 10/16	6 1/16	Park Co., Mont.	Patrick J. Gilligan	Patrick J. Gilligan	1989	73
14 11/16	8 11/16	6	Washington Co., Utah	Donald R. Seitz	Donald R. Seitz	1991	73
14 10/16	8 11/16	5 15/16	Daggett Co., Utah	Robert A. Skrzypek	Robert A. Skrzypek	1976	76
14 10/16	8 9/16	6 1/16	Montrose Co., Colo.	David E. Nesler	David E. Nesler	1987	76
14 10/16	8 10/16	6	Rio Arriba Co., N.M.	Robert J. Seeds	Robert J. Seeds	1988	76
14 9/16	8 9/16	6	Mesa Co., Colo.	Clayton C. French	Clayton C. French	1989	79
14 9/16	8 10/16	5 15/16	Nye Co., Nev.	Jesse A. Westby	Jesse A. Westby	1989	79
14 9/16	8 10/16	5 15/16	Beaver Co., Utah	Fred R. Douglas	Fred R. Douglas	1990	79
14 8/16	8 7/16	6 1/16	Carbon Co., Utah	Larry W. Grudziecke	Larry W. Grudziecke	1980	82
14 8/16	8 8/16	6 2/16	Johnson Co., Wyo.	Gary A. Roebling	Gary A. Roebling	1987	82
14 8/16	8 11/16	5 13/16	Duchesne Co., Utah	Samuel C. Carter	Samuel C. Carter	1991	82
15 12/16 *	9 6/16	6 8/16	Idaho Co., Idaho	Matthew S. Motil	Matthew S. Motil	1987	

* Final Score subject to revision by additional verifying measurements.

Pacific Walrus

Odobenus rosmarus divergens

Minimum Score 100   World's Record 145-6/8

Score	Entire Length of Loose Tusk R.	L.	Circumference of Base R.	L.	Circumference at Third Quarter R.	L.	Locality Killed	By Whom Killed	Owner	Date Killed	Rank
124 6/8	31 7/8	32 7/8	8 2/8	8 2/8	5 7/8	5 7/8	Cape Seniavin, Alaska	Picked Up	Tom Atkins	1990	1
135 2/8*	37 6/8	38.0	7 7/8	8 1/8	5 7/8	5 7/8	Bristol Bay, Alaska	Picked Up	Al Pace	1989	

* Final Score subject to revision by additional verifying measurements.

421

American Elk, *Typical Antlers*

Cervus elaphus nelsoni and related subspecies

Score	Length of Main Beam R.	L.	Inside Spread	Circumference at Smallest Place Between First and Second Points R.	L.	Number of Points R.	L.	Locality Killed	By Whom Killed	Owner	Date Killed	Rank
421 4/8	55 4/8	58 2/8	39	11 2/8	10 6/8	7	7	Gila Co., Ariz.	James C. Littleton	James C. Littleton	1985	1
420 4/8	56 4/8	56 2/8	45 6/8	9	9 2/8	7	7	Yakima Co., Wash.	Charles F. Gunnier	Charles F. Gunnier	1990	2
406 7/8	52 7/8	52 6/8	49 3/8	8 6/8	9 2/8	6	7	Duck Mt., Man.	Herb Andres	Larry L. Huffman	1980	3
394 4/8	55 2/8	54 4/8	37	10	10	6	6	Duck Mt., Man.	Melvin J. Podaima	Melvin J. Podaima	1991	4
393 5/8	56 2/8	52 4/8	42 5/8	9 1/8	9 4/8	7	7	Elmore Co., Idaho	Picked Up	Joe Adams PR	1955	5
392 3/8	54	54 4/8	41 7/8	9 4/8	10	6	6	Apache Co., Ariz.	McLean Bowman	McLean Bowman	1989	6
390 6/8	57 3/8	57 2/8	51 2/8	8 6/8	8 4/8	6	6	Apache Co., Ariz.	Robert M. Brittingham	Robert M. Brittingham	1990	7
389 5/8	55 1/8	54	45 7/8	7 7/8	8 1/8	7	7	Park Co., Mont.	Butch Kuflak	Butch Kuflak	1990	8
387 5/8	60 2/8	60	42 7/8	9	8 7/8	7	7	Cherokee Co., Iowa	C.A. Stiles	Jim Haas PR	1900	9
386 2/8	56 3/8	57 4/8	46 6/8	9 3/8	8 6/8	6	6	Carbon Co., Utah	Edward C. Jessen	Edward C. Jessen	1961	10
385 2/8	53 3/8	52 2/8	41 1/8	10 1/8	9 7/8	6	7	Apache Co., Ariz.	Herman C. Meyer	Herman C. Meyer	1991	11
382 2/8	54 2/8	56 6/8	44 2/8	9	8 4/8	7	7	Clark Co., Idaho	John Larick, Jr.	John Larick, Jr.	1963	12
381 6/8	56 1/8	55	44 4/8	9 1/8	8 5/8	7	7	Waterton River, Alta.	Keith A. Keeler	Keith A. Keeler	1989	13
381 6/8	54 3/8	52 5/8	38 4/8	9 2/8	10	7	7	Otero Co., N.M.	David U. Inge	David U. Inge	1990	13
381 5/8	54 7/8	56 3/8	40 1/8	9 3/8	8	7	6	Rich Co., Utah	Walter R. Moore	Kirk W. Moore	1935	15
381 5/8	58 2/8	57 2/8	39 5/8	9 7/8	10 1/8	6	6	Apache Co., Ariz.	McLean Bowman	McLean Bowman	1990	15
381 3/8	55 1/8	55 5/8	50	9	9 1/8	8	8	Mora Co., N.M.	Andrew J. Ortega	Andrew J. Ortega	1989	17
380 3/8	53 4/8	53 2/8	51 7/8	8 1/8	8 5/8	7	7	Rich Co., Utah	Fahy S. Robinson, Jr.	Fahy S. Robinson, Jr.	1988	18
380	50 4/8	50 3/8	35	8	8 2/8	7	7	Navajo Co., Ariz.	Gerry J. Tod	Gerry J. Tod	1990	19
379 2/8	57 1/8	55 5/8	41 6/8	8 1/8	8	6	6	Freemont Co., Wyo.	Larry C. Nicholas	Frank J. Vrablic	1976	20
379 2/8	53 2/8	53 4/8	41 4/8	8 5/8	8 7/8	6	6	Whirlpool River, Man.	Rudy R. Usick	Rudy R. Usick	1989	20
379 2/8	56 3/8	57 1/8	56	8 6/8	8 3/8	6	0	Coconino Co., Ariz.	Fred Williams	Fred Williams	1990	20
378 6/8	54 6/8	52 7/8	44 2/8	9 7/8	9 6/8	6	5	Otter Lake, Man.	Walter Giesbrecht	Walter Giesbrecht	1989	23
378 4/8	51 3/8	49 6/8	40 2/8	9 3/8	9 1/8	6	6	Park Co., Mont.	M.J. Young	M.J. Young	1967	24
378 1/8	50 1/8	50 3/8	36 2/8	11 5/8	11 1/8	8	7	Idaho Co., Idaho	Johnny Bliznak	Johnny Bliznak	1990	24
378 1/8	52 4/8	53 2/8	39 7/8	7 1/8	6 7/8	7	8	Langill Lake, B.C.	Gary D. Fodor	Gary D. Fodor	1989	26
377 3/8	49 3/8	49 7/8	40 3/8	11 2/8	10 2/8	6	6	Petroleum Co., Mont.	Jack Atcheson, Jr.	Jack Atcheson, Jr.	1990	27
377	58 5/8	56 4/8	47 4/8	8 6/8	8 1/8	7	7	Benton Co., Wash.	Daniel J. Bishop	Daniel J. Bishop	1988	28
375 7/8	52	54 6/8	37 3/8	9	8 5/8	6	6	Apache Co., Ariz.	McLean Bowman	McLean Bowman	1986	29
375 4/8	55 1/8	54	42 4/8	9	9	6	6	Skamania Co., Wash.	Kevin Schmid	Kevin Schmid	1990	30

375 3/8	58 1/8	59 1/8	37 3/8	8 4/8	8 6/8	6	6	Apache Co., Ariz.	Picked Up	H. Jack Corbin	1989	31
375 3/8	59 2/8	60 4/8	45 2/8	8 7/8	8 5/8	6	7	Apache Co., Ariz.	Michael S. Muhlbauer	Michael S. Muhlbauer	1989	31
373 3/8	52 5/8	51 7/8	49 3/8	8 4/8	7 5/8	7	7	Sevier Co., Utah	Picked Up	James R. Burr	1989	33
373 2/8	52 3/8	51 6/8	44	9 2/8	9 5/8	6	7	Petroleum Co., Mont.	David W. Kuhns	David W. Kuhns	1989	34
372 7/8	50 1/8	50 6/8	49 5/8	9 4/8	9	6	6	Grant Co., Oreg.	Robert B. Abbott	Robert B. Abbott	1989	35
372	57 6/8	57 2/8	39 6/8	9 4/8	9 2/8	6	6	Mohave Co., Ariz.	David A. Thompson	David A. Thompson	1991	36
369 2/8	54 1/8	52 2/8	41 4/8	8 6/8	9 2/8	6	6	Uintah Co., Utah	Ronald J. Wopsock	Ronald J. Wopsock	1990	37
365 5/8	58 2/8	57 1/8	43 3/8	10 2/8	10 7/8	8	7	Mescalero Co., N.M.	George Rose	George Rose	1991	38
364 2/8	54	53 5/8	40 2/8	8 4/8	8 4/8	6	6	Apache Co., Ariz.	Jacob N. Allen	Jacob N. Allen	1990	39
363 2/8	53	51 7/8	40 2/8	7 4/8	8 1/8	7	6	White Pine Co., Nev.	Richard P. Norrup	Richard P. Norrup	1990	40
360 2/8	50 4/8	53 1/8	43 4/8	10 5/8	10 2/8	6	6	Coconino Co., Ariz.	Billie F. Bechtel	Billie F. Bechtel	1984	41
410 6/8 *	55 2/8	55 4/8	42 6/8	9 7/8	9 7/8	6	6	Carbon Co., Wyo.	Unknown	William H. Tott	1945	

* Final Score subject to revision by additional verifying measurements.

American Elk, Non-Typical Antlers

Cervus elaphus nelsoni and related subspecies

Minimum Score 385 — New World's Record 447-1/8

Score	Length of Main Beam R.	L.	Inside Spread	Circumference at Smallest Place Between First and Second Points R.	L.	Number of Points R.	L.	Locality Killed	By Whom Killed	Owner	Date Killed	Rank
447 1/8	54 1/8	52 5/8	39 7/8	11	10 2/8	9	9	Gilbert Plains, Man.	James R. Berry	James R. Berry	1961	1
405 4/8	54 3/8	51 7/8	44	8 6/8	9	8	8	Granite Co., Mont.	Arthur W. Lundgren	Grace Lundgren	1946	2
403 3/8	49 5/8	58 3/8	38 2/8	9 6/8	9 6/8	8	8	Coconino Co., Ariz.	Robert B. Krogh, Jr.	Robert B. Krogh, Jr.	1983	3
403 2/8	54 5/8	52 4/8	47 4/8	8 6/8	9 2/8	9	6	Park Co., Mont.	Gary Beley	Gary Beley	1964	4
403	52 5/8	52 3/8	57 1/8	8 7/8	8 4/8	7	8	Uinta Co., Wyo.	Steven W. Condos	Norman Heater	1967	5
401 1/8	51 3/8	51 3/8	47 4/8	9 1/8	9 4/8	8	6	Fremont Co., Wyo.	Bud Cantleberry	Robert E. Cantleberry	1948	6
400 6/8	51 2/8	52	50 3/8	8 5/8	8 3/8	9	8	Madison Co., Mont.	Arthur A. Cooper	Arthur A. Cooper	1962	7
400	55 3/8	53 4/8	42 2/8	9 7/8	9 5/8	6	7	Routt Co., Colo.	William E. Goosman	William E. Goosman	1939	8
395 3/8	51 5/8	50 7/8	40 4/8	8 7/8	9	7	7	Apache Co., Ariz.	Mark W. White, Jr.	Mark W. White, Jr.	1983	9
394 1/8	58	56 6/8	44 6/8	8 7/8	8	6	8	Apache Co., Ariz.	Richard R. Childress	Richard R. Childress	1991	10
393 6/8	54 5/8	55 6/8	46 6/8	7 5/8	7 4/8	7	8	Navajo Co., Ariz.	Larry G. Van Hassle	Burke Hudnall	1990	11
393 3/8	50 2/8	48 4/8	41 2/8	9 5/8	10 1/8	8	7	Shoshone Co., Idaho	Hueh M. Kitzmiller	John M. Kitzmiller	1974	12
392 5/8	56 3/8	56 1/8	46 7/8	7 7/8	8	6	8	Coconino Co., Ariz.	John L. Hontalas	John L. Hontalas	1990	13
392 4/8	46	47 5/8	41 6/8	12	12 1/8	7	8	Otero Co., N.M.	David U. Inge	David U. Inge	1989	14
392	54 6/8	54	45 1/8	9 3/8	9 6/8	2	1	Mohave Co., Ariz.	Alfred L. McMicking	Alfred L. McMicking	1989	15
390 7/8	43 6/8	45 2/8	41	9 4/8	9 3/8	8	10	Apache Co., Ariz.	Theodore E. Dugey, Jr.	Theodore E. Dugey, Jr.	1978	16
386 2/8	44 3/8	47 4/8	43 4/8	8 7/8	9	9	6	Socorro Co., N.M.	Richard P. Gould	Richard P. Gould	1990	17
385	57 2/8	57 3/8	36 7/8	10 4/8	10 5/8	7	6	Navajo Co., Ariz.	David W. Baxter	David W. Baxter	1991	18
438 7/8*	45 3/8	48 5/8	44 5/8	8 6/8	9 4/8	10	8	Fraser River, B.C.	Ben Young	John Young	1980	
436 1/8*	55 5/8	52 2/8	68 7/8	10 1/8	11 5/8	9	10	Laramie Co., Wyo.	Joseph C. Dereemer	Charles Bird	1971	
423 4/8*	51 4/8	50 6/8	44 7/8	8 4/8	7 7/8	8	7	Granite Co., Mont.	Lee F. Tracy	Lee F. Tracy	1971	
420 4/8*	56 4/8	57 7/8	45 1/8	10 5/8	10 3/8	8	9	Yakima Co., Wash.	Stan Orr	Cary Brune	1933	
412 5/8*	51 5/8	51	43	9 3/8	9 3/8	9	8	Navajo Co., Ariz.	John A. Gulius	John A. Gulius	1990	

* Final Score subject to revision by additional verifying measurements.

424

Roosevelt's Elk

Cervus elaphus roosevelti

Minimum Score 275

New World's Record 388-3/8

Roosevelt's Elk includes trophies from: West of Highway 1-5 in Oregon and Washington; Del Norte and Humboldt Counties of California; Afognak and Raspberry Islands of Alaska; and Vancouver Island, British Columbia.

Score	Length of Main Beam R.	L.	Inside Spread	Circumference at Smallest Place Between First and Second Points R.	L.	Number of Points R.	L.	Locality Killed	By Whom Killed	Owner	Date Killed	Rank
388 3/8	44 2/8	46 7/8	36 1/8	11 2/8	11 2/8	11	8	Tsitika River, B.C.	Wayne Coe	Wayne Coe	1989	1
367	51 6/8	51 4/8	43 2/8	9 6/8	9 6/8	6	6	Mason Co., Wash.	Unknown	George B. Putnam	1900	2
351 5/8	45	45 5/8	40 2/8	9 1/8	9 7/8	8	9	Menzies Bay, B.C.	Gordon J. Birgbauer, Jr.	Gordon J. Birgbauer, Jr.	1991	3
342 1/8	52	50 4/8	34 5/8	9 5/8	10 3/8	6	7	Jefferson Co., Wash.	Ralph Warren	Ralph Warren	1972	4
341	47	47	38 7/8	8 7/8	9 3/8	8	7	Lewis Co., Wash.	Keith A. Heldreth	Keith A. Heldreth	1988	5
340 2/8	49	46 4/8	43 5/8	9 5/8	9 5/8	7	8	Clatsop Co., Oreg.	Fain J. Little	Fain J. Little	1945	6
337 7/8	52 3/8	50 3/8	34 3/8	9	9	9	9	Greenstone Creek, B.C.	Gerald L. Warnock	Gerald L. Warnock	1989	7
330	51	50 1/8	38 4/8	8 7/8	9	6	6	Nanaimo Lakes, B.C.	Picked Up	Eric D. Martin	1988	8
325 5/8	47 3/8	47 6/8	43 2/8	7 2/8	8	7	8	Wahkiakum Co., Wash.	Robert B. Seaberg	Robert B. Seaberg	1958	9
323 4/8	44	43 4/8	44	8 1/8	7 3/8	7	7	Jefferson Co., Wash.	Larry W. Haddock	Larry W. Haddock	1988	10
319 5/8	49 4/8	47 6/8	39 7/8	6 7/8	6 6/8	6	7	Clatsop Co., Oreg.	Picked Up	John T. Mee	1969	11
318 3/8	41 3/8	41 5/8	36 2/8	9	8 6/8	8	7	Grilise Creek, B.C.	Jack Foord	Jack Foord	1984	12
312 7/8	43 5/8	45 1/8	43 4/8	8	7 5/8	7	8	Clallam Co., Wash.	Donald W. Coman	Donald W. Coman	1981	13
304 1/8	39 6/8	38 1/8	31 1/8	8	7 6/8	8	8	Yamhill Co., Oreg.	Kevin E. Mishler	Kevin E. Mishler	1989	14
303 6/8	42 2/8	45 7/8	36 4/8	9 3/8	9 4/8	7	7	Gold River, B.C.	Abe Dougan	Abe Dougan	1988	15
302 6/8	49	49 1/8	38 4/8	7 7/8	7 7/8	6	6	Columbia Co., Oreg.	Picked Up	Rick A. Hood	1991	16
302 1/8	41 3/8	41 2/8	37 5/8	8 2/8	8 4/8	6	6	Wahkiakum Co., Wash.	Kyle J. Parker	Kyle J. Parker	1990	17
300 7/8	44	43 5/8	41	9 3/8	9 5/8	7	6	Vancouver Island, B.C.	William C. Holcombe	William C. Holcombe	1989	18
299 2/8	42 4/8	41 6/8	46 4/8	7 2/8	7 5/8	7	6	Columbia Co., Oreg.	Charles H. Atkins	Charles H. Atkins	1964	19
298 6/8	41 2/8	40 7/8	38 6/8	8 1/8	7 7/8	6	6	Jefferson Co., Wash.	Douglas A. Smith	Douglas A. Smith	1989	20
298 5/8	43 4/8	50 6/8	39 6/8	8	8	8	8	Clatsop Co., Oreg.	Harold O. Hundere	Harold O. Hundere	1943	21
298 2/8	47 6/8	47 2/8	40 5/8	9	9	6	6	Humboldt Co., Calif.	Eugene M. Boyd IV	Eugene M. Boyd IV	1988	22
291 1/8	41 6/8	40 4/8	43 6/8	6 7/8	6 6/8	6	6	Jefferson Co., Wash.	George R. Bernethy	George R. Bernethy	1956	23
283 1/8	37 5/8	37 2/8	30 7/8	9 1/8	9 2/8	7	7	Clallam Co., Wash.	Jesse Elder	Jesse Elder	1968	24
279 6/8	42 4/8	42 6/8	40	8 6/8	8 7/8	6	6	Tillamook Co., Oreg.	Karl F. Hale	Karl F. Hale	1985	25
371 2/8*	47 3/8	51 1/8	35 7/8	10 6/8	10 4/8	7	7	Clallam Co., Wash.	Joe Pavel	Joe Pavel	1942	

* Final Score subject to revision by additional verifying measurements.

425

Mule Deer, Typical Antlers

Odocoileus hemionus hemionus and certain related subspecies

Minimum Score 185   World's Record 226-4/8

Score	Length of Main Beam R.	L.	Inside Spread	Circumference at Smallest Place Between Burr and First Point R.	L.	Number of Points R.	L.	Locality Killed	By Whom Killed	Owner	Date Killed	Rank
207	28 3/8	29 3/8	27	5 5/8	5 4/8	5	7	Kane Co., Utah	Picked Up	John K. Springer	1986	1
206 2/8	28 6/8	28 6/8	22 4/8	6	6	9	7	Montrose Co., Colo.	Patrick E. Courtin, Jr.	Patrick E. Courtin, Jr.	1972	2
205 5/8	27 5/8	28	30 1/8	4 7/8	4 4/8	5	5	Montrose Co., Colo.	Joe M. Gardner	Z. Gardner Holland	1954	3
205 1/8	26 3/8	25 6/8	25 5/8	4 4/8	4 4/8	5	5	Morgan Co., Utah	Gale Allen	Gale Allen	1946	4
202	28	27	26	5 3/8	5 6/8	9	6	Bear Lake Co., Idaho	David L. Williams	Raymond L. Williams	1949	5
202	27 4/8	27 3/8	25 6/8	5 2/8	5 2/8	5	5	Elko Co., Nev.	Arlo M. Hummell	Arlo M. Hummell	1989	5
201 7/8	27	26	26 5/8	5 1/8	5 1/8	5	5	Union Co., Oreg.	Brian M. Erwin	Brian M. Erwin	1991	7
201 4/8	27 1/8	26 2/8	22 6/8	5 7/8	5 1/8	5	5	Adams Co., Idaho	Gary D. Lewis	Gary D. Lewis	1990	8
201	28 2/8	28 6/8	28 6/8	5	5 2/8	6	4	Summit Co., Utah	Clinton A. Larson	Clinton A. Larson	1949	9
201	26 6/8	26 1/8	24 5/8	5 1/8	5 2/8	7	5	Idaho	Unknown	Rick Stover PR	1990	9
200 4/8	28 5/8	27 5/8	28 2/8	4 7/8	4 6/8	4	5	Utah Co., Utah	Elroy A. Loveridge	Elroy A. Loveridge	1965	11
200 4/8	27 3/8	27 4/8	31	5 5/8	5 4/8	5	5	Madison Co., Mont.	Glenn S. Shelton	Glenn S. Shelton	1976	11
200 4/8	24	24 6/8	23 3/8	4 6/8	5	5	6	Dolores Co., Colo.	James L. Horneck	James L. Horneck	1988	11
200 2/8	23 6/8	24 5/8	19 3/8	5	4 7/8	5	6	Bonneville Co., Idaho	Richard A. Kelley	Richard A. Kelley	1990	14
200 1/8	24 4/8	25 4/8	26	5 2/8	5 3/8	7	6	Mohave Co., Ariz.	Jay M. Ogden	Jay M. Ogden	1990	15
200	28	27 5/8	21 6/8	5 7/8	6	6	5	Park Co., Colo.	Jim Fitzgerald	Rob Firth	1971	16
199 7/8	26 4/8	26 4/8	24 4/8	4 7/8	4 7/8	6	6	Eagle Co., Colo.	George S. Burton	Betty Burton	1967	17
199 3/8	25 5/8	26 3/8	26 4/8	4 5/8	4 3/8	5	4	San Miguel Co., N.M.	Frank Mata	Robert Cordova	1965	18
199 2/8	26 6/8	26 4/8	25 5/8	5 3/8	5 3/8	7	5	Eagle Co., Colo.	Anthony W. DeToy	Anthony W. DeToy	1978	19
199 2/8	28 5/8	27 6/8	25	5 4/8	5 4/8	5	5	Gable Mt., B.C.	Jack V. Quiring	Jack V. Quiring	1988	19
199 2/8	26 6/8	26 3/8	25 3/8	5 3/8	4 7/8	5	6	Great Sand Hills, Sask.	Howard Jackle	Howard Jackle	1991	19
198 1/8	25 1/8	26 1/8	25 7/8	5 4/8	5 4/8	5	6	Routt Co., Colo.	William E. Goswick	William E. Goswick	1968	22
198 1/8	26 6/8	27 5/8	24 5/8	5 1/8	5 1/8	6	8	Colorado	Unknown	Richard A. Heitman PR	1989	22
197 6/8	26 6/8	24 7/8	23 6/8	5 3/8	5 4/8	5	5	Botanie Lake, B.C.	Dennis R. Milton	Dennis R. Milton	1991	24
197 5/8	27	26 6/8	22 7/8	5 7/8	5	6	6	San Miguel Co., Colo.	Virgil L. Burbridge	Jerry D. Burbridge	1964	25
197 5/8	23 5/8	29 5/8	21 3/8	5	5	5	5	Eagle Co., Colo.	Joseph Sokel, Jr.	Steve J. Sokel	1965	25
197 5/8	25 4/8	26 5/8	29 4/8	5 5/8	5 5/8	5	5	Elko Co., Nev.	Manfred E. Koska	Manfred E. Koska	1966	25
197 4/8	24 6/8	27	23 4/8	6	5 7/8	8	9	Routt Co., Colo.	William E. Goswick	William E. Goswick	1969	28
197 3/8	24 7/8	24 5/8	27 2/8	4 5/8	4 4/8	5	4	Lincoln Co., Wyo.	Kim L. King	Kim L. King	1990	29
197 1/8	27	28	30	5 3/8	5 3/8	7	6	Delta Co., Colo.	B. Allan Jones	B. Allan Jones	1977	30

196 7/8	25 3/8	25 2/8	25 3/8	5	5	5	5	Lincoln Co., Wyo.	William L. Lewis	William L. Lewis	1990	31
196 4/8	24	25 1/8	24 6/8	4 5/8	4 5/8	5	7	Teton Co., Wyo.	John C. Branca III	John C. Branca III	1991	32
196 2/8	28 4/8	26	25 6/8	5 3/8	5 4/8	6	6	San Juan Co., Utah	John Rowley	John Rowley	1989	33
196	29 1/8	28 2/8	28 6/8	5 3/8	4 6/8	5	5	Elko Co., Nev.	Johnny W. Filippini	Johnny W. Filippini	1991	34
195 7/8	24 3/8	27 6/8	28	4 6/8	4 6/8	5	5	Teton Co., Wyo.	Lewis E. Sharp	Lewis E. Sharp	1990	35
195 6/8	26 3/8	28 2/8	27 3/8	5 5/8	5 4/8	7	6	Custer Co., Idaho	Sylvester Potaman	W. Douglas Lightfoot	1900	36
195 6/8	33	28	26	5 4/8	5 5/8	5	5	Grant Co., Oreg.	Gordon E. Mitchell	Gordon E. Mitchell	1982	36
195 6/8	24	26 1/8	24 5/8	5 1/8	5 1/8	5	5	Caribou Co., Idaho	John B. Kochever	John B. Kochever	1986	36
195 6/8	23 2/8	27 1/8	27 2/8	5 4/8	5 4/8	5	5	Caribou Co., Idaho	Robin W. Bechtel	Robin W. Bechtel	1989	36
195 5/8	26 3/8	25 3/8	25 3/8	5 3/8	5 3/8	5	5	Huerfano Co., Colo.	Hub R. Grounds	Hub R. Grounds	1989	40
195 5/8	26 7/8	25 7/8	25 3/8	5 4/8	5 4/8	5	5	Mesa Co., Colo.	John F. Stewart	John F. Stewart	1989	40
195 3/8	25 5/8	25 5/8	25	5 3/8	5 3/8	5	5	Garfield Co., Utah	John E. Braithwaite	John E. Braithwaite	1987	42
195 1/8	26 1/8	26 1/8	25 6/8	5 3/8	5 3/8	6	6	Rio Arriba Co., N.M.	David Shadrick	David Shadrick	1988	43
195	22 2/8	25 1/8	24 1/8	4 5/8	4 6/8	5	5	Beaver Co., Utah	Unknown	Mark R. Dotson	1969	44
195	27 1/8	26 5/8	27 1/8	5 2/8	5 5/8	6	5	Carbon Co., Utah	Thomas E. Wilson	Thomas E. Wilson	1988	44
194 5/8	26 6/8	28 3/8	28 3/8	5 5/8	5 5/8	6	5	Duchesne Co., Utah	Kate Hamilton	Raymond R. Cross	1948	46
194 5/8	21 3/8	25 2/8	24 7/8	4 5/8	4 5/8	5	6	Cabri Lake, Sask.	Dean R. Francis	Dean R. Francis	1991	46
193 6/8	22	26 7/8	25	4 4/8	4 4/8	5	6	Smoky River, Alta.	Jeffrey S. Reichert	Jeffrey S. Reichert	1989	48
193 2/8	25 2/8	24	26	6 1/8	6	6	6	Gunnison Co., Colo.	Bill Morrow	Nancy Morrow	1960	49
193 2/8	22 2/8	25 2/8	23 6/8	5 4/8	5 2/8	7	8	Franklin Co., Idaho	L. Munk & T. Braegger	Larry Munk	1990	49
192 1/8	23 3/8	26 1/8	25 4/8	4 7/8	4 7/8	6	7	Bonneville Co., Idaho	Glen M. Brown	Glen M. Brown	1949	51
191 4/8	25 4/8	25 4/8	26 3/8	5	5 2/8	5	6	Coconino Co., Ariz.	Steven G. Mallory	Steven G. Mallory	1988	52
191 3/8	24 7/8	24 7/8	25 5/8	4 7/8	4 7/8	5	5	Grant Co., N.M.	Robin W. Bechtel	Robin W. Bechtel	1988	53
191 1/8	26	26 6/8	24 5/8	4 4/8	4 6/8	5	5	Morrow Co., Oreg.	Russell D. Britt	Russell D. Britt	1990	54
191	24 3/8	25 1/8	23 3/8	4 4/8	4 3/8	6	5	Grand Co., Colo.	Zane Palmer	Zane Palmer	1981	55
190 5/8	25 1/8	25 1/8	25 1/8	5 2/8	5 2/8	6	6	Kane Co., Utah	Edward B. Franceschi, Jr.	Edward B. Franceschi, Jr.	1990	56
190 4/8	22 4/8	24 6/8	24 1/8	6 6/8	6 7/8	5	6	Douglas Co., Colo.	Harold A. Weippert	Harold A. Weippert	1990	57
190 3/8	26 4/8	25 4/8	25 4/8	4 6/8	5	5	5	Archuleta Co., Colo.	James M. Russell III	James M. Russell III	1985	58
189 3/8	21 5/8	25 6/8	25 1/8	4 6/8	4 3/8	8	8	Lincoln Co., Wyo.	Jerry A. McAllister	Jerry A. McAllister	1990	59
189 3/8	25 4/8	25	24 4/8	5 3/8	5 1/8	5	5	Custer Co., Mont.	Hugh R. Neumann	Hugh R. Neumann	1969	60
189 3/8	27 2/8	24	26	6 2/8	5 1/8	7	5	Coconino Co., Ariz.	Frederick T. Lau	Frederick T. Lau	1988	60
188 5/8	25 2/8	27 6/8	25	5 4/8	5 1/8	5	5	Caribou Co., Idaho	Robert E. Anderson	Robert E. Anderson	1990	60
188 3/8	23 1/8	25 2/8	24 7/8	4 4/8	4 5/8	6	5	Washoe Co., Nev.	Darin D. Clements	Darin D. Clements	1989	63
188 3/8	23 1/8	25 5/8	23 4/8	5	5	6	5	Tangent, Alta.	David Hirsch	David Hirsch	1964	64
188 1/8	27 3/8	25	26 2/8	5 4/8	5 2/8	5	5	Garfield Co., Utah	Johnny Parsons	Johnny Parsons	1984	65
188	21 1/8	26 6/8	26 5/8	5 4/8	4 7/8	5	5	Kit Carson Co., Colo.	Thomas Aasbo	Thomas Aasbo	1990	66
187 7/8	26 5/8	25 2/8	24 7/8	4 3/8	4 5/8	5	6	Routt Co., Colo.	Thomas N. Garvin	Thomas N. Garvin	1986	67
187 7/8	27 2/8	25 7/8	27 2/8	4 6/8	6 2/8	5	7	Pitkin Co., Colo.	Kenneth N. Tucker	Kenneth N. Tucker	1990	67
187 3/8	22 7/8	23 4/8	23 2/8	6 3/8	4 7/8	5	4	Washoe Co., Nev.	Sandra D. Cooper	Sandra D. Cooper	1991	69
187 1/8	26 1/8	23 5/8	23 3/8	4 7/8	4 7/8	5	5	Morgan Co., Utah	Terry R. Bitton	Terry R. Bitton	1989	70
186 4/8	24 1/8	25 1/8	25 1/8	4 7/8	5 1/8	8	7	Saddle Hills, Alta.	Maurice Southmayd	Maurice Southmayd	1989	71

Mule Deer, *Typical Antlers - Continued*

Score	Length of Main Beam R.	L.	Inside Spread	Circumference at Smallest Place Between Burr and First Point R.	L.	Number of Points R.	L.	Locality Killed	By Whom Killed	Owner	Date Killed	Rank
186 2/8	26	25 1/8	25 3/8	5	5 1/8	5	6	Demaine, Sask.	Bruce C. Brown	Bruce C. Brown	1990	72
186	25 7/8	26	28 4/8	5 2/8	5 1/8	5	5	Park Co., Wyo.	Darren W. Vorhies	Darren W. Vorhies	1991	73
185 5/8	26 5/8	25 7/8	17 5/8	5 2/8	5 1/8	6	5	Caribou Co., Idaho	Ralph E. Peldo	Ralph E. Peldo	1988	74
185 4/8	24	24 6/8	20 6/8	5 1/8	5 1/8	5	5	Franklin Co., Idaho	K. Bruce Kidman	K. Bruce Kidman	1988	75
185 3/8	25 3/8	25 3/8	23 5/8	4 6/8	4 4/8	5	5	Delta Co., Colo.	Mark S. Petrucci	Mark S. Petrucci	1989	76
185	21 7/8	22 2/8	18 6/8	4 3/8	4 3/8	5	5	Lincoln Co., Wyo.	Edward D. Whitmore	Edward D. Whitmore	1990	77
213 4/8*	26 7/8	26 6/8	25 2/8	5 2/8	5 2/8	5	5	Bonneville Co., Idaho	Ike Ellis	Raymond R. Cross	1986	
205 7/8*	26	27 7/8	24 3/8	5 1/8	5 1/8	5	6	Fremont Co., Idaho	Michael W.G. Neff	Michael W.G. Neff	1990	
203 6/8*	26 6/8	27 1/8	26	5 6/8	5 7/8	7	5	Beaver Co., Utah	John A. Dotson	John A. Dotson	1989	

* Final Score subject to revision by additional verifying measurements.

428

Mule Deer, Non-Typical Antlers

Odocoileus hemionus hemionus and certain related subspecies

Minimum Score 225   World's Record 355-2/8

Score	Length of Main Beam R.	L.	Inside Spread	Circumference at Smallest Place Between Burr and First Point R.	L.	Number of Points R.	L.	Locality Killed	By Whom Killed	Owner	Date Killed	Rank
321 1/8	28 1/8	25 4/8	26 5/8	6 7/8	6 7/8	17	25	Umatilla Co., Oreg.	Albert C. Peterson	Don Schaufler	1925	1
294 1/8	27 1/8	26 1/8	24 3/8	5 7/8	5 6/8	14	16	Coconino Co., Ariz.	Philip K. Coffeen	William A. Coffeen	1939	2
285 7/8	27 7/8	27 6/8	26 7/8	6	6 1/8	19	16	Adams Co., Idaho	Picked Up	Raymond R. Cross	PR 1968	3
280 2/8	29	31 2/8	29 4/8	5 1/8	5 4/8	11	16	Coconino Co., Ariz.	Unknown	Marlen D. Murphy	1941	4
274 5/8	25 1/8	26	24 2/8	5 7/8	5 6/8	11	13	Pueblo Co., Colo.	Picked Up	Butler Ranch	1988	5
273	22 1/8	24	24	5 6/8	6	10	13	Madison Co., Mont.	Ray Ypma	Ray Ypma	1946	6
269 4/8	28 3/8	28 7/8	25 7/8	5 5/8	6	14	13	Owyhee Co., Idaho	Frank Cogdill	Raymond R. Cross	1939	7
267 4/8	24	25 3/8	18 2/8	6 2/8	7 7/8	16	15	Mariposa Co., Calif.	Ray Douglas	John Douglas	1948	8
264 1/8	22 2/8	22	20 2/8	4 5/8	4 5/8	13	14	Coconino Co., Ariz.	Gilbert T. Adams, Jr.	Gilbert T. Adams, Jr.	1989	9
261 6/8	24 4/8	23 3/8	20 5/8	5 4/8	5 4/8	16	14	Gallatin Co., Mont.	Clifford R. Plum	Clifford R. Plum	1932	10
258 6/8	26	25 2/8	18 7/8	4 4/8	4 4/8	13	11	Washington Co., Utah	Brian A. Bowler	Brian A. Bowler	1989	11
258	26 5/8	29	27 6/8	5 4/8	5 3/8	14	16	Coconino Co., Ariz.	William T. Parsons	William T. Parsons	1967	12
257 5/8	25 3/8	25 2/8	24	4 7/8	5 1/8	12	13	Rio Blanco Co., Colo.	Rachael Palmer	Rachael Palmer	1970	13
256 1/8	26 2/8	27 4/8	21 6/8	4 6/8	4 5/8	15	13	Summit Lake, B.C.	Herald A. Friedenberger	Herald A. Friedenberger	1988	14
255	26 6/8	25 4/8	23 4/8	4 6/8	4 6/8	8	8	Adams Co., Idaho	Fred Bain	Raymond R. Cross	1974	15
252 5/8	20 5/8	21 7/8	18 3/8	4 5/8	4 6/8	12	13	Valley Co., Idaho	Picked Up	Raymond R. Cross	PR 1989	16
251 6/8	25 2/8	25 7/8	23	6 3/8	6	7	14	Washington Co., Utah	Richard S. Mansker	Richard S. Mansker	1990	17
251 3/8	26 7/8	26	31 1/8	5 5/8	5 3/8	18	12	Wayne Co., Utah	Chuck Simmons	Chuck Simmons	1988	18
250 4/8	26	27 7/8	27 3/8	5 4/8	6	11	9	Quesnel, B.C.	Picked Up	Paul W. Stafford	1984	19
250 4/8	29	26 7/8	30 2/8	5 4/8	5 6/8	10	13	Shoshone Co., Idaho	Ron L. Purnell	Ron L. Purnell	1987	19
249 3/8	25	24 6/8	22 6/8	5 4/8	5 6/8	18	16	Owyhee Co., Idaho	Tom Tomlinson	Raymond R. Cross	1968	21
249 2/8	26 1/8	28 4/8	29 1/8	5 6/8	5 5/8	14	10	Klamath Co., Oreg.	Fred Teeny	Rick Teeny	1947	22
248 3/8	24 4/8	25 1/8	25 1/8	5 5/8	6 2/8	10	9	Mesa Co., Colo.	Edwin Baal	Edwin Baal	1988	23
248 3/8	29 2/8	27 7/8	27 2/8	6 1/8	5 4/8	10	9	Costilla Co., Colo.	Ronald E. Lewis	Ronald E. Lewis	1988	23
247 7/8	25 6/8	26	25 3/8	5 4/8	4 3/8	19	17	Weber Co., Utah	John Lindsay	Robert R. Donaldson	1966	25
247 6/8	22 2/8	22 2/8	19 2/8	5	6 6/8	10	13	Grand Co., Utah	Bruce M. Turnbow	Bruce M. Turnbow	1967	26
247 4/8	22 6/8	27	31 6/8	6	5 5/8	14	13	Tooele Co., Utah	Murray G. Loveless	Murray G. Loveless	1949	27
247 2/8	24 3/8	24 1/8	24 7/8	5 3/8	5	13	10	Owyhee Co., Idaho	Elwin J. Saxton	Raymond R. Cross	1975	28
247 2/8	18 1/8	23 4/8	19 2/8	5	4 7/8	8	11	Elko Co., Nev.	Picked Up	Ron Druck	1980	28
246 7/8	25 6/8	26 7/8	26 5/8	5 5/8	5 5/8	10	7	Carbon Co., Utah	Sherman R. Jensen, Jr.	Sherman R. Jensen, Jr.	1965	30

Mule Deer, *Non-Typical Antlers - Continued*

Score	Length of Main Beam R.	L.	Inside Spread	Circumference at Smallest Place Between Burr and First Point R.	L.	Number of Points R.	L.	Locality Killed	By Whom Killed	Owner	Date Killed	Rank
246	26 7/8	25 3/8	26 4/8	5	4 6/8	9	13	Cherokee Co., Iowa	C.A. Stiles	Jim H. Haas	PR 1900	31
245	26 5/8	26 7/8	24 1/8	5 3/8	5 2/8	12	12	Kane Co., Utah	Koyle T. Cram	Koyle T. Cram	1966	32
243 7/8	23 3/8	23 4/8	21 3/8	4 3/8	4 4/8	11	10	Malheur Co., Oreg.	Larry L. Herron	Larry L. Herron	1983	33
243 1/8	24 4/8	24 3/8	21 4/8	5	5	12	7	Converse Co., Wyo.	William E. Goswick	William E. Goswick	1968	34
242 7/8	26 4/8	26 3/8	22 3/8	5 5/8	5 7/8	11	16	Gem Co., Idaho	Cary G. Cada	Raymond R. Cross	1975	35
242 2/8	24	25 2/8	21	6	6	9	11	Rio Arriba Co., N.M.	Elvon DeVaney	Shannon DeVaney	1971	36
241 7/8	24	25 4/8	18 5/8	5 7/8	6	14	11	Great Sand Hills, Sask.	A. Bruce LaRose	A. Bruce LaRose	1989	37
241 6/8	24 7/8	23 5/8	21 6/8	5 6/8	6	17	19	Hot Springs Co., Wyo.	Picked up	John A. Kotan, Jr.	1983	38
240 7/8	27 7/8	27 5/8	29	5 3/8	5 1/8	7	9	Rio Arriba Co., N.M.	Douglas Bryant	Douglas Bryant	1988	39
240 4/8	25 5/8	24 4/8	21 6/8	5 4/8	5 4/8	10	9	Great Sand Hills, Sask.	Emile T. Paradis	Emile T. Paradis	1989	40
238 4/8	27	27 1/8	28 7/8	6 1/8	4 6/8	17	13	Pima Co., Ariz.	Richard M. Cordora	Richard M. Cordora	1989	41
237 5/8	25 4/8	26	21 7/8	4 7/8	4 6/8	8	9	Lynx Creek, B.C.	J. Gregory Simmons	J. Gregory Simmons	1989	42
230 5/8	24 1/8	25 2/8	27 7/8	5	5 4/8	7	10	San Juan Co., Utah	Gregory S. Amaral	Gregory S. Amaral	1988	43
228 7/8	27 1/8	26 5/8	24	5 2/8	5 4/8	8	12	Franklin Co., Idaho	Michael H. Vroman	Michael H. Vroman	1986	44
228 3/8	25 3/8	24 7/8	24 4/8	5 4/8	5 5/8	8	9	Yellowstone Co., Mont.	Paul P. Reichert	Paul P. Reichert	1951	45
225 1/8	25 1/8	24 2/8	21 4/8	4 6/8	5 1/8	9	12	Smith Co., Kan.	Richard L. Quinn	Richard L. Quinn	1989	46
277*	25 7/8	24 2/8	23 6/8	5 6/8	5 7/8	11	15	Delta Co., Colo.	Robert G. Wilson	Robert G. Wilson	1989	

* Final Score subject to revision by additional verifying measurements.

Columbia Blacktail Deer

Odocoileus hemionus columbianus

Minimum Score 120

World's Record 182-2/8

Score	Length of Main Beam R.	L.	Inside Spread	Circumference at Smallest Place Between Burr and First Point R.	L.	Number of Points R.	L.	Locality Killed	By Whom Killed	Owner	Date Killed	Rank
170	23 2/8	24	20 2/8	4 3/8	4 3/8	5	5	Jackson Co., Oreg.	Wayne Despain	Wayne Despain	1989	1
167 7/8	24 3/8	26	16 1/8	6	6	7	6	Lewis Co., Wash.	Maurice D. Heldreth	Maurice D. Heldreth	1976	2
165 6/8	22 6/8	23	20 6/8	4 6/8	4 6/8	5	5	Curry Co., Oreg.	Si Pellow	Si Pellow	1988	3
160 3/8	22 7/8	23 1/8	17 7/8	4 2/8	4 1/8	5	5	Jackson Co., Oreg.	Mickey C. Haynes	Travis J. Harvey	1989	4
159 2/8	24 7/8	24	24 4/8	4 4/8	5 2/8	4	5	Whatcom Co., Wash.	Paul A. Braddock	Paul A. Braddock	1963	5
159 2/8	22 4/8	22 7/8	19 4/8	4 4/8	4 4/8	5	5	Josephine Co., Oreg.	Wayne Despain	Wayne Despain	1979	5
155 3/8	26 2/8	25 7/8	25 7/8	4 4/8	4 4/8	7	7	Jackson Co., Oreg.	Gary B. Christlieb	Gary B. Christlieb	1979	7
154 2/8	20 3/8	20 7/8	17 5/8	5	5 1/8	6	5	Jackson Co., Oreg.	Mary L. Hannah	Mary L. Hannah	1988	8
154	23 3/8	23 3/8	23 3/8	4 1/8	4 2/8	6	6	Josephine Co., Oreg.	Ryan Kinghorn	Ryan Kinghorn	1989	9
152 4/8	22	21 7/8	18 4/8	5 1/8	5	6	6	Mendocino Co., Calif.	Richard C. Martin	Richard C. Martin	1990	10
152 2/8	20 7/8	21	20 2/8	4	4 1/8	4	4	Douglas Co., Oreg.	Ronald L. Sherva	Ronald L. Sherva	1987	11
152 1/8	22 2/8	21 4/8	22	4 3/8	4 3/8	5	6	Josephine Co., Oreg.	Bob Ferreira	Bob Ferreira	1988	12
151 5/8	20 3/8	20 1/8	22 4/8	4 5/8	4 4/8	5	5	Mendocino Co., Calif.	Bill L. Conn	Bill L. Conn	1969	13
151 4/8	22 7/8	21 3/8	17 5/8	4 1/8	4 2/8	6	6	Douglas Co., Oreg.	Robert Shrode	Robert Shrode	1959	14
149 3/8	23 7/8	26 5/8	20 5/8	4 5/8	4 4/8	5	5	Tehama Co., Calif.	Bill F. Stevenson	Bill F. Stevenson	1989	15
148 5/8	21 3/8	21 5/8	18 5/8	3 7/8	4 1/8	5	5	Lane Co., Oreg.	Bill Sparks	Bill Sparks	1970	16
148 1/8	21 6/8	22 1/8	18 6/8	5	5 1/8	8	7	Trinity Co., Calif.	Dean Tackette	Dean Tackette	1981	17
147 7/8	27	26 5/8	21 3/8	5 5/8	5 4/8	0	0	Marion Co., Oreg.	James C. Tennimon	James C. Tennimon	1988	18
146 5/8	20 7/8	20 7/8	18 1/8	4 2/8	4 2/8	5	5	Clackamas Co., Oreg.	Stan K. Naylor	Stan K. Naylor	1990	19
146 2/8	21 7/8	21 6/8	16 2/8	3 7/8	3 7/8	5	5	Humboldt Co., Calif.	Charles R. Jurin	Charles R. Jurin	1988	20
146 1/8	22 4/8	22 4/8	14 5/8	4 5/8	4 3/8	0	0	Lewis Co., Wash.	Keith A. Heldreth	Keith A. Heldreth	1988	21
145 1/8	22 6/8	21 5/8	16 3/8	5	5 3/8	6	6	Pierce Co., Wash.	Robert L. Armstrong	Robert L. Armstrong	1978	22
144 5/8	20 1/8	20	18 1/8	4	4	5	5	Jackson Co., Oreg.	Dean P. Pasche	Dean P. Pasche	1988	23
144 5/8	21 5/8	21 2/8	16 1/8	4 4/8	4 2/8	5	5	Benton Co., Oreg.	Gerald L. Hibbs	Gerald L. Hibbs	1990	23
144 5/8	22 5/8	23 1/8	19 1/8	4 4/8	4 4/8	5	5	Linn Co., Oreg.	Donald J. Semolke	Donald J. Semolke	1990	23
144 4/8	21	20 7/8	15 4/8	4 1/8	4 3/8	5	5	Benton Co., Oreg.	Lance M. Holm	Lance M. Holm	1988	26
144 3/8	20 4/8	20 7/8	14 7/8	4 4/8	4 5/8	5	5	Humboldt Co., Calif.	Richard G. Van Vorst	Richard G. Van Vorst	1990	27
144 3/8	20 1/8	22	19 1/8	4 4/8	4 4/8	5	5	Alameda Co., Calif.	Anthony S. Webb	Anthony S. Webb	1990	27
143 6/8	20 6/8	20 3/8	15 4/8	5 2/8	4 7/8	5	5	Humboldt Co., Calif.	Hartwell A. Burnett	Hartwell A. Burnett	1988	29
143 3/8	19 7/8	18 7/8	18 3/8	3 4/8	3 4/8	5	5	Mendocino Co., Calif.	Larry G. Miller	Larry G. Miller	1978	30

Columbia Blacktail Deer - *Continued*

Score	Length of Main Beam R.	L.	Inside Spread	Circumference at Smallest Place Between Burr and First Point R.	L.	Number of Points R.	L.	Locality Killed	By Whom Killed	Owner	Date Killed	Rank
143 2/8	21 2/8	21 3/8	18 2/8	4 6/8	5 1/8	5	5	Josephine Co., Oreg.	Jaime L. Torres	Jaime L. Torres	1990	31
142 5/8	22	23	20 5/8	4	3 7/8	5	5	Mendocino Co., Calif.	Warren F. Coffman	Warren F. Coffman	1989	32
142 1/8	20 4/8	19 5/8	15 5/8	4 4/8	4 3/8	5	5	Lewis Co., Wash.	Michael H. Carle	Michael H. Carle	1989	33
141 3/8	21 2/8	21 7/8	16 7/8	4 3/8	4 1/8	5	5	Mendocino Co., Calif.	Gene V. Bradley	Gene V. Bradley	1988	34
141 1/8	21	21	19 3/8	4 6/8	4 5/8	5	5	Clallam Co., Wash.	David P. Sanford	David P. Sanford	1989	35
141	20 2/8	19 6/8	14	4	4	4	5	Lane Co., Oreg.	Richard Porter	Ruel Holt	1962	36
140 6/8	21	22 2/8	20 6/8	4	4	5	5	Mendocino Co., Calif.	Bill L. Conn	Bill L. Conn	1968	37
140 3/8	24 3/8	24 2/8	17 3/8	4	4 2/8	4	4	Jackson Co., Oreg.	John T. Mee	John T. Mee	1974	38
140 1/8	22	21 2/8	19 1/8	3 5/8	3 6/8	4	5	Jackson Co., Oreg.	Ronald L. Sherva	Ronald L. Sherva	1989	39
139 6/8	19 6/8	19 7/8	18 6/8	4	4	5	5	Lewis Co., Wash.	Keith A. Heldreth	Keith A. Heldreth	1989	40
139 3/8	19 7/8	19 5/8	19 5/8	3 6/8	3 6/8	5	5	Marion Co., Oreg.	Robert W. Hickman	Randall W. Hickman	1974	41
139	21 7/8	21 1/8	15 7/8	4 3/8	4 6/8	6	6	Lane Co., Oreg.	Picked Up	Ruel Holt	1964	42
139	22	21 6/8	17 2/8	4 3/8	4 1/8	4	4	Trinity Co., Calif.	Roger J. Scala	Roger J. Scala	1990	42
139	21 2/8	20 7/8	17 2/8	5	5 1/8	5	5	Polk Co., Oreg.	Jimmy L. Smithey	Jimmy L. Smithey	1990	42
138 6/8	18 4/8	18	16 2/8	3 6/8	3 7/8	5	5	Mendocino Co., Calif.	Richard L. Moore	Richard L. Moore	1988	45
138 5/8	19 3/8	19 5/8	14 6/8	5	4 7/8	5	6	Linn Co., Oreg.	Jeff B. Garber	Jeff B. Garber	1987	46
138 3/8	20 4/8	20 1/8	18 5/8	4 1/8	4 3/8	4	5	Trinity Co., Calif.	Stanley A. Apuli	Stanley A. Apuli	1991	47
138 2/8	19 5/8	20 4/8	16 2/8	4 3/8	4 3/8	5	5	Trinity Co., Calif.	Monte D. Matheson	Monte D. Matheson	1990	48
137 5/8	20 1/8	19 7/8	15 6/8	4 6/8	4 6/8	6	5	Lewis Co., Wash.	Larry L. Larson	Larry L. Larson	1978	49
137 3/8	20 4/8	21 7/8	18 7/8	4 6/8	4 5/8	5	5	Mendocino Co., Calif.	Carlton C. White	Carlton C. White	1983	50
137 1/8	20 4/8	21 1/8	19 2/8	4 4/8	4 4/8	5	7	Douglas Co., Oreg.	Jerry A. Caster	Jerry A. Caster	1989	51
136 5/8	22 4/8	21 1/8	20 1/8	3 4/8	3 6/8	4	5	Jackson Co., Oreg.	Alberto L. Garcia	Alberto L. Garcia	1988	52
136 4/8	20 2/8	20	18 4/8	4 7/8	4 5/8	5	5	Grays Harbor Co., Wash.	Joseph S. Prohaska	Stephen H. Prohaska	1952	53
136 3/8	21 4/8	21	15 3/8	5 1/8	4 7/8	5	5	Marion Co., Oreg.	Albert F. Brundidge	Albert F. Brundidge	1990	54
136 2/8	20 7/8	20 3/8	16 5/8	4 7/8	5	5	6	Clackamas Co., Oreg.	Loren R. Schilperoort	Loren R. Schilperoort	1990	55
136 1/8	19	18 6/8	14 5/8	5	5 2/8	5	6	Whatcom Co., Wash.	Dick Vander Yacht	Dick Vander Yacht	1960	56
135 5/8	20 2/8	21 2/8	15 1/8	5	4 1/8	5	5	Humboldt Co., Calif.	Michael M. Golightly	Michael M. Golightly	1990	57
135 4/8	20 6/8	20 6/8	17 4/8	4 3/8	4 3/8	5	5	Trinity Co., Calif.	Robert T. Hammaker	Robert T. Hammaker	1988	58
135 3/8	21 7/8	21 6/8	16 5/8	5 1/8	5	5	5	King Co., Wash.	Ernest Zwiefelhofer	Wayne Ferderer	1941	59
135	22 6/8	23 2/8	20	4 4/8	4 3/8	4	4	Mendocino Co., Calif.	Rodney E. Carley	Rodney E. Carley	1989	60
134 7/8	21 6/8	21 6/8	21 1/8	4 5/8	4 6/8	5	5	Josephine Co., Oreg.	Kevin N. Walch	Kevin N. Walch	1991	61
134 6/8	19 7/8	19 7/8	17 7/8	4 6/8	4 7/8	5	5	Humboldt Co., Calif.	Bettie L. Lovie	Bettie L. Lovie	1988	62

Score	Length of Main Beam R	Length of Main Beam L	Inside Spread	Circumference R	Circumference L	Points R	Points L	Locality	By Whom Taken	Owner	Date	Rank
134 2/8	18 4/8	19 4/8	13	4 5/8	4 2/8	5	5	Mendocino Co., Calif.	Gary D. Powell	Gary D. Powell	1990	63
134	21 2/8	20 5/8	16	4 4/8	4 4/8	4	4	Pierce Co., Wash.	William B. Bressler	William B. Bressler	1987	64
133 6/8	19 4/8	19 7/8	13 4/8	4 5/8	4 7/8	5	5	Douglas Co., Oreg.	Ronald L. Sherva	Ronald L. Sherva	1990	65
133 5/8	19 1/8	18 3/8	15 7/8	3 4/8	3 7/8	6	6	Siskiyou Co., Calif.	Edwin W. Masonheimer	Edwin W. Masonheimer	1978	66
133 5/8	21 1/8	21 7/8	17 7/8	4 6/8	4 7/8	6	5	Clackamas Co., Oreg.	Vick L. Ward	Vick L. Ward	1990	66
133 4/8	19 7/8	19 1/8	14 6/8	4 4/8	4 8/8	5	5	Clackamas Co., Oreg.	Scott J. Fuge	Scott J. Fuge	1990	68
133 3/8	18 3/8	18 7/8	17 3/8	4 4/8	4 7/8	5	5	Mendocino Co., Calif.	Richard L. Moore	Richard L. Moore	1989	69
133 2/8	20 2/8	20 1/8	18 2/8	4 7/8	4 7/8	5	5	Polk Co., Oreg.	Picked Up	Ron Zimmerdahl	1988	70
133 1/8	21 3/8	21 1/8	17	4 7/8	4 7/8	4	4	Jackson Co., Oreg.	Brian K. Samuel	Brian K. Samuel	1989	71
133 1/8	20 5/8	20 5/8	15 3/8	4 3/8	4 4/8	5	5	Marion Co., Oreg.	Corinne B. Olson	Corinne B. Olson	1990	71
133	23	21 6/8	16 6/8	4 3/8	4 7/8	5	5	Snohomish Co., Wash.	Burl Champeaux	Burl Champeaux	1959	73
133	19 1/8	18 4/8	18 6/8	4 3/8	4 6/8	5	5	Humboldt Co., Calif.	George B. Stiglich	George B. Stiglich	1988	73
132 7/8	21 1/8	22 5/8	17	3 2/8	3 2/8	5	5	Mendocino Co., Calif.	John E. Coughlin	John E. Coughlin	1988	75
132 6/8	22	21 7/8	15	5 3/8	4 3/8	7	7	Clatsop Co., Oreg.	Kenneth W. Heil	Kenneth W. Heil	1991	76
132 5/8	20 5/8	19 6/8	16 5/8	5 4/8	6 2/8	5	5	Mason Co., Wash.	Fred E. Champlin	Fred E. Champlin	1981	77
132 5/8	20 4/8	20 2/8	16 1/8	4 1/8	4 3/8	5	5	Siskiyou Co., Calif.	Daniel A. Rich	Daniel A. Rich	1990	77
132 3/8	20 4/8	20 4/8	16 3/8	4 1/8	4 1/8	6	5	Mendocino Co., Calif.	Richard L. Moore	Richard L. Moore	1989	79
132 3/8	22 7/8	21 6/8	16 1/8	4 1/8	4	5	5	Siskiyou Co., Calif.	Edward P. Reardon	Edward P. Reardon	1989	79
131 6/8	20 4/8	20 2/8	21 3/8	4	4 3/8	5	5	Lake Co., Calif.	Michael D. Keesee, Sr.	Michael D. Keesee, Sr.	1982	81
131 4/8	18 3/8	19	15 6/8	4 4/8	4	5	5	Skamania Co., Wash.	Fred R. Froehlich	Fred R. Froehlich	1988	82
131 4/8	21 2/8	22 4/8	15 4/8	4 2/8	4 2/8	5	4	Jackson Co., Oreg.	Yannick Y. Watkins	Yannick Y. Watkins	1990	82
131 3/8	21	20 4/8	15 1/8	4 1/8	4	5	5	Pierce Co., Wash.	Dean A. Bender	Dean A. Bender	1990	84
131 1/8	21 1/8	19 4/8	18 4/8	3 7/8	3 7/8	5	5	Tehama Co., Calif.	Richard D. Stillwell	Richard D. Stillwell	1989	85
130 7/8	17 5/8	17 5/8	16 7/8	4 2/8	4 2/8	4	5	Mendocino Co., Calif.	John W. McGehee	John W. McGehee	1989	86
130 6/8	20 4/8	20 4/8	17 6/8	4 3/8	4 3/8	5	5	Lewis Co., Wash.	Bill K. Stoner	Bill K. Stoner	1988	87
130 6/8	20 7/8	20 5/8	17 6/8	3 6/8	3 7/8	5	5	Jackson Co., Oreg.	Ann F. Pope	Ann F. Pope	1989	87
130 3/8	18 3/8	18 1/8	16 1/8	4 2/8	4 2/8	5	5	Mendocino Co., Calif.	Helen F. Ornbaun	Helen F. Ornbaun	1960	89
129 1/8	19 4/8	21 2/8	16 7/8	4 6/8	4 6/8	5	4	Lewis Co., Wash.	Kenneth J. Alwine, Sr.	Kenneth J. Alwine, Sr.	1956	90
127 7/8	20 4/8	21 2/8	15 3/8	3 3/8	3 3/8	4	4	Trinity Co., Calif.	Marlene L. Coats	Marlene & Johnny Coats	1988	91
127 4/8	20 4/8	21	18 6/8	4 5/8	4 6/8	5	5	Clatsop Co., Oreg.	Allan R. Maki	Allan R. Maki	1966	92
127 3/8	21	21 3/8	21	4 4/8	4 4/8	4	4	Mendocino Co., Calif.	Timothy Hickam	Timothy Hickam	1991	93
124 2/8	19 3/8	20 3/8	18	4	4	5	5	Santa Cruz Co., Calif.	Warren D. Huber	William C. Huber	1971	94
123 5/8	18	18 1/8	15 5/8	4 2/8	4 2/8	4	4	Trinity Co., Calif.	Monte D. Matheson	Monte D. Matheson	1988	95
123 3/8	18 7/8	17 4/8	19 6/8	4 3/8	4 3/8	5	5	Mendocino Co., Calif.	Timothy Hickam	Timothy Hickam	1990	96
123 2/8	19 1/8	18 3/8	16 2/8	4 2/8	4 2/8	4	5	Tillamook Co., Oreg.	Fain J. Little	Fain J. Little	1943	97
122 3/8	21 3/8	21 2/8	15 5/8	4 3/8	4 3/8	4	4	Columbia Co., Oreg.	Kelly P. Dering	Kelly P. Dering	1990	98
121 7/8	20 5/8	20 6/8	15 7/8	4 3/8	4 2/8	5	5	Lewis Co., Wash.	Robert E. Hill	Robert E. Hill	1988	99
120 6/8	17 6/8	18 1/8	17 2/8	4 4/8	4 4/8	5	5	Trinity Co., Calif.	Monte D. Matheson	Monte D. Matheson	1988	99
159 2/8*	20 7/8	20 7/8	18 2/8	4 3/8	4 3/8	5	6	Jackson Co., Oreg.	Jeffrey S. Sedey	Jeffrey S. Sedey	1988	100

* Final Score subject to revision by additional verifying measurements.

Sitka Blacktail Deer

Odocoileus hemionus sitkensis

Minimum Score 100

World's Record 128

Sitka blacktail deer includes trophies from coastal Alaska and Queen Charlotte Islands of British Columbia.

Score	Length of Main Beam R.	L.	Inside Spread	Circumference at Smallest Place Between Burr and First Point R.	L.	Number of Points R.	L.	Locality Killed	By Whom Killed	Owner	Date Killed	Rank
118 3/8	19	17 1/8	14 7/8	4	4 1/8	5	5	Prince of Wales Island, Alaska	Johnnie R. Laird	Johnnie R. Laird	1987	1
114 3/8	17 4/8	18 3/8	15 3/8	4 4/8	4 2/8	5	5	Hobart Bay, Alaska	Terry LaFrance	Terry LaFrance	1988	2
112 3/8	19 4/8	19 7/8	17 5/8	4 1/8	4 1/8	4	4	Prince of Wales Island, Alaska	David L. Hahnes	David L. Hahnes	1990	3
112 2/8	17 3/8	17	15 6/8	3 6/8	3 6/8	6	6	Big Salt Lake, Alaska	Roy Weatherford	Roy Weatherford	1988	4
110 7/8	17 7/8	17 6/8	12 3/8	3 5/8	3 7/8	4	4	Queen Charlotte Islands, B.C.	Gordon O. Tolman	Gordon O. Tolman	1990	5
110 5/8	16 4/8	17 1/8	14 7/8	3 5/8	3 5/8	5	5	Amook Island, Alaska	Bob Price	Bob Price	1990	6
110 4/8	20 4/8	19	17 4/8	4 2/8	3 6/8	5	4	Klawock Lake, Alaska	Chris J. Blanc	Chris J. Blanc	1983	7
110 4/8	17 4/8	16 7/8	15 7/8	3 7/8	3 7/8	6	5	Kodiak Island, Alaska	William N. Krenz	William N. Krenz	1988	7
110 2/8	18 6/8	17 6/8	14 2/8	4 1/8	4	5	5	Kodiak Island, Alaska	R. Fred Fortier	R. Fred Fortier	1988	9
110 1/8	16 3/8	16 7/8	14 1/8	4 2/8	4 1/8	5	5	Ratz Harbor, Alaska	Gerald Hedges	Gerald Hedges	1985	10
110 1/8	18 1/8	17 6/8	15 5/8	4 1/8	3 7/8	6	4	Deadman Bay, Alaska	Donald W. Simmons	Donald W. Simmons	1989	10
109 7/8	16 5/8	17 5/8	14 2/8	3 5/8	3 4/8	6	6	Kosciusko Island, Alaska	Michael C. Fezatte	Michael C. Fezatte	1983	12
109 5/8	18 2/8	18 2/8	14 7/8	3 5/8	3 6/8	4	5	Olga Bay, Alaska	Ronnie L. Aldridge	Ronnie L. Aldridge	1988	13
108 4/8	16 4/8	15	15	4 5/8	4 6/8	5	6	Cape Uyak, Alaska	Richard H. Dykema	Richard H. Dykema	1986	14
108 4/8	15 5/8	16 2/8	11 6/8	3 6/8	3 5/8	5	5	Winter Harbor, Alaska	Rocky C. Littleton	Rocky C. Littleton	1988	14
108 4/8	15 5/8	15 1/8	14 5/8	3 7/8	4	5	5	Kodiak Island, Alaska	Kenneth G. Gerg	Kenneth G. Gerg	1988	16
107 1/8	17	16 7/8	13 7/8	4	4	5	5	Copper Mt., Alaska	Lynn W. Merrill	Lynn W. Merrill	1985	17
106 5/8	18 2/8	17 5/8	16 7/8	4 1/8	4 1/8	5	4	Deadman Bay, Alaska	James L. Kedrowski	James L. Kedrowski	1989	18
105 7/8	17 4/8	17 2/8	14 1/8	3 6/8	3 7/8	4	5	Port Lions, Alaska	Dean F. Kalbfleisch	Dean F. Kalbfleisch	1988	19
105 5/8	17 6/8	17 7/8	16	3 7/8	3 6/8	5	5	Whale Pass, Alaska	Victor R. Poythress	Victor R. Poythress	1988	20
105 5/8	18 2/8	17 7/8	14 5/8	3 7/8	4	6	5	Kaiugnak Bay, Alaska	Mark B. Sippin	Mark B. Sippin	1989	20
101 7/8	15 4/8	16 1/8	13 1/8	3 5/8	3 5/8	5	5	Kodiak Island, Alaska	Stephen R. Grubb	Stepehn R. Grubb	1989	22
101 3/8	16 7/8	17	16 5/8	3 7/8	4	4	4	Kodiak Island, Alaska	Roger G. Stewart	Roger G. Stewart	1988	23
100	16 3/8	16 7/8	14	3 4/8	3 3/8	4	4	Barabara Cove, Alaska	Victor R. Poythress	Victor R. Poythress	1988	24
120 2/8*	18 7/8	18 6/8	16	3 7/8	3 7/8	5	5	Luck Lake, Alaska	Ronald A. Littleton	Ronald A. Littleton	1988	
118 5/8*	19 1/8	19 2/8	14 6/8	4 1/8	4 3/8	6	5	Prince of Wales Island, Alaska	Gerald R. Hedges	Gerald R. Hedges	1987	

* Final Score subject to revision by additional verifying measurements.

434

Whitetail Deer, *Typical Antlers*

Minimum Score 160   *Odocoileus virginianus virginianus* and certain related subspecies   World's Record 206-1/8

Score	Length of Main Beam R.	L.	Inside Spread	Circumference at Smallest Place Between Burr and First Point R.	L.	Number of Points R.	L.	Locality Killed	By Whom Killed	Owner	Date Killed	Rank
201 4/8	27 5/8	29 1/8	23	5 5/8	5 2/8	6	6	Hamilton Co., Iowa	Wayne A. Bills	Larry L. Huffman	1974	1
199 5/8	30 1/8	28	29 1/8	5 3/8	5 3/8	6	6	Edmonton, Alta.	Don McGarvey	Don McGarvey	1991	2
197 1/8	31	29 7/8	21 2/8	6 1/8	6 5/8	7	7	Macoupin Co., Ill.	Kevin L. Naugle	James H. Reimer	1988	3
196 3/8	28 7/8	30 5/8	22 1/8	6 5/8	7	7	5	Plymouth Co., Iowa	Picked Up	James H. Reimer	1952	4
194 2/8	26 5/8	25	21	4 6/8	5	6	6	Jones Co., Iowa	Unknown	Larry L. Huffman	1977	5
192 7/8	28 7/8	28 7/8	23 3/8	5 3/8	5 4/8	6	5	Pope Co., Minn.	Roger Syrstad	Roger Syrstad	1989	6
191 7/8	29 5/8	30 1/8	20 3/8	5 7/8	5 7/8	9	8	Wayne Co., Ill.	Leo E. Elliott	Leo E. Elliott	1990	7
191 3/8	24 6/8	25 1/8	25 5/8	4 7/8	5 1/8	5	5	Meade Co., Ky.	Picked Up	William N. Burrell	1977	8
190 5/8	28 6/8	28	17 6/8	5 6/8	6	5	5	Polk Co., Iowa	Richard B. Swim	Richard B. Swim	1981	9
190 3/8	27	26 7/8	20 4/8	4 5/8	4 5/8	6	7	Pettis Co., Mo.	Jesse A. Perry	Jesse A. Perry	1986	10
190 1/8	26 4/8	27	18 4/8	6 1/8	5 7/8	9	7	Randolph Co., Ill.	Kevin Leemon	Kevin Leemon	1990	11
189 5/8	26 3/8	27 3/8	25 1/8	6 2/8	6 7/8	9	7	Schuyler Co., Ill.	Picked Up	Randall E. Hacker	1990	12
189 3/8	24 6/8	24 6/8	23 6/8	5	4 7/8	7	6	Henry Co., Iowa	Lamonte A. Stark	Lamonte A. Stark	1984	13
189 1/8	26	26 5/8	17 3/8	5 6/8	5 6/8	8	9	Douglas Co., Wisc.	Bryan Lawler	Scott McFarren	1946	14
187 6/8	27 4/8	27 7/8	25 3/8	5 2/8	5 3/8	6	6	Union Co., Ky.	Charles Meuth	Larry S. Melton	1964	15
187 4/8	27	27 4/8	19 5/8	5 2/8	4 7/8	9	8	Brown Co., Ill.	Charles A. Howell	Charles A. Howell	1988	16
187 1/8	27 2/8	27 6/8	17 7/8	5	5	8	6	Montgomery Co., Ind.	Larry E. Lawson	Larry E. Lawson	1988	17
186 7/8	26 3/8	26 7/8	20 5/8	5 4/8	5 3/8	5	5	Andrew Co., Mo.	Kenneth Till	Kenneth Till	1989	18
186 6/8	29 1/8	29 7/8	23	4 6/8	4 6/8	5	5	Logan Co., Ohio	Bernard R. Hines	Bernard R. Hines	1990	19
186 4/8	27 6/8	26	22	5 1/8	5 2/8	6	7	Becker Co., Minn.	Ilo Dugger	Jeff Dugger	1930	20
186 3/8	26 1/8	26 3/8	18 6/8	4 7/8	4 7/8	7	5	Otter Tail Co., Minn.	Robert Ames	David R. Brigan	1977	21
186 3/8	28 5/8	28 4/8	20 7/8	5 3/8	5 2/8	5	5	Pike Co., Ill.	Merle L. Shull	Merle L. Shull	1985	21
186 2/8	29 4/8	29	22	4 7/8	4 6/8	6	6	Carter Co., Ky.	Herman G. Holbrooks	Herman G. Holbrooks	1989	23
186 1/8	27 4/8	26 5/8	20 7/8	5	5 5/8	5	5	St. Louis Co., Minn.	Mark O. DuLong	Mark O. DuLong	1988	24
186 1/8	26 2/8	25 4/8	22	6	5 5/8	6	5	Pope Co., Ill.	Picked Up	Jim Frailey	1990	24
185 4/8	26 2/8	26 3/8	20 2/8	4 6/8	4 6/8	5	5	Sussex Co., Del.	Herbert N. Milan	Herbert N. Milan	1978	26
185 3/8	29	28 1/8	23	4 7/8	4 7/8	9	8	Riley Co., Kan.	Robert L. Tully	Robert L. Tully	1988	27
185	25 2/8	25	19 2/8	4 6/8	4 6/8	6	6	Frio Co., Texas	Loyd Nail	Steve L. Smith	1941	28
184 6/8	26 3/8	26 2/8	24 2/8	4 6/8	4 6/8	7	6	Starr Co., Texas	Harry Richardson, Jr.	Harry Richardson, Jr.	1973	29
184 5/8	27 1/8	27 1/8	21 2/8	5 4/8	5 3/8	8	6	Paddle River, Alta.	Gregory D. Graff	Gregory D. Graff	1988	30

Whitetail Deer, *Typical Antlers - Continued*

Score	Length of Main Beam R.	L.	Inside Spread	Circumference at Smallest Place Between Burr and First Point R.	L.	Number of Points R.	L.	Locality Killed	By Whom Killed	Owner	Date Killed	Rank
184 1/8	25 3/8	25 4/8	18 1/8	4 4/8	4 5/8	6	6	Carroll Co., Ohio	Timothy F. Treadway	Timothy F. Treadway	1989	31
184	28 1/8	29 1/8	24 7/8	5	5 1/8	7	9	Allamakee Co., Iowa	William P. Mitchell	W. Mitchell & J. Bakewell	1989	32
183 4/8	29 7/8	29 3/8	23 7/8	5 4/8	5 6/8	8	8	Holmes River, B.C.	Randy Lloyd	Randy Lloyd	1991	33
183 3/8	26 7/8	26 1/8	18 7/8	4 6/8	4 7/8	5	5	McLean Co., Ky.	Larry G. Porter	Larry G. Porter	1980	34
183 3/8	28 5/8	29 5/8	18 5/8	5 4/8	5 3/8	5	5	Franklin Co., Maine	Real Boulanger	Real Boulanger	1990	34
183 2/8	29 1/8	28 3/8	20 4/8	4 4/8	4 4/8	5	6	Shawnee Co., Kan.	Mark W. Young	Mark W. Young	1990	36
183 1/8	25 3/8	26 1/8	21 3/8	5	5 4/8	7	8	Nuevo Leon, Mexico	Thomas D. Brittingham	Thomas D. Brittingham	1990	37
183	28 4/8	28 1/8	20 4/8	5 5/8	5 5/8	5	5	Union Co., Iowa	Randy G. Hall	Randy G. Hall	1986	38
183	26 6/8	28 4/8	18 5/8	5 7/8	5 5/8	5	7	Van Buren Co., Iowa	Picked Up	Timothy J. Wilson	1990	38
182 7/8	27 7/8	28 1/8	21 1/8	4 7/8	4 7/8	5	5	Iosco Co., Mich.	Harvey H. Keast	Harvey H. Keast	1938	40
182 7/8	29 1/8	28 3/8	20 1/8	5 2/8	5 3/8	7	6	Oromocto River, N.B.	Bruce MacGougan	Bruce MacGougan	1984	40
182 6/8	26	25 4/8	18	4 7/8	5	8	6	Webb Co., Texas	George Strait	George Strait	1988	42
182 6/8	28 2/8	28 6/8	19	6 3/8	6 2/8	8	6	Labette Co., Kan.	David W. Steeby	David W. Steeby	1989	42
182 6/8	27 7/8	28 4/8	19 4/8	4 6/8	4 4/8	9	7	Lee Co., Iowa	John L. Kite	John L. Kite	1990	42
182 6/8	25 3/8	25 1/8	22	4 3/8	4 3/8	6	6	Coahuila, Mexico	Manuel A. Flores Rojas	Manuel A. Flores Rojas	1990	42
182 5/8	24 6/8	26 3/8	18 1/8	5	5 1/8	5	5	Jones Co., S.D.	Richard A. Gordon	Richard A. Gordon	1989	46
182 2/8	24 4/8	25 4/8	17 2/8	5 4/8	6	6	6	Stearns Co., Minn.	Michael G. Maki	Michael G. Maki	1988	47
182 2/8	27 1/8	25 6/8	23 4/8	5 3/8	5 4/8	5	5	Hancock Co., Ill.	Robert A. Reed	Robert A. Reed	1988	47
182 1/8	26 5/8	26 7/8	18 6/8	6 4/8	6	7	7	Keokuk Co., Iowa	Willaim Musgrove	William H. Lilienthal	1977	49
182 1/8	27	26 7/8	22 1/8	5 1/8	5 2/8	5	5	Lincoln Co., Mo.	David L. Mudd	David L. Mudd	1988	49
182 1/8	28	27 4/8	25 3/8	6	6 2/8	7	6	MacCafferty Lake, Alta.	Alan S. Bell	Alan S. Bell	1990	49
182	28 1/8	28 4/8	22 6/8	4 4/8	4 5/8	5	5	St. Louis Co., Minn.	Unknown	George Flaim	1975	52
182	27 7/8	28 4/8	21 4/8	5 1/8	5 1/8	6	6	Monona Co., Iowa	Jerry W. Conover	Jerry W. Conover	1990	52
181 7/8	26 3/8	26 3/8	21 1/8	5	4 7/8	6	6	Jackson Co., Iowa	Ambrose Beck	Ambrose Beck	1963	54
181 7/8	25 4/8	26 3/8	21 1/8	5 2/8	5 2/8	5	5	Alice Lake, Alta.	Dave S. Sietz	Dave S. Sietz	1989	54
181 6/8	27 5/8	27 7/8	21 4/8	4 4/8	4 3/8	5	5	Sussex Co., Del.	Donald L. Betts	Donald L. Betts	1989	56
181 5/8	27 5/8	28 3/8	21 2/8	4 6/8	5 3/8	6	6	Bourbon Co., Kan.	Larry Daly	Larry Daly	1990	56
181 5/8	28	27 5/8	25 3/8	4 5/8	4 6/8	5	5	Blaine Co., Mont.	David A. Sprinkle	David A. Sprinkle	1989	58
181 4/8	26 6/8	26	18 2/8	5 3/8	5	7	7	Will Co., Ill.	James J.A. O'Keefe	James J.A. O'Keefe	1989	59
181 3/8	28	26 6/8	18 5/8	4 5/8	4 6/8	6	5	Polk Co., Iowa	Bob Boydston	Kevin Freymiller	1972	60
181 3/8	27 4/8	26 7/8	18 4/8	5 1/8	5 1/8	5	7	Warren Co., Ind.	Todd J. Hemke	Todd J. Hemke	1987	60

Score	L. Main Beam R	L. Main Beam L	Inside Spread	Circ. R	Circ. L	Pts. R	Pts. L	Locality	By Whom Killed	Owner	Date	Rank
181 1/8	27 1/8	27 1/8	21 6/8	5 2/8	5 4/8	7	7	Elk River, Minn.	John E. Bush	Richard L. Busse	1870	62
181 1/8	24 5/8	25 1/8	20 5/8	5 3/8	5 2/8	7	7	Wood River, Sask.	Jeremy Egan	Jeremy Egan	1990	62
181	26 1/8	25 7/8	20 2/8	5 6/8	5 6/8	4	4	St. Louis Co., Minn.	Unknown	Evelyn Case	1909	64
180 7/8	26 4/8	26 6/8	22	5 3/8	5	7	4	Wayne Co., Iowa	Richard L. Spencer	Richard L. Spencer	1990	65
180 5/8	29 6/8	29 3/8	22 5/8	4 4/8	4 4/8	5	7	Adams Co., Ill.	Kenneth E. Klauser	Kenneth E. Klauser	1990	66
180 5/8	25 6/8	25 6/8	19 3/8	4 5/8	4 3/8	5	5	Jim Hogg Co., Texas	Michael L. Vickers	Michael L. Vickers	1991	66
180 4/8	27 1/8	26 7/8	16 6/8	5	4 7/8	6	6	Adams Co., Iowa	Dale D. Blazek	Dale D. Blazek	1962	68
180 4/8	26 4/8	26 4/8	21	5 3/8	5 2/8	6	6	Henry Co., Iowa	Jeff L. Weigert	Jeff L. Weigert	1991	68
180 3/8	25 1/8	24 7/8	17 2/8	4 7/8	4 5/8	5	5	Story Co., Iowa	Richard L. Borton	Richard L. Borton	1987	70
180 2/8	24 7/8	24 7/8	20 2/8	4 7/8	4 7/8	6	7	Texas	Alfred Schroeder	John E. Hamilton	1926 PR	71
180 2/8	27 7/8	27 7/8	20 4/8	4 7/8	4 7/8	6	6	Yuma Co., Colo.	Jeff L. Mekelburg	Jeff L. Mekelburg	1989	71
180 2/8	25 3/8	25 3/8	20 4/8	4 3/8	5	5	6	Polk Co., Iowa	Jeff P. Susie	Jeff P. Susie	1990	71
180 1/8	27 4/8	27 4/8	22 4/8	4 6/8	4 6/8	7	5	Chariton Co., Mo.	Ricky Pearman	Ricky Pearman	1982	74
180 1/8	26	26	15 7/8	4 7/8	4 7/8	5	5	Jackson Co., S.D.	Timothy J. Kelley	Timothy J. Kelley	1988	74
180	26 1/8	26 7/8	19 4/8	4 4/8	5 2/8	5	6	Florence Co., Wisc.	Dale E. Samsa	Dale E. Samsa	1988	76
180	28	28	19 4/8	5 1/8	4 5/8	7	10	Pembina River, Alta.	Joe Jandl	Joe Jandl	1989	76
179 4/8	25 4/8	25 4/8	19 4/8	6	6 1/8	6	6	Clarke Co., Iowa	Rodney D. Hommer	Rodney D. Hommer	1990	78
179 4/8	28 1/8	24 1/8	22	5 4/8	5 3/8	6	6	Yankee Lake, Sask.	Leo Stieb	Leo Stieb	1990	78
179 2/8	24 6/8	25 4/8	20 6/8	4 7/8	5	7	6	Hinds Co., Miss.	Marlon Stokes	Marlon Stokes	1988	80
179	25 6/8	26 5/8	21	4 7/8	5	5	5	Monroe Co., Mo.	Tommy Garnett	Tommy Garnett	1988	81
179	26 3/8	27 2/8	19 1/8	5 1/8	5 4/8	5	5	Pictou Co., N.S.	Earl Perry	Earl Perry	1990	81
178 7/8	27 2/8	29 4/8	18 1/8	5	5	6	6	Whiteside Co., Ill.	Bernard J. Higley, Jr.	Bernard J. Higley, Jr.	1990	83
178 7/8	29 4/8	30	22 7/8	4 5/8	4 5/8	5	5	Coahuila, Mexico	Donald R. Summers	Donald R. Summers	1990	83
178 6/8	26 4/8	26 4/8	20 7/8	4	4 4/8	5	8	Texas	Unknown	Lone Star Brewing Co.	1960 PR	85
178 6/8	27 3/8	27 5/8	21 3/8	4 6/8	4 4/8	5	5	Corson Co., S.D.	Dean Little Dog	Dick Rossum	1984	85
178 6/8	28 1/8	27 3/8	21 2/8	4 7/8	4 7/8	6	6	Vilna City, Alta.	M.M. Berrien, Jr.	M.M. Berrien, Jr.	1990	85
178 5/8	26 4/8	26 4/8	21 5/8	4 7/8	4 7/8	8	7	St. Louis Co., Minn.	John Nordenstam	George Flaim	1977	88
178 5/8	25 7/8	25 7/8	18 7/8	5 1/8	5 1/8	7	5	Grundy Co., Ill.	Charles H. Frantini	Charles H. Frantini	1987	88
178 5/8	23 7/8	23 7/8	19 5/8	5 5/8	5 5/8	5	5	Jones Co., Iowa	Dennis Boots	Dennis Boots	1988	88
178 5/8	26 2/8	26 2/8	20 3/8	4 6/8	4 6/8	6	8	Riley Co., Kan.	Colt Knutson	Colt Knutson	1989	88
178 4/8	26	27 1/8	16 1/8	5 2/8	5 7/8	6	6	Yuma Co., Colo.	Terry M. Scheidecker	Terry M. Scheidecker	1979	92
178 4/8	27 1/8	25 3/8	18 2/8	5 6/8	6 2/8	10	8	Nance Co., Neb.	Robert J. Ziemba	Robert J. Ziemba	1988	92
178 3/8	25 3/8	30 4/8	17 1/8	6 2/8	4 7/8	6	6	Dubuque Co., Iowa	Clay W. Gronen	Clay W. Gronen	1978	94
178 3/8	30 4/8	28 4/8	25	4 7/8	5 6/8	6	6	Gregory Co., S.D.	Ronald L. Larson	Ronald L. Larson	1980	94
178 2/8	28 4/8	27 7/8	21 2/8	5 6/8	5 1/8	7	6	Lawrence Co., Ill.	Brian M. Dining	Brian M. Dining	1987	96
178 1/8	27 7/8	24 2/8	20 4/8	5 1/8	4 3/8	5	9	Vonda, Sask.	Orest Hilkewich	Orest Hilkewich	1980	97
178	24 2/8	28	25	4 2/8	5 1/8	6	5	Appanoose Co., Iowa	Steve G. Huff	Steve G. Huff	1988	98
177 7/8	28	26 5/8	29	5	5 1/8	9	6	Haralson Co., Ga.	Picked Up	Alfred Wright	1982	99
177 7/8	26 5/8	30 2/8	18 5/8	5 3/8	5 1/8	5	6	Vilas Co., Wisc.	Dean A. Casper	Dean A. Casper	1990	99
177 6/8	25 4/8	26 1/8	17	5	5 1/8	6	6	Pendleton Co., Ky.	Daniel Michalski	Daniel Michalski	1988	101
177 6/8	26 3/8	27 7/8	18 2/8	5 4/8	5 4/8	6	6	Antler River, Sask.	Larry Sterling	Larry Sterling	1989	101

Whitetail Deer, Typical Antlers - Continued

Score	Length of Main Beam R.	L.	Inside Spread	Circumference at Smallest Place Between Burr and First Point R.	L.	Number of Points R.	L.	Locality Killed	By Whom Killed	Owner	Date Killed	Rank
177 6/8	27 6/8	28 1/8	19 1/8	4 3/8	4 4/8	7	8	Anderson Co., Kan.	Randall R. West	Randall R. West	1990	101
177 6/8	26 4/8	26 6/8	20 7/8	4 6/8	4 4/8	5	6	Lincoln Co., Mont.	Bernard B. White	Bernard B. White	1990	101
177 5/8	27 6/8	28 5/8	18	5 5/8	5 4/8	6	6	Colquitt Co., Ga.	Timothy Carter	Timothy Carter	1990	105
177 2/8	27 5/8	28 3/8	19 4/8	4 6/8	4 6/8	7	7	Pine Co., Minn.	C. Foster & E. Kepler	Lois Youngbauer	1930	106
177 2/8	29 1/8	29 2/8	21	4 6/8	4 5/8	5	5	Buffalo Co., Wisc.	George W. Kees	George W. Kees	1957	106
177 2/8	26 5/8	27 3/8	22	4 6/8	4 4/8	7	5	Gathrie Co., Iowa	Picked Up	Dalton H. Hoover	1970	106
177 2/8	27 4/8	28 3/8	18 6/8	4 5/8	4 7/8	7	7	Clarke Co., Iowa	Richard Bassett	Richard Bassett	1989	106
177 1/8	26 7/8	27 1/8	22 1/8	5	4 7/8	5	6	Harrison Co., Ky.	Picked Up	George Simpson	1978	110
177 1/8	25 7/8	25 3/8	18 5/8	4 5/8	4 4/8	8	6	Forest Co., Wisc.	Carl S. Ernst	Carl S. Ernst	1990	110
177 1/8	27 1/8	28 6/8	21 2/8	4 6/8	4 6/8	7	5	St. Croix Co., Wisc.	Phillip R. Hovde	Phillip R. Hovde	1990	110
177 1/8	26 4/8	27	19 4/8	4 6/8	4 7/8	5	5	Cass Co., Iowa	Cleve H. Powell	Cleve H. Powell	1990	110
177	25 1/8	25 3/8	17 2/8	5	5 1/8	7	7	Rainey River, Ont.	Robert K. Hayes	Robert K. Hayes	1949	114
177	23 4/8	22 6/8	16 4/8	4 6/8	4 6/8	6	5	Harrison Co., Iowa	Craig D. Mitchell	Craig D. Mitchell	1988	114
177	28 2/8	28 1/8	18 3/8	5	5	8	6	Baltimore Co., Md.	Richard B. Traband	Richard B. Traband	1990	114
176 7/8	27 1/8	27 7/8	18 5/8	4 4/8	4 5/8	5	5	Cass Co., Ill.	Mark A. Kluckman	Mark A. Kluckman	1988	117
176 7/8	27 4/8	27 5/8	21 1/8	4 5/8	4 4/8	5	5	Warren Co., Ohio	Richard M. Barhorst	Richard M. Barhorst	1990	117
176 6/8	25 6/8	25 6/8	20 2/8	4 7/8	4 7/8	6	6	Muscatine Co., Iowa	Donald L. McCullough	Donald L. McCullough	1980	119
176 6/8	23 7/8	26 1/8	20 3/8	5 3/8	5 4/8	6	5	Linn Co., Iowa	Douglas D. Kriegel	Douglas D. Kriegel	1988	119
176 6/8	27 4/8	26 2/8	23	5	4 7/8	6	6	Sturgeon River, Alta.	Michael G. Schmermund	Michael G. Schmermund	1990	119
176 5/8	24 2/8	23 3/8	16 7/8	4 3/8	4 3/8	9	9	Welsh Co., Texas	Antonio Gonzalez	Edmundo R. Gonzalez, Jr.	1929	122
176 5/8	27 4/8	27 7/8	20 5/8	5 1/8	5 1/8	5	5	Winona Co., Minn.	Robert J. Haessig	Robert J. Haessig	1961	122
176 5/8	26 5/8	25 6/8	17 3/8	4 2/8	4 4/8	5	5	Meade Co., S.D.	Jerry Humble	Jerry Humble	1970	122
176 4/8	26 6/8	26 3/8	18 4/8	5 1/8	5 1/8	6	6	Itasco Co., Minn.	Jim Soukup	Jim Soukup	1960	125
176 4/8	25 1/8	24 1/8	19 2/8	4 6/8	4 6/8	7	8	Jim Hogg Co., Texas	Picked Up	Eddie Garza	1990	125
176 3/8	28	27	20 5/8	4 7/8	4 7/8	5	6	Montgomery Co., Iowa	Stanley D. Means	Stanley D. Means	1977	127
176 3/8	26 6/8	25 7/8	18 7/8	5 2/8	5 3/8	5	7	Fremont Co., Iowa	Scott J. Carnes	Scott J. Carnes	1987	127
176 3/8	22 3/8	24 5/8	21 7/8	5 2/8	5 1/8	6	6	Champaign Co., Ohio	David A. Owen	David A. Owen	1988	127
176 3/8	24 5/8	24 3/8	17 1/8	4 7/8	4 7/8	7	6	Round Lake, Sask.	Randy Tulloch	Randy Tulloch	1989	127
176 3/8	27 3/8	26 5/8	21 6/8	5 3/8	5 4/8	5	6	Hamilton Co., Ill.	Dennis W. Woolard, Jr.	Dennis W. Woolard, Jr.	1989	127
176 3/8	27 3/8	28 4/8	23 3/8	5 3/8	5 2/8	10	10	Cypress Hills, Sask	Dwight W. Dobson	Dwight W. Dobson	1990	127
176 2/8	25 3/8	26 4/8	22 2/8	5	5	6	6	Des Moines Co., Iowa	Virgil Landrum	Virgil Landrum	1960	133
176 2/8	26 7/8	27 7/8	21 6/8	4 4/8	4 5/8	5	5	St. Louis Co., Minn.	Picked Up	George Flaim	1978	133

Score	Main Beam R	Main Beam L	Inside Spread	Circumference R	Circumference L	Points R	Points L	Locality	Hunter	Owner	Date Killed	Rank
176 2/8	28 3/8	29 4/8	23 2/8	5 2/8	5 1/8	6	6	Aroostook Co., Maine	Daniel T. Geary	Daniel T. Geary	1989	133
176 2/8	24 5/8	23 1/8	15 6/8	6	6 2/8	7	7	Converse Co., Wyo.	Basil C. Bradbury	Basil C. Bradbury	1990	133
176 1/8	24 1/8	25 4/8	19 5/8	4 7/8	4 4/8	5	5	Jackson Co., Iowa	Roy O. Lindemier	Roy O. Lindemier	1990	137
176 1/8	27 1/8	27 4/8	23 5/8	4 7/8	5 4/8	6	5	Johnson Co., Mo.	James A. Stephens	James A. Stephens	1990	137
176	24 1/8	23 7/8	16	4 3/8	4 4/8	5	5	Ghost Lake, Alta.	Viktor Nill	Viktor Nill	1989	139
175 7/8	23 3/8	24 3/8	20 5/8	4 3/8	4 4/8	6	6	Kinney Co., Texas	Walter Griener	John L. Stein	1935	140
175 7/8	25 3/8	25 5/8	21 2/8	6	5 6/8	6	6	Haron Co., Ohio	Royal R. Chisholm	Royal R. Chisholm	1988	140
175 7/8	25 2/8	25 1/8	16 3/8	5	5 2/8	5	5	Barrhead, Alta.	Hugh L. Schmaus	Hugh L. Schmaus	1990	140
175 6/8	26 3/8	24 5/8	19 6/8	5 5/8	5 7/8	6	6	Nemaha Co., Kan.	Kevin L. Kramer	Kevin L. Kramer	1988	143
175 5/8	26 6/8	25 1/8	17 7/8	5 1/8	5 1/8	5	5	Mellette Co., S.D.	Ben Krogman	Ben Krogman	1969	144
175 4/8	26 5/8	28	20 2/8	5	5 1/8	6	6	Mille Lacs Co., Minn.	John Krol	Ronald D. Evensen	1973	145
175 4/8	26 3/8	25 7/8	21 2/8	5 1/8	5 1/8	5	5	Winnebago Co., Iowa	Joel Kingland	Joel Kingland	1975	145
175 4/8	22 4/8	26 4/8	21 4/8	5 1/8	5 1/8	5	5	Maine	Unknown	Richard Arsenault	1989	145
175 3/8	29 1/8	28 7/8	21 4/8	5 2/8	5 2/8	6	6	Wright Co., Iowa	Picked Up	Ron Schaumburg	1976	148
175 3/8	28 3/8	28 5/8	17 6/8	4 6/8	4 4/8	6	7	Carroll Co., Iowa	Edward L. Golay	Edward L. Golay	1984	148
175 2/8	27 2/8	27 3/8	15 4/8	5 2/8	6	6	8	Cherokee Co., Iowa	Unknown	James H. Reimer	1954	150
175 2/8	30	28 3/8	22	6 1/8	6 1/8	7	8	Schuyler Co., Ill.	Rodney C. Chute	Rodney C. Chute	1989	150
175	26 6/8	27 4/8	23	5 1/8	5 3/8	5	5	Henry Co., Ill.	Bradley DeMay	Bradley DeMay	1989	150
175	28 6/8	30 7/8	19 7/8	4 7/8	4 7/8	5	5	Van Buren Co., Mich.	Daryl D. Kovach	Daryl D. Kovach	1989	150
175	25 6/8	26 2/8	19 5/8	4 3/8	4 4/8	7	7	Jo Daviess Co., Ill.	Michael J. Traum	Michael J. Traum	1989	150
175	27 4/8	27 3/8	22 3/8	4 7/8	4 6/8	7	7	Roberts Co., S.D.	Rudy Duwenhoegger, Jr.	Rudy Duwenhoegger, Jr.	1966	155
175	25 7/8	26 5/8	22 4/8	5	5 1/8	6	6	Sac Co., Iowa	Randy J. Bentsen	Randy J. Bentsen	1973	155
175	27 3/8	27 6/8	20 7/8	5 5/8	5 4/8	7	7	Des Moines Co., Iowa	Gordon F. Roebeck	Gordon F. Roebeck	1987	155
175	28 4/8	28 3/8	18 2/8	4 4/8	4 4/8	6	6	LaSalle Co., Texas	Phil Lyne	Phil Lyne	1972	158
175	28 5/8	29 1/8	21 5/8	5 1/8	5	7	7	Henry Co., Iowa	Richard Doggett	Richard Doggett	1975	158
175	31 3/8	31	23 2/8	4 7/8	5	6	6	Mower Co., Minn.	Scott R. Lau	Scott R. Lau	1983	158
175	25 3/8	24 3/8	17 7/8	5 4/8	5 7/8	7	8	Hardin Co., Ohio	Roger E. Titus	Roger E. Titus	1988	158
175	27	27	21	5 2/8	5 2/8	5	7	Riverdale, Man.	David Hofer, Jr.	David Hofer, Jr.	1989	158
174 7/8	27 6/8	28 6/8	19	4 3/8	4 1/8	6	6	Lee Co., Iowa	Stephen D. McKeehan, Jr.	Stephen D. McKeehan, Jr.	1989	158
174 7/8	26 3/8	25 4/8	17	4 7/8	4 6/8	6	5	Bureau Co., Ill.	Paul S. Cobane III	Paul S. Cobane III	1990	158
174 6/8	26 1/8	26 1/8	18 4/8	5 1/8	5 1/8	7	7	Stevens Co., Wash.	Clifton W. Hamilton	Clifton W. Hamilton	1990	165
174 6/8	23 3/8	23 5/8	16 7/8	4 3/8	4 4/8	5	5	Dent Co., Mo.	Thomas P. Wylie	Thomas P. Wylie	1990	165
174 5/8	27 4/8	28	19 4/8	5 2/8	5 3/8	6	5	Lake William, N.S.	Neil G. Oickle	Neil G. Oickle	1985	167
174 5/8	27 1/8	27 2/8	20 3/8	4 5/8	4 5/8	5	5	Isanti Co., Minn.	Unknown	Pete Thiry	PR 1940	168
174 5/8	26	27 2/8	20 3/8	4 7/8	4 7/8	8	8	Des Moines Co., Iowa	Gene L. McAlister	Gene L. McAlister	1980	168
174 5/8	26	25 3/8	22 3/8	6 5/8	6 7/8	8	8	Beaver Co., Okla.	Tanner Alexander	Tanner Alexander	1990	168
174 5/8	28 6/8	28	20 4/8	5 4/8	5 5/8	5	9	Ray Co., Mo.	Dennis B. Bales	Dennis B. Bales	1990	168
174 5/8	28 2/8	28 1/8	19 1/8	5 4/8	5 5/8	5	5	Delaware Co., Ohio	Robert J. Miller	Robert J. Miller	1990	168
174 5/8	26 2/8	25 3/8	18 7/8	5 4/8	5 3/8	6	6	Buffalo Co., Wisc.	Daniel L. Scharmer	Daniel L. Scharmer	1990	168
174 5/8	25 1/8	25 5/8	30 4/8	4 4/8	5 2/8	5	5	Larimer Co., Colo.	George S. Sumter, Jr.	George S. Sumter, Jr.	1990	168
174 5/8	27 5/8	27 5/8	20 1/8	4 4/8	4 5/8	6	5	Jefferson Co., Ohio	Walter R. Sutton	Walter R. Sutton	1991	168

Whitetail Deer, *Typical Antlers* – Continued

Score	Length of Main Beam R.	Length of Main Beam L.	Inside Spread	Circumference at Smallest Place Between Burr and First Point R.	Circumference ... L.	Number of Points R.	Number of Points L.	Locality Killed	By Whom Killed	Owner	Date Killed	Rank
174 4/8	24 7/8	24 3/8	16 6/8	4 6/8	4 6/8	6	6	Marquette Co., Mich.	Henry L. Terres	Paul Terres	1944	176
174 4/8	26 4/8	25 2/8	19 4/8	5 7/8	6	5	5	Buffalo Co., Wisc.	Unknown	Douglas R. Plourde	1961	176
174 4/8	24 2/8	24 6/8	20 2/8	5 5/8	5 5/8	5	5	Jensen Reservoir, Alta.	Gary Stanford	Gary Stanford	1976	176
174 4/8	27 7/8	26 3/8	18 3/8	5 2/8	4 6/8	8	5	Lee Co., Ill.	Fred L. Schimel	Fred L. Schimel	1988	176
174 3/8	26 2/8	25 2/8	20 5/8	4 6/8	4 2/8	5	5	McCreary Co., Ky.	Richard Keeton	Richard Keeton	1982	180
174 3/8	27 1/8	27 1/8	21 3/8	6 2/8	5 7/8	5	5	Hasco Co., Minn.	Mark O. DuLong	Mark O. DuLong	1987	180
174 3/8	26 2/8	25	17 3/8	5 7/8	5 7/8	6	5	N. Saskatchewan River, Alta.	James S. Romanchuk	James S. Romanchuk	1988	180
174 3/8	25 4/8	25 4/8	19 5/8	4 3/8	4 2/8	5	5	Jackson Co., Ind.	Max E. Gambrel	Max E. Gambrel	1989	180
174 3/8	26	26 6/8	21 7/8	5 4/8	5 4/8	5	5	Hardin Co., Ohio	Ron Hamilton	Ron Hamilton	1989	180
174 3/8	27	27 6/8	22 7/8	5 2/8	5 2/8	8	7	Warren Co., Iowa	Craig O. Carpenter	Craig O. Carpenter	1990	180
174 3/8	27 7/8	28	28	5 3/8	5 3/8	5	5	Washenaw Co., Mich.	Picked Up	Comm. Bucks of Mich.	1991	180
174 2/8	28 3/8	28 2/8	22 2/8	5 4/8	5 4/8	4	4	Cass Co., Iowa	Cecil Erickson	Cecil Erickson	1975	187
174 1/8	27	26 5/8	18 4/8	4 5/8	4 4/8	5	6	Buffalo Co., Wisc.	Apolinary Sonsalla	Apolinary Sonsalla	1959	188
174 1/8	24 5/8	23 5/8	19 5/8	5 4/8	5 4/8	5	5	Blackfoot, Alta.	Thomas J. Slager	Thomas J. Slager	1969	188
174 1/8	27 3/8	26 4/8	18 1/8	5 4/8	5 4/8	5	5	Clarke Co., Iowa	Lee R. Lundstrom	Lee R. Lundstrom	1987	188
174 1/8	23 7/8	23 5/8	19 7/8	5	5	5	6	Goodhue Co., Minn.	Tom Nesserh	Tom Nesserh	1988	188
174 1/8	25	25 4/8	18 1/8	5	5	5	5	Mason Co., Ky.	Rocky L. Hamm	Rocky L. Hamm	1989	188
174 1/8	24 3/8	25 4/8	19 2/8	5 3/8	5 3/8	7	6	Day Co., S.D.	Vernon L. Skoba	Vernon L. Skoba	1989	188
174 1/8	25 5/8	25 2/8	20 7/8	4 2/8	4 2/8	6	6	Seneca Co., Ohio	Patrick J. Gillig	Patrick J. Gillig	1990	188
174	29 1/8	28 3/8	17	5 1/8	5 1/8	5	5	Jefferson Co., N.Y.	James S. Hoar	James S. Hoar	1988	195
174	27 6/8	28 4/8	19 6/8	4 3/8	4 4/8	5	5	Whitley Co., Ky.	Edward S. Pittman	Edward S. Pittman	1988	195
174	26 3/8	26 2/8	17 6/8	4 2/8	4 2/8	6	6	Harrison Co., Iowa	Ricky G. Seydel	Ricky G. Seydel	1989	195
173 7/8	27	26 1/8	19 3/8	5 6/8	5 4/8	6	5	Henry Co., Iowa	Marion L. Shappell	Marion L. Shappell	1970	198
173 6/8	25 5/8	26 1/8	22 1/8	4 7/8	4 7/8	6	5	Des Moines Co., Iowa	Richard R. Hassell	Richard R. Hassell	1979	199
173 6/8	24	24 4/8	18	4 4/8	4 4/8	6	6	Marshall Co., Minn.	Neil Jacobson	Neil Jacobson	1984	199
173 6/8	26 1/8	25	21 5/8	4 4/8	4 4/8	6	5	Winneshiek Co., Iowa	Herbert I. Amundson	Herbert I. Amundson	1985	199
173 6/8	25 5/8	25 1/8	18 4/8	5 6/8	5 6/8	5	5	Lincoln Co., Neb.	Raymond E. Blede	Raymond E. Blede	1988	199
173 6/8	29 3/8	28 4/8	20 6/8	5 4/8	5 4/8	5	5	Mahaska Co., Iowa	Gareth P. Vande Klieft	Gareth P. Vande Klieft	1988	199
173 6/8	25 6/8	26 6/8	20	4 3/8	4 3/8	5	5	Dawson Co., Neb.	Michael L. Seaman	Michael L. Seaman	1989	199
173 6/8	26 4/8	25 2/8	21 4/8	5 2/8	5 2/8	6	6	Mercer Co., Ill.	Clarence R. Howard	Clarence R. Howard	1990	199
173 5/8	27	27	19 7/8	4 2/8	4 2/8	6	5	Winona Co., Minn.	John W. Brand	John W. Brand	1969	206

Score	L. Main Beam R	L. Main Beam L	Inside Spread	Circ. R	Circ. L	Pts R	Pts L	Locality	Hunter	Owner	Date	Rank
173 5/8	25 3/8	26	18 5/8	4 7/8	4 7/8	5	6	Plymouth Co., Iowa	Pat Kenaley	Pat Kenaley	1986	206
173 5/8	25 5/8	27 2/8	18 1/8	4 5/8	4 5/8	6	6	Roseau Co., Minn.	David A. Harmon	David A. Harmon	1987	206
173 5/8	27 3/8	27 7/8	18 7/8	6 4/8	6 4/8	7	6	Pike Co., Ill.	Jimmy Howard	Jimmy Howard	1989	206
173 4/8	26 6/8	27 1/8	16	4 7/8	4 7/8	5	5	Zavala Co., Texas	Roger Morris	Alvin Morris	1931	210
173 4/8	28 4/8	28 3/8	20 5/8	5	5	7	5	St. Louis Co., Minn.	Clarence Lindstrom	Donald A. Fondrick	1960	210
173 4/8	25 3/8	25 3/8	18	5	5	6	6	Barber Co., Kan.	James R. Schreiner	James R. Schreiner	1990	210
173 3/8	28 7/8	28 1/8	19 1/8	5 2/8	4 7/8	5	6	Monona Co., Iowa	Steve D. Maher	Steve D. Maher	1986	213
173 3/8	26 6/8	26 5/8	24 7/8	4 5/8	4 4/8	5	6	Bullitt Co., Ky.	Leon R. Allen	Leon R. Allen	1988	213
173 3/8	26 3/8	26 6/8	25 7/8	4 5/8	4 5/8	6	6	Riley Co., Kan.	Russell S. Santo	Russell S. Santo	1989	213
173 3/8	25 5/8	25 7/8	19	4 1/8	4 2/8	6	6	Texas	Unknown	Marvin Schwarz	PR 1940	216
173 2/8	30 1/8	27 5/8	20 6/8	5	5	6	6	Calhoun Co., Ill.	Picked Up	Dean Diaz	1990	216
173 2/8	26 3/8	26 6/8	17 4/8	5 2/8	5 2/8	5	5	Woodbury Co., Iowa	Jim C. Jepson	Jim C. Jepson	1990	216
173 2/8	27 4/8	26 3/8	21 7/8	5 3/8	5 5/8	5	5	St. Louis Co., Minn.	Unknown	George Flaim	1934	219
173 1/8	26 7/8	26 6/8	20 5/8	4 3/8	4 2/8	5	5	Adams Co., Ohio	Mark N. Barnes	Mark N. Barnes	1986	219
173 1/8	27 7/8	27 1/8	20 7/8	4 6/8	4 5/8	4	4	Ralls Co., Mo.	Picked Up	Les James	1988	219
173 1/8	27 3/8	27 3/8	20 3/8	4 4/8	4 3/8	5	5	Allegan Co., Mich.	Charles O. Hooper	Charles O. Hooper	1990	219
173	26 4/8	26 4/8	20 7/8	4 6/8	4 7/8	8	5	Pottawatomie Co., Kan.	Donald L. Smith	Donald L. Smith	1990	219
173	25 7/8	25 7/8	22	4 7/8	4 7/8	5	5	Pope Co., Minn.	Unknown	Tom Hammer	PR 1960	219
173	25 1/8	24 7/8	18 6/8	4 7/8	5 1/8	6	5	Fairfield Co., Ohio	James Carmichael	James Carmichael	1988	224
173	27	26	20 1/8	4 2/8	4 1/8	6	7	Big Horn Co., Wyo.	Daniel D. Wood	Daniel D. Wood	1989	224
172 7/8	25 4/8	25 4/8	21 6/8	4 6/8	4 7/8	5	5	Pepin Co., Wisc.	William A. Gray	William A. Gray	1990	224
172 7/8	22 3/8	23	20	4 3/8	4 3/8	8	8	Dallas Co., Iowa	Gordon Cochran	Gordon Cochran	1982	224
172 6/8	29 3/8	28 4/8	24 7/8	4 7/8	4 7/8	4	4	Jackson Co., Iowa	Picked Up	Roy Rathje	1989	228
172 6/8	28 2/8	28	20 4/8	5 3/8	5 3/8	5	4	Louisa Co., Iowa	Merrill Flake	Monna B. Flake	1974	228
172 6/8	27 6/8	27 6/8	18	5 1/8	5 1/8	5	5	Ashland Co., Wisc.	Picked Up	David Sanborn	PR 1987	228
172 6/8	27 4/8	27	24 4/8	4 6/8	4 5/8	6	6	Henderson Co., Ill.	Larry Spiker	William H. Lilienthal	1988	230
172 6/8	27	25 5/8	22	5 4/8	5 4/8	4	5	Stafford Co., Kan.	Donald G. Fisher	Donald G. Fisher	1989	230
172 5/8	25 4/8	26	18 7/8	4 4/8	4 7/8	5	6	Bee Co., Texas	John W. Galloway	John W. Galloway	1990	230
172 5/8	25 5/8	27 1/8	21 1/8	4 3/8	4 4/8	6	7	Renville Co., Minn.	Elroy E. Kuglin	Elroy E. Kuglin	1990	230
172 5/8	27 1/8	27 3/8	20	4 6/8	4 6/8	5	5	Crawford Creek, Sask.	Scott Macnab	Scott Macnab	1990	230
172 5/8	27 3/8	24 3/8	23 5/8	4 3/8	4 3/8	7	7	San Patricio Co., Texas	Mary L. Edwards	Mary L. Edwards	1967	230
172 4/8	24	24 3/8	18 7/8	4 4/8	4 3/8	7	5	Rosebud Co., Mont.	Michael E. Gayheart	Michael E. Gayheart	1989	237
172 4/8	26 7/8	27 1/8	18 6/8	5 2/8	5 5/8	5	5	Douglas Co., Mo.	Virgil Churchill	Virgil Churchill	1990	237
172 4/8	26 2/8	25 5/8	22 3/8	5 3/8	5 3/8	5	5	Jackson Co., Iowa	Robert R. Morehead	Robert R. Morehead	1990	237
172 4/8	26 6/8	27 1/8	17 1/8	4 1/8	5 1/8	4	4	Wayne Co., Ky.	Ronald G. Sexton	Ronald G. Sexton	1990	237
172 3/8	26 4/8	26 1/8	19	5 3/8	5 2/8	5	5	Fillmore Co., Minn.	Picked Up	William H. Lilienthal	1965	237
172 3/8	29 4/8	26 5/8	20	5 2/8	5 3/8	5	6	Iron Co., Wisc.	Dale D. Tuszke	Dale D. Tuszke	1987	242
172 3/8	22	28 6/8	23 7/8	4 6/8	4 7/8	7	5	Smoky River, Alta.	Bevar C. Rose	Bevar C. Rose	1988	242
172 3/8	26 5/8	25 5/8	17 1/8	4 4/8	4 3/8	8	7	Kanabec Co., Minn.	Gregory L. Schultz	Gregory L. Schultz	1976	242
172 3/8	26 4/8	27 6/8	16 2/8	4 6/8	5	5	5	Mercer Co., Mo.	Jarin J. Simpson	Jarin J. Simpson	1988	245
172 3/8	27 7/8	26 7/8	18	5 2/8	5 6/8	7	7	Boone Co., Iowa	Kevin A. Anderson	Kevin A. Anderson	1989	245

Whitetail Deer, Typical Antlers - Continued

Score	Length of Main Beam R.	L.	Inside Spread	Circumference at Smallest Place Between Burr and First Point R.	L.	Number of Points R.	L.	Locality Killed	By Whom Killed	Owner	Date Killed	Rank
172 3/8	24 6/8	24 6/8	17 5/8	4 3/8	4 3/8	5	5	Dearborn Co., Ind.	Walter C. Drake	Walter C. Drake	1990	245
172 3/8	27	27 3/8	23 5/8	5 3/8	5 3/8	6	6	McHenry Co., Ill.	Kevin Rubow	Kevin Rubow	1990	245
172 2/8	25 6/8	26 3/8	20	5 1/8	5 1/8	5	5	Jones Co., S.D.	Walter Prahl	Walter Prahl	1960	250
172 2/8	24 7/8	25	18 2/8	5	4 7/8	6	5	Putman Co., Ga.	Spunky Thornton	Spunky Thornton	1983	250
172 2/8	27 1/8	27	22	5 3/8	5	5	5	Jefferson Co., Iowa	Paul Hagist, Jr.	Paul Hagist, Jr.	1986	250
172 2/8	26 7/8	27 6/8	26 2/8	4 7/8	4 3/8	6	5	Saunders Co., Neb.	John I. Kunert	John I. Kunert	1986	250
172 2/8	26 7/8	25 5/8	23 4/8	4 4/8	4 4/8	6	6	Scott Co., Minn.	Kenneth J. Scherer	Kenneth J. Scherer	1987	250
172 2/8	22 7/8	27 1/8	16 3/8	5 3/8	5 4/8	8	7	Rainy Lake, Ont.	Andrew Brigham	Andrew Brigham	1989	250
172 2/8	26 1/8	26 6/8	21	5 2/8	5 2/8	8	8	Norman Co., Minn.	Corey Hoseth	Corey Hoseth	1989	250
172 2/8	26	26	22	5 4/8	5	5	5	Washtenaw Co., Mich.	Guy A. Miller	Guy A. Miller	1989	250
172 2/8	25 1/8	25	18	5 2/8	5	6	6	Union Co., Ill.	Richard A. Sotiropoulos	Richard A. Sotiropoulos	1990	250
172 1/8	30 2/8	30 1/8	20 7/8	5	4 7/8	6	5	Fillmore Co., Minn.	C.J. Semmen & G. Lea	Charles J. Semmen	1961	259
172 1/8	24 1/8	24 5/8	19 6/8	5 3/8	5 3/8	7	7	Louisa Co., Iowa	John Bloomer	John Bloomer	1987	259
172 1/8	25 1/8	24 6/8	22 5/8	5 7/8	5 7/8	8	8	Lake Co., Ill.	Mark J. Kramer	Mark J. Kramer	1990	259
172 1/8	27 6/8	27 4/8	17 5/8	4 3/8	4 1/8	6	6	Dooly Co., Ga.	Marty T. McNulty	Marty T. McNulty	1990	259
172 1/8	22 7/8	22 6/8	17 5/8	5 4/8	5 5/8	6	6	Smoky River, Alta.	Lawrence Zawacki	Lawrence Zawacki	1990	259
172 1/8	27 3/8	27 3/8	22 3/8	5 3/8	5 3/8	4	4	Goose Lake, Sask.	Joe W. Schmidt	Joe W. Schmidt	1991	259
172	25 4/8	26 3/8	19 6/8	4 7/8	4 6/8	5	5	Sauk Co., Wisc.	Rudy Lehnherr	Philip J. Rouse	1946	265
172	25 6/8	26 7/8	24 2/8	5 2/8	5 1/8	6	6	Woodbury Co., Iowa	Harold Horsley	Harold Horsley	1956	265
172	25 7/8	25 6/8	18 4/8	5 3/8	5 2/8	5	7	Henderson Co., Ill.	Harry M. Carner	Harry M. Carner	1959	265
172	27 3/8	27 1/8	19 3/8	4 4/8	4 4/8	5	6	Marshall Co., Minn.	Keith D. Anderson	Keith D. Anderson	1982	265
172	29 5/8	29 4/8	22 2/8	5 4/8	5 4/8	4	4	Edwards Co., Ill.	Picked Up	George Flaim	1985	265
172	25 5/8	26 4/8	21 6/8	4 4/8	4 2/8	6	6	Henderson Co., Ky.	Gary Hancock	Gary Hancock	1990	265
172	23 7/8	23 5/8	15 5/8	4 2/8	4	5	5	Callaway Co., Mo.	Picked Up	Larry W. Quick	1990	265
171 7/8	27	27 1/8	21 4/8	6 3/8	6 5/8	6	6	Fillmore Co., Minn.	Maynard Howe	Maynard Howe	1957	272
171 7/8	26 5/8	27	19	4 7/8	4 6/8	6	5	Grundy Co., Tenn.	Wilson W. Weaver	Wilson W. Weaver	1987	272
171 7/8	27 5/8	26 6/8	21 5/8	4 4/8	4 3/8	6	6	Lucas Co., Iowa	Tim M. Whitlatch	Tim M. Whitlatch	1989	272
171 6/8	26 2/8	26	21 6/8	4 6/8	4 7/8	5	5	Garden Co., Neb.	Doreen R. Lawrence	Doreen R. Lawrence	1989	275
171 6/8	24 5/8	24 7/8	19 7/8	4 7/8	5 1/8	6	6	Tunica Co., Miss.	Delton D. Davis	Delton D. Davis	1990	275
171 5/8	26 4/8	28 4/8	20 1/8	4 6/8	5	6	6	Meeker Co., Minn.	Ronald E. Lampi	Ronald E. Lampi	1973	277
171 5/8	26	25 6/8	17 3/8	4 3/8	4 3/8	5	5	Crawford Co., Mo.	Chris Glaser	Fred Glaser	1982	277
171 5/8	25 6/8	24 6/8	21 6/8	4 6/8	4 6/8	7	5	Mercer Co., Ohio	Daniel J. Garman	Daniel J. Garman	1988	277

Score	Main Beam R	Main Beam L	Inside Spread	Circ. R	Circ. L	Pts. R	Pts. L	Locality	By Whom Killed	Owner	Date	Rank
171 5/8	26 3/8	26 4/8	18 3/8	5 5/8	5 4/8	8	9	Anderson Co., Ky.	Blaine K. Price	Blaine K. Price	1990	277
171 4/8	25 1/8	25 6/8	20 4/8	4 7/8	4 5/8	6	6	Delta Co., Mich.	Lawrence Charles	Delor J. Wellman	1941	281
171 4/8	25	25 4/8	19 2/8	4 5/8	4 6/8	5	5	Cherry Co., Neb.	Jim R. Monnier	Jim R. Monnier	1981	281
171 4/8	26 6/8	25 2/8	19 6/8	4 6/8	4 6/8	5	5	Licking Co., Ohio	Michael E. Fleitz	Michael E. Fleitz	1988	281
171 4/8	25 1/8	25 5/8	23 6/8	4 5/8	4 4/8	5	5	Washtenaw Co., Mich.	Michael C. Lamirand	Michael C. Lamirand	1988	281
171 4/8	26	26 7/8	17	5 3/8	5 2/8	6	5	Kankakee Co., Ill.	Dennis Schneider	Dennis Schneider	1988	281
171 4/8	25 5/8	25 7/8	18	4 7/8	4 7/8	6	8	Bollinger Co., Mo.	Darrell L. Bostic	Darrell L. Bostic	1989	281
171 4/8	28 2/8	27 7/8	21	4 6/8	5 4/8	6	5	Ballard Co., Ky.	Howard P. Gardner	Howard P. Gardner	1989	281
171 4/8	26 7/8	27 5/8	17 6/8	5 3/8	4 4/8	6	5	Lenawee Co., Mich.	Robert E. Knight	Robert E. Knight	1989	281
171 4/8	26 3/8	26 3/8	17 5/8	4 4/8	4 5/8	6	5	Clay Co., Kan.	Eldyn W. Peck	Eldyn W. Peck	1989	281
171 4/8	26 4/8	25 2/8	18 6/8	5 1/8	4 4/8	5	6	Scotland Co., Mo.	Harry Robeson	Harry Robeson	1989	281
171 4/8	27 7/8	28 1/8	18 2/8	4 6/8	4 5/8	5	6	Barber Co., Kan.	Stan E. Christiansen	Stan E. Christiansen	1990	281
171 4/8	25 3/8	24 3/8	21	5 2/8	4 4/8	5	5	Rock Island Co., Ill.	David Parchert	David Parchert	1990	281
171 4/8	27	26	16	4 2/8	4 2/8	6	5	Iowa	Unknown	William H. Lilienthal	PR 1991	281
171 3/8	25 2/8	25 3/8	25 2/8	4 4/8	4 3/8	7	6	Bennett Co., S.D.	Dave Risse	Dave Risse	1975	294
171 3/8	25 3/8	26 2/8	16 2/8	4 6/8	4 6/8	6	7	Pike Co., Ill.	John Shover	John Shover	1979	294
171 3/8	26 1/8	26 7/8	23 2/8	5 5/8	5 4/8	5	6	Buffalo Co., Wisc.	Donald C. Neitzel	Donald C. Neitzel	1981	294
171 3/8	25 1/8	25 7/8	18 7/8	4 6/8	4 6/8	5	5	Washington Co., Ky.	Robert F. Medley	Robert F. Medley	1988	294
171 3/8	26 5/8	25 5/8	19 6/8	5	5	6	5	Washington Co., Wisc.	Joseph E. Kohler	Joseph E. Kohler	1989	294
171 3/8	27	26 6/8	21 2/8	4 3/8	4 3/8	6	7	Custer Co., Neb.	Larry C. Beitel	Larry C. Beitel	1990	294
171 2/8	26	26	20 3/8	4 5/8	4 5/8	7	6	O'Brien Co., Iowa	George Sleeper	William H. Lilienthal	1959	300
171 2/8	29 6/8	27 4/8	18	5 5/8	5 4/8	7	7	Lucas Co., Iowa	James L. Barlow	James L. Barlow	1985	300
171 2/8	26 2/8	26 1/8	22 4/8	4 6/8	4 6/8	5	6	Ringgold Co., Iowa	John H. Good	John H. Good	1988	300
171 2/8	25 1/8	23 7/8	21 2/8	5 2/8	5 2/8	5	5	Marshall Co., Iowa	Dale E. Smith	Dale E. Smith	1988	300
171 2/8	25 5/8	25 5/8	20 6/8	5 7/8	5 6/8	6	6	Adams Co., Iowa	Gary D. Maatsch	Gary D. Maatsch	1990	300
171 1/8	26 1/8	26 2/8	19 5/8	5 5/8	5 4/8	6	6	Howard Brook, N.B.	Ralph L. Orser	Ralph L. Orser	1986	305
171 1/8	28 6/8	28 5/8	22 7/8	6 4/8	6 4/8	5	5	Van Buren Co., Iowa	Walter S. Church	Walter S. Church	1988	305
171	28 2/8	25 6/8	20	5	5	4	5	Windsor Co., Ver.	Picked Up	Alfred A. Durkee	1935	307
171	25 6/8	24 4/8	24 2/8	5 4/8	5 4/8	5	5	Brown Co., S.D.	Anthony B. Goldade	Anthony B. Goldade	1960	307
171	26 2/8	26 5/8	18 3/8	4 6/8	4 5/8	8	8	Lyman Co., S.D.	Art Zimbelmann	Art Zimbelmann	1973	307
171	27	23 4/8	20 2/8	4 3/8	4 3/8	6	6	Delaware Co., Iowa	G. Covington & A. Schnittjer	Greg Covington	1986	307
171	24 7/8	26 6/8	17 4/8	4 1/8	4 1/8	5	5	Boone Co., Ind.	Kevin L. Albert	Kevin L. Albert	1988	307
171	26 2/8	25 4/8	21 6/8	4 7/8	4 4/8	5	5	Williamson Co., Ill.	Ronnie G. Fletcher	Ronnie G. Fletcher	1988	307
171	26 2/8	26 2/8	21 4/8	5	5 1/8	5	6	Okemasis Lake, Sask.	Rick Galloway	Rick Galloway	1989	307
171	26	26 2/8	19 3/8	5 3/8	5 1/8	6	5	Wabasha Co., Minn.	Thomas J. Mullenbach	Thomas J. Mullenbach	1989	307
171	26 3/8	26	21 2/8	5 7/8	5 3/8	5	5	Nuevo Leon, Mexico	Farryl Holub	Farryl Holub	1991	307
170 7/8	25 7/8	26 3/8	21 3/8	5	5	5	5	Cass Co., Minn.	Orland Weekley	George Flaim	1929	316
170 7/8	25 6/8	25 6/8	17 5/8	5	5	5	5	McDonald Lake, N.S.	Frederick Zwarum	Frederick Zwarum	1976	316
170 7/8	23 7/8	25 5/8	22	5 5/8	5 1/8	7	7	Henry Co., Iowa	Lewis E. Dallmeyer	Lewis E. Dallmeyer	1981	316

443

Whitetail Deer, *Typical Antlers - Continued*

Score	Length of Main Beam R.	L.	Inside Spread	Circumference at Smallest Place Between Burr and First Point R.	L.	Number of Points R.	L.	Locality Killed	By Whom Killed	Owner	Date Killed	Rank
170 7/8	29	29 3/8	21 5/8	6 3/8	5 3/8	4	4	Shelby Co., Ill.	Paul Marley	Paul Marley	1985	316
170 7/8	26	26 7/8	16 3/8	4 5/8	4 5/8	5	5	Grundy Co., Mo.	Bill Zang	Bill Zang	1986	316
170 7/8	23 4/8	23 5/8	18 7/8	4 6/8	4 6/8	6	7	Polk Co., Wisc.	Timothy J. Droher	Timothy J. Droher	1988	316
170 7/8	25 2/8	26 3/8	17 3/8	4 3/8	4 3/8	6	6	Crawford Co., Wisc.	Dale M. Hanson	Dale M. Hanson	1988	316
170 7/8	26	25 5/8	21 1/8	4 7/8	4 7/8	6	6	Eau Claire Co., Wisc.	John F. Prissel	John F. Prissel	1988	316
170 7/8	26 4/8	25 7/8	17 1/8	5 5/8	5 2/8	5	5	Houston Co., Minn.	Tony S. Rostad	Tony S. Rostad	1988	316
170 7/8	28 5/8	28 6/8	26 2/8	5 3/8	5 2/8	5	5	Jackson Co., Iowa	Clarence E. Gartman	Clarence E. Gartman	1989	316
170 7/8	26 2/8	25 7/8	18 6/8	5 2/8	5	5	6	Lamont, Alta.	Allen C. Johnston	Allen C. Johnston	1989	316
170 7/8	24	25 2/8	20 1/8	5 7/8	4 7/8	6	6	Knox Co., Ill.	Carl A. Swanson	Carl A. Swanson	1989	316
170 6/8	27	26 2/8	18	4 4/8	4 3/8	6	5	Eau Claire Co., Wisc.	Kenneth W. Kling	Mrs. Kenneth W. Kling	1938	328
170 6/8	26 7/8	25 6/8	19	5 7/8	5 1/8	6	6	Coles Co., Ill.	Jeff D. Shrader	Jeff D. Shrader	1990	328
170 6/8	23 3/8	23 3/8	18	4 1/8	4 1/8	7	6	Chisago Co., Minn.	Gary Thomas	Gary Thomas	1990	328
170 5/8	23 6/8	25 7/8	17 5/8	4 4/8	4 4/8	6	6	Kinney Co., Texas	Don T. Barksdale	Marshall E. Kuykendall	1925	331
170 5/8	25 2/8	26 1/8	18 5/8	5	5 1/8	5	5	Wawota, Sask.	Benjamin F. Kregel	Benjamin F. Kregel	1965	331
170 5/8	25 2/8	26 6/8	20 2/8	6	5 7/8	7	6	Prowers Co., Colo.	Douglas W. Kuhns	Douglas W. Kuhns	1987	331
170 5/8	24 6/8	25 1/8	20 6/8	4 5/8	4 4/8	7	8	Henry Co., Iowa	Michael S. Matthews	Michael S. Matthews	1988	331
170 5/8	27 3/8	27 7/8	18 5/8	5 4/8	5 4/8	5	6	Grundy Co., Mo.	Michael C. Weathers	Michael C. Weathers	1988	331
170 5/8	27 7/8	29 4/8	23 3/8	5 3/8	5 3/8	7	8	Sawyer Co., Wisc.	Thorvald Skar	James M. Skar	PR 1990	331
170 5/8	28 4/8	28 4/8	23 3/8	5 6/8	5 5/8	4	5	Polk Co., Minn.	D. Keith Thunem, Jr.	D. Keith Thunem, Jr.	1990	331
170 4/8	25 7/8	25 7/8	18 6/8	4 6/8	5 5/8	5	6	Pend Oreille Co., Wash.	Picked Up	Eugene M. Bailey	1944	338
170 4/8	25 3/8	25 4/8	18 3/8	5 2/8	5 2/8	6	6	Monroe Co., Ga.	T.E. Land	Jerry Moseley	1958	338
170 4/8	26	25 3/8	19	4 2/8	4 2/8	8	8	Henry Co., Iowa	Gerald Bailey	Gerald Bailey	1970	338
170 4/8	27 4/8	27 2/8	20 2/8	5 4/8	5 3/8	5	5	St. Louis Co., Minn.	Unknown	David R. Brigan	1974	338
170 4/8	25 1/8	25 1/8	19	3 7/8	4 1/8	6	5	Sullivan Co., Mo.	Randy Tucker	Randy Tucker	1981	338
170 4/8	27 1/8	26 7/8	21 6/8	4 5/8	4 5/8	5	5	Washington Co., Minn.	Peter J. Mogren	Peter J. Mogren	1988	338
170 4/8	23 6/8	23 3/8	18 4/8	4 7/8	4 3/8	6	6	Bradley Co., Ark.	Joe Hairston	Joe Hairston	1989	338
170 4/8	26 4/8	28	18 5/8	4 3/8	4 3/8	6	6	Clinton Co., Iowa	Scott Jacobsen	Scott Jacobsen	1989	338
170 4/8	25 3/8	24 7/8	20	5 2/8	5 3/8	6	6	Vilas Co., Wisc.	Rick R. Lax	Rick R. Lax	1990	338
170 3/8	26 6/8	26 3/8	17 3/8	4 3/8	4 2/8	6	7	Coweta Co., Ga.	Douglas R. Freeman	Douglas R. Freeman	1978	347
170 3/8	29 5/8	29 3/8	26	5 3/8	5 1/8	4	5	Dimmit Co., Texas	McLean Bowman	McLean Bowman	1981	347
170 3/8	23 2/8	24 2/8	17	4 1/8	4 2/8	7	7	Marshall Co., Minn.	John R. O'Donnell	John R. O'Donnell	1988	347
170 3/8	25	22 6/8	18 1/8	4 5/8	4 5/8	6	5	Pottawatomie Co., Kan.	Larry C. Schroeder	Larry C. Schroeder	1988	347

170 3/8	27 4/8	27 5/8	23 1/8	5	5	5	5	Orange Co., Ind.	John W. Matthew	John W. Matthew		1989	347
170 3/8	27 5/8	27 3/8	17 7/8	5	5	5	5	Montcalm Co., Mich.	Michael R. Nelson	Michael R. Nelson		1989	347
170 3/8	27 1/8	27 5/8	20 1/8	5 1/8	4 7/8	5	5	Warren Co., Iowa	Lanny Caligiuri	Lanny Caligiuri		1990	347
170 3/8	25 2/8	25 2/8	18 7/8	5 4/8	5 4/8	7	7	Mercer Co., Mo.	Robert W. Vasey	Robert W. Vasey		1990	347
170 3/8	26 6/8	26 2/8	17 7/8	4 6/8	4 6/8	5	5	McCook Co., S.D.	Unknown	Sam A. Wilson	PR	1990	347
170 2/8	26 7/8	26 4/8	20 1/8	5 1/8	5 1/8	6	5	Shawano Co., Wisc.	Jule Vandergate	Don E. Smith		1932	356
170 2/8	25 3/8	26 3/8	19 4/8	5 2/8	5 2/8	5	5	Calhoun Co., Ark.	George M. Gorman	George M. Gorman		1961	356
170 2/8	24 7/8	24 2/8	19 6/8	5	4 7/8	5	5	Winneshiek Co., Iowa	David Hageman	David Hageman		1988	356
170 2/8	24 2/8	25 5/8	18	5	4 7/8	7	8	Pend Oreille Co., Wash.	George T. Law	George T. Law		1988	356
170 2/8	26 3/8	26 1/8	19 6/8	4 7/8	4 7/8	5	5	Whitley Co., Ky.	Shevelery C. Sturgill	Shevelery C. Sturgill		1988	356
170 2/8	26 1/8	28 3/8	25 2/8	4 2/8	4 3/8	7	7	Houston Co., Minn.	Omer M. Wangen	Omer M. Wangen		1988	356
170 2/8	24 4/8	24 6/8	19 2/8	4 1/8	4 1/8	5	5	Jackson Co., Ohio	Roger K. Saltsman	Roger K. Saltsman		1989	356
170 2/8	28 4/8	26	20 2/8	4 7/8	4 7/8	5	7	Adams Co., Ohio	R. Scott Boschert	R. Scott Boschert		1990	356
170 2/8	26	25 6/8	26 6/8	4 4/8	4 4/8	4	5	Washington Co., Maine	Phillip R. Dobbins	Phillip R. Dobbins		1990	356
170 2/8	26 2/8	25 5/8	22 6/8	4 7/8	4 6/8	5	5	Lafayette Co., Wisc.	Everette F. Mau	Everette F. Mau		1990	356
170 2/8	27 6/8	26 2/8	19 3/8	5 6/8	6	7	6	Knox Co., Ohio	Ralph D. Wiley	Ralph D. Wiley		1990	356
170 1/8	25 7/8	27 6/8	19	5 2/8	5 2/8	5	6	Minnesota	Unknown	William H. Lilienthal	PR	1950	367
170 1/8	30	27 5/8	23 1/8	4 2/8	4 2/8	6	7	Bayfield Co., Wisc.	Roy Jacobson	David R. Jacobson		1960	367
170 1/8	23 7/8	24 7/8	18 3/8	4 7/8	4 6/8	5	5	Oglethorpe Co., Ga.	Robert C. Thaxton	Robert C. Thaxton		1978	367
170 1/8	26 7/8	27	19 5/8	5 1/8	5 4/8	7	7	Breckinridge Co., Ky.	Thomas F. Dean	Thomas F. Dean		1982	367
170 1/8	28 6/8	28 1/8	23	5	5	6	7	Winona Co., Minn.	Picked Up	Gary L. Bornfleth		1987	367
170 1/8	25 6/8	25 1/8	17 5/8	5 5/8	5 5/8	5	5	Camal Co., Texas	Lyman Skolaut	Lyman Skolaut		1987	367
170 1/8	25 4/8	25 3/8	23 1/8	5	5	5	6	Lycoming Co., Pa.	Richard C. Tebbs, Jr.	Richard C. Tebbs, Jr.		1987	367
170 1/8	27 7/8	26 4/8	18 7/8	5 4/8	5 1/8	5	6	Montgomery Co., Mo.	Kenneth B. Maskey	Kenneth B. Maskey		1988	367
170 1/8	28 1/8	29 4/8	23 7/8	5 1/8	4 6/8	7	5	Douglas Co., Kan.	Picked Up	Frank Virchow		1988	367
170 1/8	23 3/8	27 4/8	20 5/8	4 6/8	4 7/8	5	5	Racine Co., Wisc.	Michael H. Poeschel	Michael H. Poeschel		1989	367
170 1/8	25 2/8	26 5/8	17 6/8	5 6/8	5 6/8	6	6	Saginaw Co., Mich.	Scott M. Hutchins	Scott M. Hutchins		1990	367
170 1/8	23 6/8	23 1/8	15 3/8	4 5/8	4 6/8	6	7	Webb Co., Texas	Gerald W. Rentz, Jr.	Gerald W. Rentz, Jr.		1990	367
170 1/8	26 6/8	26 4/8	24 2/8	5	5 1/8	6	6	La Crosse Co., Wisc.	Scott R. Wavra	Scott R. Wavra		1991	367
170	26 7/8	27 2/8	20 4/8	5 4/8	5 6/8	5	5	Jones Co., Iowa	James L. Coyle	James L. Coyle		1988	380
170	28	28 1/8	18 5/8	4 4/8	4 4/8	8	7	Dane Co., Wisc.	Patrick D. Anderson	Patrick D. Anderson		1989	380
170	28 4/8	26 7/8	20	4 4/8	4 4/8	5	5	Madison Co., Iowa	Terry L. Snyder	Terry L. Snyder		1989	380
170	26	27	19 4/8	4 6/8	4 7/8	6	5	Jackson Co., Mich.	Michael D. Fitzgerald	Michael D. Fitzgerald		1990	380
170	29 3/8	27 5/8	21	4 5/8	4 6/8	5	7	Sounding Lake, Alta.	Bill Kostenuk	Bill Kostenuk		1990	380
170	25 6/8	25 4/8	16 1/8	5 4/8	5 3/8	6	7	Tift Co., Ga.	Alan Parrish	Alan Parrish		1990	380
170	28 3/8	27 4/8	17 4/8	4 1/8	4	6	6	Worth Co., Ga.	Travis Strenth	Travis Strenth		1990	380
169 6/8	24 4/8	25 6/8	17 2/8	4 3/8	4 1/8	7	7	Duval Co., Texas	Don Harrison	Mike Pillow		1969	387
169 6/8	26 4/8	26 3/8	18	5	5	5	6	Wright Co., Minn.	Michael D. Arnold	Michael D. Arnold		1989	387
169 4/8	26 4/8	26	19	4 4/8	4 4/8	7	8	Clearwater Co., Idaho	Frederick R. Staab	Frederick R. Staab		1990	389
169 2/8	24 1/8	27 3/8	23 4/8	4 6/8	5	5	5	Webster Co., Ky.	Wayne Daugherty	Wayne Daugherty		1990	390

Whitetail Deer, *Typical Antlers - Continued*

Score	Length of Main Beam R.	L.	Inside Spread	Circumference at Smallest Place Between Burr and First Point R.	L.	Number of Points R.	L.	Locality Killed	By Whom Killed	Owner	Date Killed	Rank
169 1/8	24 6/8	23 3/8	18 6/8	6	6 1/8	9	9	Trempealeau Co., Wisc.	Thomas E. Halderson	Thomas E. Halderson	1990	391
169	25 1/8	25 4/8	20 2/8	4 2/8	4 6/8	7	7	Cass Co., Minn.	Darrell L. Shaw	Darrell L. Shaw	1968	392
169	27 2/8	27 3/8	20 3/8	5 5/8	5 5/8	6	6	Breckinridge Co., Ky.	Denny Barr	Denny Barr	1990	392
168 5/8	23 1/8	23	20 1/8	4 6/8	4 7/8	5	5	Sanders Co., Mont.	Rex Indra	Rex Indra	1988	394
168 5/8	24 6/8	24 6/8	21 6/8	4 7/8	4 7/8	6	5	Pittsylvania Co., Va.	Jack B. Singletary	Jack B. Singletary	1990	394
168 4/8	23 7/8	23 4/8	16 6/8	5 2/8	5 1/8	6	5	Grayson Co., Ky.	John D. Johnson	John D. Johnson	1989	396
168 3/8	27 4/8	27	19 2/8	5 1/8	5	5	7	Penobscot Co., Maine	John R. Hollobaugh	John R. Hollobaugh	1987	397
168 3/8	23 7/8	23 7/8	23 7/8	4 6/8	4 7/8	6	6	Cheshire Co., N.H.	Richard J. Jarvis	Richard J. Jarvis	1988	397
168 3/8	25 7/8	27 7/8	21 3/8	4 6/8	4 5/8	5	5	Reynolds Co., Mo.	Rex Mehrhoff	Rex Mehrhoff	1990	397
168 2/8	26 5/8	26 4/8	21 5/8	5 5/8	5 4/8	8	5	Crittenden Co., Ky.	Donald W. Greenwell	Donald W. Greenwell	1988	400
168 1/8	21 3/8	21 4/8	19 6/8	4 5/8	4 6/8	7	7	Flathead Co., Mont.	Peter Neumann	Peter Neumann	1989	401
168	24 5/8	26 2/8	17 4/8	4 3/8	4 4/8	6	6	Grant Co., Wisc.	Timothy G. Ginter	Timothy G. Ginter	1988	402
168	25	25	20	4 5/8	4 4/8	5	5	Golden Valley Co., N.D.	Allen L. Unruh	Allen L. Unruh	1989	402
168	28 3/8	28 7/8	21 4/8	4 5/8	4 6/8	6	5	Sullivan Co., Mo.	James E. Hines	James E. Hines	1990	402
167 7/8	25 4/8	24 3/8	18 7/8	5 3/8	5 5/8	5	6	Ozark Co., Mo.	Rex E. Jenkins	Rex E. Jenkins	1982	405
167 7/8	26 6/8	26 5/8	21 7/8	5 2/8	5 2/8	5	7	Aroostook Co., Maine	Gilbert J. Bois	Gilbert J. Bois	1990	405
167 6/8	24 7/8	25	16 4/8	4 4/8	4 4/8	7	6	Washburn Co., Wisc.	Norem L. Cain	Norem L. Cain	1990	407
167 4/8	27 3/8	26 2/8	19 7/8	4 4/8	4 3/8	6	5	Augusta Co., Va.	Terry L. Hammer	Terry L. Hammer	1982	408
167 4/8	26 1/8	26 2/8	19 4/8	4 3/8	4 3/8	5	5	Ohio Co., Ky.	Charles R. Rush	Charles R. Rush	1990	408
167 3/8	25	24 7/8	19 3/8	5 3/8	5 6/8	6	5	Adams Co., Ill.	Jay W. Brackensick	Jay W. Brackensick	1989	410
167 3/8	27 5/8	23 7/8	19 5/8	6	6 7/8	4	6	Parke Co., Ind.	Chester P. Walls	Chester P. Walls	1990	410
167 2/8	25 6/8	25 4/8	20 1/8	4 1/8	4 1/8	6	6	Dodge Co., Wisc.	Wesley F. Braunschweig	Wesley F. Braunschweig	1969	412
167 2/8	26	25 7/8	19 7/8	5	5	5	6	Pope Co., Minn.	Hans Engebretson	Hans Engebretson	1977	412
167 2/8	27 2/8	27 4/8	21 6/8	4 7/8	4 7/8	7	10	Laclede Co., Mo.	Eldar R. Krueger	Eldar R. Krueger	1989	412
167 2/8	25 2/8	25 4/8	22 3/8	5	5 2/8	3	3	Logan Co., Okla.	Paul W. Newsom	Paul W. Newsom	1990	412
167 1/8	23 4/8	23 5/8	16 3/8	4 4/8	4 3/8	6	6	Maverick Co., Texas	Frank W. McBee, Jr.	Frank W. McBee, Jr.	1989	416
167 1/8	23 4/8	24	18 5/8	5 2/8	5 2/8	6	5	McHenry Co., Ill.	Charlie H. Rand	Charlie H. Rand	1989	416
167 1/8	27	27 7/8	16 3/8	5 3/8	5 3/8	5	6	Cass Co., Minn.	Neil G. Anderson	Neil G. Anderson	1990	416
167	25 2/8	26 2/8	17 7/8	4 6/8	4 6/8	6	7	Washburn Co., Wisc.	William Dahl	Morton Dahl	1940	419
167	24 4/8	25 1/8	18 4/8	4	4	5	5	Dougherty Co., Ga.	Rhonda J. Smith	Rhonda J. Smith	1991	419
166 7/8	25 2/8	24 4/8	20 5/8	4 7/8	4 7/8	5	5	Wabasha Co., Minn.	Chalmer Boyd	Fred W. King	1947	421
166 6/8	24 3/8	23 6/8	18 6/8	4 3/8	4 3/8	5	5	DeKalb Co., Ill.	Leon Tuestad	Leon Tuestad	1990	422

Score	Length R	Length L	Inside Spread	Circ. R	Circ. L	Pts. R	Pts. L	Locality	Hunter	Owner	Date	Rank
166 5/8	25 6/8	25 5/8	19	5 5/8	5 4/8	8	7	Beaver River, Sask.	Graham Dalziel	Graham Dalziel	1989	423
166 4/8	24 1/8	24 3/8	16 4/8	4 2/8	4 3/8	5	5	Trempealeau Co., Wisc.	John J. Kokett	John J. Kokett	1963	424
166 4/8	26 6/8	26 3/8	22 3/8	5 5/8	5 5/8	5	6	Valleyview, Alta.	Wayne Yowell	Wayne Yowell	1988	424
166 4/8	24 6/8	25	21 2/8	5	5	5	5	Washburn Co., Wisc.	John D. Rindfleisch	John D. Rindfleisch	1989	424
166 3/8	28 1/8	28 6/8	18 5/8	4 2/8	4 3/8	6	8	Buffalo Co., Wisc.	Michael R. Wineski	Michael R. Wineski	1988	427
166 3/8	27 2/8	27	19 6/8	5 1/8	5 2/8	8	7	Lesliville, Alta.	R. Terrel Ross	R. Terrel Ross	1989	427
166 2/8	29 4/8	28 1/8	18 1/8	5 4/8	5 4/8	6	5	La Salle Co., Ill.	Jeffrey A. Sampson	Jeffrey A. Sampson	1990	429
166 1/8	25 3/8	27 2/8	18 1/8	4 5/8	4 4/8	5	6	Boone Co., Iowa	O. Scot DeShong	O. Scot DeShong	1990	430
165 7/8	25 1/8	26	18 4/8	5 1/8	5 1/8	5	6	Douglas Co., Wisc.	George H. Norton	Jerry Hall	1917	431
165 7/8	26 3/8	26 7/8	22 1/8	4 6/8	4 5/8	5	5	Pepin Co., Wisc.	Reuben E. Bignell	Reuben E. Bignell	1966	431
165 6/8	28 4/8	28 3/8	20 7/8	5 1/8	5 1/8	5	9	Delta Co., Mich.	Herbert Lundin	Herbert Lundin	1946	433
165 6/8	27 2/8	26 7/8	19 5/8	4 4/8	4 7/8	9	8	St. Charles Co., Mo.	Gary L. Vails	Gary L. Vails	1989	433
165 5/8	26 5/8	27 3/8	18 7/8	4 4/8	4 3/8	6	5	Richland Co., Ohio	Erwin Merkli	Erwin Merkli	1988	435
165 5/8	27 3/8	27 6/8	23 3/8	5	5	6	5	Sumter Co., Ga.	Heath Bass	Heath Bass	1989	435
165 4/8	29 1/8	28 3/8	18 1/8	4 6/8	4 7/8	5	4	Buffalo Co., Wisc.	Patrick M. Ryan	Patrick M. Ryan	1985	437
165 4/8	25 5/8	25 5/8	19 4/8	4 6/8	4 6/8	7	8	Forest Co., Wisc.	Todd Webb	Todd Webb	1986	437
165 4/8	23 4/8	24 4/8	18 7/8	5	5	6	5	Winona Co., Minn.	John I. Kunert	John I. Kunert	1990	437
165 3/8	25 3/8	25 6/8	16 6/8	5 2/8	5 5/8	6	6	Desha Co., Ark.	Calvin Walker	Calvin Walker	1956	440
165 3/8	25	25	15 5/8	4 4/8	5	7	6	Union Co., S.D.	Milton Ustad	Milton Ustad	1988	440
165 2/8	27	27	22 2/8	5 2/8	4 5/8	5	5	Winona Co., Minn.	Gary G. Dumdei	Gary G. Dumdei	1977	442
165 2/8	25 6/8	25 6/8	18	5 5/8	5 2/8	6	6	Van Buren Co., Iowa	Richard W. Steinke	Richard W. Steinke	1978	442
165 2/8	24 7/8	24 7/8	16 4/8	5	5 5/8	6	8	Cass Co., Minn.	Richard D. Dabill	Richard D. Dabill	1989	442
165 2/8	25	25	18 6/8	4 6/8	5	7	7	Dunn Co., Wisc.	Lamoine E. Roatch	Lamoine E. Roatch	1989	442
165 1/8	23 7/8	23 7/8	22 7/8	4 4/8	4 6/8	6	6	McLean Co., Ill.	Kevin A. Miner	Kevin A. Miner	1988	446
165 1/8	27 3/8	26 4/8	18 7/8	4	4 4/8	5	5	Dooly Co., Ga.	Billy W. Gilbert	Billy W. Gilbert	1990	446
165	26 2/8	26	18 3/8	4 5/8	4	7	5	Waushara Co., Wisc.	Glenn E. Mentink	Glenn E. Mentink	1988	448
164 7/8	25	25	19 3/8	5 1/8	4 6/8	8	8	Fayette Co., Iowa	Charley Daisy	Charley Daisy	1988	449
164 7/8	28 1/8	28 1/8	21 3/8	5 3/8	4 7/8	6	7	Coles Co., Ill.	Ralph Garland	Ralph Garland	1988	449
164 7/8	25 4/8	26	19 6/8	5 1/8	5 3/8	5	4	Coles Co., Ill.	Walter C. Watson	Walter C. Watson	1989	449
164 7/8	25 7/8	26 1/8	18 7/8	5 2/8	5 2/8	5	5	Spencer Co., Ky.	Mitchell McMichael	Mitchell McMichael	1990	449
164 7/8	26 7/8	26 7/8	22	4 5/8	5 2/8	7	7	Bayfield Co., Wisc.	Frances M. Steen	Frances M. Steen	1990	449
164 6/8	27 3/8	27 1/8	21 4/8	5	4 4/8	5	5	Washburn Co., Wisc.	Lawrence A. Radzak	Lawrence A. Radzak	1989	454
164 5/8	25 1/8	25 1/8	16 3/8	4 4/8	5	5	6	Koochiching Co., Minn.	George E. Nelson	George E. Nelson	1965	455
164 5/8	24 6/8	24 3/8	19 2/8	4 1/8	4 3/8	6	7	Loon Lake, Sask.	John Clark, Jr.	John Clark, Jr.	1985	455
164 5/8	25 2/8	23 7/8	19 7/8	4 3/8	4	5	5	Zavala Co., Texas	Kielly Yates	Kielly Yates	1987	455
164 4/8	25 7/8	25 7/8	19 7/8	5 2/8	4 2/8	5	6	Hillsdale Co., Mich.	Allan J. Clendening	Allan J. Clendening	1988	458
164 4/8	24 7/8	25 1/8	18	5 4/8	5 3/8	7	6	Brown Co., Texas	A.C. Ebensberger	A.C. Ebensberger	1990	458
164 3/8	23 7/8	23 7/8	22 2/8	4 4/8	5 6/8	6	5	Peers, Alta.	Anthony Burke	Anthony Burke	1990	460
164 3/8	26 1/8	25 2/8	18	4 3/8	4 4/8	7	8	Early Co., Ga.	Denny D. Morgan	Denny D. Morgan	1990	460
164 2/8	25	25	19 7/8	4 7/8	4 7/8	7	6	Love Co., Okla.	DeWayne Erwin	DeWayne Erwin	1964	462
164 2/8	23 2/8	23 2/8	22 1/8	4 4/8	4 3/8	5	7	Woods Co., Okla.	Michael D. Hartwig	Michael D. Hartwig	1987	462

Whitetail Deer, *Typical Antlers - Continued*

Score	Length of Main Beam R.	L.	Inside Spread	Circumference at Smallest Place Between Burr and First Point R.	L.	Number of Points R.	L.	Locality Killed	By Whom Killed	Owner	Date Killed	Rank
164 1/8	26 1/8	25 4/8	18 7/8	4 6/8	4 7/8	6	5	Licking Co., Ohio	Richard Allen	Richard Allen	1989	462
164 1/8	26 1/8	26 6/8	21 5/8	4 4/8	4 4/8	6	5	Fayette Co., Iowa	Clayton C. Avenson	Clayton C. Avenson	1989	462
164 1/8	28 3/8	26 2/8	21 7/8	4 7/8	4 7/8	8	7	Macoupin Co., Ill.	Paul D. Tonsor	Paul D. Tonsor	1989	462
164	22	22 2/8	17 5/8	4 3/8	4 4/8	5	6	Shawano Co., Wisc.	Roy J. Habeck	Roy J. Habeck	1958	467
164	25 5/8	24 2/8	19 7/8	4 5/8	4 4/8	9	8	Brooks Co., Texas	Si Weeks, Jr.	Si Weeks, Jr.	1981	467
164	25 6/8	23 3/8	19 2/8	4 5/8	4 4/8	5	5	Dane Co., Wisc.	Bradley Behnke	Bradley Behnke	1988	467
164	23 2/8	23 3/8	20 3/8	4 6/8	4 6/8	6	6	Peace River, Alta.	Jack Ondrack	Jack Ondrack	1989	467
163 7/8	27	26 6/8	18 7/8	5 3/8	5 3/8	5	7	Gogebic Co., Mich.	Humbert A. Landretti	Jerry D. Prosek	1958	471
163 7/8	28 2/8	25 6/8	20 1/8	5	4 7/8	5	5	Dry Lake, Ont.	Clarence C. Kauffeldt	Wallace C. Kauffeldt	1988	471
163 6/8	25 5/8	25 5/8	17 6/8	4 6/8	4 6/8	5	5	Price Co., Wisc.	Andrew P. Pohlod	Andrew P. Pohlod	1965	473
163 6/8	25	25	17 3/8	5 2/8	5	6	5	Chippewa Co., Wisc.	Rodney M. Gulich	Rodney M. Gulich	1988	473
163 6/8	22 5/8	22 3/8	17	5 3/8	5 3/8	5	5	Great Sand Hills, Sask.	Jack Clary	Jack Clary	1990	473
163 5/8	25 3/8	24 6/8	22	4 5/8	4 5/8	5	7	Unknown	Unknown	W. Douglas Lightfoot	PR 1981	476
163 5/8	25 3/8	24 3/8	19 5/8	4 3/8	4 5/8	6	7	Pierce Co., Wisc.	Jeffrey W. Gilles	Jeffrey W. Gilles	1988	476
163 5/8	24 7/8	23 7/8	17 1/8	4 4/8	4 4/8	5	5	Grafton Co., N.H.	Lester J. Downing	Lester J. Downing	1989	476
163 4/8	26 4/8	27 6/8	19 3/8	4 7/8	4 7/8	6	6	Dooly Co., Ga.	David L. Register	David L. Register	1985	479
163 3/8	25 7/8	24 1/8	21 7/8	3 7/8	4 7/8	7	6	Douglas Co., Minn.	Maynard D. Hoppe	Maynard D. Hoppe	1990	479
163 1/8	24 7/8	24 4/8	17 7/8	4 6/8	4 6/8	7	5	Haralson Co., Ga.	Picked Up	Courtney White	1980	481
163 1/8	25	24 2/8	22 2/8	5	5	6	5	Umatilla Co., Oreg.	Jeffrey A. Koorenny	Jeffrey A. Koorenny	1987	481
163 1/8	28 5/8	28	19 3/8	5 3/8	5 6/8	5	4	Jackson Co., Mich.	Robert A. Lusk	Robert A. Lusk	1988	481
163 1/8	23 1/8	24 4/8	18 3/8	5 1/8	5	5	5	Kent Co., Del.	Austin M. Carney	Austin M. Carney	1989	481
163	25 6/8	25 6/8	22	4 5/8	4 7/8	5	5	Bayfield Co., Wisc.	Michael S. Statz	Michael S. Statz	1990	485
162 7/8	26 5/8	27	22 5/8	5 2/8	5 1/8	4	4	Belknap Co., N.H.	Lawrence L. Lee, Sr.	Lawrence L. Lee, Sr.	1958	486
162 7/8	27 7/8	27 7/8	17 5/8	5 3/8	5 1/8	5	6	Camden Co., Mo.	Picked Up	Lester Capps	1984	486
162 7/8	24 3/8	25 6/8	18 7/8	4 7/8	4 5/8	6	7	Washita Co., Okla.	Bruce D. Sears	Bruce D. Sears	1988	486
162 6/8	25 7/8	25 4/8	17 4/8	4 6/8	5	6	6	Worth Co., Ga.	Ezekiel A. Woodall	Ezekiel A. Woodall	1974	489
162 6/8	26 1/8	25 2/8	17 2/8	4 4/8	4 7/8	6	5	Muscatine Co., Iowa	David W. Howell	David W. Howell	1987	489
162 4/8	24	23 1/8	18 6/8	5 1/8	5 2/8	7	7	Dooly Co., Ga.	Andy Colter	Andy Colter	1990	491
162 3/8	25 6/8	25 6/8	16 7/8	5 6/8	5 4/8	5	5	Oconto Co., Wisc.	Roland H. Ziesmer	Roland H. Ziesmer	1948	492
162 3/8	25 5/8	25 5/8	21 1/8	4 2/8	4 3/8	5	5	Dunn Co., Wisc.	LaVerne Jones	LaVerne Jones	1960	492
162 3/8	26 5/8	28 1/8	21 3/8	5	5	5	5	Tobique River, N.B.	David A. DuFresne	David A. DuFresne	1990	492
162 3/8	27 3/8	27 4/8	19 4/8	3 7/8	4	5	6	Victoria Co., Texas	Patrick S. Edwards	Patrick S. Edwards	1990	492

Score	Main Beam R	Main Beam L	Inside Spread	Circ.	Circ.	Pts. R	Pts. L	Owner	By Whom Killed	Locality	Date	Rank
162 2/8	25 7/8	25 1/8	19 5/8	4 6/8	4 6/8	7	5	Bendik B. Vik	Bendik B. Vik	Beltrami Co., Minn.	1963	496
162 2/8	26 2/8	27 2/8	20 4/8	4 2/8	4 1/8	5	5	Dan Thompson	Dan Thompson	Merrimack Co., N.H.	1990	496
162	26 2/8	26	19 2/8	4 4/8	4 4/8	5	7	Karl P. Blank, Sr.	Karl P. Blank, Sr.	Chippewa Co., Wisc.	1952	498
162	21 7/8	23	17 2/8	5 1/8	4 6/8	5	5	James D. Holder	James D. Holder	Coal Co., Okla.	1987	498
162	24 1/8	24 1/8	18	5	5	6	7	Joseph S. Stavalone	Joseph S. Stavalone	Steuben Co., N.Y.	1988	498
162	23 6/8	23 4/8	16 2/8	5 1/8	4 7/8	5	7	David M. Jones	David M. Jones	Madison Co., Ill.	1989	498
162	27 4/8	26 3/8	21 7/8	4 4/8	4 3/8	5	5	Randy E. Montague	Randy E. Montague	Grafton Co., N.H.	1989	498
162	22 1/8	23	19 6/8	3 6/8	3 7/8	6	6	Rogers Bracy	Rogers Bracy	Zavala Co., Texas	1990	498
161 7/8	25 6/8	27 1/8	18 4/8	4 7/8	4 7/8	6	6	Phillip Flanders	Phillip Flanders	Laurens Co., Ga.	1988	504
161 7/8	24 4/8	21 5/8	17 5/8	5 5/8	5 4/8	7	6	Adam T. Kupis	Adam T. Kupis	Ontario Co., N.Y.	1989	504
161 5/8	25 6/8	25 1/8	18 3/8	5 2/8	5 1/8	5	4	Forrest Kunes	Claire Kunes	Sawyer Co., Wisc.	1932	504
161 5/8	25 1/8	25 5/8	20 6/8	5 2/8	5 2/8	7	6	John S. Nelson	John S. Nelson	McHenry Co., Ill.	1988	506
161 5/8	24 1/8	24 4/8	17 1/8	4 3/8	4 4/8	5	6	David G. Van Hoosen	Daniel G. Van Hoosen	Forest Co., Wisc.	1990	506
161 5/8	23	23 3/8	18 7/8	5 5/8	5 4/8	5	6	Kenneth Rhinesmith	Kenneth Rhinesmith	Pierce Lake, Sask.	1988	506
161 4/8	26 6/8	26 1/8	16 7/8	4 6/8	5	5	6	Jeffrey J. Brabant	Jeffrey J. Brabant	Oconto Co., Wisc.	1989	509
161 4/8	27 3/8	27 7/8	20 6/8	5	5	6	5	Bradley Houdasheldt	Bradley Houdasheldt	Vinton Co., Ohio	1990	509
161 4/8	18 1/8	23 7/8	17 3/8	4 6/8	4 5/8	5	7	David Fernholz	David Fernholz	Buffalo Co., Wisc.	1982	509
161 3/8	23 7/8	23 7/8	22 1/8	5 7/8	5 7/8	8	5	Kinney Hudgens	Kinney Hudgens	Coweta Co., Ga.	1983	512
161 3/8	23 4/8	25 4/8	17 1/8	4 6/8	5	5	5	Jimmy Mullins	Jimmy Mullins	Lee Co., Va.	1988	512
161 3/8	25 4/8	24 3/8	18 4/8	4 6/8	5	5	5	Warren Walker	Warren Walker	Desha Co., Ark.	1955	512
161 2/8	24	25 1/8	19 7/8	5 4/8	5 2/8	5	7	Donald D. Ash	Donald D. Ash	Buffalo Co., Wisc.	1959	515
161 2/8	26	25 6/8	21 4/8	5 2/8	5	7	5	Dan McGee	Dan McGee	Montgomery Co., Ala.	1978	515
161 1/8	25 7/8	25 1/8	19 6/8	4 4/8	4 2/8	5	5	Kent W. Kurtz	Kent W. Kurtz	Ingham Co., Mich.	1989	515
161 1/8	25 2/8	23 3/8	16	4 6/8	4 6/8	5	6	Craig S. Brown	Craig S. Brown	Ellis Co., Kan.	1990	515
161 1/8	23 3/8	27 3/8	21 2/8	5	5 1/8	5	5	Lloyd E. Zink	Lloyd E. Zink	Des Moines Co., Iowa	1969	515
161	27 1/8	24 5/8	19 3/8	4 2/8	4 5/8	6	5	Daryl G. Zemke	Daryl G. Zemke	Washtenaw Co., Mich.	1990	520
160 7/8	25 5/8	27 4/8	19 2/8	4 4/8	4 5/8	5	5	Mike D. Roberts, Jr.	Mike D. Roberts, Jr.	Worth Co., Ga.	1989	520
160 7/8	28	21 1/8	21 1/8	4 5/8	4 6/8	5	5	Billie F. Bechtel	Billie F. Bechtel	Granite Co., Mont.	1987	522
160 5/8	21 7/8	25	17 7/8	4 5/8	4 3/8	5	5	Gary D. Ritchey	Gary D. Ritchey	Augusta Co., Va.	1990	523
160 5/8	24 6/8	27 3/8	18 5/8	4 5/8	4 6/8	5	5	Kris Huber	Kris Huber	Scott Co., Minn.	1988	523
160 5/8	24 4/8	23 1/8	20 3/8	4 6/8	4 3/8	6	9	William A. Johnson	William A. Johnson	Pittsburg Co., Okla.	1988	525
160 5/8	23 2/8	26	23 3/8	4 5/8	4 6/8	6	6	Jeffrey J. Parkison	Jeffrey J. Parkison	Jefferson Co., Iowa	1990	525
160 4/8	26 6/8	24 4/8	18 2/8	5	4 7/8	5	4	Nancy L. Schmidt	Nancy L. Schmidt	Jefferson Co., Wisc.	1987	525
160 4/8	24 6/8	26 1/8	15 6/8	4 1/8	4 1/8	5	5	Doug Borries	Doug Borries	Noxubee Co., Miss.	1988	528
160 4/8	23	23	19 4/8	5 6/8	5 6/8	5	5	Cleo L. Hoel	Cleo L. Hoel	Chippewa Co., Wisc.	1989	528
160 4/8	25 3/8	26 6/8	20 4/8	4 4/8	4 6/8	6	5	Larry D. Martin	Larry D. Martin	McLean Co., Ill.	1989	528
160 4/8	27 3/8	27 6/8	18 3/8	4 5/8	4 6/8	6	5	Burrus F. Martin	Burrus F. Martin	LeFlore Co., Okla.	1990	528
160 4/8	23 7/8	24 4/8	20 3/8	5 1/8	4 7/8	5	7	Robert R. Williams	Robert R. Williams	Pepin Co., Wisc.	1990	528
160 3/8	25 7/8	25 2/8	17 7/8	5 3/8	5	5	7	Clifford A. Citty	Clifford A. Citty	McCurtain Co., Okla.	1988	534
160 3/8	25 3/8	26 5/8	22 7/8	5 3/8	5 2/8	4	5	Dick A. Jacobs	Dick A. Jacobs	Montreal Lake, Sask.	1989	534
160 2/8	25 5/8	25 7/8	21	5	5	6	5	Wendell H. Bullard	Wendell H. Bullard	Telfair Co., Ga.	1988	536

449

Whitetail Deer, *Typical Antlers – Continued*

Score	Length of Main Beam R.	L.	Inside Spread	Circumference at Smallest Place Between Burr and First Point R.	L.	Number of Points R.	L.	Locality Killed	By Whom Killed	Owner	Date Killed	Rank
160 2/8	24 1/8	24 4/8	21	5 6/8	5 7/8	5	5	Valleyview, Alta.	Carl L. Yowell	Carl L. Yowell	1988	536
160 2/8	24 6/8	25 2/8	18 5/8	5	4 7/8	8	5	Langlade Co., Wisc.	Peter G. Clabots	Peter G. Clabots	1990	536
160 2/8	26 4/8	24 6/8	18 2/8	4 4/8	4 4/8	4	5	Otter Tail Co., Minn.	Jon S. Walker	Jon S. Walker	1990	536
160 1/8	25 2/8	25 1/8	19 2/8	5 1/8	5 4/8	5	6	Adams Co., Ill.	Gerald Giesing	Gerald Giesing	1979	540
160 1/8	26 7/8	26 1/8	22 6/8	5 2/8	5 2/8	5	6	Colquitt Co., Ga.	James L. Malone	James L. Malone	1989	540
160 1/8	24 6/8	23 3/8	17 3/8	4 7/8	4 5/8	5	6	Sawyer Co., Wisc.	Wayne L. Beckwith	Wayne L. Beckwith	1990	540
196 4/8*	27	26 1/8	22 4/8	4 5/8	4 5/8	8	7	Des Moines Co., Iowa	Michael R. Edle	Michael R. Edle	1989	
194 4/8*	26 2/8	26	18 7/8	5 6/8	5 4/8	8	9	Nipawin, Sask.	Gerald Whitehead	Gerald Whitehead	1990	
194 3/8*	29 1/8	28 6/8	23 5/8	5 1/8	5 1/8	5	5	Warren Co., Iowa	Forest H. Richardson	Forest H. Richardson	1989	

* Final Score subject to revision by additional verifying measurements.

450

Whitetail Deer, *Non-Typical Antlers*

Odocoileus virginianus virginianus and certain related subspecies

Minimum Score 185 — World's Record 333-7/8

Score	Length of Main Beam R.	L.	Inside Spread	Circ. at Smallest Place Between Burr and First Point R.	L.	Number of Points R.	L.	Locality Killed	By Whom Killed	Owner	Date Killed	Rank
279 6/8	27 6/8	26	21 6/8	6	6	13	14	Whitemud Creek, Alta.	Neil J. Morin	Neil J. Morin	1991	1
259 7/8	27	28 4/8	22 1/8	5	5 5/8	27	9	Perry Co., Ala.	Jon G. Moss	Jon G. Moss	1989	2
258 7/8	23 1/8	24 4/8	18 3/8	5 5/8	5 4/8	17	12	Cedar Co., Iowa	Picked Up	Gale Sup	1988	3
256 7/8	28 3/8	27 7/8	21	5 1/8	5 3/8	18	17	Jackson Co., Iowa	David B. Manderscheid	Larry L. Huffman	1977	4
251 4/8	26 3/8	27 5/8	22 7/8	5 4/8	5 3/8	17	14	Beltrami Co., Minn.	Rodney Rhineberger	Gale Sup	1976	5
250 2/8	24 5/8	28	16 1/8	7 1/8	7	16	12	Washington Co., Kan.	Picked Up	Gale Sup	1988	6
249 3/8	26 3/8	26 3/8	25 3/8	5 1/8	5	14	14	Rockingham Co., Va.	Jeffery W. Hensley	Jeffery W. Hensley	1990	7
248 6/8	27 4/8	28 1/8	20 5/8	6	5 7/8	18	19	Warren Co., Iowa	Larry J. Caldwell	Larry J. Caldwell	1990	8
248 4/8	28	27 4/8	23 5/8	7 7/8	7 4/8	15	13	Fulton Co., Ind.	Robert S. Sears	Robert S. Sears	1990	9
245 4/8	27 7/8	27 5/8	18 6/8	6 1/8	6 2/8	16	15	Kittson Co., Minn.	Lyndon K. Westerberg	Lyndon K. Westerberg	1990	10
245	24 3/8	25 2/8	19 1/8	5 7/8	5 4/8	11	16	Lee Co., Iowa	Carl Wenke	Craig Kohl	1972	11
244 7/8	20 7/8	20	16 1/8	4 7/8	4 2/8	18	14	Zavala Co., Texas	John R. Campbell	John L. Stein	1947	12
240 4/8	24 4/8	24 5/8	18 7/8	6 3/8	6 3/8	12	18	Tisdale, Sask.	John Law	John Law	1988	13
238 6/8	26 2/8	25 3/8	20 5/8	6 7/8	7 2/8	11	12	Fulton Co., Ill.	Neil M. Booth	Neil M. Booth	1988	14
238 2/8	24 3/8	25 2/8	22 6/8	7 2/8	7 4/8	10	11	Potter Co., S.D.	Larry Nylander	Donna Nylander	1963	15
237 6/8	23 4/8	22 3/8	15	6	6	15	12	Henderson Co., Ill.	Robert E. Todd	Robert E. Todd	1978	16
237	27 5/8	26 3/8	22 4/8	5 5/8	5 7/8	14	12	Madison Co., Iowa	Picked Up	Iowa Dept. of Natl.Resc.	PR 1989	17
235 3/8	21 7/8	22 6/8	21 6/8	6 2/8	6	13	10	Harding Co., S.D.	J.H. Krueger & R. Keeton	J.D. Andrews	1965	18
234 5/8	28 6/8	23 3/8	17 1/8	4 7/8	6 4/8	9	15	Round Lake, Ont.	Picked Up	Harry Jones	1990	19
234 1/8	26 7/8	26 3/8	20 2/8	5 5/8	6 2/8	16	14	Minnesota	Unknown	Gale Sup	PR 1985	20
233 2/8	27 7/8	25 5/8	18 6/8	4 7/8	4 7/8	9	11	Switzerland Co., Ind.	Henry Mitchell	Larry L. Huffman	1972	21
232 7/8	25 7/8	26	18 7/8	5 1/8	5	13	11	Montana	Unknown	Raymond R. Cross	PR 1950	22
232 3/8	26 3/8	19 6/8	23 2/8	4 4/8	6 7/8	11	12	Breathitt Co., Ky.	Delmar R. Hounshell	Delmar R. Hounshell	1990	23
232	30 1/8	30 7/8	18 7/8	5 1/8	5 4/8	11	8	Barron Co., Wisc.	Wayne F. Lindemans	Wayne F. Lindemans	1988	24
231 1/8	25 3/8	25 7/8	21 4/8	5 6/8	5 6/8	14	12	Henry Co., Iowa	Wendell R. Prottsman	Wendell R. Prottsman	1988	25
231	27 5/8	28	21 2/8	5 5/8	5 1/8	8	7	Cass Co., Minn.	L.S. Hanson	Joel H. Karvonen	1970	26
230 7/8	25 4/8	25 2/8	21 5/8	5 2/8	5 1/8	12	14	Provost, Alta.	Richard C. Nelson	Richard C. Nelson	1990	27
230 2/8	26 1/8	26	19 1/8	5	5 1/8	11	11	Todd Co., Minn.	John Berscheit	John Berscheit	1976	28

451

Whitetail Deer, Non-Typical Antlers - *Continued*

Score	Length of Main Beam R.	L.	Inside Spread	Circumference at Smallest Place Between Burr and First Point R.	L.	Number of Points R.	L.	Locality Killed	By Whom Killed	Owner	Date Killed	Rank
230	27 1/8	28 1/8	19 7/8	5	5	11	8	Houston Co., Minn.	Winnie Papenfuss	Winnie Papenfuss	1973	29
229 7/8	27 4/8	26 7/8	19 7/8	6 4/8	6 2/8	13	11	Jackson Co., Ind.	Larry E. Deaton	Larry E. Deaton	1990	30
228 6/8	24 3/8	24 5/8	18 1/8	6	5 5/8	18	14	Fulton Co., Ohio	Bernard Williamson III	Bernard Williamson III	1989	31
227 6/8	21 6/8	25	17	6 4/8	6	13	10	Des Moines Co., Iowa	Edgar J. Steward	Edgar J. Steward	1990	32
227 1/8	24	23 6/8	21 4/8	4 4/8	4 4/8	8	9	Dimmit Co., Texas	Stuart W. Stedman	Stuart W. Stedman	1990	33
227	26	26 2/8	21 4/8	6 1/8	6 2/8	19	14	Concordia Parish, La.	Picked Up	Sandra Leger	1969	34
226 4/8	26 1/8	24 3/8	22	6 7/8	6 5/8	12	10	Linn Co., Kan.	Jerry O. Hampton	Jerry O. Hampton	1988	35
226 2/8	26 6/8	25 3/8	24 5/8	6 2/8	6	10	11	Warren Co., Ohio	Daniel H. Detrick	Daniel H. Detrick	1989	36
226 1/8	25 3/8	24 7/8	22 3/8	5 1/8	5	12	14	Kimble Co., Texas	Coke R. Stevenson	Marguerite K. Stevenson	1934	37
225 6/8	27 3/8	26 7/8	26 3/8	4 4/8	4 2/8	7	9	La Porte Co., Ind.	David Grundy	Don Schaufler	1987	38
225 6/8	26 7/8	24 5/8	21 1/8	5 2/8	5 2/8	9	8	Yellow Medicine Co., Minn.	Glen Bullick	Glen Bullick	1989	38
225 2/8	23 2/8	23 5/8	16 7/8	6 3/8	6 1/8	13	10	Fayette Co., Iowa	Duane J. Cahoy	Duane J. Cahoy	1975	40
225 1/8	22 4/8	22 6/8	17 1/8	4 7/8	5	10	13	Burnet Co., Texas	Mr. Stevens	Mclean Bowman	1938	41
225	28 7/8	26 6/8	20 2/8	5 7/8	5 7/8	10	13	Barber Co., Kan.	Picked Up	Larry L. Huffman	1979	42
225	24 1/8	24 7/8	24 7/8	4 7/8	5	11	9	Londes Co., Miss.	Richard Herring	Richard Herring	1988	42
224 6/8	27	26 7/8	27 1/8	5 2/8	5 2/8	11	10	Mills Co., Iowa	James C. Reed	James C. Reed	1988	44
224 4/8	26	26 3/8	25 6/8	5 6/8	5 6/8	11	14	Rock Co., Wisc.	Joseph T. Fisher	Joseph T. Fisher	1988	45
224	31	31 2/8	19 2/8	5 3/8	5 2/8	11	11	Hancock Co., Ill.	Ronald A. Paul	Bill Lilienthal	1968	46
223 5/8	28	28 3/8	18 7/8	4 7/8	4 7/8	10	12	Woods Co., Okla.	Monty E. Pfleider	Monty E. Pfleider	1987	47
223 5/8	24 6/8	24 6/8	24 2/8	6	6 2/8	8	14	Wabash Co., Ill.	Tim W. Stout	Tim W. Stout	1988	47
223 3/8	22 5/8	20 5/8	12 5/8	8 1/8	8 7/8	12	12	Madison Co., Iowa	Duane Fick	Duane Fick	1972	49
223 3/8	24 7/8	26 1/8	20 2/8	5 5/8	5 5/8	11	15	Jefferson Co., Kan.	David P. Haeusler	David P. Haeusler	1990	49
223 1/8	23 6/8	24 1/8	18 3/8	5 3/8	5 4/8	21	14	McCreary Co., Ky.	James H. Sanders	James H. Sanders	1957	51
223 1/8	29 7/8	29 5/8	21 1/8	4 3/8	4 3/8	12	8	Wyandotte Co., Kan.	Randy W. Tillery	Randy W. Tillery	1988	51
223	19 7/8	19 2/8	18 2/8	7 6/8	8 2/8	6	10	Van Buren Co., Iowa	Picked Up	Wade Roberts	1979	53
222 7/8	27 5/8	28 1/8	18 6/8	5	5	9	7	Coles Co., Ill.	Kim L. Boes	Kim L. Boes	1989	54
222 3/8	27 3/8	27 5/8	22 3/8	6 5/8	6 7/8	9	7	Stearns Co., Minn.	Richard E. Sand	Richard E. Sand	1988	55
221 4/8	25	20 7/8	21 2/8	6 3/8	6 1/8	12	21	Hancock Co., Ill.	Neal C. Meyer	Neal C. Meyer	1987	56
221 3/8	29 3/8	29 5/8	19	5 5/8	5 4/8	11	10	Dewey Co., S.D.	Leo Fischer	Leo Fischer	1958	57
221 3/8	21 6/8	19 4/8	17 1/8	10	10	12	13	Anne Arundel Co., Md.	Unknown	Fred Horn	1979	57
221 2/8	28 5/8	28 7/8	22 3/8	5 5/8	5 5/8	10	11	Franklin Co., Kan.	Marvin R. Smith	Marvin R. Smith	1988	59

Score								Locality	Hunter	Owner	Date	Rank
221 1/8	27 2/8	29 4/8	22 6/8	5 5/8	5 4/8	15	14	Jefferson Co., Iowa	Daniel R. Thurman	Daniel R. Thurman	1979	60
220 5/8	28	28	21 3/8	6 2/8	6 2/8	12	8	Jefferson Co., Iowa	Mike Laux	Mike Laux	1990	61
220 3/8	27 4/8	27 1/8	19	5 1/8	4 7/8	13	13	Caldwell Co., Ky.	Loyd Holt	Loyd Holt	1984	62
219 7/8	25 4/8	25 7/8	20 4/8	5 3/8	5 3/8	11	10	Clearwater Co., Idaho	Kipling D. Manfull	Kipling D. Manfull	1989	63
219 6/8	19 1/8	23 3/8	18 4/8	4 4/8	4 6/8	15	8	Caddo Parish, La.	William D. Ethredge, Jr.	William D. Ethredge, Jr.	1988	64
219 4/8	26 5/8	26 1/8	21 2/8	5	5	11	8	Sumner Co., Kan.	Picked Up	Greg L. Hill	1987	65
218 7/8	25 3/8	22 4/8	18 7/8	4 7/8	4 7/8	12	12	Marshall Co., Iowa	Picked Up	Charles E. Lewis	1989	66
218 7/8	26 6/8	25 5/8	20 3/8	6	6	8	12	St. Joseph Co., Mich.	Picked Up	Rex A. Mayer	1989 PR	66
218 3/8	29 2/8	29 5/8	19 5/8	4 7/8	5 1/8	12	10	Fillmore Co., Minn.	Darrel R. Highum	Darrel R. Highum	1989	68
218 3/8	29 3/8	29 7/8	23 4/8	5 3/8	5 3/8	7	7	Allamakee Co., Iowa	Unknown	James H. Reimer	1963	69
218 3/8	27	26 7/8	18 6/8	5 3/8	5 4/8	8	7	Waukesha Co., Wisc.	Picked Up	Wisconsin Dept. Natl. Resc.	1986	69
217 7/8	23 4/8	23 4/8	19 4/8	4 5/8	4 5/8	11	10	Dimmit Co., Texas	Unknown	McLean Bowman	1920	71
217 5/8	26	23 2/8	18 5/8	5 5/8	5 1/8	9	16	Flagstaff, Alta.	Craig A. Miller	Craig A. Miller	1990	72
217 4/8	24 6/8	24 6/8	19 1/8	5	4 6/8	10	13	Hardin Co., Iowa	Picked Up	W.H. Lilienthal & J. Bruce	1987	73
217 3/8	22 7/8	23 6/8	13	4 6/8	4 6/8	10	11	Weston Co., Wyo.	Harry Phillips	Harry Phillips	1957	74
217 3/8	27 5/8	29 2/8	18 7/8	4 3/8	4 2/8	9	11	Dewer River, N.S.	Alan Fahey	Alan Fahey	1989	74
217 2/8	28 6/8	28 5/8	21 6/8	5 2/8	4 7/8	11	8	Clark Co., Mo.	Lawrence L. Paul	Lawrence L. Paul	1977	76
217 2/8	23 6/8	24 2/8	19	5 4/8	5 4/8	13	10	Hudson Bay, Sask.	Ron Kenyon	Ron Kenyon	1987	76
217 2/8	30	29 2/8	21 2/8	5	4 6/8	6	12	Kandiyohi Co., Minn.	Picked Up	Dean Salzl	1988	76
217	30 7/8	28 6/8	18 4/8	5 2/8	5	9	10	Dearborn Co., Ind.	Jerry L. Irvine	Jerry L. Irvine	1990	79
217	29	27 4/8	19 4/8	5 4/8	5	10	9	Pike Co., Ill.	Picked Up	James H. Reimer	1990	79
216 7/8	27 3/8	28 7/8	21 6/8	5 4/8	5 1/8	12	12	Wilson Co., Kan.	Gilbert J. McGee	Gilbert J. McGee	1988	81
216 1/8	25 2/8	23 4/8	19 6/8	5 2/8	5 1/8	13	12	Gillespie Co., Texas	J.C. Park	John L. Stein	1932	82
215 7/8	27 1/8	27 5/8	22 2/8	4 4/8	4 3/8	9	13	Wabasha Co., Minn.	Leroy Goranson	Leroy Goranson	1990	83
215 5/8	24 4/8	21 3/8	17 6/8	5 6/8	5 5/8	11	9	Huron Co., Mich.	Patrick L. Flanagan, Jr.	Patrick L. Flanagan, Jr.	1990	84
215 1/8	26 5/8	25 6/8	21 4/8	6	6	11	10	Cass Co., Ill.	David G. Bolletto	David G. Bolletto	1988	85
215 1/8	25 2/8	24	22 1/8	6 7/8	6 4/8	13	11	Winnebago Co., Ill.	Dennis F. Shipler	Dennis F. Shipler	1990	85
215	26 3/8	25 6/8	15 2/8	5 2/8	5 2/8	9	13	Fillmore Co., Minn.	Picked Up	Jeffrey S. Mackey	1968	87
214 6/8	26 6/8	28	21 6/8	5	4 7/8	8	9	Decatur Co., Iowa	Dean D. Grimm	Dean D. Grimm	1988	88
214 6/8	27	26 3/8	17 2/8	5 5/8	5 6/8	10	8	Roseau River, Man.	Darcy J. Stewart	Darcy J. Stewart	1990	88
214 2/8	22 5/8	22 5/8	16 5/8	4 6/8	4 5/8	9	12	Unknown	Unknown	Kent Austin	1991 PR	90
214	26 3/8	26 3/8	21	5 4/8	5 2/8	14	9	Hamilton Co., Iowa	Picked Up	Larry L. Huffman	1987	91
213 7/8	22 5/8	28 4/8	20 7/8	5 2/8	5 2/8	10	10	Botetourt Co., Va.	Craig A. Brogan	Craig A. Brogan	1989	92
213 7/8	23 3/8	20 7/8	18 6/8	6 3/8	6 3/8	15	11	Athabasca River, Alta.	Todd Armstrong	Todd Armstrong	1990	92
213 6/8	23 7/8	24 4/8	18 5/8	5	4 6/8	10	11	Webb Co., Texas	Unknown	John B. Collier	1961	94
213 5/8	22 7/8	22 6/8	13 5/8	3 7/8	3 6/8	9	15	Webb Co., Texas	Unknown	Miguil Harper	1950 PR	95
213 4/8	22 1/8	23 1/8	19 3/8	5	5	15	7	Texas	Unknown	Lone Star Brewing Co.	1950 PR	96
213 2/8	27 2/8	27 1/8	18 5/8	5 1/8	5	7	8	Fillmore Co., Minn.	Steven A. Johnson	Steven A. Johnson	1988	97
212 7/8	24 4/8	22 5/8	17 6/8	4 6/8	4 6/8	12	9	Boone Co., Iowa	Orlin Sorber	Ron Sorber	1973	98

Whitetail Deer, Non-Typical Antlers - Continued

Score	Length of Main Beam R.	L.	Inside Spread	Circumference at Smallest Place Between Burr and First Point R.	L.	Number of Points R.	L.	Locality Killed	By Whom Killed	Owner	Date Killed	Rank
212 6/8	24 2/8	23 2/8	19 5/8	4 2/8	4 4/8	14	9	McCurtain Co., Okla.	Robert H. Crenshaw	Robert H. Crenshaw	1988	99
212 6/8	24 3/8	28 3/8	28 3/8	5 2/8	5 1/8	11	6	Illinois	Picked Up	John Brewer	1989	99
212 6/8	24 5/8	26 7/8	24 6/8	4 7/8	5 1/8	8	14	Fremont Co., Iowa	Picked Up	Jeff Haning	1989	99
212 2/8	23 1/8	25 1/8	20 3/8	5 1/8	5	11	10	Gregory Co., S.D.	Picked Up	J.D. Andrews	1983	102
212	28 3/8	28 3/8	20 4/8	5 5/8	5	6	9	Greene Co., Iowa	Don Buswell	Don Buswell	1973	103
211 7/8	24 1/8	24 4/8	19 5/8	4 7/8	4 7/8	11	8	Van Buren Co., Iowa	Loras R. Ernzen	Loras R. Ernzen	1988	104
211 7/8	27 6/8	27	18 6/8	5 6/8	5 6/8	12	8	Waukesha Co., Wisc.	Patrick F. Cherone III	Patrick F. Cherone III	1989	104
211 6/8	26 5/8	27 7/8	18 4/8	5 1/8	4 6/8	12	12	Roseau Co., Minn.	Edward L. Quiring	Edward L. Quiring	1988	106
211 4/8	23 3/8	23	18 6/8	4 2/8	5	13	14	Worth Co., Ga.	Wade Patterson	Wade Patterson	1988	107
211 2/8	26 1/8	25 5/8	19 4/8	4 2/8	4 2/8	9	7	Stearns Co., Minn.	Ronald Steil	Ronald Steil	1983	108
211	27 3/8	28 4/8	22 2/8	6 4/8	6 3/8	10	11	Rock Co., Wisc.	Kevin C. Viken	Kevin C. Viken	1990	109
210 7/8	23 1/8	22 2/8	21 1/8	4 6/8	4 6/8	11	11	Patience Lake, Sask.	Rick Schindel	Rick Schindel	1990	110
210 6/8	26 2/8	26 7/8	21 1/8	5 5/8	5 4/8	12	9	Todd Co., Minn.	Paul E. Berscheit	Paul E. Berscheit	1990	111
210 2/8	28 4/8	27 6/8	20 4/8	5 4/8	5 6/8	11	9	Louisa Co., Iowa	Picked Up	William H. Lilienthal	1959	112
210 2/8	28 3/8	28 3/8	23 6/8	5 6/8	5 5/8	12	7	Washburn Co., Wisc.	Dennis Loreth	William H. Lilienthal	1982	112
210 1/8	25 1/8	25 1/8	20 6/8	5	5	10	9	White Co., Ark.	Chester Weathers, Sr.	Chester Weathers, Jr.	1973	114
210	26 2/8	25 1/8	19 6/8	4 5/8	4 4/8	8	7	Dallas Co., Iowa	Picked Up	William H. Lilienthal	1989	115
209 6/8	25 5/8	25 2/8	16	5 5/8	5 5/8	8	9	Oak Lake, Man.	Michael W. Leochko	Michael W. Leochko	1985	116
209 6/8	25 5/8	25	19 5/8	4 5/8	4 5/8	14	18	Pulaski Co., Ky.	Alan Sidwell	Alan Sidwell	1988	116
209 6/8	26 4/8	26 4/8	18 1/8	6	6	12	10	Union Co., Ind.	Billy G. Finch	Billy G. Finch	1989	116
209 5/8	25 4/8	25 3/8	21 5/8	5 2/8	5 3/8	10	8	Franklin Co., Va.	Timothy J. Wright	Timothy J. Wright	1989	119
209 4/8	23 3/8	23 1/8	22 5/8	4 4/8	4 5/8	10	14	Webb Co., Texas	A. Holden	McLean Bowman	1940	120
209 3/8	28 3/8	30 3/8	24 4/8	5 3/8	5 4/8	9	7	Jefferson Co., Ind.	Tim L. Brawner	Tim L. Brawner	1989	121
209 2/8	23 7/8	22	16 4/8	4 7/8	6 2/8	8	13	Clarke Co., Iowa	James C. Reed	James C. Reed	1988	122
209 1/8	23 4/8	24 4/8	16 6/8	4 3/8	4 2/8	12	14	Kenedy Co., Texas	Dick Roberts	Dick Roberts	1988	123
209 1/8	26	25 7/8	22 4/8	5	5	9	8	Monroe Co., Iowa	Kelly J. Willis	Kelly J. Willis	1988	123
209 1/8	27 6/8	30 5/8	19 6/8	6 3/8	6 3/8	8	10	Monona Co., Iowa	Vincent P. Jauron	Vincent P. Jauron	1990	123
208 7/8	27 1/8	27	23 5/8	6 3/8	6	11	13	Rideau River, Ont.	Harry Rathwell	Harry Rathwell	1988	126
208 6/8	27 1/8	26 6/8	20 4/8	5 3/8	5 1/8	7	10	Crook Co., Wyo.	Joe Engelhaupt	Joe Engelhaupt	1956	127
208 5/8	26 6/8	24 3/8	20 4/8	6 3/8	7 1/8	10	12	Woodbury Co., Iowa	Ronald J. Eickhold	Ronald J. Eickhold	1977	128
208 4/8	26 6/8	27 3/8	21 6/8	6	6 1/8	9	8	Itasca Co., Minn.	Unknown	William L. Achman	1945	129
208 4/8	22	21 1/8	17 6/8	5	5	12	13	Webb Co., Texas	Travis D. Kelly	Travis D. Kelly	1978	129

Score								Locality	Hunter	Owner	Date	Rank
208 4/8	30 5/8	30 2/8	20 6/8	5 5/8	5 5/8	7	8	Ford Co., Kan.	Picked Up	Larry L. Huffman	1985	129
208 2/8	27	26	22 2/8	5 4/8	5 3/8	10	7	St. Louis Co., Minn.	Ed Mikulich	Terry Mikulich	1964	132
208 1/8	25 2/8	26 1/8	19 6/8	4 7/8	4 7/8	9	9	Beaverhill Lake, Alta.	Dean Hrehirchuk	Dean Hrehirchuk	1989	133
208	26 3/8	26	15	4 1/8	4 1/8	14	10	Buena Vista Co., Iowa	Robert L. Vierow	Robert L. Vierow	1982	134
207 7/8	23 7/8	24 5/8	22 2/8	5 1/8	5	10	10	Monona Co., Iowa	Robert V. Dean	Vernon R. Dean	1968	135
207 5/8	25 3/8	25	20 3/8	4 7/8	4 6/8	8	14	Gentry Co., Mo.	Eric D. Sybert	Eric D. Sybert	1990	136
207 4/8	26 5/8	25 5/8	18 7/8	5 2/8	5 2/8	8	14	Comanche Co., Kan.	Picked Up	Larry L. Huffman	1984	137
207 3/8	25 7/8	25 3/8	20 2/8	4 4/8	4 4/8	10	8	Zapata Co., Texas	Romeo H. Garcia	Romeo H. Garcia	1977	138
207 3/8	23 4/8	24 3/8	17 4/8	6 2/8	6 1/8	12	9	Dane Co., Wisc.	Todd J. DeForest	Todd J. DeForest	1989	138
207 2/8	26 2/8	24 4/8	19	6	5 7/8	12	8	Unknown	Unknown	John Stein	PR 1979	140
207 2/8	26 5/8	22 7/8	18 2/8	5 3/8	6 5/8	9	11	Brown Co., Neb.	Terry J. Graff	Terry J. Graff	1987	140
207 2/8	23 4/8	25 5/8	18 7/8	6 1/8	5 3/8	7	7	Adair Co., Mo.	Kevin Elsea	Kevin Elsea	1988	140
207 2/8	26	23 7/8	20 2/8	5 6/8	6 3/8	15	10	Swan Plain, Sask.	Gary A. Markofer	Gary A. Markofer	1991	140
207	24 7/8	26	19 1/8	5 3/8	5 7/8	9	13	Cowley Co., Kan.	Joyce A. Williams	Joyce A. Williams	1983	144
206 7/8	28 1/8	24 6/8	20	5 4/8	5 2/8	13	12	Baxter Lake, Alta.	Terry F. Ermel	Terry F. Ermel	1988	145
206 7/8	26 5/8	27 1/8	21 4/8	5 1/8	5	12	14	Dodge Co., Wisc.	Steven J. Schultz	Steven J. Schultz	1989	145
206 5/8	24 3/8	25 3/8	19 7/8	6 1/8	5	11	9	Outlook, Sask.	Unknown	Dick Rossum	1971	147
206 5/8	29 6/8	24 3/8	19 6/8	5 4/8	6 1/8	8	11	Kevisville, Alta.	Brian R. McKain	Brian R. McKain	1990	147
206 3/8	24 6/8	28 5/8	22 2/8	4 5/8	5 5/8	12	10	Adams Co., Ohio	James M. Wilson	James M. Wilson	1989	149
206 3/8	24 6/8	24 7/8	14	4 5/8	4 6/8	9	9	Colquitt Co., Ga.	Picked Up	Ga. Dept. of Natl. Resc.	1990	149
206 2/8	31 5/8	29 3/8	23 4/8	4 6/8	4 4/8	8	9	Benton Co., Minn.	Kenneth R. Nodo	Kenneth R. Nodo	1987	151
206 1/8	25 1/8	26 1/8	19 7/8	5 4/8	5 5/8	10	12	Lake of the Woods Co., Minn.	Keith D. Yahnke	Keith D. Yahnke	1987	152
206 1/8	23 5/8	23	21	5 2/8	5 1/8	7	9	Union Co., Ohio	Henry W. Leistritz	Henry W. Leistritz	1989	152
205 5/8	28	27 4/8	18 6/8	6 4/8	6 3/8	10	13	Spencer Co., Ky.	Phillip W. Lawson	Phillip W. Lawson	1989	154
205 4/8	25 4/8	26 1/8	23 3/8	4 6/8	4 6/8	10	6	Ram River, Alta.	William Howard	William Howard	1988	155
205 3/8	27 1/8	25 7/8	21	6 2/8	6	8	12	Louisa Co., Iowa	Daniel Kaufman	Daniel Kaufman	1984	156
205 3/8	24 7/8	24 7/8	17 4/8	4 5/8	4 6/8	8	9	Wadena Co., Minn.	Donald R. Brockob	Donald R. Brockob	1990	156
205 3/8	25 1/8	24	15	6	7 3/8	8	12	Beltrami Co., Minn.	Matt E. Stone	Matt E. Stone	1990	156
205	26	24 5/8	22 1/8	4 5/8	5 7/8	7	11	Jo Daviess Co., Ill.	David L. Virtue	David L. Virtue	1990	159
204 7/8	26 3/8	24 5/8	18 5/8	5 4/8	4 6/8	9	12	Winona Co., Minn.	Picked Up	Gary Bornfleth	1979	160
204 6/8	27 1/8	26 4/8	19 7/8	5 3/8	5 3/8	11	8	Washington Co., Ind.	David Souder	David Souder	1988	161
204 3/8	30	26 6/8	18 7/8	6 3/8	5 4/8	13	11	Rock Island Co., Ill.	Jeff B. Davis	Jeff B. Davis	1990	162
204 2/8	25 6/8	27 2/8	21 2/8	3 4/8	6 4/8	6	11	Cass Co., Ill.	J. David Bartels	J. David Bartels	1989	163
204 1/8	27 7/8	25 7/8	18 6/8	4 7/8	3 5/8	9	8	Dodge Co., Wisc.	Wesley G. Braunschweig	Wesley G. Braunschweig	1976	164
203 6/8	28	28	19 7/8	5 7/8	4 7/8	10	9	Phillips Co., Ark.	Dolph Horton	N.V. Hyde, Jr.	1948	165
203 6/8	23	22 4/8	16 1/8	5 1/8	5 7/8	11	12	Pike Co., Ill.	Randall B. Long	Randall B. Long	1987	165
203 4/8	27 5/8	27 5/8	18 3/8	5 1/8	4 7/8	9	8	Jones Co., Ga.	Curtis F. Long	Mrs. Curtis F. Long	1965	167
203 4/8	22 2/8	22 2/8	18 6/8	6 3/8	5 2/8	9	9	Lincoln Co., Mont.	Sean M. Blackley	Sean M. Blackley	1990	167
203 4/8	24	27 2/8	19 6/8	4 7/8	5 7/8	8	11	Upper Cutbank, B.C.	William E. Eckert	William E. Eckert	1990	167
203 3/8	24 6/8	25 3/8	19 1/8	5 1/8	5 4/8	9	10	Appanoose Co., Iowa	Clem A. Herman	Clem A. Herman	1990	167

Whitetail Deer, Non-Typical Antlers – Continued

Score	Length of Main Beam R.	L.	Inside Spread	Circumference at Smallest Place Between Burr and First Point R.	L.	Number of Points R.	L.	Locality Killed	By Whom Killed	Owner	Date Killed	Rank
203 3/8	27 4/8	26 4/8	16	5 4/8	5 5/8	8	9	St. Louis Co., Minn.	Eino W. Nurmi	Eino W. Nurmi	1934	171
203 1/8	27	20 1/8	19 5/8	5 4/8	5 4/8	10	9	Fulton Co., Ill.	Picked Up	Mitchell Hoffman	1989	172
203	26 3/8	25 4/8	18 4/8	4 5/8	5	10	8	Madison Co., Iowa	Joe Bruns	Tim Bruns	1967	173
203	28 4/8	27 3/8	21 7/8	5 5/8	5 5/8	9	8	Guthrie Co., Iowa	Ronald R. Hoyt	Ronald R. Hoyt	1974	173
203	27	23 6/8	18 1/8	5 2/8	5 4/8	8	9	Lee Co., Iowa	Wayne L. McClain	Wayne L. McClain	1980	173
203	24	23 6/8	15	4 6/8	4 7/8	9	12	Wayne Co., Ky.	Jack L. Keith	Jack L. Keith	1990	173
202 7/8	27 7/8	26 2/8	18	5 2/8	5 3/8	12	7	Du Page Co., Ill.	Picked Up	E. Dolf Pfefferkorn	1962	177
202 7/8	24 4/8	24 3/8	19	6	5 7/8	10	10	Kingman Co., Kan.	Picked Up	Michael L. Piaskowski	1966	177
202 6/8	25 1/8	24 5/8	20 7/8	5 7/8	5 7/8	9	14	Warren Co., Iowa	Leland Cortum	Leland Cortum	1969	179
202 6/8	25	25 1/8	17 7/8	5 4/8	5 3/8	9	10	Chautauque Co., Kan.	John L. Brown	John L. Brown	1990	179
202 5/8	26 7/8	26 7/8	23 1/8	4 5/8	4 5/8	9	10	Kleberg Co., Texas	Richard J. Mills	Richard J. Mills	1926	181
202 4/8	24 7/8	24 6/8	23 6/8	4 7/8	5	10	11	Texas	Unknown	Lone Star Brewing Co. PR	1920	182
202 4/8	26 2/8	25 3/8	22 1/8	5 1/8	5 2/8	9	8	Spokane Co., Wash.	Unknown	Dick Rossum PR	1989	182
202 3/8	26 2/8	25 4/8	18 1/8	4 7/8	4 6/8	10	7	Cass Co., Minn.	Hollace Brockoff	Hollace Brockoff	1976	184
202 3/8	25 7/8	24 6/8	22 7/8	5 6/8	6	9	13	Delaware Co., Ohio	Duane E. Robinson	Duane E. Robinson	1980	184
202 3/8	26 7/8	28 7/8	22 7/8	6 1/8	6 7/8	10	9	Douglas Co., Minn.	Timothy C. Sukke	Timothy C. Sukke	1988	184
202 2/8	28 4/8	28 3/8	20 1/8	6 2/8	5 7/8	8	10	Oglethorpe Co., Ga.	J. Richard Mocko	J. Richard Mocko	1983	187
202 2/8	25 4/8	24 3/8	17 5/8	5	5 1/8	9	9	Lenawee Co., Mich.	Fredrick M. Hood, Jr.	Fredrick M. Hood, Jr.	1988	187
202	25 3/8	19 6/8	18 3/8	6 3/8	6 3/8	10	10	Monona Co., Iowa	Gary W. Anfinson	Gary W. Anfinson	1988	189
202	24	24	19 2/8	5 5/8	5 4/8	12	10	Roberts Co., S.D.	Ronnie A. Bucklin	Ronnie A. Bucklin	1988	189
201 7/8	27 4/8	27 4/8	20 1/8	5 3/8	5 5/8	8	7	Anderson Co., Kan.	Arthur O. Bell	Arthur O. Bell	1990	191
201 6/8	24 1/8	24 1/8	19 3/8	4 2/8	4 1/8	12	12	Texas	Unknown	Lone Star Brewing Co. PR	1920	192
201 5/8	25 2/8	24 6/8	18 7/8	5 7/8	5 6/8	8	7	Van Buren Co., Iowa	Randy Kramer	Randy Kramer	1989	192
201 5/8	25 5/8	26 6/8	21 6/8	4 7/8	5	10	10	Howard Co., Mo.	Gregory A. O'Brian	Gregory A. O'Brian	1983	194
201 5/8	26 4/8	26 4/8	24 7/8	5 1/8	5	8	8	Clinton Co., Mo.	David E. Eads	David E. Eads	1989	194
201 4/8	28 3/8	27 6/8	17 7/8	4 6/8	4 7/8	7	8	Clayton Co., Iowa	Paul C. Crawford	Paul C. Crawford	1987	196
201 4/8	24 7/8	26 1/8	20 2/8	6 6/8	6 3/8	8	8	Allamakee Co., Iowa	Daniel J. Gallagher	Daniel J. Gallagher	1989	196
201 3/8	24 1/8	23 5/8	17 3/8	5 3/8	5 4/8	11	14	Wakulla Co., Fla.	Clark Durrance	Clark Durrance	1941	198
201 3/8	26 6/8	24 1/8	19 3/8	5 5/8	5 3/8	13	9	Swift Co., Minn.	Joel T. Schmidt	Joel T. Schmidt	1973	198
201 1/8	25 2/8	26 6/8	20 1/8	5 4/8	5 1/8	9	9	Jackson Co., Mich.	Steven G. Crocker	Steven G. Crocker	1989	200
201	26 1/8	25	22 5/8	4 6/8	4 6/8	10	7	Crawford Co., Wisc.	Lloyd C. Rickleff	Lloyd C. Rickleff	1989	201
201	25 5/8	26 1/8	22 2/8	5 7/8	5 7/8	9	9	Wilkenson Co., Ga.	E. Dwaine Davis	E. Dwaine Davis	1990	201

Score								Locality				
200 7/8	22 7/8	24 6/8	20 7/8	8	9 1/8	13	10	Randolph Co., Mo.	Gale Sup	Picked Up	1986	203
200 7/8	24	22 5/8	22 1/8	5 1/8	6 3/8	7	8	Davis Co., Iowa	Roger G. Pettit	R.G. Pettit & W. Van Mersberger	1988	203
200 7/8	25 3/8	25 1/8	20	5 1/8	5 2/8	12	10	Morgan Co., Ky.	Greg Powers	Greg Powers	1989	203
200 7/8	26 1/8	22 7/8	18 3/8	4 7/8	5 1/8	13	8	Davison Co., S.D.	Louis W. Cooper	Louis W. Cooper	1990	203
200 6/8	25 1/8	26	13 7/8	6 5/8	6 5/8	10	8	Sask.	Ron Lavoie	Picked Up	1989	207
200 5/8	26 7/8	26 7/8	18 6/8	5 7/8	5 6/8	10	10	Washington Co., Iowa	Bruce Guy	Bruce Guy	1973	208
200 5/8	26 2/8	26 2/8	14	4 5/8	4 7/8	9	6	Texas Co., Okla.	Jeffrey T. Wright	Jeffrey T. Wright	1987	208
200 5/8	24 6/8	24 6/8	22 2/8	5 4/8	5 5/8	9	10	Harper Co., Kan.	Robert A. Thomas	Robert A. Thomas	1990	208
200 4/8	26 2/8	27 1/8	19 6/8	4 1/8	4 7/8	8	8	Kleberg Co., Texas	Charles Hoge	Charles Hoge	1976	211
200 4/8	25 5/8	27 5/8	16 6/8	4 5/8	4 5/8	7	10	Howard Co., Iowa	Victor J. Buresh	Victor J. Buresh	1990	211
200 3/8	25 2/8	22 1/8	21 4/8	5 1/8	5 2/8	11	9	Fremont Co., Wyo.	Wallace M. Oldman	Wallace M. Oldman	1989	213
200 2/8	26 2/8	26	19	5	5 2/8	14	13	Delaware Co., Ohio	Franklin D. Ronk	Franklin D. Ronk	1990	214
200 1/8	24 3/8	25 4/8	18 2/8	5 1/8	5 2/8	7	12	Dallas Co., Ala.	H. Lloyd Morris	H. Lloyd Morris	1989	215
200	19 5/8	18 1/8	17 1/8	4 7/8	5 1/8	11	6	Crook Co., Wyo.	Ralph R. Van Beck	Ralph R. Van Beck	1989	216
200	27	25 6/8	22 3/8	5 4/8	5 2/8	12	11	Boone Co., Ind.	John E. Wright	John E. Wright	1989	216
200	25 5/8	26 1/8	18 2/8	4 6/8	4 6/8	7	8	Stearns Co., Minn.	David L. LaVoi	David L. LaVoi	1990	216
199 7/8	27	23 3/8	19 7/8	5 7/8	5	11	8	Knox Co., Ill.	Rodney G. Eklund	Rodney G. Eklund	1990	219
199 5/8	24 7/8	22	21 2/8	5 7/8	5 7/8	8	8	Baraga Co., Mich.	Kenneth J. Harjala	William Simula	1925	220
199 5/8	25 5/8	25 1/8	18 4/8	6 2/8	6 4/8	12	8	Clinton Co., Iowa	Arlo Ketelsen	Arlo Ketelsen	1985	220
199 5/8	25 5/8	26 1/8	24 6/8	4 5/8	5 1/8	12	10	Pend Oreille Co., Wash.	John C. Kroker	John C. Kroker	1989	220
199 4/8	25 7/8	25 4/8	19 7/8	6 4/8	7 2/8	20	13	Gregory Co., S.D.	Adeline Gnirk	Fred Gnirk	1958	223
199 4/8	26 2/8	28	17 5/8	5	5 1/8	11	8	St. Francis Co., Mo.	Henry A. Hull	Henry A. Hull	1984	223
199 4/8	27 5/8	28	22 2/8	5 4/8	5 3/8	8	8	Linn Co., Iowa	Don J. Jilovec	Don J. Jilovec	1988	223
199 3/8	27 2/8	22 3/8	20 4/8	5 4/8	5 4/8	9	11	Chisago Co., Minn.	Jeff Benson	Helmer Benson	1965	226
199 3/8	22 3/8	20	20 1/8	6 1/8	6	9	11	Morgan Co., Ill.	David W. Roehrs	David W. Roehrs	1979	226
199 3/8	20	17 1/8	18 5/8	6	6 1/8	12	17	Van Buren Co., Mich.	Michael A. DeRosa	Michael A. DeRosa	1989	226
199 2/8	24 6/8	25 4/8	14	4 7/8	4 7/8	9	13	Richland Co., Mont.	Raymond Schmierer	Aron Schmierer	1952	229
199 2/8	29 1/8	28 1/8	21 3/8	5 2/8	5 2/8	8	7	Todd Co., Minn.	Wayne V. Jensen	Wayne V. Jensen	1965	229
199 1/8	26 3/8	26	24 2/8	5	5	11	11	Meade Co., S.D.	Donald Trohkimoinen	Donald Trohkimoinen	1966	231
199	23 2/8	22 4/8	15 2/8	5 4/8	5 4/8	10	10	Harrison Co., Iowa	Chester R. Hilton	Chester R. Hilton	1958	232
199	26 1/8	26 3/8	19 6/8	5 5/8	4 3/8	8	10	Jackson Co., Iowa	John T. Kremer	John T. Kremer	1983	232
199	23 7/8	23 2/8	18	4 4/8	4 6/8	8	8	Crawford Co., Wisc.	Jeff Sheckler	Jeff Sheckler	1989	232
198 7/8	27	23 7/8	17 7/8	4 6/8	6 2/8	13	11	Logan Co., Ky.	Oscar Howard	Oscar Howard	1989	235
198 6/8	24 6/8	26 7/8	24	5 7/8	6 2/8	9	5	Lake of the Woods Co., Minn.	Gerald K. Sorenson	Gerald K. Sorenson	1977	236
198 6/8	25 4/8	25 3/8	19 2/8	6 2/8	6	13	11	Rappahannock Co., Va.	Chris K. Foster	Chris K. Foster	1989	236
198 6/8	25 5/8	24 7/8	19 3/8	4 7/8	4 7/8	8	10	Jefferson Co., Wisc.	Wayne Perry	Picked Up	1989	236
198 6/8	22 5/8	24 5/8	15	6 5/8	5 5/8	11	11	Peoria Co., Ill.	Roger Woodcock	Roger Woodcock	1989	236
198 5/8	25 5/8	25 6/8	21 3/8	5 5/8	5 7/8	9	12	Hamilton Co., Ill.	Thomas D. Flannigan	Thomas D. Flannigan	1989	240
198 5/8	28 5/8	27 2/8	22 1/8	5 5/8	6 2/8	8	6	Franklin Co., Ill.	Freddie Cooper	Freddie Cooper	1990	240

Score	Length of Main Beam R.	L.	Inside Spread	Circumference at Smallest Place Between Burr and First Point R.	L.	Number of Points R.	L.	Locality Killed	By Whom Killed	Owner	Date Killed	Rank
198 5/8	22	22	20 2/8	4 6/8	4 6/8	9	9	Dawsons Creek, B.C.	Philip D. Springer	Philip D. Springer	1990	240
198 4/8	26	26 4/8	21	4 6/8	4 6/8	13	9	Forest Co., Wisc.	John Lehner	Eric Lehner	1946	243
198 4/8	24	23 5/8	19	5 5/8	5 6/8	11	11	Itasca Co., Minn.	Wayne W. Blesi, Jr.	Wayne W. Blesi, Jr.	1968	243
198 4/8	26 1/8	26 7/8	22 5/8	6	5 4/8	8	8	Perry Co., Ohio	Donald J. Griggs	Donald J. Griggs	1988	243
198 3/8	25 7/8	26 6/8	19 5/8	4 6/8	5	9	9	Rappahannock Co., Va.	Collis W. Dodson, Jr.	Collis W. Dodson, Jr.	1966	246
198 2/8	27 3/8	27 4/8	22 2/8	6 1/8	6 3/8	5	8	Unknown	Unknown	John Stein	1968 PR	247
198 2/8	26 4/8	26 6/8	17 6/8	4 6/8	5 1/8	7	8	Madison Co., Iowa	Dan L. Bush	Dan L. Bush	1987	247
198 1/8	25 6/8	26 2/8	20 2/8	4 6/8	4 6/8	10	8	Carrot River, Sask.	Wayne W. Karling	Wayne W. Karling	1989	249
198 1/8	25	24 1/8	24 4/8	5 3/8	5 5/8	6	6	Unknown	Unknown	Rick Stover	1990 PR	249
198	26	26 7/8	20	5	4 6/8	7	11	McLeod Co., Minn.	Owen L. Knacke	Owen L. Knacke	1990	251
198	27	27 4/8	20 4/8	5 6/8	5 7/8	10	9	Jo Daviess Co., Ill.	Victor W. Rogers	Victor W. Rogers	1990	251
197 7/8	25	25 5/8	25 1/8	5 3/8	5 4/8	12	11	St. John River, N.B.	James A. Perruso	James A. Perruso	1988	253
197 7/8	24 7/8	24 6/8	19 6/8	5 4/8	5	10	9	Riley Co., Kan.	Gary L. Schroller	Gary L. Schroller	1990	253
197 6/8	24 5/8	24 4/8	13 4/8	4 6/8	4 4/8	11	9	Prowers Co., Colo.	Samuel S. Pattillo	Samuel S. Pattillo	1988	255
197 5/8	24	24	17 5/8	5 2/8	4 6/8	11	9	Pennington Co., S.D.	Lynn Williams	Dick Rossum	1958	256
197 5/8	26 5/8	27 3/8	20 5/8	5	5	8	9	Monona Co., Iowa	Picked Up	Larry Koch	1987	256
197 5/8	28 4/8	29 3/8	22 5/8	5 1/8	4 5/8	10	8	Stephenson Co., Ill.	Richard M. Keller	Richard M. Keller	1988	256
197 5/8	28 2/8	27 1/8	19	5 3/8	5 4/8	7	7	Thurston Co., Neb.	Picked Up	Rudy Reichelt	1989	256
197 5/8	24 7/8	25 1/8	16 7/8	4 5/8	4 7/8	7	9	McDonough Co., Ill.	Jeffrey W. Foxall	Jeffrey W. Foxall	1990	256
197 4/8	27 1/8	27	20 1/8	5 2/8	5 3/8	9	9	Boone Co., Iowa	Grant E. Saunders	Grant E. Saunders	1990	261
197 3/8	29 1/8	27 2/8	18	4 7/8	5 3/8	8	11	Anoka Co., Minn.	Dale M. Zimmerman	Dale M. Zimmerman	1990	262
197 2/8	23	24	20	6 2/8	5 6/8	10	8	Chouteau Co., Wash.	J. Burton Long	J. Burton Long	1975	263
197 2/8	27 4/8	26 3/8	20	5	5	12	11	Tiudish River, N.S.	Clayton Ward	Clayton Ward	1982	263
197 1/8	27 4/8	27 3/8	18 3/8	4 5/8	4 5/8	9	9	Clay Co., Texas	Dale L. Coleman	Dale L. Coleman	1988	265
197 1/8	22 6/8	24 4/8	17 3/8	6 3/8	4 5/8	8	6	Caldwell Co., Mo.	James B. Nickels	James B. Nickels	1990	265
197	27 2/8	26 3/8	20 4/8	4 4/8	4 5/8	7	13	Cook Co., Minn.	Edwin F. Niemeyer	Helen Niemeyer	1947	267
196 7/8	26 2/8	27 1/8	20 6/8	4 7/8	5 1/8	11	12	St. Louis Co., Minn.	James A. Guist	James A. Guist	1963	268
196 7/8	22 6/8	22 1/8	17 1/8	4 2/8	4 4/8	11	9	Trigg Co., Ky.	Homer Stevens, Jr.	Homer Stevens, Jr.	1986	268
196 7/8	23	23 1/8	23 1/8	6	5 6/8	8	9	Yazoo Co., Miss.	Eddie J. Alias, Jr.	Eddie J. Alias, Jr.	1989	268
196 6/8	28 2/8	28	21	5 2/8	5 3/8	7	8	McHenry Co., Ill.	Timothy A. Schulze	Timothy A. Schulze	1989	271
196 5/8	28 7/8	25 4/8	22	5 4/8	4 6/8	10	12	Westchester Co., N.Y.	Picked Up	John J. Vitale	1968	272
196 5/8	30 2/8	30 3/8	20 5/8	5 4/8	5 6/8	9	7	Langlade Co., Wisc.	Thomas G. Jahnke	Thomas G. Jahnke	1990	272

Score	Main Beam R	Main Beam L	Inside Spread	Circ. R	Circ. L	Points R	Points L	Locality	By Whom Killed	Owner	Date Killed	Rank
196 4/8	25 6/8	26 4/8	25 3/8	4 6/8	4 6/8	9	8	Jackson Co., Ohio	Francis L. Ray	Francis L. Ray	1988	274
196 3/8	25 1/8	25 2/8	17 6/8	4 6/8	4 5/8	9	6	Webb Co., Texas	R. Blair James	R. Blair James	1954	275
196 3/8	25 4/8	26 5/8	20 1/8	6 1/8	6	12	11	Magaguadowic Lake, N.B.	Albert Fawcett	Albert Fawcett	1988	275
196 3/8	27	26 1/8	17 7/8	5 6/8	5 7/8	8	7	Hougton Co., Mich.	Picked Up	Robert L. Marr	1990	275
196 2/8	25 4/8	25 7/8	19 6/8	5 5/8	5 3/8	10	11	Winneshiek Co., Iowa	Picked Up	William H. Lilienthal	1940	278
196 2/8	23 2/8	23 1/8	17 5/8	4 7/8	5 2/8	11	7	Lake of the Woods Co., Minn.	Ralph Rehder	Ralph Rehder	1951	278
196 2/8	24	24 5/8	18 6/8	5 5/8	5 3/8	11	10	Crook Co., Wyo.	Donald W. Clements	Colleen B. Clements	1958	278
196 1/8	29 3/8	29 2/8	22 4/8	5 1/8	5	10	10	Crow Wing Co., Minn.	LeRoy E. Pelarski	LeRoy E. Pelarski	1975	282
196	24 4/8	26	17 2/8	5 6/8	5 7/8	11	10	McCreary Co., Ky.	Jack W. Bailey	Jack W. Bailey	1976	283
196	25	24 7/8	20	4 6/8	4 6/8	8	8	Forest Co., Wisc.	Aaron E. Huettl	Aaron E. Huettl	1939	283
195 7/8	26 5/8	24 7/8	17 7/8	5 4/8	5 3/8	10	9	Dubuque Co., Iowa	Terry D. Freese	Terry D. Freese	1990	285
195 7/8	21 4/8	21 6/8	20 6/8	4 5/8	4 4/8	9	10	La Salle Co., Texas	Steve A. Meyer	Steve A. Meyer	1968	285
195 7/8	30	30 1/8	21 4/8	5	4 7/8	7	8	Jackson Co., Mich.	Picked Up	Ronald D. Murphy	1984	285
195 6/8	23 1/8	23 4/8	19	4 7/8	4 7/8	9	9	Latah Co., Idaho	Cecil H. Cameron	Cecil H. Cameron	1989	288
195 6/8	28 6/8	30 7/8	23 4/8	6	5 7/8	7	8	Illinois	Unknown	Ed Feist	1945	288
195 6/8	28 2/8	29 5/8	22	5 4/8	5 4/8	7	8	Douglas Co., Wisc.	Unknown	Buckhorn of Gordon, Inc.	PR 1970	288
195 6/8	21 7/8	25 7/8	16 4/8	5 7/8	6 3/8	14	8	Greenwater Creek, Sask.	Picked Up	Edward R. Mielke	1988	288
195 5/8	26 6/8	24 4/8	17 2/8	4 4/8	4 3/8	9	10	Coal Co., Okla.	Todd Tobey	Todd Tobey	1988	292
195 4/8	21 4/8	22 4/8	16 7/8	4 4/8	4 4/8	11	14	Menard Co., Texas	Don N. Jones, Jr.	Ray Cooper	1987	293
195 4/8	28 5/8	27 3/8	21 2/8	4	4	8	7	Fillmore Co., Minn.	Jim Sletten	Mrs. Jim Sletten	1974	293
195 4/8	26 3/8	27 2/8	20 2/8	4 7/8	5 1/8	11	9	Kanabec Co., Minn.	Kenneth L. Smith	Kenneth L. Smith	1976	293
195 4/8	26 2/8	27 6/8	17 4/8	5	5	10	8	Peoria Co., Ill.	Jerry T. Wyatt	Jerry T. Wyatt	1989	293
195 4/8	21 4/8	23 4/8	15 2/8	4 2/8	6 1/8	11	8	Jessamine Co., Ky.	Tony W. Drury	Tony W. Drury	1991	293
195 3/8	26 3/8	26	20 7/8	5 7/8	6	9	8	Scott Co., Iowa	Jeffrey Rasche	Jeffrey Rasche	1989	297
195 3/8	24 7/8	23	18 2/8	5 2/8	5 1/8	9	11	N. Saskatchewan River, Alta.	Thomas J. Procinsky	Thomas J. Procinsky	1990	297
195 2/8	24	24 4/8	20	5	5 1/8	8	8	Chitek Lake, Sask.	Charles E. Gambino	Charles E. Gambino	1990	299
195 2/8	11 7/8	12 4/8	16 7/8	4	4 4/8	21	16	Grimes Co., Texas	Walter Schroeder, Jr.	Walter Schroeder, Jr.	1990	299
195 1/8	25 5/8	23 4/8	18	4 4/8	4 3/8	15	13	Bonner Co., Idaho	George B. Hatley	George B. Hatley	1939	301
195 1/8	23 4/8	23 5/8	15 3/8	4 7/8	4 5/8	8	8	Macon Co., Ga.	Wesley Jones	Wesley Jones	1986	301
195 1/8	26 7/8	25 5/8	20 5/8	5 1/8	5 2/8	8	7	Massac Co., Ill.	Kent Sommer	Kent Sommer	1989	301
195	25 6/8	27 5/8	20 3/8	5 3/8	5 4/8	11	13	Guthrie Co., Iowa	Tom C. Klever	Tom C. Klever	1982	304
195	25 4/8	25	18 6/8	4 5/8	4 5/8	10	9	Clarke Co., Iowa	Picked Up	Jeff Jorgenson	1985	304
195	23 1/8	21 4/8	17 1/8	4 4/8	4 4/8	9	10	Kenedy Co., Texas	Phil Lyne	Phil Lyne	1986	304
195	25 3/8	22 6/8	20 6/8	5 3/8	5 6/8	9	8	Henderson Co., Ill.	George S. Worley	William H. Lilienthal	1989	304
195	25 6/8	26 1/8	17	4 3/8	4 3/8	9	8	Goodhue Co., Minn.	Darrin L. Goplen	Darrin L. Goplen	1990	304
194 4/8	28 2/8	28 2/8	19 1/8	5 2/8	5 1/8	11	7	Marshall Co., Minn.	Timothy F. Johnson	Timothy F. Johnson	1988	309
194 2/8	28 7/8	28 7/8	24 1/8	5	5	9	5	Mercer Co., Mo.	Dennis D. Schmidt	Dennis D. Schmidt	1989	310

459

Whitetail Deer, Non-Typical Antlers - Continued

Score	Length of Main Beam R.	L.	Inside Spread	Circumference at Smallest Place Between Burr and First Point R.	L.	Number of Points R.	L.	Locality Killed	By Whom Killed	Owner	Date Killed	Rank
193 7/8	28 6/8	28 7/8	19	5 5/8	5 5/8	7	10	Lee Co., Ga.	John T. Marbury	John T. Marbury	1990	311
193 4/8	26 5/8	25 1/8	16 1/8	5 1/8	4 7/8	9	13	Juneau Co., Wisc.	Maurice Sterba	Maurice Sterba	1955	312
193 4/8	26 3/8	25 2/8	20 2/8	4 7/8	5 1/8	7	8	Edgar Co., Ill.	Jerry R. David	Jerry R. David	1988	312
193	27 4/8	27 1/8	19 7/8	6 1/8	5 2/8	8	7	Lake Co., Ill.	Steven Derkson	Steven Derkson	1989	314
192 7/8	26 7/8	26 7/8	19 6/8	5 3/8	5 1/8	7	7	Minnesota	Picked Up	Gary W. Haeckel	PR 1991	315
192 6/8	25 3/8	27 1/8	18 2/8	6 7/8	7 2/8	10	9	Brown Co., Ill.	Thomas March	Thomas March	1990	316
192 2/8	26 1/8	25	16 6/8	4 4/8	4 4/8	6	6	Kleberg Co., Texas	Cissy H. Taub	Cissy H. Taub	1983	317
192 2/8	28	26 5/8	32 6/8	5 4/8	5 4/8	9	9	Somerset Co., Maine	Ryan Snell	Ryan Snell	1990	317
191 6/8	27 5/8	26 4/8	17 4/8	5	5	9	9	Davis Co., Iowa	Harry E. Nicholson, Jr.	Harry E. Nicholson, Jr.	1988	319
191 4/8	24 7/8	25 1/8	23 3/8	5	4 6/8	9	8	Hancock Co., Maine	Douglas D. Adamson	Douglas D. Adamson	1988	320
191 3/8	24 2/8	25 2/8	23 1/8	6	6	9	8	Douglas Co., Ill.	Jackie L. Norman	Jackie L. Norman	1990	321
191 2/8	23 5/8	24 1/8	16	4 3/8	4 3/8	9	8	Worth Co., Ga.	Mike D. Roberts, Sr.	Mike D. Roberts, Sr.	1963	322
191 2/8	23 6/8	23 2/8	17 1/8	4 5/8	5	9	10	Alger Co., Mich.	David Walther	David Walther	1990	322
191 1/8	26 3/8	27 3/8	17 6/8	4 5/8	4 5/8	10	9	Rockingham Co., N.H.	Theron G. Young, Sr.	Theron G. Young, Sr.	1945	324
191 1/8	24 3/8	26	17	5	4 6/8	9	9	Custer Co., Neb.	Robert D. Brestel	Robert D. Brestel	1989	324
190 7/8	26 1/8	27 2/8	21	6 3/8	6 1/8	9	11	Wright Co., Minn.	Keith A. Rudolph	Keith A. Rudolph	1989	326
190 6/8	24 7/8	23 5/8	18 2/8	4 3/8	4 1/8	7	11	Marathon Co., Wisc.	August F. Bisping	August F. Bisping	1945	327
190 5/8	26 1/8	25 6/8	21 6/8	5 2/8	5 3/8	9	8	Monroe Co., Mo.	Michael F. Strunk	Michael F. Strunk	1989	328
190 4/8	26 6/8	28 4/8	19	6	5 7/8	8	9	Piscataquis Co., Maine	Robert J. Pelletier	Robert J. Pelletier	1988	329
190 4/8	26 4/8	27 1/8	20	5	5 2/8	13	14	Osage Co., Kan.	Philip E. Spencer	Philip E. Spencer	1990	329
190	23 5/8	26 7/8	19 6/8	5 6/8	4 7/8	11	6	Breckenridge Co., Ky.	John M. Pollock	John M. Pollock	1987	331
189 7/8	24 5/8	26 1/8	18 7/8	5	5 2/8	9	10	Chisholm, Alta.	Prosper L. Boisvert	Prosper L. Boisvert	1990	332
188 7/8	22 6/8	24 1/8	17 4/8	4 3/8	4 4/8	9	10	Medina Co., Texas	David T. Wallace	J. Claude Wallace	PR 1917	333
188 7/8	26 1/8	25 7/8	20 3/8	5	5 2/8	10	12	Pine Co., Minn.	Peter Feider	Peter Feider	1974	333
188 4/8	25 3/8	29 3/8	19	5 1/8	5	11	7	Bayfield Co., Wisc.	Henry Schmidt	Jeffery Schmidt	1939	335
188 3/8	26 2/8	27 2/8	19 4/8	4 4/8	4 5/8	5	10	Minnedosa River, Man.	Mark Usick	Mark Usick	1986	336
188 2/8	23 3/8	24 4/8	19 7/8	4 4/8	4 6/8	13	9	Surry Co., Va.	George M. Summerfield	George M. Summerfield	1989	337
188 1/8	24 7/8	25 1/8	21 3/8	5 2/8	5 3/8	9	7	Aroostook Co., Maine	Fritjof Jacobson	Fritjof Jacobson	1939	338
188	24 6/8	23 3/8	16 4/8	5	5	9	7	N. Saskatchewan River, Alta.	William N. Toth	William N. Toth	1988	339

Score							Locality	Owner	By whom killed or picked up	Date	
187 5/8	27 1/8	27 3/8	18 7/8	4 4/8	4 5/8	6	8	Hancock Co., W.Va.	Shawn J. Sargent	Shawn J. Sargent	1990	340
187 4/8	21 2/8	15 2/8	20 5/8	4 7/8	4 6/8	10	13	Pend Oreille Co., Wash.	Picked Up	Eugene Bailey	1946	341
187 4/8	23 5/8	24 4/8	19 2/8	5	5 2/8	7	10	Mahaska Co., Iowa	Jason W. Fox	Jason W. Fox	1989	341
187 4/8	21 1/8	21 3/8	15 3/8	6	6	9	14	McDonald Co., Mo.	William J. Mustain	William J. Mustain	1989	341
187 2/8	25 3/8	25 5/8	22 5/8	5 3/8	5 7/8	9	9	Langlade Co., Wisc.	Carl J. McIlquham	Carl J. McIlquham	1988	344
187 1/8	19 2/8	20 6/8	30 5/8	4 7/8	4 6/8	10	8	Cape Brenton, N.S.	Bernard T. Langlais	Bernard T. Langlais	1989	344
187 1/8	26 4/8	28 2/8	19 6/8	5 2/8	5 3/8	8	9	Oneida Co., Wisc.	Dean F. Look	Dean F. Look	1989	346
187	25 6/8	27	17 7/8	5 1/8	5 3/8	6	7	Woodford Co., Ill.	David K. Jacobs	David K. Jacobs	1989	347
187	23 2/8	24 7/8	18	7	6	12	10	Coffey Co., Kan.	Ty A. Pyle	Ty A. Pyle	1989	347
186 7/8	21 5/8	22 3/8	20 5/8	5 2/8	6 2/8	8	9	La Porte Co., Ind.	David W. Nelson	David W. Nelson	1988	349
186 7/8	25 5/8	25	18 7/8	4 4/8	4 4/8	8	9	Roseau Co., Minn.	John R. Franke	John R. Franke	1990	349
186 7/8	24	24 3/8	17 5/8	4 7/8	4 1/8	8	6	Latah Co., Idaho	Tami M. VanNess	Tami M. VanNess	1990	349
186 6/8	26 2/8	26 5/8	23 2/8	5 7/8	5 7/8	9	6	Concordia Parish, La.	T.B. Jones	William T. Beasley PR	1950	352
186 4/8	23 6/8	26 3/8	18 3/8	5	5	8	6	Calhoun Co., Mich.	Robert G. Day	Robert G. Day	1988	353
186 4/8	21 4/8	24	20 7/8	4 7/8	5 1/8	8	8	Clayton Co., Iowa	Francis C. O'Donnell	Francis C. O'Donnell	1988	353
186 2/8	23 1/8	22 5/8	17 6/8	5 7/8	5 7/8	8	10	Traverse Co., Minn.	Terry L. Miller	Terry L. Miller	1987	355
186 2/8	24 2/8	24 2/8	17 3/8	5	4 7/8	8	10	Red Deer River, Alta.	Lorne Proudfoot	Lorne Proudfoot	1990	355
186	23 3/8	22 7/8	17 7/8	4 4/8	4 7/8	7	7	Washington Co., Neb.	Stephen W. Blankenship	Stephen W. Blankenship	1988	357
186	23 3/8	23 4/8	16 7/8	4 6/8	4 6/8	7	7	Pike Co., Mo.	Billy Boston	Billy Boston	1990	357
185 5/8	25 6/8	26	20	4 4/8	4 4/8	7	9	Lincoln Co., Wisc.	Fred H. Storm	Fred H. Storm	1977	357
185 5/8	21 7/8	19 7/8	19	5 7/8	5 6/8	7	10	Forest Co., Wisc.	Earl V. Conradt	Earl V. Conradt	1988	359
185 5/8	22 7/8	23	22 4/8	4 6/8	4 6/8	7	9	Polk Co., Minn.	Delphus H. Hanson	Delphus H. Hanson	1988	359
185 1/8	24	26 5/8	16 5/8	5 1/8	5 4/8	11	9	Bayfield Co., Wisc.	Charles Hermansen	Donald Ash	1914	359
268*	25 4/8	25	18	4 3/8	4 7/8	15	16	Idaho	Unknown	James H. Reimer PR	1982	362

* Final Score subject to revision by additional verifying measurements.

461

Coues' Whitetail Deer, *Typical Antlers*

Minimum Score 100   *Odocoileus virginianus couesi*   World's Record 143

Score	Length of Main Beam R.	L.	Inside Spread	Circumference at Smallest Place Between Burr and First Point R.	L.	Number of Points R.	L.	Locality Killed	By Whom Killed	Owner	Date Killed	Rank
133	20 6/8	19 7/8	18	3 7/8	3 7/8	6	6	Pima Co., Ariz.	Michael E. Duperret	M.E. Duperret & J.K. Volk	1990	1
120 3/8	19 6/8	19 3/8	16 7/8	4 2/8	4	5	4	Sonora, Mexico	J. Marvin Smith III	J. Marvin Smith III	1990	2
119 6/8	19 3/8	19 4/8	13 2/8	3 7/8	3 6/8	5	5	Hidalgo Co., N.M.	Frank L. Riley	Frank L. Riley	1990	3
114 4/8	18	17 5/8	15	4 2/8	4 1/8	4	4	Gila Co., Ariz.	Dallas J. Duhamell, Jr.	Dallas J. Duhamell, Jr.	1990	4
111 1/8	17 5/8	17 4/8	14 5/8	4 1/8	4 1/8	5	5	Cochise Co., Ariz.	Harvey G. Ward, Jr.	Harvey G. Ward, Jr.	1988	5
110 4/8	18	18 4/8	14 2/8	3 3/8	3 2/8	4	4	Sonora, Mexico	Ricardo Andrade	Ricardo Andrade	1988	6
110	18 1/8	17 6/8	14 5/8	4 6/8	5	4	6	Cochise Co., Ariz.	Bill Saathoff	Bill Saathoff	1987	7
109 3/8	19 6/8	19 3/8	14 5/8	3 4/8	3 4/8	5	4	Sonora, Mexico	Mitchell A. Thorson	Mitchell A. Thorson	1988	8
108 1/8	15 5/8	15 5/8	14 1/8	4 2/8	4 1/8	5	5	Gila Co., Ariz.	Frank J. Cecelic	Frank J. Cecelic	1989	9
107 4/8	16 7/8	15 1/8	12	4 2/8	4 4/8	4	4	Hidalgo Co., N.M.	Clyde G. Kain	Clyde G. Kain	1990	10
104 4/8	16 6/8	16 7/8	15 1/8	4 3/8	4 2/8	5	5	Graham Co., Ariz.	Robin W. Bechtel	Robin W. Bechtel	1984	11
134 4/8 *	20 5/8	21 1/8	16	4 5/8	4 3/8	5	5	Grant Co., N.M.	Victor Giacoletti, Jr.	Victor Giacoletti, Jr.	1981	

* Final Score subject to revision by additional verifying measurements.

Coues' Whitetail Deer, Non-Typical Antlers

Odocoileus virginianus couesi

Minimum Score 105

World's Record 158-4/8

Score	Length of Main Beam R.	L.	Inside Spread	Circumference at Smallest Place Between Burr and First Point R.	L.	Number of Points R.	L.	Locality Killed	By Whom Killed	Owner	Date Killed	Rank
155	19	20	16 6/8	4 7/8	4 5/8	9	8	Gila Co., Ariz.	Charles E. Erickson, Jr.	Charles E. Erickson, Jr.	1988	1
132 3/8	17 4/8	17 1/8	13 7/8	5	5	6	8	Gila Co., Ariz.	Dale J. Little	Dale J. Little	1989	2
131 2/8	16 1/8	18	13 5/8	6 6/8	5	9	8	Gila Co., Ariz.	Nathan E. Ellison	Nathan E. Ellison	1958	3
125 7/8	18 7/8	17 7/8	12 1/8	4	4	6	8	Arizona	Picked Up	Michael J. Tamboli	PR 1976	4
124	17 6/8	16 4/8	12 7/8	4	4 2/8	7	6	Arizona	Unknown	George L. Cooper	1977	5
122 2/8	17 7/8	16 5/8	13 4/8	4 4/8	4 4/8	4	7	Santa Cruz Co., Ariz.	Clifton E. Cox	Clifton E. Cox	1980	6
112 4/8	16 1/8	15 5/8	14 7/8	4	4 1/8	4	6	Graham Co., Ariz.	Picked Up	Billie F. Bechtel	PR 1990	7
107 5/8	15	15 2/8	12 6/8	4	4	5	5	Graham Co., Ariz.	Noel S. Allen	Noel S. Allen	1989	8
106 6/8	16 5/8	16 4/8	12	3 3/8	3 4/8	5	8	Sonora, Mexico	Lonnie L. Ritchey	Lonnie L. Ritchey	1988	9
105 3/8	18 1/8	18	15 2/8	4 3/8	4 3/8	4	4	Graham Co., Ariz.	Robin W. Bechtel	Robin W. Bechtel	1986	10
134 3/8*	21 3/8	21	16 6/8	4 5/8	4 4/8	8	5	Cochise Co., Ariz.	Brian Childers	Brian Childers	1990	
130 1/8*	17	18 3/8	14 5/8	4 3/8	4 5/8	8	4	Yavapai Co., Ariz.	David K. Moore	David K. Moore	1988	

* Final Score subject to revision by additional verifying measurements.

463

Canada Moose

Alces alces americana and Alces alces andersoni

Minimum Score 185   World's Record 242

Three categories of moose are recognized for the records keeping, with boundaries based on geographic lines. Canada moose includes trophies from Canada (except for the Yukon and Northwest Territories), Minnesota, Maine, North Dakota, New Hampshire, and Vermont.

Score	Greatest Spread	Length of Palm R.	L.	Width of Palm R.	L.	Circumference of Beam at Smallest Place R.	L.	Number of Normal Points R.	L.	Locality Killed	By Whom Killed	Owner	Date Killed	Rank
221 4/8	66	40 1/8	41	15 7/8	15	7 5/8	8 1/8	16	15	Logan Mt., Que.	Charles R. Roy	C.R. Roy & R. Roy	1988	1
219 7/8	65 5/8	40 1/8	44 2/8	16 4/8	16 4/8	7 4/8	7 6/8	16	13	East West Lake, Ont.	Kurt Skalitzky	Kurt Skalitzky	1989	2
214 6/8	57	46 2/8	41 7/8	15 1/8	15 3/8	7 7/8	7 7/8	14	14	Red Lake, Ont.	Dan K. Brumm	D.K. Brumm & J. Krizsan	1991	3
213	59	42	41 7/8	15	14 3/8	7 3/8	7 7/8	14	14	Candle Lake, Sask.	Roger Mann	Roger Mann	1989	4
212	58 4/8	41 7/8	43 5/8	13 6/8	15 5/8	7 1/8	7 7/8	14	14	Taku River, B.C.	William A. Van Alstine	William A. Van Alstine	1990	5
211 4/8	54	45 1/8	44 7/8	13 4/8	13 1/8	8 3/8	7 6/8	15	13	Sheslay River, B.C.	Daniel E. Gorecki	Daniel E. Gorecki	1989	6
211	59 6/8	40 6/8	38 7/8	15 5/8	15 4/8	8 6/8	8 2/8	15	13	Mojikit Lake, Ont.	Charles R. Salfer	Charles R. Salfer	1987	7
210	53 4/8	42 3/8	39 2/8	18 4/8	19	7 4/8	7 5/8	13	15	Cold Fish Lake, B.C.	Glenroy G. Livingston	Glenroy G. Livingston	1990	8
209 7/8	53 3/8	44 5/8	45 7/8	12 5/8	12 6/8	7 3/8	7	15	14	Cutbank River, Alta.	Alan D. Taylor	Alan D. Taylor	1970	9
209 7/8	57 5/8	44 3/8	41	16 6/8	14 7/8	7 4/8	7 2/8	13	15	Dease River, B.C.	Michael D. Rochette	Michael D. Rochette	1988	9
209 5/8	68 3/8	41	41	13 3/8	13 4/8	7 6/8	7 7/8	10	9	Liard River, B.C.	Ronald B. Barker	Ronald B. Barker	1990	11
208 3/8	58 7/8	43 4/8	44 4/8	14	15 3/8	7 2/8	7 7/8	10	19	Taku River, B.C.	Robert J. Matyas	Robert J. Matyas	1989	12
208 2/8	61 4/8	40 4/8	40 1/8	15 2/8	13 5/8	8 3/8	8 1/8	12	12	Coos Co., N.H.	Charles A. Covey, Sr.	Charles A. Covey, Sr.	1990	13
208	61 4/8	41 2/8	42 7/8	16	16	7 7/8	7 5/8	12	11	Legend Lake, Alta.	Reg Berry	Reg Berry	1977	14
206 7/8	61 7/8	44 5/8	40 7/8	14 7/8	14 3/8	7 6/8	7 6/8	9	17	Notikewin River, Alta.	Denis Drainville	Denis Drainville	1987	15
206 5/8	59 5/8	41 1/8	43 4/8	14 3/8	15 4/8	8	8	10	12	Peerless Lake, Alta.	Janet E. Spinks	Jonathan Spinks	1989	16
205 2/8	61 4/8	41	40 5/8	16	16 3/8	7 4/8	7 2/8	9	8	Serpentine River, Nfld.	Picked Up	Gerard Beaulieu	1989	17
203 7/8	52 3/8	41 6/8	41 1/8	13 5/8	13 2/8	7 4/8	7 6/8	13	14	Kakwa River, Alta.	Dean A. Estes	Dean A. Estes	1987	18
203 4/8	55 6/8	38 4/8	40	13 2/8	13 2/8	8 1/8	8 4/8	14	15	Pink Mt., B.C.	John L. London	John L. London	1966	19
203 3/8	59 3/8	38 3/8	38 3/8	13 5/8	13 5/8	7 1/8	7 1/8	14	17	Teslin Lake, B.C.	Russ LaFreniere	Russ LaFreniere	1988	20
202 4/8	60 2/8	43	46 4/8	11 6/8	13 3/8	7 3/8	7 6/8	9	14	Glundebery Creek, B.C.	Neil Lawson	Neil Lawson	1988	21
202 2/8	63 2/8	38	37	13	13 6/8	7 5/8	7 4/8	12	12	Wreck Cove Lakes, N.S.	Donald J. Sauveur	Donald J. Sauveur	1988	22
202 1/8	54 3/8	40 7/8	41 1/8	14 6/8	15 3/8	7 2/8	7 2/8	11	11	Halfway River, B.C.	M. Toby Hobek	M. Toby Hobek	1990	23
200 7/8	56 5/8	41	38	12 3/8	16	7 6/8	7 7/8	15	14	Aroostook Co., Maine	Ernest L. Leighton	Ernest L. Leighton	1988	24
200 7/8	63 3/8	42 7/8	39	13 3/8	14 4/8	8	8	9	9	Swan Lake, B.C.	Gary A. Markofer	Gary A. Markofer	1990	24

464

Score										Locality	Hunter	Owner	Year	Rank
200 5/8	66 5/8	36	37 2/8	14 6/8	15 3/8	7 3/8	7 2/8	9	11	Low Fog Creek, B.C.	Delmar L. Achenbach	Delmar L. Achenbach	1989	26
200 4/8	57 6/8	38 3/8	39	14 4/8	15	9 7/8	8 4/8	10	10	Kedahda Lake, B.C.	Brian Bergen	Brian Bergen	1990	27
199 1/8	64	37 7/8	37	12 5/8	16 2/8	7 1/8	7 3/8	12	17	Kechika River, B.C.	John R. Shotzberger	John R. Shotzberger	1990	28
199 1/8	56 3/8	43 1/8	41 5/8	13	14	6 6/8	6 6/8	10	13	Victoria Creek, B.C.	Bradley Bowden	Bradley Bowden	1986	29
198 5/8	57 1/8	40 3/8	40 3/8	16 4/8	16 3/8	8	8	9	6	Lake Nipigon, Ont.	Ohne L. Raasch	Ohne L. Raasch	1991	30
198 2/8	57	40 7/8	38 6/8	11 4/8	12 7/8	7 3/8	7 5/8	13	13	Heart Mts., B.C.	Richard E. Radavich	Richard E. Radavich	1989	31
197 4/8	47 6/8	40 2/8	47 6/8	13 1/8	14 4/8	8 1/8	7 4/8	14	16	Inverness River, Alta.	Steve C. Klask	Steve C. Klask	1988	32
197 2/8	58 4/8	17 1/8	17 2/8	39 1/8	37 2/8	6 5/8	6 6/8	8	8	St. Louis Co., Minn.	Paul W. Anthony	Minn. Dept. of Natl. Resc.	1906	33
197 2/8	59 4/8	36 3/8	34 5/8	15 5/8	14	7 3/8	7 2/8	13	13	Hayes River, Man.	John R. Schleicher	John R. Schleicher	1990	33
196 4/8	57 4/8	41	42 6/8	13 6/8	10 6/8	7 6/8	7 7/8	10	13	Swan Lake, B.C.	Patricia Markofer	Patricia Markofer	1989	35
196	49 6/8	41	40 4/8	13 3/8	14 3/8	7 2/8	7 4/8	12	15	Birchwood Creek, Alta.	Gert B. Nielsen	Gert B. Nielsen	1990	36
195 5/8	57 7/8	36 6/8	40 6/8	12 5/8	16 4/8	7 4/8	7 7/8	12	13	Pink Mt., B.C.	Michael H. LaViolette	Michael H. LaViolette	1989	37
194	64 2/8	33 1/8	33	15 6/8	13 3/8	8	8	12	12	Somerset Co., Maine	Carl J. Moore	Carl J. Moore	1991	38
193 2/8	51	36 7/8	36 6/8	13 3/8	14	7	7 1/8	14	15	Robinsons, Nfld.	Picked Up	Aloysious Alexander	1966	39
191 6/8	61	41 4/8	37	14 6/8	13 4/8	6 7/8	7	9	8	Kaltin River, B.C.	Dan F. Holleman	Dan F. Holleman	1964	40
191 2/8	52 2/8	37 6/8	43 2/8	16 6/8	14 7/8	7 5/8	7 4/8	10	12	Tetsa River, B.C.	Nicholas Misciagna	Nicholas Misciagna	1989	41
190	56 2/8	36 2/8	36 5/8	13	14 2/8	6 6/8	6 5/8	12	11	Jackinnes Lake, Ont.	Frank McFarquhar	Frank McFarquhar	1986	42
188 3/8	56 3/8	38 3/8	33 7/8	14 1/8	13 3/8	6 6/8	6 6/8	15	12	Pink Mt., B.C.	John T. Crooks	John T. Crooks	1988	43
187 5/8	57 1/8	35 1/8	37 1/8	12 4/8	12 2/8	6 7/8	6 7/8	11	13	Turnagain River, B.C.	Glenn Hisey	Glenn Hisey	1978	44
185	54	39 1/8	42 6/8	12 1/8	13 5/8	7 2/8	7 4/8	7	9	Halfway River, B.C.	David Templeton	David Templeton	1986	45
185	50 6/8	36 7/8	39 3/8	12	12 1/8	7 2/8	7 2/8	12	11	Firebag River, Alta.	Steve Herhei	Steve Herhei	1989	45
220 1/8*	59 7/8	44 6/8	44 1/8	17	16 1/8	7	6 7/8	13	18	Squaw Rapids Dam, Sask.	Dennis Flikinger	Dennis Flikinger	1981	45

* Final Score subject to revision by additional verifying measurements.

Alaska-Yukon Moose

Alces alces gigas

Alaska-Yukon Moose includes trophies from Alaska, the Yukon Territory, and the Northwest Territories.

Score	Greatest Spread	Length of Palm R.	L.	Width of Palm R.	L.	Circumference of Beam at Smallest Place R.	L.	Number of Normal Points R.	L.	Locality Killed	By Whom Killed	Owner	Date Killed	Rank
234 2/8	71 4/8	49 2/8	47 6/8	13 7/8	14 7/8	7 7/8	7 6/8	12	14	Beluga Lake, Alaska	Eugene J. Smart	Eugene J. Smart	1989	1
234 2/8	66 6/8	47 7/8	45 4/8	16 1/8	15	8 2/8	8 3/8	15	17	Salcha River, Alaska	Robert C. Lang	Robert C. Lang	1991	1
232 5/8	69 7/8	47 3/8	48 7/8	18 1/8	17	8	8	9	10	Lake Clark, Alaska	Wyatt B. Peek	Wyatt B. Peek	1987	3
232 2/8	66 2/8	50 4/8	49 4/8	16 4/8	14 6/8	7 6/8	7 6/8	12	11	Wien Lake, Alaska	James E. Guist	James E. Guist	1988	4
232 1/8	67 3/8	45 7/8	45 2/8	17	16 7/8	8 7/8	8 6/8	12	12	Amos Lakes, Alaska	Buddy R. Donaldson	Buddy R. Donaldson	1990	5
231 7/8	69 5/8	45 7/8	49 7/8	16 5/8	17 3/8	8 2/8	8 1/8	11	13	Wood River, Alaska	Robert Kennedy	Robert Kennedy	1989	6
231 6/8	65	45 5/8	46 6/8	18 5/8	18 4/8	7 6/8	8	13	12	Koyukuk River, Alaska	Don N. Bunker	Don N. Bunker	1990	7
231 4/8	67 4/8	46	44 4/8	17 2/8	17	7 5/8	7 4/8	13	15	Wood River, Alaska	H. Peter Blount	H. Peter Blount	1989	8
230 5/8	60 1/8	50	47 4/8	14 7/8	14 4/8	7 5/8	7 2/8	16	16	Hart River, Yukon	Charles H. Menzer	Charles H. Menzer	1988	9
230 5/8	70 3/8	49 7/8	50	13 7/8	12 4/8	7 7/8	7 6/8	13	10	Talkeetna River, Alaska	Wayne DiSarro	Wayne DiSarro	1989	9
229 7/8	73	43 5/8	43	17 4/8	15 7/8	8 3/8	8 2/8	12	12	Fortymile River, Alaska	Brian Yamamoto	Brian Yamamoto	1988	11
228 4/8	68 4/8	47 1/8	47 5/8	15 4/8	15 3/8	7 5/8	7 5/8	10	10	Flattop Mt., Alaska	John F. Walchli	John F. Walchli	1991	12
228	64 4/8	53 4/8	48 3/8	15 5/8	15 3/8	8 4/8	8 4/8	10	11	Cinder River, Alaska	John S. Pangbron	John S. Pangbron	1990	13
227 7/8	69 1/8	46	44 4/8	14 1/8	15	9	9 1/8	13	12	Koyukuk River, Alaska	James R. Ryffel	James R. Ryffel	1986	14
227 6/8	61 2/8	49 3/8	45 2/8	17 6/8	22	9 5/8	9 2/8	11	11	Seward Pen., Alaska	Andrew Pellessier	Homer Westmark	1990	15
227	74 2/8	44 6/8	48 4/8	15 1/8	17 3/8	8 4/8	8 4/8	8	14	Alaska Pen., Alaska	John A. Schumacher	John A. Schumacher	1987	16
226 7/8	66 5/8	47	48	15 3/8	19	7 6/8	8	10	11	Alaska Pen., Alaska	Michael Z. Abrams	Michael Z. Abrams	1989	17
226 4/8	73 2/8	45 3/8	42 7/8	16 6/8	17 5/8	8	8 4/8	9	10	Koyukuk River, Alaska	Paul H. Ruesch	Paul H. Ruesch	1990	18
225 6/8	67 2/8	43 3/8	44 4/8	17 2/8	18 2/8	8 5/8	8 4/8	10	12	Kugururok River, Alaska	H.I.H. Prince Abdorreza Pahlavi	H.I.H. Prince Abdorreza Pahlavi	1988	19
225 2/8	65	39 6/8	43 4/8	22 1/8	19 2/8	9 1/8	10 7/8	16	12	Dog Salmon River, Alaska	Marvin D. Fuller	Marvin D. Fuller	1988	20
225 1/8	62 5/8	46 2/8	53 5/8	17 7/8	18 4/8	8 1/8	8 2/8	9	10	King Salmon River, Alaska	Michaelangelo P. Ripepi	Michaelangelo P. Ripepi	1989	21
224 6/8	62 6/8	47 3/8	46	19	15 4/8	7 4/8	7 4/8	13	14	Earn Lake, Yukon	Julian D. Weiant	Julian D. Weiant	1978	22
224 5/8	65 1/8	44 6/8	40 3/8	20 6/8	20 4/8	7 7/8	8 3/8	12	12	Kandik River, Yukon	Charles W. Brammer	Charles W. Brammer	1988	23
224 1/8	61 7/8	49 3/8	48 7/8	12 6/8	13	7 5/8	7 5/8	12	12	Fifteen Mile River, Yukon	Larry Lee	Larry Lee	1990	24
221 7/8	61 6/8	45 3/8	44 2/8	15 4/8	15 5/8	7 7/8	7 2/8	13	15	Johnson River, Alaska	Thomas L. Clyde	Thomas L. Clyde	1989	25

Score										Locality	Owner	Hunter	Year	Rank
220 7/8 *	69 7/8	44 4/8	44 4/8	14 7/8	17	8 1/8	8 1/8	8	10	Braided Creek, Alaska	John T. Gardner, Jr.	John T. Gardner, Jr.	1988	26
219 4/8	64 4/8	43	50 5/8	17 7/8	15 1/8	8 2/8	8 5/8	11	12	Brooks Range, Alaska	Joseph Evancho	Joseph Evancho	1991	27
218 5/8	60 5/8	45 1/8	45 5/8	12 5/8	14	8 2/8	8 2/8	13	14	Alaska Range, Alaska	Daniel C. Boardman	Daniel C. Boardman	1974	28
216 2/8	68 2/8	43 7/8	41 1/8	16 5/8	17 2/8	7 2/8	7 6/8	13	10	Kobuk River, Alaska	Locie L. Murphy	Locie L. Murphy	1990	29
216	64 2/8	43 4/8	51	14 4/8	14 2/8	8 5/8	8 1/8	10	13	Pass Creek, Alaska	Raymond E. Hovis	Raymond E. Hovis	1989	30
215 4/8	56 2/8	48 4/8	45 7/8	15 2/8	22 1/8	7 4/8	7 4/8	12	11	Tustemena Lake, Alaska	William O. West	William O. West	1989	31
215 3/8	65 7/8	42 4/8	44 7/8	14 1/8	15	7 3/8	7 1/8	11	11	Mackenzie Mts., N.W.T.	Ralph Fleegle	Ralph Fleegle	1988	32
214 2/8	66	44 6/8	42 7/8	15 4/8	14	7 2/8	7 3/8	14	10	Iliamna Lake, Alaska	John Jondal	John Jondal	1988	33
212 5/8	64 5/8	43 2/8	43 1/8	14	13 6/8	8 4/8	8 1/8	9	9	Iliamna Lake, Alaska	Roscoe Blaisdell	Roscoe Blaisdell	1990	34
212 2/8	65 2/8	38 2/8	38 1/8	15 6/8	18 1/8	7 5/8	7 5/8	12	13	Hartman River, Alaska	John L. Lundin	John L. Lundin	1988	35
212 1/8	66 1/8	39 3/8	43 5/8	13 1/8	13 4/8	7 4/8	7 4/8	15	13	North Klondike River, Yukon	Bruce F. Gilbert	Bruce F. Gilbert	1988	36
212 1/8	64 5/8	42	41	11 7/8	12 1/8	8	7 7/8	13	15	Alaska Range, Alaska	Mark J. Bowersox	Mark J. Bowersox	1989	36
212	56 6/8	47 1/8	47 4/8	12 2/8	13	8 2/8	8 2/8	10	10	Squirrel River, Alaska	Tom Suedmeier	Tom Suedmeier	1988	38
211 6/8	64	38 4/8	37 4/8	16 2/8	16 6/8	8 1/8	8 1/8	12	13	Japan Hills, Alaska	George P. Williams	George P. Williams	1990	39
210 6/8	67	39 1/8	40	12 4/8	13 3/8	7 4/8	7 2/8	13	14	Natla River, N.W.T.	Delbert E. Rieckers	Delbert E. Rieckers	1990	40
210 3/8	57 5/8	46 2/8	43 6/8	15 3/8	15 4/8	9 4/8	9 4/8	8	8	Fifteen Mile River, Yukon	Fred Mack	Fred Mack	1990	41
242 5/8 *	67 5/8	50	50 4/8	17 5/8	17 7/8	7 7/8	8 2/8	14	12	Alaska Pen., Alaska	William L. Porteous	William L. Porteous	1991	
240 1/8 *	69 1/8	49 2/8	47 4/8	14 2/8	15	7 6/8	7 6/8	17	16	Fortymile River, Alaska	Roger D. Delaney	Roger D. Delaney	1988	
237 2/8 *	73 2/8	43	44	16 6/8	15 6/8	8 2/8	8 2/8	17	15	Alaska Pen., Alaska	Gregory C. McCann	Gregory C. McCann	1990	
235 6/8 *	71 4/8	45 6/8	45 4/8	17 4/8	18 5/8	7 7/8	7 7/8	11	12	Alaska Pen., Alaska	John F. Nash, Jr.	John F. Nash, Jr.	1989	
234 4/8 *	66 2/8	46 6/8	45 5/8	18 5/8	19 7/8	7 4/8	7 4/8	13	13	Alaska Range, Alaska	Bill Brown, Jr.	Bill Brown, Jr.	1987	

* Final Score subject to revision by additional verifying measurements.

Wyoming or Shiras Moose

Alces alces shirasi

Minimum Score 140

World's Record 205-4/8

Wyoming moose includes trophies taken in Colorado, Utah, Idaho, Montana, Wyoming, and Washington.

Score	Greatest Spread	Length of Palm R.	L.	Width of Palm R.	L.	Circumference of Beam at Smallest Place R.	L.	Number of Normal Points R.	L.	Locality Killed	By Whom Killed	Owner	Date Killed	Rank
183 4/8	57 2/8	36 7/8	35 4/8	11 5/8	14 4/8	7	7	9	13	Sublette Co., Wyo.	Norb Voerding	Barney J. Voerding	1940	1
178 5/8	47 7/8	34 3/8	38 3/8	12 7/8	13	7 1/8	7 4/8	12	11	Sheridan Co., Wyo.	Jack A. Wilkinson	Jack A. Wilkinson	1991	2
173 7/8	46 5/8	37 3/8	36 7/8	9 6/8	10 3/8	7	7	10	11	Gallatin Co., Mont.	Rolf S. Dull	Rolf S. Dull	1988	3
170 6/8	54 2/8	39	29 6/8	11 6/8	11 2/8	6 5/8	6 2/8	12	11	Cache Co., Utah	Jim Vanderbeek	Jim Vanderbeek	1990	4
170 4/8	49 2/8	35 5/8	34 6/8	11 3/8	10 3/8	6 5/8	6 4/8	11	9	Teton Co., Wyo.	W.R. Titterington	W.R. Titterington	1989	5
169	46 4/8	36	33 5/8	11 4/8	12 7/8	6 2/8	6 1/8	10	11	Caribou Co., Idaho	Richard M. Hydzik	Richard M. Hydzik	1988	6
166 3/8	50 3/8	35 2/8	33 5/8	10 6/8	9 2/8	6 2/8	6 1/8	9	9	Lincoln Co., Wyo.	T. Jefferson Cook	T. Jefferson Cook	1988	7
166 2/8	43 4/8	31 2/8	32 4/8	14 1/8	15 1/8	6	6 3/8	10	11	Morgan Co., Utah	Michael F. Gleason	Michael F. Gleason	1990	8
166	42 4/8	39 6/8	38 2/8	8 7/8	9 1/8	6 5/8	6 7/8	9	8	Flathead Co., Mont.	Kathy A. Nagel	Kathy A. Nagel	1988	9
165 3/8	53 7/8	39 3/8	33 6/8	8 6/8	7 4/8	6 4/8	6 6/8	11	8	Lincoln Co., Wyo.	Brad H. Jacobs	Brad H. Jacobs	1990	10
164 7/8	45 1/8	33 4/8	37 3/8	10	11 2/8	7 4/8	7 3/8	10	9	Fremont Co., Idaho	David F. Burk	Eugene H. Putnam	1973	11
164 2/8	43 6/8	34 2/8	33 5/8	9	10 3/8	6 5/8	6 5/8	12	11	Sublette Co., Wyo.	Kenneth D. Rupp	Kenneth D. Rupp	1988	12
163 7/8	49 7/8	31 7/8	34 5/8	41 3/8	11 3/8	6 3/8	6 3/8	11	9	Park Co., Mont.	William D. West	William D. West	1990	13
163 2/8	46 6/8	33 7/8	32 1/8	9 3/8	10	6 7/8	6 6/8	10	10	Bonneville Co., Idaho	Judith A. Gordon	Judith A. Gordon	1988	14
162 6/8	49 4/8	34 3/8	33 2/8	9 3/8	9 1/8	6 3/8	6 7/8	9	8	Mineral Co., Mont.	Shawn R. Andres	Shawn R. Andres	1991	15
162 4/8	49	33 3/8	36 3/8	10	11 7/8	6 3/8	6 5/8	7	14	Lincoln Co., Mont.	Kurt Spencer	Kurt Spencer	1991	16
161 4/8	46	32 6/8	36 2/8	8 5/8	8 7/8	6 3/8	6 3/8	11	11	Bonneville Co., Idaho	Richard H. Meservey	Richard H. Meservey	1989	17
161	37 2/8	34 3/8	33 1/8	10 4/8	12 1/8	6 2/8	6 4/8	12	13	Lincoln Co., Mont.	Charles M. Miller	Charles M. Miller	1990	18
160 7/8	40 5/8	34	32 6/8	11 7/8	11 1/8	7 3/8	7 7/8	9	9	Lincoln Co., Wyo.	Julian E. Sjostrom	Julian E. Sjostrom	1990	19
160 5/8	53 5/8	30 2/8	35 6/8	9	12 7/8	6 1/8	6 1/8	8	10	Caribou Co., Idaho	Dale E. Lindstrom	Dale E. Lindstrom	1988	20
160 5/8	49 5/8	31 5/8	31 1/8	7 6/8	10 6/8	6 5/8	6 5/8	10	11	Bonneville Co., Idaho	Gary L. Sant	Gary L. Sant	1991	20
159 4/8	42 6/8	30 2/8	30 6/8	11 6/8	14	6 3/8	6 5/8	12	10	Weber Co., Utah	Neal W. Darby	Neal W. Darby	1989	22
159 1/8	47 3/8	31	30 2/8	12 6/8	14	5 7/8	5 7/8	9	7	Teton Co., Wyo.	Eugene E. Hafen	Eugene E. Hafen	1989	23
159	48	35 1/8	31	9 4/8	9 5/8	7	7 7/8	10	8	Sheridan Co., Wyo.	Bradley C. Wichman	Bradley C. Wichman	1990	24
158 6/8	40 6/8	27 3/8	34 3/8	13 6/8	12 4/8	6 2/8	6 1/8	13	13	Gallatin Co., Mont.	Fred Moger	Lance Hossack	1951	25
157 6/8	46 4/8	29 2/8	31 2/8	10	10 7/8	6 4/8	6 3/8	10	14	Morgan Co., Utah	John L. Estes	John L. Estes	1987	26
157 5/8	41 5/8	33 3/8	34 1/8	10 2/8	9 5/8	6 1/8	6 1/8	9	12	Madison Co., Idaho	Lawrence Buckland	Lawrence Buckland	1987	27
156 6/8	45 6/8	34 2/8	34 4/8	10	9 2/8	6	6 3/8	6	7	Lincoln Co., Wyo.	Bryan Dexter	Bryan Dexter	1989	28

Score										Locality	Hunter	Owner	Date	Rank
156	43 4/8	31 2/8	29 1/8	11 2/8	10	6 1/8	6 2/8	13	11	Bonneville Co., Idaho	Bruce J. Thomson	Bruce J. Thomson	1990	29
155 5/8	52 7/8	29 4/8	31 2/8	8	8	5 7/8	5 7/8	10	8	Summit Co., Utah	Michelle R. Liechty	Michelle R. Liechty	1989	30
155 4/8	48 4/8	31	31 7/8	12 6/8	9 1/8	5 5/8	5 7/8	9	8	Lincoln Co., Mont.	H.E. Thompson, Jr.	H.E. Thompson, Jr.	1984	31
155 1/8	48 5/8	31 6/8	33 2/8	8 6/8	9 4/8	6 6/8	6 6/8	6	9	Teton Co., Wyo.	John J. King	John J. King	1988	32
155 1/8	43 3/8	31 4/8	28 3/8	11 2/8	12 2/8	6 2/8	6 2/8	11	10	Cache Co., Utah	Brian R. Nosker	Brian R. Nosker	1988	32
155 1/8	45 3/8	32 5/8	32 6/8	8 5/8	8	6 3/8	6 2/8	8	9	Beaverhead Co., Mont.	Katharine F. Heffner	Katharine F. Heffner	1990	32
153	47 4/8	29 3/8	30	10	11	6 3/8	6 3/8	7	10	Doggett Co., Utah	Ben L. Seegmiller	Ben L. Seegmiller	1989	35
147 7/8	46 7/8	30 6/8	31 2/8	9 4/8	8 5/8	6 1/8	6 3/8	5	5	Caribou Co., Idaho	Willard J. Teuscher	Willard J. Teuscher	1990	36
146 1/8	43 5/8	27 4/8	27 2/8	11	9 5/8	6 4/8	6 3/8	9	9	Teton Co., Wyo.	Charles J. Martin	Charles J. Martin	1989	37
145 2/8	51 2/8	27 7/8	31	9 4/8	9	6 1/8	6 1/8	6	4	Idaho Co., Idaho	Dell E. Jemmett	Dell E. Jemmett	1991	38
143 6/8	41 2/8	26	27 5/8	11 1/8	9 7/8	6 3/8	6 3/8	10	9	Teton Co., Wyo.	Nancy Bodenhamer	Nancy Bodenhamer	1990	39
143 5/8	46 3/8	25 7/8	30	9	9 4/8	5 5/8	5 7/8	8	8	Caribou Co., Idaho	Brian D. Washburn	Brian D. Washburn	1990	40
141 4/8	44 2/8	27 3/8	25	12 2/8	9 7/8	5 7/8	5 6/8	8	9	Rich Co., Utah	Sharon G. Green	Sharon G. Green	1989	41
140 2/8	43 2/8	21 7/8	24 5/8	10 7/8	12	5 5/8	6	10	11	Teton Co., Wyo.	Harry L. Deuser	Harry L. Deuser	1988	42
186 2/8*	48 2/8	35 1/8	34 5/8	13 2/8	13 4/8	6 6/8	6 6/8	14	14	Bonneville Co., Idaho	Jacque J. Steele	Jacque J. Steele	1989	
179 6/8*	52	35 2/8	38	12 6/8	14 3/8	6 7/8	7	9	10	Flathead Co., Mont.	Michael Clanton	Michael Clanton	1988	
177 6/8*	48 2/8	35 6/8	36 4/8	12 4/8	12	7	7	10	11	Bonneville Co., Idaho	Ramona C. Mitchell	Ramona C. Mitchell	1988	
176 3/8*	53 1/8	33	33 5/8	11 1/8	13 6/8	6 2/8	6 1/8	11	14	Bingham Co., Idaho	Michael B. Messick	Michael B. Messick	1988	

* Final Score subject to revision by additional verifying measurements.

Mountain Caribou

Rangifer tarandus caribou

Mountain caribou includes trophies from Alberta, British Columbia, southern Yukon Territory, and the Mackenzie Mountains of the Northwest Territories.

Score	Length of Main Beam R.	L.	Inside Spread	Circumference at Smallest Place Between Brow and Bez Points R.	L.	Length of Brow Points R.	L.	Width of Brow Points R.	L.	Number of Points R.	L.	Locality Killed	By Whom Killed	Owner	Date Killed	Rank
449 4/8	37 7/8	37 4/8	30 2/8	5 7/8	5 7/8	17 5/8	13 3/8	10 6/8	9 3/8	33	40	Fire Lake, Yukon	James R. Hollister	James R. Hollister	1989	1
440	55 5/8	55 3/8	46 2/8	6	5 5/8	21	21	5 4/8	3 4/8	17	17	Carcajou River, N.W.T.	David P. McBrayer	David P. McBrayer	1990	2
426 5/8	48 4/8	51 1/8	38 2/8	6 7/8	7	15 2/8	14 5/8	8	10	18	17	Pelly Mts., Yukon	Knut Wittfoth	Knut Wittfoth	1989	3
425 6/8	52 6/8	54 5/8	47	6 4/8	6 4/8	18 4/8	21 1/8	2 5/8	16	15	13	Kechika Range, B.C.	Victor E. Moss	Victor E. Moss	1988	4
414 1/8	55	54 6/8	42 6/8	6 2/8	6 2/8	12 7/8	18 2/8	1/8	15 1/8	18	13	Johiah Lake, B.C.	Harold G. Vriend	Harold G. Vriend	1990	5
412 6/8	51 2/8	50 7/8	40 6/8	6 4/8	6 4/8	21 6/8	5 6/8	19 1/8	1/8	15	25	Kechika Range, B.C.	Tom Andres	Tom Andres	1991	6
412	47 7/8	52 4/8	40	6 5/8	6 7/8	17 7/8	16 1/8	12 4/8	5 1/8	14	14	Cassiar Mts., B.C.	Peter E. Paulos	Peter E. Paulos	1988	7
411 7/8	40 1/8	43 3/8	39 1/8	7 4/8	8 1/8	18	13 6/8	13 1/8	8 5/8	18	21	Fire Lake, Yukon	James C. Wondzell	James C. Wondzell	1991	8
411 2/8	49 2/8	49 1/8	30 7/8	6	6 2/8	17 2/8	18 3/8	11 6/8	11 2/8	21	20	Watson Lake, Yukon	John Csepp	John Csepp	1988	9
407 7/8	50 1/8	45 2/8	36 5/8	7 3/8	8	17 1/8	13 4/8	10	9 2/8	20	19	Mackenzie Mts., N.W.T.	John K. Miller	John K. Miller	1989	10
407 6/8	48 6/8	49 2/8	37 3/8	6 4/8	6 5/8	15 4/8	18 7/8	10 2/8	18 6/8	20	20	Buttle Creek, Yukon	Roy McLeod	Kerry Wagantall	1991	11
406 5/8	47 5/8	45 3/8	36 5/8	8 3/8	8 2/8	6 7/8	17	1/8	14 4/8	17	14	Tay Lake, Yukon	Ray J. Dennehy	Ray J. Dennehy	1988	12
404 2/8	51 1/8	51 3/8	36 4/8	6	6	21 5/8	10 3/8	17 5/8	1/8	22	22	Mackenzie Mts., N.W.T.	Michael B. Murphy	Michael B. Murphy	1991	13
404	41	40	39 1/8	6 2/8	5 4/8	17	18	12 1/8	15 6/8	14	22	Teslin Lake, B.C.	Peter Hohn	Peter Hohn	1988	14
403 3/8	46	45 4/8	32 5/8	7 1/8	7	15 7/8	16	12 3/8	9 4/8	15	17	Ross River, B.C.	Gail W. Holderman	Gail W. Holderman	1989	15
402	42 7/8	42 4/8	35 6/8	7 1/8	6 5/8	18 4/8	12 7/8	11 4/8	1/8	14	19	Tuya Lake, B.C.	Robert G. Frew	Robert G. Frew	1988	16
400	42 1/8	41	29	7	7	16 1/8	14 2/8	10 4/8	6 1/8	17	22	Little Rancheria River, B.C.	Allan Edwards	Allan Edwards	1988	17
399 7/8	43 2/8	41	37 5/8	7 1/8	6 5/8	18 3/8	18 6/8	12 3/8	16 2/8	16	15	Mackenzie Mts., N.W.T.	James J. McBride	James J. McBride	1989	18
397 3/8	50	49	35	6 7/8	6 5/8	17	17 3/8	8 6/8	11 6/8	17	15	Mackenzie Mts., N.W.T.	Bob Donnelly	Bob Donnelly	1988	19
396 7/8	44 1/8	43 5/8	35 3/8	6 7/8	6 7/8	17	15 1/8	3 2/8	12 5/8	21	15	Divide Lake, N.W.T.	Delbert E. Rieckers	Delbert E. Rieckers	1990	20
395 7/8	48 3/8	48 4/8	37 6/8	8 1/8	8 3/8	15 2/8	17 4/8	1/8	10 4/8	17	15	O'Grady Lake, N.W.T.	Ralph Fleegle	R. Fleegle & D. Fleegle	1988	21
394 6/8	45 4/8	46 4/8	36 4/8	6 4/8	6 4/8	17 7/8	16 1/8	6 3/8	14 4/8	16	15	Keele River, N.W.T.	Anthony T. Brazil	Anthony T. Brazil	1991	22
394 2/8	51 1/8	52	41 1/8	7 2/8	7 6/8	10 5/8	19 1/8	13 2/8	1/8	21	13	Cry Lake, B.C.	Ritchey Elliott	Catherine Mulvahill	1987	23
393 6/8	45 4/8	43 4/8	39	7 6/8	6 6/8	14 4/8	15 7/8	8 7/8	12	16	17	Mackenzie Mts., N.W.T.	Steven S. Bruggeman	Steven S. Bruggeman	1988	24
393 4/8	47 3/8	42 6/8	38 2/8	6 6/8	6 6/8	15 4/8	2 2/8	8 7/8	1/8	15	18	Mackenzie Mts., N.W.T.	James K. McCasland	James K. McCasland	1988	24
393 3/8	47 1/8	50 4/8	42 1/8	5 3/8	5 4/8	18 3/8	10 6/8	11	1 5/8	16	18	Mackenzie Mts., N.W.T.	Lonnie L. Ritchey	Lonnie L. Ritchey	1990	26
392 2/8	41 1/8	46	29 6/8	7 5/8	6 7/8	3	16 3/8	1/8	13	20	14	Fire Lake, Yukon	Michael L. Haydock	Michael L. Haydock	1989	27
391 1/8	48	46 2/8	37 1/8	6 6/8	6 3/8	19	17	6	10 4/8	16	15	Cassiar Mts., B.C.	Stan McKay	Stan McKay	1990	28

391 1/8	49 1/8	47	36 4/8	6 6/8	6 7/8	14 6/8	13 3/8	8 7/8	2 5/8	16	17	Lonesome Creek, N.W.T.	Frank J. Kukurin	Frank J. Kukurin	1989	29
390 4/8	57 3/8	57 6/8	42 1/8	5 7/8	5 7/8	2 4/8	19	11 1/8	12 2/8	15	17	Mountain River, N.W.T.	Jack R. Cook	Jack R. Cook	1981	30
390	56 7/8	58 3/8	42 3/8	6 3/8	7	18 6/8	5 3/8	11 1/8	1/8	15	18	Mackenzie Mts., N.W.T.	John R. Young	John R. Young	1985	31
385 2/8	49 7/8	49 4/8	42 3/8	6 3/8	6 2/8	18 1/8	19 2/8	12 6/8	6 2/8	15	14	Plateau Creek, B.C.	Steven M. Herndon	Steven M. Herndon	1990	32
384 2/8	43 3/8	46 6/8	39 4/8	6 6/8	6 6/8	15 4/8	15	6 4/8	11 7/8	14	18	Mackenzie Mts., N.W.T.	Spencer J. Vaa	Spencer J. Vaa	1991	33
382 2/8	54 7/8	55 5/8	35 3/8	5 3/8	5 5/8	17 1/8	4 6/8	13 3/8	1/8	18	12	Cranswick River, N.W.T.	William S. Perry	William S. Perry	1988	34
381 7/8	42 1/8	40 4/8	21 2/8	5 3/8	5 3/8	17	16 1/8	2 7/8	15 5/8	18	23	Divide Lake, N.W.T.	Robert P. Neville	Robert P. Neville	1991	35
378 2/8	45 4/8	46 7/8	37 4/8	6 6/8	7 1/8	18 1/8	9 5/8	12 1/8	1/8	21	19	Mackenzie Mts., N.W.T.	Robert G. Burkhouse	Robert G. Burkhouse	1990	36
377 6/8	52 4/8	51	35 4/8	5 7/8	5 7/8	2	16 1/8	1/8	9 4/8	17	18	Mackenzie Mts., N.W.T.	Wayne H. Kinglsey	Wayne H. Kinglsey	1990	37
377 2/8	45 4/8	45 2/8	32 7/8	6 5/8	6 5/8	18 6/8	15 7/8	8 2/8	5 4/8	15	13	Mountain Lake, N.W.T.	Everett C. Ramsay	Everett C. Ramsay	1990	38
377 1/8	45 7/8	47 7/8	35 7/8	6 7/8	6 4/8	15 1/8	8 7/8	10 4/8		20	16	Mountain River, N.W.T.	Walter A. Tilley	Walter A. Tilley	1991	39
376 7/8	41 1/8	40 6/8	27 3/8	6 4/8	6 5/8	17	16 4/8	15 2/8	3 4/8	21	21	Divide Lake, N.W.T.	John T. Wenders	John T. Wenders	1989	40
373 1/8	49 3/8	50 4/8	35 6/8	6 5/8	6 2/8	17	17 4/8	8 1/8	9	21	13	Ice Lakes, Yukon	Robert W. Tekulve	Robert W. Tekulve	1990	41
371 4/8	48 6/8	44 6/8	34 4/8	7 1/8	7 4/8	9 3/8	18 2/8	1 7/8	14 4/8	12	15	Pelly Mts., Yukon	Roger H. Wotring	Roger H. Wotring	1990	42
371 4/8	48 2/8	45 3/8	38 1/8	5 6/8	6	2 6/8	16 1/8	1/8	10 3/8	13	15	Mackenzie Mts., N.W.T.	George Skaggs	George Skaggs	1991	42
369 1/8	49 2/8	50 5/8	32 6/8	6 6/8	6 4/8	18 1/8	1 5/8	14 2/8	1/8	11	13	Einarson Lake, Yukon	Timothy K. Rushing	Timothy K. Rushing	1989	44
365 7/8	47 3/8	49 6/8	42 6/8	7 3/8	7	14 6/8	3 1/8	6 3/8	1/8	23	10	Divide Lake, N.W.T.	Donald P. Lamm	Donald P. Lamm	1989	45
360	41 1/8	40 3/8	25 7/8	7 3/8	7 6/8	18 5/8	10 7/8	15 1/8	1/8	18	14	Lincoln Lake, B.C.	Phillip D. Wagner	Phillip D. Wagner	1991	46
438 4/8*	43	42 2/8	33 2/8	6 5/8	7 1/8	19 4/8	18 1/8	14 3/8	5 2/8	18	24	Mackenzie Mts., N.W.T.	Monte Sorgard	Monte Sorgard	1988	

* Final Score subject to revision by additional verifying measurements.

Woodland Caribou

Rangifer tarandus caribou

Minimum Score 265

World's Record 419-5/8

Woodland caribou includes trophies from Nova Scotia, New Brunswick, and Newfoundland.

Score	Length of Main Beam R.	L.	Inside Spread	Circumference at Smallest Place Between Brow and Bez Points R.	L.	Length of Brow Points R.	L.	Width of Brow Points R.	L.	Number of Points R.	L.	Locality Killed	By Whom Killed	Owner	Date Killed	Rank
341 2/8	37 6/8	38 1/8	31	5 3/8	5 3/8	16 4/8	18 4/8	11	17	15	20	Grey River, Nfld.	Karl Dore	Karl Dore	1984	1
338 3/8	37 7/8	41 3/8	35	4 7/8	5 1/8	15 2/8	14 7/8	13 1/8	12 3/8	17	12	Avalon Pen., Nfld.	Picked Up	Gerard Beaulieu	PR 1970	2
322 1/8	40 7/8	42 5/8	30 4/8	6	6 1/8	18	14 7/8	14 6/8	10 7/8	15	12	Avalon Pen., Nfld.	Unknown	Gerard Beaulieu	PR 1991	3
315 1/8	39 1/8	36	33 6/8	5 2/8	5	15 1/8	15 2/8	12 7/8	10 1/8	15	13	Hinds Plains, Nfld.	Picked Up	Gerard Beaulieu	1977	4
314 2/8	47 7/8	47 3/8	24 7/8	5 7/8	5 7/8	12 7/8	13 1/8	9 7/8	3	13	12	Mt. Howley, Nfld.	Picked Up	Tom Rose	1988	5
305 7/8	38 1/8	39 7/8	32 3/8	5	5	2	16 1/8	1/8	13 6/8	15	18	Grey River, Nfld.	Jeffrey J. Eichhorst	Jeffrey J. Eichhorst	1980	6
305 5/8	36 4/8	33	25 5/8	4 5/8	4 6/8	13 1/8	13	11 7/8	10 6/8	17	17	Long Range Mts., Nfld.	Collins F. Kellogg, Sr.	Collins F. Kellogg, Sr.	1989	7
304	38	40	33 5/8	5 1/8	5 2/8	12 1/8	12 2/8	4 4/8	10 6/8	13	14	Avalon Pen., Nfld.	Unknown	Gerard Beaulieu	PR 1991	8
301 1/8	39 6/8	40 6/8	29 1/8	5 3/8	5	13 3/8	13 3/8	8 3/8	12 5/8	11	14	Parsons Pond, Nfld.	Gerard Beaulieu	Gerard Beaulieu	1991	9
289 2/8	35 5/8	34 4/8	30 2/8	5 5/8	5 7/8	13	15 4/8	8	10 4/8	14	18	Goose Pond, Nfld.	C.A. Banfield	C.A. Banfield	1989	10
286 6/8	35 3/8	33	27 3/8	5 2/8	5 5/8	13 5/8	14 3/8	10 4/8	11 3/8	12	16	Dashwoods Pond, Nfld.	Kerry Kammer	Kerry Kammer	1990	11
276 5/8	36 5/8	38	33 5/8	5 2/8	5 2/8	13 1/8	15 1/8	7 7/8	8 4/8	9	15	Long Range Mts., Nfld.	Jerald E. Mason	Jerald E. Mason	1991	12
270 2/8	28	26 5/8	25 3/8	5 6/8	6 2/8	9 6/8	1 7/8	4 5/8	1/8	15	15	LaPoile, Nfld.	William T. Bohensky	William T. Bohensky	1986	13
268 7/8	33 2/8	27 3/8	27	5 3/8	8 6/8	11 1/8	10 4/8	7 7/8	7 1/8	14	19	Shanadithit Brook, Nfld.	Stan R. Godfrey	Stan R. Godfrey	1989	14

Barren Ground Caribou

Rangifer tarandus granti

Minimum Score 375

Barren ground caribou includes trophies from Alaska, northern Yukon Territory, Saskatchewan, Manitoba, and Ontario.

Score	Length of Main Beam R.	L.	Inside Spread	Circumference at Smallest Place Between Brow and Bez Points R.	L.	Length of Brow Points R.	L.	Width of Brow Points R.	L.	Number of Points R.	L.	Locality Killed	By Whom Killed	Owner	Date Killed	Rank
440	50	50 1/8	41 3/8	6 1/8	6 5/8	17 5/8	16 1/8	12 5/8	10 6/8	23	30	Mulchatna River, Alaska	Ted J. Forsi	Ted J. Forsi	1988	1
434 6/8	53 2/8	51 5/8	35 2/8	6	6 2/8	24 6/8	11 4/8	14 7/8	1/8	30	16	Alinchak Bay, Alaska	Rodney R. Havens	Rodney R. Havens	1991	2
433 4/8	50 2/8	50 7/8	33 5/8	6 6/8	6 1/8	19 1/8	22 7/8	10	14 5/8	16	21	Seventy Mile River, Alaska	Bronk Jorgensen	Bronk Jorgensen	1989	3
432 1/8	54	53 3/8	49 7/8	6	5 7/8	10 1/8	22 3/8	1/8	15 5/8	15	25	Wide Bay, Alaska	Roy C. Jablonski	Roy C. Jablonski	1990	4
429 6/8	51 1/8	49 7/8	40 3/8	8 6/8	8 7/8	14 3/8	14 6/8	22 1/8	9 6/8	20	16	Mulchatna River, Alaska	William Leffingwell	William Leffingwell	1990	5
429 4/8	54 2/8	54 4/8	42 6/8	5 7/8	6	17 6/8	15 6/8	10 2/8	7	17	17	Mulchatna River, Alaska	Bruce C. Wassom	Bruce C. Wassom	1991	6
429	50 3/8	51 6/8	48 6/8	5 4/8	6	18 6/8	17 7/8	8 6/8	10 3/8	19	18	Pinochle Creek, Alaska	William B. Ripley	William B. Ripley	1989	7
428 1/8	54 5/8	54 3/8	44 2/8	5 7/8	5 7/8	20 1/8	20 1/8	13 3/8	14 4/8	16	18	Tutna Lake, Alaska	Robert W. Roessel	Robert W. Roessel	1987	8
427 4/8	57 2/8	53 7/8	42 7/8	7 4/8	7 3/8	21 2/8	18 2/8	10 6/8	10 4/8	17	17	Aniak River, Alaska	Lad R. Neilson	Lad R. Neilson	1991	9
426	54 2/8	58 2/8	40 6/8	5 6/8	5 4/8	2 7/8	18	1/8	13 6/8	27	18	Bear Creek, Alaska	Douglas E. Christiansen	Douglas E. Christiansen	1988	10
426	52 3/8	53	36 3/8	7 1/8	6 6/8	16 1/8	7	11 3/8	1/8	20	25	Hart River, Yukon	Peter C. Elarde, Jr.	Peter C. Elarde, Jr.	1990	10
425 3/8	49 4/8	50 3/8	39 2/8	5 6/8	5 5/8	19 4/8	16 1/8	6 6/8	9 5/8	15	16	Taylor Mts., Alaska	Val B. Jones	Val B. Jones	1990	12
424 7/8	53 7/8	54 6/8	41 6/8	7	6 7/8	21 7/8	18 7/8	11	13 7/8	14	13	Post River, Alaska	Roger E. Austin	Roger E. Austin	1988	13
423 7/8	57 1/8	57	41 5/8	5 6/8	5 4/8	11 4/8	19 3/8	1/8	17 7/8	23	17	Mulchatna River, Alaska	Monte R. Ford	Monte R. Ford	1988	14
423 6/8	53 4/8	52 1/8	39 3/8	6 2/8	6 4/8	18 4/8	18 4/8	8 1/8	14 4/8	22	18	Port Heiden, Alaska	James A. Prince, Jr.	James A. Prince, Jr.	1988	15
422 3/8	47	52 3/8	49	7 3/8	6	17 3/8		14 6/8		16	27	Hoholitna River, Alaska	Bradley A. Finch	Bradley A. Finch	1990	16
421 7/8	50 1/8	50 5/8	36 6/8	6 6/8	7 5/8	16 5/8	15 7/8	11 3/8	1 4/8	15	20	Mosquito Creek, Alaska	Tom Teague	Tom Teague	1989	17
421 6/8	50 2/8	50 4/8	38 2/8	5 7/8	5 5/8	3 5/8	16 6/8	1	14 3/8	12	21	Cinder River, Alaska	Jerry A. Wilkinson	Jerry A. Wilkinson	1972	18
418	48	47 2/8	39 4/8	5 2/8	5 4/8	15 2/8	22 4/8	4 5/8	14 1/8	17	21	Becharof Lake, Alaska	Robert D. Lewallen	Robert D. Lewallen	1989	19
417 7/8	52 6/8	54 5/8	45 5/8	6 4/8	5 7/8	16 4/8	20 6/8	1/8	13 7/8	23	17	Shotgun Creek, Alaska	Norman C. Wilslef	Norman C. Wilslef	1989	20
417 6/8	57 4/8	57	50 1/8	6 2/8	6 4/8	18 5/8	16 4/8	11 3/8	7 7/8	16	13	Nushagak River, Alaska	John M. Glover	John M. Glover	1988	21
415 7/8	64	63 1/8	45 4/8	6	6 2/8	17 4/8	21 1/8	8	10 7/8	19	12	Becharof Lake, Alaska	Alfred T. Bachman	Alfred T. Bachman	1989	22
414 3/8	52 2/8	50 3/8	42 6/8	5 6/8	6 2/8	18 2/8	18 1/8	11 1/8	6 3/8	16	17	Tutna Lake, Alaska	Jim S. Campbell	Jim S. Campbell	1987	23
414 2/8	53 4/8	53 6/8	36 1/8	6 5/8	5 6/8	14 4/8	14 2/8	15 2/8	5 7/8	13	14	Taylor Mts., Alaska	Robert J. Allen	Robert J. Allen	1989	24
414 1/8	52 5/8	50 6/8	37 7/8	6 3/8	5 7/8	19	15 3/8	6 6/8	9 3/8	21	18	Iliamna Lake, Alaska	Richard J. Sands	Richard J. Sands	1989	25
414	48 6/8	48 1/8	39 7/8	6 3/8	6 3/8	17 1/8	21	14 2/8	13 6/8	14	20	Johnson River, Alaska	Donald W. Bunselmeier	Donald W. Bunselmeier	1988	26
412 3/8	44 2/8	44 5/8	30 3/8	4 7/8	5 7/8	17 7/8	19	4 4/8	17 7/8	20	21	Squirrel River, Alaska	Jack D. Adams	Jack D. Adams	1991	27

Barren Ground Caribou - *Continued*

Score	Length of Main Beam R.	L.	Inside Spread	Circumference at Smallest Place Between Brow and Bez Points R.	L.	Length of Brow Points R.	L.	Width of Brow Points R.	L.	Number of Points R.	L.	Locality Killed	By Whom Killed	Owner	Date Killed	Rank
410	51 7/8	50 7/8	40 2/8	5 5/8	5 7/8	19 4/8	19 6/8	7 5/8	11 1/8	17	18	Cinder River, Alaska	Joe B. Owen	Joe B. Owen	1990	28
409 5/8	48	47 1/8	35 6/8	6 3/8	7 4/8	13 7/8	18 4/8	11 1/8	13 1/8	19	25	Alaska Range, Alaska	James C. Forrest	James C. Forrest	1988	29
409 5/8	44 5/8	48 1/8	28 1/8	6	6 1/8	17 6/8	17 7/8	14 7/8	9 2/8	23	23	Hicks Lake, Alaska	Raymond S. George	Raymond S. George	1990	29
409 2/8	51 3/8	56 7/8	39	6 1/8	6	29 1/8	6 6/8	15 7/8	1	22	13	King Salmon, Alaska	Jerry Ida	Jerry Ida	1990	31
409 1/8	48 2/8	51 5/8	43 6/8	6	6 1/8	18 5/8	19 1/8	14 7/8	5 4/8	20	17	Iliamna Lake, Alaska	Picked Up	Richard A. Link	1990	32
408	46 1/8	48 2/8	32 4/8	6 2/8	6 2/8	15 5/8	16 6/8	10	13 7/8	25	30	Aniak River, Alaska	Renn G. Neilson	Renn G. Neilson	1991	33
407 7/8	50 6/8	47 1/8	38 3/8	6 3/8	6 2/8	19 4/8	20 3/8	4 2/8	13 5/8	17	17	Post Lake, Alaska	Lyle D. Fett	Lyle D. Fett	1988	34
407 7/8	48 1/8	50 4/8	42 7/8	5 6/8	5 7/8	19 5/8	19 1/8	12 3/8	9 6/8	18	18	Mulchatna River, Alaska	Harold L. Biggs	Harold L. Biggs	1990	34
407 6/8	55 7/8	54 5/8	30 5/8	6	6 1/8	16 7/8	18 1/8	12 2/8	17 3/8	18	25	Old Man Creek, Alaska	Gary A. French	Gary A. French	1991	36
407 2/8	53 2/8	52 2/8	44 1/8	6 2/8	6 2/8	12 3/8	19 5/8	1/8	18 4/8	25	14	Brooks Range, Alaska	Carol Kilian	Carol Kilian	1987	37
407	51 3/8	49 2/8	42	5 5/8	6 1/8	20 5/8	19 3/8	11 3/8	13 3/8	13	16	Dog Salmon River, Alaska	Jack A. Wilkinson	Jack A. Wilkinson	1989	38
406 1/8	56 5/8	56 5/8	51 2/8	6 2/8	5 5/8	19 1/8		15		15	16	Kvichak River, Alaska	John J. Jondal	John J. Jondal	1991	39
406	49 5/8	50 6/8	50 6/8	6 2/8	5 5/8	18	7 3/8	13 2/8	5	23	17	Alaska Pen., Alaska	Harace R. Morgan	Harace R. Morgan	1980	40
405 6/8	53 7/8	52	43	6 2/8	7 4/8	18 7/8	19	17 1/8	12	18	16	Taylor Mts., Alaska	John Burcham	John Burcham	1988	41
405 2/8	52 2/8	55 1/8	37 2/8	5 6/8	6 1/8	3	22 5/8	1/8	17	23	13	Lake Clark, Alaska	Jeff LaBour	Jeff LaBour	1991	42
404 7/8	52 4/8	49 3/8	41 2/8	8 1/8	7 6/8	17 4/8	17 7/8	14	7 4/8	15	14	Iliamna Lake, Alaska	M.E. Wackler	M.E. Wackler	1990	43
404 6/8	53 6/8	51 7/8	46	6 3/8	7 6/8	16 2/8	11 5/8	11 5/8	7 7/8	17	12	Mulchatna River, Alaska	Daryl Stanley	Daryl Stanley	1988	44
404 4/8	50 3/8	50 2/8	41 7/8	5 6/8	5 2/8	14 6/8	17 4/8	9 2/8	12 1/8	23	22	Becharof Lake, Alaska	Bill Cade	Bill Cade	1984	45
404 4/8	48 2/8	50 7/8	44 1/8	6 4/8	6 1/8	14	16 7/8	7 7/8	11	15	17	Moose Creek, Alaska	Dee Sanderson	Chuck J. Sanderson	1988	45
404 4/8	48 7/8	45 6/8	31 7/8	7 1/8	7 2/8	14 2/8	15 4/8	11 6/8	1/8	19	17	Chilchitna River, Alaska	Mark S. Woltanski	Mark S. Woltanski	1988	45
404 1/8	53 5/8	51 6/8	39 6/8	7 3/8	6 7/8	15 4/8	18 1/8	1/8	15 5/8	19	24	Kvichak River, Alaska	John Jondal	John Jondal	1988	48
403 6/8	51	49 6/8	46 3/8	6 2/8	6 6/8	16 5/8	18 4/8	7 2/8	8 4/8	15	19	Alaska Pen., Alaska	J. Leslie Rainey	J. Leslie Rainey	1989	49
402 4/8	47 6/8	49 6/8	44 4/8	6 4/8	6 1/8	17 5/8	17 5/8	10 4/8	13	15	14	Moose Lake, Alaska	Walter R. Willey	Walter R. Willey	1991	50
400 5/8	58	59	43 3/8	5 3/8	5	19 3/8	16 5/8	10 4/8	11 1/8	18	20	Cinder River, Alaska	Brian Peterson	Brian Peterson	1988	51
399 3/8	55 3/8	53 1/8	43 1/8	6 2/8	6 2/8	17 6/8	17 5/8	7	10 5/8	13	16	Post River, Alaska	Roy D. Wallis	Roy D. Wallis	1990	52
397 4/8	50 5/8	50	32	5 3/8	5 2/8	19	20 6/8	14 5/8	2 3/8	14	21	Talkeetna Mts., Alaska	Stephen E. Sherman	Stephen E. Sherman	1965	53
394 7/8	51 1/8	53 6/8	41 3/8	5 5/8	5 2/8	7 2/8	19 1/8	1/8	13 4/8	21	19	Tutna Lake, Alaska	Patricia H. Abel	Patricia H. Abel	1983	54
394 4/8	49 7/8	53 5/8	37 2/8	6 3/8	6 7/8	17 6/8	20 7/8	11 2/8	10 3/8	16	20	Lower Ugashik Lake, Alaska	Bruce M. Swanson	Bruce M. Swanson	1989	55

Score										No. Points	Locality	Hunter	Owner	Date Killed	Rank
393 5/8	52 5/8	54	42 3/8	7 5/8	7 3/8	7 5/8	12 4/8	17 7/8	1/8	19	Mulchatna River, Alaska	Debora D. Ford	Debora D. Ford	1988	56
393 4/8	50 3/8	52 5/8	42 6/8	6 6/8	7 2/8	6 6/8	13 6/8	19 4/8	13 1/8	17	King Salmon River, Alaska	Anthony J. Ripepi	Anthony J. Ripepi	1989	57
393 3/8	47 5/8	48 1/8	39 6/8	6 2/8	6 2/8	6 2/8	20 4/8	18	13 1/8	14	Dick Creek, Alaska	Scott A. Jordan	Scott A. Jordan	1989	58
391	53 5/8	53 4/8	26 7/8	6 7/8	6 7/8	6 7/8	14 3/8	17	6 7/8	17	Billy Creek, Alaska	James J. Potts	James J. Potts	1981	59
387 4/8	41 1/8	41	29 6/8	5 3/8	5 3/8	5 4/8	15	15 6/8	11	23	Hoholitna River, Alaska	Noel T. Schroeder	Noel T. Schroeder	1989	60
387 4/8	52 4/8	52	31 3/8	6 6/8	6 5/8	8 6/8	18	3	6/8	15	Alaska Range, Alaska	Lorraine K. Harrison	Lorraine K. Harrison	1991	61
385 6/8	50 4/8	49 5/8	40 7/8	6	6 1/8	6 1/8	15 3/8	15 4/8	14 5/8	17	Sharp Mt., Alaska	Robert F. Hart	Robert F. Hart	1990	62
384 6/8	50 2/8	48 1/8	38	5 7/8	5 4/8	5 4/8	16 4/8	2 7/8	1/8	18	Nushagak River, Alaska	Michael C. DeNeut	Michael C. DeNeut	1990	63
384	53	54 6/8	41 5/8	6 4/8	6 2/8	6 2/8	17 7/8	18 2/8	13 1/8	13	Kenai, Alaska	James E. Chapman	James E. Chapman	1990	64
383	41 2/8	40 3/8	29 6/8	7 1/8	7	7	17 3/8	2 7/8	12 7/8	15	Bonnet Plume River, Yukon	Donald J. Craite	Donald J. Craite	1991	65
382 1/8	55 3/8	56 1/8	38	7 1/8	6 4/8	6 4/8	16 3/8	17 5/8	13	17	Squirrel River, Alaska	Brett J. Kmiecik	Brett J. Kmiecik	1988	66
382 1/8	51 1/8	52 1/8	49 2/8	6 4/8	6	6	20	2 6/8	13	12	Beaver Creek, Alaska	Michael J. Masters	Michael J. Masters	1990	66
381 7/8	49 1/8	52 1/8	36 7/8	6 1/8	6 3/8	6 3/8	13 2/8	12	11	14	Cinder River, Alaska	Richard C. Klimes	Richard C. Klimes	1987	68
380 5/8	61 2/8	62 2/8	36 5/8	5 5/8	5 4/8	5 4/8	15 3/8	19 1/8	7 1/8	13	Naknek River, Alaska	Glenn E. Hisey	Glenn E. Hisey	1984	69
380 2/8	58	51 2/8	46	4 6/8	5	5	11 4/8	18 1/8	1/8	11	Alaska Pen., Alaska	Norman A. Spring	Norman A. Spring	1989	70
380 1/8	52 7/8	53 1/8	30 5/8	6 2/8	6	6	15 2/8	15 7/8	8 2/8	15	Brooks Range, Alaska	Stan J. Neitling, Jr.	Stan J. Neitling, Jr.	1989	71
375 4/8	49 6/8	49 3/8	28 2/8	6 3/8	6 5/8	6 5/8	15 1/8	21 1/8	16 2/8	25	Stony River, Alaska	James E. Spaide	James E. Spaide	1989	72
375	49 4/8	48 3/8	40 7/8	5 4/8	5 5/8	5 5/8	16	5 3/8	1/8	15	Old Man Creek, Alaska	Roger French	Roger French	1991	73
464 6/8*	54 1/8	56 1/8	34 5/8	7 6/8	6 6/8	6 1/8	19 4/8	19 6/8	11 4/8	17	Sharp Mt., Alaska	Frank Lobitz	Frank Lobitz	1988	
434 2/8*	49	50 2/8	49	6	6 1/8	6 1/8	19 7/8	22 3/8	4 5/8	17	Mulchatna River, Alaska	C. Wayne Dolezal	C. Wayne Dolezal	1991	

* Final Score subject to revision by additional verifying measurements.

Central Canada Barren Ground Caribou

Rangifer tarandus groenlandicus

Minimum Score 330   New World's Record 412-6/8

Central Canada barren ground caribou occur on Baffin Island and the mainland of N.W.T., with geographic boundaries of the Mackenzie River to the west; the north edge of the continent to the north (excluding any islands except Baffin Island); Hudson's Bay to the east; and the southern boundary of N.W.T. to the south.

Score	Length of Main Beam R.	L.	Inside Spread	Circumference at Smallest Place Between Brow and Bez Points R.	L.	Length of Brow Points R.	L.	Width of Brow Points R.	L.	Number of Points R.	L.	Locality Killed	By Whom Killed	Owner	Date Killed	Rank
412 6/8	50 2/8	49 3/8	36 2/8	4 5/8	4 6/8	18 6/8	20	6 3/8	15 7/8	19	17	MacKay Lake, N.W.T.	James H. Wooten	James H. Wooten	1989	1
401 1/8	53	52 5/8	40	5 6/8	5 6/8	17	17 1/8	12	11	15	14	Courageous Lake, N.W.T.	Richard B. Limbach	Richard B. Limbach	1989	2
389 7/8	43 7/8	53 3/8	39 4/8	4 7/8	5	14	12 4/8	8 5/8	5 5/8	16	15	Desteffany Lake, N.W.T.	Gordon W. Russell	Mike Howden	1989	3
386 3/8	43 1/8	42 6/8	38	6 1/8	5 3/8	15 3/8	14 7/8	11 1/8	9 4/8	20	18	Tsoko Lake, N.W.T.	Picked Up	Roger A. Hansen	1989	4
384 3/8	49	50 2/8	39	5	5 3/8	17	14 6/8	12 5/8	13 4/8	21	21	Lake Providence, N.W.T.	John Branneky	John Branneky	1991	5
383 7/8	50 4/8	50 2/8	31 4/8	6 2/8	7 2/8	9 4/8	15 4/8	2/8	15	28	16	Rendez-vous Lake, N.W.T.	Michael L. Chaffin	Michael L. Chaffin	1988	6
383 6/8	50 3/8	50 3/8	40 7/8	5 2/8	5 3/8	18 5/8	17 4/8	6 2/8	12 6/8	17	14	Rendez-vous Lake, N.W.T.	Shawn R. Andres	Shawn R. Andres	1991	7
383 1/8	55	54	36 2/8	4 6/8	5	16 5/8	2 4/8	12 7/8	1/8	12	17	Little Marten Lake, N.W.T.	Roger J. Larson	Roger J. Larson	1989	8
382 4/8	53 4/8	55 4/8	30 2/8	6	5 5/8	15	13 5/8	7	10 4/8	15	15	Desteffany Lake, N.W.T.	Steve MacKenzie	Steve MacKenzie	1989	9
382 6/8	47 3/8	47 3/8	32 2/8	4 6/8	5 1/8	18 3/8	19 4/8	5 6/8	14 1/8	18	17	Rendez-vous Lake, N.W.T.	James C. Johnson	James C. Johnson	1990	10
382 3/8	49 7/8	44 6/8	31 3/8	5	5 6/8	13 7/8	13 2/8	13 3/8	12 4/8	26	20	Courageous Lake, N.W.T.	Patrick T. Stanosheck	Patrick T. Stanosheck	1989	11
381 4/8	51 4/8	52 7/8	33 3/8	5	5 2/8	17 4/8	19	12 1/8	16 1/8	22	17	Lake Providence, N.W.T.	Vicki L. St. Germaine	Vicki L. St. Germaine	1989	12
381	52	54 1/8	35 4/8	6	6 2/8	15 6/8	19	11 1/8	15 7/8	17	15	Little Marten Lake, N.W.T.	Scott D. Fink	Scott D. Fink	1988	13
380 6/8	48 2/8	49 1/8	34 5/8	5	4 7/8	15 2/8	16	12 3/8	16 2/8	20	17	Courageous Lake, N.W.T.	Brian G. Edgerton	Brian G. Edgerton	1990	14
380 2/8	49 2/8	50 1/8	40	6	6 2/8	18 6/8	16	15 1/8	3 1/8	15	19	MacKay Lake, N.W.T.	Richard B. Martin	Richard B. Martin	1990	15
379 4/8	51 4/8	50	36 3/8	5 1/8	5 2/8	19 4/8	18 6/8	16 6/8	13 2/8	16	16	Courageous Lake, N.W.T.	Gordon B. Knipe	Gordon B. Knipe	1989	16
379 1/8	53 1/8	49 6/8	35	6	6 1/8	18 1/8	16 7/8	15 2/8	7 3/8	13	16	Courageous Lake, N.W.T.	Lester I. Pearmine	Lester I. Pearmine	1989	16
378 4/8	50 4/8	52 4/8	38 2/8	5 2/8	5 1/8	15 4/8	14	9 3/8	9 1/8	17	12	Courageous Lake, N.W.T.	James A. Erickson	James A. Erickson	1989	18
376 4/8	48 5/8	46 6/8	37 7/8	6	6 2/8	15 7/8		11		19	15	MacKay Lake, N.W.T.	David Emken	David Emken	1990	19
374 7/8	57 1/8	55 3/8	41 2/8	5 7/8	5 7/8	22 2/8	2 7/8	19 1/8	1/8	13	17	Little Marten Lake, N.W.T.	Scott D. Fink	Scott D. Fink	1988	20

Score												Locality	Hunter	Owner	Date	Rank
373 5/8	52 5/8	53 4/8	43 3/8	6	6 3/8	11	11 5/8	18 4/8	17 6/8	15	13	Courageous Lake, N.W.T.	Wayne H. Kingsley	Wayne H. Kingsley	1989	21
373 1/8	52 1/8	53 6/8	38 7/8	5 2/8	5	9 4/8	11 7/8	15 5/8	15 4/8	14	14	Point Lake, N.W.T.	Gary A. Bingham	Gary A. Bingham	1989	22
372 7/8	56 3/8	56 4/8	47 5/8	5 3/8	5 6/8	13 6/8	1/8	17 5/8	2 4/8	14	13	Little Marten Lake, N.W.T.	Ronald V. Hurlburt	Ronald V. Hurlburt	1989	23
372 5/8	48 2/8	48 7/8	32 2/8	5 3/8	5	12	8	15 5/8	16 5/8	18	16	Courageous Lake, N.W.T.	Charles L. Cleis	Charles L. Cleis	1990	24
372 2/8	48 2/8	47 3/8	36 1/8	5 1/8	5 1/8	9 4/8	11 6/8	14 6/8	15 7/8	19	16	MacKay Lake, N.W.T.	Ronald L. Chapman	Ronald L. Chapman	1990	25
371 7/8	49	48 3/8	32 6/8	4 7/8	5 1/8	6/8	14 6/8	5 6/8	17 6/8	16	22	Little Marten Lake, N.W.T.	David J. Richey, Sr.	David J. Richey, Sr.	1990	26
371 1/8	50 3/8	48 4/8	44	5 6/8	5 7/8	11 5/8	2 5/8	17 1/8	15 4/8	15	15	MacKay Lake, N.W.T.	Dan Brockman	Dan Brockman	1990	27
371	47 3/8	43 5/8	36 5/8	4 6/8	4 6/8	14 6/8	14 6/8	17 1/8	17 1/8	19	17	MacKay Lake, N.W.T.	Phillip Henry	Phillip Henry	1988	28
370 7/8	55 5/8	57 3/8	32 7/8	5 7/8	5 7/8	9 4/8	11 7/8	17	19 7/8	16	17	Muskox Lake, N.W.T.	Neill A. Murphy	Fred Freidmeyer	1978	29
368 7/8	56	56 4/8	43 7/8	5 6/8	6	6/8	13 6/8	10 7/8	16 5/8	16	17	Courageous Lake, N.W.T.	Kent T. Michaelson	Kent T. Michaelson	1988	30
368 7/8	58 4/8	56 1/8	36 4/8	5 2/8	5 3/8	14	14	16 1/8	17 3/8	17	21	Courageous Lake, N.W.T.	Richard Fitch	Richard Fitch	1989	30
368 3/8	48	49 4/8	29 4/8	10	7 1/8	1/8	11 4/8	10 7/8	16 1/8	12	15	Courageous Lake, N.W.T.	Kent T. Michaelson	Kent T. Michaelson	1988	32
367	51	49 4/8	35 7/8	5	5 6/8	12 2/8	4 3/8	16 7/8	15 2/8	19	17	MacKay Lake, N.W.T.	James L. White	James L. White	1989	33
365 5/8	54 2/8	52 2/8	32 4/8	5	5 1/8	13 2/8	8 2/8	16 3/8	14 2/8	15	14	Little Marten Lake, N.W.T.	Ralph Madden	Ralph Madden	1989	34
365 2/8	48	46 3/8	28 4/8	5 6/8	5 5/8	17 3/8		17 1/8		26	23	Snare River, N.W.T.	William M. Leitner	William M. Leitner	1987	35
364 6/8	51 3/8	51 3/8	36 3/8	5 5/8	5 2/8	10		15 7/8		16	13	Point Lake, N.W.T.	Rodger E. Warwick	Rodger E. Warwick	1991	36
363 6/8	46 7/8	47 6/8	37 7/8	6 1/8	6 2/8	13 2/8	1/8	12 5/8	4 5/8	16	14	MacKay Lake, N.W.T.	Gary A. Jackson	Gary A. Jackson	1988	37
362 2/8	50 3/8	53 3/8	28 4/8	4 7/8	4 7/8	6 5/8	8	13 6/8	15 6/8	12	16	Courageous Lake, N.W.T.	Larry H. Beller	Larry H. Beller	1991	38
362	53 4/8	54	36 4/8	6	5 5/8	14	13 6/8	19	16 4/8	13	18	Little Marten Lake, N.W.T.	William H. Oliver	William H. Oliver	1990	39
361 2/8	53 6/8	53 6/8	41 2/8	5 1/8	4 7/8	14 5/8	1/8	17 2/8	9 2/8	14	10	Point Lake, N.W.T.	Neil Harles	Neil Harles	1991	40
361 1/8	51 2/8	51 5/8	31 7/8	5 7/8	6 2/8	13	10 4/8	17 6/8	16 2/8	18	11	Courageous Lake, N.W.T.	Paul E. Opfermann	Paul E. Opfermann	1988	41
360 3/8	49 4/8	50 3/8	38	5 1/8	4 5/8	14 4/8	18 3/8	18 7/8	19 6/8	19	16	Point Lake, N.W.T.	Sharon Ziegenhagen	Sharon Ziegenhagen	1988	42
360 2/8	52 3/8	53 2/8	33 5/8	5 1/8	5 2/8	7 7/8	13 7/8	17 2/8	19 1/8	13	15	Obstruction Rapids, N.W.T.	George Bishop	George Bishop	1989	43
359 6/8	47	46 2/8	39 6/8	5 1/8	5 2/8	1/8	5 2/8	2 5/8	15 4/8	13	17	Ellice River, N.W.T.	Gerald L. Warnock	Gerald L. Warnock	1988	44
357	49 3/8	48 2/8	28 6/8	5	5 5/8	5 2/8	16 1/8	13 1/8	18 2/8	16	21	MacKay Lake, N.W.T.	Robert C. Harrison	Robert C. Harrison	1987	45
356 5/8	47 7/8	45 3/8	33 6/8	5 7/8	5	6 4/8	12 2/8	19 7/8	18	15	16	Bathurst Inlet, N.W.T.	George R. Skaggs	George R. Skaggs	1988	46
356 5/8	51 2/8	49 2/8	36 7/8	5 4/8	5 3/8	1/8	16 1/8	8 1/8	18 2/8	16	13	Little Marten Lake, N.W.T.	Lloyd R. Broadwater	Lloyd R. Broadwater	1989	47
356 1/8	51	54 3/8	31 7/8	5 4/8	5 3/8	7 7/8	10 3/8	17	16 4/8	17	9	Little Marten Lake, N.W.T.	Barry J. Mitchell	Barry J. Mitchell	1988	48
355 5/8	48 6/8	51	30 2/8	4 5/8	5 3/8	1 2/8	14 4/8	17 3/8	20 7/8	14	15	Lake Providence, N.W.T.	Robert L. Kammerer	Robert L. Kammerer	1991	49
355 5/8	44 5/8	43 5/8	42 7/8	5	4 5/8	6 4/8	6 4/8	13 3/8	14 3/8	16	18	Rendez-vous Lake, N.W.T.	Shawn R. Andres	Shawn R. Andres	1991	50
353 2/8	51 5/8	51 5/8	32 7/8	6 3/8	6 4/8	11 5/8	11 1/8	16 1/8	16 2/8	16	21	Rendez-vous Lake, N.W.T.	Roy C. Ewen	Roy C. Ewen	1988	51

Central Canada Barren Ground Caribou - *Continued*

Score	Length of Main Beam R.	L.	Inside Spread	Circumference at Smallest Place Between Brow and Bez Points R.	L.	Length of Brow Points R.	L.	Width of Brow Points R.	L.	Number of Points R.	L.	Locality Killed	By Whom Killed	Owner	Date Killed	Rank
348 3/8	42 5/8	42 4/8	27 7/8	5 5/8	5 1/8	17 2/8	17 5/8	17 3/8	15 5/8	17	15	Rendez-vous Lake, N.W.T.	William Mitchell	William Mitchell	1991	52
348	53 1/8	48	38	5 4/8	5 4/8	18 2/8	2 6/8	16 7/8	1/8	17	15	MacKay Lake, N.W.T.	Fred S. Youngblood	Fred S. Youngblood	1989	53
347 1/8	40 7/8	42 4/8	37 1/8	5	5	18 1/8	4	15 4/8	1/8	17	20	Point Lake, N.W.T.	Sharon Ziegenhagen	Sharon Ziegenhagen	1988	54
346 7/8	49 4/8	50 2/8	35 3/8	4 6/8	4 5/8	17 1/8	16 2/8	12 3/8	11 7/8	18	15	Little Marten Lake, N.W.T.	Jack R. Cook	Jack R. Cook	1989	55
346 1/8	45	44 7/8	33 5/8	5	5 6/8	19 2/8	2 3/8	15 4/8	1/8	13	15	Big Lake, N.W.T.	Dan Murphy	Dan Murphy	1979	56
345 7/8	46 4/8	47 7/8	46 7/8	5 4/8	4 7/8	6 7/8	17 3/8	1/8	13 3/8	11	11	Lake Providence, N.W.T.	Wayne Stewart	Wayne Stewart	1991	57
345 2/8	44 5/8	43	33 3/8	4 4/8	5 5/8	13 1/8	12 6/8	7 6/8	5 4/8	14	17	MacKay Lake, N.W.T.	Thomas J. Reardon	Thomas J. Reardon	1987	58
345	47 4/8	47	31	5	5	6	19	1/8	15 7/8	10	17	MacKay Lake, N.W.T.	W.J. Burns	W.J. Burns	1991	59
344 7/8	51 7/8	48 7/8	41 6/8	4 5/8	4 6/8	14 5/8	1 7/8	12 4/8	1/8	17	17	Lake Providence, N.W.T.	Craig A. Ross	Craig A. Ross	1987	60
343 7/8	53 7/8	52	37 5/8	6 5/8	6	18 5/8	6/8	14	1/8	11	15	MacKay Lake, N.W.T.	Carolyn A. Godfrey	Carolyn A. Godfrey	1990	61
342 5/8	47 3/8	43	47 3/8	5 3/8	5 2/8	16 4/8	13 4/8	12 5/8	7 3/8	20	15	Lac de Gras, N.W.T.	Frank E. Baldwin	Frank E. Baldwin	1990	62
342 1/8	54 6/8	55 4/8	39 7/8	5 2/8	5 5/8	10	14 7/8	1/8	10	13	16	Ellice River, N.W.T.	Jerald E. Mason	Jerald E. Mason	1989	63
336 2/8	45 5/8	47 1/8	27 3/8	6 2/8	5 7/8	2 5/8	17 5/8	1/8	14 3/8	14	16	MacKay Lake, N.W.T.	Stanley R. Godfrey	Stanley R. Godfrey	1990	64
333 4/8	44 5/8	46 3/8	33 2/8	5 4/8	5 5/8	11 2/8	16 1/8	5 1/8	10	9	10	Parry Pen., N.W.T.	Mark B. Sippin	Mark B. Sippin	1988	65
332 7/8	49 7/8	51	31 2/8	5 4/8	5 3/8	1	16 2/8	1/8	13 1/8	19	20	Point Lake, N.W.T.	Linda Warwick	Linda Warwick	1991	66
407 2/8 *	54 1/8	54 4/8	36 4/8	5 5/8	5 5/8	19 7/8	17 7/8	15	15 4/8	16	21	Kugaryuak River, N.W.T.	James G. Empey	James G. Empey	1990	
395 2/8 *	63	61 3/8	37 7/8	5 3/8	6 3/8	17 4/8	15 1/8	13 7/8	9 3/8	18	17	Little Marten Lake, N.W.T.	Daniel Butzler	Daniel Butzler	1989	
393 1/8 *	48	51 2/8	43 6/8	7 1/8	5	15 2/8	14 4/8	6 5/8	10	14	14	Courageous Lake, N.W.T.	Daniel R. Herring	Daniel R. Herring	1987	

* Final Score subject to revision by additional verifying measurements.

Quebec-Labrador Caribou

Rangifer tarandus from Quebec and Labrador

Minimum Score 365

World's Record 474-6/8

Score	Length of Main Beam R.	L.	Inside Spread	Circumference at Smallest Place Between Brow and Bez Points R.	L.	Length of Brow Points R.	L.	Width of Brow Points R.	L.	Number of Points R.	L.	Locality Killed	By Whom Killed	Owner	Date Killed	Rank
424 1/8	55 2/8	55 3/8	47 6/8	6 2/8	5 5/8	16 3/8	18 3/8	9 4/8	14 6/8	18	22	Serigny River, Que.	Brad Case	Brad Case	1989	1
416	52	50 3/8	50	5 3/8	5 2/8	21 2/8	20 7/8	14	15 5/8	17	20	Lake Consigny, Que.	Ricardo L. Garza	Ricardo L. Garza	1989	2
410 7/8	50 7/8	51 2/8	54	5 1/8	5 1/8	19 5/8	17 5/8	13 5/8	13 4/8	19	23	Caniapiscau Lake, Que.	Stephen C. Lockhart	Stephen C. Lockhart	1988	3
410 4/8	52 4/8	51 6/8	48 6/8	6	6 2/8	18	16 5/8	12	10 7/8	18	20	Pons River, Que.	Don Young	Don Young	1988	4
407 7/8	50 3/8	50	45 3/8	5 6/8	5 6/8	17 3/8	18 7/8	13 4/8	11	18	21	Lake Moyer, Que.	Jeffrey S. Baker	Jeffrey S. Baker	1988	5
404 2/8	53 3/8	50 4/8	46	5 6/8	5 6/8	19 4/8	13 7/8	14 5/8	2	18	16	George River, Que.	Paul Bambara	Paul Bambara	1985	6
403 3/8	47 3/8	50 2/8	43	5 5/8	5 3/8	20 7/8	11 1/8	16 2/8	1/8	28	17	Samuel Lake, Que.	James R. Blankenheim	James R. Blankenheim	1989	7
401 3/8	49 4/8	49	49 4/8	4 6/8	4 4/8	10 7/8	18 6/8	1 6/8	13	15	22	Ungava Bay, Que.	C. Gordon Demeritt	C. Gordon Demeritt	1988	8
397 6/8	48 5/8	49 4/8	47	5 1/8	5	19 4/8	18	16	10 4/8	22	16	Lac Vallerenne, Que.	Charles J. Spies	Charles J. Spies	1988	9
396	55 2/8	57 2/8	42 5/8	5 3/8	5 1/8	21 5/8	21 3/8	8 3/8	16 2/8	17	20	Ungava Bay, Que.	Edwin L. DeYoung	Edwin L. DeYoung	1989	10
395	47 7/8	51 7/8	44 6/8	5 6/8	5 4/8	8 7/8	18	1/8	14 4/8	19	24	George River, Que.	Kurt Roenspies	Kurt Roenspies	1990	11
394 5/8	54 6/8	52 7/8	48 5/8	5 3/8	5 5/8	17	17 3/8	13	12 4/8	15	17	Ungava Bay, Que.	Norbert D. Bremer	Norbert D. Bremer	1989	12
394 4/8	44 1/8	44 2/8	38 2/8	5 7/8	6 2/8	13 5/8	17 6/8	10	13 5/8	22	21	Rogers Lake, Que.	Gregg D. Dunkel	Gregg D. Dunkel	1988	13
393 2/8	55 3/8	56 4/8	48 4/8	5 5/8	5 7/8	18 7/8	18 2/8	9 7/8		15	19	Lake Natuak, Que.	Dale Stangil	Dale Stangil	1989	14
392 6/8	52 5/8	52 4/8	52 5/8	5 6/8	5 7/8	19 1/8	17 5/8	6 4/8	8 7/8	20	17	Lake Consigny, Que.	Thomas L. Vaux	Thomas L. Vaux	1988	15
390 4/8	49 6/8	52 2/8	48 5/8	4 7/8	4 5/8	17 2/8	10 7/8	10 5/8	10 5/8	18	18	Caniapiscau River, Que.	John W. Flies	John W. Flies	1990	16
389 6/8	56 6/8	55 4/8	44 4/8	5 2/8	5 4/8	13 3/8	18 4/8	1	15 1/8	13	21	Echo Lake, Que.	James T. Luxem	James T. Luxem	1989	17
388 6/8	53 3/8	57 6/8	42	7 1/8	5 7/8	18 5/8	17 4/8	13 2/8	1 7/8	23	13	George River, Que.	Rodney A. Scott	Rodney A. Scott	1990	18
387 7/8	56 6/8	57 1/8	46 7/8	5 7/8	7 1/8	18 3/8	16 1/8	5 7/8	10 5/8	14	14	Abloviak Fjord, Que.	Frederick S. Fish	Frederick S. Fish	1989	19
387 4/8	44 4/8	47 2/8	45 2/8	5 3/8	5 1/8	16 5/8	18 6/8	12	9 5/8	22	20	Whale River, Que.	Michael Karboski	Michael Karboski	1988	20
386 4/8	52 4/8	53	53	5 4/8	5 2/8	12 1/8	17 2/8	1/8	13 5/8	14	15	Pons River, Que.	George D. Berger	George D. Berger	1991	21
385 6/8	49 6/8	58 1/8	48 6/8	5 2/8	5	4 5/8	20 4/8	1/8	13 6/8	16	17	Koksoak River, Que.	Donald E. Eberman	Donald E. Eberman	1990	22
385	53 7/8	55 1/8	54 4/8	5 2/8	5 1/8	19 3/8	16 3/8	12 3/8	11 5/8	24	19	Delay River, Que.	Dan E. Stimmell	Dan E. Stimmell	1990	23
384 2/8	47 4/8	51 4/8	40 6/8	6	5 3/8	16 7/8		13 5/8		20	16	Pons Lake, Que.	Jonathan S. Warke	Jonathan S. Warke	1991	24
383 7/8	47 3/8	49 5/8	46 7/8	4 6/8	5 1/8	15	19 3/8	10 6/8	15 5/8	18	23	Lake Loudin, Que.	Roger M. Schmitt	Roger M. Schmitt	1988	25
383 2/8	50 2/8	50 7/8	50 1/8	5 7/8	6 1/8	4 5/8	16 1/8	1/8	12 4/8	16	19	Abloviak Fjord, Que.	Steven N. Mitchell	Steven N. Mitchell	1991	26
382 5/8	50 4/8	50 5/8	33	5 6/8	5 4/8	17 1/8	15 1/8	10 5/8	7 7/8	13	17	Lake Diane, Que.	Wayne R. Martka	Wayne R. Martka	1990	27
381 6/8	53 7/8	51 2/8	42 2/8	4 6/8	4 6/8	18 2/8	15 4/8	15 1/8	6 5/8	15	13	Pons River, Que.	Chris S. Marshall	Chris S. Marshall	1990	28
381 2/8	49 3/8	50 5/8	45 5/8	5 1/8	5 2/8	16 2/8	14 5/8	9 1/8	8 5/8	17	18	Wayne Lake, Que.	Vincent P. Cina, Sr.	Vincent P. Cina, Sr.	1990	29
381	53 5/8	55 7/8	48 6/8	4 7/8	5 1/8	18 3/8	19	13 4/8	4 7/8	14	17	Ungava Bay, Que.	Jeff S. Koster	Jeff S. Koster	1990	30

Quebec-Labrador Caribou - Continued

Score	Length of Main Beam R.	L.	Inside Spread	Circumference at Smallest Place Between Brow and Bez Points R.	L.	Length of Brow Points R.	L.	Width of Brow Points R.	L.	Number of Points R.	L.	Locality Killed	By Whom Killed	Owner	Date Killed	Rank
380 4/8	55	55 5/8	50 3/8	5 1/8	5 2/8	17 3/8	11 3/8	13 4/8	1/8	17	15	Pons River, Que.	Ronald S. Newman	Ronald S. Newman	1990	31
380 3/8	60 2/8	59 7/8	50 6/8	5 4/8	5 7/8	18 4/8	20 5/8	4 7/8	15 3/8	13	14	Tunulik River, Que.	Thomas L. Cash	Thomas L. Cash	1988	32
379 7/8	49	50 2/8	50 2/8	5	5 1/8	3 7/8	17	1/8	11 3/8	17	16	Baleine River, Que.	Michael C. Dysh	Michael C. Dysh	1990	33
379 6/8	42 7/8	47 2/8	41 6/8	5 7/8	6	14 4/8	15 5/8	9 6/8	8 5/8	20	21	Wade Lake, Lab.	Unknown	Gerard Beaulieu	1985	34
379 3/8	62 2/8	64 2/8	41	6	6	1 1/8	23 6/8		17 2/8	11	14	Ungava Bay, Que.	Bruce E. Cepicky	Bruce E. Cepicky	1988	35
378 3/8	45 6/8	50 1/8	41	4 5/8	4 7/8	17 7/8	15 6/8	17 2/8	7 4/8	19	19	Wendell Lake, Que.	Terry E. Lefever	Terry E. Lefever	1988	36
377 1/8	53 6/8	54 5/8	48	5 1/8	5 3/8	18 7/8	18 2/8	12 2/8	7 6/8	16	16	Rainbow Lake, Que.	David J. Richey, Sr.	David J. Richey, Sr.	1990	37
376 7/8	48 1/8	49 6/8	51	4 7/8	4 7/8	4 3/8	20 1/8		9 2/8	18	18	Lake Lachine, Que.	Edward A. Mertins	Edward A. Mertins	1990	38
375 5/8	61 4/8	58 6/8	41	5 3/8	5 2/8	6 5/8	20 3/8	16		27	22	Du Gue River, Que.	Arden Bancroft	Arden Bancroft	1989	39
375 3/8	51 4/8	52 3/8	46 4/8	4 4/8	4 5/8	16 6/8	18 1/8	4 3/8	11 5/8	18	17	Caniapiscau River, Que.	Gerald A. Gredell	Gerald A. Gredell	1987	40
375	53 4/8	52 3/8	36	5 1/8	5 2/8	12 4/8	19 1/8	1/8	16	18	15	Tunulik River, Que.	Kenneth G. Straub	Kenneth G. Straub	1989	41
372 5/8	46 3/8	43 2/8	37 6/8	6 4/8	6 2/8	17 2/8	16 6/8	8 2/8	13 7/8	20	26	Ungava Bay, Que.	Si Pellow	Si Pellow	1988	42
371 7/8	52 3/8	52 2/8	44 7/8	5	4 7/8	17 2/8	18 7/8	3	16 5/8	16	16	Tunulik River, Que.	Dale Carruth	Dale Carruth	1990	43
370 5/8	52	54	40 3/8	7 6/8	6	3	16 4/8	12 3/8	13 3/8	29	20	Tunulik River, Que.	Fred Buthe	Fred Buthe	1990	44
369 7/8	52 5/8	50 6/8	50 6/8	5 5/8	5 7/8	13	19 6/8	1	15 7/8	18	32	Caniapiscau River, Que.	Lawrence M. Yacubian	Lawrence M. Yacubian	1991	45
367 1/8	47 7/8	50 6/8	48 1/8	5	5	15 1/8	13 3/8	9 5/8	4 7/8	17	19	Tunulic River, Que.	Dave Franklin	Dave Franklin	1989	46
365 7/8	49 2/8	50 6/8	52 5/8	6 6/8	6 4/8	13 4/8	15 1/8	6 6/8	9 6/8	13	12	Aigneau Lake, Que.	Louis A. Waltz	Louis A. Waltz	1989	47
427 1/8*	48 6/8	48 3/8	44 4/8	5 4/8	5 7/8	23 4/8	22 6/8	10 3/8	19 4/8	33	26	Serigny River, Que.	Douglas E. Billings	Douglas E. Billings	1989	
414*	57 4/8	55	57	5 3/8	5 3/8	13 5/8	14 7/8	6 3/8	7 5/8	10	11	Ungava Bay, Que.	Jurgen Blattgerste	Jurgen Blattgerste	1990	
411*	51	55	46 7/8	6 7/8	6 3/8	4 1/8	17 1/8	13 1/8	13 7/8	17	17	Delay River, Que.	Nunzio Canduci	Nunzio Canduci	1988	

* Final Score subject to revision by additional verifying measurements.

Pronghorn

Antilocapra americana americana and related subspecies

Minimum Score 80 · World's Record 93-4/8

Score	Length of Horn R.	L.	Circumference of Base R.	L.	Circumference at Third Quarter R.	L.	Inside Spread	Tip to Tip Spread	Length of Prong R.	L.	Locality Killed	By Whom Killed	Owner	Date Killed	Rank
92 6/8	16 6/8	16 4/8	7 7/8	7 1/8	3 1/8	3 1/8	12 4/8	9 5/8	7 4/8	7 4/8	Coconino Co., Ariz.	Sam Jaksick, Jr.	Sam Jaksick, Jr.	1991	1
91	17 7/8	17 5/8	6 7/8	6 7/8	2 5/8	2 5/8	14	8 2/8	7 1/8	7 3/8	Humboldt Co., Nev.	Steve W. Dustin	Steve W. Dustin	1990	2
90 6/8	16 3/8	16 4/8	7	7 3/8	3 4/8	3 4/8	13 2/8	8 6/8	6 1/8	5 7/8	Natrona Co., Wyo.	Richard J. Guthrie	Richard J. Guthrie	1989	3
89 6/8	18 7/8	19	6 1/8	6	3	3	12 4/8	8	6	5 6/8	Colfax Co., N.M.	Hudson DeCray	Hudson DeCray	1989	4
89 2/8	17 4/8	17 1/8	7 2/8	7 1/8	2 4/8	2 4/8	12 5/8	8 6/8	7	7 1/8	Washoe Co., Nev.	Jaime L. Fuentes	Jaime L. Fuentes	1990	5
89 2/8	15 4/8	15 4/8	6 6/8	6 6/8	2 6/8	2 6/8	10	4 4/8	8	8	Washoe Co., Nev.	Marjorie A. Puryear	Marjorie A. Puryear	1990	5
89 2/8	17 2/8	17 1/8	7 4/8	7 4/8	2 6/8	2 6/8	11 7/8	4 7/8	6 2/8	5 7/8	Mora Co., N.M.	Michael R. Memmer	Michael R. Memmer	1991	5
89	16 2/8	16 2/8	6 7/8	6 6/8	2 6/8	2 6/8	10 7/8	4 5/8	6 4/8	6 4/8	Catron Co., N.M.	Picked Up	Charles A. Grimmett	1989	8
88 6/8	16 5/8	16 5/8	6 3/8	6 6/8	3 1/8	3 1/8	15 6/8	12 6/8	5 7/8	5 7/8	Catron Co., N.M.	Gerald Roland Gold	Gerald Roland Gold	1990	9
88 6/8	16 3/8	16 3/8	7 3/8	7 2/8	3 1/8	3 1/8	13 6/8	12 4/8	6 2/8	5 7/8	Socorro Co., N.M.	Grant L. Perry	Grant L. Perry	1991	9
88 4/8	18 1/8	18 2/8	7	7 1/8	3 2/8	3 1/8	10	5 7/8	5 4/8	5 3/8	Coconino Co., Ariz.	Arthur R. Dubs	Arthur R. Dubs	1990	11
88 4/8	18	18	6 6/8	6 6/8	3	3	11 4/8	6 1/8	5 4/8	5 3/8	Cochise Co., Ariz.	Tom R. Braun	Tom R. Braun	1991	11
88 2/8	18 2/8	18 2/8	6 7/8	7	2 7/8	2 7/8	16 4/8	12 1/8	5 6/8	5 4/8	Carbon Co., Utah	James M. Machac	James M. Machac	1989	13
88 2/8	17 6/8	18 1/8	6 7/8	6 7/8	3	3	11 3/8	6 4/8	5 4/8	5 2/8	Mohave Co., Ariz.	Peter E. Mangelsdorf	Peter E. Mangelsdorf	1989	13
88 1/8	17 2/8	17 2/8	7	7	2 6/8	2 6/8	17 3/8	14	6 2/8	6 2/8	Carter Co., Mont.	Carl T. Clapp	Carl T. Clapp	1955	15
87 6/8	15 3/8	15 3/8	7 2/8	7 7/8	2 6/8	2 6/8	13 6/8	11 7/8	7 1/8	7	Fremont Co., Wyo.	Karey H. Stebner	Karey H. Stebner	1991	16
87 2/8	19 1/8	18 4/8	7 2/8	7 2/8	2 6/8	2 6/8	14 3/8	8 2/8	7 1/8	7	Humboldt Co., Nev.	Jared R. Nuffer	Jared R. Nuffer	1988	17
87 2/8	16 4/8	16 5/8	6 6/8	7 1/8	2 4/8	2 4/8	11 7/8	8	5 5/8	5 7/8	Washoe Co., Nev.	Pierre M. Leautier	Pierre M. Leautier	1989	17
87 2/8	17 6/8	18 1/8	6 4/8	6 4/8	2 6/8	2 7/8	10 7/8	3 4/8	7 6/8	6 4/8	Catron Co., N.M.	Roy Holdridge	Roy Holdridge	1991	17
87	15 6/8	16	6 7/8	7 1/8	3 2/8	3 2/8	10 2/8	5 6/8	5 6/8	6	Cochise Co., Ariz.	David J. Braun	David J. Braun	1984	20
87	16 2/8	16 6/8	6 7/8	6 6/8	2 4/8	2 6/8	11 5/8	6 7/8	6 1/8	6 2/8	Catron Co., N.M.	Laurie Scott	Laurie Scott	1987	20
87	16 4/8	17 4/8	6 7/8	6 5/8	3	3	10 5/8	5 7/8	6 3/8	6 2/8	Yavapai Co., Ariz.	Robbie A. Jochim	Robbie A. Jochim	1989	20
87	16 5/8	16 6/8	7 5/8	7 5/8	3 1/8	3 2/8	9 1/8	2 6/8	5 3/8	5 3/8	Chouteau Co., Mont.	Darrell J. Woodahl	Darrell J. Woodahl	1990	20
86 6/8	14 2/8	14 4/8	7 1/8	7	3 3/8	3 2/8	6	2 2/8	6 1/8	6 2/8	Perkins Co., S.D.	Scott R. Dell	Scott R. Dell	1990	24
86 6/8	17	17 3/8	7 1/8	7	2 7/8	2 7/8	11 3/8	5 2/8	5 7/8	5 7/8	Coconino Co., Ariz.	Ben E. Stayner	Ben E. Stayner	1991	24
86 6/8	16 6/8	16 3/8	6 4/8	6 7/8	2 5/8	2 4/8	13 3/8	11 1/8	6 1/8	6 1/8	Fremont Co., Wyo.	Glen H. Taylor	Glen H. Taylor	1991	24
86 4/8	16 6/8	16 4/8	7	7	2 4/8	2 4/8	11 2/8	7 5/8	6 5/8	6 5/8	Fremont Co., Wyo.	Gerald G. Korell	Gerald G. Korell	1989	27
86 4/8	16	16	6 7/8	6 5/8	3 1/8	3 1/8	8 7/8	5 7/8	6	6 1/8	Hay Lake, Sask.	Gerald W. Bien	Gerald W. Bien	1990	27
86 4/8	16 6/8	16 7/8	6 7/8	6 5/8	3 1/8	3 1/8	9	2 4/8	5 5/8	5 5/8	Billings Co., N.D.	Greg A. Ganje	Greg A. Ganje	1990	27
86 4/8	17 3/8	17 7/8	6 4/8	6 4/8	2 3/8	2 1/8	14 6/8	13	6 5/8	7	Malheur Co., Oreg.	Nicholas J. Vidan	Nicholas J. Vidan	1991	27

Pronghorn - Continued

Score	Length of Horn R.	L.	Circumference of Base R.	L.	Circumference at Third Quarter R.	L.	Inside Spread	Tip to Tip Spread	Length of Prong R.	L.	Locality Killed	By Whom Killed	Owner	Date Killed	Rank
86 2/8	17 5/8	17 2/8	6 5/8	6 4/8	2 7/8	2 7/8	15 6/8	13 4/8	4 7/8	5	Coconino Co., Ariz.	Scott J. Reger	Scott J. Reger	1988	31
86 2/8	15 3/8	15 4/8	7 1/8	7 1/8	2 4/8	2 4/8	12 1/8	10	7 7/8	6 6/8	Sweetwater Co., Wyo.	Brian T. Gabbitas	Brian T. Gabbitas	1990	31
86 2/8	16 4/8	16 4/8	7 3/8	7 3/8	2 5/8	2 6/8	9 2/8	4	6 2/8	5 3/8	Sweetwater Co., Wyo.	Daniel Daugherty	Daniel Daugherty	1991	31
86	16 2/8	16 2/8	7	6 7/8	2 5/8	2 6/8	11 7/8	7 6/8	6 3/8	6 7/8	Sierra Co., N.M.	Vicki L. Leonard	Vicki L. Leonard	1987	34
86	16	15 6/8	7	6 6/8	3 1/8	3	13 4/8	10 6/8	6 1/8	6 2/8	Lassen Co., Calif.	David A. Tye	David A. Tye	1987	34
86	14 4/8	14 2/8	8 1/8	8 1/8	3	2 7/8	12	10	6	5 5/8	Rosebud Co., Mont.	William E. Butler	William E. Butler	1989	34
86	16 1/8	16	6 7/8	7	3 3/8	3 1/8	11	7 5/8	6 3/8	5 5/8	Catron Co., N.M.	B&C National Collection	B&C National Collection	1990	34
86	17	16 6/8	6 5/8	6 5/8	2 7/8	2 6/8	10 6/8	5 5/8	5 5/8	6 6/8	Garfield Co., Utah	Lynn M. Greene	Lynn M. Greene	1991	34
86	16 2/8	16 4/8	7	7	2 6/8	2 6/8	8 7/8	8 2/8	6 4/8	6 4/8	Sweetwater Co., Wyo.	William H. Miller	William H. Miller	1991	34
86	17 2/8	18	6 4/8	6 4/8	2 5/8	2 7/8	9 5/8	3 4/8	5 5/8	5 4/8	Socorro Co., N.M.	Joseph C. Sawyers	Joseph C. Sawyers	1991	34
85 6/8	16	16 2/8	6 4/8	6 4/8	2 6/8	2 4/8	9	3	6 7/8	6 7/8	Sweetwater Co., Wyo.	Steven J. Vanlerberghe	Steven J. Vanlerberghe	1988	41
85 6/8	15 7/8	15 7/8	7 6/8	7 6/8	2 6/8	2 6/8	8 6/8	2 3/8	5 5/8	5 5/8	Sweetwater Co., Wyo.	Duane M. Smith	Duane M. Smith	1989	41
85 6/8	16 6/8	16 6/8	6 5/8	6 5/8	2 7/8	3	10 6/8	9 4/8	6	6	Carbon Co., Wyo.	Herman A. Hatfield	Herman A. Hatfield	1990	41
85 6/8	17	16 7/8	7	7	2 5/8	2 5/8	11	4 7/8	5 4/8	5 4/8	Mora Co., N.M.	Michael J. Loomis	Michael J. Loomis	1990	41
85 6/8	16 3/8	16 5/8	6 2/8	6 2/8	2 5/8	2 5/8	8	1 7/8	6 6/8	6 6/8	Emery Co., Utah	Jerry L. Oveson	Jerry L. Oveson	1991	41
85 4/8	16 5/8	16 5/8	6 6/8	6 6/8	2 6/8	2 5/8	15 1/8	11 1/8	5 4/8	5 5/8	Butte Co., Idaho	Picked Up	S. Eric Krasa	1988	46
85 4/8	16 6/8	16 6/8	6 6/8	6 4/8	3	2 7/8	9 2/8	5 1/8	5 4/8	5 5/8	Millard Co., Utah	David J. Carter	David J. Carter	1989	46
85 4/8	16 5/8	16 6/8	6 7/8	6 7/8	2 6/8	3	7	1 1/8	6	6	Rosebud Co., Mont.	John A. Hill	John A. Hill	1989	46
85 4/8	16 4/8	16 4/8	6 6/8	6 6/8	3	3	11 2/8	5	5 7/8	5 7/8	Coconino Co., Ariz.	Lester E. Bradley	Lester E. Bradley	1990	46
85 4/8	16	16 2/8	7 1/8	7 1/8	3	3	12 5/8	8 3/8	6	5 4/8	Harney Co., Oreg.	Van G. Decker	Van G. Decker	1990	46
85 4/8	16 5/8	16 5/8	6 4/8	6 4/8	2 7/8	2 6/8	12 6/8	7 7/8	5 4/8	5 5/8	Coconino Co., Ariz.	Don R. Drew	Don R. Drew	1990	46
85 4/8	16 6/8	16 7/8	7	7	2 6/8	2 6/8	12 5/8	8 5/8	4 4/8	4 2/8	Washoe Co., Nev.	Gregg A. Menter	Gregg A. Menter	1991	46
85 2/8	16 4/8	16 3/8	6 6/8	6 6/8	2 7/8	2 6/8	7 1/8	2 2/8	6 3/8	5 7/8	Navajo Co., Ariz.	Robert A. Dodson	Robert A. Dodson	1989	53
85 2/8	16 4/8	16 4/8	6 6/8	6 4/8	2 7/8	3	7 5/8	2 6/8	7	5 4/8	Natrona Co., Wyo.	J. Brendan Bummer	J. Brendan Bummer	1990	53
85 2/8	15	14 7/8	7 1/8	7 1/8	3	2 7/8	10 3/8	7 3/8	6 3/8	5 7/8	McKenzie Co., N.D.	Michael A. Palmer	Michael A. Palmer	1990	53
85 2/8	16 7/8	16 6/8	6 5/8	6 3/8	2 7/8	2 7/8	12 3/8	7 4/8	5 6/8	6	Baker Co., Oreg.	Gordon C. Van Patten	Gordon C. Van Patten	1990	53
85	16 5/8	16	6 6/8	6 6/8	2 6/8	2 6/8	13 2/8	9 6/8	5 2/8	5 3/8	Campbell Co., Wyo.	O.P. Nicholson	Johnson Co. Museum	1937	57
85	16 1/8	16	6 6/8	6 6/8	2 7/8	2 7/8	13 1/8	8 2/8	4 4/8	4 4/8	Garfield Co., Mont.	Jeff M. Busse	Jeff M. Busse	1988	57
85	16 6/8	16 7/8	6 6/8	6 6/8	3	3	11 4/8	8 3/8	5	5	Rosebud Co., Mont.	Daniel D. Ova	Daniel D. Ova	1988	57
85	15 5/8	15 3/8	6 6/8	6 7/8	2 6/8	2 6/8	9 4/8	4 3/8	6 6/8	6 6/8	Sweetwater Co., Wyo.	Ronald L. Barber	Ronald L. Barber	1989	57
85	17 5/8	18 1/8	6 6/8	6 3/8	2 7/8	2 7/8	10 7/8	3 1/8	5 3/8	5 2/8	Coconino Co., Ariz.	John L. Neely	John L. Neely	1989	57
85	15 7/8	15 1/8	7 7/8	7 7/8	2 5/8	2 4/8	7 3/8	4 5/8	6 4/8	6 3/8	Sweetwater Co., Wyo.	Mary A. Barbour	Mary A. Barbour	1990	57

Score											Locality	Hunter	Owner	Year	Rank
84 6/8	16 3/8	16 1/8	6 3/8	6 4/8	3	3 1/8	13 2/8	11 2/8	6 7/8	6 7/8	Sweetwater Co., Wyo.	Melvin E. Killman	Melvin E. Killman	1989	63
84 6/8	16 4/8	16	6 4/8	6 4/8	2 5/8	2 6/8	11 1/8	6 3/8	6 4/8	7 1/8	Lassen Co., Calif.	Gary Caraccioli	Gary Caraccioli	1990	63
84 6/8	15 6/8	16	6 7/8	6 7/8	2 6/8	2 6/8	7 7/8	3 7/8	6 7/8	6 6/8	Natrona Co., Wyo.	Warren N. Pearce	Warren N. Pearce	1990	63
84 6/8	15 2/8	15 3/8	7 4/8	7 4/8	2 5/8	2 5/8	11 3/8	9 6/8	7	5 7/8	Carbon Co., Wyo.	Myron J. Wakkuri	Myron J. Wakkuri	1990	63
84 6/8	16 4/8	16 3/8	7 7/8	7 7/8	3	2 6/8	8 4/8	3 7/8	6 5/8	5 7/8	Cochise Co., Ariz.	David J. Braun	David J. Braun	1991	63
84 6/8	17 1/8	16 7/8	6 5/8	6 5/8	2 4/8	2 4/8	12 4/8	3 6/8	6 5/8	6 5/8	Coconino Co., Ariz.	Jerrell F. Coburn	Jerrell F. Coburn	1991	63
84 6/8	16 3/8	16 4/8	6 4/8	6 4/8	2 6/8	2 6/8	7 4/8	1 7/8	4 5/8	5 3/8	Fremont Co., Wyo.	Karen L. Jenson	Karen L. Jenson	1991	63
84 6/8	14 4/8	15	7 4/8	7 1/8	2 5/8	2 5/8	7 7/8	11 7/8	5 6/8	5 3/8	Converse Co., Wyo.	Michael R. Land	Michael R. Land	1991	63
84 6/8	16 1/8	15 7/8	6 6/8	6 6/8	3 1/8	2 7/8	14 5/8	7 1/8	5 6/8	5 5/8	Mora Co., N.M.	Linda J. McBride	Linda J. McBride	1991	63
84 6/8	16 2/8	16 2/8	6 5/8	6 5/8	3	3	11 7/8	7 7/8	6 6/8	6 6/8	Lake Co., Oreg.	Patrick R. McConnell	Patrick R. McConnell	1991	63
84 6/8	17 4/8	17 5/8	7 1/8	7	2 3/8	2 3/8	10 2/8	5 2/8	5 5/8	7	Mora Co., N.M.	Robert Model	Robert Model	1991	63
84 6/8	17	16 4/8	6 4/8	6 4/8	3 2/8	3	13 4/8	11 6/8	6 6/8	4 6/8	Lincoln Co., N.M.	Jay B. Robert	Jay B. Robert	1991	63
84 4/8	17 1/8	17 1/8	7	7	2 7/8	2 6/8	11 6/8	6 4/8	6	5 4/8	Washoe Co., Nev.	Tracy A. Tripp	Tracy A. Tripp	1989	75
84 4/8	14 7/8	15 1/8	7 3/8	7 3/8	2 7/8	2 7/8	8 6/8	8 2/8	4 2/8	4 7/8	Fremont Co., Wyo.	Lyle D. Fruchey	Lyle D. Fruchey	1990	75
84 4/8	17 1/8	17	6 1/8	6 2/8	2 7/8	2 7/8	12 2/8	4 6/8	5 5/8	5 6/8	Humboldt Co., Nev.	Shawn R. Hall	Shawn R. Hall	1990	75
84 4/8	16 1/8	15 6/8	7	7	3	2 4/8	11 7/8	6 4/8	6 3/8	6 2/8	Cutbank Creek, Alta.	Cameron C. Owen	Cameron C. Owen	1990	75
84 4/8	16 3/8	16 5/8	6 4/8	6 3/8	2 5/8	2 6/8	13 4/8	9 7/8	5 7/8	7	Mora Co., N.M.	Kenneth L. Ebbens	Kenneth L. Ebbens	1991	75
84 4/8	16 7/8	17	6 6/8	6 6/8	2 7/8	2 7/8	12 7/8	6 1/8	6 4/8	6 2/8	Hudspeth Co., Texas	Larry R. Price	Larry R. Price	1991	75
84 4/8	16 6/8	16 6/8	6 7/8	6 7/8	2 5/8	2 6/8	15	11 6/8	5	5 2/8	Union Co., N.M.	Walter R. Schreiner, Jr.	Walter R. Schreiner, Jr.	1991	75
84 2/8	16	16	6 6/8	6 6/8	2 2/8	2 6/8	10	4	6	6 5/8	Yavapai Co., Ariz.	Brian Murray	Brian Murray	1988	82
84 2/8	15 7/8	15 1/8	7 1/8	7 1/8	2 5/8	2 5/8	10 1/8	6 3/8	7 1/8	7 5/8	Fremont Co., Wyo.	Boyd E. Sharp, Jr.	Boyd E. Sharp, Jr.	1989	82
84 2/8	16 4/8	16 2/8	6 5/8	6 5/8	2 5/8	2 6/8	11 6/8	7 3/8	6 5/8	6 4/8	Mora Co., N.M.	Scott Steinkruger	Scott Steinkruger	1989	82
84 2/8	17 1/8	16 3/8	7 1/8	7 1/8	2 4/8	2 4/8	12	7 7/8	6 7/8	6 2/8	San Miguel Co., N.M.	Larry R. Griffin	Larry R. Griffin	1990	82
84 2/8	15 4/8	15 6/8	7 2/8	7 2/8	2 4/8	2 5/8	9 6/8	5	7 2/8	5 7/8	Carbon Co., Mont.	Patrick I. Kalloch	Patrick I. Kalloch	1990	82
84 2/8	16 7/8	16 6/8	6 2/8	6 5/8	2 6/8	2 6/8	8 5/8	1 3/8	6	5 5/8	Harney Co., Oreg.	Douglas J. Modey	Douglas J. Modey	1990	82
84 2/8	15 7/8	15 7/8	6 6/8	6 7/8	2 4/8	2 4/8	9 3/8	8 4/8	6 3/8	6 2/8	Sweetwater Co., Wyo.	Kurt D. Olson	Kurt D. Olson	1990	82
84 2/8	15 2/8	15	6 6/8	6 6/8	2 6/8	2 5/8	11 1/8	8	6 4/8	7 1/8	Carbon Co., Wyo.	Robert G. Wimpenny	Robert G. Wimpenny	1990	82
84 2/8	16	15 5/8	7 5/8	7 5/8	2 3/8	2 3/8	12 6/8	12 6/8	5 5/8	5	Fremont Co., Wyo.	Carl A. Engler	Carl A. Engler	1991	82
84 2/8	17 7/8	17 3/8	6 5/8	6 5/8	2 6/8	2 6/8	12 4/8	8 2/8	5 4/8	5	Quay Co., N.M.	Marvin S. Keating	Marvin S. Keating	1991	82
84 2/8	17 4/8	17 3/8	7	7	2 6/8	2 6/8	11 7/8	6 6/8	5 3/8	5 7/8	Mora Co., N.M.	Ralph C. Stayner	Ralph C. Stayner	1991	82
84 2/8	16 3/8	16 4/8	6 7/8	6 7/8	2 5/8	2 6/8	9 7/8	5 3/8	5 5/8	5 3/8	Dawson Co., Mont.	Jeff S. Trangmoe	Jeff S. Trangmoe	1991	82
84	16 7/8	17 2/8	6 6/8	6 2/8	2 6/8	2 5/8	12 2/8	7 3/8	5 2/8	5 2/8	Sierra Co., N.M.	Mike W. Leonard	Mike W. Leonard	1985	93
84	15 5/8	15 2/8	6 6/8	6 6/8	2 6/8	3	11 1/8	11 4/8	5 7/8	5 7/8	Harney Co., Oreg.	James E. Baley	James E. Baley	1987	93
84	17	16 7/8	6 5/8	6 5/8	2 4/8	2 4/8	8 6/8	8 6/8	5 7/8	5 7/8	Custer Co., Mont.	Don A. Bryendl	Don A. Bryendl	1988	93
84	16 3/8	16 3/8	6 6/8	6 6/8	2 7/8	2 7/8	11 3/8	8	5 3/8	5 3/8	Elko Co., Nev.	Larri R. Naveran	Larri R. Naveran	1988	93
84	15 6/8	15 7/8	6 6/8	6 6/8	2 6/8	2 6/8	11 3/8	6 1/8	6 4/8	5 5/8	Navajo Co., Ariz.	Alan K. Nulliner	Alan K. Nulliner	1989	93
84	17 4/8	17 4/8	6 6/8	6 6/8	2 4/8	2 4/8	14 6/8	8 5/8	5 6/8	4 6/8	Washoe Co., Nev.	Roger D. Puccinelli	Roger D. Puccinelli	1989	93
84	14 7/8	15 6/8	7	7	2 3/8	2 4/8	13 1/8	10 7/8	7 4/8	7	Lassen Co., Calif.	Larry R. Brower	Larry R. Brower	1990	93
84	16 2/8	16 2/8	6 4/8	6 4/8	2 6/8	2 6/8	10 6/8	7 2/8	6 4/8	5 5/8	Coconino Co., Ariz.	William B. Bullock	William B. Bullock	1991	93
84	15	15 2/8	7 2/8	7 2/8	2 7/8	2 7/8	10 4/8	5 2/8	7 2/8	5 3/8	Fremont Co., Wyo.	John J. Weust	John J. Weust	1991	93
83 6/8	15 7/8	15 7/8	6 4/8	6 3/8	3 1/8	3	9 6/8	3 5/8	6	6	Hudspeth Co., Texas	A. Alan Griffin	A. Alan Griffin	1988	103

483

Pronghorn - Continued

Score	Length of Horn R.	L.	Circumference of Base R.	L.	Circumference at Third Quarter R.	L.	Inside Spread	Tip to Tip Spread	Length of Prong R.	L.	Locality Killed	By Whom Killed	Owner	Date Killed	Rank
83 6/8	16 3/8	16 3/8	6 4/8	6 4/8	2 4/8	2 4/8	9 1/8	4 3/8	5 6/8	6 4/8	Harney Co., Oreg.	Lyle W. Crawford	Lyle W. Crawford	1990	103
83 6/8	16 2/8	16 3/8	7	7 1/8	2 5/8	2 6/8	10 2/8	5 3/8	5 3/8	5 5/8	Harney Co., Oreg.	John S. Hansen	John S. Hansen	1990	103
83 6/8	17	17 7/8	6 6/8	6 6/8	3 1/8	3	16	11 7/8	4 5/8	4 1/8	Washoe Co., Nev.	P.D. Kiser	P.D. Kiser	1990	103
83 6/8	15 4/8	15 2/8	7 2/8	7 2/8	2 3/8	2 3/8	13 4/8	10	5 6/8	5 6/8	Yavapai Co., Ariz.	Michael J. Rusing	Michael J. Rusing	1990	103
83 6/8	16 4/8	16 6/8	6 5/8	6 5/8	2 4/8	2 4/8	9 6/8	6	5 6/8	5 7/8	Carbon Co., Wyo.	Rod F. Waeckerlin	Rod F. Waeckerlin	1990	103
83 6/8	15 7/8	16	6 3/8	6 4/8	2 6/8	2 6/8	11 4/8	6 7/8	5 6/8	6 2/8	Yavapai Co., Ariz.	Roland J. Chooljian	Roland J. Chooljian	1991	103 •
83 6/8	16 5/8	16 7/8	6 4/8	6 4/8	2 7/8	3	11 7/8	7	5 2/8	5	Humboldt Co., Nev.	Sam Lair	Sam Lair	1991	103
83 4/8	17 2/8	17 4/8	6 3/8	6 5/8	2 7/8	2 7/8	8 4/8	1 6/8	4 6/8	4 6/8	Foremost, Alta.	Brian J. Gathercole	Brian J. Gathercole	1988	111
83 4/8	16 3/8	16 2/8	6 1/8	6 1/8	2 6/8	2 6/8	16 1/8	13 7/8	6	6	Wildhorse, Alta.	Ralph L. Cervo	Ralph L. Cervo	1989	111
83 4/8	16 5/8	16 7/8	6 4/8	6 5/8	2 6/8	2 6/8	9	3 6/8	5 1/8	5 3/8	Colfax Co., N.M.	David M. Lackie	David M. Lackie	1989	111
83 4/8	15 5/8	15 3/8	7	6 6/8	2 4/8	2 3/8	11 6/8	7 2/8	6	6 3/8	Sweetwater Co., Wyo.	Charles R. Monroe	Charles R. Monroe	1989	111
83 4/8	17 2/8	17 2/8	6 2/8	6 2/8	2 6/8	2 6/8	10	4 3/8	6	5 2/8	Maple Creek, Sask.	Lynn P. Needham	Lynn P. Needham	1989	111
83 4/8	15 7/8	15 6/8	6 2/8	6 3/8	2 5/8	2 5/8	10 2/8	6 4/8	7	6 3/8	Carbon Co., Utah	John R. Stevens	John R. Stevens	1989	111
83 4/8	15 5/8	16	6 5/8	6 4/8	2 7/8	2 6/8	15 5/8	12 4/8	5 7/8	5 2/8	Colfax Co., N.M.	Louie Alcon	Louie Alcon	1990	111
83 4/8	15 5/8	15 5/8	6 6/8	6 6/8	2 7/8	2 4/8	15 5/8	12 4/8	6 3/8	6 3/8	Socorro Co., N.M.	Michael T. Miller	Michael T. Miller	1990	111
83 4/8	15 5/8	15 6/8	7	6 7/8	2 7/8	2 7/8	8 5/8	3 2/8	5 5/8	5 5/8	Moffat Co., Colo.	Brad A. Winder	Brad A. Winder	1990	111
83 4/8	16 4/8	16 6/8	6 2/8	6 1/8	2 5/8	2 5/8	8 7/8	3 2/8	6	6	Hudspeth Co., Texas	Carl H. Green	Carl H. Green	1991	111
83 4/8	18 3/8	18	5 7/8		2 4/8	2 3/8	10 3/8	8 7/8	6	5 6/8	Hudspeth Co., Texas	Eduardo Padilla	Eduardo Padilla	1991	111
83 4/8	16 4/8	16 4/8	6 4/8	6 4/8	2 5/8	2 6/8	11 7/8	6 6/8	5 5/8	5 5/8	Elko Co., Nev.	Eugene E. Schain	Eugene E. Schain	1991	111
83 4/8	17 3/8	17 2/8	6 5/8	6 4/8	2 5/8	2 3/8	10	5	5 5/8	5 2/8	Humboldt Co., Nev.	William J. Swartz, Jr.	William J. Swartz, Jr.	1991	111
83 4/8	15 7/8	16	6 6/8	7	3	3	14 7/8	11 5/8	6	6	Mora Co., N.M.	Jeffrey D. Warren	Jeffrey D. Warren	1991	111
83 2/8	17 1/8	17 2/8	6 2/8	6 2/8	2 6/8	2 6/8	10 1/8	4 5/8	5 6/8	5 2/8	Coconino Co., Ariz.	H. Keith Neitch	H. Keith Neitch	1988	125
83 2/8	17 2/8	17 2/8	6	6	2 4/8	2 4/8	9 6/8	6 6/8	5 3/8	5 5/8	Mora Co., N.M.	Patrick F. Taylor	Patrick F. Taylor	1988	125
83 2/8	16 6/8	16	6 2/8	6 2/8	3 1/8	2 7/8	13 6/8	9 3/8	4 3/8	3 6/8	Hartley Co., Texas	Ernie Davis	Ernie Davis	1989	125
83 2/8	16	15	7	7	2 7/8	3 3/8	8 4/8	2 3/8	5 5/8	5 5/8	Rosebud Co., Mont.	Anthony J. Emmerich	Anthony J. Emmerich	1989	125
83 2/8	17 1/8	16 1/8	6 2/8	6 3/8	2 4/8	2 4/8	12 6/8	9 2/8	6 2/8	6 2/8	Sweet Grass Co., Mont.	Daniel Phariss	Daniel Phariss	1989	125
83 2/8	16 3/8	15 1/8	6 2/8	6 3/8	2 4/8	2 7/8	10 3/8	7	6 3/8	6 2/8	Rosebud Co., Mont.	Gary M. Van Dyke	Gary M. Van Dyke	1989	125
83 2/8	15 1/8	15 1/8	6 7/8	6 6/8	2 7/8	2 7/8	6 7/8	1 4/8	5	4 6/8	Natrona Co., Wyo.	Dean Albanis	Dean Albanis	1990	125
83 2/8	14 2/8	14 4/8	6 6/8	6 6/8	2 6/8	2 7/8	10 5/8	5 5/8	7 7/8	7	Modoc Co., Calif.	David T. Eveland	David T. Eveland	1990	125
83 2/8	16 2/8	16 2/8	6 4/8	6 4/8	2 5/8	2 5/8	9 4/8	4	5	5 1/8	Washoe Co., Nev.	Steve F. Holmes	Steve F. Holmes	1990	125
83 2/8	14 5/8	15	7	7	3 4/8	3 2/8	11 4/8	10 5/8	5 4/8	5	Uinta Co., Wyo.	John W. McGehee	John W. McGehee	1990	125
83 2/8	16	16	6 6/8	6 6/8	2 7/8	3	10	6 7/8	5	4 7/8	Carter Co., Mont.	Donald W. Mindemann, Jr.	Donald W. Mindemann, Jr.	1990	125

Score									Locality	Hunter	Owner	Date Killed	Rank
83 2/8	16 1/8	7 1/8	2 6/8	2 5/8	13 1/8	9 7/8	5 5/8	5 6/8	Carbon Co., Wyo.	Thomas W. Popham	Thomas W. Popham	1990	125
83 2/8	16 4/8	6 5/8	2 6/8	2 6/8	9 6/8	6 5/8	5 5/8	5 2/8	Natrona Co., Wyo.	Robert B. Poskie	Robert B. Poskie	1990	125
83 2/8	16 1/8	6 6/8	2 7/8	3	13 6/8	9 5/8	5 7/8	5 7/8	Carbon Co., Wyo.	Robert H. Ruegge	Robert H. Ruegge	1990	125
83 2/8	17 1/8	6 6/8	2 7/8	2 7/8	12 3/8	7 7/8	5 7/8	6 1/8	Custer Co., Mont.	Eric S. Doeden	Eric S. Doeden	1991	125
83 2/8	17	6 7/8	2 4/8	2 4/8	11 6/8	6 3/8	5 7/8	5 2/8	Fremont Co., Wyo.	John M. Dunsworth	John M. Dunsworth	1991	125
83 2/8	17 3/8	7	2 5/8	2 5/8	14 1/8	10 3/8	5 5/8	5 5/8	Harney Co., Oreg.	Patricia A. Kaiser	Patricia A. Kaiser	1991	125
83 2/8	16 7/8	6 3/8	2 4/8	2 5/8	11 4/8	6 4/8	5 5/8	5 6/8	Colfax Co., N.M.	Robert J. Seeds	Robert J. Seeds	1991	125
83 2/8	15 7/8	6 2/8	2 5/8	2 5/8	9 6/8	6 6/8	5 5/8	5 5/8	Mineral Co., Nev.	Victor Trujillo	Victor Trujillo	1991	125
83 2/8	17 2/8	6 2/8	3 2/8	2 7/8	15 3/8	12 2/8	5 6/8	5 6/8	Coconino Co., Ariz.	Billie F. Bechtel	Billie F. Bechtel	1988	144
83	17	6 2/8	3	3	14 4/8	10	5	5 5/8	Sierra Co., N.M.	Steven A. Berry	Steven A. Berry	1988	144
83	17 4/8	6	3	3	16 4/8	16 4/8	4 5/8	4	Washakie Co., Wyo.	Gordon E. Deromedi	Gordon E. Deromedi	1988	144
83	16 2/8	6 4/8	3 1/8	3 1/8	16 2/8	16 4/8	4 5/8	4 5/8	Fremont Co., Wyo.	Douglas R. Dow	Douglas R. Dow	1988	144
83	16	6 4/8	2 6/8	2 6/8	14 6/8	11	5 4/8	5 2/8	Jackson Co., Colo.	Douglas A. Weimer	Douglas A. Weimer	1988	144
83	15 6/8	6 6/8	2 6/8	2 6/8	15 4/8	8 4/8	5 5/8	5 2/8	Carbon Co., Wyo.	Gary Duggins	Gary Duggins	1989	144
83	16	7	2 3/8	2 4/8	13 1/8	9 7/8	6 2/8	6 3/8	Sheridan Co., Wyo.	Tom W. Housh	Tom W. Housh	1989	144
83	16 5/8	6 7/8	2 1/8	2 1/8	13 7/8	13 7/8	4 7/8	4 5/8	Navajo Co., Ariz.	Ray V. Pogue	Ray V. Pogue	1989	144
83	16 3/8	6 3/8	3 5/8	3 5/8	16 2/8	16 2/8	6	6	Moffat Co., Colo.	Mike Wallers	Mike Wallers	1989	144
83	15 6/8	6 1/8	2 7/8	2 7/8	16 5/8	15 2/8	5 4/8	5 2/8	Carbon Co., Wyo.	Robert G. Wimpenny	Robert G. Wimpenny	1989	144
83	16 4/8	6 4/8	2 5/8	2 5/8	15 7/8	15 3/8	5 7/8	5 7/8	Socorro Co., N.M.	David A. Berry	David A. Berry	1990	144
83	15 7/8	7 1/8	2 4/8	2 4/8	11 6/8	7 6/8	4 6/8	4	Fremont Co., Wyo.	Tom Covert	Tom Covert	1990	144
83	17	6 4/8	2 6/8	2 6/8	13 1/8	8 5/8	5 7/8	5	Perkins Co., S.D.	Dick D. Knock	Dick D. Knock	1990	144
83	15 4/8	6 4/8	2 4/8	2 4/8	9 4/8	6	6 7/8	6 6/8	Greenlee Co., Ariz.	Paul E. Palmer	Paul E. Palmer	1990	144
83	16 1/8	7 2/8	3 1/8	3	11 2/8	7	5	4 7/8	Mora Co., N.M.	Gerald W. Pullin	Gerald W. Pullin	1990	144
83	16 3/8	6 2/8	2 6/8	2 6/8	9 3/8	6 1/8	5 7/8	5 6/8	Lincoln Co., N.M.	Robert M. Rogulic	Robert M. Rogulic	1990	144
83	16 2/8	6 5/8	2 5/8	2 5/8	9 2/8	4	5 5/8	5 6/8	Carbon Co., Wyo.	Roger M. Green	Roger M. Green	1991	144
83	17	6 5/8	2 6/8	2 7/8	10 1/8	5 5/8	5 3/8	5 3/8	Uinta Co., Wyo.	Florence Kitchel	Florence Kitchel	1991	144
83	17 3/8	6 2/8	3 1/8	3 1/8	10	10 7/8	4 7/8	4 7/8	Carbon Co., Wyo.	Gerald A. Steele	Gerald A. Steele	1991	144
82 7/8	15 7/8	6 2/8	2 5/8	2 5/8	10 7/8	11 7/8	6 1/8	5 7/8	Lemhi Co., Idaho	Richard W. Feagan	Richard W. Feagan	1988	163
82 7/8	17	6 6/8	2 6/8	2 6/8	10 3/8	2	5 6/8	5 6/8	Washoe Co., Nev.	David E. Messmann	David E. Messmann	1988	163
82 7/8	17 3/8	6 3/8	2 6/8	2 6/8	12 4/8	9 7/8	4 7/8	4 6/8	Humboldt Co., Nev.	Christopher C. Hornbarger	Christopher C. Hornbarger	1989	163
82 6/8	16	6 6/8	3	3	8 6/8	4 1/8	5 7/8	5 7/8	Campbell Co., Wyo.	Richard H. Stasiak	Richard H. Stasiak	1989	163
82 6/8	17 4/8	6 6/8	2 4/8	2 6/8	11	5 5/8	6	4 7/8	Fremont Co., Wyo.	Ronald E. Cebuhar	Ronald E. Cebuhar	1990	163
82 6/8	16 2/8	6 3/8	2 6/8	2 6/8	12 1/8	8 7/8	6 1/8	6 1/8	Catron Co., N.M.	H. James Tonkin, Jr.	H. James Tonkin, Jr.	1990	163
82 6/8	16 2/8	7	2 4/8	2 6/8	13 3/8	9 6/8	5	5	Harney Co., Oreg.	Garry L. Whitmore	Garry L. Whitmore	1990	163
82 6/8	16 3/8	6 1/8	3	3	8	1 6/8	5 2/8	5 7/8	Cypress Lake, Sask.	Jack Clary	Jack Clary	1991	163
82 6/8	15 4/8	6 4/8	2 5/8	2 6/8	9 1/8	4 6/8	5 5/8	5 6/8	Carbon Co., Wyo.	Rebecca J. Miller	Rebecca J. Miller	1991	163
82 6/8	16	6 6/8	2 4/8	2 6/8	9	4 3/8	5 7/8	5	Natrona Co., Wyo.	Charles P. Weber	Charles P. Weber	1991	163
82 4/8	16 2/8	6 4/8	2 5/8	2 6/8	9 4/8	3 5/8	5 6/8	5 6/8	Sweetwater Co., Wyo.	Eric M. Berg	Eric M. Berg	1965	172
82 4/8	17 1/8	6 2/8	2 4/8	2 6/8	11 6/8	6 6/8	5 6/8	6 2/8	Humboldt Co., Nev.	Michael K. McBeath	Michael K. McBeath	1988	172
82 4/8	17 1/8	6	2 5/8	2 6/8	9 5/8	7 7/8	6 1/8	5 5/8	Custer Co., Idaho	Ronald E. Pruyn	Ronald E. Pruyn	1988	172

Score	Length of Horn R.	L.	Circumference of Base R.	L.	Circumference at Third Quarter R.	L.	Inside Spread	Tip to Tip Spread	Length of Prong R.	L.	Locality Killed	By Whom Killed	Owner	Date Killed	Rank
82 4/8	17 1/8	15 7/8	6 4/8	6 4/8	3 1/8	2 7/8	8 5/8	6 2/8	6	5 7/8	Yavapai Co., Ariz	Chris Skoczylas	Chris Skoczylas	1988	172
82 4/8	16 5/8	16 2/8	6 5/8	6 5/8	2 3/8	2 3/8	11 1/8	7 2/8	6 2/8	6 1/8	Fremont Co., Wyo.	Ben L. Adamson	Ben L. Adamson	1989	172
82 4/8	15 2/8	15 1/8	6 4/8	6 2/8	3 1/8	3 1/8	14 1/8	12 6/8	5 4/8	5 5/8	Box Elder Co., Utah	Curtis K. Blasingame	Curtis K. Blasingame	1989	172
82 4/8	15 5/8	15 5/8	6 2/8	6 4/8	3 4/8	2 7/8	9 2/8	3	5 5/8	5 4/8	Graham Co., Ariz.	Daniel C. Hicks	Daniel C. Hicks	1989	172
82 4/8	15 6/8	15 6/8	6 3/8	6 3/8	2 7/8	2 7/8	8 4/8	3 4/8	5 7/8	5 6/8	Colfax Co., N.M.	Roy G. Jones	Roy G. Jones	1989	172
82 4/8	14 5/8	14 4/8	7 1/8	7	2 5/8	2 4/8	12 6/8	11 5/8	6 6/8	6 5/8	Fremont Co., Wyo.	James M. Machac	James M. Machac	1989	172
82 4/8	14 5/8	14 5/8	7 2/8	7 2/8	2 5/8	2 4/8	13 2/8	11	6 3/8	6 3/8	Carbon Co., Wyo.	Lance E. Novak	Lance E. Novak	1989	172
82 4/8	14 2/8	14 3/8	6 6/8	6 6/8	3	3	13 5/8	12 6/8	5 4/8	5 5/8	Jackson Co., Colo.	Loren D. Reid	Loren D. Reid	1989	172
82 4/8	16 4/8	16 6/8	6 6/8	6 6/8	2 6/8	2 5/8	11 1/8	9 1/8	5	5 1/8	Humboldt Co., Nev.	Richard Vanderkous	Richard Vanderkous	1989	172
82 4/8	14 6/8	15	6 6/8	6 6/8	2 4/8	2 4/8	12 1/8	8 3/8	6 2/8	6 3/8	Converse Co., Wyo.	Larry E. Zumbrum	Larry E. Zumbrum	1989	172
82 4/8	15 4/8	15 2/8	7 4/8	7 3/8	2 4/8	2 4/8	8 3/8	3 2/8	5 4/8	5 5/8	Natrona Co., Wyo.	Robert W. Genner	Robert W. Genner	1990	172
82 4/8	15 2/8	15 2/8	6 5/8	6 5/8	2 6/8	2 7/8	9 5/8	4 7/8	5 4/8	5 3/8	McKenzie Co., N.D.	Nathan S. Gilbertson	Nathan S. Gilbertson	1990	172
82 4/8	17 1/8	17	6	5 7/8	2 4/8	2 4/8	13 6/8	9 7/8	6 3/8	6	San Juan Co., Utah	Wayne A. Hines	Wayne A. Hines	1990	172
82 4/8	15 5/8	15 6/8	6 5/8	6 4/8	3	3 6/8	12 5/8	11 7/8	5 2/8	5 5/8	Converse Co., Wyo.	Farrell M. McQuiddy	Farrell M. McQuiddy	1990	172
82 4/8	15 6/8	15 4/8	7 1/8	7 1/8	2 5/8	2 5/8	12 2/8	8 2/8	6 6/8	6 5/8	Fremont Co., Wyo.	James J. Person	James J. Person	1990	172
82 4/8	17 6/8	17 6/8	6 7/8	7	2 5/8	2 5/8	9 7/8	3 3/8	5 2/8	5	Mora Co., N.M.	Gilbert T. Adams	Gilbert T. Adams	1991	172
82 4/8	16 3/8	16 4/8	7	6 7/8	2 6/8	2 5/8	10 1/8	5 6/8	6 3/8	6 2/8	Box Elder Co., Utah	Roudy Christensen	Roudy Christensen	1991	172
82 4/8	15 5/8	16	6 1/8	6	2 2/8	2 3/8	15 4/8	15 2/8	5 6/8	5 5/8	Sweetwater Co., Wyo.	Robert S. Lund	Robert S. Lund	1991	172
82 4/8	17 2/8	17	6 3/8	6 3/8	2 3/8	2 4/8	10 1/8	4 7/8	5 5/8	5 1/8	Mora Co., N.M.	Dan E. McBride	Dan E. McBride	1991	172
82 4/8	17	16 6/8	6 5/8	6 5/8	2 4/8	2 4/8	9	2 6/8	4 7/8	4 7/8	Mora Co., N.M.	Kenneth G. Planet	Kenneth G. Planet	1991	172
82 4/8	16 3/8	16 5/8	6 2/8	6 2/8	2 5/8	2 5/8	9 7/8	5	5 5/8	5 4/8	Washoe Co., Nev.	Dean C. Tischler	Dean C. Tischler	1991	172
82 2/8	17 2/8	17 2/8	6 3/8	6 3/8	2 7/8	2 6/8	11 3/8	5 5/8	6 1/8	6 2/8	Weld Co., Colo.	James Gertson, Jr.	Howard E. Bates	1955	197
82 2/8	14 6/8	15 4/8	6 7/8	7 1/8	2 6/8	2 7/8	10 3/8	4 6/8	5 6/8	5 7/8	Mohave Co., Ariz.	Ronald D. Wood	Ronald D. Wood	1987	197
82 2/8	14 7/8	14 7/8	6 4/8	6 5/8	2 6/8	2 5/8	8 1/8	5 3/8	5 6/8	5 7/8	Rosebud Co., Mont.	Cory Nissen	Cory Nissen	1988	197
82 2/8	16 2/8	15 7/8	6	6	2 5/8	2 6/8	7 7/8	2 6/8	6 4/8	6 4/8	Carbon Co., Wyo.	Robert Depellegrini	Robert Depellegrini	1989	197
82 2/8	16 2/8	16 6/8	6 4/8	6 1/8	2 5/8	2 4/8	9 5/8	3 4/8	6 3/8	6 4/8	Fremont Co., Wyo.	John A. Monje	John A. Monje	1989	197
82 2/8	16 1/8	15 5/8	6 6/8	6 6/8	2 6/8	2 5/8	12 1/8	5 5/8	6 1/8	6 2/8	Natrona Co., Wyo.	Valentine Novicki II	Valentine Novicki II	1989	197
82 2/8	17	16 7/8	6 1/8	6 5/8	2 5/8	2 4/8	16 3/8	12 1/8	5	5 5/8	Middle Creek Res., Alta.	Donald P. Penner	Donald P. Penner	1989	197
82 2/8	16	15 5/8	6 6/8	6 5/8	2 6/8	2 6/8	14 2/8	10 1/8	5 4/8	5 3/8	Washoe Co., Nev.	Robert E. Hill	Robert E. Hill	1990	197
82 2/8	14 4/8	14 4/8	6 6/8	6 6/8	3 1/8	3	10 5/8	6 6/8	6	5 2/8	Colfax Co., N.M.	Virgil A. Lair	Virgil A. Lair	1990	197
82 2/8	16 2/8	16 5/8	6 6/8	6 5/8	3 1/8	3 1/8	9 3/8	7 1/8	4 5/8	4 5/8	Weston Co., Wyo.	Scott H. Eia	Scott H. Eia	1991	197
82 2/8	18 7/8	19 4/8	5 6/8	5 5/8	2 3/8	2 3/8	17 7/8	15 4/8	4 5/8	4 5/8	Modoc Co., Calif.	Rod Eisenbeis	Rod Eisenbeis	1991	197

Score	Length of Horn R	Length of Horn L	Circ. of Base R	Circ. of Base L	Circ. 3rd Qtr. R	Circ. 3rd Qtr. L	Length of Prong R	Length of Prong L	Tip to Tip Spread	Inside Spread	Locality	Killed By	Owner	Date	Rank
82 2/8	15 6/8	15 6/8	7 7/8	7 4/8	2 5/8	2 4/8	6 7/8	6 7/8	9 7/8	5 4/8	Natrona Co., Wyo.	Brian G. Elliott	Brian G. Elliott	1991	197
82 2/8	17	16 7/8	6 6/8	6 6/8	2 4/8	2 4/8	6 6/8	6 2/8	9	6 1/8	Dewey Co., S.D.	Alan Ruhlman	Alan Ruhlman	1991	197
82	15 7/8	15 7/8	6 3/8	6 2/8	3	3	7	6 7/8	14 4/8	5 7/8	Billings Co., N.D.	Curtis D. Decker	Curtis D. Decker	1988	210
82	17 1/8	17 1/8	6 4/8	6 4/8	2 6/8	2 3/8	6 4/8	6 4/8	11 5/8	6 3/8	Fremont Co., Wyo.	Timothy A. Kiefer	Timothy A. Kiefer	1988	210
82	16	16	6 4/8	6 4/8	2 6/8	2 4/8	6 4/8	6 4/8	11	6 4/8	Harding Co., N.M.	Andrew J. Ortega	Andrew J. Ortega	1988	210
82	14 3/8	14 6/8	7 2/8	6 3/8	2 3/8	2 4/8	7 2/8	7	11 5/8	7 2/8	Carbon Co., Wyo.	Becky Strand	Becky Strand	1988	210
82	16 7/8	16 7/8	6 3/8	6 4/8	2 5/8	2 5/8	6 3/8	6 4/8	11 2/8	6 4/8	Mora Co., N.M.	H.P. Wood	H.P. Wood	1988	210
82	14 4/8	14 6/8	7 6/8	7 6/8	2 6/8	2 6/8	7 6/8	7 6/8	10 6/8	5 6/8	Sweetwater Co., Wyo.	Mark E. Gillespie	Mark E. Gillespie	1989	210
82	16 2/8	16	6 5/8	6 5/8	2 4/8	2 4/8	6 5/8	6 7/8	10 6/8	5 5/8	Washoe Co., Nev.	James E. Puryear	James E. Puryear	1989	210
82	16 2/8	16 2/8	6 4/8	6 3/8	2 4/8	2 3/8	6 4/8	6 4/8	9 5/8	5 5/8	Lincoln Co., Wyo.	Michael H. Romney	Michael H. Romney	1989	210
82	15 5/8	15 5/8	6 1/8	6 2/8	2 7/8	2 7/8	6 1/8	6 2/8	8 6/8	5	Natrona Co., Wyo.	Victor Colonna	Victor Colonna	1990	210
82	15 3/8	15 2/8	6 3/8	6 4/8	2 6/8	2 7/8	6 3/8	6 4/8	8 2/8	4	Albany Co., Wyo.	Phil Darnell	Phil Darnell	1990	210
82	15	15	7 1/8	7	2 4/8	2 3/8	6 5/8	6 1/8	8 4/8	4	Carbon Co., Wyo.	Allen A. Ehrke	Allen A. Ehrke	1990	210
82	16 7/8	16 7/8	6 7/8	7	2 6/8	2 5/8	6 6/8	6 7/8	9 6/8	5 5/8	Washakie Co., Wyo.	Jake Hanson	Jake Hanson	1990	210
82	15 7/8	16	6 3/8	6 2/8	2 4/8	2 4/8	6 3/8	6 2/8	10 3/8	5	Mora Co., N.M.	Todd S. Hyden	Todd S. Hyden	1990	210
82	17 4/8	17 3/8	6 2/8	6 1/8	2 4/8	2 4/8	6 2/8	6 1/8	8 2/8	4 7/8	Washoe Co., Nev.	Paul J. Jesch	Paul J. Jesch	1990	210
82	17	17	6 6/8	6 6/8	3	3	6 6/8	6 6/8	9 2/8	3 5/8	Lincoln Co., N.M.	Steve A. Marasovich, Jr.	Steve A. Marasovich, Jr.	1990	210
82	16 5/8	16 3/8	6 1/8	6 1/8	2 4/8	2 4/8	6 1/8	6 1/8	16 3/8	12 3/8	Slope Co., N.D.	Todd M. Quinn	Todd M. Quinn	1990	210
82	17 6/8	17 4/8	6 2/8	6 3/8	2 6/8	2 5/8	6 2/8	6 3/8	8 7/8	4 5/8	Hudspeth Co., Texas	E. Scott Smith	E. Scott Smith	1990	210
82	16	16	6 4/8	6 4/8	2 4/8	2 5/8	6 4/8	6 4/8	10 4/8	6 1/8	Albany Co., Wyo.	James T. Sprinkle	James T. Sprinkle	1990	210
82	15 7/8	15 5/8	6 4/8	6 1/8	2 5/8	2 5/8	6 4/8	6 1/8	9 7/8	5	Washoe Co., Nev.	James D. Jones	James D. Jones	1991	210
82	15 4/8	15 4/8	7 2/8	7 3/8	2 7/8	2 7/8	7 2/8	7 3/8	10 6/8	4 3/8	Lassen Co., Calif.	Joseph D. Nolan	Joseph D. Nolan	1991	210
82	16 3/8	16 4/8	6 6/8	6 5/8	2 5/8	2 5/8	6 6/8	6 5/8	9 7/8	5 4/8	Converse Co., Wyo.	Rick P. Sakovitz	Rick P. Sakovitz	1991	210
82	13 4/8	13 2/8	7 1/8	7 1/8	2 6/8	2 7/8	7 1/8	7 1/8	11 7/8	6 3/8	Carbon Co., Wyo.	Andrew W. Serres	Andrew W. Serres	1991	210
81 6/8	16 5/8	16 6/8	6 4/8	6 4/8	2 6/8	2 6/8	6 4/8	6 4/8	14 4/8	5 2/8	Catron Co., N.M.	Shelton I. Pricer	Shelton I. Pricer	1987	232
81 6/8	15 4/8	15 4/8	7 1/8	7 1/8	2 4/8	2 4/8	7 1/8	7 1/8	11 4/8	4 4/8	Washoe Co., Nev.	Roger E. Hillygus	Roger E. Hillygus	1990	232
81 6/8	15 5/8	15 5/8	6 6/8	6 4/8	2 4/8	2 5/8	6 6/8	6 4/8	8 3/8	5 3/8	Carbon Co., Wyo.	Loren R. Tri	Loren R. Tri	1990	232
81 4/8	15 1/8	15 1/8	6 3/8	6 3/8	2 4/8	2 4/8	6 3/8	6 3/8	12 1/8	6 4/8	Lake Co., Oreg.	Ralph Buckingham	Ralph Buckingham	1988	235
81 4/8	14 6/8	15	6 7/8	6 7/8	2 5/8	2 5/8	6 7/8	6 7/8	8 6/8	5 5/8	Colfax Co., N.M.	LeGrand C. Kirby III	LeGrand C. Kirby III	1989	235
81 4/8	16 4/8	16 3/8	6 1/8	6 1/8	2 3/8	2 3/8	6 1/8	6 1/8	1 7/8	6 4/8	Mora Co., N.M.	Kenneth L. Ebbens	Kenneth L. Ebbens	1990	235
81 2/8	16 3/8	16 3/8	6 1/8	6 2/8	2 6/8	2 6/8	6 1/8	6 2/8	10	5 5/8	Sweetwater Co., Wyo.	Jeffrey L. Hoving	Jeffrey L. Hoving	1991	235
81 2/8	15 2/8	15 4/8	6 5/8	6 4/8	2 7/8	2 7/8	6 5/8	6 4/8	9 6/8	6	Sweetwater Co., Wyo.	Bruce E. Cepicky	Bruce E. Cepicky	1989	239
81 2/8	16 3/8	17	6 1/8	6 1/8	2 3/8	2 3/8	6 1/8	6 1/8	9 3/8	6	Emery Co., Utah	Monte E. Tucker	Monte E. Tucker	1989	239
81 2/8	16 7/8	16 7/8	6 1/8	6	2 6/8	2 6/8	6 1/8	6	8 7/8	6 3/8	Mora Co., Utah	S. Kim Bonnett	S. Kim Bonnett	1989	239
81 2/8	15 5/8	15 5/8	6 7/8	6 6/8	2 6/8	2 6/8	6 7/8	6 6/8	11 4/8	5 7/8	McCone Co., Mont.	Jerry D. Curtiss	Jerry D. Curtiss	1990	239
81 2/8	15 7/8	15 7/8	6 4/8	6 4/8	2 6/8	2 6/8	6 4/8	6 4/8	9 6/8	5	Union Co., N.M.	Orville L. Harris	Orville L. Harris	1990	239
81 2/8	16 3/8	16 4/8	6 1/8	6 1/8	2 7/8	2 7/8	6 1/8	6 1/8	12	5 3/8	Socorro Co., N.M.	Stephen J. McGaughey	Stephen J. McGaughey	1990	239
81	16 1/8	16	6 6/8	6 6/8	2 6/8	2 6/8	6 6/8	6 6/8	8 7/8	4 1/8	Uintah Co., Utah	Ben M. Murray	Ben M. Murray	1990	245
81	15 3/8	15	6 5/8	6 5/8	2 6/8	2 6/8	6 5/8	6 5/8	12 3/8	5	Musselshell Co., Mont.	Omer Ware	Omer Ware	1989	245
81	16 7/8	16 7/8	5 7/8	5 7/8	2 5/8	2 5/8	5 7/8	5 7/8	11 6/8	6	Valley Co., Mont.	Kevin L. Wieberg	Kevin L. Wieberg	1989	245
81	16	16	6 1/8	6 2/8	2 4/8	2 4/8	6 1/8	6 2/8	8 3/8	6	Carbon Co., Wyo.	Raymond R. Thomma, Jr.	Raymond R. Thomma, Jr.	1990	245

Pronghorn - Continued

Score	Length of Horn R.	L.	Circumference of Base R.	L.	Circumference at Third Quarter R.	L.	Inside Spread	Tip to Tip Spread	Length of Prong R.	L.	Locality Killed	By Whom Killed	Owner	Date Killed	Rank
80 6/8	15	14 6/8	7 1/8	6 2/8	2 5/8	2 6/8	13 2/8	8 7/8	6	5 6/8	Fremont Co., Wyo.	J.R. Hansen	J.R. Hansen	1989	249
80 6/8	15 2/8	15	6 1/8	6 2/8	3	3	9 1/8	6	5 6/8	5 6/8	Box Elder Co., Utah	Merrell A. Hurd	Merrell A. Hurd	1989	249
80 6/8	15	15 2/8	6 6/8	6 6/8	2 5/8	2 7/8	7 5/8	7 4/8	5 3/8	5 5/8	Orion, Alta.	John Luthi	John Luthi	1989	249
80 6/8	14 6/8	15 1/8	7 1/8	7	2 5/8	2 6/8	12	7 2/8	6	5 7/8	Uinta Co., Wyo.	David J. White	David J. White	1990	249
80 4/8	15	14 6/8	6 4/8	6 4/8	2 5/8	2 4/8	12 6/8	10 2/8	6	5 6/8	Custer Co., Mont.	Brandon P. Taylor	Brandon P. Taylor	1990	253
80 4/8	15 5/8	15 7/8	6 4/8	6 2/8	2 5/8	2 6/8	13	11	5 4/8	5 4/8	Carbon Co., Wyo.	Jim E. Jairell	Jim E. Jairell	1991	253
80 4/8	14 1/8	14 1/8	7	7	3 1/8	3	10 1/8	8 3/8	5 5/8	5 3/8	Jackson Co., Colo.	Beryl J. Palmer	Beryl J. Palmer	1991	253
80 2/8	15 5/8	15 3/8	6 3/8	6 6/8	2 6/8	3	10 2/8	4 4/8	5 6/8	5	Box Elder Co., Utah	Carol Conroy	Carol Conroy	1988	256
80 2/8	16 7/8	16 7/8	6 4/8	6	3	2 7/8	10 4/8	5 4/8	4 4/8	4	Coconino Co., Ariz.	Noel S. Allen	Noel S. Allen	1989	256
80 2/8	15 4/8	15 2/8	6	6	2 4/8	2 4/8	8 1/8	2 6/8	6 1/8	6 1/8	Rosebud Co., Mont.	Steven L. Rogers	Steven L. Rogers	1989	256
80 2/8	15 3/8	15 3/8	6 4/8	6 4/8	2 4/8	2 4/8	13 2/8	9 3/8	5 6/8	6 1/8	Fremont Co., Wyo.	Gary P. Stewart	Gary P. Stewart	1989	256
80 2/8	15 1/8	15 4/8	6 7/8	6 6/8	2 4/8	2 6/8	9	6	5	4 7/8	Fremont Co., Wyo.	Russell W. Korp	Russell W. Korp	1990	256
80 2/8	15 4/8	15 4/8	6 1/8	6 1/8	2 6/8	2 6/8	10 6/8	8 2/8	5 6/8	5 7/8	Mora Co., N.M.	Edward J. Moxley	Edward J. Moxley	1990	256
80 2/8	17	16 6/8	6 1/8	6 1/8	2 4/8	2 5/8	11 6/8	8 1/8	5 6/8	5 5/8	Socorro Co., N.M.	James E. Smith, Jr.	James E. Smith, Jr.	1990	256
80 2/8	15 7/8	16	6 2/8	6 1/8	2 4/8	2 4/8	10 2/8	5 5/8	5 3/8	5 1/8	Humboldt Co., Nev.	Kenneth G. Detweiler	Kenneth G. Detweiler	1991	256
80 2/8	15	16 5/8	6 1/8	6 7/8	2 7/8	3	12 4/8	10	6 2/8	5 3/8	Hudspeth Co., Texas	Jarl E. Hanson	Jarl E. Hanson	1991	256
80 2/8	14 4/8	14 1/8	7	6 4/8	2 6/8	2 6/8	10 2/8	7 7/8	5 5/8	5 4/8	Custer Co., Mont.	John W. Hitch	John W. Hitch	1991	256
80 2/8	15 5/8	15 3/8	6 4/8	6 4/8	2 4/8	2 4/8	15 2/8	10 2/8	5 6/8	5 6/8	Dewey Co., S.D.	James H. Lohrman	James H. Lohrman	1991	256
80 2/8	16 6/8	16 6/8	6 1/8	6 1/8	2 5/8	2 5/8	13 1/8	7 5/8	4 5/8	5	Converse Co., Wyo.	Clayton H. Maue	Clayton H. Maue	1991	256
80 2/8	15 5/8	15 4/8	6 6/8	6 5/8	2 6/8	2 6/8	14 4/8	10 5/8	5 5/8	5 5/8	Elko Co., Nev.	L. William Traverso	L. William Traverso	1991	256
80	15 4/8	15	6	5 6/8	2 7/8	2 7/8	10 5/8	6 1/8	5 5/8	5 6/8	Catron Co., N.M.	Mike Steele	Mike Steele	1989	269
80	15	15	6 5/8	6 7/8	2 5/8	2 5/8	8 2/8	6 2/8	5 6/8	6 2/8	Forty Mile Coulee, Alta.	Ronald M. Steels	Ronald M. Steels	1989	269
80	14 6/8	14 2/8	7 3/8	6 7/8	2 7/8	2 5/8	10 1/8	6 1/8	6	6 5/8	Natrona Co., Wyo.	David M. Crum	David M. Crum	1990	269
80	16 4/8	16 4/8	6 4/8	6 3/8	2 4/8	2 5/8	13 1/8	10	4 6/8	4 7/8	Coconino Co., Ariz.	Kenneth D. Smith	Kenneth D. Smith	1990	269
80	16 2/8	16 2/8	6 1/8	6 4/8	2 3/8	2 4/8	9 6/8	3 2/8	5 2/8	5 7/8	Mora Co., N.M.	Kerry Egan	Kerry Egan	1991	269
80	16 1/8	16 3/8	6 5/8	6 4/8	2 4/8	2 5/8	13	7 7/8	5 6/8	4 4/8	Washoe Co., Nev.	John P. Nolan	John P. Nolan	1991	269

Bison

Minimum Score 115

Bison bison bison and Bison bison athabascae

World's Record 136-4/8

Trophies from the lower 48 states are acceptable only for records, not awards, and only from states that recognize bison as wild and free-ranging and for which a hunting license and/or big-game tag is required for hunting.

Score	Length of Horn R.	L.	Circumference of Base R.	L.	Circumference at Third Quarter R.	L.	Greatest Spread	Tip to Tip Spread	Locality Killed	By Whom Killed	Owner	Date Killed	Rank
128 4/8	18 7/8	18 6/8	15 1/8	14 7/8	7 6/8	7 4/8	31	23 5/8	Custer Co., S.D.	Stephanie Altimus	Wildl. Mus. of the West	1989	1
128	21 5/8	20 4/8	14 5/8	14 4/8	6 6/8	5 7/8	23 7/8	27	Custer Co., S.D.	Larry L. Altimus	Larry L. Altimus	1990	2
126 6/8	20 7/8	21 1/8	14 2/8	14 4/8	6 2/8	6 2/8	30 3/8	19 6/8	Garfield Co., Utah	Holland D. Butler	Holland D. Butler	1990	3
126 4/8	18 7/8	18 7/8	15	14 6/8	6 5/8	6 2/8	29	22	Park Co., Mont.	Picked Up	Matthew J. Young	1990	4
125 2/8	18 6/8	19	14 2/8	14 1/8	8	7 6/8	31 6/8	26 2/8	Park Co., Mont.	Richard Olson	Richard Olson	1989	5
124 2/8	18 3/8	18 3/8	15 4/8	15 4/8	6 5/8	7 2/8	29 4/8	23 7/8	Delta Junction, Alaska	Gary D. Wolfe	Gary D. Wolfe	1990	6
123	16 4/8	17	14 5/8	14 6/8	8	7	27 6/8	24	Custer Co., S.D.	Jerry Ippolito	Jerry Ippolito	1990	7
122 6/8	18 4/8	18 3/8	14 5/8	14 5/8	6 5/8	7 1/8	29 3/8	21 1/8	Park Co., Mont.	Picked Up	James J. Darr	1991	8
122 4/8	18 4/8	18 5/8	14 6/8	14 2/8	6 6/8	6	25	23 7/8	Custer Co., S.D.	Donald F. Senter	Donald F. Senter	1989	9
122	19 6/8	19 6/8	15 1/8	15 4/8	5 6/8	5 3/8	29 4/8	21 3/8	Goodpastor River, Alaska	Charles W. Jackson	Charles W. Jackson	1989	10
122	19 1/8	19 4/8	15 2/8	15 4/8	5 2/8	5 3/8	30 4/8	25 3/8	Gerstle River, Alaska	Richard Voss	Richard Voss	1990	10
121 6/8	18 6/8	18 6/8	13 4/8	13 3/8	7 4/8	7 3/8	32 4/8	30 3/8	Custer Co., S.D.	Thomas H. Coe	Thomas H. Coe	1991	12
121 2/8	16 7/8	17 2/8	13 5/8	13 4/8	7 1/8	7 1/8	30 4/8	25 3/8	Custer Co., S.D.	Bradley D. Hanson	Bradley D. Hanson	1988	13
120 6/8	15 1/8	14 4/8	14 3/8	14 2/8	9	8 2/8	28	25	Custer Co., S.D.	Douglas M. Dreeszen	Douglas M. Dreeszen	1988	14
120 6/8	17 3/8	16 6/8	14 6/8	14 3/8	6 6/8	6 3/8	27	20	Park Co., Mont.	Matthew P. Wheeler	Matthew P. Wheeler	1989	14
119 2/8	19 6/8	19 3/8	14 4/8	14 4/8	5	5 1/8	26 6/8	15 4/8	San Juan Co., Utah	Janice N. Wahlstrom	Janice N. Wahlstrom	1979	16
119 2/8	17 4/8	17 2/8	14	14 4/8	6 4/8	5 5/8	28 3/8	21 5/8	Coconino Co., Ariz.	James R. Brown	James R. Brown	1988	16
119 2/8	19	17 7/8	15 1/8	15	5 7/8	5 5/8	31 7/8	27 6/8	Park Co., Mont.	Mike Cadwell	Mike Cadwell	1988	16
118 2/8	18 1/8	18 7/8	15 1/8	15	5 4/8	5 6/8	30 5/8	23 5/8	Teton Co., Wyo.	Steven C. Kobold	Steven C. Kobold	1990	19
117 6/8	17 4/8	16 4/8	14 5/8	14 5/8	6	6 6/8	27 4/8	23	Park Co., Mont.	Tom Roe	Tom Roe	1988	20
116 6/8	19 1/8	18 5/8	14 3/8	14 3/8	5	5 6/8	30 5/8	25	Post River, Alaska	Elizabeth A. Bassney	Elizabeth A. Bassney	1990	21
116 2/8	19 4/8	19 3/8	13 6/8	13 3/8	5 1/8	4 7/8	27 3/8	18 5/8	Garfield Co., Utah	Jed D. Topham	Jed D. Topham	1989	22
115 6/8	15 3/8	17	14 6/8	14 3/8	6 4/8	6	25 5/8	21	Park Co., Mont.	Hilary J. Benbenek	Hilary J. Benbenek	1989	23
115	18 2/8	19 2/8	14 4/8	12 4/8	7 2/8	6	30	23 2/8	Custer Co., S.D.	Picked Up	J.D. Andrews	1987	24

Rocky Mountain Goat

Oreamnos americanus americanus and related subspecies

Minimum Score 47 World's Record 56-6/8

Score	Length of Horn R.	L.	Circumference of Base R.	L.	Circumference at Third Quarter R.	L.	Greatest Spread	Tip to Tip Spread	Locality Killed	By Whom Killed	Owner	Date Killed	Rank
54 2/8	10 5/8	10 5/8	6 2/8	6 2/8	2		7 5/8	6 7/8	Mt. Meehaus, B.C.	Denis J. Chagnon	Denis J. Chagnon	1989	1
54 2/8	11 6/8	12	5 5/8	5 4/8	1 7/8	1 7/8	7 7/8	5 5/8	Yes Bay, Alaska	Wally L. Grover	Wally L. Grover	1991	1
53 6/8	10 6/8	10 5/8	6	6	2	2	8 3/8	8 2/8	Telegraph Creek, B.C.	Steven M. Gross	Steven M. Gross	1991	3
53	10 7/8	10 7/8	5 7/8	6	1 7/8	2	8 6/8	8 5/8	Toms Creek, B.C.	Tommy B. Lee, Jr.	Tommy B. Lee, Jr.	1988	4
53	11	11 3/8	5 5/8	5 6/8	2	2	8 1/8	7 5/8	Morice River, B.C.	Elizabeth D. Saunders	Rob Saunders	1989	4
53	10 7/8	10 6/8	6	6	1 7/8	1 7/8	7 1/8	6 2/8	Skeena River, B.C.	Russil Tanner	Russil Tanner	1990	4
52 4/8	10 6/8	10 7/8	5 3/8	5 3/8	2	2 1/8	7 3/8	6 6/8	Granite Basin Lake, Alaska	Scott D. Hansen	Scott D. Hansen	1988	7
52 2/8	11 1/8	11 1/8	5 5/8	5 5/8	1 7/8	1 7/8	6 7/8	6	Mt. Meehaus, B.C.	George A. Angello, Jr.	George A. Angello, Jr.	1988	8
52 2/8	11	10 5/8	5 4/8	5 4/8	1 7/8	1 7/8	9 5/8	9 3/8	Little Oliver Creek, B.C.	James K. Hansen	James K. Hansen	1988	8
52 2/8	10 5/8	10 6/8	5 6/8	5 6/8	2	2	10	9 7/8	Sheslay River, B.C.	Steve Parks	Steve Parks	1988	8
52 2/8	10 2/8	10 2/8	5 4/8	5 4/8	2 1/8	2 1/8	6 7/8	6 2/8	Cassiar Mts., B.C.	Debbie S. Sanowski	Debbie S. Sanowski	1989	8
52 2/8	10 2/8	10 3/8	5 7/8	5 7/8	1 7/8		7 7/8	6 6/8	Lynn Canal, Alaska	Charles F. Roy	Charles F. Roy	1990	8
52	9 7/8	9 4/8	5 7/8	5 6/8	2 2/8	2 2/8	5 3/8	5 2/8	Yes Bay, Alaska	Roddy Shelton	Roddy Shelton	1987	13
52	10	10 1/8	5 7/8	5 7/8	2 1/8	2 1/8	8	7	Shemes River, B.C.	Russil Tanner	Russil Tanner	1990	13
51 6/8	10 1/8	10 1/8	5 5/8	5 5/8	2	2	7	6 3/8	Chita Creek, B.C.	Anthony D. Tindall	Anthony D. Tindall	1989	15
51 6/8	10	9 6/8	5 4/8	5 4/8	2 1/8		6 6/8	6 2/8	Snohomish Co., Wash.	Terry L. Wagner	Terry L. Wagner	1990	15
51 4/8	11 1/8	11	5 4/8	5 4/8	1 6/8	1 7/8	7 4/8	7 4/8	Maiyuk Creek, B.C.	John P. Katrichak	John P. Katrichak	1988	17
51 4/8	9 5/8	9 5/8	6	6	2 1/8	2	7 4/8	7	Sheslay River, B.C.	Daniel E. Gorecki	Daniel E. Gorecki	1989	17
51 4/8	10	10 1/8	6	6	1 7/8	1 7/8	7 7/8	7 7/8	Bradley Lake, Alaska	Paul H. Ross	Paul H. Ross	1989	17
51 4/8	9 7/8	10	6	6	2	2	6 7/8	6 3/8	Beaverhead Co., Mont.	Shawn M. Probst	Shawn M. Probst	1990	17
51 2/8	9 7/8	9 7/8	5 5/8	5 6/8	2	2	6 2/8	5 3/8	Snehumption Creek, B.C.	Raymond C. Croissant	Raymond C. Croissant	1989	21
51	10 1/8	10	6	6		1 7/8	7 1/8	7 1/8	Serrated Peak, B.C.	Philip E. Blacher, Jr.	Philip E. Blacher, Jr.	1989	22
51	10 4/8	10 7/8	5 4/8	5 4/8	1 7/8	2	6 2/8	5 5/8	Cleveland Pen., Alaska	Lynn K. Herbert	Lynn K. Herbert	1989	22
50 6/8	9 5/8	9 5/8	5 6/8	5 6/8	2	2	8	7 5/8	Klastline River, B.C.	Glenn E. Hisey	Glenn E. Hisey	1979	24
50 6/8	10 1/8	9 7/8	5 4/8	5 4/8	1 7/8	1 7/8	8 2/8	7 7/8	Okanogan Co., Wash.	Monica M. Knight	Monica M. Knight	1987	24
50 6/8	10 2/8	10 3/8	5 5/8	5 5/8	1 7/8	1 7/8	6 5/8	6 1/8	Chouteau Co., Mont.	Craig L. Nowak	Craig L. Nowak	1990	24
50 2/8	9 2/8	9 2/8	5 7/8	5 7/8	1 7/8	1 7/8	7 1/8	6 6/8	Sicintine Range, B.C.	Roger L. Pock	Roger L. Pock	1988	27
50	10 2/8	10 1/8	5 7/8	5 6/8	1 6/8	1 7/8	6 3/8	5	Bradfield Canal, Alaska	James L. Beskin	James L. Beskin	1989	28
50	10 1/8	9 7/8	5 2/8	5 2/8	2	2	7 4/8	6 3/8	Snobomish Co., Wash.	Jeffrey J. Nelson	Jeffrey J. Nelson	1989	28

Score									Locality	Owner	By whom taken	Date	Rank
50	10 4/8	10 2/8	5 5/8	5 4/8	1 7/8	1 6/8	6 2/8	5 7/8	King Co., Wash.	Spencer C. Davis	Spencer C. Davis	1990	28
50	9 1/8	9 3/8	5 6/8	5 6/8	2	2	7 3/8	7 1/8	Thunder Mt., B.C.	Jimmy E. Dixon	Jimmy E. Dixon	1990	28
49 6/8	9 4/8	9 4/8	5 6/8	5 6/8	2	1 7/8	7 3/8	7 3/8	Bradley Lake, Alaska	Michael L. Ross	Michael L. Ross	1989	32
49 4/8	10 3/8	9 7/8	5 6/8	5 5/8	1 6/8	1 7/8	7 4/8	7	Gallatin Co., Mont.	Doug Columbik	Doug Columbik	1990	33
49 4/8	10 2/8	10 7/8	5 3/8	5 4/8	1 6/8	1 7/8	8 1/8	7 1/8	Fredrickson Lake, B.C.	Robert W. Dager	Robert W. Dager	1990	33
49 4/8	10 1/8	10 4/8	5 5/8	5 5/8	1 6/8	1 6/8	8 7/8	8 4/8	Dawson Creek, B.C.	Charles H. Eddy	Charles H. Eddy	1991	33
49 4/8	10 2/8	10 1/8	5 5/8	5 6/8	1 5/8	1 5/8	6 3/8	5 6/8	Powell Co., Mont.	Daniel T. Morgan	Daniel T. Morgan	1990	36
49	10	10	5 5/8	5 5/8	1 6/8	1 7/8	8	7 7/8	Sheep Creek, Alaska	Miles Collier	Miles Collier	1988	37
48 6/8	9 6/8	9 6/8	5 5/8	5 4/8	1 6/8	1 6/8	6 1/8	4 5/8	Endicott Arm, Alaska	Thomas H. Pitts	Lorraine Harrison	1988	37
48 6/8	10 4/8	9 7/8	5 5/8	5 4/8	1 7/8	1 7/8	7 1/8	6 6/8	Kinskuch Lake, B.C.	Randy L. Dietrich	Randy L. Dietrich	1990	39
48 4/8	10	10 1/8	5 4/8	5 5/8	1 6/8	2	6 6/8	5 7/8	Gallatin Co., Mont.	Dale L. Martin	Dale L. Martin	1990	39
48 4/8	10 1/8	9 7/8	5 5/8	5 4/8	1 7/8	1 5/8	7 7/8	7 4/8	Kenai Peninsula, Alaska	Cecil R. Jones	Cecil R. Jones	1988	41
48 2/8	9 2/8	9 6/8	5 4/8	5 3/8	1 6/8	1 6/8	6 3/8	5 4/8	Pelly Lake, B.C.	Russ L. Martin	Russ L. Martin	1989	41
48 2/8	10	9 4/8	5 4/8	5 6/8	1 6/8	1 7/8	7 3/8	7 1/8	Inklin River, B.C.	William H. Moyer	William H. Moyer	1990	43
48	9 4/8	9 3/8	5 6/8	5 4/8	1 6/8	1 6/8	6 5/8	6 1/8	Sawyer Creek, B.C.	John C. Shifflett	John C. Shifflett	1991	43
48	9 5/8	9 4/8	5 4/8	5 5/8	1 6/8	1 6/8		7 1/8	Maria Creek, B.C.	K. James Malady III	K. James Malady III	1989	45
47 6/8	9 4/8	9 6/8	5 2/8	5 2/8	1 7/8	1 7/8	7	6 4/8	Driftpile Creek, B.C.	David J. Craite	David J. Craite	1990	45
47 6/8	9 5/8	9	5 4/8	5 3/8	1 7/8	1 7/8	6 5/8	6 3/8	Carmen Mt., B.C.	Stanley W. Janusiewicz	Stanley W. Janusiewicz	1990	45
47 6/8	9	10 2/8	5 1/8	5 1/8	1 5/8	1 5/8	6 6/8	5 3/8	Horn Cliffs, Alaska	Brent R. Akers	Brent R. Akers	1989	48
47 4/8	10 5/8	9	5 5/8	5 4/8	1 6/8	1 6/8	6 1/8	5 7/8	Terror Lake, Alaska	Patricia A. Stewart	Patricia A. Stewart	1989	48
47 4/8	9	10	5	5	1 6/8	1 7/8	7	5 5/8	Chugach Mts., Alaska	William J. Swartz, Jr.	William J. Swartz, Jr.	1982	50
47 2/8	10	9 7/8	5	5	1 7/8	1 5/8	6 7/8	6 4/8	Chouteau Co., Mont.	Jerry E. Copenhaver	Jerry E. Copenhaver	1987	51
47	9 6/8	9 4/8	5 3/8	5 3/8	1 5/8	1 6/8	7 5/8	7 2/8	Bear Creek, B.C.	William A. Brooks, Sr.	William A. Brooks, Sr.	1989	51
47	9 4/8	9 3/8	5 4/8	5 4/8	1 6/8	1 5/8	7 3/8	6 6/8	Park Co., Wyo.	Paul L. Scott, Jr.	Paul L. Scott, Jr.	1989	51
47	9 7/8	8 7/8	5 6/8	5 5/8	1 6/8	1 6/8	6 2/8	5 2/8	Yakima Co., Wash.	Lee M. Shetler	Lee M. Shetler	1989	51
54*	11 4/8	11 5/8	5 5/8	5 5/8	1 7/8	1 7/8	8 4/8	7 5/8	Cleveland Pen., Alaska	Chris Guggenbrickler	C. & T. Guggenbrickler	1987	
53 4/8*	11 3/8	11 3/8	5 5/8	5 5/8	2	2	8 2/8	7 7/8	Yakataga Cape, Alaska	William F. Sherman	Thomas M. Bradley	1990	

491

* Final Score subject to revision by additional verifying measurements.

Muskox

Ovibos moschatus moschatus and certain related subspecies

Minimum Score 105 — World's Record 125-2/8

Score	Length of Horn R.	L.	Width of Boss R.	L.	Circumference at Third Quarter R.	L.	Greatest Spread	Tip to Tip Spread	Locality Killed	By Whom Killed	Owner	Date Killed	Rank
125	30 2/8	31 6/8	10 4/8	10 1/8	5	6 3/8	31 4/8	30 5/8	Bay Chimo, N.W.T.	Stephen A. Kroflich	Stephen A. Kroflich	1990	1
122 4/8	27 6/8	27 6/8	10 7/8	11	5 6/8	5 5/8	30 2/8	29 4/8	Rendez-vous Lake, N.W.T.	William R. Powers	William R. Powers	1991	2
119 4/8	28 7/8	29 1/8	9 5/8	10	5 4/8	5 4/8	29 1/8	28 7/8	McNaughton River, N.W.T.	Picked Up	Robert D. Jones	1991	3
118 6/8	27 5/8	28 2/8	10 4/8	9 7/8	5	5 2/8	29 3/8	28 3/8	Bay Chimo, N.W.T.	Doyle V. Toliver	Doyle V. Toliver	1989	4
118 4/8	28 3/8	29 1/8	9 3/8	9 3/8	5 4/8	5 7/8	32	31 6/8	Perry Island, N.W.T.	Lawrence T. Epping	Lawrence T. Epping	1990	5
117	29 5/8	29 6/8	9 7/8	9 3/8	5	5 5/8	30 3/8	29 4/8	Perry Island, N.W.T.	Robert D. Jones	Robert D. Jones	1989	6
116 6/8	26 3/8	26 3/8	10 2/8	10 4/8	5 5/8	5 6/8	27 2/8	25 6/8	Ellice River, N.W.T.	George M. Dirgo	George M. Dirgo	1991	7
116 6/8	26	26 6/8	9 7/8	9 7/8	4 7/8	5 4/8	24 4/8	22 2/8	Rendez-vous Lake, N.W.T.	Picked Up	Hubert R. Kennedy	PR 1991	7
115 6/8	28 2/8	27 5/8	10 1/8	10	5 7/8	5 5/8	27 1/8	26 6/8	Perry Island, N.W.T.	Delbert E. Rieckers	Delbert E. Rieckers	1988	9
115 6/8	28 3/8	29 5/8	9 6/8	9 4/8	4 3/8	5 1/8	28 5/8	26 3/8	Rendez-vous Lake, N.W.T.	Hubert R. Kennedy	Hubert R. Kennedy	1990	9
114 6/8	25 4/8	25 7/8	9 7/8	9 6/8	5 2/8	5 4/8	28 3/8	27 7/8	Kent Pen., N.W.T.	Archie J. Nesbitt	Archie J. Nesbitt	1989	11
114 7/8	27 6/8	25 5/8	9 7/8	10 7/8	6 2/8	5 5/8	26 6/8	26 1/8	Ellice River, N.W.T.	Gary Loghry	Gary Loghry	1990	12
114 2/8	26 6/8	27 4/8	10 4/8	10 7/8	5	5 6/8	26	24 4/8	Rendez-vous Lake, N.W.T.	James C. Johnson	James C. Johnson	1991	12
113 4/8	28 2/8	27 2/8	9 5/8	9 3/8	5 7/8	5 1/8	28 1/8	27 4/8	Bathurst Inlet, N.W.T.	George R. Skaggs	George R. Skaggs	1988	14
113	27 6/8	27 1/8	9 4/8	9	5 4/8	5 6/8	30	29 6/8	Bay Chimo, N.W.T.	David B. Dentoni, Sr.	David B. Dentoni, Sr.	1990	15
112 6/8	28 4/8	26 7/8	10 6/8	11 4/8	5 6/8	4 5/8	25 1/8	23 3/8	Paulatuk, N.W.T.	Picked Up	Roger A. Hansen	1988	16
111 6/8	25 4/8	26 3/8	9 6/8	9 3/8	5 4/8	5 7/8	29 1/8	29	Ellice River, N.W.T.	William G. Farley	William G. Farley	1990	17
111 6/8	26 4/8	26 3/8	9 2/8	9	5	4 7/8	27 7/8	27 4/8	Nunivak Island, Alaska	Danny Pankoski	Danny Pankoski	1991	17
111 2/8	26 4/8	26 6/8	8 4/8	8 6/8	6	5 7/8	26 3/8	25 6/8	Nunivak Island, Alaska	Willard G. Waite	Willard G. Waite	1989	19
111 2/8	27	27 1/8	8 3/8	8 1/8	5 4/8	5 5/8	27 7/8	27 5/8	Nunivak Island, Alaska	David L. Richards	David L. Richards	1990	19
111 2/8	26 2/8	26 6/8	9 5/8	10	5 1/8	5 5/8	23	21 1/8	Rendez-vous Lake, N.W.T.	Mark A. Adams	Mark A. Adams	1991	19
111 2/8	26 7/8	28 1/8	9	9 6/8	4 5/8	5 3/8	28 1/8	27 5/8	Coppermine, N.W.T.	Robert W. Kubick	Robert W. Kubick	1991	19
110	26 2/8	25 2/8	9 7/8	9 6/8	5	5 7/8	28 7/8	28 4/8	Pelly Island, N.W.T.	Jurgen Blattgerste	Jurgen Blattgerste	1990	23
109 4/8	26 1/8	26 3/8	8 1/8	8	5 3/8	5 5/8	26 3/8	25 4/8	Canning River, Alaska	Gregory L. Venable	Gregory L. Venable	1990	24

Score									Location	Owner	Hunter	Year	Rank
109 4/8	25 3/8	26 5/8	9 2/8	9	5 4/8	5 7/8	28 1/8	27 6/8	Nunivak Island, Alaska	David R. Lautner	David R. Lautner	1991	24
109	26	26 4/8	9	8 6/8	5 4/8	5 4/8	27 7/8	26 5/8	Ellice River, N.W.T.	Gerald L. Warnock	Gerald L. Warnock	1988	26
109	27 3/8	26 6/8	8 2/8	8 4/8	5 2/8	4 5/8	26 2/8	25 5/8	Nunivak Island, Alaska	Butch Hautanen	Butch Hautanen	1989	26
109	26 2/8	24 3/8	9 2/8	9 2/8	5 4/8	5 7/8	28 1/8	28	Ellice River, N.W.T.	Thomas D. Suedmeier	Thomas D. Suedmeier	1989	26
108 6/8	26 2/8	26 4/8	8 1/8	8 1/8	5 3/8	5 2/8	26 6/8	26 4/8	Nunivak Island, Alaska	William C. Cloyd	William C. Cloyd	1991	29
108 6/8	27 7/8	27	7 6/8	7 7/8	5 6/8	5 1/8	26 6/8	26 4/8	Nunivak Island, Alaska	Joseph E. Hardy	Joseph E. Hardy	1991	29
108 6/8	26 7/8	28	9	8 6/8	4 1/8	5 1/8	26 3/8	26	Nunivak Island, Alaska	Loren B. Hollers	Loren B. Hollers	1991	29
108 4/8	25 3/8	27 4/8	7 7/8	8	5	5	28 5/8	28 3/8	Nunivak Island, Alaska	Jerry M. Wylie	Jerry M. Wylie	1989	32
108 2/8	25 3/8	27	8 5/8	8 5/8	5 3/8	5 3/8	29	28 2/8	Ellice River, N.W.T.	Jerald E. Mason	Jerald E. Mason	1989	33
108 2/8	25 7/8	25 7/8	9 3/8	9 3/8	4 7/8	6	25 3/8	24 2/8	Lady Franklin Point, N.W.T.	Perry Harwell	Perry Harwell	1990	33
108	26 1/8	26 1/8	8 4/8	8 4/8	5 1/8	5 1/8	26 7/8	26 3/8	Nunivak Island, Alaska	Terrance E. Burlew	Terrance E. Burlew	1990	35
108	27	25 5/8	8 7/8	8 7/8	6 1/8	4 7/8	28 5/8	28 2/8	Queen Mand Gulf, N.W.T.	Archie J. Nesbitt	Archie J. Nesbitt	1990	35
107 6/8	25 2/8	25 5/8	9 5/8	9 4/8	5	5 4/8	25 4/8	23 7/8	Perry River, N.W.T.	Robert L. Killett	Robert L. Killett	1989	37
107 4/8	25 2/8	26	8 4/8	8 4/8	5 4/8	5	28	27 2/8	Cape Mohican, Alaska	Tommy L. Ramsey	Tommy L. Ramsey	1990	38
106 4/8	25 6/8	26 2/8	8 4/8	8 2/8	4 7/8	4 7/8	26 2/8	25 3/8	Nunivak Island, Alaska	Richard McIntyre	Richard McIntyre	1988	39
106 4/8	26 4/8	26 4/8	8 1/8	8	4 7/8	5	26	25 3/8	Saddlerochit River, Alaska	Donald L. Willis	Donald L. Willis	1990	39
106 2/8	25 4/8	26 5/8	9 1/8	9	5	5 7/8	26 6/8	26 6/8	Nunivak Island, Alaska	Elwin J. Lawler	Elwin J. Lawler	1990	41
106 2/8	25 7/8	25 2/8	8 5/8	8 6/8	5 7/8	5 1/8	26 7/8	25 6/8	Canning River, Alaska	Carl L. Yowell	Carl L. Yowell	1990	41
105 4/8	25 4/8	25 6/8	9 5/8	9 4/8	5 1/8	5 1/8	26 4/8	25 4/8	Sachs Harbor, N.W.T.	William H. Bynum	William H. Bynum	1989	43
105 4/8	26 4/8	27	8 6/8	8 2/8	4 5/8	4 5/8	24 3/8	23 2/8	Bluenose Lake, N.W.T.	George P. Mann	George P. Mann	1990	43
105 2/8	25 6/8	27	9 2/8	9 1/8	4 4/8	5 1/8	26 5/8	26	Gjaa Haven, N.W.T.	James J. McBride	James J. McBride	1991	45
105	27 1/8	27 5/8	8 1/8	7 7/8	4 4/8	4 6/8	27 7/8	27 1/8	Nelson Island, Alaska	Thomas W. Oates	Unknown	PR 1992	46
120*	28 5/8	28 3/8	10 6/8	10 7/8	5 4/8	5 2/8	28 4/8	27	Rendez-vous Lake, N.W.T.	Jim Moellman	Jim Moellman	1989	
118 2/8*	27 2/8	27 2/8	10 6/8	10 4/8	5 2/8	5 4/8	26 7/8	24 4/8	Rendez-vous Lake, N.W.T.	Victor E. Moss	Victor E. Moss	1989	
117 2/8*	28 7/8	27 5/8	10 1/8	10 2/8	6 3/8	5 2/8	29	28 4/8	Perry River, N.W.T.	Dennis Ader	Picked Up	1990	

* Final Score subject to revision by additional verifying measurements.

Bighorn Sheep

Minimum Score 175   Ovis canadensis canadensis and certain related subspecies   World's Record 208-1/8

Score	Length of Horn R.	L.	Circumference of Base R.	L.	Circumference at Third Quarter R.	L.	Greatest Spread	Tip to Tip Spread	Locality Killed	By Whom Killed	Owner	Date Killed	Rank
202	46 6/8	45 1/8	15 2/8	15 3/8	10 4/8	10 4/8	22 6/8	22 5/8	Canmore, Alta.	Picked Up	Alberta Fish & Wildl. Div.	1987	1
200 7/8	45 7/8	49 2/8	15 2/8	15 2/8	9 1/8	9 1/8	28 5/8	28 1/8	Deer Lodge Co., Mont.	Lester A. Kish	Lester A. Kish	1990	2
197 5/8	41 1/8	42 4/8	15 7/8	16 1/8	11	11	22 3/8	22 3/8	Deer Lodge Co., Mont.	Arthur R. Dubs	Arthur R. Dubs	1987	3
197 1/8	42	41 5/8	16 5/8	16 4/8	10 5/8	10 6/8	23 5/8	23 2/8	Granite Co., Mont.	Lee Hart	Lee Hart	1990	4
196 7/8	43	40 7/8	16 3/8	16 2/8	9 7/8	10 1/8	20 5/8	20	Granite Co., Mont.	Keith J. Koprivica	Keith J. Koprivica	1990	5
195 3/8	44 5/8	43 4/8	15 4/8	15 7/8	9	9	24 7/8	23 2/8	Missoula Co., Mont.	Leonard G. Thompson	Leonard G. Thompson	1990	6
193 5/8	43 1/8	41 2/8	15 2/8	15 4/8	10 4/8	10 4/8	22 4/8	19 4/8	Sheep River, Alta.	Gary H. Cain	Gary H. Cain	1990	7
193 4/8	39	39 4/8	16 4/8	16 3/8	10 6/8	10 7/8	26 7/8	23 2/8	Silver Bow Co., Mont.	Thomas R. Webster	Thomas R. Webster	1990	8
193 2/8	39 7/8	39 7/8	16 5/8	16 4/8	10	10	22 4/8	19 1/8	Sanders Co., Mont.	Jerry Landa	Jerry Landa	1989	9
193 1/8	40 1/8	39 2/8	16 3/8	16 4/8	10 3/8	10 3/8	19 7/8	15	Ewin Creek, B.C.	Gary N. Goode	Gary N. Goode	1989	10
192 7/8	40 6/8	41 3/8	16 2/8	16 3/8	10	9 5/8	21 3/8	21 3/8	Granite Co., Mont.	Raymond J. Dvorak	Raymond J. Dvorak	1989	11
192 3/8	40 6/8	40 7/8	15 4/8	15 5/8	10 5/8	10 5/8	20 5/8	17 6/8	Granite Co., Mont.	Robert L. Sandman	Robert L. Sandman	1991	12
192	43 3/8	42 7/8	15 5/8	15 6/8	9	9 6/8	24 2/8	24 2/8	Wallowa Co., Oreg.	H. James Tonkin	H. James Tonkin	1991	13
191 7/8	41 3/8	40 6/8	15 6/8	15 7/8	8 6/8	9 4/8	24 3/8	21 7/8	Missoula Co., Mont.	Carl W. Schmidt	Carl W. Schmidt	1989	14
191 1/8	43 2/8	43 3/8	16	15 7/8	8 1/8	8 2/8	25 1/8	25 3/8	Wolverine Creek, Alta.	James R. Gaines	James R. Gaines	1990	15
191 1/8	44	40 1/8	15 6/8	15 4/8	9	9	21 6/8	21 6/8	Sheep River, Alta.	Harvey Pyra	Harvey Pyra	1991	15
190 7/8	39 6/8	41 1/8	15 7/8	16	9 4/8	9 1/8	23 4/8	18 7/8	Sanders Co., Mont.	Terri Stoneman	Terri Stoneman	1988	17
190 6/8	42 3/8	41 5/8	15 5/8	15 5/8	8 7/8	8 7/8	25 5/8	25 7/8	Missoula Co., Mont.	Arthur R. Dubs	Arthur R. Dubs	1986	18
190 6/8	40 6/8	39 4/8	15 6/8	15 7/8	10 3/8	9 7/8	23	17 3/8	Granite Co., Mont.	Scott A. Campbell	Scott A. Campbell	1990	18
189 5/8	39 4/8	42 3/8	15 4/8	15 3/8	9 7/8	10 1/8	22 3/8	21 4/8	Deer Lodge Co., Mont.	Lawrence A. Jany	Lawrence A. Jany	1990	20
189 2/8	40 7/8	40 3/8	16 6/8	16 6/8	8 1/8	8 2/8	26	25 6/8	Sanders Co., Mont.	Linda Phillips	Linda Phillips	1989	21
188 7/8	44 7/8	39 6/8	15 7/8	15 7/8	8 4/8	8 2/8	26 6/8	26 4/8	Silver Bow Co., Mont.	Jerry J. Joseph	Jerry J. Joseph	1990	22
188 5/8	40 5/8	39 2/8	15 2/8	15 3/8	10 3/8	10 2/8	20 6/8	18 2/8	Sanders Co., Mont.	Richard L. Grimes	Richard L. Grimes	1990	23
188 3/8	40 4/8	39 3/8	15 2/8	15 4/8	10 7/8	11	23 6/8	20 6/8	Granite Co., Mont.	Larry J. Antonich	Larry J. Antonich	1990	24
188 3/8	40	39 7/8	16	16	9	8 7/8	25 1/8	20 1/8	Sheep River, Alta.	Katherine A. Pyra	Katherine A. Pyra	1991	24
188 1/8	40 1/8	40 4/8	15 1/8	15 2/8	10 1/8	10	23 3/8	23 1/8	Blaine Co., Mont.	Curtis L. Kostelecky	Curtis L. Kostelecky	1991	26
187 6/8	40 1/8	39 7/8	16	16	9 6/8	8 4/8	21	12	Ghost River, Alta.	Gerald Molnar	Gerald Molnar	1988	27
187 4/8	35	37 4/8	16 1/8	16 2/8	10 7/8	10 7/8	24 4/8	23 5/8	Deer Lodge Co., Mont.	Dorothy A. Pennington	Dorothy A. Pennington	1991	28
187 2/8	36 3/8	37 1/8	16 5/8	16 5/8	9 7/8	9 7/8	22 4/8	20	Thornton Creek, Alta.	John Gehan	John Gehan	1988	29
187	39 3/8	39 7/8	16	15 7/8	8 7/8	8 5/8	22	22 4/8	Granite Co., Mont.	Norman C. Dunkle	Norman C. Dunkle	1989	30

Score									Locality	Name	By Whom Taken	Date	Rank
187	39	38 4/8	15 2/8	15 2/8	10 3/8	11	22 1/8	22 1/8	Sanders Co., Mont.	William J. Kuchera	William J. Kuchera	1990	30
187	40 4/8	39 4/8	15 5/8	15 5/8	10	9 6/8	20 4/8	17 4/8	Granite Co., Mont.	Pearl Foust	Pearl Foust	1991	30
186 7/8	40 1/8	38 4/8	16 1/8	16	9	9	24 3/8	19	Ghost River, Alta.	D. James Turner	D. James Turner	1990	33
186 6/8	41 2/8	40 2/8	15	15	9 6/8	9 6/8	22 5/8	18 7/8	Tornado Creek, B.C.	Clive J. Endicott	Clive J. Endicott	1988	34
186 6/8	39 4/8	37 5/8	15 2/8	15 3/8	11 1/8	10 5/8	22 3/8	20 3/8	Sanders Co., Mont.	Bill Mitchell	Bill Mitchell	1988	34
186 6/8	41 1/8	41 1/8	15 4/8	15 4/8	8 5/8	8 6/8	22 3/8	21 6/8	Granite Co., Mont.	Carol K. Chudy	Carol K. Chudy	1991	34
186 6/8	39 4/8	40	15 3/8	15 4/8	10 1/8	9 1/8	20 4/8	15	Sheep River, Alta.	Percy Pyra	Percy Pyra	1991	34
186 5/8	41	40 7/8	16 1/8	16 1/8	8	8 6/8	23 6/8	23 6/8	Beaverhead Co., Mont.	Gary L. Peltomaa	Gary L. Peltomaa	1989	38
186 4/8	40 1/8	39 7/8	16 2/8	16 3/8	8 6/8	8 4/8	21 7/8	20 4/8	Mt. Assiniboine, B.C.	Shirley A. Malbery	Shirley A. Malbery	1990	39
186 1/8	39 5/8	38	15 3/8	15 3/8	9 6/8	10 2/8	20 4/8	20 4/8	Cougar Mt., Alta.	Alan E. Schroeder	Alan E. Schroeder	1989	40
186	40 6/8	40 2/8	15 4/8	15 4/8	9 7/8	9	22	22	Line Creek, B.C.	Sam W. Stephenson	Sam W. Stephenson	1991	41
185 7/8	40 3/8	41	15 6/8	15 6/8	8 4/8	8 5/8	21 5/8	21	Botanie Creek, B.C.	William J. Pincock	William J. Pincock	1988	42
185 6/8	39 6/8	38 4/8	15 2/8	15 2/8	9 7/8	9 6/8	20 4/8	20	Granite Co., Mont.	James M. Milligan	James M. Milligan	1990	43
185 4/8	40 5/8	39 3/8	16 4/8	16 3/8	8 7/8	8 3/8	21 7/8	20	Deer Lodge Co., Mont.	Douglas C. Landers	Douglas C. Landers	1987	44
185 3/8	38 1/8	40 6/8	15 7/8	15 7/8	9 4/8	9 3/8	22 6/8	21 7/8	Sanders Co., Mont.	Chad R. Jones	Chad R. Jones	1990	45
185 1/8	38	38 5/8	16 4/8	16 2/8	8 5/8	9	25 1/8	22 6/8	Blaine Co., Mont.	Mark K. Weiser	Mark K. Weiser	1989	46
184 4/8	36 7/8	37 5/8	15 4/8	15 4/8	10 1/8	10 5/8	24 6/8	23 7/8	Granite Co., Mont.	Kevin R. Bouley	Kevin R. Bouley	1988	47
184 1/8	39	38 1/8	15 7/8	16	9 5/8	9 5/8	25	23 5/8	Silver Bow Co., Mont.	John D. Truzzoline	John D. Truzzoline	1990	48
184	40 4/8	43 4/8	15	15	8 2/8	8 3/8	25 5/8	25 4/8	Deer Lodge Co., Mont.	Dave Bisch	Dave Bisch	1988	49
184	39	40 2/8	14 4/8	14 4/8	10 2/8	10 4/8	22	19 7/8	Mineral Co., Mont.	Ronald A. Snyder	Ronald A. Snyder	1991	49
183 7/8	41	41 1/8	15 1/8	15 1/8	8 4/8	8 2/8	24 3/8	24 3/8	Sanders Co., Mont.	Lyndell C. Stahn	Lyndell C. Stahn	1988	51
183 7/8	39 2/8	39 3/8	16	16 1/8	8 2/8	8 2/8	21 5/8	18 3/8	Garfield Co., Wash.	Klaus H. Meyn	Klaus H. Meyn	1990	51
183 4/8	39 1/8	37 5/8	16 6/8	16 4/8	8 1/8	7 6/8	22 6/8	14 2/8	Chauncey Creek, B.C.	Stewart Cockshutt	Stewart Cockshutt	1990	53
183 4/8	39 2/8	38 6/8	16 1/8	16 1/8	8	8	21 7/8	21 3/8	Galatea Creek, Alta.	Karlo Miklic	Karlo Miklic	1990	53
183 3/8	37 2/8	37 2/8	16 4/8	16 4/8	7 7/8	7 7/8	20 5/8	18 4/8	Mt. Sparrowhawk, Alta.	Gregory Kondro	Gregory Kondro	1989	55
183 3/8	37 4/8	37 4/8	16 1/8	16 1/8	9 5/8	9 6/8	22 6/8	19 4/8	Silver Bow Co., Mont.	Travis R. Schuessler	Travis R. Schuessler	1990	55
183 2/8	39 5/8	36 3/8	16 2/8	16 3/8	8 7/8	8 5/8	28 2/8	28 2/8	Granite Co., Mont.	Scott R. Rossow	Scott R. Rossow	1988	57
183 2/8	39 4/8	39 6/8	15 3/8	15 4/8	9 1/8	9 1/8	20 2/8	18 2/8	Simpson River, B.C.	Robert T. White	Robert T. White	1988	57
183 1/8	39	39	15 2/8	15 2/8	9 4/8	9 4/8	21 4/8	18 6/8	Prospect Creek, Alta.	Bruce E. Williams	Bruce E. Williams	1989	57
183 1/8	36 1/8	40 2/8	16	15 7/8	8 7/8	9	20 2/8	20 3/8	Deer Lodge Co., Mont.	Jeffrey R. Shellenberg	Jeffrey R. Shellenberg	1990	60
182 7/8	37 6/8	38 5/8	16 4/8	16 4/8	8 7/8	8 1/8	22 1/8	17	Line Creek, B.C.	Kevin J. Galla	Kevin J. Galla	1989	61
182 6/8	42	40 4/8	16	16	7	7 1/8	25 7/8	25 3/8	Deer Lodge Co., Mont.	Kirk G. Stovall	Kirk G. Stovall	1990	62
182 4/8	39 3/8	39 3/8	15 5/8	15 5/8	9 7/8	8 4/8	21 5/8	19	Sanders Co., Mont.	Thorne R. Johnson	Thorne R. Johnson	1989	63
182 3/8	38 7/8	39 2/8	15 6/8	15 6/8	9 4/8	8 7/8	20 6/8	20 2/8	Pigeon Mt., Alta.	Len Guldman	Len Guldman	1990	64
182 2/8	39 3/8	39 7/8	16 1/8	15 7/8	8	7 7/8	23 3/8	23 5/8	Beaverhead Co., Mont.	Raymond L. Cote	Raymond L. Cote	1989	65
182 2/8	38 5/8	38 7/8	15 1/8	15 1/8	9 3/8	9 6/8	19 7/8	19 1/8	Silver Bow Co., Mont.	John T. LaPierre	John T. LaPierre	1990	65
182 1/8	39	39 3/8	16 1/8	16 1/8	7 6/8	7 6/8	22 4/8	22 3/8	Silver Bow Co., Mont.	Eric L. Jacobson	Eric L. Jacobson	1990	67
182	39 4/8	39 6/8	15	15	9 4/8	9 4/8	22 3/8	20 3/8	Sanders Co., Mont.	Kevin K. Harris	Kevin K. Harris	1988	68
182	37 5/8	37 6/8	16 2/8	16 2/8	8 2/8	8 2/8	20 4/8	19 4/8	Wigwam River, B.C.	Grant W. Markoski	Grant W. Markoski	1990	68
181 6/8	40 5/8	39 5/8	15 2/8	15 2/8	8 4/8	8 4/8	26	24 4/8	Teton Co., Wyo.	Richard L. Grabowski	Richard L. Grabowski	1989	70
181 5/8	38 3/8	39 7/8	14 7/8	14 7/8	9 1/8	8 4/8	22 2/8	22 2/8	Blaine Co., Mont.	Betty L. Ramsey	Betty L. Ramsey	1989	70

Bighorn Sheep - *Continued*

Score	Length of Horn R.	L.	Circumference of Base R.	L.	Circumference at Third Quarter R.	L.	Greatest Spread	Tip to Tip Spread	Locality Killed	By Whom Killed	Owner	Date Killed	Rank
181 5/8	36 7/8	35 5/8	16	16	9 5/8	10 4/8	23 3/8	22 5/8	Lewis & Clark Co., Mont.	Pamela J. Bennett	Pamela J. Bennett	1989	72
181 5/8	39 7/8	38 2/8	15 6/8	15 4/8	8 4/8	8 7/8	21 7/8	20 1/8	Teton Co., Mont.	Neil L. Hamm	Neil L. Hamm	1990	72
181 4/8	35 7/8	36 7/8	16 3/8	16 3/8	8 5/8	9 2/8	22 3/8	21	Granite Co., Mont.	Bronwyn M. Price	Bronwyn M. Price	1989	74
181 3/8	38 5/8	40 2/8	14 5/8	14 7/8	9 2/8	9 1/8	22 6/8	22 1/8	Wallowa Co., Oreg.	Michael L. Taylor	Michael L. Taylor	1987	75
181 3/8	37 3/8	39 2/8	15	15 1/8	9 7/8	9 5/8	20 2/8	16 4/8	Fairholme Range, Alta.	Eldon Hoff	Eldon Hoff	1989	75
181 3/8	39 3/8	39	15	15 1/8	10 2/8	9 6/8	23 3/8	21 4/8	Grant Co., N.M.	Dan Pocapalia	Dan Pocapalia	1990	75
181 2/8	41 3/8	39 5/8	15 4/8	15 3/8	7 5/8	7 6/8	21	21	Granite Co., Mont.	Tom J. Lewis	Tom J. Lewis	1989	78
181 2/8	40	40 6/8	15 1/8	15	7 6/8	7 6/8	21 4/8	21	Ghost River, Alta.	Mike Michalezki	Mike Michalezki	1991	78
181	39 1/8	41 1/8	15	15	7 7/8	8 1/8	22 4/8	22 4/8	Kindersley Creek, B.C.	Karl Dorr	Karl Dorr	1989	80
180 7/8	39 2/8	38 1/8	14 5/8	14 6/8	9 3/8	9 4/8	22 6/8	22 2/8	Clearwater River, Alta.	Kevin Peters	Kevin Peters	1989	81
180 7/8	40 5/8	37 4/8	16	16 3/8	7 7/8	7 6/8	25 5/8	25 3/8	Sanders Co., Mont.	Raymond J. Smith	Raymond J. Smith	1990	81
180 7/8	38 7/8	39 4/8	15	15	9 2/8	9 1/8	19 4/8	15 4/8	Line Creek, B.C.	Kevin J. Galla	Kevin J. Galla	1991	81
180 6/8	38 7/8	37 7/8	16 7/8	16 2/8	7 5/8	7 6/8	24 4/8	24	Sanders Co., Mont.	Bob L. Jacks	Bob L. Jacks	1990	84
180 5/8	38 7/8	40 2/8	14 4/8	14 2/8	9 5/8	10	21 6/8	21	Lemhi Co., Idaho	Eugene L. Chesler	Eugene L. Chesler	1990	85
180 5/8	39 4/8	38 7/8	15 5/8	15 3/8	8 2/8	8 1/8	21 2/8	19 6/8	Blaine Co., Mont.	Mark D. Farnam	Mark D. Farnam	1990	85
180 3/8	38 6/8	40 1/8	15 1/8	15 1/8	8 6/8	9 3/8	20 1/8	19	Bow Lake, Alta.	Robert D. Layton	Robert D. Layton	1942	87
180 3/8	38	38 1/8	15 5/8	15 5/8	8 3/8	9 3/8	19 3/8	19 3/8	Ravalli Co., Mont.	Terry Frey	Terry Frey	1988	87
180 3/8	35 1/8	37 2/8	15 5/8	15 4/8	9 4/8	9 7/8	24	15 6/8	Greenlee Co., Ariz.	James A. Gerrettie II	James A. Gerrettie II	1988	87
180 3/8	40 4/8	40 3/8	14 6/8	15	8 1/8	8	25 6/8	25 6/8	Chouteau Co., Mont.	Scott D. Rubin	Scott D. Rubin	1989	87
180 3/8	38 4/8	38 5/8	15 1/8	15 3/8	8 7/8	8 7/8	23 1/8	22 4/8	Deer Lodge Co., Mont.	Max E. Leishman	Max E. Leishman	1990	87
180 3/8	41 6/8	32 5/8	16 4/8	16 4/8	9 1/8	7 3/8	25	22 4/8	Beaverhead Co., Mont.	James M. Linscott	James M. Linscott	1990	87
180 2/8	38	39 2/8	14 4/8	14 4/8	10 2/8	10 4/8	21	14	British Columbia	James T. Wilson	Kevin D. O'Connell	1928	93
180 2/8	39 5/8	39 5/8	15 3/8	15 4/8	7 7/8	7 6/8	21 1/8	19 1/8	Invermere, B.C.	Lyle O. Fett	Lyle O. Fett	1982	93
180 2/8	37 6/8	37 4/8	15	15	10 1/8	9 5/8	20 1/8	12 7/8	Ewin Creek, B.C.	Bob Hildebrandt	Bob Hildebrandt	1988	93
180 2/8	38 2/8	38 2/8	15 2/8	15 3/8	8 5/8	8 6/8	19 5/8	16 3/8	Cross River, B.C.	Daryl Stech	Daryl Stech	1988	93
180 2/8	39 1/8	39 1/8	14 5/8	14 4/8	9 1/8	9 1/8	22	20 2/8	Lincoln Co., Mont.	Bradley S. Osler	Bradley S. Osler	1989	93
180 2/8	35 3/8	35 7/8	15 5/8	15 6/8	9 7/8	10	21 1/8	14 2/8	Warden Rock, Alta.	Brian N. Holthe	Brian N. Holthe	1990	93
180 1/8	36 2/8	38 1/8	14 1/8	15 4/8	9 5/8	9 6/8	19 2/8	17 4/8	Granite Co., Mont.	Scott M. Willumsen	Scott M. Willumsen	1989	99
180 1/8	40	39 5/8	14 1/8	14 2/8	9 2/8	9 1/8	22 6/8	22 4/8	Lemhi Co., Idaho	JoAnn Basso	JoAnn Basso	1990	99
180 1/8	37 4/8	37 3/8	15 2/8	15 2/8	9 2/8	9	22 7/8	18 2/8	Clear Creek Co., Colo.	Charles W. Hanawalt	Charles W. Hanawalt	1990	99
180	37 1/8	39 5/8	15 6/8	15 5/8	7 7/8	8 1/8	21 6/8	21 6/8	Beaverhead Co., Mont.	Kory McGavin	Kory McGavin	1988	102

180	38 2/8	40	14 4/8	14 6/8	9 2/8	9 1/8	21 7/8	20 6/8	Lewis & Clark Co., Mont.	Brian J. Boehm	Brian J. Boehm	1989	102
180	38 1/8	37 5/8	15 3/8	15 2/8	9 1/8	9	23 1/8	22 4/8	Deer Lodge Co., Mont.	Michael P. Lorello	Michael P. Lorello	1990	102
180	37 4/8	37	15 3/8	15 5/8	9 2/8	9 1/8	21	17 4/8	Granite Co., Mont.	Thomas I. Jenni	Thomas I. Jenni	1991	102
179 2/8	39 2/8	39 2/8	16	16	7 3/8	7 7/8	20 4/8	19	Cross River, B.C.	Warren K. Winkler	Warren K. Winkler	1991	106
179 1/8	37 7/8	37 6/8	15	15 1/8	9 2/8	9 4/8	20 3/8	21 4/8	Deer Lodge Co., Mont.	Chad Gochanour	Chad Gochanour	1988	107
178 7/8	38	38 5/8	15 1/8	15 1/8	8 6/8	9	22 3/8	21 7/8	Sanders Co., Mont.	Aivars O. Berkis	Aivars O. Berkis	1989	108
178 5/8	40	38 5/8	15 1/8	15 2/8	8 2/8	7 7/8	22 1/8	21	Taseko Lakes, B.C.	George F. Dennis, Jr.	George F. Dennis, Jr.	1990	109
177 6/8	35 2/8	36	15 2/8	15 2/8	9 4/8	9 5/8	22 3/8	22 3/8	Lewis & Clark Co., Mont.	Rusten L. Barnes	Rusten L. Barnes	1990	110
177	36 4/8	36 6/8	15 4/8	15 4/8	8 3/8	8 4/8	17 3/8	16 3/8	Simpson River, B.C.	Frank J. Blaha, Jr.	Frank J. Blaha, Jr.	1990	111
176 6/8	39 4/8	37 2/8	15 7/8	15 5/8	7 3/8	7 6/8	21 5/8	17 6/8	Simpson River, B.C.	Frank J. Blaha, Jr.	Frank J. Blaha, Jr.	1991	112
176	36 6/8	36 2/8	15	15 1/8	9	9 1/8	22 5/8	21 2/8	Harney Co., Oreg.	Red Iler	Red Iler	1991	113
198 2/8*	40 6/8	44 4/8	17 2/8	17 4/8	8 6/8	9	23 6/8	18 6/8	Asotin Co., Wash.	Michael W. Houser	Michael W. Houser	1989	
198*	42 4/8	43 4/8	16 5/8	16 5/8	10	9 4/8	25	18 4/8	Wallowa Co., Oreg.	Todd B. Jaksick	Todd B. Jaksick	1988	

* Final Score subject to revision by additional verifying measurements.

497

Desert Sheep

Minimum Score 165

Ovis canadensis nelsoni and certain related subspecies

World's Record 205-1/8

Score	Length of Horn R.	L.	Circumference of Base R.	L.	Circumference at Third Quarter R.	L.	Greatest Spread	Tip to Tip Spread	Locality Killed	By Whom Killed	Owner	Date Killed	Rank
197 1/8	42 3/8	41 6/8	16 1/8	16 1/8	10 5/8	11	26	26	Graham Co., Ariz.	Arthur R. Dubs	Arthur R. Dubs	1988	1
190 3/8	41	43 7/8	15 3/8	15 5/8	9 1/8	9 1/8	23 7/8	23 7/8	Arizona	Unknown	Bruce R. Kemp, Sr.	1903	2
186 3/8	41 7/8	39	15 7/8	16	9 3/8	9 4/8	24	22 3/8	Gila Co., Ariz.	Steven E. Wright	Steven E. Wright	1990	3
185 3/8	38 3/8	39 4/8	16 1/8	16 1/8	8 7/8	9	23 2/8	19 6/8	Baja Calif., Mexico	Robert L. Williamson	Robert L. Williamson	1987	4
184 6/8	42 6/8	41	15	15 1/8	8 4/8	8 3/8	27 1/8	26 6/8	Nye Co., Nev.	Alfred L. Raiche, Sr.	Alfred L. Raiche, Sr.	1988	5
180 4/8	36 7/8	37 5/8	16 2/8	16 2/8	9 4/8	9 5/8	21 5/8	17 3/8	Yuma Co., Ariz.	Weldon A. Rogers	Weldon A. Rogers	1990	6
179 2/8	38 3/8	40 1/8	15 1/8	15 2/8	9 3/8	9 3/8	23 4/8	23	Clark Co., Nev.	Tammy H. Bawcom	Tammy H. Bawcom	1988	7
179 1/8	39 5/8	40	14 4/8	14 4/8	9	9	25 1/8	24 5/8	Clark Co., Nev.	Gary D. Selmi	Gary D. Selmi	1989	8
178 2/8	38 6/8	36 2/8	14 2/8	14 2/8	10 1/8	10 4/8	23 5/8	22 4/8	Clark Co., Nev.	Kenneth A. Brunk	Kenneth A. Brunk	1989	9
177 7/8	34 2/8	38 1/8	16 2/8	16 1/8	8 3/8	8 4/8	24	23 3/8	Graham Co., Ariz.	William N. Willis	William N. Willis	1989	10
177 4/8	36 5/8	35 5/8	15 2/8	15 2/8	9 3/8	9 5/8	20 7/8	20 3/8	Pima Co., Ariz.	Mark D. Morris	Mark D. Morris	1990	11
176 6/8	39 6/8	37	14 6/8	14 6/8	9 4/8	9	21 7/8	22 1/8	Clark Co., Nev.	Douglas E. Wendt	Douglas E. Wendt	1989	12
176 4/8	35 2/8	34 7/8	15 1/8	15	9 6/8	10 2/8	19 2/8	21 2/8	Yuma Co., Ariz.	Gail Ferguson	Gail Ferguson	1988	13
176 1/8	37	34 7/8	15 6/8	16	8 4/8	8 4/8	22 4/8	22 4/8	Pima Co., Ariz.	Don Petersen	Don Petersen	1988	14
175 1/8	34 4/8	36 5/8	15	15	10	9 6/8	23 2/8	22	Clark Co., Nev.	William J. Conner	William J. Conner	1989	15
175	35 5/8	36 4/8	14 6/8	14 6/8	9 5/8	9 5/8	20 6/8	20 2/8	Baja Calif., Mexico	Craig Leerberg	Craig Leerberg	1990	16
174 7/8	35 7/8	35 4/8	15 5/8	15 5/8	8 4/8	8 5/8	19 6/8	19 6/8	Clark Co., Nev.	Cleldon E. Nelson	Cleldon E. Nelson	1987	17
174	37 2/8	38 2/8	14 3/8	14 2/8	8 7/8	8 7/8	22	17 5/8	Clark Co., Nev.	H. James Tonkin, Jr.	H. James Tonkin, Jr.	1990	18
173 5/8	35 4/8	36 3/8	15 6/8	15 4/8	8 2/8	8 7/8	21	20 4/8	Baja Calif., Mexico	John P. Reilly	John P. Reilly	1989	19
173 3/8	36 4/8	35 1/8	14 6/8	14 7/8	8 7/8	9	23 4/8	22 5/8	Maricopa Co., Ariz.	James D. Thorne	James D. Thorne	1989	20
173 2/8	35 4/8	35 6/8	15 1/8	15 1/8	8 6/8	9 1/8	26 1/8	25 4/8	Lincoln Co., Nev.	Ken G. Gerg	Ken G. Gerg	1990	21
173 1/8	36 5/8	36	14 7/8	14 7/8	9 5/8	9 5/8	24	24	Lincoln Co., Nev.	Michael D. Rowe	Michael D. Rowe	1988	22
172 7/8	34 4/8	34 1/8	15	15	9 5/8	9 7/8	22 1/8	18 7/8	Gila Co., Ariz.	Picked Up	Michael T. Miller	1990	23
172 6/8	36 4/8	35	15 2/8	15 3/8	8 7/8	8 4/8	19 1/8	22	Gila Co., Ariz.	Richard P. Carlsberg	Richard P. Carlsberg	1989	24
172 4/8	36 6/8	37 6/8	14 4/8	14 1/8	8 6/8	9 3/8	29 5/8	28 4/8	Mohave Co., Ariz.	Densel M. Strang	Densel M. Strang	1989	25
172 4/8	35 6/8	35 4/8	14 7/8	14 7/8	9 6/8	9 5/8	20 3/8	17 7/8	Lincoln Co., Nev.	Craig S. Boyack	Craig S. Boyack	1990	25
172 2/8	37 3/8	37 1/8	14 2/8	14 4/8	8 5/8	8 4/8	20 3/8	19 6/8	Clark Co., Nev.	Verner J. Fisher, Jr.	Verner J. Fisher, Jr.	1988	27
172 2/8	35 3/8	34 3/8	15 3/8	15 1/8	9	8 7/8	22 2/8	22 2/8	Baja Calif., Mexico	Fred Fortier	Fred Fortier	1989	27
172 2/8	36 4/8	36 4/8	14	13 7/8	10	10 1/8	19 6/8	21 1/8	Clark Co., Nev.	Nicholas J. Coussoulis	Nicholas J. Coussoulis	1990	27
172 1/8	35 5/8	35 5/8	14 7/8	15	9 2/8	8 6/8	20 6/8	20 6/8	Baja Calif., Mexico	Greg A. Strait	Greg A. Strait	1989	30

Score								Locality	Owner	By Whom Collected	Date	Rank
172	36 7/8	37 3/8	15 1/8	14 7/8	8 5/8	8 6/8	25 7/8	25 7/8	Clark Co., Nev.	Dan Pocapalia	Dan Pocapalia	1988	31
171 5/8	34 6/8	34 7/8	14 7/8	15	9	8 4/8	22 3/8	18	Yuma Co., Ariz.	Miles R. Brown	Miles R. Brown	1989	32
171 5/8	33 7/8	33 3/8	15 1/8	15 2/8	9 6/8	10 7/8	22	23 6/8	Lincoln Co., Nev.	James D. Buonamici	James D. Buonamici	1989	32
171 4/8	35 4/8	35	14 4/8	14 4/8	10	10 2/8	21 4/8	20 2/8	San Bernardino Co., Calif.	Leon A. Pimentel	Leon A. Pimentel	1989	34
171 1/8	35 5/8	36 6/8	14 7/8	14 6/8	8 2/8	8 3/8	22	21 4/8	Yuma Co., Ariz.	Robert J. Cordes III	Robert J. Cordes III	1988	35
171	36 1/8	35 5/8	14 7/8	14 7/8	8 2/8	8 2/8	26 5/8	26	Mohave Co., Ariz.	Michael L. Gwaltney	Michael L. Gwaltney	1990	36
170 7/8	34 1/8	35 4/8	15 4/8	15 4/8	8 4/8	8 7/8	22 6/8	19 3/8	Yuma Co., Ariz.	Gary L. Major	Gary L. Major	1989	37
170 6/8	36 3/8	37 7/8	13 6/8	14	8 4/8	8 6/8	24	24	Clark Co., Nev.	Lacel Bland	Picked Up	1991	38
170 4/8	34 7/8	35 7/8	15 1/8	15	8 7/8	8 3/8	18 7/8	19 4/8	Baja Calif., Mexico	Edward J. Huxen	Edward J. Huxen	1988	39
170 4/8	34 5/8	32 1/8	15 2/8	15 3/8	8 6/8	8 5/8	23 6/8	23	Lincoln Co., Nev.	Robert Del Porto	Robert Del Porto	1989	39
170 3/8	36 2/8	36 1/8	14	14	8 4/8	9 2/8	20 6/8	18	La Paz Co., Ariz.	Rick P. Palmer	Rick P. Palmer	1989	41
170	36 2/8	36	15	14 7/8	9 6/8	9 6/8	22 3/8	21 4/8	Yuma Co., Ariz.	Cheryl Machac	Cheryl Machac	1988	42
169 6/8	37 7/8	37	13 6/8	14	9 1/8	9	20 7/8	18 4/8	San Bernardino Co., Calif.	Charles E. Cook	Charles E. Cook	1989	43
169 6/8	38 2/8	36	13 3/8	13 5/8	9 3/8	9 3/8	23	21 7/8	Clark Co., Nev.	Harold D. Humes	Harold D. Humes	1990	43
169 5/8	33	34 5/8	15 7/8	15 1/8	8 4/8	8 5/8	18 6/8	18 4/8	Coconino Co., Ariz.	Terry S. Marcum	Terry S. Marcum	1990	45
169 4/8	34 4/8	34 2/8	14 6/8	14 6/8	9 4/8	9 1/8	23 3/8	20 4/8	San Bernardino Co., Calif.	Jefre R. Bugni	Jefre R. Bugni	1989	46
169 4/8	35	35 2/8	15 1/8	15 1/8	8 1/8	8 5/8	22 5/8	21 5/8	Baja Calif., Mexico	Steven D. Bacon	Steven D. Bacon	1990	46
169 2/8	32 2/8	34 4/8	15 3/8	15 4/8	10	9 2/8	21 2/8	20	Coconino Co., Ariz.	Warren K. Winkler	Warren K. Winkler	1990	46
169	33 4/8	34 4/8	15 1/8	15 2/8	8 7/8	8 6/8	21 3/8	21	La Paz Co., Ariz	Jim F. Phelps	Jim F. Phelps	1988	49
168 5/8	35 4/8	34	15	15	8 5/8	8 2/8	22 1/8	16 1/8	Maricopa Co., Ariz.	C. Ames Thompson	C. Ames Thompson	1988	50
168 4/8	35 5/8	34 4/8	15	15	8	8	24 1/8	22 1/8	Clark Co., Nev.	Joseph Machac	Joseph Machac	1989	51
168 1/8	34 7/8	35 5/8	14 6/8	14 7/8	8 3/8	8 5/8	25 2/8	24 4/8	Mohave Co., Ariz.	Louise B. Ellison	Louise B. Ellison	1984	52
168	35 6/8	36 5/8	14 6/8	14 6/8	7 6/8	7 3/8	23	21 1/8	Clark Co., Nev.	Richard L. Deane	Richard L. Deane	1988	53
168	33 6/8	32 4/8	14 6/8	14 7/8	9 1/8	9 1/8	25 3/8	24 5/8	Mohave Co., Ariz.	Joseph D. Lynch	Joseph D. Lynch	1987	54
168	35 2/8	35 5/8	14 1/8	14 2/8	8 7/8	8 7/8	19 6/8	17 3/8	Baja Calif., Mexico	Mclean Bowman	Mclean Bowman	1989	54
165 5/8	32 5/8	35 2/8	14 2/8	14 2/8	9 4/8	8 7/8	23 4/8	23 6/8	Lincoln Co., Nev.	Hilding Lund	Hilding Lund	1985	56
188 3/8 *	40 2/8	39 3/8	15 5/8	15 5/8	10 2/8	10 1/8	24 6/8	23 6/8	Yuma Co., Ariz.	Randy W. Smith	Randy W. Smith	1988	

* Final Score subject to revision by additional verifying measurements.

Dall's Sheep

Ovis dalli dalli and Ovis dalli kenaiensis

Score	Length of Horn R.	L.	Circumference of Base R.	L.	Circumference at Third Quarter R.	L.	Greatest Spread	Tip to Tip Spread	Locality Killed	By Whom Killed	Owner	Date Killed	Rank
180 3/8	46 6/8	45 5/8	13	13	6 5/8	6 6/8	28 3/8	28 3/8	Hartman River, Alaska	Carl E. Jacobson	Carl E. Jacobson	1989	1
173 4/8	41 7/8	41 5/8	13 6/8	14	6 6/8	6 6/8	26 4/8	26 4/8	Troublesome Creek, Alaska	David G. Urban	David G. Urban	1991	2
172 3/8	41 4/8	41 7/8	14 1/8	14 2/8	6 4/8	6 6/8	23	22 7/8	Mackenzie Mts., N.W.T.	Dan L. Johnerson	Dan L. Johnerson	1989	3
170 5/8	39 3/8	41 3/8	14	14	7	6 4/8	19 2/8	18 6/8	S. Nahanni River, N.W.T.	Lionel G. Heinrich	Lionel G. Heinrich	1987	4
170 3/8	40 6/8	40 3/8	13 7/8	13 7/8	6 7/8	6 6/8	23 7/8	23 7/8	Alaska Range, Alaska	James W. Thompson	James W. Thompson	1986	5
170 2/8	38 2/8	37 6/8	13 3/8	13 7/8	8 2/8	9 2/8	21	20 5/8	Robertson River, Alaska	John W. Redmond	John W. Redmond	1970	6
170 2/8	41 7/8	41 1/8	14	14	6 5/8	6 6/8	21 4/8	21 2/8	Mackenzie Mts., N.W.T.	Alan Means	Alan Means	1991	6
168 6/8	42 2/8	41 6/8	13 4/8	13 4/8	5 7/8	5 7/8	26 3/8	26 3/8	Mackenzie Mts., N.W.T.	J. Wesley Jones	J. Wesley Jones	1990	8
167 5/8	40 3/8	41 6/8	14 3/8	14	6	6	28 4/8	28 4/8	Brooks Range, Alaska	James B. Leet	James B. Leet	1989	9
167 2/8	42 2/8	41 4/8	14	14	6 2/8	5 4/8	26 7/8	26 7/8	Hulahula River, Alaska	Robert D. Boutang	Robert D. Boutang	1989	10
167	36	37 4/8	13 4/8	13 4/8	8 5/8	8 4/8	21	21	Brooks Range, Alaska	G. Todd Ralstin	G. Todd Ralstin	1989	11
166 4/8	43 2/8	42 6/8	13 2/8	13 3/8	5 3/8	5 5/8	27 7/8	27 7/8	Godlin River, N.W.T.	John R. Connelly	John R. Connelly	1990	12
165 3/8	38 2/8	40 5/8	13 6/8	13 6/8	6 1/8	6 1/8	22 7/8	22 4/8	Nisling River, Yukon	Joe W. Carroll	Joe W. Carroll	1980	13
165 1/8	40 7/8	40	13 2/8	13 2/8	5 5/8	5 5/8	26 3/8	26 3/8	Chandalar River, Alaska	Charles E. White	Charles E. White	1988	14
165 1/8	39 6/8	39 5/8	13 6/8	13 4/8	6 3/8	6 2/8	25	24 7/8	Ruby Range, Yukon	George L. Tickell	George L. Tickell	1989	14
165	40	40	12 5/8	12 7/8	7 2/8	7 2/8	21	21	Alaska Range, Alaska	Donald W. Bunselmeier	Donald W. Bunselmeier	1988	16
165	36	43	14 2/8	14 3/8	5 5/8	6 2/8	25 1/8	25 1/8	White Mts., Alaska	Edward B. Crain II	Edward B. Crain II	1989	16
163 6/8	41 3/8	37 7/8	14	13 7/8	5 2/8	5 4/8	23 4/8	20 6/8	Kuskokwim River, Alaska	Basil T. Moore, Jr.	Basil T. Moore, Jr.	1990	18
163 4/8	40 2/8	39 6/8	13 2/8	13 2/8	6	6	24 4/8	24 2/8	Ruby Range, Yukon	Theodore E. Dugey, Jr.	Theodore E. Dugey, Jr.	1982	19
163 3/8	38 2/8	41	14	14 1/8	5 6/8	5 6/8	32 3/8	32	Carcajou River, N.W.T.	Lee M. Wahlund	Lee M. Wahlund	1986	20
163 3/8	41 7/8	41 6/8	13 1/8	13 1/8	5 2/8	5 2/8	24 5/8	24 5/8	Mackenzie Mts., N.W.T.	Ralph Fleegle	Ralph Fleegle	1991	20
161 6/8	38 3/8	38 1/8	13 1/8	13 4/8	6 4/8	6 3/8	27 1/8	27 1/8	Alaska Range, Alaska	James L. Kedrowski	James L. Kedrowski	1987	22
161 2/8	40 2/8	35 6/8	14 1/8	13 7/8	5 4/8	5 6/8	24 1/8	24 1/8	Robertson River, Alaska	Douglas J. Miller	Douglas J. Miller	1989	23
160 4/8	39 4/8	39	12 7/8	12 7/8	6 3/8	6 1/8	24 6/8	24 4/8	Sanpete Creek, Yukon	Mark Farnam	Mark Farnam	1988	24
160 3/8	35 1/8	41	13 1/8	13 1/8	6 2/8	6 2/8	26	26	Brooks Range, Alaska	Stan J. Neitling, Jr.	Stan J. Neitling, Jr.	1989	25
184 7/8*	43 2/8	43 7/8	14 4/8	15	7 3/8	7 1/8	26 1/8	26 1/8	Brooks Range, Alaska	Paul S. Zaczkowski	Paul S. Zaczkowski	1990	
183 4/8*	45 5/8	46 1/8	14 4/8	13 4/8	8 2/8	8 1/8	23	22 3/8	Brooks Range, Alaska	Terry M. Webb	Terry M. Webb	1990	
176 1/8*	41	40 1/8	14 4/8	14 1/8	8	7 1/8	25 5/8	25 3/8	Swift River, Alaska	Guy J. Turner	Guy J. Turner	1989	

* Final Score subject to revision by additional verifying measurements.

Stone's Sheep

Ovis dalli stonei

Minimum Score 165   World's Record 196-6/8

Score	Length of Horn R.	L.	Circumference of Base R.	L.	Circumference at Third Quarter R.	L.	Greatest Spread	Tip to Tip Spread	Locality Killed	By Whom Killed	Owner	Date Killed	Rank
176	41 2/8	40 2/8	14 2/8	14 4/8	8 1/8	8 1/8	21 6/8	21 1/8	Tuchodi Lakes, B.C.	Terry Filas	Terry Filas	1989	1
174 5/8	36 7/8	39	14 6/8	14 6/8	8 3/8	8 4/8	20 7/8	20 2/8	Prophet River, B.C.	Craig R. Johnson	Craig R. Johnson	1989	2
174 4/8	40	40 2/8	15	15	6 7/8	6 7/8	22 6/8	21	Dall Lake, B.C.	Darrell Orth	Darrell Orth	1990	3
174 2/8	39 7/8	39 1/8	15 1/8	15 1/8	6 7/8	6 6/8	22 5/8	22 5/8	Toad River, B.C.	Bill Hicks, Jr.	Bill Hicks, Jr.	1990	4
174 2/8	38 2/8	39 2/8	15 4/8	15 6/8	6 7/8	6 6/8	26 6/8	26 4/8	Redfern Lake, B.C.	Wilf Klingsat	Wilf Klingsat	1990	4
172 5/8	38 7/8	40	14 7/8	14 7/8	6 6/8	6 6/8	24 4/8	23	Blue Sheep Lake, B.C.	John Deromedi	John Deromedi	1989	6
172	41 7/8	40 6/8	13 5/8	13 4/8	6 7/8	6 5/8	23	23	Toad River, B.C.	Steve Best	Steve Best	1988	7
171 7/8	42 3/8	39 6/8	14 1/8	14 2/8	6 2/8	6 3/8	23 5/8	23 5/8	Toad River, B.C.	Larry Jenkins	Larry Jenkins	1988	8
171 6/8	42 4/8	42 6/8	14	14 2/8	6 3/8	6	24 7/8	24 7/8	Rock Island Lake, B.C.	William K. Mortlock	William K. Mortlock	1988	9
170 6/8	41 6/8	37 6/8	14	14 1/8	6 6/8	7	25 5/8	25 5/8	Tuchodi Lakes, B.C.	Larry Tooze	Larry Tooze	1986	10
170 5/8	41 1/8	42 6/8	14 1/8	14 1/8	6 1/8	6 4/8	25 4/8	25 4/8	Sharktooth Mt., B.C.	Steven J. DeRicco	Steven J. DeRicco	1990	11
169 3/8	40 4/8	41 5/8	13 5/8	13 4/8	6 3/8	6 3/8	25	25	Cullivan Creek, B.C.	Russell LeSage	Russell LeSage	1991	12
166 7/8	41 1/8	42 2/8	13 3/8	13 4/8	5 4/8	6	27 6/8	27 4/8	Toad River, B.C.	Anna M. Blattgerste	Anna M. Blattgerste	1990	13
166 5/8	40 4/8	41 5/8	14	14 2/8	5 5/8	5 5/8	25 2/8	25 2/8	Fox Mt., Yukon	George F. Dennis, Jr.	George F. Dennis, Jr.	1990	14
177 2/8*	43 3/8	42 3/8	14 6/8	14 6/8	6 5/8	6 6/8	26 5/8	26 2/8	Cassiar Mts., B.C.	Larry C. Fisher	Larry C. Fisher	1991	
175*	44	45 4/8	13 5/8	13 6/8	6 4/8	6 4/8	26	26	Anvil Range, Yukon	John A. Capdeville	John A. Capdeville	1991	
174 7/8*	38 2/8	38 3/8	13 7/8	14	9 3/8	9 1/8	19 6/8	17	Summit Lake, B.C.	John D. Chalk III	John D. Chalk III	1989	

* Final Score subject to revision by additional verifying measurements.

501

Score Charts
of the
Official Scoring System
for
North American
Big Game Trophies

OFFICIAL SCORING SYSTEM FOR NORTH AMERICAN BIG GAME TROPHIES

Records of North American
Big Game

BOONE AND CROCKETT CLUB

P.O. Box 547
Dumfries, VA 22026

Minimum Score:	Awards	All-time
Alaska brown	26	28
black	20	21
grizzly	23	24
polar	27	27

BEAR

Kind of Bear __Grizzly__

Sex __Male__

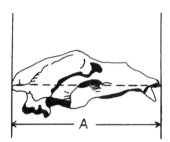

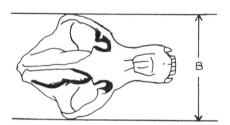

SEE OTHER SIDE FOR INSTRUCTIONS	Measurements
A. Greatest Length Without Lower Jaw	17 3/16
B. Greatest Width	9 15/16
FINAL SCORE	27 2/16

Exact Locality Where Killed: __Inglutalik Creek, Alaska__

Date Killed: 4/16/91 By Whom Killed: __Theodore Kurdziel, Jr.__

Present Owner: __Theodore Kurdziel, Jr.__

Address:

Guide Name and Address: __Bob Hannon__

Remarks: (Mention Any Abnormalities or Unique Qualities)

I certify that I have measured the above trophy on _____ May 6 _____ 19 92 ____

at (Address) _____ Milwaukee Public Museum _____ (City) __Milwaukee__ (State) WI ____

and that these measurements and data are, to the best of my knowledge and belief, made in accordance with the

instructions given.

Witness: ____Frank Cook_____ Signature: ____Howard Hanson_____

B&C OFFICIAL MEASURER

I.D. Number

504

Measurements are taken with calipers or by using parallel perpendiculars, to the nearest one-sixteenth of an inch, without reduction of fractions. Official measurement cannot be taken until skull has dried for at least sixty days after the animal was killed. All adhering flesh, membrane and cartilage must be completely removed before official measurements are taken.

A. Greatest Length is measured between perpendiculars parallel to the long axis of the skull, without the lower jaw and excluding malformations.

B. Greatest Width is measured between perpendiculars at right angles to the long axis.

* * * * * * * * * * * * * * * * *

FAIR CHASE STATEMENT FOR ALL HUNTER-TAKEN TROPHIES

To make use of the following methods shall be deemed as UNFAIR CHASE and unsportsmanlike, and any trophy obtained by use of such means is disqualified from entry.

    I. Spotting or herding game from the air, followed by landing in its vicinity for pursuit;

    II. Herding or pursuing game with motor-powered vehicles;

    III. Use of electronic communications for attracting, locating or observing game, or guiding the hunter to such game;

    IV. Hunting game confined by artificial barriers, including escape-proof fencing; or hunting game transplanted solely for the purpose of commercial shooting.

* * * * * * * * * * * * * * * * *

I certify that the trophy scored on this chart was not taken in UNFAIR CHASE as defined above by the Boone and Crockett Club. I further certify that it was taken in full compliance with local game laws of the state, province, or territory.

Date: _____ Signature of Hunter: _____

(Have Signature Notarized by a Notary Public)

505

Records of North American
Big Game

BOONE AND CROCKETT CLUB

P.O. Box 547
Dumfries, VA 22026

Minimum Score:	Awards	All-time
cougar	14-8/16	15
jaguar	14-8/16	14-8/16

COUGAR AND JAGUAR

Kind of Cat ___Cougar___

Sex ___Male___

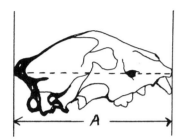
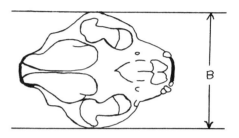

SEE OTHER SIDE FOR INSTRUCTIONS	Measurements
A. Greatest Length Without Lower Jaw	9 2/16
B. Greatest Width	6 12/16
FINAL SCORE	15 14/16 *

Exact Locality Where Killed: Walla Walla Co., Wash.	
Date Killed: 12/17/88 By Whom Killed: Robert A. Klicker	
Present Owner: Robert A. Klicker	
Address:	
Guide Name and Address: Claude Scott	
Remarks: (Mention Any Abnormalities or Unique Qualities)	

I certify that I have measured the above trophy on ___April 24,___ 19 __89__

at (Address) _____ (City) __Walla Walla__ (State) __WA__

and that these measurements and data are, to the best of my knowledge and belief, made in accordance with the

instructions given.

Witness: _____ Signature: ___Gail Martin___

B&C OFFICIAL MEASURER

*Score verified by the 21st Awards Judges Panel.

I.D. Number

INSTRUCTIONS FOR MEASURING COUGAR AND JAGUAR

Measurements are taken with calipers or by using parallel perpendiculars, to the nearest one-sixteenth of an inch, without reduction of fractions. Official measurements cannot be taken until the skull has dried for at least sixty days after the animal was killed. All adhering flesh, membrane and cartilage must be completely removed before official measurements are taken.

A. Greatest Length is measured between perpendiculars parallel to the long axis of the skull, without the lower jaw and excluding malformations.

B. Greatest Width is measured between perpendiculars at right angles to the long axis.

* * * * * * * * * * * * * * * * *

FAIR CHASE STATEMENT FOR ALL HUNTER-TAKEN TROPHIES

To make use of the following methods shall be deemed as UNFAIR CHASE and unsportsmanlike, and any trophy obtained by use of such means is disqualified from entry.

I. Spotting or herding game from the air, followed by landing in its vicinity for pursuit;

II. Herding or pursuing game with motor-powered vehicles;

III. Use of electronic communications for attracting, locating or observing game, or guiding the hunter to such game;

IV. Hunting game confined by artificial barriers, including escape-proof fencing; or hunting game transplanted solely for the purpose of commercial shooting.

* * * * * * * * * * * * * * * * *

I certify that the trophy scored on this chart was not taken in UNFAIR CHASE as defined above by the Boone and Crockett Club. I further certify that it was taken in full compliance with local game laws of the state, province, or territory.

Date: _____ Signature of Hunter: _____

(Have Signature Notarized by a Notary Public)

OFFICIAL SCORING SYSTEM FOR NORTH AMERICAN BIG GAME TROPHIES

Records of North American
Big Game

BOONE AND CROCKETT CLUB

P.O. Box 547
Dumfries, VA 22026

Minimum Score:	Awards	All-time
Atlantic	95	95
Pacific	100	100

WALRUS

Kind of Walrus: Pacific

Sex: Male

SEE OTHER SIDE FOR INSTRUCTIONS		Column 1	Column 2	Column 3
A. Greatest Spread	10 3/8	Right Tusk	Left Tusk	Difference
B. Tip to Tip Spread	8			
C. Entire Length of Loose Tusk		31 7/8	32 7/8	1
D-1. Circumference of Base		8 2/8	8 2/8	
D-2. Circumference at First Quarter		8 7/8	8 6/8	1/8
D-3. Circumference at Second Quarter		7 5/8	7 5/8	
D-4. Circumference at Third Quarter		5 7/8	5 7/8	
TOTALS		62 4/8	63 3/8	1 1/8

Enter Total of Columns 1 and 2	125 7/8	Exact Locality Where Killed:	Cape Seniavin, Alaska
Subtract Column 3	1 1/8	Date Killed: PU 1990 — By Whom Killed:	Picked Up
FINAL SCORE	124 6/8	Present Owner:	Tom Atkins
		Guide Name and Address:	
		Remarks:	

I certify that I have measured the above trophy on _____ July 22, 19 90 _____

at (Address) _____ (City) Anchorage _____ (State) AK _____

and that these measurements and data are, to the best of my knowledge and belief, made in accordance with the

instructions given.

Witness: Pat Deis _____ Signature: Ron Deis _____

B&C OFFICIAL MEASURER

I.D. Number

508

INSTRUCTIONS FOR MEASURING WALRUS

All measurements must be made with a 1/4-inch, flexible steel tape to the nearest one-eighth of an inch. Wherever it is necessary to change direction of measurement, mark a control point and swing tape at this point. Enter fractional figures in eighths, without reduction. Tusks must be removed from mounted specimens for measuring. Official measurement cannot be taken until tusks have dried for at least sixty days after the animal was killed.

A. Greatest Spread is measured between perpendiculars at a right angle to the center line of the skull.

B. Tip to Tip Spread is measured between tips of tusks.

C. Entire Length of Loose Tusk is measured over outer curve from base to a point in line with tip.

D-1 Circumference of Base is measured at a right angle to axis of tusk. Do not follow edge of contact between tusk and skull.

D. 2-3-4 Divide measurement C of longer tusk by four. Starting at base, mark both tusks at these quarters (even though the other tusk is shorter) and measure circumferences at these marks.

* * * * * * * * * * * * * * * *

FAIR CHASE STATEMENT FOR ALL HUNTER-TAKEN TROPHIES

To make use of the following methods shall be deemed as UNFAIR CHASE and unsportsmanlike, and any trophy obtained by use of such means is disqualified from entry.

I. Spotting or herding game from the air, followed by landing in its vicinity for pursuit;

II. Herding or pursuing game with motor-powered vehicles;

III. Use of electronic communications for attracting, locating or observing game, or guiding the hunter to such game;

IV. Hunting game confined by artificial barriers, including escape-proof fencing; or hunting game transplanted solely for the purpose of commercial shooting.

* * * * * * * * * * * * * * * *

I certify that the trophy scored on this chart was not taken in UNFAIR CHASE as defined above by the Boone and Crockett Club. I further certify that it was taken in full compliance with local game laws of the state, province, or territory.

Date: _____ Signature of Hunter: _____

(Have Signature Notarized by a Notary Public)

OFFICIAL SCORING SYSTEM FOR NORTH AMERICAN BIG GAME TROPHIES

Records of North American
Big Game

BOONE AND CROCKETT CLUB

P.Q. Box 547
Dumfries, VA 22026

Minimum Score: Awards All-time
360   375

TYPICAL
AMERICAN ELK (WAPITI)

DETAIL OF POINT
MEASUREMENT

	Abnormal Points	
	Right Antler	Left Antler
E. Total of Lengths of Abnormal Points		

SEE OTHER SIDE FOR INSTRUCTIONS				Column 1	Column 2	Column 3	Column 4
A. No. Points on Right Antler	7	No. Points on Left Antler	7	Spread Credit	Right Antler	Left Antler	Difference
B. Tip to Tip Spread	44 7/8	C. Greatest Spread	50 0/8				
D. Inside Spread of Main Beams	45 7/8	(Credit May Equal But Not Exceed Longer Antler)		45 7/8			
F. Length of Main Beam					55 1/8	54 0/8	1 1/8
G-1. Length of First Point					17 6/8	18 7/8	1 1/8
G-2. Length of Second Point					17 1/8	16 6/8	3/8
G-3. Length of Third Point					15 1/8	12 3/8	2 6/8
G-4. Length of Fourth (Royal) Point					22 3/8	23 3/8	1
G-5. Length of Fifth Point					16 2/8	16 6/8	4/8
G-6. Length of Sixth Point, If Present					5 1/8	5 4/8	3/8
G-7. Length of Seventh Point, If Present					--	--	--
H-1. Circumference at Smallest Place Between First and Second Points					7 7/8	8 1/8	2/8
H-2. Circumference at Smallest Place Between Second and Third Points					6 3/8	6 3/8	--
H-3. Circumference at Smallest Place Between Third and Fourth Points					6 7/8	6 7/8	--
H-4. Circumference at Smallest Place Between Fourth and Fifth Points					6 4/8	6 1/8	3/8
TOTALS				45 7/8	176 4/8	175 1/8	7 7/8

Enter Total of Columns 1, 2, and 3	397 4/8	Exact Locality Where Killed:	Park County, Montana	
Subtract Column 4	7 7/8	Date Killed: 11/22/90	By Whom Killed:	Butch Kuflak
Subtotal	389 5/8	Present Owner:	Butch Kuflak	
Subtract (E) Total of Lengths of Abn. Points		Guide Name and Address:	Tom Wilkes	
FINAL SCORE	389 5/8	Remarks:		

510

I certify that I have measured the above trophy on ___ May 6, _____ 19 92

at (address) __Milwaukee Public Museum_____ City Milwaukee ___ State WI ___
and that these measurements and data are, to the best of my knowledge and belief, made in accordance with the
instructions given.

Witness: __Larry Streiff_____ Signature __Stanley R. Godfrey_____

B&C OFFICIAL MEASURER

I.D. Number

INSTRUCTIONS FOR MEASURING TYPICAL AMERICAN ELK (WAPITI)

All measurements must be made with a 1/4-inch flexible steel tape to the nearest one-eighth of an inch. Wherever it is necessary to change direction of measurement, mark a control point and swing tape at this point. (Note: a flexible steel cable can be used to measure points and main beams only.) Enter fractional figures in eighths, without reduction. Official measurements cannot be taken until the antlers have dried for at least 60 days after the animal was killed.

A. Number of Points on Each Antler: to be counted a point, the projection must be at least one inch long, with length exceeding width at one inch or more of length. All points are measured from tip of point to nearest edge of beam as illustrated. Beam tip is counted as a point but not measured as a point.

B. Tip to Tip Spread is measured between tips of main beams.

C. Greatest Spread is measured between perpendiculars at a right angle to the center line of the skull at widest part, whether across main beams or points.

D. Inside Spread of Main Beams is measured at a right angle to the center line of the skull at widest point between main beams. Enter this measurement again as Spread Credit if it is less than or equal to the length of longer antler; if longer, enter longer antler length for Spread Credit.

E. Total of Lengths of all Abnormal Points: Abnormal Points are those non-typical in location (such as points originating from a point or from bottom or sides of main beam) or pattern (extra points, not generally paired). Measure in usual manner and record in appropriate blanks.

F. Length of Main Beam is measured from lowest outside edge of burr over outer curve to the most distant point of what is, or appears to be, the main beam. The point of beginning is that point on the burr where the center line along the outer curve of the beam intersects the burr, then following generally the line of the illustration.

G. 1-2-3-4-5-6-7 Length of Normal Points: Normal points project from the top or front of the main beam in the general pattern illustrated. They are measured from nearest edge of main beam over outer curve to tip. Lay the tape along the outer curve of the beam so that the top edge of the tape coincides with the top edge of the beam on both sides of point to determine the baseline for point measurement. Record point length in appropriate blanks.

H. 1-2-3-4 Circumferences are taken as detailed for each measurement.

* * * * * * * * * * * * * * * * * *

FAIR CHASE STATEMENT FOR ALL HUNTER-TAKEN TROPHIES

To make use of the following methods shall be deemed as UNFAIR CHASE and unsportsmanlike, and any trophy obtained by use of such means is disqualified from entry.

   I. Spotting or herding game from the air, followed by landing in its vicinity for pursuit;

  II. Herding or pursuing game with motor-powered vehicles;

 III. Use of electronic communications for attracting, locating or observing game, or guiding the hunter to such game;

 IV. Hunting game confined by artificial barriers, including escape-proof fencing; or hunting game transplanted solely for the purpose of commercial shooting.

* * * * * * * * * * * * * * * * * *

I certify that the trophy scored on this chart was not taken in UNFAIR CHASE as defined above by the Boone and Crockett Club. I further certify that it was taken in full compliance with local game laws of the state, province, or territory.

Date _____ Signature of Hunter _____

(Have signature notarized by a Notary Public)

OFFICIAL SCORING SYSTEM FOR NORTH AMERICAN BIG GAME TROPHIES

Records of North American
Big Game

BOONE AND CROCKETT CLUB

P.O. Box 547
Dumfries, VA 22026

Minimum Score: Awards All-time
385   385

NON-TYPICAL
AMERICAN ELK (WAPITI)

	Abnormal Points	
	Right Antler	Left Antler
	4 6/8	26 7/8
	1 3/8	4 2/8

DETAIL OF POINT
MEASUREMENT

E. Total of Lengths of Abnormal Points	37 2/8

SEE OTHER SIDE FOR INSTRUCTIONS	Column 1	Column 2	Column 3	Column 4
	Spread Credit	Right Antler	Left Antler	Difference
A. No. Points on Right Antler 9 — No. Points on Left Antler 9				
B. Tip to Tip Spread 45 1/8 — C. Greatest Spread 52 7/8				
D. Inside Spread of Main Beams 39 7/8 — (Credit May Equal But Not Exceed Longer Antler)	39 7/8			
F. Length of Main Beam		54 1/8	52 5/8	1 4/8
G-1. Length of First Point		15 7/8	16 4/8	5/8
G-2. Length of Second Point		16 2/8	16 2/8	
G-3. Length of Third Point		28 2/8	24 4/8	3 6/8
G-4. Length of Fourth (Royal) Point		21 1/8	22 4/8	1 3/8
G-5. Length of Fifth Point		18 5/8	20	1 3/8
G-6. Length of Sixth Point, If Present		8 7/8	3 7/8	5
G-7. Length of Seventh Point, If Present				
H-1. Circumference at Smallest Place Between First and Second Points		11	10 2/8	6/8
H-2. Circumference at Smallest Place Between Second and Third Points		7 1/8	7 1/8	
H-3. Circumference at Smallest Place Between Third and Fourth Points		7 1/8	7 1/8	
H-4. Circumference at Smallest Place Between Fourth and Fifth Points		8 7/8	7 5/8	1 2/8
TOTALS	39 7/8	197 2/8	188 3/8	15 5/8

Enter Total of Columns 1, 2, and 3	425 4/8	Exact Locality Where Killed:	Gilbert Plains, Man.
Subtract Column 4	15 5/8	Date Killed: 1961 — By Whom Killed:	James Berry
Subtotal	409 7/8	Present Owner:	James Berry
Add (E) Total of Lengths of Abnormal Points	37 2/8	Guide Name and Address:	
FINAL SCORE	447 1/8	Remarks:	

512

I certify that I have measured the above trophy on _____ May 6, 1992

at (address) ___Milwaukee Public Museum_____ City Milwaukee State WI
and that these measurements and data are, to the best of my knowledge and belief, made in accordance with the
instructions given.

Witness: __C. Randall Byers_____ Signature _____John O. Cook III_____

B&C OFFICIAL MEASURER

I.D. Number

INSTRUCTIONS FOR MEASURING NON-TYPICAL AMERICAN ELK (WAPITI)

All measurements must be made with a 1/4-inch flexible steel tape to the nearest one-eighth of an inch. Wherever it is necessary to change direction of measurement, mark a control point and swing tape at this point. (Note: a flexible steel cable can be used to measure points and main beams only.) Enter fractional figures in eighths, without reduction. Official measurements cannot be taken until the antlers have dried for at least 60 days after the animal was killed.

A. Number of Points on Each Antler: to be counted a point, the projection must be at least one inch long, with length exceeding width at one inch or more of length. All points are measured from tip of point to nearest edge of beam as illustrated. Beam tip is counted as a point but not measured as a point.

B. Tip to Tip Spread is measured between tips of main beams.

C. Greatest Spread is measured between perpendiculars at a right angle to the center line of the skull at widest part, whether across main beams or points.

D. Inside Spread of Main Beams is measured at a right angle to the center line of the skull at widest point between main beams. Enter this measurement again as the Spread Credit if it is less than or equal to the length of longer antler; if longer, enter longer antler length for Spread Credit.

E. Total of Lengths of all Abnormal Points: Abnormal Points are those non-typical in location (such as points originating from a point or from bottom or sides of main beam) or pattern (extra points, not generally paired). Measure in usual manner and record in appropriate blanks.

F. Length of Main Beam is measured from lowest outside edge of burr over outer curve to the most distant point of what is, or appears to be, the main beam. The point of beginning is that point on the burr where the center line along the outer curve of the beam intersects the burr, then following generally the line of the illustration.

G. 1-2-3-4-5-6-7 Length of Normal Points: Normal points project from the top or front of the main beam in the general pattern illustrated. They are measured from nearest edge of main beam over outer curve to tip. Lay the tape along the outer curve of the beam so that the top edge of the tape coincides with the top edge of the beam on both sides of point to determine the baseline for point measurement. Record point length in appropriate blanks.

H. 1-2-3-4 Circumferences are taken as detailed for each measurement.

* * * * * * * * * * * * * * * * * *

FAIR CHASE STATEMENT FOR ALL HUNTER-TAKEN TROPHIES

To make use of the following methods shall be deemed as UNFAIR CHASE and unsportsmanlike, and any trophy obtained by use of such means is disqualified from entry.

I. Spotting or herding game from the air, followed by landing in its vicinity for pursuit;
II. Herding or pursuing game with motor-powered vehicles;
III. Use of electronic communications for attracting, locating or observing game, or guiding the hunter to such game;
IV. Hunting game confined by artificial barriers, including escape-proof fencing; or hunting game transplanted solely for the purpose of commercial shooting.

* * * * * * * * * * * * * * * * * *

I certify that the trophy scored on this chart was not taken in UNFAIR CHASE as defined above by the Boone and Crockett Club. I further certify that it was taken in full compliance with local game laws of the state, province, or territory.

Date _____ Signature of Hunter _____

(Have signature notarized by a Notary Public)

Records of North American
Big Game

BOONE AND CROCKETT CLUB

P.O. Box 547
Dumfries, VA 22026

Minimum Score: Awards All-time
275   290

ROOSEVELT'S ELK

Crown Points	
Right Antler	Left Antler
11 2/8	12 7/8
2 5/8	
2 0/8	
7 2/8	

I. Add to Total   36 0/8

Abnormal Points	
Right Antler	Left Antler
1 5/8	

DETAIL OF POINT
MEASUREMENT

E. Total of Lengths
of Abnormal Points   1 5/8

SEE OTHER SIDE FOR INSTRUCTIONS				Column 1	Column 2	Column 3	Column 4
				Spread Credit	Right Antler	Left Antler	Difference
A. No. Points on Right Antler	11	No. Points on Left Antler	8				
B. Tip to Tip Spread	39 0/8	C. Greatest Spread	46 4/8				
D. Inside Spread of Main Beams	36 1/8	(Credit May Equal But Not Exceed Longer Antler)		36 1/8			
F. Length of Main Beam					44 2/8	46 7/8	2 5/8
G-1. Length of First Point					15 7/8	18 1/8	2 2/8
G-2. Length of Second Point					16 6/8	17 1/8	3/8
G-3. Length of Third Point					19 6/8	20 4/8	6/8
G-4. Length of Fourth (Royal) Point					17 0/8	15 5/8	1 3/8
G-5. Length of Fifth Point					12 2/8	12 2/8	
G-6. Length of Sixth Point, If Present					Ø	3 7/8	
G-7. Length of Seventh Point, If Present					Ø	Ø	
H-1. Circumference at Smallest Place Between First and Second Points					11 2/8	11 2/8	Ø
H-2. Circumference at Smallest Place Between Second and Third Points					7 7/8	7 3/8	4/8
H-3. Circumference at Smallest Place Between Third and Fourth Points					7 3/8	7 5/8	2/8
H-4. Circumference at Smallest Place Between Fourth and Fifth Points					7 0/8	6 4/8	4/8
TOTALS				36 1/8	159 3/8	167 1/8	8 5/8

Enter Total of Columns 1, 2, 3 and (I)	398 5/8	Exact Locality Where Killed: Tsitika River, B.C.
SUBTRACT Column 4	8 5/8	Date Killed: 11/4/89 By Whom Killed: Wayne Coe
Subtotal	390	Present Owner: Wayne Coe
SUBTRACT (E) Abn. Pts.	1 5/8	Guide Name and Address:
FINAL SCORE	388 3/8	Remarks:

I certify that I have measured the above trophy on ___May 6___ 19 _92_

at (address) ___Milwaukee Public Museum___ City _Milwaukee_ State _WI_
and that these measurements and data are, to the best of my knowledge and belief, made in accordance with the instructions given.

Witness: ___Larry Streiff___ Signature ___Michael C. Cupell___

B&C OFFICIAL MEASURER

I.D. Number

INSTRUCTIONS FOR MEASURING ROOSEVELT'S ELK

All measurements must be made with a 1/4-inch flexible steel tape to the nearest one-eighth of an inch. Wherever it is necessary to change direction of measurement, mark a control point and swing tape at this point. (Note: a flexible steel cable can be used to measure points and main beams only.) Enter fractional figures in eighths, without reduction. Official measurements cannot be taken until the antlers have dried for at least 60 days after the animal was killed.

A. Number of Points on Each Antler: to be counted a point, the projection must be at least one inch long, with length exceeding width at one inch or more of length. All points are measured from tip of point to nearest edge of beam as illustrated. Beam tip is counted as a point but not measured as a point.

B. Tip to Tip Spread is measured between tips of main beams.

C. Greatest Spread is measured between perpendiculars at a right angle to the center line of the skull at widest part, whether across main beams or points.

D. Inside Spread of Main Beams is measured at a right angle to the center line of the skull at widest point between main beams. Enter this measurement again as the Spread Credit if it is less than or equal to the length of longer antler; if longer, enter longer antler length for Spread Credit.

E. Total of Lengths of all Abnormal Points: Abnormal Points are those non-typical in location (such as points originating from a point or from bottom or sides of main beam) or pattern (extra points, not generally paired). Measure in usual manner and record in appropriate blanks. **Note: do not confuse with Crown Point that may occur at base of Royal.**

F. Length of Main Beam is measured from lowest outside edge of burr over outer curve to the most distant point of what is, or appears to be, the main beam. The point of beginning is that point on the burr where the center line along the outer curve of the beam intersects the burr, then following generally the line of the illustration.

G. 1-2-3-4-5-6-7 Length of Normal Points: Normal points project from the top or front of the main beam in the general pattern illustrated. They are measured from nearest edge of main beam over outer curve to tip. Lay the tape along the outer curve of the beam so that the top edge of the tape coincides with the top edge of the beam on both sides of point to determine the baseline for point measurement. Record point length in appropriate blanks.

H. 1-2-3-4 Circumferences are taken as detailed for each measurement.

I. Crown Points: From the well-defined Royal on out to end of beam, all points other than the normal points in their typical locations are Crown Points. This includes points occurring on the Royal, on other normal points, and on Crown Points. Measure and record in appropriate blanks provided and add to score below.

* * * * * * * * * * * * * * * * *

FAIR CHASE STATEMENT FOR ALL HUNTER-TAKEN TROPHIES

To make use of the following methods shall be deemed as UNFAIR CHASE and unsportsmanlike, and any trophy obtained by use of such means is disqualified from entry.

   I. Spotting or herding game from the air, followed by landing in its vicinity for pursuit;

   II. Herding or pursuing game with motor-powered vehicles;

   III. Use of electronic communications for attracting, locating or observing game, or guiding the hunter to such game;

   IV. Hunting game confined by artificial barriers, including escape-proof fencing; or hunting game transplanted solely for the purpose of commercial shooting.

* * * * * * * * * * * * * * * * *

I certify that the trophy scored on this chart was not taken in UNFAIR CHASE as defined above by the Boone and Crockett Club. I further certify that it was taken in full compliance with local game laws of the state, province, or territory.

Date _____ Signature of Hunter _____

(Have signature notarized by a Notary Public)

Records of North American Big Game	BOONE AND CROCKETT CLUB	P.O. Box 547 Dumfries, VA 22026

Minimum Score: Awards   All-time
   mule   185   195
   Columbia   120   130
   Sitka   100   108

TYPICAL
MULE AND BLACKTAIL DEER

Kind of Deer   **Columbia Blacktail**

DETAIL OF POINT MEASUREMENT

	Abnormal Points	
	Right Antler	Left Antler
E. Total of Lengths of Abnormal Points		

SEE OTHER SIDE FOR INSTRUCTIONS				Column 1	Column 2	Column 3	Column 4
A. No. Points on Right Antler	5	No. Points on Left Antler	5	Spread Credit	Right Antler	Left Antler	Difference
B. Tip to Tip Spread	15 6/8	C. Greatest Spread	22 4/8				
D. Inside Spread of Main Beams	20 2/8	(Credit May Equal But Not Exceed Longer Antler)		20 2/8			
F. Length of Main Beam					23 2/8	24	6/8
G-1. Length of First Point, If Present					3 3/8	3 3/8	
G-2. Length of Second Point					15 1/8	16 6/8	1 5/8
G-3. Length of Third Point, If Present					7 5/8	7	5/8
G-4. Length of Fourth Point, If Present					9 5/8	10 5/8	1
H-1. Circumference at Smallest Place Between Burr and First Point					4 3/8	4 3/8	
H-2. Circumference at Smallest Place Between First and Second Points					4 1/8	4 1/8	
H-3. Circumference at Smallest Place Between Main Beam and Third Point					3 5/8	3 4/8	1/8
H-4. Circumference at Smallest Place Between Second and Fourth Points					4 4/8	4 4/8	
TOTALS				20 2/8	75 5/8	78 2/8	4 1/8

Enter Total of Columns 1, 2, and 3	174 1/8	Exact Locality Where Killed:	Jackson Co., Oreg.
Subtract Column 4	4 1/8	Date Killed: 3/10/89 By Whom Killed:	Wayne Despain
Subtotal	170	Present Owner:	Wayne Despain
Subtract (E) Total of Lengths of Abn. Points		Guide Name and Address:	
FINAL SCORE	170	Remarks:	

I certify that I have measured the above trophy on _____ May 6, _____ 19 92

at (address) ____ Milwaukee Public Museum _____ City Milwaukee ____ State WI ____
and that these measurements and data are, to the best of my knowledge and belief, made In accordance with the
Instructions given.

Witness: ____ Larry Streiff _____ Signature: ____ Jack Graham _____

B&C OFFICIAL MEASURER [ ][ ][ ][ ]

I.D. Number

INSTRUCTIONS FOR MEASURING TYPICAL MULE AND BLACKTAIL DEER

All measurements must be made with a 1/4-Inch flexible steel tape to the nearest one-eighth of an inch. Wherever
it is necessary to change direction of measurement, mark a control point and swing tape at this point. (Note: a
flexible steel cable can be used to take point and beam length measurements only.) Enter fractional figures in
eighths, without reduction. Official measurements cannot be taken until antlers have dried for at least 60 days
after the animal was killed.

A. Number of Points on Each Antler: to be counted a point, the projection must be at least one inch long, with
length exceeding width at one inch or more of length. All points are measured from tip of point to nearest edge
of beam as illustrated. Beam tip is counted as a point but not measured as a point.

B. Tip to Tip Spread is measured between tips of main beams.

C. Greatest Spread is measured between perpendiculars at a right angle to the center line of the skull at widest
part, whether across main beams or points.

D. Inside Spread of Main Beams is measured at a right angle to the center line of the skull at widest point
between main beams. Enter this measurement again as Spread Credit if it is less than or equal to the length of
longer antler; if longer, enter longer antler length for Spread Credit.

E. Total of Lengths of all Abnormal Points: Abnormal Points are those non-typical in location such as points
originating from a point (exception: G-3 originates from G-2 in perfectly normal fashion) or from bottom or sides
of main beam, or any points beyond the normal pattern of five (including beam tip) per antler. Measure each
abnormal point in usual manner and enter in appropriate blanks.

F. Length of Main Beam is measured from lowest outside edge of burr over outer curve to the most distant point of
what is, or appears to be, the Main Beam. The point of beginning is that point on the burr where the center line
along the outer curve of the beam intersects the burr, then following generally the line of the illustration.

G. 1-2-3-4 Length of Normal Points: Normal points are the brow and the upper and lower forks as shown in the
illustration. They are measured from nearest edge of beam over outer curve to tip. Lay the tape along the outer
curve of the beam so that the top edge of the tape coincides with the top edge of the beam on both sides of point
to determine the baseline for point measurement. Record point lengths in appropriate blanks.

H. 1-2-3-4 Circumferences are taken as detailed for each measurement. If brow point is missing, take H-1 and H-
2 at smallest place between burr and G-2. If G-3 is missing, take H-3 halfway between the base and tip of second
point. If G-4 is missing, take H-4 halfway between second point and tip of main beam.

* * * * * * * * * * * * * * * * *

FAIR CHASE STATEMENT FOR ALL HUNTER-TAKEN TROPHIES

To make use of the following methods shall be deemed as UNFAIR CHASE and unsportsmanlike, and any trophy obtained
by use of such means is disqualified from entry.

    I. Spotting or herding game from the air, followed by landing in its vicinity for pursuit;

    II. Herding or pursuing game with motor-powered vehicles;

    III. Use of electronic communications for attracting, locating or observing game, or guiding the
       hunter to such game;

    IV. Hunting game confined by artificial barriers, including escape-proof fencing; or hunting game
       transplanted solely for the purpose of commercial shooting.

* * * * * * * * * * * * * * * * *

I certify that the trophy scored on this chart was not taken In UNFAIR CHASE as defined above by the Boone and
Crockett Club. I further certify that it was taken in full compliance with local game laws of the state,
province, or territory.

Date: _____ Signature of Hunter: _____

                               (Have signature notarized by a Notary Public)

517

Records of North American
Big Game

BOONE AND CROCKETT CLUB

P.O. Box 547
Dumfries, VA 22026

Minimum Score: Awards All-time
225   240

NON-TYPICAL
MULE DEER

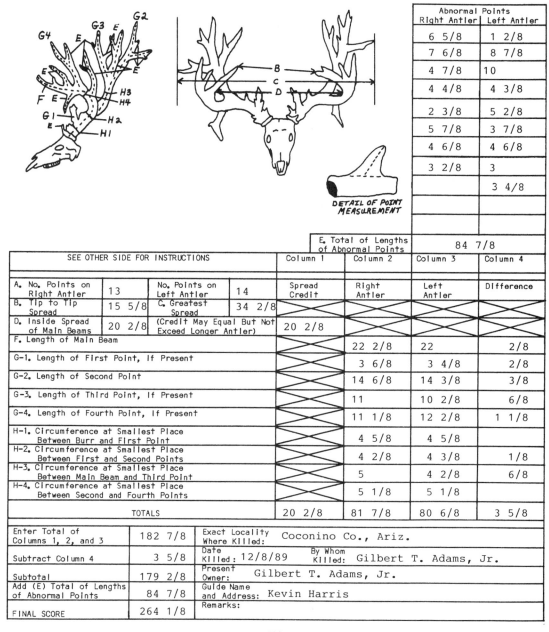

DETAIL OF POINT
MEASUREMENT

Abnormal Points	
Right Antler	Left Antler
6 5/8	1 2/8
7 6/8	8 7/8
4 7/8	10
4 4/8	4 3/8
2 3/8	5 2/8
5 7/8	3 7/8
4 6/8	4 6/8
3 2/8	3
	3 4/8

E. Total of Lengths of Abnormal Points	84 7/8

SEE OTHER SIDE FOR INSTRUCTIONS				Column 1	Column 2	Column 3	Column 4
A. No. Points on Right Antler	13	No. Points on Left Antler	14	Spread Credit	Right Antler	Left Antler	Difference
B. Tip to Tip Spread	15 5/8	C. Greatest Spread	34 2/8				
D. Inside Spread of Main Beams	20 2/8	(Credit May Equal But Not Exceed Longer Antler)	20 2/8				
F. Length of Main Beam					22 2/8	22	2/8
G-1. Length of First Point, If Present					3 6/8	3 4/8	2/8
G-2. Length of Second Point					14 6/8	14 3/8	3/8
G-3. Length of Third Point, If Present					11	10 2/8	6/8
G-4. Length of Fourth Point, If Present					11 1/8	12 2/8	1 1/8
H-1. Circumference at Smallest Place Between Burr and First Point					4 5/8	4 5/8	
H-2. Circumference at Smallest Place Between First and Second Points					4 2/8	4 3/8	1/8
H-3. Circumference at Smallest Place Between Main Beam and Third Point					5	4 2/8	6/8
H-4. Circumference at Smallest Place Between Second and Fourth Points					5 1/8	5 1/8	
TOTALS				20 2/8	81 7/8	80 6/8	3 5/8

Enter Total of Columns 1, 2, and 3	182 7/8	Exact Locality Where Killed:	Coconino Co., Ariz.
Subtract Column 4	3 5/8	Date Killed: 12/8/89 By Whom Killed:	Gilbert T. Adams, Jr.
Subtotal	179 2/8	Present Owner:	Gilbert T. Adams, Jr.
Add (E) Total of Lengths of Abnormal Points	84 7/8	Guide Name and Address:	Kevin Harris
FINAL SCORE	264 1/8	Remarks:	

518

I certify that I have measured the above trophy on _____ May 6,   19 92

at (address) _____ Milwaukee Public Museum _____ City Milwaukee ____ State WI
and that these measurements and data are, to the best of my knowledge and belief, made in accordance with the
instructions given.

Witness: __ Dennis Shirley _____ Signature: __ C. Randall Byers _____

INSTRUCTIONS FOR MEASURING NON-TYPICAL MULE DEER

I.D. Number

All measurements must be made with a 1/4-inch flexible steel tape to the nearest one-eighth of an inch. Wherever
it is necessary to change direction of measurement, mark a control point and swing tape at this point. (Note: a
flexible steel cable can be used to measure points and main beams only.) Enter fractional figures in eighths,
without reduction. Official measurements cannot be taken until antlers have dried for at least 60 days after the
animal was killed.

A. Number of Points on Each Antler: to be counted a point, the projection must be at least one inch long, with
the length exceeding width at one inch or more of length. All points are measured from tip of point to nearest
edge of beam as illustrated. Beam tip is counted as a point but is not measured as a point.

B. Tip to Tip Spread is measured between tips of main beams.

C. Greatest Spread is measured between perpendiculars at a right angle to the center line of the skull at widest
part, whether across main beams or points.

D. Inside Spread of Main Beams is measured at a right angle to the center line of the skull at widest point
between main beams. Enter this measurement again as the Spread Credit if it is less than or equal to the length
of longer antler; if longer, enter longer antler length for Spread Credit.

E. Total of Lengths of all Abnormal Points: Abnormal Points are those non-typical in location such as points
originating from a point (exception: G-3 originates from G-2 in perfectly normal fashion) or from bottom or sides
of main beam, or any points beyond the normal pattern of five (including beam tip) per antler. Measure each
abnormal point in usual manner and enter in appropriate blanks.

F. Length of Main Beam is measured from lowest outside edge of burr over outer curve to the most distant point of
what is, or appears to be, the main beam. The point of beginning is that point on the burr where the center line
along the outer curve of the beam intersects the burr, then following generally the line of the illustration.

G. 1-2-3-4 Length of Normal Points: Normal points are the brow and the upper and lower forks, as shown in the
illustration. They are measured from nearest edge of main beam over outer curve to tip. Lay the tape along the
outer curve of the beam so that the top edge of the tape coincides with the top edge of the beam on both sides of
point to determine the baseline for point measurement. Record point lengths in appropriate blanks.

H. 1-2-3-4 Circumferences are taken as detailed for each measurement. If brow point is missing, take H-1 and
H-2 at smallest place between burr and G-2. If G-3 is missing, take H-3 halfway between the base and tip of
second point. If G-4 is missing, take H-4 halfway between second point and tip of main beam.

* * * * * * * * * * * * * * * * * *

FAIR CHASE STATEMENT FOR ALL HUNTER-TAKEN TROPHIES

To make use of the following methods shall be deemed as UNFAIR CHASE and unsportsmanlike, and any trophy obtained
by use of such means is disqualified from entry.

   I. Spotting or herding game from the air, followed by landing in its vicinity for pursuit;

  II. Herding or pursuing game with motor-powered vehicles;

 III. Use of electronic communications for attracting, locating or observing game, or guiding the
      hunter to such game;

 IV. Hunting game confined by artificial barriers, including escape-proof fencing; or hunting game
      transplanted solely for the purpose of commercial shooting.

* * * * * * * * * * * * * * * * * *

I certify that the trophy scored on this chart was not taken in UNFAIR CHASE as defined above by the Boone and
Crockett Club. I further certify that it was taken in full compliance with local game laws of the state,
province, or territory.

Date: _____ Signature of Hunter: _____

(Have signature notarized by a Notary Public)

OFFICIAL SCORING SYSTEM FOR NORTH AMERICAN BIG GAME TROPHIES

Records of North American
Big Game

BOONE AND CROCKETT CLUB

P.O. Box 547
Dumfries, VA 22026

Minimum Score:	Awards	All-time
whitetail	160	170
Coues'	100	110

TYPICAL
WHITETAIL AND COUES' DEER

Kind of Deer __whitetail__

DETAIL OF POINT
MEASUREMENT

	Abnormal Points	
	Right Antler	Left Antler
E. Total of Lengths of Abnormal Points		

SEE OTHER SIDE FOR INSTRUCTIONS				Column 1	Column 2	Column 3	Column 4
				Spread Credit	Right Antler	Left Antler	Difference
A. No. Points on Right Antler	6	No. Points on Left Antler	6				
B. Tip to Tip Spread	23 7/8	C. Greatest Spread	31 5/8				
D. Inside Spread of Main Beams	29 1/8	(Credit May Equal But Not Exceed Longer Antler)		29 1/8			
F. Length of Main Beam					30 1/8	28	2 1/8
G-1. Length of First Point, If Present					7 2/8	8 3/8	1 1/8
G-2. Length of Second Point					12	12 4/8	4/8
G-3. Length of Third Point					9 6/8	9 6/8	
G-4. Length of Fourth Point, If Present					5 6/8	5 6/8	
G-5. Length of Fifth Point, If Present					1 6/8	1 1/8	5/8
G-6. Length of Sixth Point, If Present							
G-7. Length of Seventh Point, If Present							
H-1. Circumference at Smallest Place Between Burr and First Point					5 3/8	5 3/8	
H-2. Circumference at Smallest Place Between First and Second Points					4 7/8	4 7/8	
H-3. Circumference at Smallest Place Between Second and Third Points					6	6 3/8	3/8
H-4. Circumference at Smallest Place Between Third and Fourth Points					5 1/8	5 1/8	
TOTALS				29 1/8	88	87 2/8	4 6/8

Enter Total of Columns 1, 2, and 3	204 3/8	Exact Locality Where Killed:	Edmonton, Alta.	
Subtract Column 4	4 6/8	Date Killed: 9-20-91	By Whom Killed:	Don McGarvey
Subtotal	199 5/8	Present Owner: Don McGarvey		
Subtract (E) Total of Lengths of Abn. Points		Guide Name and Address:		
FINAL SCORE	199 5/8*	Remarks:		

*Score verified by 21st Awards Judges Panel.

520

I certify that I have measured the above trophy on _____ November 20, 19 88 _____

at (address) _____ City _____ State _____
and that these measurements and data are, to the best of my knowledge and belief, made in accordance with the
instructions given.

Witness: __Brian Burrows_____ Signature: __Ryk Visscher_____

B&C OFFICIAL MEASURER

I.D. Number

INSTRUCTIONS FOR MEASURING TYPICAL WHITETAIL AND COUES' DEER

All measurements must be made with a 1/4-inch flexible steel tape to the nearest one-eighth of an inch. Wherever
it is necessary to change direction of measurement, mark a control point and swing tape at this point. (Note: a
flexible steel cable can be used to measure points and main beams only.) Enter fractional figures in eighths,
without reduction. Official measurements cannot be taken until antlers have dried for at least 60 days after the
animal was killed.

A. Number of Points on Each Antler: to be counted a point, the projection must be at least one inch long, with
the length exceeding width at one inch or more of length. All points are measured from tip of point to nearest
edge of beam as illustrated. Beam tip is counted as a point but not measured as a point.

B. Tip to Tip Spread is measured between tips of main beams.

C. Greatest Spread is measured between perpendiculars at a right angle to the center line of the skull at widest
part, whether across main beams or points.

D. Inside Spread of Main Beams is measured at a right angle to the center line of the skull at widest point
between main beams. Enter this measurement again as the Spread Credit if it is less than or equal to the length
of longer antler; if longer, enter longer antler length for Spread Credit.

E. Total of Lengths of all Abnormal Points: Abnormal Points are those non-typical in location (such as points
originating from a point or from bottom or sides of main beam) or extra points beyond the normal pattern of
points. Measure in usual manner and enter in appropriate blanks.

F. Length of Main Beam is measured from lowest outside edge of burr over outer curve to the most distant point of
what is, or appears to be, the main beam. The point of beginning is that point on the burr where the center line
along the outer curve of the beam intersects the burr, then following generally the line of the illustration.

G. 1-2-3-4-5-6-7 Length of Normal Points: Normal points project from the top of the main beam. They are
measured from nearest edge of main beam over outer curve to tip. Lay the tape along the outer curve of the beam
so that the top edge of the tape coincides with the top edge of the beam on both sides of the point to determine
the baseline for point measurements. Record point lengths in appropriate blanks.

H. 1-2-3-4 Circumferences are taken as detailed for each measurement. If brow point is missing, take H-1 and
H-2 at smallest place between burr and G-2. If G-4 is missing, take H-4 halfway between G-3 and tip of main
beam.

* * * * * * * * * * * * * * * * * *

FAIR CHASE STATEMENT FOR ALL HUNTER-TAKEN TROPHIES

To make use of the following methods shall be deemed as UNFAIR CHASE and unsportsmanlike, and any trophy obtained
by use of such means is disqualified from entry.

    I. Spotting or herding game from the air, followed by landing in its vicinity for pursuit;

    II. Herding or pursuing game with motor-powered vehicles;

    III. Use of electronic communications for attracting, locating or observing game, or guiding the
       hunter to such game;

    IV. Hunting game confined by artificial barriers, including escape-proof fencing; or hunting game
       transplanted solely for the purpose of commercial shooting.

* * * * * * * * * * * * * * * * * *

I certify that the trophy scored on this chart was not taken in UNFAIR CHASE as defined above by the Boone and
Crockett Club. I further certify that it was taken in full compliance with local game laws of the state,
province, or territory.

Date: _____ Signature of Hunter: _____

(Have signature notarized by a Notary Public)

Records of North American
Big Game

BOONE AND CROCKETT CLUB

P.O. Box 547
Dumfries, VA 22026

Minimum Score:	Awards	All-time
whitetail	185	195
Coues'	105	120

NON-TYPICAL
WHITETAIL AND COUES' DEER

Kind of Deer __Coues'__

Abnormal Points	
Right Antler	Left Antler
5 1/8	4 2/8
3 1/8	1 2/8
6 3/8	2 6/8
1 5/8	

DETAIL OF POINT MEASUREMENT

E. Total of Lengths of Abnormal Points	24 4/8

SEE OTHER SIDE FOR INSTRUCTIONS				Column 1	Column 2	Column 3	Column 4
				Spread Credit	Right Antler	Left Antler	Difference
A. No. Points on Right Antler	9	No. Points on Left Antler	8				
B. Tip to Tip Spread	11 5/8	C. Greatest Spread	20				
D. Inside Spread of Main Beams	16 6/8	(Credit May Equal But Not Exceed Longer Antler)		16 6/8			
F. Length of Main Beam					19	20	1
G-1. Length of First Point, If Present					3 5/8	4 1/8	4/8
G-2. Length of Second Point					9 6/8	9	6/8
G-3. Length of Third Point					8 6/8	4 3/8	4 3/8
G-4. Length of Fourth Point, If Present					2 4/8	4 7/8	2 3/8
G-5. Length of Fifth Point, If Present							
G-6. Length of Sixth Point, If Present							
G-7. Length of Seventh Point, If Present							
H-1. Circumference at Smallest Place Between Burr and First Point					4 7/8	4 5/8	2/8
H-2. Circumference at Smallest Place Between First and Second Points					4 2/8	4	2/8
H-3. Circumference at Smallest Place Between Second and Third Points					4 7/8	5	1/8
H-4. Circumference at Smallest Place Between Third and Fourth Points					5	4 7/8	1/8
TOTALS				16 6/8	62 5/8	60 7/8	9 6/8

Enter Total of Columns 1, 2, and 3	140 2/8	Exact Locality Where Killed:	Gila Co., Ariz.
Subtract Column 4	9 6/8	Date Killed: 12-16-88 By Whom Killed:	Charles E. Erickson, Jr.
Subtotal	130 4/8	Present Owner:	Charles E. Erickson, Jr.
Add (E) Total of Lengths of Abnormal Points	24 4/8	Guide Name and Address:	
FINAL SCORE	155	Remarks:	

I certify that I have measured the above trophy on _____ May 6, 19 92

at (address) Milwaukee Public Museum _____ City Milwaukee State WI
and that these measurements and data are, to the best of my knowledge and belief, made in accordance with the instructions given.

Witness: Glenn E. Hisey _____ Signature: Walter H. White

<table>
<tr><td></td><td>B&C OFFICIAL MEASURER</td><td></td><td></td><td></td><td></td></tr>
</table>

INSTRUCTIONS FOR MEASURING NON-TYPICAL WHITETAIL AND COUES' DEER   I.D. Number

All measurements must be made with a 1/4-inch flexible steel tape to the nearest one-eighth of an inch. Wherever it is necessary to change direction of measurement, mark a control point and swing tape at this point. (Note: a flexible steel cable can be used to measure points and main beams only.) Enter fractional figures in eighths, without reduction. Official measurements cannot be taken until antlers have dried for at least 60 days after the animal was killed.

A. Number of Points on Each Antler: to be counted a point, the projection must be at least one inch long, with the length exceeding width at one inch or more of length. All points are measured from tip of point to nearest edge of beam as illustrated. Beam tip is counted as a point but not measured as a point.

B. Tip to Tip Spread is measured between tips of main beams.

C. Greatest Spread is measured between perpendiculars at a right angle to the center line of the skull at widest part, whether across main beams or points.

D. Inside Spread of Main Beams is measured at a right angle to the center line of the skull at widest point between main beams. Enter this measurement again as the Spread Credit if it is less than or equal to the length of longer antler; if longer, enter longer antler length for Spread Credit.

E. Total of Lengths of all Abnormal Points: Abnormal Points are those non-typical in location (such as points originating from a point or from bottom or sides of main beam) or extra points beyond the normal pattern of points. Measure in usual manner and enter in appropriate blanks.

F. Length of Main Beam is measured from lowest outside edge of burr over outer curve to the most distant point of what is, or appears to be, the main beam. The point of beginning is that point on the burr where the center line along the outer curve of the beam intersects the burr, then following generally the line of the illustration.

G. 1-2-3-4-5-6-7 Length of Normal Points: Normal points project from the top of the main beam. They are measured from nearest edge of main beam over outer curve to tip. Lay the tape along the outer curve of the beam so that the top edge of the tape coincides with the top edge of the beam on both sides of the point to determine the baseline for point measurement. Record point lengths in appropriate blanks.

H. 1-2-3-4 Circumferences are taken as detailed for each measurement. If brow point is missing, take H-1 and H-2 at smallest place between burr and G-2. If G-4 is missing, take H-4 halfway between G-3 and tip of main beam.

* * * * * * * * * * * * * * * * *

FAIR CHASE STATEMENT FOR ALL HUNTER-TAKEN TROPHIES

To make use of the following methods shall be deemed as UNFAIR CHASE and unsportsmanlike, and any trophy obtained by use of such means is disqualified from entry.

   I.   Spotting or herding game from the air, followed by landing in its vicinity for pursuit;

   II. Herding or pursuing game with motor-powered vehicles;

  III. Use of electronic communications for attracting, locating or observing game, or guiding the hunter to such game;

  IV. Hunting game confined by artificial barriers, including escape-proof fencing; or hunting game transplanted solely for the purpose of commercial shooting.

* * * * * * * * * * * * * * * * *

I certify that the trophy scored on this chart was not taken in UNFAIR CHASE as defined above by the Boone and Crockett Club. I further certify that it was taken in full compliance with local game laws of the state, province, or territory.

Date: _____ Signature of Hunter: _____

(Have signature notarized by a Notary Public)

OFFICIAL SCORING SYSTEM FOR NORTH AMERICAN BIG GAME TROPHIES

Records of North American
Big Game

BOONE AND CROCKETT CLUB

P.O. Box 547
Dumfries, VA 22026

Minimum Score:	Awards	All-time
Alaska-Yukon	210	224
Canada	185	195
Wyoming	140	155

MOOSE

Kind of Moose __Wyoming__

DETAIL OF POINT
MEASUREMENT

SEE OTHER SIDE FOR INSTRUCTIONS	Column 1	Column 2	Column 3	Column 4
A. Greatest Spread	47 7/8	Right Antler	Left Antler	Difference
B. Number of Abnormal Points on Both Antlers				
C. Number of Normal Points		12	11	1
D. Width of Palm		12 7/8	13	1/8
E. Length of Palm Including Brow Palm		34 3/8	38 3/8	4
F. Circumference of Beam at Smallest Place		7 1/8	7 4/8	3/8
TOTALS	47 7/8	66 3/8	69 7/8	5 4/8

Enter Total of Columns 1, 2, and 3	184 1/8	Exact Locality Where Killed:	Sheridan Co., Wyo.
Subtract Column 4	5 4/8	Date Killed: 10/3/91 By Whom Killed:	Jack A. Wilkinson
FINAL SCORE	178 5/8	Present Owner:	Jack A. Wilkinson
		Guide Name and Address:	Randy Reese
		Remarks:	

I certify that I have measured the above trophy on _____ May 6, 19 92 _____

at (Address) __Milwaukee Public Museum__ (City) __Milwaukee__ (State) WI ____

and that these measurements and data are, to the best of my knowledge and belief, made in accordance with the

Instructions given.

Witness: __Micahel C. Cupell__   Signature: __Jack Graham__

B&C OFFICIAL MEASURER

I.D. Number

524

INSTRUCTIONS FOR MEASURING MOOSE

All measurements must be made with a 1/4-inch flexible steel tape to the nearest one-eighth of an inch. Enter fractional figures in eighths, without reduction. Official measurements cannot be taken until antlers have dried for at least sixty days after animal was killed.

A. Greatest Spread is measured between perpendiculars in a straight line at a right angle to the center line of the skull.

B. Number of Abnormal Points on Both Antlers: Abnormal points are those projections originating from normal points or from the upper or lower palm surface, or from the inner edge of palm (see illustration). Abnormal points must be at least one inch long, with length exceeding width at one inch or more of length.

C. Number of Normal Points: Normal points originate from the outer edge of palm. To be counted a point, a projection must be at least one inch long, with the length exceeding width at one inch or more of length.

D. Width of Palm is taken in contact with the under surface of palm, at a right angle to the length of palm measurement line. The line of measurement should begin and end at the midpoint of the palm edge, which gives credit for the desirable character of palm thickness.

E. Length of Palm Including Brow Palm is taken in contact with the surface along the underside of the palm, parallel to the inner edge, from dips between points at the top to dips between points (if present) at the bottom. If a bay is present, measure across the open bay if the proper line of measurement, parallel to inner edge, follows this path. The line of measurement should begin and end at the midpoint of the palm edge, which gives credit for the desirable character of palm thickness.

F. Circumference of Beam at Smallest Place is taken as illustrated.

* * * * * * * * * * * * * * * * *

FAIR CHASE STATEMENT FOR ALL HUNTER-TAKEN TROPHIES

To make use of the following methods shall be deemed as UNFAIR CHASE and unsportsmanlike, and any trophy obtained by use of such means is disqualified from entry.

I. Spotting or herding game from the air, followed by landing in its vicinity for pursuit;

II. Herding or pursuing game with motor-powered vehicles;

III. Use of electronic communications for attracting, locating or observing game, or guiding the hunter to such game;

IV. Hunting game confined by artificial barriers, including escape-proof fencing; or hunting game transplanted solely for the purpose of commercial shooting.

* * * * * * * * * * * * * * * * *

I certify that the trophy scored on this chart was not taken in UNFAIR CHASE as defined above by the Boone and Crockett Club. I further certify that it was taken in full compliance with local game laws of the state, province, or territory.

Date: _____ Signature of Hunter: _____

(Have Signature Notarized by a Notary Public)

Records of North American
Big Game

BOONE AND CROCKETT CLUB

P.O. Box 547
Dumfries, VA 22026

Minimum Score:	Awards	All-time
barren ground	375	400
mountain	360	390
Quebec-Labrador	365	375
woodland	265	295
Central Canada		
barren ground	330	345

CARIBOU

Kind of Caribou Mountain

DETAIL OF POINT
MEASUREMENT

SEE OTHER SIDE FOR INSTRUCTIONS		Column 1	Column 2	Column 3	Column 4
A. Tip to Tip Spread	27 4/8	Spread Credit	Right Antler	Left Antler	Difference
B. Greatest Spread	38				
C. Inside Spread of Main Beams	30 2/8 (Credit May Equal But Not Exceed Longer Antler)	30 2/8			
D. Number of Points on Each Antler Excluding Brows			30	29	1
Number of Points on Each Brow			10	4	
E. Length of Main Beam			37 2/8	37 4/8	2/8
F-1. Length of Brow Palm or First Point			17 5/8	13 6/8	
F-2. Length of Bez or Second Point			22 4/8	22 7/8	3/8
F-3. Length of Rear Point, If Present			9 4/8	8 6/8	6/8
F-4. Length of Second Longest Top Point			19 4/8	22 1/8	2 5/8
F-5. Length of Longest Top Point			26	26	
G-1. Width of Brow Palm			10 6/8	9 3/8	
G-2. Width of Top Palm			6	9 4/8	3 4/8
H-1. Circumference at Smallest Place Between Brow and Bez Points			5 7/8	5 7/8	
H-2. Circumference at Smallest Place Between Bez and Rear Point, If Present			5 3/8	5 3/8	
H-3. Circumference at Smallest Place Before First Top Point			4 7/8	5	1/8
H-4. Circumference at Smallest Place Between Two Longest Top Palm Points			11 6/8	18 2/8	6 4/8
TOTALS		30 2/8	217	217 3/8	15 1/8

Enter Total of Columns 1, 2, and 3	464 5/8	Exact Locality Where Killed:	Fire Lake, Yukon	
Subtract Column 4	15 1/8	Date Killed: 9-17-89	By Whom Killed:	James R. Hollister
FINAL SCORE	449 4/8*	Present Owner:	James R. Hollister	
		Guide Name and Address:	Leon Jules	
		Remarks:		

*Score vertified by the 21st Awards Judges Panel.

I certify that I have measured the above trophy on _____ April 2, _____ 19 90 _____

at (address) _____ City Baker City State OR

and that these measurements and data are, to the best of my knowledge and belief, made in accordance with the instructions given.

Witness: ___ Hope T. Buckner _____ Signature ___ Eldon Buckner _____

B&C OFFICIAL MEASURER

I.D. Number

INSTRUCTIONS FOR MEASURING CARIBOU

All measurements must be made with a 1/4-inch flexible steel tape to the nearest one-eighth of an inch. Wherever it is necessary to change direction of measurement, mark a control point and swing tape at this point. (Note: a flexible steel cable can be used to measure points and main beams only.) Enter fractional figures in eighths, without reduction. Official measurements cannot be taken until antlers have dried for at least 60 days after the animal was killed.

A. Tip to Tip Spread is measured between tips of main beams.

B. Greatest Spread is measured between perpendiculars at a right angle to the center line of the skull at widest part, whether across main beams or points.

C. Inside Spread of Main Beams is measured at a right angle to the center line of the skull at widest point between main beams. Enter this measurement again as Spread Credit if it is less than or equal to the length of longer antler; if longer, enter longer antler length for Spread Credit.

D. Number of Points on Each Antler: To be counted a point, a projection must be at least one-half inch long, with length exceeding width at the point of measurement. Beam tip is counted as a point but not measured as a point. There are no "abnormal" points in caribou.

E. Length of Main Beam is measured from lowest outside edge of burr over outer curve to the most distant point of what is, or appears to be, the main beam. The point of beginning is that point on the burr where the center line along the outer curve of the beam intersects the burr.

F. 1-2-3 Length of Points are measured from nearest edge of beam on the shortest line over outer curve to tip. Lay the tape along the outer curve of the beam so that the top edge of the tape coincides with the top edge of the beam on both sides of point to determine the baseline for point measurement. Record point lengths in appropriate blanks.

F. 4-5 Length of Points are measured from the tip of the point to the top of the beam, then at a right angle to the lower edge of beam. The Second Longest Top Point cannot be a point branch of the Longest Top Point.

G-1 Width of Brow is measured in a straight line from top edge to lower edge, as illustrated, with measurement line at a right angle to main axis of brow.

G-2 Width of Top Palm is measured from midpoint of lower rear edge of main beam to midpoint of a dip between points, at widest part of palm. The line of measurement begins and ends at midpoints of palm edges, which gives credit for palm thickness.

H. 1-2-3-4 Circumferences are taken as described for measurements. If brow point is missing, take H-1 at smallest point between burr and bez point. If rear point is missing, take H-2 and H-3 measurements at smallest place between bez and first top point. Do not depress the tape into any dips of the palm or main beam.

* * * * * * * * * * * * * * * * *

FAIR CHASE STATEMENT FOR ALL HUNTER-TAKEN TROPHIES

To make use of the following methods shall be deemed as UNFAIR CHASE and unsportsmanlike, and any trophy obtained by use of such means is disqualified from entry.

  I. Spotting or herding game from the air, followed by landing in its vicinity for pursuit;

  II. Herding or pursuing game with motor-powered vehicles;

  III. Use of electronic communications for attracting, locating or observing game, or guiding the hunter to such game;

  IV. Hunting game confined by artificial barriers, including escape-proof fencing; or hunting game transplanted solely for the purpose of commercial shooting.

* * * * * * * * * * * * * * * * *

I certify that the trophy scored on this chart was not taken in UNFAIR CHASE as defined above by the Boone and Crockett Club. I further certify that it was taken in full compliance with local game laws of the state, province, or territory.

Date _____ Signature of Hunter _____

(Have signature notarized by a Notary Public)

OFFICIAL SCORING SYSTEM FOR NORTH AMERICAN BIG GAME TROPHIES

Records of North American
Big Game

BOONE AND CROCKETT CLUB

P.O. Box 547
Dumfries, VA 22026

Minimum Score: Awards All-time
80   82

PRONGHORN

SEE OTHER SIDE FOR INSTRUCTIONS		Column 1	Column 2	Column 3
A. Tip to Tip Spread	9 5/8	Right Horn	Left Horn	Difference
B. Inside Spread of Main Beams	12 4/8			
IF Inside Spread Exceeds Longer Horn, Enter Difference		✕	✕	--
C. Length of Horn		16 4/8	16 4/8	--
D-1. Circumference of Base		7 2/8	7 1/8	1/8
D-2. Circumference at First Quarter		7 6/8	7 6/8	--
D-3. Circumference at Second Quarter		4 4/8	4 4/8	--
D-4. Circumference at Third Quarter		3 1/8	3 1/8	--
E. Length of Prong		7 3/8	7 4/8	1/8
TOTALS		46 4/8	46 4/8	2/8

Enter Total of Columns 1 and 2	93	Exact Locality Where Killed: Coconino Co., Arizona	
Subtract Column 3	2/8	Date Killed: 9/10/91	By Whom Killed: Sam Jaksick, Jr.
FINAL SCORE	* 92 6/8	Present Owner: Sam Jaksick, Jr.	
		Guide Name and Address: Tony Grimmett	
		Remarks:	

I certify that I have measured the above trophy on November 12,   19 91

at (Address) _____ (City) Gilbert _____ (State) AZ

and that these measurements and data are, to the best of my knowledge and belief, made in accordance with the

instructions given.

Witness: _____ Signature: Robin Bechtel

B&C OFFICIAL MEASURER

*Score verified by 21st Awards Judges Panel.

I.D. Number

528

INSTRUCTIONS FOR MEASURING PRONGHORN

All measurements must be made with a 1/4-inch, flexible steel tape to the nearest one-eighth of an inch. Wherever it is necessary to change direction of measurement, mark a control point and swing tape at this point. Enter fractional figures in eighths, without reduction. Official measurement cannot be taken until horns have dried for at least sixty days after the animal was killed.

A. Tip to Tip Spread is measured between tips of horns.

B. Inside Spread of Main Beams is measured at a right angle to the center line of the skull, at widest point between main beams.

C. Length of Horn is measured on the outside curve on the general line illustrated. The line taken will vary with different heads, depending on the direction of their curvature. Measure along the center of the outer curve from tip of horn to a point in line with the lowest edge of the base, using a straight edge to establish the line end.

D-1 Measure around base of horn at a right angle to long axis. Tape must be in contact with the lowest circumference of the horn in which there are no serrations.

D. 2-3-4 Divide measurement C of longer horn by four. Starting at base, mark both horns at these quarters (even though the other horn is shorter) and measure circumferences at these marks. If the prong interferes with D-2, move the measurement down to just below the swelling of the prong. If the prong interferes with D-3, move the measurement up to just above the swelling of the prong.

E. Length of Prong: Measure from the tip of the prong along the upper edge of the outer curve to the horn; then continue around the horn to a point at the rear of the horn where a straight edge across the back of both horns touches the horn, with the latter part being at a right angle to the long axis of horn.

* * * * * * * * * * * * * * * * *

FAIR CHASE STATEMENT FOR ALL HUNTER-TAKEN TROPHIES

To make use of the following methods shall be deemed as UNFAIR CHASE and unsportsmanlike, and any trophy obtained by use of such means is disqualified from entry.

I. Spotting or herding game from the air, followed by landing in its vicinity for pursuit;

II. Herding or pursuing game with motor-powered vehicles;

III. Use of electronic communications for attracting, locating or observing game, or guiding the hunter to such game;

IV. Hunting game confined by artificial barriers, including escape-proof fencing; or hunting game transplanted solely for the purpose of commercial shooting.

* * * * * * * * * * * * * * * * *

I certify that the trophy scored on this chart was not taken in UNFAIR CHASE as defined above by the Boone and Crockett Club. I further certify that it was taken in full compliance with local game laws of the state, province, or territory.

Date: _____ Signature of Hunter: _____

(Have Signature Notarized by a Notary Public)

Records of North American
Big Game

BOONE AND CROCKETT CLUB

P.O. Box 547
Dumfries, VA 22026

Minimum Score: Awards All-time
115   115

BISON

Sex   Male

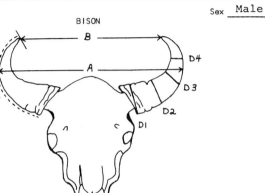

SEE OTHER SIDE FOR INSTRUCTIONS		Column 1	Column 2	Column 3
A. Greatest Spread	31	Right Horn	Left Horn	Difference
B. Tip to Tip Spread	23 3/8			
C. Length of Horn		18 7/8	18 6/8	1/8
D-1. Circumference of Base		15 1/8	14 7/8	2/8
D-2. Circumference at First Quarter		12 7/8	12 4/8	3/8
D-3. Circumference at Second Quarter		10 6/8	10 5/8	1/8
D-4. Circumference at Third Quarter		7 6/8	7 4/8	2/8
TOTALS		65 3/8	64 2/8	1 1/8

Enter Total of Columns 1 and 2	129 5/8	Exact Locality Where Killed: Custer County, South Dakota
Subtract Column 3	1 1/8	Date Killed: 12/14/89 By Whom Killed: Stephanie Altimus
FINAL SCORE	128 4/8	Present Owner: Wildlife Museum of the West
		Guide Name and Address: Fred Matthews and Larry Altimus
		Remarks:

I certify that I have measured the above trophy on May 6   19 92

at (Address) Milwaukee Public Museum   (City) Milwaukee   (State) WI

and that these measurements and data are, to the best of my knowledge and belief, made in accordance with the

instructions given.

Witness: Frank Cook   Signature: Stan Godfrey

B&C OFFICIAL MEASURER

I.D. Number

All measurements must be made with a 1/4-inch, flexible steel tape to the nearest one-eighth of an inch. Wherever it is necessary to change direction of measurement, mark a control point and swing tape at this point. Enter fractional figures in eighths, without reduction. Official measurement cannot be taken until horns have dried for at least sixty days after the animal was killed.

A. Greatest Spread is measured between perpendiculars at a right angle to the center line of the skull.

B. Tip to Tip Spread is measured between tips of horns.

C. Length of Horn is measured from the lowest point on underside over outer curve to a point in line with tip. Use a straight edge, perpendicular to horn axis, to end the measurement, if necessary.

D-1 Circumference of Base is measured at a right angle to axis of horn. Do not follow the irregular edge of horn; the line of measurement must be entirely on horn material, not the jagged edge often noted.

D. 2-3-4 Divide measurement C of longer horn by four. Starting at base, mark both horns at these quarters (even though the other horn is shorter) and measure circumferences at these marks, with measurements taken at right angles to horn axis.

* * * * * * * * * * * * * * * * * *

FAIR CHASE STATEMENT FOR ALL HUNTER-TAKEN TROPHIES

To make use of the following methods shall be deemed as UNFAIR CHASE and unsportsmanlike, and any trophy obtained by use of such means is disqualified from entry.

    I. Spotting or herding game from the air, followed by landing in its vicinity for pursuit;

    II. Herding or pursuing game with motor-powered vehicles;

    III. Use of electronic communications for attracting, locating or observing game, or guiding the hunter to such game;

    IV. Hunting game confined by artificial barriers, including escape-proof fencing; or hunting game transplanted solely for the purpose of commercial shooting.

* * * * * * * * * * * * * * * * * *

I certify that the trophy scored on this chart was not taken in UNFAIR CHASE as defined above by the Boone and Crockett Club. I further certify that it was taken in full compliance with local game laws of the state, province, or territory.

Date: _____ Signature of Hunter: _____

(Have Signature Notarized by a Notary Public)

Records of North American
Big Game

BOONE AND CROCKETT CLUB

P.O. Box 547
Dumfries, VA 22026

Minimum Score: Awards All-time
47   50

ROCKY MOUNTAIN GOAT

Sex __Male__

SEE OTHER SIDE FOR INSTRUCTIONS		Column 1	Column 2	Column 3
A. Greatest Spread	7 2/8	Right Horn	Left Horn	Difference
B. Tip to Tip Spread	5 2/8			
C. Length of Horn		11 6/8	12	2/8
D-1. Circumference of Base		5 4/8	5 4/8	
D-2. Circumference at First Quarter		4 7/8	4 7/8	
D-3. Circumference at Second Quarter		3 1/8	3 2/8	1/8
D-4. Circumference at Third Quarter		1 7/8	1 7/8	
TOTALS		27 1/8	27 4/8	3/8

Enter Total of Columns 1 and 2	54 5/8	Exact Locality Where Killed: Yes Bay, Alaska
Subtract Column 3	3/8	Date Killed: 8/24/91 By Whom Killed: Wally L. Grover
FINAL SCORE	54 2/8	Present Owner: Wally L. Grover
		Guide Name and Address:
		Remarks:

I certify that I have measured the above trophy on _____ May 6, 1992

at (Address) __Milwaukee Public Museum__ (City) __Milwaukee__ (State) WI

and that these measurements and data are, to the best of my knowledge and belief, made in accordance with the

instructions given.

Witness: __Larry Streiff__   Signature: __Jack Graham__

B&C OFFICIAL MEASURER

I.D. Number

532

INSTRUCTIONS FOR MEASURING ROCKY MOUNTAIN GOAT

All measurements must be made with a 1/4-inch, flexible steel tape to the nearest one-eighth of an inch. Wherever it is necessary to change direction of measurement, mark a control point and swing tape at this point. Enter fractional figures in eighths, without reduction. Official measurement cannot be taken until horns have dried for at least sixty days after the animal was killed.

A. Greatest Spread is measured between perpendiculars at a right angle to the center line of the skull.

B. Tip to Tip Spread is measured between tips of horns.

C. Length of Horn is measured from the lowest point in front over outer curve to a point in line with tip.

D-1 Circumference of Base is measured at a right angle to axis of horn. Do not follow irregular edge of horn.

D. 2-3-4 Divide measurement C of longer horn by four. Starting at base, mark both horns at these quarters (even though the other horn is shorter) and measure circumferences at these marks.

* * * * * * * * * * * * * * * *

FAIR CHASE STATEMENT FOR ALL HUNTER-TAKEN TROPHIES

To make use of the following methods shall be deemed as UNFAIR CHASE and unsportsmanlike, and any trophy obtained by use of such means is disqualified from entry.

    I. Spotting or herding game from the air, followed by landing in its vicinity for pursuit;

   II. Herding or pursuing game with motor-powered vehicles;

 III. Use of electronic communications for attracting, locating or observing game, or guiding the hunter to such game;

 IV. Hunting game confined by artificial barriers, including escape-proof fencing; or hunting game transplanted solely for the purpose of commercial shooting.

* * * * * * * * * * * * * * * *

I certify that the trophy scored on this chart was not taken in UNFAIR CHASE as defined above by the Boone and Crockett Club. I further certify that it was taken in full compliance with local game laws of the state, province, or territory.

Date: _____ Signature of Hunter: _____

                                 (Have Signature Notarized by a Notary Public)

Records of North American
Big Game

BOONE AND CROCKETT CLUB

P.O. Box 547
Dumfries, VA 22026

Minimum Score: Awards All-time
105 105

MUSKOX

Sex __Male__

SEE OTHER SIDE FOR INSTRUCTIONS		Column 1	Column 2	Column 3
A. Greatest Spread	31 4/8	Right Horn	Left Horn	Difference
B. Tip to Tip Spread	30 5/8			
C. Length of Horn		30 2/8	31 6/8	1 4/8
D-1. Width of Boss		10 4/8	10 1/8	3/8
D-2. Width at First Quarter		6 6/8	7	2/8
D-3. Circumference at Second Quarter		10 3/8	11 4/8	1 1/8
D-4. Circumference at Third Quarter		5	6 3/8	1 3/8
TOTALS		62 7/8	66 6/8	4 5/8

Enter Total of Columns 1 and 2	129 5/8	Exact Locality Where Killed:	Bay Chimo, N.W.T.
Subtract Column 3	4 5/8	Date Killed: 8-24-90	By Whom Killed: Stephen A. Kroflich
FINAL SCORE	125	Present Owner:	Stephen A. Kroflich
		Guide Name and Address:	Philip Kadlun
		Remarks:	

I certify that I have measured the above trophy on _____ May 6, 19 92

at (Address) __Milwaukee Public Museum__ (City) __Milwaukee__ (State) __WI__

and that these measurements and data are, to the best of my knowledge and belief, made in accordance with the

instructions given.

Witness: __Howard Hanson__   Signature: __C. Randall Byers__

B&C OFFICIAL MEASURER

I.D. Number

All measurements must be made with a 1/4-inch, flexible steel tape and adjustable calipers to the nearest one-eighth of an inch. Wherever it is necessary to change direction of measurement, mark a control point and swing tape at this point. Enter fractional figures in eighths, without reduction. Official measurement cannot be taken until horns have dried for at least sixty days after the animal was killed.

A. Greatest Spread is measured between perpendiculars at a right angle to the center line of the skull.

B. Tip to Tip Spread is measured between tips of horns by using large calipers, which are then read against a yardstick.

C. Length of Horn is measured along center of upper horn surface, staying within curve of horn as illustrated, to a point in line with tip. Attempt to free the connective tissue between the horns at the center of the boss to determine the lowest point of horn material on each side, near the top center of the skull. Hook the tape under the lowest point of the horn and measure the length of horn, with the measurement line maintained in the center of the upper surface of horn following the converging lines to the horn tip.

D-1 Width of Boss is measured with calipers at greatest width of base, with measurement line forming a right angle with horn axis. It is often helpful to measure D-1 before C, marking the midpoint of the boss as the correct path of C.

D. 2-3-4 Divide measurement C of longer horn by four. Starting at base, mark both horns at these quarters (even though the other horn is shorter). Then, using calipers, measure width of boss at D-2, making sure the measurement is at a right angle to horn axis and in line with the D-2 mark. Circumferences are then measured at D-3 and D-4, with measurements being taken at right angles to horn axis.

* * * * * * * * * * * * * * * * *

FAIR CHASE STATEMENT FOR ALL HUNTER-TAKEN TROPHIES

To make use of the following methods shall be deemed as UNFAIR CHASE and unsportsmanlike, and any trophy obtained by use of such means is disqualified from entry.

I. Spotting or herding game from the air, followed by landing in its vicinity for pursuit;

II. Herding or pursuing game with motor-powered vehicles;

III. Use of electronic communications for attracting, locating or observing game, or guiding the hunter to such game;

IV. Hunting game confined by artificial barriers, including escape-proof fencing; or hunting game transplanted solely for the purpose of commercial shooting.

* * * * * * * * * * * * * * * * *

I certify that the trophy scored on this chart was not taken in UNFAIR CHASE as defined above by the Boone and Crockett Club. I further certify that it was taken in full compliance with local game laws of the state, province, or territory.

Date: _____ Signature of Hunter: _____

(Have Signature Notarized by a Notary Public)

Records of North American Big Game	BOONE AND CROCKETT CLUB	P.O. Box 547 Dumfries, VA 22026

Minimum Score:	Awards	All-time		Kind of Sheep	Bighorn
bighorn	175	180	SHEEP		
desert	165	168			
Dall's	165	170			
Stone's	165	170			

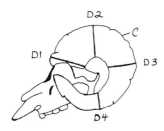
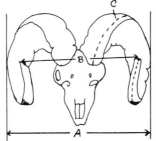

MEASURE TO A POINT IN LINE WITH HORN TIP

SEE OTHER SIDE FOR INSTRUCTIONS		Column 1	Column 2	Column 3
A. Greatest Spread (Is Often Tip to Tip Spread)	22 6/8	Right Horn	Left Horn	Difference
B. Tip to Tip Spread	22 5/8			
C. Length of Horn		46 5/8	45 1/8	✕
D-1. Circumference of Base		15 2/8	15 3/8	1/8
D-2. Circumference at First Quarter		15 1/8	15 1/8	
D-3. Circumference at Second Quarter		14 2/8	14 2/8	
D-4. Circumference at Third Quarter		10 4/8	10 4/8	
TOTALS		101 6/8	100 3/8	1/8

Enter Total of Columns 1 and 2	202 1/8	Exact Locality Where Killed: Canmore, Alberta
Subtract Column 3	1/8	Date Killed: Dec. 1987 By Whom Killed: Picked Up
FINAL SCORE	202 *	Present Owner: Alberta Fish & Wildlife Division
		Guide Name and Address:
		Remarks:

I certify that I have measured the above trophy on _____ July 30 _____ 19 88 _____

at (Address) _____ (City) Stony Plain (State) Alberta

and that these measurements and data are, to the best of my knowledge and belief, made in accordance with the

instructions given.

Witness: L.S. Weshart _____ Signature: John G. Stelfox _____

B&C OFFICIAL MEASURER

*Score verified by 21St Awards Judges Panel.

I.D. Number

All measurements must be made with a 1/4-inch, flexible steel tape to the nearest one-eighth of an inch. Wherever it is necessary to change direction of measurement, mark a control point and swing tape at this point. Enter fractional figures in eighths, without reduction. Official measurement cannot be taken until horns have dried for at least sixty days after the animal was killed.

A. Greatest Spread is measured between perpendiculars at a right angle to the center line of the skull.

B. Tip to Tip Spread is measured between tips of horns.

C. Length of Horn is measured from the lowest point in front on outer curve to a point in line with tip. Do not press tape into depressions. The low point of the outer curve of the horn is considered to be the low point of the frontal portion of the horn, situated above and slightly medial to the eye socket (not the outside edge). Use a straight edge, perpendicular to horn axis, to end measurement on "broomed" horns.

D-1 Circumference of Base is measured at a right angle to axis of horn. Do not follow irregular edge of horn; the line of measurement must be entirely on horn material, not the jagged edge often noted.

D. 2-3-4 Divide measurement C of longer horn by four. Starting at base, mark both horns at these quarters (even though the other horn is shorter) and measure circumferences at these marks, with measurements taken at right angles to horn axis.

* * * * * * * * * * * * * * * * * *

FAIR CHASE STATEMENT FOR ALL HUNTER-TAKEN TROPHIES

To make use of the following methods shall be deemed as UNFAIR CHASE and unsportsmanlike, and any trophy obtained by use of such means is disqualified from entry.

    I. Spotting or herding game from the air, followed by landing in its vicinity for pursuit;

    II. Herding or pursuing game with motor-powered vehicles;

    III. Use of electronic communications for attracting, locating or observing game, or guiding the hunter to such game;

    IV. Hunting game confined by artificial barriers, including escape-proof fencing; or hunting game transplanted solely for the purpose of commercial shooting.

* * * * * * * * * * * * * * * * * *

I certify that the trophy scored on this chart was not taken in UNFAIR CHASE as defined above by the Boone and Crockett Club. I further certify that it was taken in full compliance with local game laws of the state, province, or territory.

Date: _____ Signature of Hunter: _____

                                            (Have Signature Notarized by a Notary Public)